THE GREAT IDEAS ANTHOLOGIES

This is a volume in the Arno Press series

THE GREAT IDEAS ANTHOLOGIES

CONTEMPORARY IDEAS IN HISTORICAL PERSPECTIVE
THE HUMANITIES TODAY
THE SCIENCES TODAY
THE SOCIAL SCIENCES TODAY

THE HUMANITIES TODAY

Edited by
Robert M. Hutchins and Mortimer Adler

Introduction by John Van Doren

ARNO PRESS
A New York Times Company
New York / 1977

First publication, 1977 by Arno Press Inc.
© 1977 by Encyclopaedia Britannica, Inc.
Published by arrangement with Encyclopaedia
  Britannica, Inc.

THE GREAT IDEAS ANTHOLOGIES
ISBN for complete set: 0-405-07170-1
See last pages of this volume for titles.

Manufactured in the United States of America

———◆———

Library of Congress Cataloging in Publication Data
Main entry under title:

The Humanities today.

   (The Great ideas anthologies)
   Selected essays from the Great ideas today, 1961-1974.
   Bibliography: p.
   Includes index.
   1. Humanities--Addresses, essays, lectures.
I. Hutchins, Robert Maynard, 1899-   II. Adler,
Mortimer Jerome, 1902-   III. Great ideas today.
IV. Series.
AZ221.H85   001.3'08   75-4298
ISBN 0-405-07172-8

INTRODUCTION

The Humanities Today is one of three volumes published at the same time — the others being devoted, respectively, to the sciences and the social sciences — which bring together the writings of noted authorities on recent developments in the world of learning and ideas, described so far as possible in layman's language, for the benefit of the lay reader. A fourth volume, *Contemporary Issues*, offers discussions of a controversial nature about matters of common interest by persons of relevant background or known concern.

All of these pieces were first printed in *The Great Ideas Today*, an annual publication of the Great Books Division of Encyclopaedia Britannica, Inc., which has appeared every year since 1961. Each issue of this annual, a hard-bound volume of approximately 500 pages, contains a symposium on a topic of current importance, three or four essays devoted to recent developments in the arts and sciences, and an examination of some classic work or traditional subject in contemporary terms. It is intended primarily for readers of Britannica's *Great Books of the Western World* (usually referred to in the pages that follow as GBWW), a 54-volume set of works representing the tradition of western thought from Homer to Freud, and including a topical index, known as the Syntopicon, with references arranged under one or another of what are called the Great Ideas. In offering *The Great Ideas Today* each year to the owners of this set, the editors have in mind that the tradition it embodies accounts for much of what goes on in the contemporary world, and the contributors to the volume, in commenting upon contemporary developments, endeavor to show how that is so. The title of the work reflects a further conviction that it is in terms of the ideas in the Syntopicon that the body of thought comprised by this tradition can be most easily grasped, and that it is by such means that we perceive our connection with the past and bring some coherence to the present.

It is not required, of course, that every reader of these collections be familiar with *The Great Ideas Today*, or that he have *Great Books of the Western World* conveniently at hand. Footnotes occasionally point to such sources, and most of the articles are followed by Notes to the Reader suggesting further study through the Syntopicon, but no special knowledge is assumed. Nor are the pieces to be taken simply as expressions of the editorial purpose with which they were originally commissioned. The views they present are those of their authors, who are mostly men of acknowledged eminence in their chosen fields, and who were offered certain guidelines as to how their subjects should be treated but were left to decide what they should actually say. Each piece therefore stands on its own as a discussion of a current discipline or some aspect of contemporary life, and can be read as such.

Inevitably, many of the pieces show some evidence of the fact that they were written in a particular year, their authors having been asked to summarize developments that concerned them as of that time. This was particularly true in the first issues of *The Great Ideas Today*, when the annual character of the volume was more strictly adhered to than it has been since — which accounts for the fact that fewer pieces have been selected from those early issues than from later ones. Such datedness is mostly superficial, however, and where it is more serious it is apt to be corrected in the course of a later discussion of the same subject by a different contributor. When an essay seemed in some crucial respect to be no longer current, it was left out of these collections, but it was not rejected for its passing references to a year that is now gone by. For those who wish to know what has happened in certain fields since these writings were first published, each collection includes an added bibliography of important works on the subjects covered that have recently appeared.

As the content of the various pieces is partly determined by the annual occasions for which they were written, so their style reflects a concern with the particular audience they were designed to reach. This may be said to comprise not only those persons who receive *The Great Ideas Today* but all who, beyond any special competence they happen to have, take a sober interest in what goes on in the world and are willing to read at substantial length about it. Not a great deal is written for such an audience, whose requirements lie somewhere between journalism and the academic — between, in other words, what is conveyed by those who can write of contemporary developments only as events, not being learned in their subject matter, and those who speak as to the initiate, assuming knowledge of the things they discuss. If most of the contributors to these volumes are themselves academics, and some are journalists, yet they have taken a view of their material and adopted a manner of presenting it which is nowadays untypical of their professions. The result is a series of reports that, while intended for the general reader and avoiding special terminology, provide as comprehensive and detailed an account as such limitations allow of the progress of the disciplines, the development of ideas, and the tendencies of thought in our time.

*　　*　　*　　*　　*　　*

Of the writings assembled here, two are concerned with theology, four with philosophy, four (one of which is a symposium) with the arts, and one each with archeology and classical studies. Such a distribution among what in general are called the humanities is the result of no particular design and is not comprehensive, but it reflects the fact that some disciplines are more given than others to the task of saying what they are about, and the further fact that in the last decade or so some of them have been more inclined than usual to undertake such work. There would not, perhaps, have been two essays devoted to theology in a volume of this sort if it were not for the profound self-examination that recent events have forced upon organized religion, and in particular upon Christianity. It is from a sense that a crisis has lately occurred in the life of the churches that Professor Gilkey addresses himself to what he regards as the central problem, at least for Protestants, which has to do with the reality of God and the question whether it is possible for there to be any significant talk about him. And M. Gilson, in "The Idea of God and the Difficulties of Atheism," takes up the same question from a different point of view that leads him to ask what the intellectual and moral consequences must be if we insist, as many people nowadays do, that there is no God, or that if there was one once, he is now dead.

The need that philosophy has felt to explain itself in recent years has not seemed so critical, but it has been real. Hence W. T. Jones, in undertaking to give an account of the course the discipline has followed over the twentieth century, sees it as a protracted and on the whole futile struggle to escape the limits of the Kantian formulations from which it comes. Similarly, Professors Henry B. Veatch and Moltke S. Gram, in a survey of contemporary academic philosophy that notes two main lines of development — analytical philosophy and phenomenology and existentialism — traces both to the "transcendental turn" that is seen to have occurred with Kant, and points out the difficulties that result for any theory of ethics. In other philosophical essays, V. J. McGill surveys the contemporary literature on the subject of happiness, in particular the dispute that has arisen — of which the classic protagonists are Aristotle and Kant — as to whether happiness can, or should, constitute the norm of human action; and Chaim Perelman, in "The New Rhetoric," discusses a branch of rhetoric that was originally formulated by Aristotle but has since been largely ignored — a branch, Professor Perelman suggests, which may be called the rhetoric of argumentation, and in which he sees a theory of practical reasoning appropriate to the solution of practical problems.

Among the essays on the arts, two are by Mark Van Doren. One of them, prepared at the request of the editors of *The Great Ideas Today*, undertakes in reflective terms to suggest which of the works of literature published so far in the twentieth century may possibly last. Another discusses Chaucer's *Canterbury Tales* as a poem, or more exactly as a group of stories in verse, to be read by anyone — in modern English if necessary — for the special and apparently permanent power it has, notwithstanding its medieval setting, to affect and entertain. A third discussion of literature is also concerned with poetry, but the kind is lyric and contemporary and the writers — for there are three, rather than one — are themselves poets of distinction who speak variously of their art as it is practised in these times. These essays, by Louis Simpson, James Dickey, and Stephen Spender, are followed by selections of each poet's own verse.

Only one essay, by Roy McMullen, deals with other arts than literature, and it encompasses no fewer than three of them — music, painting, and sculpture. In each case Mr. McMullen tries to suggest what the distinctively modern aspect of the art is and how it has developed in the course of the century — a difficult work to do without drifting so far into talk of history, movements, and influences that the arts themselves become lifeless things to comprehend; but Mr. McMullen manages to stay close to his material, and the resulting essay is both competent and genuinely helpful. It is Mr. McMullen's conviction, incidentally, that recent developments in the arts of which he treats are very much an outgrowth of "the great ideas of the Western tradition," which he regards as "thoroughly relevant."

The remaining essays are concerned not with modern but with ancient times, and they cover some of the same ground, but the disciplines they represent are different, and the effort is to show that both have changed in recent years. Thus Leonard Cottrell relates how archeology has in our time, through new techniques, become at once "the adjunct of written history" and the source of information about an immeasurably older human past; and M. I. Finley, in "New Developments in Classical Studies," examines what through the brilliant work of certain scholars we have lately learned about classical antiquity, as distinct from what we once thought we knew. It should perhaps be explained that this last essay was written just before the theories of Hans Georg Wunderlich with respect to the palace of Knossos in Crete were first published (see the bibliography at the end of this volume for a subsequent book by Wunderlich), and so does not comment upon what has been perhaps the most sensational of new developments in the field.

John Van Doren

In presenting this volume, as with the other collections of material on different subjects that appear along with it, the editors acknowledge the assistance of those who have helped over the years to get out *The Great Ideas Today* — in particular, Peter C. Wolff, Otto A. Bird, and John Van Doren, and in general, the editorial production staff of Encyclopaedia Britannica, Inc. They wish also to thank Wayne Moquin, who for each of these collections prepared the bibliography of recent works that will be found at the end.

HUMANITIES BIBLIOGRAPHY

Batlock, Gregory. *Notes on a New Theory of Art*. New York: Dutton, 1971

Bronowski, J. *The Identity of Man*. New York: Doubleday, 1971

Bloom, Harold. *The Anxiety of Influence: A Theory of Poetry*, New York: Oxford, 1973

Cameron, Kenneth Neill. *Humanity and Society*. Bloomington: Indiana University Press, 1971

Collins, Peter. *Architectural Judgment*. Montreal: McGill-Queens University Press, 1971

Cornman, James W. *Materialism and Sensations*. New Haven: Yale, 1971

Craig, David. *The Real Foundations: Literature and Social Change*. New York: Oxford, 1974

Edwards, Thomas R. *Imagination and Power: A Study of Poetry on Public Themes*. New York: Oxford, 1971

Egbert, Donald Drew. *Social Radicalism and the Arts: Western Europe*. New York: Knopf, 1970

Escarpit, Robert. *Sociology of Literature*. Frank Cass, Ltd., 1971

Feibleman, James K. *The Quiet Rebellion: The Making and Meaning of the Arts*. New York: Horizon, 1972

Fingesten, Peter. *The Eclipse of Symbolism*. Columbia: University of South Carolina Press, 1970

Hamburger, Michael. *The Truth of Poetry: Tensions in Modern Poetry from Baudelaire to the 1960s*. New York: Harcourt, 1970

Holmes, Arthur F. *Faith Seeks Understanding*. Grand Rapids: Eerdmans, 1971

Hospers, John, ed. *Artistic Expression*. New York: Appleton, 1971

Jarvie, I. C. *Movies and Society*. New York: Basic Books, 1970

Johes, Howard Mumford. *Revolution and Romanticism*. Cambridge: Harvard, 1974

Krieger, Murray. *The Classic Vision: The Retreat from Extremity in Modern Literature*. Baltimore: Johns Hopkins, 1971

Kreitter, Hans and Shulamith Kreiter. *Psychology of the Arts.* Durham: Duke University Press, 1972

Leone, Mark P., ed. *Contemporary Archaeology: A Guide to Theory and Contributions.* Carbondale: Southern Illinois University Press, 1973

Lynch, William F. *Images of Faith: An Exploration of the Ironic Imagination.* South Bend: Notre Dame Press, 1973

Osborne, Harold. *Aesthetics and Art Theory.* New York: Dutton, 1970

Panofsky, Erwin. *Idea: A Concept in Art Theory.* Columbia: University of South Carolina Press, 1968

Polanyi, Michael. *Knowing and Being.* Chicago: University of Chicago Press, 1969

Porter, Thomas E. *Myth and Modern American Drama.* Detroit: Wayne State U. Press. 1973

Richardson, John Adkins. *Modern Art and Scientific Thought.* Urbana: University of Illinois Press, 1971

Santillana, Giorgio de, and Hertha von Dechend. *Hamlet's Mill: An Essay on Myth and the Frame of Time.* Boston: Gambit, 1969

Scholes, Robert. *Structuralism in Literature.* New Haven: Yale

Sircello, Guy. *Mind and Art: An Essay on the Varieties of Expression.* Princeton: Princeton University Press

Smart, Ninian. *The Religious Experience of Mankind.* New York: Scribners, 1971

Spears, Monroe K. *Dionysius and the City: Modernism in Twentieth Century Poetry.* New York: Oxford, 1970

Tilghman, Benjamin R., ed. *Language and Aesthetics: Contributions to the Philosophy of Art.* Lawrence: Kansas University Press, 1973

Voss, Arthur. *The American Short Story.* Norman: University of Oklahoma Press, 1973

Weightman, John. *The Concept of the Avant-Garde.* Freeport, N. Y.: Library Press, 1973

Wollheim, Richard. *On Art and the Mind.* Cambridge: Harvard, 1974

Wunderlich, Hans Georg. *The Secret of Crete.* New York: Macmillan, 1974

Recent Books by
Great Ideas Today Authors

W. T. Jones, *The Sciences and the Humanities:* Conflict and Reconciliation (1965)

Henry B. Veatch, *For an Ontology of Morals:* A Critique of Contemporary Ethical Theory (1971)

V. J. McGill, *Schopenhauer* (1971)

Langdon B. Gilkey, *Naming the Whirlwind:* The Renewal of God-Language (1969)
Religion and the Scientific Future: Reflections on Myth, Science, and Theology (1970)

James Dickey, *Deliverance* (1970)
Eye-Beaters, Blood, Victory, Madness, Buckhead and Mercy (1970)
Sorties: Journals and New Essays (1971)

Louis Simpson, *North of Jamaica* (1972)

Stephen Spender, *Year of the Young Rebels* (1969)
Generous Days (1971)
The New Realism (1972)
World Within World: The Autobiography of Stephen Spender (1974)

Roy McMullen, *Art, Affluence, and Alienation:* The Fine Arts Today (1968)
The World of Marc Chagall (1968)
Victorian Outsider (1973)

M. I. Finley, co-author of *History of Sicily*, 3 vols. (1968)

CONTENTS

The Widening Gyre: Philosophy in the Twentieth Century

W. T. Jones

Born in Natchez, Mississippi, in 1910, W. T. Jones was educated at Swarth-more, from which he graduated in 1931; at Oxford University, where he was a Rhodes Scholar (1931–34); and at Princeton, from which he received a doctorate in philosophy in 1937. In 1938 he joined the faculty of Pomona College, Claremont, California, where he became a professor in 1950, and which he has recently left to become professor of philosophy at the California Institute of Technology (he was elected a trustee of Pomona upon his departure). During the Second World War he served in the naval reserves and subsequently taught social and political philosophy at the U.S. Naval War College (1953–54). He is the author of *Morality and Freedom in Kant* (1941), *Masters of Political Thought* (1947), *Approaches to Ethics* (1962), *The Romantic Syndrome* (1962), and other works, as well as of a highly useful and very readable *History of Western Philosophy* (4 volumes, 1952). Professor Jones lives in Claremont.

Turning and turning in the widening gyre
The falcon cannot hear the falconer;
Things fall apart; the center cannot hold;
Mere anarchy is loosed upon the world. . . .
                    —W. B. Yeats, *The Second Coming*

The Kantian paradigm

At the turn of the century the leading philosophers were Bradley and Bosanquet in Britain, Bergson in France, and James and Royce in this country. Were they to return to Oxford and Harvard and the Sorbonne today they would encounter few familiar signposts: not only the topics that engage philosophers but even the ways of "doing" philosophy have changed so much that they would feel lost indeed.

Has there then been a revolution in philosophy in the twentieth century? Many philosophers would say that there has been, but if we think of earlier debates—those that divided Plato from the Sophists, the Thomists from the Scotists, the Aristotelians from the Cartesians—we may suspect that this contemporary estimate of the contemporary scene is an exaggeration. In every period, for contemporaries, it is the disagreements, rather than the agreements, that command attention. But gradually, as the time passes, the similarities, not the differences, come into focus. Since there is no reason to think that the twentieth century is exempt from such perspectival foreshortening, later generations, looking back on us from a distance, will probably decide that twentieth-century philosophy is less revolutionary than twentieth-century philosophers now judge it to be.

Indeed, all the disagreements, from major engagements to minor skirmishes, have been conducted within, around, or over what may be called the Kantian paradigm. When Kant's *Critique of Pure Reason* was published in 1781, the dominant philosophical school was a form of metaphysical and epistemological dualism. According to this way of thinking, there are two sorts of entities in the universe: minds and material objects. A mind knows objects (and other minds) by means of mental states (variously called "ideas," "representations," "impressions," "phantasms") that are caused by these objects and that resemble them. Despite differences on many points, the Lockeians and the Cartesians agreed that the mind is directly acquainted only with its own states, that is, its ideas are its only means of access to the outside world.

The difficulty with this view, as Hume pointed out, is that if the mind knows only its own states, its own states are all that it knows. Suppose that there exist a number of photographs claiming to be likenesses of Richard Nixon, but that Nixon himself, immured in the White House, has been seen by no man. In these circumstances, it is obviously impos-

3

sible to say that any of the photographs is the likeness of Nixon it claims to be. Similarly, if we have access only to ideas, we can compare ideas with each other but never with the external reality they claim to represent. Indeed, we can never know that an external world, or that other minds than ours, exist. Hume did not argue that only Hume exists. On the contrary, he believed in the existence of other minds and of an external world. But these beliefs, which he shared with all men, he held to be incapable of proof. So far from being supported by evidence, they are merely the expressions of "a blind and powerful instinct of nature." It is not reason or logic, but only "custom," that is "the great guide of human life."

It was at this point, where the whole post-Renaissance philosophy threatened to collapse in solipsism and skepticism, that Kant came on the scene. Since Hume had demonstrated the breakdown of the hypothesis that truth consists in the mind's being in agreement with objects, Kant proposed to try the opposite hypothesis that truth consists in the agreement of objects with minds. That is, he proposed to abandon the old view that the mind passively records what is "out there" and to try instead the hypothesis that it selects and structures what is out there. This in turn required him to suppose that the mind contains selecting and organizing principles and that it is possible to learn what those principles are. If we can ascertain this, as Kant believed he could, it follows that an absolutely certain knowledge of nature can be had—not an absolutely certain knowledge of particular facts but of the basic structure of nature as far as we can experience it. For the basic structure of nature so considered is a product of the mind's activity, not something independent of that activity.*

It follows that particular causal laws such as "all bodies gravitate" or "friction causes heat" are only probable, because they depend on empirical observation—that is, they are arrived at a posteriori. But the basic law that every event has a cause, on which the whole procedure of physics rests, is a priori, i.e., certain, because the human mind structures its experience in a cause-effect way. Within the range of that structure it can be sure of its ground. And while the extent of its assured knowledge may seem limited in scope, yet Kant believed that the mind's organizing and synthesizing activities were sufficient to justify and warrant the fundamental principles of Newtonian physics, above all the principle of the uniformity of nature, as to which Hume had maintained that our belief rests on mere blind instinct rather than on logic or evidence.

Kant described his hypothesis about the knower and his relation to the objects of his knowledge as a Copernican revolution. Just as Copernicus had shifted the frame of reference from the earth to the sun, so Kant shifted the frame of reference from objects to the mind. What Copernicus brought about admittedly was an enormous shift in perspective, with momentous consequences; in calling his own hypothesis "Copernican,"

Kant was claiming that it was an equally revolutionary shift in perspective. In this estimate he was correct, but, paradoxically, his hypothesis had an almost directly opposite effect. Whereas Copernicus's astronomical hypothesis had demoted the earth (and with it man) from the center to the periphery, Kant's epistemological hypothesis brought man, the knower, back to the center.

Most pre-Kantian philosophers had conceived the mind as a receptor of impressions from outside. In Locke's phrase, it was a *tabula rasa,* a blank tablet, until experience wrote upon it. They granted, of course, that the mind could combine in various ways (e.g., in accordance with the "laws" of association) the materials it received from the outside world, but they held that in its essential nature the mind was passive. The Kantian revolution transformed all this. The mind was no longer a Cartesian substance contemplating other Cartesian substances from a distance. It was not a "thing" at all but an activity, a number of "transcendental syntheses." And from this epistemological change there followed a profound metaphysical change: The so-called objective world (the objects of the mind's experience, not the world of things-in-themselves) is a construct, a product of the synthesizing activity of mind working upon and organizing the materials of sense (what Kant called the "sensuous manifold"). For this reason, views of the Kantian type are sometimes called constructivist theories.

From the beginning, reactions to the constructivism that Kant introduced were varied, but always strong. For some, it was a liberating thing. In *The Prelude,* for instance, Wordsworth emphasizes the active, synthesizing power of the mind in true Kantian fashion. When "the infant Babe" stretches out his hand toward a flower, he does not experience merely the physical flower out there; "already love . . . hath beautified that flower" for him. He has synthesized his response to his mother's loving, protective care into the material object. The babe is already "creator and receiver both," and what is true of the babe is even truer of the poet.[1] Thus, by assigning a positive function to what Coleridge called "the primary Imagination," the Kantian revolution allowed the poet to exalt his role. No longer merely a pleasing imitator of nature, he is a creative god, albeit only a minor one, in his own right.

---

* As a rough analogy, think of the relation between a camera, the film it contains, and the objects photographed by it. The film does not record indiscriminately what is "out there," for mediating between the film and the object is a system of lenses with varying focal lengths. If we know what focal length has been chosen by the photographer, we can make a number of a priori (i.e., absolutely certain) judgments about what has been photographed. Suppose that the stop has been set at $f/4$ and that the distance has been set at nine feet. Though we cannot say, prior to seeing the developed film, what object has been photographed, we *can* say that whatever was nearer than nine feet and further than twelve feet will be out of focus. We know this, prior to seeing the developed film, (1) because the camera is a selecting and organizing medium between the film and object photographed and (2) because we know the principles by which this selection and organization occur.

For others, Kantianism had a profoundly disturbing effect. Nietzsche quotes a letter of Heinrich von Kleist's:

> *Not long ago I became acquainted with Kant's philosophy; and now I must tell you of a thought in it, inasmuch as I cannot fear that it will upset you as profoundly and painfully as me. We cannot decide whether that which we call truth is really truth or whether it merely appears that way to us. If the latter is right, then the truth we gather here comes to nothing after our death; and every aspiration to acquire a possession which will follow us even into the grave is futile. . . . My only, my highest aim has sunk, and I have none left.*[2]

These very different responses to Kantianism, representing very different temperaments, can be traced through the whole subsequent history of philosophy. For those who experienced a strong metaphysical urge, "despair of truth," as Nietzsche wrote, was a likely response. "As soon as Kant would begin to exert a popular influence, we should find it reflected in the form of a gnawing and crumbling skepticism and relativism."[3] For such philosophers the main question was "How can objectivity be saved?" Saving objectivity obviously depended on being able to keep at a minimum the role mind plays in constructing the world-of-experience. But the course of nineteenth-century philosophy demonstrated that, once the camel of constructivism got its nose within the philosophical tent, it was very hard to prevent the rest of the animal from following.

Hegel was the first to expand the constructivist role of mind. Whereas Kant had conceived his twelve categories as timeless features of all of mind's activities everywhere, Hegel argued that mind has a history. It passes through a sequence of stages, to each of which there corresponds a particular form, or level, of experience. It is true that Hegel believed that these levels of experience succeed each other according to a standard pattern such that each later level of experience includes all the earlier levels, while transcending them. Thus there was still, according to Hegel, something a priori about human experience, namely the sequential pattern of development that the history of culture reveals. The next step was precisely to attack this remnant of apriority.

According to Marx, the various worlds of experience, so far from revealing a pattern of spiritual development, reflect, and so are relative to, changing modes of economic production and exchange. Nietzsche was even more relativistic: "We invent the largest part of the thing experienced," he wrote. "We are much greater artists than we know." That is, what each of us experiences (our world) is not merely a function of the social class of which we are members; it is a function of personal interests, and hence varies from individual to individual. "Most of the conscious thinking of a philosopher is secretly guided by his instincts and forced along certain lines. . . . every great philosophy up to now has been . . . a type of involuntary and unaware memoirs." Science, Nietzsche thought, is no better off than philosophy: "Physics, too, is only an interpretation of the universe, an arrangement of it (to suit us, if I may be so bold!), rather than a clarification."[4]

Meanwhile, and independently of this process of relativizing the categories, other philosophers pointed out that if things-in-themselves are unknowable, there can be no evidence that they exist. F. H. Bradley expressed a commonly held opinion in his gibe at Herbert Spencer's unknowable:

> *I do not wish to be irreverent, but Mr. Spencer's attitude towards his Unknowable strikes me as a pleasantry, the point of which lies in its unconsciousness. It seems a proposal to take something for God simply and solely because we do not know what the devil it can be.*[5]

Bradley replaced the Unknowable with "Absolute," but since this Absolute was supposed to transcend all finite (i.e., human) experience, it is not easy to see in what way it was an improvement on unknown things-in-themselves. Do we, for instance, have a "positive idea" of the Absolute? Bradley was obliged to admit that

> *fully to realize the existence of the Absolute is for finite beings impossible. In order thus to know we should have to be, and then we should not exist. This result is certain, and all attempts to avoid it are illusory.*[6]

He did indeed claim that we can nonetheless "gain some idea of its main features"—it is all-inclusive; it is one; it is a system—but he confessed that this idea, though "true as far as it goes," inevitably remains "abstract and incomplete." This was the best Bradley could do, and it was not enough to satisfy what we may call the falcon's metaphysical urge, that is, his urge to find a center about which to orient his flight.

Bradley's *Appearance and Reality* was published in 1893. Thus by the end of the century the Kantian strategy of substituting a human center for the old external and objective center was increasingly perceived by philosophers as a failure. What Kant had thought of as a single, firm center around which the falcon could orient his flight, because it was rooted in the universal and necessary characteristics of the human mind, had become a plurality of individual centers—and so no true center.

The revival of realism: G. E. Moore

At the turn of the century a vigorous counterattack was launched. It was based on a theory of the nature of consciousness advocated by Brentano and Meinong, which appealed because it made possible a radical departure from the whole idealistic, constructivist paradigm. The most influential of this group of publications—at least in English-speaking countries—was G. E. Moore's "The Refutation of Idealism" (1903).

The heart of Moore's refutation was his account of the structure of human experience. Instead of being a product, experience is the simple juxtaposition of two radically different sorts of elements: the object of experience (what is experienced) and the act, or activity, of experiencing this object. Anybody, Moore maintained, who attends carefully to very simple experiences—such as the difference between an experience of a blue sense-datum and an experience of a green sense-datum—will see that these two elements, and only these two elements, are involved. They are also the elements, and the only elements, involved in more complex perceptions and in cognition, though in such cases the presence of these elements, and the distinction between them, is less obvious and can, therefore, be overlooked by a careless observer.

> *We all know that the sensation of blue differs from that of green. But it is plain that if both are sensations they also have some point in common. What is it that they have in common? . . . The element that is common to them all . . . is consciousness. . . . The sensation of blue includes in its analysis, besides blue, both a unique element "awareness" and a unique relation of this element to blue. . . . Introspection [enables] me to decide that . . . I am aware of blue, and by this I mean, that my awareness has to blue . . . the simple and unique relation the existence of which alone justifies us in distinguishing knowledge of a thing from the thing known, indeed in distinguishing mind from matter.*[7]

There is no problem, Moore thought, about the nature of the element blue as it occurs in the experience: blue is just blue, no more or less, one item among the millions of items in the universe, but the item of which we happen, at this moment, to be aware. But what about consciousness, the other element in experience? The difficulty is that consciousness is "transparent."

> *The moment we try to fix our attention upon consciousness and to see what, distinctly, it is, it seems to vanish. . . . When we try to introspect the sensation of blue, all we can see is the blue: the other element is as if it were diaphanous. Yet it can be distinguished if we look attentively enough.*[8]

And now, supposing we have looked attentively, what does consciousness contribute to experience? Moore's answer is that it contributes absolutely nothing; it does not alter blue in any way. It merely selects blue—this particular item from amongst the millions of other items in the universe —and holds it before the mind.

8

Whenever I have a mere sensation or idea, the fact is that I am then aware of something which is equally and in the same sense not an inseparable aspect of my experience. . . . There is, therefore, no question of how we are to "get outside the circle of our own ideas and sensations." Merely to have a sensation is already to be outside that circle. It is to know something which is as truly and really not a part of my experience, as anything which I can ever know.[9]

This, then, was Moore's mode of escape from the solipsism and skepticism in which, as Hume had shown, Cartesianism ended, and it wholly by-passed the Kantian revolution. Hume had pointed out that if what we know are only our own ideas, then we can never "get out of the circle of our own ideas." Whereas Kant's strategy for escaping from this dilemma had been to suggest that some of our ideas are a priori organizing elements in experience, rather than images of the world outside our experience, Moore's was to maintain that in an act of awareness there is no intermediary idea at all. Consciousness in its essential nature is consciousness *of.* When we are conscious of blue, we are not contemplating some mental image that is somehow supposed to resemble blue; we are contemplating blue.

The universe, of course, contains not only items like blue and green; it contains in fact

an immense variety of different kinds of entities. For instance: My mind, any particular thought or perception of mine, the quality which distinguishes an act of volition from a mere act of perception, the Battle of Waterloo, the process of baking, the year 1908, the moon, the number 2, the distance between London and Paris, the relation of similarity—all of these are contents of the Universe, all of them are or were contained in it.[10]

These items divide into two main classes—items that are "mental" (or "psychical") and items that are not. Some of the items that are not mental are physical objects; some are not. But all of these items have the characteristic of being, in their nature, independent of minds. They exist (they are what they are) even if they are not for any consciousness at all. What is more, this objective and public world which is thus revealed to view is just the world that common sense believes in. Finally, that all this is true Moore held to be obvious to anyone who takes the trouble to look carefully at his experience.

It would be difficult to exaggerate the effect of this analysis on those, like Russell, who had been disturbed by the subjectivism of idealism:

G. E. Moore . . . took the lead in rebellion, and I followed, with a sense of emancipation. . . . With a sense of escaping from prison, we allowed ourselves to think that grass is green, that the sun and

> *stars would exist if no one was aware of them [and that] mathematics could be* quite *true, and not merely a stage in dialectic.*[11]

It was not long, however, before both Moore and Russell began to see grave difficulties with the new position. How, for instance, are sense-data related to physical objects? When, for instance, I see a dime and a quarter lying on the ground in front of me, I am (they thought) obviously not directly aware of the whole of either coin—I don't see the other side of either, still less the inside of either. Further, if the coins are a little way off, I am directly aware of two elliptical sense-data (though the coins themselves are round) and, if the dime happens to be nearer than the quarter, the sense-datum associated with the dime may be larger than the sense-datum associated with the quarter.

Moore saw that one way of dealing with this problem would be to define a physical object (e.g., the coin) as the whole set of sense-data that all possible observers would experience under all possible conditions of observation. Then the obscure and puzzling relation of "being a property of" would be replaced by the straightforward and readily understood relation of "being a member of a class": the elliptical sense-datum would be simply one element among others in the well-ordered set of sense-data which together constituted the coin. This, as we shall see, is the type of solution for which Russell opted, but since Moore's main aim was to "vindicate" common sense against speculative philosophy, and since he believed that common sense holds material objects to be more than mere collections of sense-data, he could not take this way out. As he wrote, "on this view, though we shall still be allowed to say that the coins *existed* before I saw them, are *circular* etc., all these expressions, if they are to be true, will have to be understood in a Pickwickian sense."[12]

What, then, is the alternative for a realist? In the end, Moore said, he inclined to a position "roughly identical . . . with Locke's view," that some, at least, of the sense-data "resemble" the physical objects which are their "source." But, as Moore recognized, this seems indistinguishable from just that representative theory of perception which Moore's own original formulations were designed to avoid: "How can I ever come to know that these sensibles have a 'source' at all? And how do I know that these 'sources' are circular?" Moore confessed that he did not know how to answer these questions. If, along with our experience of sensibles, there were an "immediate awareness" that the sources exist and are circular, the problem would of course be solved. But *is* there such an immediate awareness? The most Moore felt he could say was that there is no conclusive evidence that there is not.[13]

This is not the only difficulty in which realism was involved: When a color-blind man looks at a traffic signal, where are the gray sense-data that he sees? If they are objective, as Moore's theory must hold them to be, they must be somewhere in physical space. Are they in the same region of space as the red and green sense-data that the man with normal vision sees? How can this be? And what about the silvery circular sense-datum that we see when we look at the moon? Where is it? Out there, where the moon itself is, 250,000 miles away?

Still another nest of problems emerged in connection with developments of modern physics. For physics the coin was neither the solid material object that common sense believes it to be nor yet the collection of sense-data that, as we have seen, one philosophical theory held it to be. On the contrary, for physics, it seemed, the coin was mostly empty space, occupied here and there by electrical charges. Thus arose what Sir Arthur Eddington called "the two-tables problem": What is the relation between the table of physics and the table of common sense? If the former is real, must not the latter be an illusion? This was one of the questions to which Russell addressed himself.

Russell

Temperamentally, Moore and Russell differed markedly; it is hardly surprising, therefore, that, despite their agreement on the basic "realistic" thesis, their philosophical theories developed in very different directions. Moore, as we have seen, took his stand on common sense—so much so that he declared that neither the world nor the sciences had ever suggested to him "any philosophical problems. What has suggested philosophical problems to me is things which other philosophers have said about the world or the sciences."[14] He used what he called "analysis" to vindicate common sense by showing that the problems about which philosophers typically worry are the results of muddle and confusion.

Russell, in contrast, "came to philosophy through . . . the wish to find some reason to believe in the truth of mathematics."[15] The difference is fundamental. His introduction to Euclid, when he was eleven, was a "great event," though he was—characteristically—disappointed to discover that the axioms "had to be accepted without proof." What "delighted" him chiefly in mathematics was "the restfulness of mathematical certainty."[16] The animating drive of Russell's philosophy was, in fact, a "quest for certainty" as strong as Descartes's—the quest for a much more certain certainty than those deliverances of common sense that satisfied Moore. But whereas Descartes could assume both the certainty of mathematics and also its applicability to the real world, the intervening period of idealism complicated the situation for Russell. He saw that if idealism were correct, mathematics was but a stage in the Hegelian dialectic and so was contradicted and superseded by successively higher stages. Russell was attracted to the realistic distinction between consciousness and its objects not because it seemed to validate common sense but because it seemed to validate mathematics, by revealing a set of entities, wholly independent of the mind and its synthesizing activities, that are simply there, before the mathematician's mind when he is thinking mathematically.

What else, in addition to the universals contemplated in mathematics, is included in the inventory of the universe? Russell's view evolved over time. Indeed, according to his critics, "evolved" is too generous; his views, they say, changed about as frequently as Picasso's styles in painting. But throughout all these changes he clung to (1) the distinction which, like Moore, he drew between those objects about whose existence we are absolutely certain because we are directly aware of them, and those which we know about, or believe in, by inference, and (2) the desire, in the interest of simplicity and certainty, to reduce as much as possible the numbers of inferred entities. Initially, Russell allowed that the universe also contains, in addition to universals, sense-data, minds, and physical objects. Later, he decided that physical objects could be eliminated, and still later that acts of consciousness—and with them the minds in which these acts were thought to occur—could also go:

> *If there is a subject, it can have a relation to the patch of colour, namely, the sort of relation which we might call awareness. . . . The subject, however, appears to be a logical fiction, like mathematical points and instants. It is introduced, not because observation reveals it, but because it is linguistically convenient and apparently demanded by grammar. . . . The functions that [nominal entities of this kind] appear to perform can always be performed by classes or series or other logical constructions, consisting of less dubious entities. If we are to avoid a perfectly gratuitous assumption, we must dispense with the subject as one of the actual ingredients of the world.*[17]

These conclusions, so far from the common sense of Moore, reflect the main drive of Russell's philosophy: to find an absolutely secure basis for the world that science describes and that we experience in ordinary perception. The data of direct awareness are, he thought, such a basis; since we are not directly aware either of minds or of physical objects— since these are, at best, only inferred entities—he looked for ways to eliminate them from the inventory of real constituents of the universe.

He did not want, of course, to write them off as "mere appearance"— that would mean admitting that physics and psychology were not about the real world. The way to deal with minds and physical objects was to show that they are logical (or grammatical) fictions. Because the grammar and vocabulary of ordinary language are, as Russell thought, very muddled, having grown in a higgledy-piggledy manner, we do not realize that they are fictions, but suppose them all—such nouns as *man* and such descriptive phrases as "the author of *Waverley*"—to denote entities in the real world. By means of what he called "logical construction" Russell held it is possible to replace such nouns and phrases by other terms that *do* denote real entities. Russell's "logical construction" is very different from the constructivism of idealism, which was, of course, anathema to him. What Russell meant is better suggested by such terms as *reduction* or *symbolic substitution*.

Russell first developed this method, whatever it be called, in connection with a problem concerning judgments about nonexistent objects. What is the judgment "Round squares do not exist" about? It is easy, in such a judgment as "Lions roar," to say what the judgment is about: it is about lions and what is asserted is that lions roar. But "Round squares do not exist" cannot be handled in this way, for round squares do not exist and, what is more, the judgment explicitly says that they do not. Hence, if we suppose that there must be round squares in order for there to be an object judged about (just as lions must exist to be the objects judged about), we contradict ourselves. It was from Meinong that Moore and Russell adopted their basic realist premise that in every act of consciousness (and this of course includes acts of judging) there is an object that is independent of, and distinct from, the act. Meinong himself was a sufficiently determined realist to say that there must be an object judged about even in judgments of nonexistence, and he sought to escape from the dilemma just outlined by arguing that while round squares do not exist, they nevertheless subsist. Since it did not take Moore and Russell long to become extremely suspicious of subsistence, if realism was to be saved another analysis of judgments of nonexistence had to be found, which would eliminate the apparent need to suppose that such judgments have nonexistent, but subsistent, objects.

Consider, then, such a phrase as "the author of *Waverley*." It is a mistake, Russell said, to suppose that "the author of *Waverley*" denotes some objectively real entity included in the inventory of items in the universe. "The author of *Waverley*" does not denote what "Scott" denotes, because if it did, "The author of *Waverley* was Scott" would be a tautology, and it is not a tautology because it could be false. The fact is, Russell maintained, that "the author of *Waverley*" does not *denote* anything. What, then, do sentences containing this phrase, such as "The author of *Waverley* was Scott," mean? Well, "The author of *Waverley* was Scott" means that "one and only one man wrote *Waverley*, and he was Scott."

Note that when we get *clear* as to what it means to say that the author of *Waverley* was Scott, the phrase "the author of *Waverley*" has been eliminated from the sentence: we mean just what we meant when we said, "The author of *Waverley* was Scott," but we have now said what we mean in such an unambiguous way that nobody can fall into the error of supposing that the universe contains an entity named "the author of *Waverley*." Russell deals with judgments of nonexistence in an exactly parallel way: "round square," for instance, is a descriptive phrase that does not any more denote an existent object than does the descriptive phrase "the author of *Waverley*." A correct analysis of "Round squares do not exist" eliminates this phrase from the sentence, just as a correct analysis of "The author of *Waverley* was Scott" eliminates that phrase from that sentence.[18]

To return from logic to ontology, words like *matter, physical object, electron, molecule,* Russell held, are also to be treated as descriptive phrases, that is, as terms which do not name anything, and which therefore can be eliminated, rather than as the names of entities of whose existence we are less than certain since their existence depends on the correctness of inferences from what we directly experience. It will be seen how much, even from very early in his career, Russell was concerned with language, not however with rehabilitating common sense language but with constructing a new, pure language in which certainty is achievable, because the terms in this language denote only entities about whose existence there can be no doubt.

What are these entities? Russell's answer was that the ultimate constituents of the universe are not physical objects (tables, chairs, the sun, the moon) but

> a multitude of entities which . . . I shall call "particulars." . . .
> The particulars are to be conceived, not on the analogy of bricks
> in a building, but rather on the analogy of notes in a symphony.
> The ultimate constituents of a symphony (apart from relations)
> are the notes, each of which lasts only for a very short time. We
> may collect together all the notes played by one instrument: these
> may be regarded as the analogues of the successive particulars
> which common sense would regard as successive states of one
> "thing." But the "thing" ought to be regarded as no more "real"
> or "substantial" than, for example, the role of the trombone.[19]

Since each note, in this analogy, corresponds to a sense-datum that some observer has directly experienced, a physical object (e.g., the moon) is not a single, persistent entity located 250,000 miles away from us; the moon is a vast assemblage of sense-data of many different shapes, sizes, and colors, the assemblage that all possible observers have experienced and will yet experience of the moon. Each observer's sense-data fall into a pattern, or "perspective," like the pattern of notes that constitute the role of the trombone. My sense-data of the moon are within my private three-dimensional spatial perspective, and every other observer's are within *his* private perspective, all of these private spaces fitting into the public space of the real world.[20]

This analysis applies also to the problem as to where, on the realistic thesis, illusions and hallucinations are, e.g., to Moore's worry about where the gray sense-data experienced by the color-blind man are located. Russell's answer was that they lie in the private three-dimensional

14

space of the color-blind man, but that this space (along with the private three-dimensional spaces of men with normal vision) fits into public space. Russell's solution is, as Moore would say, "Pickwickian." Whether a Pickwickian solution is thought to be satisfactory is perhaps a matter of temperament, but it is important to see that Russell's solution, however Pickwickian, is also only programmatic. He did not actually carry through a "logical construction," or "elimination," of matter, still less of mind. He merely sketched out the lines along which such a construction might possibly be worked out. If the program could be carried through to completion, the falcon would be firmly reoriented in a real world— certainly not the commonsensical world of Moore, and admittedly a neutral, value-free world which the falcon might not much enjoy—but still a real world.

But *can* Russell's program be completed? That is the question, and Russell himself could not answer it. He had wanted, with Descartes, to vindicate the claims of physics; in the end, he confessed that he believed in the world of physics "without good grounds."

Logical positivism

Russell's program of logical construction (or reduction) was launched in the years just before World War I. A similarly ambitious but much more radical program was launched by a group of thinkers in Vienna in the years following that war. These thinkers, who initially called themselves the Vienna Circle and later, as the group expanded, became known as logical positivists, differed much among themselves, but for the purposes of this sketch it will be more useful to concentrate, so far as possible, on the beliefs and attitudes which they shared. In the first place, they were all passionately antimetaphysical. In this respect they differed from Moore and Russell, both of whom had aimed at ascertaining the true nature of reality. The positivists, in contrast, held that realism, as much as idealism, is nonsense. The positivist, they held, does not contradict metaphysicians, but merely says, "I don't understand you. What you say asserts nothing at all!"[21]

The second point on which all positivists agreed was that it is only in the sciences—and especially in physics—that we have anything that can properly be called *knowledge*. If we want—and who does not?—to increase the amount of reliable information available to us, we should therefore extend the use of scientific method in all domains and by its means test every assertion, eliminating any that do not measure up. Why is it that science yields reliable information? It is because all assertions made in the sciences are warranted by experiment and controlled observation. For instance, when the existence of an ether pervading space was questioned, physicists designed an experiment that would settle the issue.

They reasoned that if the ether were present and if a beam of light were first transmitted across and then along the direction of the flow of ether, there would be a discernible difference in the times of transmission. Since no difference was in fact observed, they concluded that the ether does not exist. The term *ether* should therefore be eliminated from the vocabulary of science as a meaningless word.

Generalizing from what they thus took to be the essential feature of scientific method, the positivists formulated what came to be called the Verifiability Principle. This asserted that the method of verifying a proposition is the meaning of that proposition. Since it follows that propositions for which no means of verification exist are literally meaningless, the positivists saw that they had in their hands an instrument that would totally destroy metaphysics, once and for all. To the earliest positivists the Verifiability Principle seemed "the justified unassailable nucleus" of their whole position, and all the positivists adopted the principle in one form or another. It proved anything but unassailable, however, as we shall shortly see.

There is a third point on which all positivists agreed. This was the importance of "modern" logic and the analysis it made possible. Here, of course, they learned much from Russell. The aim of logical analysis, according to the positivists, is to clarify the statements that are made in the sciences, in order to reveal their true cognitive content. We have seen that, though "The author of *Waverley* was Scott" is true, unwary readers —even the literary historian who makes the assertion—may attribute a false cognitive content to it until its precise cognitive content has been exposed by analysis. The positivists recognized that scientists could go astray in a similar way. Without a logical analysis there was a danger that physicists themselves—let alone philosophers and laymen—might misread such a true statement as "Electrons exist" and attribute a metaphysical content to it.

Underlying logical analysis as Russell and the positivists practiced it was the conviction that, when language has been correctly analyzed, it will be isomorphic with the world; the linguistic relational structures that are exposed by means of analysis exactly mirror the relational structures that characterize the world. As Russell wrote in his introduction to Wittgenstein's *Tractatus*, "There must . . . be something in common between the structure of the sentence and the structure of the fact."[22]

The *Tractatus* was intended to display the isomorphism that, as Wittgenstein and Russell believed, must exist between the basic structure of sentences and the basic structure of facts. Wittgenstein had been impressed by an account of a trial arising out of an automobile accident, in which the lawyers used dolls and miniature cars to represent the real people and automobiles involved in the accident.[23] It seemed to Wittgenstein that propositions must represent the world in the same way. "We picture facts to ourselves," he wrote, and the picture "must have something in common with what it depicts."[24] What it has in common is "its pictorial form."[25] Because the doll used in the trial occupied the same place in the miniature car that the man occupied in the real car, it represents the accident truly. "A picture agrees with reality or fails to agree; it is correct or incorrect, true or false."[26] Just as it is in virtue of pictorial form that pictures are either true or false, so it is in virtue of logical form that propositions are true or false.

What, then, is the basic logical form of propositions? Since "every statement about complexes can be resolved into a statement about their constituents,"[27] eventually analysis must terminate on simple, unanalyzable elements: "It is obvious that the analysis of propositions must bring us to elementary propositions which consist of names in immediate combination."[28] Each such name is a "primitive sign," since it is incapable of further "dissection." Accordingly, "the meanings of primitive signs" must be "explained by means of elucidations," since further analysis is impossible. "Elucidations are propositions that contain the primitive signs."[29] Since the names that occur in elucidations "are like points," the function of elucidations is to draw our attention to those simple, atomic facts pointed to by the names the elucidations contain.[30]

The *Tractatus* was a work on logic, not on ontology. Hence Wittgenstein thought it sufficient to show what follows from the nature of logic about the sort of basic structure the world must have. For instance, "The world divides into facts,"[31] and each of these facts is completely independent of every other. And again, "Each item can be the case or not the case while everything else remains the same."[32] Since the positivists, in contrast, were interested in logic chiefly as a preliminary for, and a clarification of, science, they had to go beyond the *Tractatus* and formulate a program for ascertaining in detail what the basic structure actually is. Accordingly, they proposed, first, to reduce all complex scientific statements to elementary statements, and second, to provide elucidations for these elementary statements. But what, exactly, is the nature of an elucidation? According to Russell, an elucidation was the report of the occurrence of a sense-datum, but sense-data seemed too subjective to the positivists, and, after a good deal of backing and filling, most of them decided that elucidations were what they called "protocol sentences."

A protocol sentence records an observation—either a simple observation or, as in the following example proposed by Otto Neurath, one of the early positivists, an observation of an observation—

> *Otto's protocol at 3:17 o'clock:* [*At 3:16 o'clock Otto said to himself: (at 3:15 o'clock there was a table in the room perceived by Otto)*].[33]

Analysis begins from a sentence in the "system language" in which

17

scientific assertions are formulated—say, the sentence, "The ether does not exist." From this one deduces a sentence in the protocol language—say the sentence, "If the ether does not exist, then no time difference is observed by Michelson and Morley." One then compares this sentence with the actual protocols of Michelson and Morley. Michelson: "No time difference observed." Morley: "No time difference observed." Accordingly, the sentence in the system language, "The ether does not exist," *means* "No time difference observed." That is, it means the protocol sentences that verify it.

Applying this method of analysis to sentences about God (the atheist's assertion that he does not exist, as well as the theist's that he exists), about the Absolute, about ultimate reality, it was easy to *show* that, since they are unverifiable, they are meaningless. Equally so are all normative sentences, for instance, those about the good and the beautiful. Some of the positivists were content simply to write off all sentences containing normative predicates as pseudostatements, but others allowed them a kind of use after all. Thus, "Capital punishment is wrong" tells us nothing whatever about the world, but it permits the speaker to express his disapproval of capital punishment, and it may persuade listeners to disapprove of capital punishment also. Carnap was even willing to allow a kind of use for metaphysical statements: "They serve for the *expression of the general attitude of a person towards life . . .* his emotional and volitional reaction to the environment, to society, to the tasks to which he devotes himself, to the misfortunes that befall him." Metaphysics is a kind of poetry, but since it lacks the expressive power of poetry, metaphysics is "inadequate."[34]

Thus, the positivists proposed to put the falcon at ease by assuring him that what he thought were real problems are only pseudoproblems. They believed they could relieve his metaphysical itch by eliminating all meaningless words from his vocabulary and by clarifying all the meaningful words in it. When their program was fully carried out, the falcon would find himself living in a world in which all the questions he could ask would be answerable by a unified science in terms of protocol sentences in the language of physicalism. This point of view was effectively stated by Wittgenstein near the end of the *Tractatus:*

> *Doubt can exist only where a question exists, a question only where an answer exists, and an answer only where something can be said. . . . The solution of the problem of life is seen in the vanishing of the problem.*[35]

Wittgenstein was eventually to find that a different therapy was needed, but even before he realized this, the positivist program had collapsed, for the Verifiability Principle, which had looked so straightforward, proved to involve one puzzle after another.

For instance, are the sentences in the protocol language incorrigible?

The positivists first assumed, and subsequently hoped to show, that they are. Thus, for "Otto" in the protocol sentence quoted above, it is possible to substitute "the body at such-and-such a place," and for the report of perceiving a table, it is possible to substitute a description of some movement by the body in question. For instance, the body might be instructed, whenever it perceives a table, to push a button or a lever, instead of reporting that it perceived one. But even this radical behaviorism did not save the incorrigibility of protocol sentences, according to Neurath:

> There is no way of taking conclusively established pure protocol sentences as the starting point of the sciences. . . . *We are like sailors who must rebuild their ship on the open sea, never able to dismantle it in dry-dock and to reconstruct it there out of the best materials. . . . Vague linguistic conglomerations always remain in one way or another as components of the ship. If vagueness is diminished at one point, it may well be increased at another.*[36]

But if it be allowed that protocol sentences are corrigible, then they require verification, and to admit that they require verification is to become involved in an infinite regress. System sentences are to be verified by other protocol sentences, which are to be verified by other protocol sentences, and these in their turn by still others. No process of verification can ever be completed.

To put this differently: the positivist program had assumed that the whole structure of science could be firmly based on a set of incorrigible protocol sentences, like a ladder resting securely on the ground. It now looked as if the sciences were a floating spiral, open at both ends.

> *In unified science we try to construct a non-contradictory system of protocol sentences and non-protocol sentences. . . . When a new sentence is presented to us we compare it with the system at our disposal, and determine whether or not it conflicts with that system. If the sentence does conflict with the system, we may discard it as useless (or false). . . . One may, on the other hand,* accept *the sentence and so change the system that it remains consistent even after the adjunction of the new sentence. The sentence would then be called "true."*[37]

Readers of this passage were astonished to find a positivist reverting to the idealist theory that the truth of a proposition depends on the degree of its coherence in a system.

As another example of the difficulties the Verifiability Principle encountered, consider the question, "What is the status of the Verifiability Principle itself?" On the positivist view, all meaningful sentences are either analytic (i.e., tautologies) or are verifiable by empirical means. Clearly, the principle is not analytic. Is it, then, an empirical generalization and, if so, how can it be verified? A. J. Ayer, whose *Language, Truth, and Logic* had been an early and influential exposition of positivism, finally came around to saying:

> *The Vienna Circle tended to ignore this difficulty: but it seems to me fairly clear that what they were in fact doing was to adopt the verification principle as a convention. . . . It became prescriptive with the suggestion that . . . only statements which were capable of being either true or false should be regarded as literally meaningful.*[38]

But if the Verifiability Principle is only a recommendation, or suggestion, that the terms *meaningful* and *meaningless* be used in a certain way, then the whole positivistic program as it had been originally conceived has really been abandoned. There is no longer one ideal language, whose structure is revealed by logical analysis and which, when revealed, exactly mirrors the world. Rather, there are now a variety of languages, none of which is isomorphic with the world, and all of which can be recommended on different grounds.

This radical change in point of view was also implicit in a distinction Carnap came to draw between what he called internal and external questions regarding language. Carnap pointed out that

> *we must distinguish two kinds of questions of existence: first, questions of the existence of certain entities* . . . within the [linguistic] framework; *we call them* internal questions; *and second, questions concerning the existence or reality* of the system of entities as a whole, *called* external questions.[39]

The scientific system provides rules for answering internal questions, so that, once we have accepted this system, we can decide whether King Arthur existed, whether unicorns and centaurs are real or imaginary, and whether there is a piece of white paper on my desk now. But these are all questions that are internal to the "thing language," and

> *To accept the thing world means nothing more than to accept a certain form of language. . . . The thing language . . . works indeed with a high degree of efficiency for most purposes of everyday life. . . . However, it would be wrong to describe this situation by saying: "The fact of the efficiency of the thing language is confirming evidence for the reality of the thing world"; we should rather say instead: "This fact makes it advisable to accept the thing language." . . . Let us be . . . tolerant in permitting linguistic forms.*[40]

We have now traced, from its start at the beginning of the century, one more or less continuously developing line of philosophical thought. It had begun as a revolt against idealism, but by midcentury, it had almost completely reversed itself and was, in many respects, more idealistic than realistic. Though it had not returned to the idealist doctrine of the relativity of experience to categories or conceptual forms, it had now affirmed a not very different version of relativism—the relativity of "the world" to language. Since thought and language are intimately related, the shift of attention from the former to the latter is less significant than might appear. What is chiefly significant is that once more the attempt had been abandoned to establish an objective reality independent of man. In a word, we have witnessed a return to a linguistic version of the Kantian paradigm.

What other philosophical developments occurred during this half-century? Three must be mentioned even in a sketch like this: the philosophy of organism, instrumentalism, and phenomenology-existentialism.

Whitehead

The philosophy of organism was philosophy in the grand manner—philosophy on the same scale as Hegel's and therefore an anachronism in the twentieth century. But in contrast to Hegel it was conceived in the realistic spirit that had animated Moore and Russell and the other opponents of idealism. Of course, Moore's interest in common sense beliefs left him indifferent to Whitehead's vast speculative synthesis, but it may be said that Whitehead attempted to do what Russell would have liked to do, had Russell not set himself so high a standard for certainty. Whitehead's deepest conviction was that "the ultimate natures of things lie together in a harmony which excludes mere arbitrariness."[41] He was a rationalist in the sense that he held this harmony to be *intelligible* to the human mind. The function of philosophy is to "seek the form in the facts," to make explicit the pattern that is otherwise only implicitly present in the social system and so only "ignorantly entertained." But because "we are finite beings," grasp of the pattern "in its totality . . . is denied us."[42] Because philosophy is an "attempt to express the infinity of the universe in terms of the limitations of language,"[43] every formulation of the pattern will itself sooner or later descend into the "inactive commonplace." Hence the work of philosophy is never finished.

These sentences show that Whitehead's view of language was diametrically opposed to the view of Russell, the positivists, and the tractarian Wittgenstein that the business of philosophy is to construct an ideal language that is isomorphic with the facts into which the world divides. Because he saw philosophy as "akin to poetry" and to mysticism, rather than to logic,[44] Whitehead could afford to be speculative, as Russell could not.

Whitehead also shared the interest of almost all twentieth-century philosophers in science. But he modeled his theory less on what he took to be the implications of scientific method (as with the positivists) than on what he took to be the discoveries of physics in this century. He thought that the science of the eighteenth and nineteenth centuries had had a deleterious impact on man's view of himself and of the world he lived in. It had, he thought, "bifurcated" nature. On the one side was man, with his hopes and fears, his thoughts and emotions. On the other side was nature, but nature, according to nineteenth-century physics, "is a dull affair, soundless, scentless, colourless; merely the hurrying of material, endlessly, meaninglessly."[45] Such a physics, Whitehead believed, was responsible for Eddington's two-tables problem, and the trouble, he thought, was that most men had concluded that science requires them to admit that the table of perception is not real, but only a subjective product of the interaction between light waves, optic nerve, and cortex. On this view, "the poets are entirely mistaken"; it is we, not the nightingale, to whom Keats should have addressed his Ode. But Whitehead held the poets to have been correct in believing that nature carries with it "a message of tremendous significance" and that it "cannot be divorced from its aesthetic values." Or from its moral implication. For the occurrence of every event is fully determined by the occurrence of antecedent events, according to the theories of nineteenth-century physics, and is therefore in principle predictable. But if the molecules blindly run, as nineteenth-century physics proclaimed they do, then, Whitehead pointed out, since "the human body is a collection of molecules . . . the human body blindly runs," and free will and moral responsibility are "swept away."[46]

It was thus the poetic, moral, and humanistic view of man and the universe that Whitehead wanted to rehabilitate, and he thought that recent developments in science—especially relativity theory and quantum physics—provided a way of doing so. He believed that the basic concepts of the "new" physics could be generalized to form a "categoreal" scheme providing a unified, instead of a bifurcated, account of the world. This scheme, which involved a "category of the ultimate," eight "categories of existence," twenty-seven "categories of explanation," and nine "categoreal obligations," is much too complex and difficult for a short summary, but perhaps it will be possible at least to suggest how the bifurcation of nature was to be healed.

The ultimate constituents of the universe, according to the scheme, are neither Russell's "particulars" nor material things nor egos: they are events, and each event is the "grasping into unity," or "prehending," of other events. It is easy to understand the notion of "prehending into unity" at the human level—to perceive a castle across the valley or a planet in the sky is to prehend these objects and myself into the unity of a single experience. But Whitehead held that an electron is equally a center of prehensive activity; to limit the activity of prehending to the human level of conscious perception and cognition would be to abandon realism and lapse into the idealism that Whitehead wanted to avoid. Thus the castle and the planet are prehending (feeling) me whilst I am perceiving them. What are the castle and the planet and I save three of the endless variety of standpoints from which, and into which, they, and I, are prehended, or felt? Every event in the universe is prehending every other of the "simultaneous events throughout the rest of the universe." What makes each event unique is that each feels all other events from a particular standpoint, or in a particular "perspective."

Further, a prehending center is not merely a passive contemplator of all the other manifold "aspects of nature" from its particular point of view. Each center is a life, a process having a beginning and ending in a consummation: this, again, is as true of an electron as of a human life, and for the same reason. Each involves a principle of selection and exclusion; each is "a unit of emergent value." Hence, whereas nineteenth-century physics had regarded the physical world as inert matter, fundamentally different from man, quantum physics (at least in Whitehead's view) requires us to think of nature as involving processes that, even at the most elementary level, are not different in kind from human cognition and volition.

Thus Whitehead offered the falcon what, presumably, it longed for— a world whose nature was such that the falcon could feel at home in it. Why, then, did the philosophy of organism not "take on"? One answer, surely, is that it was too difficult to be readily understood. But that is not the whole answer. Another reason is that in the 1920s and 1930s, when Whitehead was developing his theory, positivism was at the height of its influence, and not merely among philosophers. Whitehead wrote as if the Verifiability Principle had never been heard of; at a time when philosophers were contracting their horizons and concentrating on "piecemeal, detailed and verifiable results," he indulged in speculation on a large scale. But perhaps the most fundamental reason is that he really did not appreciate the depths of the falcon's distress. Whitehead, who had been born in 1861, was a civilized, cultivated English gentleman. If he experienced those "deep disquietudes" that are the center of Wittgenstein's later writings and the main preoccupation of the protagonists of Sartre's novels, he did not show it in his writings. Because his theory did not meet the mood of the times, it missed what was to become the wave of the future.

Dewey and instrumentalism

The philosophy of organism was virtually the work of one man. In contrast, instrumentalism had its origins in the work of James and Peirce, and was carried forward by many writers, during the first half of the century. Nonetheless, Dewey was so clearly its preeminent figure that it is fair to concentrate our attention on his views. Like almost all philosophers, of whatever school, Dewey was impressed by the sciences, but whereas Whitehead had focused on science as giving us clues to the ontological pattern hidden behind the flux of change, and the positivists had focused on science as a procedure for eliminating nonsense and advancing knowledge, Dewey focused on science as an instrument for improving men's "traffic with nature" and so making their lives "freer and more secure."

The fact that Dewey's emphasis was on results, rather than—as was the case with most of his contemporaries—on truth, is fundamental for understanding instrumentalism. "The two limits of every unit of thinking," he wrote,

> *are a perplexed, troubled or confused situation at the beginning and a cleared-up, unified, resolved situation at the close. . . . In between [are] states of thinking.*[47]

That is, thinking starts only when something blocks an ongoing activity (a man out for a walk in the country comes to a stream too wide to be jumped); thinking ends when action can be resumed (the man recalls having seen a log a short way back, fetches the log, finds that it is indeed long enough to bridge the stream, and so continues his walk). Thinking, in this case, has produced "a situation that is clear, coherent, settled, harmonious." Of course the situation will not *stay* coherent and harmonious. New problems are bound to arise—that is what life is. But we can hope, by reflective self-criticism, to learn how to improve our problem-solving techniques and so solve our problems more efficiently. "Improving our problem-solving techniques" is advancing from common sense, rule-of-thumb, trial-and-error methods to scientific methods (quantification, controlled experimentation, etc.); "learning how by reflective self-criticism to improve" is logic. That is, the norms in terms of which various human activities are assessed and evaluated are not abstract, ideal rules imposed from outside as infallible judges; rather, they arise from critical reflection on these activities and what they accomplish. Logic, in a word, is a human activity and, like all other human activities, it reflects human needs, and it changes in response to changes in them.

Thus Dewey's conception of logic differed radically from Russell's. The Russellians thought Dewey psychologized logic; he thought they etherealized it. They held logic to be the analysis of propositions, an analysis that terminates in logical simples. "A proposition has one and only one complete analysis," Wittgenstein wrote.[48] For Dewey, in contrast, so far from there being only one complete analysis, it made more sense to talk about "logics" than about "logic." Since logic is but the reflective criticism of actual problem-solving techniques, there are as many logics as there are different kinds of problems that need solving. There is, for instance, a logic of historical studies, which is the critical assessment, by historians, of their own methods of interpreting documents, and this logic is quite different from the logic of physics. And, so far from logic being terminating in logical simples, there are no such simples; or rather, there are simples, of course, but they are merely the end products of a particularly abstract and rarified activity, the activity of logical analysis. They have no superior ontological status.

> *Realism argues that we [must] admit that something eulogistically termed Reality . . . is but a complex made up of fixed, mutually independent simples. . . . For instrumentalism, however, the alleged . . . results of abstraction and analysis are perfectly real; but they are real, like everything else, where they are real. . . . But there is no reason for supposing that they exist elsewhere in the same manner.*[49]

When, for instance, do we experience a blue sense-datum? Typically, when it is the stain by which we recognize a cellular structure. But recognition of a cellular structure is part of one of those "units of thinking" that are intermediate between a confused and a cleared-up situation. Sense-data, in a word, "are not objects but means, instrumentalities, of knowledge: things by which we know rather than things known." The realist has erected sense-data into the ultimate constituents of the universe only because he "ignores the contextual situation. . . . [His sense-data] exist only within the procedure."[50]

So too for the protocol sentences of the positivists. Since the aim of the positivists was to put science on a secure basis, they were naturally disturbed when their protocol sentences proved to be corrigible. But Dewey, for his part, took it for granted that sentences in the protocol language, as well as sentences in the system language (to use, for the moment, the language of the positivists), are corrigible. Nothing can be absolutely secure, not even science. But science is secure enough if, by its means, we manage continuously to improve our ongoing traffic with nature and with other men.

Thus our metaphor of a spiral open at both ends, in contrast to a ladder resting firmly on the ground, would have been congenial to Dewey. If challenged by the realists to characterize the nature of this spiral, Dewey would not have evaded them by adopting the positivists' line, "To ask about the nature of Reality is a meaningless question"; he would have answered, "It is experience." And what is experience? It is not a passing show at which we are merely spectators. We are primarily agents, doers, not observers, and the concepts by which we organize experience are not more than instruments that we revise or discard if they prove to be ineffective tools in our traffic with nature.

Experience is thus anything but the object of consciousness-of. Consciousness, for Dewey, is not a transparent element that *contains* experience; it occurs *within* experience, and just at those points where problems arise that impede action. Hence consciousness "is only a very small and shifting portion of experience." [51]

And, just as we find consciousness in experience and facts in experience, so also we find values in experience. "Experience actually presents esthetic and moral traits." Such traits are as real as are "the traits found by physical inquiry." They all stand "on precisely the same level" ontologically speaking, in that all are found in experience. Indeed, in a way, values are prior: "Things are objects to be treated, used, acted upon and with, enjoyed and endured, even more than things to be known. They are things *had* before they are things cognized." [52]

Thus Dewey rejected both the old metaphysical notion of a realm of transcendent values and also the positivist claim that sentences about values are noncognitive. Such sentences may of course be expressive and persuasive, but they are also as factual as are statements about any other facts. Just as a fact is an element in our experience that has—so far—survived criticism, so a value is an enjoying that has proved to be—so far—a satisfaction. Some philosophers have argued that in order to escape subjectivism and to be able to draw a real "distinction between likings and that which is worth liking, between the desired and the desirable, between the is and the ought," it is necessary to be armed with an absolutely valid criterion. This is not the case. Whenever we weigh the claim of some liking by the test of experience, we make a viable distinction between "genuine, valid goods" and "counterfeit goods."

But to make use of the test of experience is simply to apply science (conceived as the method of intelligent inquiry) to questions about values, which have too long been the preserve of theology and other dogmatisms.

> *What the method of intelligence . . . will accomplish, if once it be tried, is for the result of trial to determine. . . . To claim that intelligence is a better method than its alternatives, authority, imitation, caprice and ignorance, prejudice and passion, is hardly an excessive claim.* [53]

Dewey was, as these lines show, both an optimist and a democrat. He believed in democracy because it is

> *the best means so far found, for realizing ends that lie in the wide domain of human relationships and the development of human personality. . . .*
>
> *The foundation of democracy is faith in the capacities of human nature; faith in human intelligence and in the power of pooled and coöperative experience. It is not belief that these things are*

26

complete but that if given a show they will grow and be able to generate progressively the knowledge and wisdom needed to guide collective action.[54]

To many people today this faith in the efficacy of "pooled intelligence" will sound naïve. Not everybody any longer shares Dewey's confidence that the problems created by technology can by technology be solved. And what about the alienation and dissociation of sensibility that so many people feel today? Here again Dewey's diagnosis may seem superficial. He thought there is nothing new in these anxieties. Indeed, since they stem from man's relative inability to control his environment, they were much more characteristic of primitive than of twentieth-century man. But wherever and whenever, for whatever reason, man has "distrusted himself," he has sought "to get beyond and above himself." This pathetic quest for certainty, this desire to escape from contingency, not only explains belief in gods; it also explains the philosopher's belief in a transcendent reality that is "universal, fixed and immutable," and also his insistence on absolute truths, absolute values, absolutely reliable sense-data, or an ideal language that is isomorphic with the world.

Moderate anxiety is of course reasonable—after all, the world is an uncertain place—and it is also socially useful. In contrast to dogmatic assurance, it is a spur to improving our instruments of control. But extreme anxiety is unreasonable, since it ignores the empirical evidence that intelligent inquiry does indeed pay off.

Of course, the acceptability of this account depends on the falcon's being contented to live in the relativistic and uncertain world that Dewey allows him. It depends, that is, on anxiety's not being existential, on its not being rooted in the divisiveness of consciousness or in the fact that we have been "thrown" into an indifferent and absurd universe. Dewey himself would have thought that belief in the absurdity of man's existence is neurotic; existentialist critics can reply that Dewey was insensitive to man's deepest needs and blind to his real nature. Who is correct? We can only say that, for the present at least, the culture as a whole seems to have moved away from Dewey's view of man.

Phenomenology-existentialism

Like realism, the phenomenological movement started at the turn of the century, from Brentano's and Meinong's assertion that consciousness is directional, or intentional, in nature. Unlike realism, which had a relatively short life, the phenomenological movement is still very vigorous and has spread from Germany, where it was launched, to the rest of the continent and to the United States. In this sketch we shall concentrate mainly on Husserl, the "father" of phenomenology, but we shall also note some representative subsequent developments at the hands of Heidegger and Sartre.

Though Husserl's starting point was the same as Russell's and Moore's, phenomenology developed in a very different way. First, as regards consciousness itself: From the fact that consciousness is always consciousness-of and that there is no mediating idea between the mind and its object, the realists concluded that consciousness can be ignored; with their interest in validating science, they concentrated on the object, which the new intentional view of consciousness had shown to be uncontaminated, as they maintained, by mind and its "constructions." And their contention was later reinforced by a behaviorism which, starting with James, sanctioned by Russell, and supported by the positivists' Verifiability Principle, held that sentences containing assertions about inner states can be eliminated and replaced by sentences about bodily states.

For Husserl this was an appalling mistake. In his view, if one attends carefully, one discovers that, so far from being directly aware only of sense-data, one is directly aware of an immense variety of entities and acts. Husserl maintained that the realists—and all previous philosophers —wholly overlooked this vast realm because observation of it requires the cultivation of a special attitude which he called "phenomenological reduction."

Second, unlike most of the philosophers we have considered, Husserl was utterly opposed to recent developments in science—indeed, to the whole development of science since Galileo. Scientific method, which Dewey admired because of its practical achievements, Husserl condemned because he regarded it as based on a series of false assumptions. Einstein's theories, for instance, are about an "idealized and naïvely objectivized nature." He "does nothing to reformulate the space and time in which our actual life takes place." [55] And what is bad enough in the natural sciences is still worse in psychology. Aping physics and chemistry, it tries to be as external and as quantified as if its object were nature, not man. In a word, it studies behavior, not "the proper essence of spirit."

Some of what Husserl says about science could have been written by Whitehead, who was as critical as Husserl of the metaphysical assumptions that led scientists to bifurcate nature, or, in Husserl's terminology, to ignore "the environing world of life." But Husserl would have had no use for the philosophy of organism. It was, from his point of view, as "relativistic" as all earlier philosophies had been. Just as realism of the Russellian type had presented us with only a limited view of reality— one relative to its assumption about the atomicity of the world and to the way it draws the distinction between direct acquaintance and inferential knowledge, so Whiteheadian realism presents us with a different but equally limited view of reality—one relative to Whitehead's assumptions about the interconnectedness of all things.

Whereas such considerations led Whitehead to conclude that completely objective knowledge, even in science, is impossible, Husserl simply decided that we must free ourselves from all presuppositions and so achieve, not merely one more view of reality, but a face-to-face confrontation with reality itself in all its purity. A science based on such a presuppositionless confrontation with reality itself would be apodictically certain, and such a science must somehow be possible, since (according to Husserl's reasoning) to deny its possibility is to fall into contradiction. For consider: Do the relativists, who argue that there is no absolutely valid knowledge, claim that their arguments are valid? They must do so, but then they are asserting what they deny. They are maintaining that they have an absolutely valid knowledge that there is no absolutely valid knowledge.

It is easy to see how Dewey would have replied to this line of reasoning. He would have pointed out that an objectively valid science is not at all necessary to render our traffic with nature freer and more secure. For that we need only a progressively improving science. We would need an absolutely objective science only if it were reasonable to hope to render our traffic with nature absolutely free and absolutely secure. But what do *absolutely free* and *absolutely secure* mean? Such terms, Dewey would have said, merely reflect the insecurity and instability of those like Husserl who resort to them.

A quest for certainty was indeed the ruling passion of Husserl's life. In 1906, for instance, he entered in his diary, "I have been through enough torments from lack of clarity and from doubt that wavers back and forth. . . . I must win clarity, else I cannot live; I cannot bear life unless I can believe that I shall achieve it."[56] Thus Husserl shared Russell's animating drive, but whereas Russell sadly confessed that most of what he believed he believed "without grounds," Husserl concluded not only that an absolutely objective science must, logically, be possible but that it was actually within his grasp. He held that what transcendentally reduced observation accomplishes is precisely the stripping away of all presuppositions. This stripping away, progressively, of presuppositions brings one into the presence of reality itself, and a science starting from such a presuppositionless confrontation with reality will indeed be objectively valid.

But what is transcendentally reduced observation? And what is the nature of that absolutely pure reality encountered in it? To begin with, Husserl contrasted the stance, or attitude, that he desires us to adopt with what he called "the natural standpoint." In this standpoint

I am aware of a world, spread out in space endlessly, and in time becoming and become, without end. . . . [Moreover,] this world is not there for me as a mere world of facts and affairs, but, with the same immediacy, as a world of values, a world of goods, a practical

29

world . . . *with value-characters such as beautiful or ugly, agreeable or disagreeable, pleasant or unpleasant. . . . To know [this world] more trustworthily, more perfectly than the naïve lore of experience is able to do . . . is the goal of the* sciences of the natural standpoint.[57]

It would be hard to find a better description of what Dewey called "experience" or of what Moore thought of as the world of common sense. But whereas they saw no reason for shifting out of the natural standpoint—indeed, they saw every reason for remaining in it—Husserl's whole philosophy depends on making such a shift.

Instead now of remaining at this standpoint, we propose to alter it radically . . . we set it as it were "out of action," *we* "disconnect it," "bracket it." *It still remains there like the bracketed in the bracket, like the disconnected outside the connexional system.*[58]

Bracketing, at least as far as this passage goes, thus amounts to suspending judgment—neither believing nor disbelieving. Now it is obvious that if I succeed in suspending my belief in everything that can possibly be suspended, then whatever survives suspension is indubitable and hence apodictically certain.

What can remain over when the whole world is bracketed? . . . Consciousness in itself has a being of its own which in its absolute uniqueness of nature remains unaffected by the phenomenological disconnexion. *It therefore remains over as a "phenomenological residuum," as a region of Being which is in principle unique, and can become in fact the field of a new science —the science of Phenomenology.*[59]

"Residuum" is an unfortunate term; it is not true that a part of the content of experience is lost in the course of bracketing and that a part remains. No content is lost; everything remains. Yet, as a result of bracketing, everything is different.

Let us suppose that we are looking with pleasure in a garden at a blossoming apple-tree, at the fresh young green of the lawn, and so forth. . . . Between . . . the real man or the real perception on the one hand, and the real apple-tree on the other, there subsist real relations. . . . Let us now pass over to the phenomenological standpoint. The transcendent world enters its "bracket." . . . Together with the whole physical and psychical world the real subsistence of the objective relation between perception and perceived is suspended; and yet a relation between perception and perceived (as likewise between the pleasure and that which pleases) is obviously left over, a relation which in its essential nature comes before us in "pure immanence." [60]

That is to say, when I "bracket" the apple tree, I merely suspend my belief in its independent existence as an object. I continue to experience myself experiencing (and taking pleasure in) its fresh green color, and I can now concentrate my attention on this relationship between my experiencing and that which I experience—a relationship that I was likely to ignore as long as I was in the natural standpoint and busily reflecting on what I could do with the tree: when the apples would be ripe, how much they would bring in the market, and so on.

As a result of bracketing, my attitude has become wholly disinterested; I observe that which I never before observed, the essential nature of "pure" consciousness. In this transcendentally reduced observation I encounter a multitude of mental acts—perceivings, thinkings, imaginings, dreamings, and the like—and a multitude of different objects intended by these diverse acts. Suppose, for instance, that I bracket the experience that in the natural standpoint we call looking at a die. What do I find?

> *I see in pure reflection that "this" die is given continuously as an objective unity in a multiform and changeable multiplicity of manners of appearing, which belong determinately to it. These, in their temporal flow, . . . flow away in the unity of a synthesis, such that in them "one and the same" . . . identical die appears, now in "near appearances," now in "far appearances." . . . Thus the near-thing, as "the same," appears now from this "side," now from that; and the "visual perspectives" change. . . . Always we find the feature in question as a unity belonging to a passing flow of "multiplicities."* [61]

This account of what we actually experience when we look at a die can be compared with Moore's account of what we see when we look at two coins. Husserl's account is surely far more reliable; Moore's is colored by an unconscious presupposition about the superior ontological status of atomistic, encapsulated sense-data, each itself and not another thing. But Husserl's better reporting of his viewing of the die as it actually occurs hardly requires a phenomenological reduction. Dewey, for instance, or Whitehead could have given, and indeed did give, similar descriptions of sense perception, without the aid of bracketing.

Husserl's next move was to report his observation of "essences" in transcendentally reduced experience. What is an essence? It is that about an object that makes it this sort of object rather than another sort of object—that about a die that makes it a die and not an apple tree, that about an apple tree that makes it an apple tree and not a die. It was fortunate for Husserl that he was able to observe essences, because he did not want to have to allow that we are directly aware merely of appearances of an object; to admit this would have involved him in all the puzzles that plagued realism. What, for instance, is the relation between an appearance of a die and the die that is presumably its cause?

One of the great virtues of phenomenology, in Husserl's view, was that transcendentally reduced experience "consists in the self-appearance, the self-exhibiting, the self-giving" of objects themselves. That is, in transcendentally reduced experience we do not have to infer the existence of a die that is not directly present from data that are directly present; we directly intuit the essence of the die (as it appears).

So much, by way of brief summary, for intentional objects, i.e., the objective pole of pure consciousness. But we not only observe the die (or the apple tree); we also observe ourselves examining the die and enjoying the apple tree. And what is more, just as we observe, not the appearance of the apple tree, but the apple tree as it appears, so we observe, not the appearances of our enjoying, but our enjoying as it appears. Similarly, of course, for all the other mental (intentional) acts—perceiving, thinking, dreaming, imagining, and the rest. The essence of these acts is self-evidently present to us in transcendentally reduced experience, just as the essence of the die, the essence of the apple tree, and the essence of physical objects generally are also directly present to us.

These directly present, and therefore self-evident, intentional acts and intentional objects were to be the basis for the "objectively valid science" that was Husserl's goal. But unfortunately this science remained as programmatic as the very different program of the positivists. Instead, Husserl's energy was distracted into the Pandora's box of metaphysical and epistemological problems which he thought his phenomenological method had forever eliminated.

The method he devised was supposed at one stroke to settle all the disputes that had ravaged post-Cartesian philosophy. All parties to these disputes started from the common presupposition that there is a basic distinction between the mental and the physical. One ended up by saying that everything is mental (the idealists); the other by saying that everything is physical (behaviorists, materialists, naturalists). Husserl claimed to have shown that the distinction which resulted in all of these irreconcilable theories, so far from being basic, is wholly unwarranted: transcendental reduction reveals that we are not dealing with independently existing minds nor with independently existing objects; we are dealing, instead, with the subjective and objective poles of pure consciousness.

In a way, this was Dewey's position—that minds and objects are occurrences within experience, but for Dewey they are "emergents" there, not revealed there in all their essential purity, and of course Dewey was quite ready to accept the constructivist, and so relativist, implications of this account. Since Husserl was not, his solution was, even within his own philosophical development, in unstable equilibrium. This instability results from a deep conflict at the heart of Husserl's thought between phenomenology as a method of describing experience accurately and phenomenology as a quest for certainty.

Phenomenology as description has had a salutary effect on the social sciences. By calling attention to "experiential variables," it has counterbalanced a tendency in psychology to think exclusively in terms of experimental variables and a stimulus-reflex model; by emphasizing "social reality" as it is perceived and actually lived by people, it has corrected a tendency in sociology to concentrate exclusively on overt, "observable" interactions.

But description, however accurate, can never establish the certainty of what is described. It can, indeed, express *feelings* of certainty, and these feelings can be explored and described in detail. But description never makes it certain that these apparent certainties are what they claim to be. This might not disturb psychologists or sociologists, especially those with instrumentalist leanings, but it was a fatal limitation for a philosopher, like Husserl, who was in search of an objectively valid science. Hence Husserl came increasingly to incline toward a Kantian type of solution to the problem of a priori knowledge: the findings of phenomenological description were to be guaranteed by the activities of a transcendental ego. But where Kant had held that this ego and its categorical syntheses are *behind* experience, Husserl held that they are *in* experience. And whereas Kant had only to present logical arguments that justify our inferring the existence of these syntheses, Husserl's phenomenological method, which he never thought of abandoning, required him to *find* the synthesizing operations of the transcendental ego in experience. Since these operations did not appear in transcendentally reduced observation as he had previously practiced it, more and more rigorous bracketing, a more and more narrow focusing on "pure" consciousness, became necessary.

Though Husserl thought this would bring to light the "hidden achievements" of the ego, few of even the most devout phenomenologists were prepared to go along with him. To them, the whole line of reasoning seemed too idealistic. From Husserl's point of view, the fact that the transcendental ego's activities were supposedly revealed in experience saved him from the nineteenth-century version of idealism. But from the point of view of his phenomenologist critics, the transcendental ego ruined everything. Husserl wrote about its activities as "constituting" the experiental world; they saw little difference between constituting and constructing. Thus phenomenology, like its great rival, positivism—both of which had been launched as efforts to break out of the Kantian paradigm—threatened to collapse back into it.

Moreover, to many phenomenologists Husserl's version of phenomenology was too intellectualistic. For Husserl, man was chiefly an observer, a spectator, of reality, and this bias naturally colored his account of the subjective pole of pure consciousness. The phenomenologists who resisted the development of his thought in that respect shared Dewey's

33

emphasis on man as a doer, not merely knower, but since they did not share Dewey's optimism and practicality, their conception of man as a doer differed radically from his. These phenomenologists perceived man as an alien, cast into an indifferent universe where he is forced to act and to choose, rather than as a social being competent to solve the social problems he confronts.

Thus the phenomenological movement underwent a dual development. First, there was an attempt to found an ontology on the basis of phenomenological description; second, there was a shift from the conception of the self as knower to an existential interpretation of consciousness, in which the self is regarded as a moral and social agent, living, acting, and suffering in the world. Since most phenomenologists shared these ontological and existential concerns, the two developments were closely related. In this connection we will briefly consider the theories of Heidegger and Sartre.

As regards the return to ontology, it is noteworthy that Heidegger's chief work, *Being and Time,* opens with a quotation from Plato:

> *For manifestly you have long been aware of what you mean when you use the expression "being." We, however, who used to think we understood it, have now become perplexed.*

Heidegger then asks:

> *Do we in our time have an answer to the question of what we really mean by the word "being"? Not at all. . . . Our aim in the following treatise is to work out the question of the meaning of Being and to do so concretely.*[62]

This, Heidegger thought, required a wholly new approach. The entire development of philosophy since Descartes was obviously a blind alley. Descartes's introduction of the fatal distinction between knower and known had led Kant to abandon Being (which Kant had called "things-in-themselves") and to concentrate on the phenomenal world. From that time on, Heidegger argued, philosophy had wallowed in subjectivism, and though the so-called realists claimed to tell us about the real world, they had not the slightest idea what Being is—they were merely interested in establishing the objectivity of the physical world in order to vindicate the claims of physics.

The Aristotelian-Scholastic tradition, for its part, Heidegger regarded as little better than the post-Cartesian philosophy. It is true that this tradition at least gave a preeminent place to metaphysics, the science of Being, but Heidegger held that the philosophers who represented this tradition concentrated their attention on the various species and genera of being, not on Being itself; it seemed to him that so far as these philosophers thought at all about Being as such, they took it to be only the highest genus, the most universal of concepts.

Metaphysics thinks about beings as beings. Wherever the question is asked what beings are, beings as such are in sight. Metaphysical representation owes this sight to the light of Being. The light itself, i.e., that which such thinking experiences as light, does not come within the range of metaphysical thinking; for metaphysics always represents beings only as beings . . . the light itself is considered sufficiently illuminated as soon as we recognize that we look through it whenever we look at beings.[63]

In another metaphor Heidegger proposed that if the sciences are the branches of a tree of which the roots are metaphysics, then Being is the ground, the soil, in which these roots grow. Just as the root "sends all nourishment and strength" into the tree and ignores the ground in which it lives and on which it depends, so metaphysics "remains concerned with beings and does not devote itself to Being as Being."[64] And just as the light (alternatively, in the other metaphor, the nourishing soil) is always there, waiting to be looked *at,* instead of being looked *with,* so Being is always present to us, waiting for us to feel its presence in our lives. Thus, as Plato said, we all know what we mean by Being. "We always conduct our activities in an understanding of Being";[65] we have simply forgotten where—and above all, how—to look.

Since our oblivion to the absence of the "involvement of Being in human nature" has "determined the entire modern age," since it has left us forsaken and "more and more exclusively [abandoned] to beings," Heidegger conceived it to be his mission to "go back into the ground of metaphysics." "If our thinking should succeed, . . . it might well help to bring about a change in human nature."[66] But how do we, who "used to understand Being," come to understand it once again? The answer is that it is possible to reach Being only through beings, and above all through the being of human beings, for, after all, man is the being who cares about Being.

It is easy to see why, given this approach, Husserlian phenomenology would initially appeal to the young Heidegger—it claimed to undercut Cartesian dualism and so to eliminate both idealism and realism, and in transcendentally reduced experience it claimed to put us in direct contact with the true reality that, in our ordinary experience, we completely overlook.

Again, Husserl seemed to Heidegger correct in emphasizing that the clue to an understanding of Being is human experience. But Husserl seemed mistaken in concentrating on "pure consciousness"—not only because to emphasize consciousness led him down the road to idealism but also because "purity" overlooks man's existential and moral involvement in the world. Hence, instead of characterizing "that sphere of being in which man stands as man" by Husserl's term "consciousness," Heidegger dramatized his difference from Husserl by characterizing it as

"Dasein" (presence). This is not, he says, "simply a matter of using different words." What is at stake is "to get men to think about the involvement of Being in human nature," and by thinking of this involvement, to come to understand the nature of Being itself.[67]

But what is there about the mode of man's existential involvement in the world that provides a key to Being? In the first place, to say that man is existentially involved in the world is to say that he lives in a world not of merely neutral objects but of things that are "ready-to-hand." And this is true not merely of the things he deliberately constructs for his use but of natural objects. "The wood is a forest of timber, the mountain a quarry of rock; the river is water-power, the wind is wind 'in the sails.' "[68] So far, Heidegger is merely repeating what Husserl had said about the "environing world of life" in contrast to that "idealized and naïve" world that physics and behavioristic psychology presuppose. But for Heidegger the fact that our environing life world is "ready-to-hand" is relatively unimportant. Far more important, this environing life world is one into which we have been "thrown" and in which therefore we are strangers.

Our experience of the world as alien and of ourselves as thrown into it generates an anxiety from which we seek to escape. "In the face of its thrownness Dasein flees to the relief which comes with the supposed freedom of the they-self."[69] In less-Heideggerian language, instead of living an authentic life in which we courageously confront the ineradicable loneliness, facticity, and alienation of human existence, we retreat into an inauthentic social existence whose daily round is determined by what "they" (other people) expect of us. But there is one fact about human existence which nobody can elude—death.

> *Dasein cannot outstrip the possibility of death. Death is the possibility of the absolute impossibility of Dasein. . . . As such, death is something* distinctively *impending. . . . Thrownness into death reveals itself to Dasein in a more primordial and impressive manner in that state-of-mind which we have called "anxiety." . . . Anxiety in the face of death must not be confused with fear in the face of one's demise. This anxiety is not an accidental or random mood of "weakness" in some individual; but, as a basic state-of-mind of Dasein, it amounts to the disclosedness of the fact that Dasein exists as thrown Being* towards *its end.*[70]

What this seems to mean, to revert again to non-Heideggerian language, is that our knowledge that we are inevitably to die and that the being of human beings is therefore "impossible" makes us aware that, by contrast, it is precisely the character of the Being of Being that it *cannot* die.

However this may be, it is clear that, at the time *Being and Time* appeared, Heidegger believed that it would be possible, using as clues such insights as these about human existence, to give a formal account of Being. But the second part of *Being and Time* was first postponed and then cancelled, as he came to feel that anything like a formal, philosophical exposition of Being is impossible. Poets, he thought, were better than philosophers at revealing Being, but in the end he concluded that even they must fail.

"Language," he wrote, is "the house of Being," and since there are many languages, Being has many houses. "If man by virtue of his language dwells within the claim and call of Being, then we Europeans presumably dwell in an entirely different house than Eastasian man. . . . And so, a dialogue from house to house remains nearly impossible."[71] Indeed, it is not merely a matter of communication—it is not merely impossible for participants in the dialogue to say *to each other* what Being is; one cannot *say* what Being is; one can only hint. And the best hint, it turns out, is silence.

> *The course of such a dialogue would have to have a character all its own, with more silence than talk. Above all, silence about silence.*[72]

Thus, by the phenomenological route we seem to have reached the conclusion already reached by the positivistic route: that the ideal of a language isomorphic with reality is an illusion. And not only this. The pursuit of sheer immediacy has led Heidegger a long way beyond Husserl's bracketing of pure "consciousness" to a community of mutual silence.

While Heidegger was thus converting Husserl's "rigorous science" into something hardly distinguishable from mysticism, Sartre was subjecting it to a different pattern of pressures, especially, perhaps, the pressure of atheism. What is a world without God? What is man's role in such a world?

In attempting to answer these questions Sartre started from Husserl's central thesis that reality consists in consciousness-of, but he launched a frontal attack on the transcendental ego. It seemed to him that Husserl had mistakenly introduced it because, with Kant, he supposed that a synthesizing activity is necessary to make mine all those consciousnesses-of that I experience as mine. Now it is true that ordinarily I am at an "unreflected level" where I am conscious only of the object and unaware of being conscious of it, and this of course is why Husserl supposed that a special unifying consciousness is necessary. But since, as Sartre pointed out, I can at any moment move from the unreflected to the "reflective level," where I am conscious of being conscious of the object, it is evident that every consciousness of an object is *also* a consciousness of self. Hence Husserl's transcendental ego is unnecessary; it has no raison d'être.

Getting rid of the transcendental ego not only eliminated idealism and reestablished the possibility of ontology; it also eliminated the notion of a self that, being somehow the source of our psychic life, is both responsible for what we do and also a limitation on our human freedom. At the subjective pole there is now only pure spontaneity. "Genuine spontaneity must be perfectly clear: it *is* what it produces and can be nothing else."[73] There are thus no limitations, either psychological or ontological, on what I may become.

> *This monstrous spontaneity is at the origin of numerous psychas-thenic ailments. Consciousness is frightened by its own spontaneity. . . . This is clearly seen in an example from Janet. A young bride was in terror, when her husband left her alone, of sitting at the window and summoning the passers-by like a prostitute. Nothing in her education, in her past, nor in her character could serve as an explanation of such a fear. . . . She found herself monstrously free.*[74]

If freedom leads to anxiety and despair that may require psychiatric treatment, it is also a challenge and an opportunity. Most of us flee from freedom and live the roles provided for us by our family, our education, and the social class to which we belong. We never know despair; we never have any real moral problem, for the answers to our questions are provided by society. But we are hardly men. "Human life begins," as Orestes says in Sartre's play *The Flies,* "on the other side of despair."

But man is not only free; he is conscious. We have to ask then, "What sort of being is consciousness-being?" It is, says Sartre, "for-itself." To understand its nature we must contrast it with being-in-itself, the sort of being an oak tree or an ashtray has. The in-itself is "massive," "solid," "glued to itself"; it is "undivided singleness." It simply is what it is. In contrast, the for-itself "is what it is not and is not what it is." By this characteristically enigmatic phrase Sartre calls attention to the fact that men, unlike oak trees and ashtrays, can imagine possibilities that are not —for instance, a homosexual can imagine being a heterosexual; a waiter can imagine being a capitalist. Further, a homosexual is not just a homo-sexual; a waiter is not just a waiter. Each has other roles, and is aware, when acting out any particular role, of the other roles in his repertory of roles. This awareness cannot but affect the homosexual's or the waiter's playing of his role as homosexual or waiter. Hence man is almost always *acting,* rather than living. He is in "bad faith."

That man's mode of life is not one of undivided singleness like that of the ashtray, that men can imagine alternatives, consider possibilities, and critically reflect on what they are doing, no philosopher would deny. "The unexamined life," Socrates declared, "is not worth living," * and many philosophers have prized consciousness precisely because (as they would say) it enriches life with additional dimensions. Not so Sartre. The characters in his novels detest consciousness and the distancing, or mediation, it introduces into experience. So in *The Reprieve* Daniel, a homosexual, asks,

> *Why can't I be what I am,* be *a pederast, villain, coward, a loath-*
> *some object that doesn't even manage to exist? . . . Just* to be. *In*
> *the dark, at random! To be homosexual just as the oak is oak. To*
> *extinguish myself. Extinguish the inner eye.*[75]

But he cannot; he is doomed to the divided, for-itself mode of being. Thus consciousness, like the recognition of freedom, is a source of despair.

There is still another source of despair. Man is a questioner who demands final, absolutely complete and definitive answers. Only a God who knows all could give such answers. Therefore, man yearns to be God. But alas!—not only is man not God; God does not, and cannot, exist. This is easily proved. The concept of God is the concept of being wholly in-itself-for-itself. But being wholly for-itself is entire consciousness and being wholly in-itself is absolute unconsciousness. It follows that the concept of God—of a being that is both entirely conscious and absolutely unconscious—is a logical contradiction. Nevertheless, man, poor pathetic man, passionately longs to be God—that is, he longs to encompass a contradiction that cannot exist. Since this hope is absurd, man is doomed to disappointment. He is in fact "a useless passion."[76]

Poor falcon!

Philosophical Investigations and beyond

Having now reached midcentury by another route, we must consider Wittgenstein's bombshell and some of the fallout from it. The *Tractatus,* which had appeared in 1921, had been a major influence on the positivists, as we have seen. Thereafter Wittgenstein published nothing, but it was known that his views had undergone a transformation and various versions of his new theory had circulated without his permission. In 1953, two years after his death, *Philosophical Investigations* appeared, probably the most influential philosophical work of this century.

Philosophical Investigations begins with a devastating critique of the picture theory of language—the theory which, as we have seen, had been a central feature of the *Tractatus.* If Wittgenstein had been led to adopt the picture theory by an account he had read of a trial in which miniature cars represented the cars in an automobile accident, he is said to have suddenly come to see the inadequacy of the picture theory when an Italian friend made a typical Neapolitan gesture and asked, "What does *that* picture?"

The *Investigations* does not maintain simply that the picture theory presented in the *Tractatus* is mistaken; if that were the difficulty, the

---

* *GBWW*, Vol. 7, p. 210.

remedy might be to provide another, better focused picture. No; the *Investigations* maintains that the picture of language as a picture is a lens through which we have been looking at the world, but without realizing that there is this lens between our eyes and reality. In other words (though Wittgenstein does not say so), the *Investigations* uncovered an unconscious presupposition of exactly the kind that Husserl believed could be uncovered only by bracketing. And the picture theory did not only distort the view set forth in *Tractatus*; it also distorted the views of Russell and of the positivists. As Wittgenstein noted, in the *Tractatus* he had written, "The general form of propositions is: This is how things are." And now he commented:

> *That is the kind of proposition that one repeats to oneself count-less times. One thinks that one is tracing the outline of the thing's nature over and over again, and one is merely tracing round the frame through which we look at it.*[77]

Pictures, it might be said, hold us captive.

The picture, in this case, is of course the picture of language as a picture. This picture is not *wholly* false. If the question be asked whether the description of language as a picture is "appropriate," the answer is,

> *Yes, it is appropriate, but only for this narrowly circumscribed region, not for the whole of what you were claiming to describe.*
> *It is as if someone were to say: "A game consists in moving objects about on a surface according to certain rules . . ."—and we replied: You seem to be thinking of board games, but there are others. You can make your definition correct by expressly restrict-ing it to those games.*[78]

Similarly, as regards language. Anyone who reviews the immense variety of ways in which people actually use language—

> *Giving orders, and obeying them—*
> *Reporting an event—*
> *Speculating about an event—*
> *Making up a story; and reading it—*
> *Play-acting—*
> *Singing catches—*
> *Guessing riddles—*
> *Asking, thanking, cursing, greeting, praying—*[79]

will see not only that the picture theory does not cover the whole range and variety of usages but that no description, no theory, can do so. Suppose someone were to reply that it is a general description of language to say that every word signifies something. But what, Wittgenstein asks, does such a general description amount to?

> *Think of the tools in a tool-box: there is a hammer, pliers, a saw, a screw-driver, a rule, a glue-pot, glue, nails and screws.— The functions of words are as diverse as the functions of these objects. (And in both cases there are similarities.) . . .*
>
> *When we say: "Every word in language signifies something" we have so far said* nothing *whatever; unless we have explained* exactly *what* distinction we wish to make. . . .
>
> *Imagine someone's saying: "All tools serve to modify something. Thus the hammer modifies the position of the nail, the saw the shape of the board, and so on."—And what is modified by the rule, the glue-pot, the nails?—"Our knowledge of a thing's length, the temperature of the glue, and the solidity of the box."—Would anything be gained by this assimilation of expressions?* [80]

This passage is a good example of Wittgenstein's new technique of philosophizing that was to have so great an influence on the next generation of philosophers. He did not *argue;* he produced counterexamples to any generalization that might be put forward. He said in effect, "Yes; your generalization covers such-and-such cases, but it does not cover such-and-such other cases. The reason you have not realized that you have overgeneralized is that the cases covered by your generalization seem to you especially important. But to someone else, in a different context, other cases will seem equally, or more, important."

The passage shows something else. The overgeneralizer has not only overgeneralized; he makes the generalization look plausible only by stretching language artificially, often to the point of absurdity. ("Our knowledge of a thing's length is modified by the rule.") Wittgenstein held that stretching language in this way in the interest of achieving generality was typical of philosophy as it had been practiced in the past. This was why, as Moore had complained, philosophy departed so far from common sense. Wittgenstein's aim was to dissolve traditional philosophical problems by showing that these problems arise only when, in the interest of some special philosophical demand, such as the demand for generality, language is stretched artificially. Everybody knows what language is, just as everybody knows what a tool is. There is no puzzle about language (or about tools) until philosophers, assuming that language (and tools) must have a "nature," look for that nature and cannot find it.

Alternatively, and in a characteristic metaphor, philosophical problems arise when language loses traction, when the wheels spin without taking hold. The problems disappear as soon as language is put back into traction. Language is in traction when it is a part of some goal-directed social activity, an activity whose end is furthered by the language the participants in this activity use in communicating with one another. Suppose a man is building with building stones and that he has an assistant whose job is to bring him the stones as he needs them. "For this

41

purpose they use a language consisting of the words 'block,' 'pillar,' 'slab,' 'beam'. . . . Conceive this as a complete primitive language."[81]

In order to emphasize that language is instrumental to some goal-directed activity, Wittgenstein called the whole enterprise into which language and action are "interwoven," a "language game." Since language is instrumental to a goal-directed activity, language is effective (is "good" language) if it furthers that activity. This is why a language consisting only of the words *block, pillar, slab,* and *beam* can be a complete language; it is complete if, by calling out these words from time to time, the builder gets the materials he needs. It follows that there are as many different languages as there are "games," i.e., different kinds of goal-directed activities. (This is why there is no "essence," or "nature," of language to be found by philosophical analysis.) Hence Wittgenstein's injunction: look, not to the meaning, but to the use: Don't look for the meaning, for there is no one meaning that is *the* meaning. Look, instead, at the way the word is actually being used in the language game that is under discussion; that use is its meaning in *this* game.

For millenia, philosophers have argued over the "status" of universals —is the universal "game," for instance, *ante rem, in re,* or *post rem?* Instead of adding to this sterile debate, as it seemed to him, Wittgenstein proposed to dissolve the whole problem: the only reason anybody could have for believing in the existence of universals at all is his desire for certainty, his desire to have a rule that makes it absolutely certain whether any particular object is, or is not, a member of a class—for instance, the class of games. But Wittgenstein held that such rules have no use except to satisfy this special need.

> I can *give the concept "number"* [or *"horse," or "cow," or "game"*] *rigid limits, . . . but I can also use it so that the extension of the concept is* not *closed by a frontier. . . .*
> *"But then"* [asks the worried traditional philosopher] *"the use of the word is unregulated, the 'game' we play with it is unregulated."—It is not everywhere circumscribed by rules; but no more are there any rules for how high one throws the ball in tennis, or how hard; yet tennis is a game for all that and has rules too.*[82]

A definition of *game*, a rule for deciding whether a particular activity is, or is not, a game, is like a signpost. A satisfactory signpost is one that guides travelers along their way; if too many travelers misread a signpost and lose their way, it can be made less ambiguous. But no signpost can be designed that is absolutely unambiguous, that could never be misread by anybody under any circumstances. Similarly, for the definition of *game:* this can be revised as needed, but it cannot be, and it need not be, decisive for all possible cases. It is, therefore, theoretically possible always to doubt whether some particular activity is, *for sure,* a game. But is such doubt reasonable? We are not in doubt merely *because it is possible for us to* imagine *a doubt. I can easily imagine someone always doubting before he opened his front door whether an abyss did not yawn behind it, and making sure about it before he went through the door (and he might on some occasion prove to be right)—but that does not make me doubt in the same case.*[83]

If this sounds familiar, it should: Dewey had said it all earlier. Wittgenstein—at least the Wittgenstein of the *Investigations*—shared Dewey's belief, first, that concepts are instruments and, second, that nobody would fail to see that this is the case whose view was not distorted by an almost neurotic quest for certainty. If one looks at the world without this distorting lens, what one sees is not universals but merely "family resemblances." Consider, for example, some of the activities we call "games."

I mean board-games, card-games, ball-games, Olympic games, and so on. What is common to them all?—Don't say: "There must *be something common, or they would not be called 'games' "—but* look and see *whether there is anything common to all. . . . Don't think, but look!—Look for example at board-games, with their multifarious relationships. Now pass to card-games; here you find many correspondences with the first group, but many common features drop out, and others appear. . . . Look at the parts played by skill and luck; and at the difference between skill in chess and skill in tennis. . . .*

And the result of this examination is: we see a complicated network of similarities overlapping and criss-crossing. . . .

I can think of no better expression to characterize these similarities than "family resemblances"; for the various resemblances between members of a family: build, features, colour of eyes, gait, temperament, etc. etc. overlap and criss-cross in the same way.[84]

Family resemblances, then, are what we see when we actually look. So much for all those essences and other verities that Husserl supposed to be disclosed in transcendentally reduced observation.

And what applies to *essence* and to *universal* applies to all those other words that are the special favorites of philosophers—*knowledge, being, object, I, proposition, name.* Each of these has generated seemingly insoluble puzzles because philosophers have never asked themselves the simple question "Is the word ever actually used in this way in the language game which is its original home?" The answer, of course, is that it is not. "What *we* do," in contrast, "is to bring words back from their metaphysical to their everyday use."[85]

As an example of "what *we* do," consider the word *analysis.* Analysis decomposes a complex into its simple constituents. But

> *What are the simple constituent parts of a chair?—The bits of wood of which it is made? Or the molecules, or the atoms? . . . We use the word "composite" (and therefore the word "simple") in an enormous number of different and differently related ways.*[86]

Thus an answer to the question "What are the simples that analysis yields?" depends on the circumstances. Given a specification of the circumstances, language is in traction when questions about analysis are asked. But *philosophical* talk about an analysis that yields "ultimate simples" or "logical atoms" is spinning; it is out of traction because no circumstances are, or can be, specified.

As to "ideal language": of course the mathematical calculi of the logicians are useful for special purposes, but to call them "ideal"

> *is liable to mislead, for it sounds as if these languages were better, more perfect, than our everyday language; and as if it took the logician to shew people at last what a proper sentence looked like.*[87]

What Wittgenstein said about the subject-to-revision character of definitions and signposts applies equally to logic. Where did logicians get the idea that "there can't be any vagueness in logic"? The "crystalline purity" that they believe they *find* in logic is actually a requirement that slipped in unnoticed at the start of their investigation, a requirement that is but the reflection of the logician's quest for certainty.

In this attack on what he called the "subliming" of logic, Wittgenstein again sounds like Dewey; he is also like Dewey in wanting to reform philosophy. But their emphases are different. Dewey wanted to reform philosophy in order to improve our traffic with nature; Wittgenstein wanted to reform philosophy in order to free us from "the bewitchment of our intelligence by language." But there is another and deeper difference. Wittgenstein thought that our intelligence has been bewitched by language because we suffer from "deep disquietudes"—among them, the passion to say the unsayable. In a way this was what the positivists had maintained: To hold that metaphysics is nonsense is a way of holding that metaphysicians have been trying to say the unsayable. But what a different way of saying this Wittgenstein's way of saying it is!

The positivists' way of saying it reflects their lack of interest in—some would want to say "insensitivity to"—the unsayable, a lack of interest (insensitivity) that Dewey shared. In contrast, Wittgenstein's way of saying it shows that he shared this passion. In this respect, he reminds us—to our surprise—of Heidegger. But he wanted to *cure* people of this passion, not, as with Heidegger, to render them open to "the claim and call of Being."

Wittgenstein's notion of philosophy as therapy—at the opposite pole from the old notion of philosophy as the most general of the sciences—

caught the attention of John Wisdom, who developed it further. The positivists were correct, Wisdom thinks, in comparing metaphysics with poetry, but this is not—as they thought—to derogate it. When a poet writes that "the red rose is a falcon and the white rose is a dove," he is certainly using language in an odd way, for red roses are red roses and white roses are white roses. But the "verbal impropriety" of this kind of talk is "not without a purpose." [88] Its purpose is to reveal "what is known and hidden"—in this case, a similarity between doves and white roses, and between falcons and red roses, that we might otherwise overlook. So, too, for philosophical talk to the effect, for instance, that "time is unreal" or that "everything is determined." What aspects of our lives and of the world does the oddity of philosophical talk forcefully bring to our attention? This talk, however abstract and arid it may sound, has in it "echoes from the heart." [89] In this respect philosophy is like psychoanalysis. The metaphysician, like the psychiatrist,

> seeks to bring into the light those models from the past which for good and evil so powerfully influence our lives in the present, so powerfully distort reality and so powerfully illuminate it. . . . In the labyrinth of metaphysics are the same whispers as one hears when climbing Kafka's staircases to the tribunal which is always one floor further up.[90]

Though we try to hurry away from such whispers or to drown them in chatter, we would do better to return and "force the accusers to speak up. . . . We can hardly do this by ourselves. But there are those who will go with us and, however terrifying the way, not desert us."

It was not, however, this aspect of *Philosophical Investigations* that attracted most philosophers. Those who had participated in the positivists' program for eliminating metaphysics but who had been disappointed by the failure of the Verifiability Principle to do the job assigned it naturally welcomed Wittgenstein's linguistic method of dissolving philosophical problems. Those who had been influenced by Moore's defense of ordinary beliefs were impressed by Wittgenstein's advocacy of ordinary language. Thus it came about that refinement and extended application of the method of analysis inaugurated in *Philosophical Investigations* became the chief occupation of almost all philosophers who did not belong to the phenomenological-existentialist camp.

One notable exception is Wilfrid Sellars, who has continued the realistic tradition, but in a very sophisticated form. "The aim of philosophy," Sellars declares,

> is to understand how things in the broadest possible sense of the term hang together in the broadest possible sense of the term. . . . To achieve success in philosophy would be, to use a contemporary term of phrase, to "know one's way around" with respect to . . .

45

such radically different items as "cabbages and kings," numbers and duties, possibilities and finger snaps, aesthetic experiences and death.[91]

Since all of these items fall within the scope of one or another of the special sciences, philosophy differs from science only in its greater generality. It is in fact only "the 'eye on the whole' which distinguishes . . . the philosopher from the persistently reflective specialist."[92]

It is impossible here to discuss the details of the synoptic view at which Sellars believes philosophy must aim. For us, the points to note are, first, that he believes it possible to obtain a view of the world that is true of the world, not merely relative to some conceptual scheme or other, and, second, that he holds this true view to be the view that quantum physics is gradually disclosing.

More representative of contemporary philosophizing is the work of J. L. Austin and Gilbert Ryle. Austin's critique of sense-data theories is a good example of the so-called "ordinary-language" philosophy in action, especially if it be contrasted with Dewey's approach. Where Dewey invited our attention to experience (When do we, as a matter of fact, actually experience sense-data?), Austin invited our attention to the way in which Englishmen actually use such words as *illusion* and *delusion*.

It will be recalled that to Moore and Russell it seemed absolutely unquestionable that there is a distinction between what is directly perceived and what is not directly perceived but only inferred. Austin undermined this distinction, which was the starting point for all versions of realism, by simply listing the circumstances in which people distinguish between directly perceiving something and indirectly perceiving something. What are these circumstances? Well, we "contrast the man who saw [a] procession directly with the man who saw it *through a periscope;* or we might contrast the place from which you can watch the door directly with the place from which you can see it only *in the mirror.*"[93] Examination of usage shows that we talk about perceiving something indirectly when there is "some kink in direction"—when we are "not looking straight at the object in question." That is all there is to the distinction: philosophical use of it to maintain that we don't directly perceive a coin, but only a sense-datum, when we are looking straight at the coin from a few feet away is "not only false but simply absurd."[94]

If Austin attacked philosophical usage of individual terms, Ryle concentrates on whole clusters of such terms, undertaking to show that philosophical problems arise because terms belonging to different "categories" are mistakenly grouped together. But his approach is still linguistic, and the underlying assumption is that ordinary usage is the criterion for evaluating philosophical usage. As Austin wrote, "One can't abuse ordinary language without paying for it."[95]

The Concept of Mind is a good example of Ryle's method. He begins by pointing out that this book "does not give new information about minds. We possess already a wealth of information about minds," information furnished not by philosophers but by scientists. Instead, the book is intended "to rectify the logical geography of the knowledge which we already possess." [96] Rectifying the logical geography means learning which concepts "correlate" with one another and which do not.

To put this differently and more formally, every proposition has certain "logical powers," meaning that it is "related to other propositions in various discoverable ways." [97] Ascertaining the logical powers of a concept—say, the concept of "existence"—is like ascertaining the boundaries of a right of way across a field: just as the boundaries of the right of way indicate where one is permitted to walk and where one is forbidden to walk, so a concept's logical powers indicate which of the sentences in which this concept occurs are meaningful and which are nonsensical. Thus we can say (1) There exists a cathedral in Oxford; (2) There exists a three-engined bomber; (3) There exists a square number between 9 and 25. Anyone who didn't understand, at least "by wont," that "existence" in these three sentences has very different logical powers might find himself saying, "The square of 4 is older than the square root of 5," which is nonsense. And it is nonsense because the concept of existence (1) correlates with, and the concept of existence (3) does not correlate with, such concepts as the concept of "aging," the concept of "younger than," and the concept of "coming into being at a particular point of time."

In such a case as this the difference in logical powers is obvious, and indeed people do know "by wont" the logical powers of most of the concepts they use. Thus they can "appraise [another man's] performances, assess his progress, understand his words and actions, discern his motives and see his jokes." [98] Unfortunately, for three hundred years we have been trying to "coordinate" all this genuine knowledge about the mind and how it works by means of a set of abstract ideas, inherited from Descartes, whose "logical cross-bearings" have never been determined. Concepts like "intellect," "emotion," and "will" have been mistakenly correlated with the concept of "substance," or "thing," a concept that has a very different set of logical powers, thus producing muddles as bad as the muddle that would be created by trying to correlate the existence of square numbers with aging.

It is important to Ryle that, though we may lack explicit knowledge of "the rules governing the logical behavior of propositions," [99] we nevertheless know their use "by wont." This means that philosophical criticism does not operate in terms of an ideal standard of the kind Wittgenstein attacked. Instead, it only uncovers the correlations implicit in ordinary, everyday languages. Philosophers in the past have confused themselves and ordinary people by failing to determine the correlations that actually obtain among the concepts we all use all the time; it is up to philosophy in the future to undo the damage.

47

Since the new philosophy does this by exposing the absurdities to which mistaken correlations lead, it may seem destructive. But the *reductio ad absurdum* arguments that it uses against muddled "galaxies of abstract ideas" are "neither more nor less nihilist than are threshing operations."[100] When the chaff has been eliminated, the grain remains.

Meanwhile, in the very heart of ordinary-language territory a revival of metaphysics has occurred. The initiator of this development is P. F. Strawson, who does what he calls "descriptive metaphysics," in contrast to "revisionary metaphysics." Whereas revisionary metaphysics is concerned to produce a better structure of our thought (and therefore shares a certain similarity of aims with positivism and ideal-language theory, which are concerned to produce a better structure of our language), "descriptive metaphysics is content to describe the actual structure of our thought."[101]

Thus descriptive metaphysics conforms to Wittgenstein's injunction: "We must do away with all *explanation,* and description alone must take its place."[102] But it differs from ordinary ordinary-language philosophy in that, though it too starts from "the actual use of words," it does not stop there. The structure that the descriptive metaphysician seeks "does not readily display itself on the surface of language, but lies submerged." It is obvious that Strawson would be dissatisfied with the analytical techniques of Wittgenstein and Austin, for they deliberately stay at the surface of actual usage. But it might be thought that he would find the approach of Ryle more satisfactory. The trouble is, however, that Ryle's "galaxies" of abstract ideas are so near the surface that they change through time. Strawson's whole procedure presupposes that "there is a massive central core of human thinking . . . [of] categories and concepts which, in their most fundamental character, change not at all."[103]

Here again, then, philosophy has returned to the Kantian paradigm, and not to the later, relativizing versions of idealism but to something very close to Kant's contention that there is an a priori structure in which all minds everywhere share. Thus Strawson has duplicated the Kantian move of offering the falcon a human, instead of an objective, center about which to orient his flight. The ordinary-language philosophers provide such a center, too, but in a less obvious way. In their analyses ordinary language has become in effect a kind of supreme court of final appeal. Or, to revert to a metaphor we have used before, for them ordinary language is a firm basis on which the ladder of thought and action can securely rest.

But with philosophy thus coming round again almost full circle, we are bound to ask ourselves whether the proposed center is likely to remain fixed. Will the shift from a nonlinguistic to a linguistic formulation be enough to prevent history from repeating itself? How secure a basis will ordinary language prove to be?

48

It would seem that, for most ordinary-language philosophers, ordinary language is their own language, the language of upper-class Englishmen (and Americans). Most linguistic analysts also operate as if this ordinary language is static and unchanging. It is true that Austin and Ryle both recognize that, as Ryle says, "new theory-shaping ideas are struck out from time to time ... by men of genius" and that, as a result, the logical powers of these new "crucial ideas" have to be determined and coordinated with the old.[104] Thus—in their view but in Strawson's terminology—philosophy cannot be merely descriptive; it has to be revisionist, if only because "men of genius" are constantly changing Strawson's unchanging core.

Though Austin and Ryle recognize, as it were officially, that language changes, change is not in the focus of attention for them or for most ordinary-language philosophers. Their practice is better represented by Austin's observation that "the ordinary 'concepts' employed by English speakers ... have evolved over a long time: that is, they ... have faced the test of practical experience, of continual hard use, better than their vanished rivals."[105] Hence Strawson's warning against "tampering"— usages that have won out in an evolutionary struggle for survival have a fitness that philosophers are seldom able to improve on. "Tampering ... is not so easy as is often supposed [and] is not justified or needed so often as is often supposed."[106]

But what do poets and other men of genius do but "tamper" with the language? It is no accident that linguistic analysts usually ignore poetry when they are looking for examples of usage, for to emphasize the cognitively meaningful "oddity" of poetry and philosophy, as Wisdom does, is to call attention to the fact that language is an open spiral, not a firm floor.

Nor is it just a matter of the openness of even the most ordinary of ordinary English; we have also to consider the implications of Wittgenstein's deep remark that "to imagine a language means to imagine a form of life." That is, since language expresses and articulates the beliefs that underlie some social group's way of living, different social groups have different languages. Wittgenstein was perhaps thinking chiefly of differences in such everyday practices as buying apples, weighing cheese, or calling for slabs, but this view of the relation between a language and a form of life also applies, if it applies at all, to the relation between (say) the Hopi language and the Hopi form of life. Agreements about the nature of time, about values, about the structure of the world can be reached within a particular form of life, but not across forms of life. "What has to be accepted, the given, is—so one could say—*forms of life*."[107] We are back once more to Heidegger's many houses, with Europeans and East Asians—not to mention Hopis—dwelling in entirely different houses.

But is this relativistic conclusion correct? About this, as about so much else, there is no agreement. Linguists such as Chomsky and anthropologists such as Levi-Strauss, who believe that there is a universal "deep structure," support Strawson's thesis—if there are as many houses as there are languages, it is nonetheless true that all of these houses have a common architectural plan.

Surprisingly, few philosophers have seriously considered this question, but Quine is one who has, and he has reached the opposite conclusion. Suppose, he says, that an anthropologist or a linguist observes that a native uses the word *gavagai* whenever he (the observer) would use the word *rabbit,* and never uses *gavagai* when the observer would not use the word *rabbit.* Can the observer conclude that *rabbit* and *gavagai* have the same meaning? No; it is true that the two words are "stimulus-synonymous," but it is impossible to devise any test by which the observer could ascertain whether the native *means* by *gavagai* just what the observer means by *rabbit.* What the observer means by *rabbit* is the whole rabbit.

> *Who knows but what the objects to which [*"gavagai"*] applies are not rabbits after all, but mere stages, or brief temporal segments, of rabbits. . . . Or perhaps the objects to which "gavagai" applies are all and sundry undetached parts of rabbits. . . . When from the sameness of stimulus meanings of "Gavagai" and "Rabbit" the linguist leaps to the conclusion that a gavagai is a whole enduring rabbit, he is just taking for granted that the native is enough like us to have a brief general term for rabbits and no brief general term for rabbit stages or parts.*[108]

The fact is that every term, even the simplest, is "theory-laden," and there is no way to tell whether *rabbit* and *gavagai* are laden by the same theory or by different theories, for any evidence by which one might seek to determine this is itself theory-laden. We can never free ourselves from all theories and face the facts themselves in their purity. "We can never do better than occupy the standpoint of some theory or other, the best we can muster at the time." [109]

Wittgenstein had declared that he wanted to help the fly escape from the fly bottle. That is, he wanted to help man free himself from the "bewitchment" of language. He wrote as if he thought that the way to escape from the fly bottle is to get back to ordinary language, and, as we have seen, many linguistic philosophers have assumed that there exists such an easy way out. But it now looks as if this may itself be a linguistic illusion. Though the fly may escape from this or that fly bottle, he only lands in another: perhaps there is no common ground, no common world, outside all fly bottles.

Thus there is no agreement even on the question of whether agreement is in principle possible or in principle impossible. Here it seems fair to characterize twentieth-century philosophy as a widening gyre.

[1] W. Wordsworth, *The Prelude,* bk. 2, lines 233, ff.

[2] Quoted by Nietzsche in *Schopenhauer as Educator,* in *Existentialism from Dostoevsky to Sartre,* trans. and ed. W. Kaufmann (New York: Meridian Books, 1956), p. 103.

[3] Ibid., p. 102.

[4] F. Nietzsche, *Beyond Good and Evil,* trans. M. Cowan (Chicago: Henry Regnery Co., 1955), pp. 101, 3, 6, 15.

[5] F. H. Bradley, *Appearance and Reality* (Oxford: Oxford University Press, Clarendon Press, 1930), p. 111, note 1.

[6] Ibid., p. 140.

[7] G. E. Moore, "The Refutation of Idealism," in *Philosophical Studies* (Patterson, N.J.: Littlefield, Adams & Co., 1959), pp. 17, 24–26.

[8] Ibid., pp. 20, 25.

[9] Ibid., p. 27.

[10] G. E. Moore, "The Subject-matter of Psychology," in *Proceedings of the Aristotelian Society* (London: Williams and Norgate, 1910), 10:36.

[11] B. Russell, "My Mental Development" in *The Philosophy of Bertrand Russell,* ed. P. A. Schilpp (Evanston, Ill.: Library of Living Philosophers, 1946), p. 12.

[12] G. E. Moore, "The Status of Sense-Data," in *Philosophical Studies,* p. 190.

[13] Ibid., pp. 195–96.

[14] G. E. Moore, "An Autobiography" in *The Philosophy of G. E. Moore,* 2d ed., ed. P. A. Schilpp (New York: Tudor Publishing Co., Library of Living Philosophers, 1952), p. 14.

[15] B. Russell, "Logical Atomism," in *Contemporary British Philosophy,* ed. J. H. Muirhead (New York: The Macmillan Co., 1924), p. 359.

[16] B. Russell, "My Mental Development," in Schilpp, p. 7.

[17] B. Russell, *The Analysis of Mind* (London: George Allen & Unwin, 1921), pp. 141–42.

[18] B. Russell, "Knowledge by Acquaintance and Knowledge by Description," in *Mysticism and Logic* (London: Penguin Books, Pelican Books, 1953), pp. 212–14.

[19] B. Russell, "The Ultimate Constituents of Matter," in *Mysticism and Logic,* pp. 124–25.

[20] Ibid., p. 133.

[21] M. Schlick, "Positivism and Realism," in *Logical Positivism,* ed. A. J. Ayer (Glencoe, Ill.: The Free Press, 1959), p. 107.

[22] B. Russell, "Introduction," in *Tractatus Logico-Philosophicus,* by L. Wittgenstein (London: Routledge & Kegan Paul, 1961), p. x.

[23] G. H. von Wright, "Biographical Sketch," in *Ludwig Wittgenstein: A Memoir,* by Norman Malcolm (London: Oxford University Press, 1958), pp. 7–8.

[24] L. Wittgenstein, *Tractatus,* sec. 2.1, 2.16.

[25] Ibid., sec. 2.17.

[26] Ibid., sec. 2.21.

[27] Ibid., sec. 2.0201.

[28] Ibid., sec. 4.221.

[29] Ibid., sec. 3.26, 3.263.

[30] Ibid., sec. 3.144.

[31] Ibid., sec. 1.2.

[32] Ibid., sec. 1.21.

[33] O. Neurath, "Protocol Sentences," in *Logical Positivism,* p. 202.

[34] R. Carnap, "The Elimination of Metaphysics through Logical Analysis of Language," in *Logical Positivism,* pp. 78–79.

[35] L. Wittgenstein, *Tractatus,* sec. 6.51, 6.521.

[36] O. Neurath, *Logical Positivism,* p. 201.

[37] Ibid., p. 203.

[38] A. J. Ayer, "Editor's Introduction," in *Logical Positivism,* p. 15.

[39] R. Carnap, "Empiricism, Semantics, and Ontology," in *Meaning and Necessity,* 2d ed., enl. (Chicago: University of Chicago Press, Phoenix Books, 1958), p. 206.

[40] Ibid., pp. 208, 221.

41 A. N. Whitehead, *Science and the Modern World* (New York: The Macmillan Co., 1925), p. 27.

42 A. N. Whitehead, *Modes of Thought* (New York: The Macmillan Co., Capricorn Books, 1938), p. 58.

43 A. N. Whitehead, *Essays in Science and Philosophy* (New York: Philosophical Library, 1948), p. 15.

44 A. N. Whitehead, *Modes of Thought,* p. 237.

45 A. N. Whitehead, *Science and the Modern World,* p. 80.

46 Ibid., pp. 127, 113–14.

47 J. Dewey, *How We Think* (Boston: D. C. Heath & Co., 1933), p. 107.

48 L. Wittgenstein, *Tractatus,* sec. 3.25.

49 J. Dewey, *Essays in Experimental Logic* (New York: Dover Publications, 1953), pp. 37–38.

50 Ibid., pp. 39, 41, 43.

51 Ibid., p. 6.

52 J. Dewey, *Experience and Nature* (Chicago: Open Court Publishing Co., 1929), pp. 96, 21.

53 Ibid., p. 437.

54 J. Dewey, "Democracy and Educational Administration," in *Intelligence in the Modern World,* ed. J. Ratner (New York: Random House, The Modern Library, 1939), pp. 400–402.

55 E. Husserl, "Philosophy and the Crisis of European Man," in *Phenomenology and the Crisis of Philosophy,* trans. Q. Lauer (New York: Harper & Row, Harper Torchbooks, 1965), p. 186.

56 Quoted in H. Spiegelberg, *The Phenomenological Movement,* 2d ed. (The Hague: Martinus Nijhoff, 1965), 1:82.

57 E. Husserl, *Ideas: A General Introduction to Pure Phenomenology,* trans. W. R. Boyce Gibson (New York: The Macmillan Co., 1931), sec. 27, 30.

58 Ibid., sec. 31.

59 Ibid., sec. 33.

60 Ibid., sec. 88.

61 E. Husserl, *Cartesian Meditations,* trans. D. Cairns (The Hague: Martinus Nijhoff, 1960), pp. 39–40.

62 M. Heidegger, *Being and Time,* trans. J. Macquarrie and E. Robinson (London: SCM Press, 1962), p. 19.

63 M. Heidegger, "The Way Back into the Ground of Metaphysics," in *Existentialism from Dostoevsky to Sartre,* p. 207.

64 Ibid., p. 208.

65 M. Heidegger, *Being and Time,* p. 25.

66 M. Heidegger, "The Way Back . . . ," pp. 211, 209.

67 Ibid., p. 213.

68 M. Heidegger, *Being and Time,* p. 100.

69 Ibid., p. 321.

70 Ibid., pp. 294–95.

71 M. Heidegger, "A Dialogue on Language," in *On the Way to Language,* trans. P. D. Hertz (New York: Harper & Row, 1971), p. 5.

72 Ibid., p. 52.

73 J.-P. Sartre, *The Transcendence of the Ego,* trans. F. Williams and R. Kirkpatrick (New York: Farrar, Straus & Giroux, Noonday Press, 1957), p. 79.

74 Ibid., pp. 99–100.

75 J.-P. Sartre, *The Reprieve,* trans. E. Sutton (New York: Bantam Books, 1968), p. 101.

76 J.-P. Sartre, *Being and Nothingness,* trans. H. Barnes (New York: Philosophical Library, 1956), p. 615.

77 L. Wittgenstein, *Philosophical Investigations,* trans. G. E. M. Anscombe (New York: The Macmillan Co., 1953), sec. 114.

78 Ibid., sec. 3.

79 Ibid., sec. 23. (Some of Wittgenstein's examples have been omitted.)

80 Ibid., sec. 11–14.

81 Ibid., sec. 2.

82 Ibid., sec. 68.

83 Ibid., sec. 84.

84 Ibid., sec. 66–67.

85 Ibid., sec. 116.

86 Ibid., sec. 47.

87 Ibid., sec. 81.

88 J. Wisdom, "Philosophy, Anxiety and Novelty," in *Philosophy and Psycho-Analysis* (Oxford: Basil Blackwell, 1953), p. 112.

89 J. Wisdom, "Philosophy and Psycho-Analysis," in *Philosophy and Psycho-Analysis*, p. 181.

90 J. Wisdom, "Philosophy, Metaphysics and Psycho-Analysis," in *Philosophy and Psycho-Analysis*, pp. 276, 282.

91 W. Sellars, "Philosophy and the Scientific Image of Man," in *Frontiers of Science and Philosophy*, ed. R. G. Colodny (Pittsburgh: University of Pittsburgh Press, 1962), p. 37.

92 Ibid., p. 39.

93 J. L. Austin, *Sense and Sensibilia*, ed. G. J. Warnock (New York: Oxford University Press, 1964), p. 15.

94 Ibid., p. 19.

95 Ibid., p. 15.

96 G. Ryle, *The Concept of Mind* (New York: Barnes and Noble, 1971), p. 7.

97 G. Ryle, *Philosophical Arguments: An Inaugural Lecture* (Oxford: Clarendon Press, 1945), p. 7.

98 Ibid., p. 7.

99 Ibid., p. 8.

100 Ibid., p. 6.

101 P. F. Strawson, *Individuals* (Garden City, N.Y.: Doubleday & Co., Anchor Books, 1963), p. xiii.

102 L. Wittgenstein, *Philosophical Investigations*, sec. 109.

103 P. F. Strawson, *Individuals*, p. xiv.

104 G. Ryle, *Philosophical Arguments*, p. 20.

105 J. L. Austin, "Three Ways of Spilling Ink," reprinted in *Approaches to Ethics*, 2d ed., ed. W. T. Jones, F. Sontag, M. O. Beckner, and R. J. Fogelin (New York: McGraw-Hill Book Co., 1969), p. 654.

106 J. L. Austin, *Sense and Sensibilia*, p. 63.

107 L. Wittgenstein, *Philosophical Investigations*, p. 226.

108 W. van O. Quine, *Word and Object* (Cambridge, Mass.: M.I.T. Press, 1960). pp. 51–52.

109 Ibid., p. 22.

NOTE TO THE READER

The history of the issues raised by Professor Jones's review of twentieth-century philosophy can easily be traced in *GBWW*. Hume's analysis of causation, which prompted, in part, the revolutionary philosophy of Kant, is contained in Section VII, Parts I and II, of his *Enquiry Concerning Human Understanding*, which appears in Volume 35; while all of Kant's major works, of which the most pertinent is the *Critique of Pure Reason*, are contained in Volume 42. The idealism of Hegel, against which Moore and Russell rebelled, is implicit in his *Philosophy of History*, for which see Volume 46.

Relevant discussions of the questions raised by Professor Jones may be found in the *Syntopicon*. In Chapter 66, on PHILOSOPHY, see Topics 1 and 1b, which treat the scope of philosophy and its relation to mathematics. See also, in the same chapter, Topic 3a, which deals with the foundations of philosophy in experience and common sense, and Topic 3d, on the methodological reformation of philosophy. In Chapter 45, on LANGUAGE, see Topic 1a on the role of language in thought, Topic 2a on the hypothesis of one natural language for all men, and Topic 5b on meaningless and absurd speech.

Henry B. Veatch and Moltke S. Gram are philosophers and university professors. Professor Veatch has had a long and distinguished teaching career. After graduating from Harvard University in 1932, he studied for two years at Heidelberg, and then returned to Harvard, where he received his doctorate in 1936. The following year he returned to his native state, Indiana (he was born in Evansville September 26, 1911), and began his teaching career at Indiana University, where he remained until 1965—the last four years as Distinguished Service Professor. He went to Northwestern University in 1965 and last year was appointed John Evans Professor of Philosophy. Besides a book on ethics, entitled *Rational Man* (1962), he has written extensively on the philosophy of logic. His latest book, *Two Logics* (1969), also provides the basis for a general theory of the humanities.

Professor Gram was born in Waterloo, Iowa, April 23, 1938. He did his undergraduate work at Indiana University, where he received his bachelor's degree in 1960. He did graduate studies at Heidelberg, Johns Hopkins, and Indiana, taking his doctorate from the last in 1965. His first teaching assignment was at Northwestern University, where he served for four years. This past year he received an appointment to the department of philosophy at the University of Iowa. Professor Gram has worked extensively in German philosophy, especially that of Kant, on which he has published two books: *Kant: Disputed Questions* (1967) and *Kant, Ontology and the A Priori* (1968).

*H. B. Veatch
and
M. S. Gram*

Philosophy and Ethics

In any synoptic account of present-day academic philosophy in the United States—i.e., philosophy as it is practised and purveyed by our contemporary American college and university professors[1]—one can scarcely fail to recognize the situation as being pretty much one of "either-or": either one is a so-called analytic philosopher, or one is a phenomenologist and/or existentialist. Nor is this well-nigh dichotomous division of schools confined only to the United States, but rather, like so many other things in American culture, it is little more than yet another duty-free import from Great Britain and from Western Europe. For in Great Britain today, particularly England, it would seem that only one philosophy is predominant—that particular variant of analytic philosophy known as "linguistic analysis" or "Oxford analysis"; and on the continent, particularly in West Germany and in France, one encounters but little else in academic philosophy save variations on the still dominant theme of phenomenology and existentialism.[2]

Suppose now that one were seeking to understand these rival philosophical tendencies or schools, not in terms of mere dates and chronology, or in terms of any mere taxonomy of names and movements, but rather in terms of the structural relationships and interconnections of the philosophical ideas involved, then one might well use as a touchstone for the interpretation of both movements their common heritage from Immanuel Kant. Not that either movement is particularly conscious of, or willing to acknowledge, this heritage from Kant; indeed, since neither movement is scarcely so much as on speaking terms with the other, they would doubtless both alike be shocked at being told that they had a common ancestor. Yet for all of this, it would seem hardly deniable that the analytic philosophers, no less than the phenomenologists, have sooner or later and almost without exception been led to make what might be called "the transcendental turn" in philosophy—a turn originally not just recommended but even invented by Kant.*

As to what such a turn amounts to, one might perhaps try characterizing

---

* *The Critique of Pure Reason; GBWW,* Vol. 42, esp. p. 7a–d.

it loosely by saying that those philosophers who have made such a turn find themselves no longer disposed toward regarding philosophy as an enterprise directed toward achieving what in an old-fashioned parlance might be called a knowledge of "the nature of things," i.e., a knowledge of things as they are in themselves and in their very being; rather the business of philosophy becomes one of trying to understand things not as they are in themselves but only as they are for us—as they appear to us, as we take them to be, and as they present themselves to us. And what is it that determines that things shall appear to us or present themselves to us, not as they are in themselves, but only under certain guises and in forms that are entirely relative to us and to our human modes of apprehending them? The answer is that it is precisely the conditions of our human knowledge and cognition that are thus determinative of the way things are for us or appear to us.

Thus in Kant's own view, it will be recalled, it was what he called the a priori forms of intuition and the pure categories of the understanding that constitute the conditions of our human knowledge and understanding. Moreover, it is in virtue of just these conditions that what Kant called the phenomenal world, or, in other words, the everyday empirical world of both science and common sense, takes on no less than the ordered and substantial character that this world obviously has. And yet there is no reason in principle why the conditions of our human knowledge and understanding should necessarily be just those that Kant thought they were. No, rather than so-called forms of intuition or categories of the understanding, it could be that it is but our human moods and attitudes that are the conditions of things appearing to us in the ways they do rather than in other ways. Or perhaps it is the peculiar features of our human language and logic that are responsible for our coming to see and understand things only as patterned and structured by such logico-linguistic features. Yes, it might be no less than our human purposes and resolves in virtue of which the world in which we find ourselves takes on only such sense and meaning as we bestow upon it. Still, whatever the particular way may be in which the conditions of human knowing may be conceived, the fact remains that on this view the knowledge that we human beings have of the world and of reality is always but a conditioned knowledge. That is to say, it is never the realities of things just as such that we may be said to see and know, but only these realities as conditioned by our modes of seeing and understanding. Accordingly, it is this thesis of the relative and conditioned character of our human knowledge that constitutes what we have chosen to call that transcendental turn in philosophy, which characterizes so much of modern thought from Kant right down to the present day.

To be sure, it would be a mistake to interpret this particular sort of turn or shift of emphasis in philosophy that stems from Kant as meaning that philosophical propositions are no more than claims about how we know things. Rather they are, even on the transcendental turn as Kant understood it, claims about things as distinct from the ways we have of knowing them. Accordingly, what distinguishes the Kantian version of the transcendental turn is just that the restriction Kant placed on philosophical propositions prevents us from talking about the world apart from the way it appears to us.

Such, then, is the historical root of the transcendental turn.[3] But does this notion have any defensible parallel in the movements of contemporary philosophy? We think it does. To be sure, the notion cannot be bodily transferred from the peculiarities of Kant's philosophical program to contemporary philosophy. There is, however, an important family resemblance between the role that that notion played in Kant's thought and the role that it plays in both contemporary analytic philosophy and in phenomenology or phenomenology-cum-existentialism.

The transcendental turn and analytic philosophy

Proceeding forthwith to a consideration first of analytic philosophy, it should be noted to begin with that what has come to be called analytic philosophy was not—in its origins, at least—a philosophy of the transcendental turn at all. In the hands of such people as Russell and Moore, it was a thoroughgoing realism.[4] Thus Russell was convinced, in the period of his so-called logical atomism, that a process of logical analysis would show both (1) what the true logical structures of ordinary English sentences were and (2) that such logical structures were in turn analyzable into certain ultimate atomic components, which exactly corresponded to things or entities in the real world that were the actual atomic components of the facts which the sentences or propositions were about. To take a crude example, to say that a is north of b is to make a statement reducible to the logical structure of a dyadic proposition, aRb. Each of the elements in that proposition is held to correspond to an item in the fact which that proposition represents; a and b, that is to say, stand for real entities in the world (Russell calls them atomic particulars) which in the present case are related to one another in that one is north of the other; accordingly, just as items a and b in the proposition stand for real particulars in the world, so also the symbol R in the proposition stands for the real relation that holds between a and b.[5]

Nevertheless, this early realism of analytic philosophy, according to which the constituents of an atomic proposition stand in a one-to-one correspondence with the constituents of the corresponding fact—this realism was soon shattered as a result of three quite different and largely independent philosophical tendencies which are still very much alive and with us and indeed might even be said to now dominate the current philosophical scene.

57

The first of these was a tendency that arose more or less within the context of developments in formal logic and that, for want of a better identification, might be associated with the name of Rudolf Carnap.[6] For one thing, Carnap distinguished between what he called material and formal modes of speech: the former contains expressions that refer to extralinguistic entities, whereas expressions of the latter type refer only to various kinds of linguistic expression. Wheeling up this distinction, Carnap trained it directly upon the very foundations of Russell's realism, particularly upon Russell's contention that the logical structure of any atomic sentence of our language must needs correspond directly to, and even mirror, the structure of the corresponding fact. For example, as we have already noted, in a sentence such as "This is to the left of that," the terms *this* and *that* may be taken to refer to extralinguistic entities called particulars, and *to the left of* to refer to a real entity, which might be called simply a relational universal. But Carnap would summarily dismiss this entire account as involving a simple confusion of the formal with the material mode of speech. For terms like *particular* and *universal* signify only linguistic expressions and do not refer to extralinguistic entities at all. Consequently, philosophical sentences of the sort "There exist particulars" or "There exist universals" are what Carnap would call pseudo-object sentences: they appear to refer to extralinguistic entities of a certain kind but really are only syntactical sentences in disguise.[7]

Moreover, the upshot of such a critique was that the very foundations of Russell's thoroughgoing realism in logic and philosophy were quite effectively blasted. On the Carnapian view, the logical structure of propositions in no wise requires the existence of special kinds of extralinguistic entities—e.g., particulars and universals or relations—corresponding to the structure of the proposition. Quite the contrary, the formation rules of a given logical system—those rules that prescribe what a well-formed proposition is for that system—are entirely a matter of arbitrary choice. "In logic there are no morals," Carnap declared in *The Logical Syntax of Language* (1934); and, in consequence, countless alternative logics and formal systems can be proliferated almost at will. And if one were then to inquire, "But what is that logical structure that is the proper structure of the world and of the facts in the world?" Carnap's answer would be that the world does not have any logical structure of its own at all. Or, what comes down to the same thing, the facts of the world have only such a logical structure as we choose to confer upon them. But with this the transcendental turn has already been made and made decisively: it is not the structure of the world in itself that we can ever hope to know and understand but only its structure relative to us and to our human ordering schemes and systems of logic.

However, the transcendental turn is not only evidenced in the theory of formal logic. A similar development occurred with respect to inductive logic, and this time the name to conjure with is not that of Carnap but of Sir Karl Popper. In his book *The Logic of Scientific Discovery,* Popper sought not to solve the problem of induction but rather to break its back. He repudiated induction as a means of scientific discovery. His argument—and the argument which brought about a transcendental turn in inductive logic—was this: Induction as a logical procedure is indefensible just because any attempt to infer from particular observed cases anything like a properly universal law is an inference which, when cast in syllogistic form, involves a fallacy of illicit minor. And to suppose that a scientific hypothesis can be verified as a result of events that have been predicted on the basis of that hypothesis is to commit the fallacy of affirming the consequent.[8]

Instead of induction, Popper recommended as the only proper method of scientific discovery a procedure that has now come to be known as the hypothetico-deductive method. According to this method, one begins by recognizing that the observed facts and regular occurrences in nature stand in need of explanation. Silver melts at 960.5°C.; the planets are observed at regularly recurrent positions at regular intervals of time—but why? What is the explanation of such phenomena? The answer is that since scientific explanations are not the sorts of things that can be found or discovered in the facts, it must be we ourselves who make up or devise the relevant explanations. Thus, to cite a classic example, given certain data as to the observed positions of the planets at different times, Johannes Kepler simply drew upon his own fertile mathematical imagination to come up with the notion of an orbit in the shape, not of a circle, but of an ellipse, as a possible explanation of why a given planet should be in the various positions it had been observed to be in at different times. Moreover, once such an explanatory hypothesis as Kepler's theory of the elliptical orbits of the planets has been thus devised, it is Popper's contention that the business of the scientific investigator must not be thought to be one of trying to verify such a hypothesis or of showing that in fact a given planet may at such and such a moment of time be observed to be in just the position that was predicted on the hypothesis of its orbit being an ellipse. No, for such an attempted "verification" of the hypothesis would be but another attempt at induction and would involve once more the fallacy of affirming the consequent.

Accordingly, rather than to try to verify the hypothesis, the real business of the scientist, Popper thinks, is to try to falsify it. Since there are certain deducible consequences from any hypothesis, the scientist should concern himself with trying to find out not whether such consequences do occur but rather with whether they do not occur. For if a deducible consequence of a hypothesis fails to occur, then the hypothesis is clearly falsified, and falsified in accordance with the perfectly impeccable logical procedure, not of affirming, but rather of denying the consequent.

Popper supposes that by putting forward this hypothetico-deductive method as the only proper method of scientific discovery, he has quite broken its back, by simply and deftly renouncing the use of induction in science altogether. But what Popper never seems to have realized is that in thus obviating the traditional problem of induction, he is forced, unwillingly and unwittingly, to make the transcendental turn.

Indeed, there are at least three features of the hypothetico-deductive method, at least as this is expounded by Popper, that would appear to make the transcendental turn quite ineluctable for anyone wishing so to construe the nature of scientific discovery. The first such feature has to do with how one arrives at such an explanatory hypothesis in the first place. For Popper is careful to insist that there is nothing about the observed facts in the case that could be said to make such a hypothesis logically plausible or from which it could be logically inferred. If there were, then the inference could only be an inductive one, and this is the very thing that Popper wishes to get away from. Clearly, then, if the propounding of an explanatory hypothesis is in no sense a logical process, or governed in any way by canons of sound reasoning, then it would appear to be more like an act of free creation or imaginative invention—comparable, say, to the composition of a symphony or thinking up a plot for a novel. And Popper does liken the devising of hypotheses in science to just such things. As soon as one views the matter in this light, scientific hypotheses cease to have the look of genuine accounts of the nature of things, or of the way things are in themselves, and take on instead the cast of just so many ways we human beings have of picturing things to ourselves and of causing them to appear to us, not as they are in themselves, but only as they are relative to us and to the imaginative constructions that we place upon them.

The same conclusion, moreover, is reinforced by the second feature of Popper's hypothetico-deductive method, which, to put it bluntly, is simply this: No explanatory hypothesis or scientific theory can ever properly be regarded as a true statement about what is in the world. Indeed, such a view of a theory is excluded when Popper says that the only way in which a theory can come into contact with the world is by such of its logical consequences as can be falsified. For what this means is that reality can reject a view but cannot tell us whether the view we have is really adequate to it: there can be, in other words, indefinitely many different theories that are capable of generating the same experimental consequences. And if this is so, then we can never know whether any theory that we have is a true description of the world. Thus Popper says that "Theories are our own inventions, our own ideas; they are not forced upon us, but are our own self-made instruments of thought."[9] It is true, of course, that Popper goes on in the very next sentence to say that theories can clash with reality and so may be held to be mistaken. But this does not show that any theory can be known to be a true picture of the way the world is. The most it shows is that certain theories are not true pictures of reality, not that we can ever know which theory is such a picture; hence, any theory that has not been disconfirmed is as much a statement about the way in which we choose to look at the world as it is about the world. In fact, it can be argued, although Popper is at pains to avoid this conclusion, that any theory we adopt is in part an expression of our determination to view reality in one way rather than another. For, after all, if there is nothing to decide between a number of competing theories that we have not disconfirmed or falsified, the reason that we decide to adopt one rather than another is not dictated by the facts but rather by human decision.[10]

We come now to feature number three of Popper's account of the logic of scientific discovery and of scientific knowledge in general. Already we have noted how, in the context of such a method of discovery, explanatory theories in science—and by extension in philosophy as well—are not based on the facts or in any way derived from the facts; rather they represent but so many different ways of seeing the facts. That is to say, given a different theory or explanatory hypothesis in either science or philosophy, the facts themselves will be seen in a different light; indeed, they will even appear as, and be seen as, different facts. And with this, one would seem compelled to take a step beyond Popper, a step that any number of younger philosophers of science have taken and taken decisively. The step is this. Granted that the facts are seen as being of this character or that, depending upon the particular overall scientific theory or conceptual scheme into which they have been integrated, then it will no longer be possible to have the sort of unequivocal falsification of theories and hypotheses that Popper had envisaged. So-called crucial experiments simply become out of the question. Why? Because the relevant facts will no longer have an independent character of their own; rather they will be, as the current expression has it, completely "theory laden"; and as such, so far from being able to stand out in conflict with the relevant theory, and so to offer evidence of its falsity, they will have no features, no nature, no characteristics of any kind save those that have been bestowed upon them by the theory. In short, just as Popper had maintained that overarching scientific theories were in no wise to be inferred or derived from the facts, so now it would appear that they are not subject to even being falsified by the facts. As a result, the change from one all-embracing scientific theory to another—say, from the Ptolemaic to the Copernican system—is never warranted by evidence that is logically decisive. Instead, such sea changes in the history of science and of human culture generally are to be understood simply as "revolutions," or as radical changes of fashion and mode, for which no logically compelling grounds or reasons can be given at all.

But what could be more telling evidence than this of the transcendental turn? Things, the world, the facts, are never seen or known for what they are in themselves; instead, they are seen or known only as our arbitrarily constructed theories and conceptual schemes permit us to see and to know them.

Finally, there is a third tendency in analytic philosophy which has contributed even more to that radical, and yet comparatively unnoticed, shift of ground in analytic philosophy from its original realism to what is today a kind of transcendental philosophy. This third tendency is associated directly with the interest contemporary analytic philosophers have in ordinary language. That such an interest is in part the result of an abandonment of an original concern with extralinguistic matters can be shown as follows. When G. E. Moore undertook to defend common sense against philosophical paradox, in his British Academy Lecture "Proof of an External World," what he took himself to be doing was to defend the reality of what one might call the everyday, ordinary world of things that exist in their own right and quite independently of when or whether we human beings happen to be perceiving them.[11] But the accomplishment for which Moore was celebrated was, it was later pointed out, misinterpreted by Moore himself. This was the thesis advanced by Norman Malcolm in his well-known essay "Moore and Ordinary Language."[12] When Moore thought he was defending the commonsense view of the world and hence was arguing about the characteristics that things in the world have, what he was in fact doing was giving a defense of ordinary language and hence was arguing about the characteristics of our discourse about things.

Consider the following example. Some philosophers have claimed that there are no material things, holding as they do that what we take to be material things are really classes of sense data. Moore seeks to answer this by saying that, if this claim is right, it would follow that none of the propositions by which we ordinarily seek to describe material objects are true. For if material objects do not exist, then no proposition that assumes their existence—as, indeed, any commonsense description does—can be true. Thus, what is wrong with certain philosophical theories, according to Moore, is that they entail conclusions that conflict with the very data— viz., the commonsense objects of our everyday world—of which they are supposed to be an account. And since we have a choice here to reject either a theory having such a consequence or the existence of the data that such a theory is meant to explain, Moore's conclusion was that we must reject the theory.

On all this Malcolm comments that Moore was mistaken to think that he was engaged in showing something about the character of the world. What Moore was really showing was something about what is or is not the correct use of certain locutions or expressions which occur in ordinary language. For what is it that our so-called sophisticated philosophers are doing, Malcolm asks, when they utter paradoxical pronouncements to the effect that "Time is unreal" or "There are no material bodies"? They are really maintaining that whenever we make assertions such as "After getting up this morning, I first shaved and then later went down to breakfast," or "There was a great mass of boulders and uprooted trees blocking the trail," what we are saying is false; and the reason statements of this sort are always false is presumably because they involve the use of temporal expressions or expressions denoting the existence of material objects. However, Malcolm counters by insisting that such statements cannot be held to be always false on the ground that they are self-contradictory, because they are not. And if, he continues, our sophisticated philosophers hold such statements are always false, because of the existence of empirical evidence to the effect that the sorts of situations described in these statements never have occurred and never will occur, then it is patently clear that there is and can be no such empirical evidence. Accordingly, Malcolm concludes, ordinary statements of the kind cited above, so far from being examples of incorrect usage, on the ground that they are always false, are rather examples of a usage that is entirely acceptable and correct.

But note what the upshot of this entire line of argument of Malcolm's would appear to be, so far as Moore's defense of common sense is concerned. Having shown that philosophers who attack common sense are really attacking the legitimacy of linguistic expressions and locutions in ordinary use, the rebuttal of these philosophers must accordingly take the form of showing that "ordinary use is correct use." Consequently, while Moore thought that he was arguing, for instance, about the existence of material things, his arguments were really no more than demonstrations about what is proper language. In other words, to say that a philosophical thesis ("There are no material bodies") is false is to say, not that there are material bodies, but rather that the thesis in question violates ordinary language. But with this, it is clear that a transcendental turn has taken place: a philosophical claim is held to be not a claim about what is in the world so much as a claim about what is proper language.

Moreover, this tendency we have just traced in Malcolm's famous essay is reinforced by the work of Ludwig Wittgenstein, particularly in his *Philosophical Investigations* (1953). Wittgenstein's views in this work were in part a reaction to a theory of language and meaning he had propounded in the *Tractatus logico-philosophicus* (1921). This latter book contained a theory—not wholly unlike the theory of Russell's mentioned above—according to which descriptive language is meaningful because it is like a picture or mirror or map, which represents the order of nature or the way things are in the world. But Wittgenstein came to reject that theory in favor of a conception of language as like a game: To be meaningful is to function in a certain way in the context of a language game. Thus meaning does not have any essential connection with picturing or representing something. What is essential is the use or purpose governing the employment of language. And this is given, not by correlating elements of the world, but rather by delineating the role that a kind of language has in the context of usage.

The attention given to the myriad uses of language is, however, but one manifestation of the transcendental turn in analytic philosophy. What caused the turn was in fact a commitment made at another level. The Wittgenstein of the *Tractatus* had argued (1) that all descriptive sentences are reducible without remainder to sentences that are logically atomic, and (2) that sentences that are logically atomic are meaningful only because they picture atomic facts in the world. On this view, accordingly, descriptive sentences have meaning only because there is something in the world that they represent. This theory of meaning has gone down in literature as the Picture or, later on, the Bearer Theory of Meaning. But there were two ways in which this was attacked by later analytic philosophers—ways that necessitated the transcendental turn. The first line of attack was to point out that there are uses of language that are meaningful but that are not properly descriptive at all and hence not reducible to collections of atomic sentences. Examples of this kind of use are, of course, not far to seek: the ethical and aesthetic uses of language offer the most prominent examples. Thus compare the following sentences:

> *The view from the top was extensive.*
> *The view from the top was sublime.*[13]

Clearly, sublimity would seem not to be an objective quality or feature of the landscape in the way in which being extensive most certainly is. And yet if there is no actual property in the world that a word like *sublime* may be said to represent, then a sentence such as the second one above would seem quite irreconcilable with the Picture Theory of Meaning.

Moreover, still another type of example that illustrates the severe limitation of scope infecting the Picture Theory is the doctrine of so-called performatory utterances which was first propounded by J. L. Austin. There are occasions, Austin reported, on which we utter such sentences as "I apologize to you," or "I do" (when the speaker is participating in the appropriate role in a marriage ceremony), or "I bet you that it will not happen." These and innumerable other kindred sentences have the characteristic—devastating to the Picture Theory of Meaning—that they cannot in principle be reduced to one or more sentences that are descriptive of any state of affairs, even though such sentences are grammatically indicative. And if this is so, the Picture Theory fails as an account even of all sentences which are grammatically indicative. The reason that performative sentences cannot be construed as descriptive is this: In apologizing, or saying "I do" at a marriage ceremony, or making a wager,

I am not describing a state of affairs but rather calling one into being. When you describe something, what you are describing would be the case whether you choose to describe it in one way or another or whether you choose to describe it at all. When you apologize, or say "I do," or wager, none of these things would be the case unless you uttered the sentences declaring that you were doing one or the other of them. Performative utterances, unlike descriptive utterances, are one and all, cases of making something so by saying it. And this put a dent in the Picture Theory which most analysts thought irreparable.

The Picture Theory was undercut in a second and more direct way: later analysts repudiated the view that *any* sentence, descriptive or not, has meaning because it mirrors or pictures what is in the world. And this attack was, ironically, initiated by Wittgenstein himself in the *Philosophical Investigations*. There were two prongs to the attack. First of all, it was argued that descriptive sentences would have meaning even if what they mirror or represent in the world were destroyed. Thus I can say "Excalibur has a sharp blade" and be understood, even if Excalibur were completely destroyed. [Cf. *Phil. Invest.*, ¶ 39.] But if a paradigm case of a descriptive sentence like this can be meaningful without necessarily picturing or mirroring anything, it must be false to say, as the Picture Theory requires us to say, that such sentences are meaningful only if they picture something in the world.

The other part of the attack was Wittgenstein's repudiation of simples. One of the main props of the Picture Theory was that the atomic sentences to which descriptive discourse was reducible mirrored a complex of things, each of which was simple. Thus, to analyze the molecular sentence "This is red" into its component atomic sentences was to trace back the referents of the words in the sentences to expressions that referred to things that could not be further analyzed. This was an obvious requirement of the theory: if atomic sentences could, *per impossibile,* contain expressions referring to things that were further analyzable, then they would not be atomic sentences. But what if there are no simples? The result would be that the Picture Theory is false. That there are no simples, Wittgenstein undertook to show as follows. He points out that what is taken to be simple for one purpose can be regarded as composite for another. [Cf. *Phil. Invest.*, ¶ 47.] The squares comprising a chessboard are simple when we consider them in the context of a chess game. But they can with equal legitimacy be called composite if we ask about the number of square inches of which the board is constituted. The conclusion of the argument is that there are no simples just because what is simple is a function of the language game that is being played. And if what is simple can, on any such interpretation, be further analyzed, it would follow, Wittgenstein reasoned, that there are no atomic constituents that can be mirrored by atomic sentences. But if this is the case, the whole Picture Theory must be abandoned: to say that there are no simples is to say that there are no atomic sentences. And since the Picture Theory of Meaning was made to depend upon the existence of such sentences, any repudiation of such sentences would be a repudiation of the theory itself.

The transcendental turn was completed, then, with the repudiation of the Picture Theory of Meaning. To ask about the meaning of a word or a sentence cannot, if the later Wittgenstein was right, consist in finding anything in the world that corresponds to it. An account of the meaning of any utterance must take the form of a description of what we do when we use words. It will include the inferences we make with them, the occasions on which we apply or refuse to apply them, and the purposes we seek to carry out when we use them. In short, philosophy is about language, not about the world. Or perhaps the latter assertion should be amended to read: philosophy is not about the world as it is in itself but about the world only as the latter is determined by, and seen through, our linguistic uses and ways of talking about it. As a result, when one leafs through today's philosophical books and periodicals to see just what it is that contemporary philosophers are doing, and what they are occupying themselves with, one may be somewhat astonished to find titles such as "On 'Trying'," "On the Meaning of 'Ought', 'If', 'So', and 'Because'," "Language and Morals," "Language and Philosophy," "Logic and Language," etc., etc.

Still, a skeptical observer of this rather odd-seeming philosophical scene might remain puzzled. For why, he might ask, must the business of philosophy be thought to be simply with language and linguistic uses? Even granting that as analytic philosophy has developed and evolved, it has come to seem increasingly fruitless for philosophers to busy themselves with trying to know the nature of things or the way the world is, still, why suppose that the only alternative for philosophers is to try to know about language? For one thing, is not language the preserve of linguists and philologists? And for another thing, are not the meanings of our words and the uses of various linguistic expressions constantly changing, so that to engage in repeated and interminable discussions about the use of the verb *to know* or the meaning of expressions like *voluntary* and *involuntary* would seem to be little more than sophisticated triviality?

To such a challenge, the contemporary linguistic analyst is likely to respond by once more falling back on the transcendental turn—this time in an unmistakably explicit way. For instance, Prof. Stanley Cavell, one of the younger American analysts, in an interchange with Prof. Benson Mates, was forced to face up to the issue of what might be termed the necessity or binding character of various linguistic uses and meanings.[14] Citing as typical examples of the sort of assertions linguistic philosophers are wont to make, Cavell calls attention to the following two statements, which he simply labels S: "We do not say, 'I know. . .' unless we mean that we have great confidence . . ."; and again, "When we ask whether an action is voluntary we imply that the action is fishy." Now why is such a meaning of *know* or of *voluntary* anything more than a mere accident of English usage that happens to prevail in the mid-twentieth century, and that is obviously subject to change and alteration? After all, there is surely nothing self-contradictory about the notion of an action being voluntary and yet not fishy at all. To this Cavell replies, "When (if) you feel that S is necessarily true, that it is a priori, you will have to explain how a statement which is obviously not analytic *can* be true a priori."[15] But presto! with this declaration Cavell has but raised all over again— albeit this time in the context of the Wittgensteinian philosophy of linguistic analysis—Kant's old question, which is no less than the very point of departure of *The Critique of Pure Reason:* "How are synthetic judgments a priori possible?"*

Moreover, should one still have doubts whether, with the raising of this question, analytic philosophy, at least in its so-called linguistic phase, has indeed taken the transcendental turn and so committed itself to being but another variant of Kantianism, one has only to read Cavell's own subsequent comment on the same issue, respecting the enterprise of linguistic analysis: "When I am impressed with the necessity of statements like S, I am tempted to say that they are categorial—about the concept of an action *überhaupt.* . . . This would account for our feeling of their necessity: they are instances (not of Formal, but) of Transcendental Logic."[16] Now what is this, indeed, if not Immanuel Kant *redivivus!*

The transcendental turn and phenomenology and existentialism

Turning attention now to the second of those two dominant trends in contemporary philosophy—phenomenology and existentialism—may one say of the latter two, no less than of analytic philosophy, that they, too, are marked by what we have chosen to label as the transcendental turn in philosophy? In answer, we would simply observe that whereas analytic philosophy is something of a Johnny-come-lately so far as transcendentalism is concerned—and sometimes even makes the turn halfheartedly, and seemingly unconsciously, and as if it were reluctant even to admit that it had made the turn at all—in phenomenology the turn is not only admitted and acknowledged but actually provides at once the starting point and the continuing basis for the entire philosophical enterprise of phenomenology's founder, Edmund Husserl. For the initial question that Husserl asked in philosophy was literally the question as to the very "possibility of a cognition that 'gets at' (*treffen*) the things themselves. . . . How can we be sure that cognition accords with things as they exist in themselves, that it 'gets at them'?"[17] And to his own question Husserl gives

---

* *GBWW*, Vol. 42, pp. 1 ff.

an emphatically negative answer: Not only is it impossible for us ever to be sure that our knowledge accords with things as they exist in themselves, but also it is irrelevant and unnecessary for us even to concern ourselves with any such unattainable will-o'-the-wisp as a knowledge of things as they are in themselves. For why worry about a knowledge of this sort—especially since such knowledge is quite unattainable? Instead, why not simply bracket the question of what things are like in themselves and confine ourselves to knowing about things merely as they present themselves to us and as they appear to us. In other words, in Kantian terms, it is again a knowledge of phenomena—not of noumena—that philosophy, in the sense of phenomenology, is to aim at.

The transcendental turn in phenomenology is effected as follows. First, Husserl distinguishes between facts and essences.[18] What we are given to start with are the ordinary entities of experience like tables, chairs, ethical experience, and other selves. What interests the phenomenologist, however, is not these things in their particularity but rather their meaning, sense, or essence; hence, judgments in phenomenology are about essences, not things that have these essences. In this sense, then, knowledge given by phenomenological explication or analysis is universal: the judgments about, say, perceptual objects like chairs are not about this or that chair but rather about what it means to be a chair.

But this is only the first step toward the transcendental turn. It is accompanied by another step which, according to Husserl, must be taken if we are to explain how knowledge of senses or essences is to be attained. All judgments about such things as essences are, for Husserl, both universal and indubitable.[19] But the ability to make indubitable judgments about essences demands that we change the subject of the judgment from the entity as it is in itself, or apart from our knowledge of it, and restrict the subject to the appearance it gives to the person knowing it. As long as judgments about essence purport to be about objects as they are in themselves, they can be mistaken: for such judgments can be falsified by future experience of the object that is the subject of the judgment. And this would be incompatible with the requirement that judgments about essences be indubitable. That requirement is fulfilled, however, once we say that what we are judging is not an object in itself but only the object as it appears to us—the object understood as an appearance. In this case, the judgment we make cannot be overturned by any future experience: What we are judging about is presented to us in its totality. For this reason, no future experience will count for or against our judgment about the subject that we judge. To restrict our judgments to things as appearances is to render these judgments certain, in just the sense that such judgments do not purport to be claims about anything that exists outside that appearance and hence anything that could be advanced as evidence against the certainty of that judgment. But this completes the transcendental turn: what we are offered is a network of judgments about a network of appearances, not about things that appear.

Moreover, this program of phenomenological description, which Husserl would prescribe as being a proper program for philosophy, is correlated with an insistence upon another feature of the situation that Husserl thought to be no less important for phenomenology. For no sooner does one renounce the enterprise of trying to know things for what they are in themselves, than one must also acknowledge that the way in which things appear to us, or present themselves to us, is not to be explained by the natures and characters of such things in themselves. Instead, as Husserl remarked in that same early treatise from which we quoted above, one can no longer say that "the things once more exist in themselves and 'send their representatives into consciousness'."[20] Rather, it must be the case that the objects of our experience, or, better, objects as we experience them, must themselves be *constituted* in being experienced. Accordingly, in addition to a program of phenomenological description of things or objects just as they appear, the philosopher or phenomenologist must also concern himself with the actual constitution of those objects that takes place in the very process of their being experienced.

So much by way of a brief account of the dominant strain of transcendentalism in Husserlian phenomenology: a transcendentalism that continues to be operative in the work of practising phenomenologists of the more or less strict Husserlian type right down to the present day—thinkers of the stamp of Aron Gurwitsch, for example.[21] Nevertheless, if such a phenomenology is to be brought up to date in terms of its more recent development at the hands of thinkers like Heidegger and Sartre and Merleau-Ponty, it behooves us to consider how the mainstream of phenomenology, as it continued and still continues to flow from its source in Husserl, soon became infused with a tributary stream of what might be called Kierkegaardian existentialism.

It was one of Kierkegaard's most telling theses that human knowledge, at least as we are familiar with it in the science, the scholarship, and even the philosophy of modern Western culture, has tended to be a purely objective knowledge. That is to say, it is a knowledge which might be said to occupy itself wholly with, and to exhaust itself completely in, the object known, thus leaving out of account entirely the human subject that achieves the knowledge and actually does the knowing. For instance, to take some very simple and trivial examples: insofar as I know, within the context of Euclidean geometry, that the square of the hypotenuse of a right triangle is equal to the sum of the squares of the other two sides— or, in the context of biology, that, as an animal develops, its ontogeny recapitulates its phylogeny—it is quite irrelevant to the truth of such pieces of knowledge how I, as the knowing subject, happen to feel about them, or whether such a knowledge makes a real difference to me personally or affects my life in any way.

To put the point just a bit differently, one might say that in the entire range of modern science and scholarship it is a matter of indifference and even irrelevance whether such objective knowledge makes the slightest difference to the life of the person who happens to have such knowledge: quite patently, one's competence and even brilliance as a physicist are not affected in the least by whether one is a saint or a scoundrel; and as for modern musicology or Chaucerian scholarship or comparative literature or business administration or medicine or mechanical engineering or whatnot, such types and kinds of objective knowledge are not even supposed to have any very direct bearing on the kind of person or human being that one becomes as a result of acquiring such knowledge.

Accordingly, Kierkegaard recommended and even preached a knowledge that would be "subjective" and not merely objective. And by "subjective" in this connection he understood a knowledge that not only would make a difference to the knowing subject but that in the very fact of its coming to be known would implicate the knower in an act of commitment, of personal responsibility, and even of being and existing as an authentic individual. Thus, to know that $2 + 2 = 4$, or that silver melts at 960.5°C., is one thing or one kind of knowledge; but to know that my redeemer liveth, or that Christ died for our sins, is a knowledge of a very different kind. For in the latter case, I can hardly be said to know in the sense of knowing ordinary objective truths or facts; rather, I know only in faith, and at the risk of being utterly mistaken, and in an act of courage and devotion that commits me in my entire way of being and existing. In short, it is a knowledge that does make a difference to me, the knower, which I cannot even achieve as knowledge without myself being or becoming a certain kind of person, without my actually being and existing in a certain way.

Let this existentialist stream be merged with this stream of Husserlian phenomenology, and the result will be that that very "constitution" of objects and of the world, which we have seen to be consequent upon Husserl's having made the transcendental turn, now becomes a constitution for which we human beings must assume a responsibility.[22] It is in part our doing and a doing that we have committed ourselves to and cannot shirk responsibility for. Thus, what in everyday parlance might be spoken of as "the world of the eighteenth century," or "the world of the mathematician," or "the world of modern man," or "the world of the ancient Greeks," or "your world," or "my world," or "the world of the schizoid," etc.—these all represent ways in which things or objects present themselves to us or appear to us, and yet at the same time ways of appearing or modes of constitution that we have had a hand in and for which we must assume a certain responsibility. In other words, it is not as if, our cognitive faculties just happening to be built in a certain way, whatever comes to be known through such faculties must therefore automatically reflect the distortions of such a cognitive medium, much as ordinary objects will quite automatically appear as fantastically elongated or grotesquely fattened when looked at through the medium of certain kinds of lenses. No, it is rather that our world, or even our immediate situation, presents itself to us in the way it does because of our own existential resolve, or lack of resolve, to take things in a certain way, to see them in this light rather than that.

To be sure, when one turns to consider the work of Heidegger, it might strike one at first that the overall scheme of the transcendental turn just would not fit the peculiar amalgam of phenomenology and existentialism that is the philosophy of Martin Heidegger. For as Heidegger's most significant recent interpreter in English, Father Richardson,[23] never tires of pointing out, Heidegger's dominant and all-pervading concern throughout his entire philosophical enterprise is with Being. And, superficially at least, a concern with Being would hardly seem reconcilable with a program such as Husserl's, which, as we have seen, might well be construed as involving the counsel to give up any and all concerns with the very being of things and to concentrate simply on the phenomena, or on things as they appear rather than as they are.

Not only that, but Heidegger himself constantly inveighs against what he calls the subject-object dichotomy, as a result of which philosophers have tended to think of the problem of knowledge much in the way Husserl did, as being a problem of how a knowing subject, which is self-contained and, as it were, closed in upon itself, could ever get outside itself so as to know things as they are in themselves. Such a way of envisaging the problem, Heidegger says, is radically mistaken; and equally mistaken presumably—or if not mistaken, then gratuitous and irrelevant—would be any resort to the transcendental turn through which thinkers like Kant and Husserl suppose they can solve the problem. No, as Heidegger sees it, a being of the kind that could be properly called "human being" (Dasein) is not a self-contained subject at all but rather a being which is simply a being-in-the-world, a being with and among things in a world, a being which is nothing but a "transcendence"—that is to say, a being that is ever outside of and beyond itself with other beings, as well as a being that is literally ahead of itself in its projection toward the future and also behind itself in its retention of the past.

Nevertheless, despite such seeming evidence of Heidegger's efforts to obviate the transcendental turn, a somewhat closer inspection reveals that it is no less than just such a turn that is fundamental to Heidegger's whole philosophical undertaking. For in that very concern with Being, which in Heidegger's eyes is the mark and sign of human being, the task and the challenge with which human being is confronted is just that of getting from beings to Being. Thus we are all familiar enough with how anything and everything that we encounter in our human existence—fish and fowl and good red herring; ships and shoes and sealing wax; the earth, the sky, the waters; the sun, the moon, the stars—these all *are;* they are all beings. Yet, Heidegger asks, "Why should there be any being of any kind and not rather just nothing at all?" The very question itself suggests that beings owe their being to Being; their being is not something which can be simply taken for granted but rather is derivative as proceeding from Being.

Nor would there seem to be anything more commonplace in the history of Western philosophy than just such a notion of beings being derived from Being, or of all things being dependent upon a first cause or a supreme being. Yet such is not at all the way in which Heidegger conceives of the derivation of beings from Being. Quite the contrary, he insists that this same Being from which all beings derive their being must not be construed as itself a being of any kind. That is to say, it is not *a* being at all: it is not in any sense another being, not even a being that is totally other than all those beings that are derivative from it. ". . . [It] is not God, nor [some] ground of the world. Being is broader than all beings—and yet is nearer to man than all beings, whether they be rocks, animals, works of art, machines, angels, or God. Being is what is nearest [to man]. Yet [this] nearness remains farthest removed from him. . . ."[24]

What, then, may Being be, if it is not a being? It is, Father Richardson suggests, simply a light or a lighting up, in and through which beings may come to be and be seen. Moreover, as this light, or lighting process, which renders beings unconcealed (*unverborgen*), Being itself remains concealed (*verborgen*).[25] For were Being, in its lighting up of beings, to become unconcealed or disclosed or lighted up itself, it would thereby cease to be Being and become a being. Accordingly, in its lighting process, Being may be said both to show itself and to hide itself in the very beings which it discloses and illuminates.

It should be noted, however, that in this lighting up and disclosure of beings by Being, the disclosure must needs be a disclosure to something, and the something can only be a being—man or human being. Clearly, though, beings cannot be disclosed to human beings, unless human being is open to such a disclosure of beings by Being. And this openness of human being to the disclosure of beings turns out to be—at least on Heidegger's account—a "constitution," perhaps not in quite the sense in which that word is to be understood in a Husserlian context, and yet not in an entirely alien sense either. For what Heidegger seems to feel is most requisite in this connection is some explanation of what there is about human being that enables it to be open to or receptive of the lighting up of beings by Being. This receptivity he interprets almost as if it were a kind of facility for constitution, in consequence of which it will be beings that come to be lighted up or illuminated for man by Being. More specifically, it is a set of what might be called existential determinants (*Existenzialien*) in human being that comprise the conditions under which beings can be disclosed and lighted up and so become beings for human being.

For example, one such existential determinant of human being is what Heidegger calls "facticity." In virtue of this, human being feels or experiences itself as in a world of beings that were already there before him and over which as human being he had no control; the world thus presents itself to man or human being as something into which he has been thrown or hurled, entirely willy-nilly. Another such existential determinant is "existentiality," in virtue of which man experiences himself as possibility, and as actually being out ahead of himself in his projects for the future, with the result that the beings of man's world present themselves to him as being for this purpose or that, and as adapted to various human ends and concerns. Finally, there is that existential determinant according to which human being is simply "forfeit"[26] to the world of beings in which he finds himself. Whether as experiencing himself as thrown into the world, or as out ahead of it and beyond it in his projects, man or human being is wholly occupied, or, better, preoccupied, with the beings of his world. He may thus be said to be forfeit to them in a total forgetfulness of Being, which is the primal source not only of beings but also of human being, and which it is the peculiar business and responsibility of human being to pass beyond mere beings in order to attain.

But what now of this world of beings, into which human being experiences itself as being thrown, and to which it is forfeit, and which provides the setting for all our human projects? Is it a world which exists quite independently of that human being which is said to be open to it; or is it not rather a world which is entirely correlative to, and inseparable from, human being, and such that the beings that make up this world, though they be lighted up by Being, are nonetheless constituted by human being in virtue of those very existential determinants that are the conditions of man's very openness to beings in the first place? For Heidegger, of course, it is only in the latter way, and not in the former, that the world and the beings that are lighted up in it are to be understood. While it is true that Heidegger repeatedly boasts of having overcome the subject-object dichotomy, what he intends thereby is no more than a rejection of an independent subject or ego, existing in itself and set over against an equally self-existent world of objects. Rather than this, Heidegger insists upon a strictly correlative structure of man and world: no human being without being-in-the-world, and no world without its being the world of or for human being.

Accordingly, as contrasted with what he says about Being, everything that Heidegger says about beings is consequent upon his having taken what we have been calling the transcendental turn in philosophy. Beings, that is to say, are "constituted," and have the features and characters that they do have, partly in virtue of the existential conditions of their being present to, and lighted up for, human being, and partly in virtue of the way in which human being takes them or lets them be present to

73

himself. Not only that, but present-day Heideggerian scholarship[27] seems almost entirely occupied with tracing out the consequences for our human concourse with beings, of the existential determinants in terms of which such beings are constituted, as well as of our human freedom within the limits of such determinants to take or to construe beings in one way rather than another. Why, for instance, in the history of Western thought, we have fallen into the habit of taking beings as ultimate and so of disregarding the all-important "ontological difference" between beings and Being; or why truth, and more particularly historical truth, is to be regarded not as something settled and unchanging but rather as having as many faces as there are human beings to seize it and make it their own— these and other like themes are the stock-in-trade of contemporary thinkers under the influence of Heideggerian transcendentalism.

Turning now briefly to Sartre and the Sartrians, as well as to Merleau-Ponty, it quickly becomes manifest that, in their case no less than in that of Heidegger, it is the transcendental turn that provides one with the key to understanding the distinctive sort of philosophical enterprise that these thinkers are all engaged in pursuing in their individually different ways. To be sure, in Sartre's case, one finds no comparable concern to that of Heidegger to get beyond beings to Being; nor is Sartre's human being, or human consciousness, quite so hedged about with existential determinants as a result of which the phenomenal world, or the world for man, is shot through with certain pervasive features of the kind Heidegger terms "ontological." Rather, consciousness for Sartre is much more free in its determination of the phenomenal world or world for man. Indeed, Sartre even insists that consciousness is not just free but is freedom. In consequence, in Sartre's work one sees exhibited in a most striking way that uniting of the notion of a constitution of phenomenal objects, which stems from Husserl, with the notion of the freedom and responsibility of the constituting subject, which stems from Kierkegaard and the existentialists.

To come, however, to some of the salient details of Sartre's philosophy, it might first be noted that the world of phenomena for Sartre—the world as it is constituted by, and appears to, consciousness—is quite firmly set in a fixed and definite ontological setting. At the one pole is being, or what Sartre calls the in-itself, which just is and is in itself and is what it is—an undifferentiated mass of inert, characterless, pointless, purposeless entity: "Uncreated, without reason for being, without any connection with another being, being-in-itself is *de trop* for eternity."[28] At the other pole is consciousness, or the for-itself. And what is it? It is nothingness; or, perhaps better, it is a mere negating or distancing of itself from being. Rather than being any sort of substance or self or person or being, consciousness is a not-being, precisely in the sense that, in being conscious of anything or any being, consciousness is perforce other than that being of which it is conscious. And so it is not that being, or any being, being rather nothing but a distancing of itself from any and all being. Nor is consciousness anything in itself, being instead always outside itself—being, that is to say, always consciousness of something other than itself. And so it is that consciousness is inescapably and irretrievably beyond itself, and on the other side of itself, and thus with the things and being that it is conscious of and yet that it itself is not.

Further, consciousness negates being in that in being conscious of something, it is conscious of one thing or of some things and not others. It thus, as it were, separates things out from the undifferentiated mass of beings and so differentiates beings from one another in its very act of discerning them. Indeed, one commentator brings out the result of this negating effect of consciousness by thus characterizing Sartre's notion of knowledge:

> . . . *the best word to define knowledge seems to be the verb "to realize" in the double ontological signification of this word: e.g., I* realize *the difficulty of my position, and I* realize *a project. To know is to realize in this twofold sense: through knowledge I* realize *that there is being (am aware of being), and also I* realize *being in the sense that I make that which appears. Sartre would say: through my knowledge I make that "there is" being. This is a dangerous expression, for it sounds very idealistic, and yet Sartre is not an idealist in the strict sense of the word. His knowledge of the world does not create the being of the world but makes the world "appear" . . . not in the idealistic sense, but in the sense that our knowledge makes the world appear, organizes the world, divides, specifies, and categorizes things.*[29]

Nor must it be overlooked that in thus making the world appear, in organizing the world, in dividing, specifying, and categorizing things, consciousness, or the for-itself, is free. For example, Sartre uses the telling illustration of the moon which is still not full, from which a quarter is still lacking. Yet what does it mean, he asks, to speak of the moon as not full, or as lacking something? In itself, it is neither complete nor incomplete, neither full nor lacking: it is only insofar as we project the moon as full, or imagine the crescent to be completed, that there is any completeness or incompleteness in the situation at all.[30] Such a projection or completion of the full moon, however, is entirely our project, or a project of consciousness; and one in respect to which consciousness is absolutely free. Oh, it's true. Sartre recognizes, that we find ourselves always in situations or in predicaments which in a sense are not at all of our own making or choosing: I am born a Negro or a white man; in the country or in town; crippled or whole; rich or poor—and clearly I have no choice as regards these factual situations, the like of which we all find ourselves committed to and into which we are thrown, as it were. Even so, Sartre insists, I am completely free as to how I comport myself in the face of such situations, and even in what I take them to be. For example, he observes how "a particular crag which manifests a profound resistance if I wish to displace it, will be on the contrary a valuable aid if I want to climb upon it to look over the countryside."[31] In itself, of course, it is completely neutral: it is neither a help nor a hindrance; indeed, it is not even a crag that is easy or difficult to climb. For the latter presupposes the existence of picks and piolets and the entire technique of mountain-climbing: without these a crag would not even be a crag. In other words, the character of things, and the way they appear, is a function of the way we take them to be; and how we take them is a function of our free projects as men.

When one turns from Sartre to Merleau-Ponty, one finds the latter sharply criticizing Sartre for overdoing this latter freedom bit. It's not that we are completely free with respect to facts and how we take them, Merleau-Ponty would say; nor are we completely determined by the facticity of our world or our situation either. Rather we are both at once: we are free and determined; our condition is one of radical and irremediable ambiguity, in other words. Moreover, the ambiguity that characterizes us as human subjects is paralleled by a like ambiguity in the objects and the world which appear to us. For our world is both our world and yet not a world of our making, at one and the same time. Nor is it possible to draw a sharp distinction between the sense that we give and bestow upon things, and the character that such things have independently of us. Here again the ambiguity is as impenetrable as it is irremediable. Indeed, one cannot even draw the sharp line of demarcation that Sartre does between consciousness or the for-itself on the one hand, and the in-itself on the other. Rather, for Merleau-Ponty it is fruitless and even impossible to distinguish between what things are in themselves and what they are for us; instead there is only the phenomenal world or the world that appears; and what is it but a thoroughgoing ambiguity?

Nevertheless, for the purposes of this brief survey of the contemporary situation in philosophy, it is really not so important how the Sartrians differ from Heidegger, or the partisans of Merleau-Ponty from Sartre, or the Heideggerians from the followers of Husserl. For the decisive consideration is the more-or-less shared way in which all of these thinkers would appear to do philosophy, not to mention their more-or-less common conception of what they take the nature of philosophic activity to be. It isn't the business of philosophy, these thinkers insist, to engage in metaphysical speculations about the Absolute or as to the ultimate nature of things or the causes of things; nor is its business with such scientific constructions as positrons, alpha particles, or curved space. These last are not the sorts of things that we encounter or that present themselves to us in our lived world of everyday human experience. Moreover, whatever one may eventually want to say about the ontological status of, and the evidence for, the scientific universe, or even for the various universes of different systems of metaphysics, what the phenomenologists and existentialists keep coming back to is the fact that a universe conceived in this sophisticated manner is in no wise the actual world that we live in as human beings. And it is no less than our lived human world, precisely as we experience it and live it, that these thinkers want to savor and describe. Not only that, but if one asks why things happen and occur as they do in this lived world of human experience, and what their causes are, this question, the phenomenologists would say, is not to be treated in the manner of traditional scientific, or even philosophical, questions as to why the infant death rate is declining, or what it is that causes an eclipse, or what makes grass green. No, the question is to be answered in terms of what there is about the human subject, or *Dasein,* or consciousness, or the for-itself, that determines our human world to have the character that it does have. In other words, philosophy for the phenomenologists is an enterprise that can be understood, not to say practised, only after one has taken the transcendental turn.

The transcendental turn and analytical ethics

The roots of the transcendental turn in the context of contemporary ethical theory[32] are to be found in two arguments which G. E. Moore gives in his *Principia Ethica* (1903). There Moore undertakes to show both that *good* is indefinable and that, in claiming that anything is good, we are assigning a peculiar kind of property to it. Consider the arguments Moore gives for these claims. In *Principia Ethica* (Chap. 1, Sec. 13) he argues that *good* cannot be defined, where by *definition* Moore means that reduction of a complex entity into its components. That *good* cannot be defined in this way, Moore claims to show as follows:

1. *Although good is defined as XY, we may always significantly ask of anything that is XY: "That is XY, but is it good?"*
2. *If the definition of good as XY is true, then we would be able to substitute "XY" for "good" in the above question without changing the sense of that question. But the result of making such a substitution is this: "That is XY, but is it XY?"*
3. *Unlike "That is XY, but is it good?" the question "That is XY, but is it XY?" is not significant; therefore the two questions cannot have the same sense.*
4. *But if "Good is XY" were a true definition, the two questions would have the same sense. But since they do not, that definition or any other must be false; hence, good is indefinable.*

There are two immediate consequences of this argument. First of all, it undercuts all attempts to account for the existence of what is denoted by the predicate ". . . is good" in terms of pleasure, the fitness of an

77

organism to survive, virtue, or any other of the myriad things to which ethical theorists had tried to reduce goodness. What this shows is that, however we justify the predication of goodness, we cannot justify it by showing that the things we take to be good have this property in virtue of something in the world.

But there is another consequence of this argument which Moore does not draw: If we can always significantly ask whether anything is good, then the relation between saying that a thing has any property and that it is good is purely contingent. Thus we cannot justify predicating goodness of anything because of any properties that it may have, for it will always be possible to affirm that a thing possesses any property that it does and consistently to deny that it possesses the property of goodness. And this raises one of the questions that has dominated ethical theory since Moore. If we cannot justify the predication of goodness of anything in the world by way of the properties it possesses, can we ever be said to have any reason or justification for saying that anything is good? If what is said to make something good is compatible with the withdrawal of the predicate from the thing in question, then it would seem to follow that the possession of *any* property by a thing would be a reason for calling that thing good. And this amounts to saying that there is no property the possession of which justifies calling the thing possessing it good.

Let us consider Moore's argument for the second claim we singled out above; the claim, namely, that the meaning of the word *good* is a peculiar property which the word *good* denotes. The argument, as it is stated in *Principia Ethica* (Chap. 1, Sec. 13, and Chap. 2, Sec. 26), runs as follows:

1. *"Good" must denote either a complex or a simple property, or the word is meaningless.*
2. *The word is not meaningless, and since it is indefinable, it does not denote a complex property.*
3. *But then "good" must denote a simple property.*
4. *A property is either natural or nonnatural. If it is the former, it can be conceived to exist in time by itself; if the latter, it cannot be so conceived.*
5. *"Goodness" cannot be conceived to exist in time all by itself but, rather, requires natural properties to support it.*
6. *Therefore, goodness is a nonnatural property.*

This is Moore's argument to show both that good is a property and that it is a nonnatural property.[33]

These arguments precipitated a crisis in contemporary ethical theory. Moore held both that typically ethical judgments expressed something true or false and that there was something in the world—what Moore called a nonnatural property—that made these judgments true or false. But what if typically ethical judgments really had no truth value at all?

What if it could be shown that all Moore had succeeded in doing was to demonstrate that there was not anything in the world that could show ethical judgments to be true or false? Subsequent ethicists were agreed that Moore had shown that ethical predicates were unique and thus could not be reduced to something else. But they were also agreed that Moore had not shown that ethical predicates denoted or referred to anything in the world which could be adduced to show that ethical judgments had a truth value.

This reaction to Moore began the transcendental turn in ethical theory. C. L. Stevenson's *Ethics and Language* (1944) and *Facts and Values* (1963) were perhaps the first attempts to effect such a turn: arguing that it is possible to describe anything completely and still be in doubt about its goodness, Stevenson concluded not that goodness is a peculiar kind of property but that it is not a property at all. What Moore and others had wrongly called a property, Stevenson analyzed into a kind of linguistic usage. There are, for Stevenson, two components in statements of the form "X is good." There is, first, an emotive component which expresses the approval of X; and there is, second, an imperative component directing others to do likewise. But this implies that typically ethical judgments lack a truth value: they are neither true nor false, because there is nothing called a typically ethical property in the world that would render them true or false. We can, on this view, persuade others to have the attitudes we have to things about which we make ethical judgments; but we cannot cite anything about the description of the things to which we have the attitude we do such that it would be impossible to have the opposite atti-tude toward it. And this move in ethical theory is an example of what we have been calling the transcendental turn: ethicists after Moore have been mainly concerned with examining how typically ethical locutions function in our discourse, and they have been concerned to exhibit the logical structure of justification in ethics.

Recent analytic ethical theorists have tried to remove the difficulties brought about by the transcendental turn, while still accommodating the facts on which it is based. Their concern has, accordingly, been twofold. First, they have tried to show that the distinction between descriptive and evaluative uses of language does not imply that ethical predicates are merely expressions of attitudes. Second, they have argued that a firm dis-tinction between descriptive and evaluative language does not destroy the possibility of rational argument in ethics. Both of these concerns derive from the kind of turn that Stevenson's arguments forced ethicists—how-ever reluctantly—to take.

R. M. Hare has addressed himself—first in *The Language of Morals* (1961) and more recently in *Freedom and Reason* (1965)—to both of these issues. The two most relevant parts of his theory are, accordingly, his analysis of *good* and his defense of the universalizability thesis as a basis of rational argument in ethics. Consider, first, his analysis of *good,* the general strategy of which is this: There is an indestructible difference between descriptive and nondescriptive uses of language. Moreover, there are decisive objections to Stevenson's account of this distinction. And, finally, there is ample evidence from the careful observation of ordinary language that (1) the meaning of *good*, which is invariant from context to context, is that it is the most general word of commendation, (2) commendation is accomplished in ordinary language by expressions in the imperative, and (3) the criteria or properties in virtue of which we apply the predicate *good* to things change from context to context.[34] Hare's objection to Stevenson's account of good as expressive or emotive rests on a distinction, honored by ordinary language, between telling somebody what to do and getting or influencing him to do something. Since we can, according to Hare, instruct somebody to do something without trying to influence him to do it, it cannot be right to say that the characteristic ethical use of *good* is persuasive.[35]

But there is still, on Hare's view, a crucial distinction between descriptive and nondescriptive (i.e., evaluative) uses of language, the nature of which Stevenson misdescribes. The argument for that distinction runs as follows:

1. *Assume that "good" is by definition C, where "C" stands for a set of either natural or nonnatural characteristics.*

2. *It follows from (1) that the sentence "x is a good K" is synonymous with "x is a K and x is C," where "K" stands for a description of x.*

3. *But these two sentences are not synonymous—which shows that no value of C can define "good."*[36]

The strategy of the foregoing argument is to show that, if we try to define *good* by any set of natural or other characteristics, we cannot say of anything that it is good. We can say only that it has the characteristics it has. And since saying that something is good is to say something more than that the thing has certain characteristics, the word *good* does not refer to a characteristic of anything. Since Hare's view is that *good* is commendatory, he would state the conclusion thus: If we define *good* in terms of any number of characteristics a good thing has, we will never be able to commend that thing for having those characteristics. But we must be able to distinguish between a thing's possession of certain characteristics and our commendation of those characteristics. Any position according to which it is impossible to do this must be false. And, if we grant Hare's further premise—the premise, namely, that the meaning of *good* is that it is the most general word of commendation—it readily follows that the nondescriptive use of *good* is commendatory.

What has been given so far, however, is only a general account of valuation. What remains to be given is an account of distinctively ethical evaluation. Hare seeks to account for this kind of evaluation by simply extending the analysis he gives of *good* to the domain of ways of life or, derivatively, of human characteristics. He holds that *good* means the same thing when it is used to commend ways of life as it does when we commend other things. What is different is the criteria of application. The restrictions placed on the application of the notion to ways of life are, of course, the same as they are in other contexts: it is logically impossible to give the same description of two ways of life while commending one and refusing to commend the other; and in this context as elsewhere no conjunction of natural or nonnatural characteristics can deductively imply a judgment of goodness. But otherwise the use of *good* in evaluating human behavior is the same as in evaluating things like, say, hockey sticks or paring knives.[37]

It remains to be asked how this account of the use of *good* meets the difficulty which the transcendental turn brought with it. Hare does not speak to this point directly, but there are several things about his account which might be thought to show that the ascription of ethical predicates like *good* has an other-than-emotive justification. For one thing, Hare sharply separates commending from influencing and propaganda. To tell somebody what he ought to do certainly does not entail that one is merely conniving to get him to do something. And this does, on the face of it, set off the giving of reasonable injunctions from setting about to manipulate an interlocutor. For another, Hare is careful to argue that the criteria of application of ethical words are inextricable parts of the use of such words: "When we make a moral judgment about something, we make it *because* of the possession by it of certain non-moral properties."[38] This indicates that, although the meaning of *good* is commendatory, the word cannot be deployed without criteria and, consequently, that the application of the word is not capricious but is founded in something that exists independently of our choice to commend or not to commend.

The advantages of Hare's account of ethical terms are, nonetheless, weakened by a fundamental disanalogy in his account of valuation. Hare holds that the analysis he gives of valuation in typically nonethical contexts can be transferred bodily to typically ethical contexts: what is true of the machinery of valuation in the context of hockey sticks and other nonhuman furniture of the world is true of the evaluation of ways of life. But this move creates the illusion of objectivity in the case of ways of life that simply is not present—at least in the same way in which it is present in nonethical contexts.

Consider the example of a good hockey stick. The criteria of a good hockey stick are objective and independent of our choice. What is not independent of our choice is whether we adopt the end of desiring a good hockey stick. But once we have adopted the end of wanting such a device, we are not at liberty to *choose* which instrument fulfills the end of being a good hockey stick. To commend in a context like this is just to *find out* as over against choosing what these criteria are. In this sense, then, the application of the word *good* in nonethical contexts has an objectivity removed from caprice that the use of the same word does not have in typically moral contexts. Thus it is not a matter of choice that we accept one instrument and reject another when we are choosing a good hockey stick. But it *is* a matter of choice that we adopt one style of life and reject another. And so the possibility of justification, present in the context of adopting things in nonethical contexts, appears to end when adoption is transferred to ways of life.

Hare does, indeed, appear to recognize this: "But when I *subscribe* to the principle [i.e., the principle governing a way of life], I do not state a fact, but make a moral decision."[39] If this is true, however, one of the problems of the transcendental turn has yet to be solved or, alternatively, shown to be insoluble. Since we are at liberty to choose criteria for the application of the word *good* with respect to alternative life styles, in a way in which we are not at liberty to do for the application of that word with respect to things other than life styles, it remains to be shown how we can justify the application of the predicate *good* in the latter context.

Consider the second problem that Hare inherits from his predecessors. If ethical judgments are prescriptive, and, further, if no prescriptive conclusion can be derived from any set of purely descriptive premises, then what is to distinguish sound from shoddy ethical reasoning? The same point can be put this way: If you grant, as Hare does, that there is no logical tie between any prescriptive use of language and statements of fact, how can we rule out any prescription as immoral? Hare's answer to this question is to tell us what makes a principle moral. A principle is moral when it is both universalizable and prescriptive.[40] We have already seen why one condition of a moral principle is that it be prescriptive: this is just a consequence of Hare's more general position that any evaluative use of language is prescriptive. But this alone does not distinguish moral from immoral principles; hence, Hare requires that a moral principle also be universalizable. And what this amounts to, according to Hare, is this: We cannot logically ascribe the predicates in universalizable judgments to one object and refuse to ascribe them to any other object having the same description. Thus to say that object x is good implies that any other object having the same properties of x is likewise good. If this condition is not honored, then we can derive a contradiction from the application of any predicate. For to apply any predicate to one object and refuse to apply it to another object of the same description is both to apply and not to apply the predicate to the original object.

Now the universalizability thesis, thus stated, is a logical claim. It is, that is, a claim about the meanings of words. But Hare transfers the principle to moral judgments, saying that "it does not make much difference whether we say that it [the universalizability thesis] is a second-order statement about the logical properties of moral judgments, or that it is a first-order, but analytic, moral judgment."[41] And he goes on to argue that the universalizability thesis will rule out principles that are immoral. Hare recognizes that there are principles governing life styles that, though mutually exclusive, nonetheless satisfy the universalizability test. But this, for Hare, does not show the inadequacy of the test. It merely indicates how divergent morally permissible ideals can be. And that we choose to live by one such ideal rather than another is not a matter of reasoning but rather of decision.[42]

Let us consider an example of the application of the universalizability test discussed by Hare to a particular moral principle.[43] The principle is that adopted by many Nazis—that all Jews ought to be exterminated. (Call it P.) Hare regards this as immoral and seeks to show that it is as follows:

1. *P is prescriptive.*
2. *P is universalizable: Everybody ought to be exterminated who has the characteristics in virtue of which the Jews ought to be exterminated.*
3. *But (2) incorporates the desire to exterminate anyone without exception having those characteristics.*
4. *It follows from (3) that, "if he is sincere and clear headed, [the Nazi] desires that he himself should be exterminated if he were to come to have the characteristics of Jews."*[44]
5. *It is a "fortunate contingent fact" that those who desire (4), even among Nazis, would be extremely rare.*
6. *Therefore, those Nazis who grasp (4) are obliged to repudiate P.*

The foregoing example exposes a serious difficulty in the universalizability thesis. That thesis was introduced by Hare to account for the distinction between moral and immoral principles of action. It was meant to explain how we can give rational justification of principles. But in the present example—and innumerable others can be constructed exactly like it—the application of the principle merely assumes that step (4) would be rejected as irrational from the start. Now it may, indeed, be the case that (4) does formulate an irrational desire. But if it does, then what counts as rational or irrational principles is not the result of the application of the universalizability test. That such a proposition is irrational is presupposed and not certified by the universalizability test. And Hare does not tell us on what grounds we would defend the irrationality of (4). Yet a large class of ethical judgments is concerned to pronounce desires like that expressed in (4) as unjustified, irrational, or even immoral. And if this is so, then a large class of ethical propositions lies outside the scope of the universalizability test

It is, accordingly, no accident that other contemporary moral philosophers have been dissatisfied both with Hare's account of goodness and his account of ethical reasoning. As diverse as the alternatives to Hare are, they have one thing in common: they are all attempts to show that there is a closer connection between ethical predicates and the world than the transcendental turn claims. P. T. Geach, in "Good and Evil," argues that *good* is used descriptively both in and out of ethical contexts.[45] He undertakes to assimilate the use of *good* to that of such terms as *big* and *small:* such words have a definite sense in each context. Thus *good* is descriptive, although it functions this way only when used with reference to kinds or classes. And Geach holds, accordingly, that it is a mistake to say, as some previous moral philosophers have said, that because *good* by itself is not descriptive, it is not descriptive at all.

What Geach wants to hold is that the term *good* has a definite sense in all contexts but that the sense changes from context to context. But it would seem that, in order to be able to say this, Geach would also have to say that there is nothing that is common to all of these contexts. True, his major point is that *good* describes, not alone, but only in the context of some natural kind or other. But while this is true enough—and something that Hare not only admits but accounts for by distinguishing between the meaning and the criteria for the application of a term—the question that Geach does not raise is whether the term that describes only by specification of a context has any sense that is not completely specified by that context. If it has, then he must give an account of what it is. If it lacks such a sense, then Geach would appear to have obliterated Hare's important distinction between describing a thing and saying that it is good.

Kurt Baier, in his *Moral Point of View,* propounds another alternative to the transcendental turn.[46] Attacking the conclusions that other ethicists have drawn from the descriptive-evaluative distinction, Baier argues that you can verify statements of value in every way in which you can verify descriptive statements. To say, for example, that *a* is faster than *b*, while it is factual, is—in one respect, at least—no different from saying that *a* is better than *b:* in both cases you are ranking things, and this requires reference to a criterion of correct ranking. But the difficulties with ranking outside of ethics are no different from those inside ethics; hence, Baier concludes that ethical claims can have a truth value.

Ethical argumentation is not, for Baier, mere persuasion, because there are beliefs that govern ethical reasoning which can be true or false. Baier calls these consideration-making beliefs, defining them as statements or reasons for doing something (every such belief takes the form: "Do so and so because . . .").[47] Such sentences are meant to restore rationality to ethical justification, for they can function as major premises in ethical arguments (thus making such reasoning deductive) and can be shown to be true or false by some standard. But what is this standard? Baier says that such beliefs can be seen to be true when they are seen "to be required or acceptable *from the moral point of view.*"[48] To adopt such a point of view is to elect only those ends that can be rationally willed by everybody and to which there are no exceptions on grounds of inclination. But this merely perpetuates the problem of the transcendental turn: do we have any reason to reject those ends that, though they meet the restrictions of the moral point of view, would still be counted as immoral ends? Baier's answer is that there are certain fundamental consideration-making beliefs and that they are true because those who refuse to adopt them "must even be said to be mad."[49] But this move solves the problem of the transcendental turn by pointing out that it is advantageous to *say* that some of the consideration-making beliefs founding one's culture are true. Some would deny that this is a solution at all.

Julius Kovesi's *Moral Notions* (1967) represents one such denial.[50] Like Baier before him, Kovesi attacks the descriptive-evaluative distinction. But he holds, unlike Baier, that the distinction has been used by philosophers as an inadequate account of the very different distinction between the formal and material elements in our use of language.[51] Such elements, so far from being present only in ethical locutions, are to be found in many so-called descriptive locutions as well. Just as we are able, for example, to cite as instances of a table things with very different shapes, sizes, and colors, so we call things good that have very different properties. The material elements of tables differ widely, while the formal element—that in virtue of which tables are given their name—does not vary. And the same point can be made about predicates like *good*. And so, if we hold that object-words like *table* can occur in sentences that are true or false, why should we deny that typically ethical predicates can occur in sentences in exactly the same way? Moral words, then, are in the same boat as other words: if we refuse to say that moral words can be used to describe something, we must also refuse to say that a host of other words can be used in this way.

The possibility of identifying the formal element in ethical predicates enables us, on Kovesi's account, to make true statements about what is good. But statements about formal elements are, for Kovesi, statements about functions; and these reduce, on his account, to statements about the criteria of application of the term we use to refer to something.[52] That any array of different things can be grouped under one functional description is not, then, the result of something that is in the world but rather the result of our linguistic conventions: the objectivity of ethical discourse is made to stand and fall with the public character of linguistic conventions. Kovesi can thus say that moral judgments "simply are not about the world."[53] But this, so far from dealing effectively with the problem of the transcendental turn, tacitly concedes that the problem is insoluble: The strategy is to hope that what has been conceded at one level—that ethical predicates are not about the world—can be recovered if we translate ethical statements into statements about language.

There remains another attempt to reverse the transcendental turn, the author of which accepts the presuppositions of that turn but denies that such a turn is the logical outcome of them. D. H. Monro defends a naturalistic analysis of ethical predicates which runs like this: "*x* is good" is equivalent to "(a) *x* has a given external characteristic *p* and (b) *p* is approved (by me or by men in general)."[54] What distinguishes this version from the usual naturalistic analysis is not the attempt to show that goodness is, after all, analyzable but that we can preserve rationality in approval or disapproval. Monro does this by showing that we can apply the universalizability test to our expressions of approval or disapproval: if anything has properties in virtue of which it is approved or disapproved, anything else having the same properties must also be approved or disapproved. Thus Monro can say that "whenever we express our emotions not merely by grunts, groans, or smiles but by projecting them onto the objects that evoke them . . . , we do imply that the same emotion will be roused by similar objects."[55] Monro concludes that expressions of emotion are not unrelated to their objects: just as we cannot consistently apply a predicate to one object and refuse to apply that predicate to other objects having the same properties, so we cannot consistently express approval for one object and withhold approval from anything else having the same description.

But this criterion can be satisfied by moral and nonmoral approvals alike. Recognizing this, Monro proposes to distinguish distinctively moral principles from others by claiming that the former are not only universalizable but also that they are what he calls overriding. To say that a principle is overriding is, for Monro, to say that acting on it takes precedence over acting on any other principle.[56] This may succeed in separating moral from nonmoral principles; but it does not succeed in separating moral from immoral principles. It is still possible, for example, to say that a principle is overriding but immoral. And there is no way, on Monro's account, to justify one rather than another overriding principle except to say that it expresses something beyond which there is nowhere else to go. And the consequence would seem to follow that Monro has introduced no more ultimate rationality into ethical deliberation than Stevenson, Hare, Baier, Geach, and Kovesi before him: what he has shown is that we cannot give or withhold expression of approval *inconsistently*. And this does not prevent us from rationally approving of anything at all so long as the approval we express is consistent.

This also aligns Monro with those with whom he professes to disagree. For all the ethicists we have been considering so far have, each in his separate way, been attempting to restore a descriptive content to ethical predicates and thus to show that there is an ontological foundation for attributing a predicate like goodness to something. But the way in which this is done leaves it an open question whether there is, after all, any such foundation for the application of ethical predicates. For whether you call it a fundamental moral belief, a decision of principle, a consideration-making belief, or an overriding principle, the problem that confronts all of these solutions is the same: we are not given a reason for condemning some principles that most or all men would condemn as immoral so long as the principles under consideration are consistently held. Perhaps this is too much to ask of moral philosophy. But if it is, then it should be admitted that the moral decisions we make are somehow ultimately irrational, because we cannot rationally condemn people who make the contrary decision so long as they hold to it consistently.[57]

The transcendental turn and phenomenological-existentialist ethics

In turning to a consideration of recent developments in ethics within the context of contemporary phenomenology and existentialism, one can hardly fail to be struck by the fact that while philosophers of this persuasion are forever given to making ethical judgments, they are scarcely ever given to writing about ethics. Neither Heidegger nor Sartre nor Merleau-Ponty—to mention only the more obvious "greats" in this philosophical tradition—has ever written an ethics. Nor is it generally agreed that they have even laid down the very principles for an ethics, which their followers might then someday eventually develop. True, Heidegger, as is well known, distinguishes between authentic and inauthentic existence.[58] Sartre, in his novels and plays, as well as in his articles, and even in *Being and Nothingness,* does not hesitate to satirize various modes and types of human behavior, castigating this person for being a "coward," that one for being a "stinker,"[59] another for being a "serious man," and all for being "in bad faith." Besides, both Sartre and Merleau-Ponty have engaged in no end of political discussion, pouring out streams of articles, pamphlets, and even books of polemics against the enormities of capitalism and bourgeois society generally, as well as against historical Marxism, particularly that form of it to which the dirty label of "Stalinist" might be attached.[60] But why in all of this has there never appeared anything that these philosophers would themselves claim was an ethics? Or why have not more of their followers undertaken to supply what would seem to be such an obvious lack on the part of their masters?[61]

The answer, we believe, is to be found in that peculiar kind of transcendental philosophy that is so much a part of the warp and woof of contemporary phenomenology and existentialism. And by way of illustration, let us consider just briefly a certain seeming sort of ethical investigation that one not infrequently finds undertaken in the context of phenomenology of the stricter and less existentialist variety. Such investigations might be loosely characterized as aiming at what one might call a phenomenology of values, or "a phenomenology of moral experience."[62] After all, there is no denying that in the experience of human beings things do appear to us, at least under certain circumstances and in certain contexts, as being morally colored, shall we say. Thus, in our awareness of most natural phenomena, such as that of water flowing downhill, for example, it is hardly the case that we experience this as being in any way right or wrong, or good or bad. But that the Soviet armies should move into Czechoslovakia, or that certain personal friends or associates should be found to be secretly conniving to defame us or undermine our reputations, or that the United States should be maintaining a presence in Vietnam—these are things that we cannot very well avoid experiencing save as morally colored, i.e., as defensible or indefensible, or as noble or vile, as reprehensible or commendable, etc. Accordingly, given the fact that in certain reaches of human experience things do appear or present themselves to us not as morally neutral but as morally colored, the phenomenologist can rightly claim that these ways of appearing that things have in so-called moral experience are just as deserving of phenomenological description as are the ways of appearing that things have in aesthetic experience, or in the experience of everyday life, or in scientific experience, or in religious experience or whatnot.

Unfortunately, however justified the phenomenologist may be in thus seeking to provide a phenomenological description of moral experience, and indeed of the entire range of value phenomena, such an undertaking is still far from being an ethics. It is one thing to know that things do in fact appear to us under the guise of good or bad or of right or wrong, etc.; it is another thing to recognize that such distinctions have some sort of a real basis, which not only justifies us but even obligates us to observe them and abide by them in our day-by-day conduct and behavior. Moreover, it is precisely the latter sort of concern, rather than the former, that is the proper business of ethics. Accordingly, the phenomenologist, having made the transcendental turn, can only find it difficult if not impossible to get beyond the phenomena of ethics to the reality. And doubtless this accounts for the fact that in recent years pure phenomenologists seem to have pretty much given up any and all attempts at developing an ethics.

But what about the existentialists? For we have already noted in our discussion of the contemporary situation in philosophy generally that pure phenomenology has in recent years often given place to a phenomenology mixed with existentialism. What, then, is one to say about ethics in the context of such a phenomenology-cum-existentialism?

Again, it might be recalled how in our foregoing discussion of contemporary philosophy in general, it was pointed out that the characteristic influence of existentialism on those who make the transcendental turn is to shift the seat or locus of the transcendental activity of "world constitution" to the individual human subject. So, likewise, when it comes to ethics, it would not be inaccurate to say that the effect of the existentialist ferment in phenomenology has been to regard that moral coloration, which our human experience in certain of its reaches does indeed have, as being something that the individual human subject has bestowed upon things and is himself responsible for. That is to say, we human beings create our own values; and, as Sartre and so many other existentialist writers would have it, in so doing, man creates himself.

What then, is the import of this characteristic existentialist move, so far as the rehabilitation of ethics is concerned? Initially, of course, it is only too clear that existential phenomenology makes the transcendental turn no less than does pure phenomenology: values, moral distinctions, standards of conduct are held not to pertain to things as they are in themselves but only to things as they appear to us. At the same time, the existentialist has in effect shifted the locus or center of ethical concern from what we might call values in things and in the world to the human subject who creates such values and bestows them upon things, and who is thus responsible for the sense and meaning that things come to have for him, but which they do not have just in themselves.

Putting it very crudely, it is as if the existentialist were saying that it really is of no importance to ethics whether a certain social order, let us say, which men have come to regard as being just, is really just or not; or whether a certain way of life or pattern of behavior, which men have come to esteem, is really estimable or not. No, what matters ethically, and all that matters ethically, are the human decisions and resolves, as a result of which certain ways of life or institutions of society have taken on the value and significance that they have. For what of the human choices and decisions and commitments that were the sources of such estimates and evaluations: were they authentic, were they genuine, were they what they should have been? These are the only properly ethical questions, as the existentialists see it, questions that have their point and locus simply with reference to the human subject in his choices, his decisions, and his evaluative activity generally.

And how would the existentialists say that such properly ethical questions are to be answered? After all, in much of traditional ethics, it is supposed that in order that a man's choices and decisions be the right ones, he must first know what the good is, and what he as a human being ought to do and be, and how he should conduct himself. Not so, though, the existentialists. Instead, they would repudiate the whole idea of knowledge as being a guide to action. For such an idea makes for an ethics of the type known as that of "the serious man," a type that has been repeatedly satirized in existentialist literature, beginning with Kierkegaard and coming down to Sartre and Simone de Beauvoir. For the serious man is said to be just such a one as must first know what course of action he ought to take before deciding to take it. Yet thus to try to base one's ethical choices and decisions on anything like knowledge and understanding is, the existentialist would say, at once ridiculous and wrongheaded. It is wrongheaded because there simply can be no objective knowledge of what is really right or wrong, or good or bad: these are distinctions that we ourselves create, and hence they are not distinctions that are already there and, as it were, simply waiting to be known. Indeed, the transcendental turn in existentialist ethics precludes any knowledge of this sort. But, also, the serious man's procedure is as ridiculous as it is wrongheaded. For as Kierkegaard so amusingly observes:

> *The serious man continues: If he were able to obtain certainty with respect to such a good, so as to know that it is really there, he would venture everything for its sake. The serious man speaks like a wag; it is clear enough that he wishes to make fools of us like the raw recruit who takes a run in preparation for jumping into the water, and actually takes the run and gives the leap a go-by. When the certainty is there he will venture all. But what then does it mean to venture? A venture is the precise correlative of an uncertainty; when the certainty is there the venture becomes impossible. If our serious man acquires the definite certainty that he seeks he will be unable to venture all; for even if he gives up everything, he will under such circumstances venture nothing—and if he does not get certainty, our serious man says in all earnest that he refuses to risk anything, since that would be madness. In this way the venture of our serious man becomes merely a false alarm. If what I hope to gain in venturing is itself certain, I do not risk or venture, but make an exchange. Thus in giving an apple for a pear, I run no risk if I hold the pear in my hand while making the exchange.*[63]

And so at last it begins to emerge just what it is that, in the eyes of the existentialist, guarantees the genuineness and authenticity of our choices and decisions. It is not that they are made in the light of knowledge and understanding but rather that they are made at a risk and as a venture, precisely in the absence of knowledge. Nor is this really to say any more than that such authentic choices are free choices, in the existentialist sense of freedom. For if there are no objectively based guidelines for human life and existence, no values or obligations written into the very nature of things, then assuredly man is free, and free precisely in the sense, as Sartre puts it, of being "condemned to be free."[64] That is to say, in making decisions and choices man has nothing to appeal to, nothing that he can fall back on for guidance, nothing that he can turn to by way of finding out what he should do and be or how he should conduct himself. Instead, he must simply decide, and decide in a full awareness of the sheer and total risk that he is running, there being no principles or maxims of any kind that can serve him either by way of guidance or of justification. Likewise, he must decide, and decide in full awareness of his own sole and absolute responsibility for his decisions. After all, there being no things "twixt heaven and earth," or even in heaven or earth, that a man can even dream of appealing to for support or guidance in such a philosophy,[65] it follows that a man's decisions are entirely his own, and decisions for which no one other than he himself is responsible.

In summary, then, may not one say that existentialist ethics amounts

90

to but little more than an ethics that calls for free and authentic choices? What one chooses would appear to be of no moment, but only how one chooses, viz., freely and authentically. As Kierkegaard puts it, "it is not so much a question of choosing the right as of the energy, the earnestness, the pathos with which one chooses . . . it is not yet a question of the choice of something in particular, it is not a question of the reality of the thing chosen, but of the reality of the act of choice." [66]

But what is this, then, if not seemingly an ethics almost without content, an ethics whose one ultimate imperative is simply the imperative to be free? And if, indeed, this is the case, then it is little wonder that the so-called existential phenomenologists should have traditionally been so ready with ethical pronouncements and yet so chary about ever discussing ethics. Nevertheless, just in the last two or three years, in this country at least, there would appear to be a slight change in this respect. For there have appeared two books, as well as an occasional article or two, which, although they are not impressive as to quantity, are very much so as regards quality, and which do address themselves directly to questions of existentialist ethics. As to the books, the one by Hazel Barnes, entitled *An Existentialist Ethics* (1967), and the other by Frederick A. Olafson, entitled *Principles and Persons: An Ethical Interpretation of Existentialism* (1967),[67] they do not profess to present systems of existentialist ethics (as if there could be any such thing), so much as apologiae designed to show that there is an existentialist ethics after all. To give a taste of the character of these books, we perhaps could not do better than simply to summarize three of the stock difficulties that seem to attach to any attempt to make of existentialism an ethics and then to indicate which of these books addresses itself to these issues.

1. The first difficulty might be stated thus: On what grounds does the existentialist justify the value that he places on freedom itself? For, having made the transcendental turn, the existentialist then insists that the things and happenings of the world are neither good nor bad, neither right nor wrong, in themselves. Rather such is but the way things sometimes present themselves to us or appear to us. Moreover, the reason they thus make their appearances to us under this guise of value is because we human beings freely bestow such values upon them. And yet what about this very freedom itself, this very power to bestow a significance and importance upon things? Is that something whose value itself comes from this same freedom to bestow value? If so, then it would begin to look as if the entire existentialist account of value were somehow trying to hoist itself by its own bootstraps. On the other hand, if our own human freedom is not something that we give value to but rather something that has value in itself and absolutely and in its own right, then this would seem to involve a serious compromising of the transcendental turn itself, to say nothing of being inconsistent with the entire existentialist account of how values arise in the world.

Now it is to just this difficulty, among others, that Professor Barnes addresses herself in her book. As to how successfully she meets the difficulty, we do not propose to comment. And yet one wonders if she may not be found to have defended an ethics of freedom only by inadvertently turning the supposedly free man into a type very much like that of Kierkegaard's serious man.

2. If that human freedom, by which as men we are said to make ourselves, is a freedom which in the final analysis is subject to no norms or standards, save such as are of our own free invention and manufacture, or if in our free choices what is ethically relevant is not what we choose but rather simply that we choose and choose freely, then will this not make for a complete and utter relativism in ethics? After all, considered with respect to the content of our choices, it would appear to make not the slightest difference whether one's choice be for the way of life of a Hitler or for that of a St. Francis; rather, all that would matter presumably would be "the energy, the earnestness, the pathos with which one chooses."

With respect to this issue and its attempted resolution from the standpoint of existentialist ethics, the reader might be referred, not so much to either of the two books just mentioned, but rather to a very interesting article by John Wild, entitled "Authentic Existence: A New Approach to 'Value Theory.' "[68] Again, in Wild's case, no less than in that of Barnes, one wonders whether in his efforts to free existentialist ethics from the charge of relativism, Wild may not have had to fall back on an appeal to our common human nature as men, a tactic which smacks rather of the ethics of the serious man than of that of existentialism.

3. Finally, if in an existentialist ethics, that which is held to be of supreme value for a human being is no more and no less than one's own free, subjective commitment to one's freely chosen goals, as well as one's continued affirmation and vindication of that same freedom of oneself, then why should anyone have the slightest regard for the needs and interests of other human beings? What possible obligations can a man have to human beings other than himself?

To this issue in regard to existentialist ethics Olafson addresses himself in some of his most effectively argued pages. What he suggests is that Sartre and others, in making their enigmatic pronouncements to the effect that "in choosing myself I choose man," may really be appealing to the principle of the so-called universalizability of moral judgments which, as we have already noted, is a marked feature of much recent ethics in the analytic tradition. Indeed, Olafson's whole book is directed toward showing how, despite great differences in language and terminology, some of the leading ideas of existentialist ethics parallel many of those of recent analytic ethics. Need we add that our own concluding comment would be that such a parallelism is ultimately traceable to that common partiality of both of these schools for the transcendental turn in philosophy?

1 This limitation means that we must leave out of account a number of contemporary philosophical activities which have had a certain popular appeal, but little effect on academic philosophy—e.g., the work of Herbert Marcuse, Teilhard de Chardin, the partisans of "situation ethics," etc. We shall further limit ourselves by not discussing surveys of the literature as, for example, William K. Frankena's "Ethics," in *Philosophy in the Mid-Century*, 4 vols., ed. Raymond Klibansky (Firenze: Nuova Italia, 1958), 3: 42 ff.; Geoffrey Warnock's *Contemporary Moral Philosophy* (New York: St. Martin's Press, 1967); and Mary Warnock's *Existentialist Ethics* (New York: St. Martin's Press, 1967).

2 An exception might be the new development of so-called structuralism in French philosophy, as represented by such thinkers as Lévi-Strauss and Louis Althusser.

3 It might be remarked that of those comparatively few contemporary tendencies in American philosophy that are not marked by the transcendental turn at all, many are explicitly pre-Kantian or even anti-Kantian in their philosophical allegiances. Two recent books, for instance, which display a predominantly Aristotelian or Thomistic realism in philosophy, as contrasted with a more Kantian type of transcendentalism, are *An Interpretation of Existence* by Joseph Owens (Milwaukee, Wis.: Bruce Publishing Co., 1968), and *Two Logics: The Conflict Between Classical and Neo-Analytic Philosophy* by Henry Veatch (Evanston, Ill.: Northwestern University Press, 1969).

4 Cf. G. E. Moore, "Proof of an External World," *British Academy Proceedings*, vol. 25 (1939), pp. 273–300; also "A Defense of Common Sense," in *Contemporary British Philosophy* (second series), ed. J. H. Muirhead (London: The Macmillan Co., 1926), pp. 193–223.

5 Cf. Bertrand Russell, "The Philosophy of Logical Atomism," in *Logic and Knowledge*, ed. Robert C. Marsh (London: George Allen & Unwin, 1956), pp. 177–281. This Russellian program of logical atomism has been continued and brilliantly developed by Gustav Bergmann. See *Meaning and Existence* (Madison: University of Wisconsin Press, 1960), *Logic and Reality* (Madison: University of Wisconsin Press, 1964), and *Realism* (Madison: University of Wisconsin Press, 1967). The work of Professor Bergmann and his school constitutes a notable exception to the philosophical developments that we are about to describe under the heading of the transcendental turn.

6 Cf. *The Logical Syntax of Language*, trans. Amethe Smeaton (Paterson, N.J.: Littlefield, Adams & Co., 1959), esp. pp. 284 ff.

7 Ibid., pp. 297–99. For a parallel line of argument, *see* Gilbert Ryle's "Systematically Misleading Expressions," in *Essays on Logic and Language* (first series), ed. Antony Flew (Oxford: Basil Blackwell & Mott, 1951).

8 Karl R. Popper, *The Logic of Scientific Discovery* (New York: Sciences Editions, 1961), pp. 59 ff. Cf. N. R. Hanson, *Patterns of Discovery* (Cambridge: Cambridge University Press, 1958), for a similar view.

9 *Conjectures and Refutations* (New York: Basic Books, 1962), p. 117.

10 This view of change in scientific theories has been worked out historically by Thomas S. Kuhn, *The Structure of Scientific Revolutions* (Chicago: University of Chicago Press, 1962). For the broader metaphysical implications of this view of theory construction, *see* Wilfrid Sellars, *Science, Perception and Reality* (London: Routledge & Kegan Paul, 1963), and *Philosophical Perspectives* (Springfield, Ill.: Charles C. Thomas, Publishers, 1967).

11 See *Philosophical Studies* (Paterson, N.J.: Littlefield, Adams & Co., 1959).

12 Reprinted in *Ordinary Language*, ed. V. C. Chappell (Englewood Cliffs, N.J.: Prentice-Hall, 1964), pp. 5–23.

13 These examples are taken from P. H. Nowell-Smith, *Ethics* (Baltimore, Md.: Penguin Books, 1954), p. 70.

14 *See* Benson Mates, "On the Verification of Statements About Ordinary Language," in Chappell, op. cit., pp. 64–74; and Stanley Cavell, "Must We Mean What We Say?" in Chappell, pp. 75–112.

15 Cavell, p. 85.

16 Ibid., p. 86.

17 *The Idea of Phenomenology*, trans. William P. Alston and George Nakhnikian (The Hague: Nijhoff, 1964), p. 1.

18 Ibid., Lecture III.

19 Ibid.

20 Ibid., p. 10.

21 Cf. *The Field of Consciousness* (Pittsburgh, Pa.: Duquesne University Press, 1964), and *Studies in Phenomenology and Psychology* (Evanston, Ill.: Northwestern University Press, 1966).

22 The tension between these two themes of description and active constitution is skillfully brought out by Paul Ricoeur, *Husserl: An Analysis of His Phenomenology*, trans. E. G. Ballard and L. E. Embree (Evanston, Ill.: Northwestern University Press, 1967).

23 William J. Richardson, S.J., *Heidegger*, preface by Martin Heidegger (The Hague: Nijhoff, 1963).

24 Heidegger, *Brief über den Humanismus* (1947), quoted in Richardson, op. cit., p. 6.

25 Richardson, op. cit., p. 5.

26 This is Marjorie Grene's way of rendering Heidegger's notion *Verfallensein;* see her *Martin Heidegger* (New York: Hillary House, 1957), p. 25.

27 For an excellent new book in explanation and assessment of Heidegger, written not in the manner of a Heideggerian but rather in that of one schooled in analytic philosophy, *see* Richard Schmitt, *Martin Heidegger on Being Human* (New York: Random House, 1969).

28 J. P. Sartre, *Being and Nothingness*, trans. Hazel E. Barnes (New York: Philosophical Library, 1956), Introduction.

29 Wilfred Desan, *The Tragic Finale: An Essay on the Philosophy of Jean-Paul Sartre* (Cambridge, Mass.: Harvard University Press, 1954), p. 49.

30 Cf. *Being and Nothingness*, p. 86.

31 Ibid., p. 482.

32 To guard against possible misunderstanding, it should be noted that, so far as Kant himself was concerned, the transcendental turn in his philosophy was not extended to cover the domain of ethics. Instead, in his eyes moral duty is incumbent upon man as he really is; hence the moral law is not relative to our human situation only as it appears to us to be and is structured for us by our modes of understanding. For this reason, contemporary analysts and phenomenologists, insofar as they make the transcendental turn even in doing ethics, are decidedly un-Kantian.

33 It is true that Moore later abandoned this way of distinguishing goodness from other properties. In "The Conception of Intrinsic Value" (*Philosophical Studies*, pp. 253–75), he distinguishes between intrinsic and nonintrinsic qualities, saying that an intrinsic property forms part of the complete description of an object, while a nonintrinsic property does not. This statement is, for our purposes, equivalent to the one he gives in *Principia Ethica*, for both distinguish between properties that require others in order to exist and those that do not.

34 R. M. Hare, *The Language of Morals* (Oxford: Clarendon Press, 1961), pp. 94 ff.

35 Ibid., pp. 14–15.

36 Ibid., pp. 84–85.

37 Ibid., p. 145.

38 R. M. Hare, *Freedom and Reason* (New York: Oxford University Press, 1965), p. 21.

39 *The Language of Morals*, p. 196.

40 *Freedom and Reason*, pp. 17 and 47.

41 Ibid., p. 33.

42 Ibid., p. 150: "It is as if a man were regarding his own life and character as a work of art, and asking how it should be completed."

43 Ibid., pp. 169–75.

44 Ibid., p. 170.

45 In *Theories of Ethics*, ed. Philippa Foot (London: Oxford University Press, 1967), pp. 64–73. Cf. Hare's reply, "Geach: Good and Evil," in the same volume, pp. 74–82.

46 *The Moral Point of View* (Ithaca, N.Y.: Cornell University Press, 1958; abridged ed. with a new preface, New York: Random House, 1965).

47 Ibid., pp. 29–30. (All references to this work will be to the second edition.)

48 Ibid., p. 91.

49 Ibid., p. 144.

50 *Moral Notions* (New York: Humanities Press, 1967), p. 11; cf. p. 25.

51 Ibid., p. 4.

52 Ibid., p. 124.

53 Ibid., p. 148; cf. pp. 30 and 68.

54 *Empiricism and Ethics* (Cambridge: Cambridge University Press, 1967), p. 233.

55 Ibid., p. 161.

56 Ibid., pp. 208 ff.

57 It would be seriously misleading were we to leave the impression that over the course of recent years no books at all have appeared in the English-speaking world that have attempted to challenge, if not the transcendental turn in ethics itself, then at least that thesis as to the ultimate irrationality of ethics, which in many ways might be said to be the basic and continuing theme of contemporary analytic ethics. Professor Brand Blanshard's Gifford Lectures, published in 1961 under the title *Reason and Goodness* (London: George Allen & Unwin; New York: The Macmillan Co.), represent a masterly critique of the up-until-then dominant tendencies in Anglo-American ethics and a vigorous reaffirmation of the possible rationality and even rationalism of ethics. In the same year a comparatively slight book by H. B. Veatch entitled *Rational Man* (Bloomington: Indiana University Press, 1962) appeared, which sought to argue for a rational basis of ethics, more or less along the lines of traditional Aristotelian realism. Two books by G. H. von Wright, *Norm and Action* (London: Routledge & Kegan Paul, 1963), and *The Varieties of Goodness* (London: Routledge & Kegan Paul, 1963), seek to show respectively that moral discourse admits of strict logical formalization and that moral philosophy is not conceptually autonomous. Although both of these theses go counter to much of what is to be found in contemporary analytic ethics, it is doubtful whether, even if sound, they involve anything like a serious challenge to the transcendental turn itself. Of far greater import, however, is a book that has just appeared, subsequent even to the composition of the present article, which styles itself quite correctly as a reaffirmation of an "ethics of common sense," and which engages in a detailed and telling critique of many of the major tendencies in current analytic ethics. This is Mortimer Adler's *The Time of Our Lives* (New York: Holt, Rinehart & Winston, 1970).

58 Heidegger, of course, explicitly denies that this distinction is of ethical import.

59 Cf. J. P. Sartre, *Existentialism,* trans. Bernard Frechtman (New York: Philosophical Library, 1947), p. 55.

60 On the social thought of Sartre and Merleau-Ponty, mention might be made of two recent books: the one by Wilfrid Desan, *The Marxism of Jean Paul Sartre* (New York: Doubleday & Company, 1965); the other by Albert Rabil, Jr., *Merleau-Ponty: Existentialist of the Social World* (New York: Columbia University Press, 1967).

61 There have been two books which might be said to have attempted to supply this lack in the case of Sartre: Simone de Beauvoir, *The Ethics of Ambiguity,* trans. Bernard Frechtman (New York: Philosophical Library, 1948); Francis Jeanson, *Le Problème Moral et la Pensée de Sartre* (Paris: Editions du Seuil, 1965).

62 For an example of such an undertaking, *see* Maurice Mandelbaum, *The Phenomenology of Moral Experience* (Chicago: Free Press, 1955).

63 *Concluding Unscientific Postscript,* trans. David F. Swenson and Walter Lowrie (Princeton, N.J.: Princeton University Press, 1941), p. 380.

64 *Existentialism,* p. 27.

65 For a brilliant and, in our judgment, quite devastating new critique of Heidegger, which exploits the theme that there is no rational basis to which Heidegger can appeal in his philosophy and that consequently the entire import of his philosophy is simply one of nihilism, *see* Stanley Rosen, *Nihilism: A Philosophical Essay* (New Haven, Conn.: Yale University Press, 1969).

66 Søren Kierkegaard, *Either/Or,* vol. 2, trans. Walter Lowrie (Princeton, N.J.: Princeton University Press, 1944), p. 149, quoted in Calvin O. Schrag, *Existence and Freedom* (Evanston, Ill.: Northwestern University Press, 1961), pp. 191–92.

67 Although in this brief review of contemporary ethics, we shall consider these books simply with respect to the way they attempt to speak to certain of the more commonly recognized difficulties of existentialist ethics, it must not be thought that such a treatment is adequate to the scope of either book. On the contrary, Professor Barnes's book seeks to set existentialist ethics in the context of contemporary culture as a whole, contrasting it with all sorts of current and more or less semiphilosophical tendencies—e.g., Ayn Rand's objectivism, the New Left, the contemporary cult of Eastern philosophy

and mysticism, the new theologians, etc. As for Professor Olafson's book, it seeks, on the one hand, to view existentialist ethics from the historical perspective of the long tradition of voluntarism in Western thought; and on the other hand, in its more critical parts, it seeks to show how many of the themes of contemporary existentialist ethics parallel themes in analytic ethics. Indeed, even though Olafson does not use the term, it is obvious from his discussion that the community of themes among these two contemporary schools of ethics is really traceable to their common partiality for the transcendental turn in philosophy generally.

68 This appears in a volume entitled *An Invitation to Phenomenology*, ed. James M. Edie (Chicago: Quadrangle Books, 1965), pp. 59–77. In somewhat the same connection and much to the same effect might be mentioned a book by a European, W. A. Luijpen, translated by H. J. Koren and published in this country under the title *Phenomenology of Natural Law* (Pittsburgh, Pa.: Duquesne University Press, 1967). This is a sustained and capable undertaking, designed to show how by virtue of making the transcendental turn it is possible for an existential-phenomenological ethics not only to obviate the charge of relativism but even to incorporate into itself much of traditional natural law.

NOTE TO THE READER

The "transcendental turn" around which Professors Veatch and Gram organize their review of recent work in ethics had its beginning in the work of Kant, as they note. Kant's thought is well represented in *Great Books of the Western World,* the whole of Vol. 42 being devoted to it.

Although Ethics as such does not constitute one of the 102 ideas into which the *Syntopicon* is divided, the subject itself, at least from its beginnings with Plato and Aristotle down to the twentieth century, is abundantly covered. As the reader will find by consulting the INVENTORY OF TERMS, Ethics receives two considerable entries, one on the science of Ethics, the other on its subject matter. Under these two entries, the reader can find his way to all the leading discussions that the set of *Great Books* contains on these subjects.

The Contemporary Status

of a Great Idea

The Idea of Happiness

V. J. McGILL

WITH AN INTRODUCTION BY THE EDITORS

V. J. McGILL

For this year's assessment of the current status of a great idea, the editors have asked Professor V. J. McGill to review and report on recent literature dealing with the subject of happiness. Dr. McGill has just completed a detailed analysis of the controversy about happiness from the time of the ancient Greeks down to the present. The editors have asked him to report the most recent developments in that controversy.

Dr. McGill received his B.A. degree from the University of Washington and his Ph.D. from Harvard University. He taught philosophy at both universities, at St. John's College, Annapolis, Maryland, at Barnard College, and, from 1929 to 1954, at Hunter College. He is an editor of the quarterly, Philosophy and Phenomenological Research. *At present, Dr. McGill is Professor of Philosophy at San Francisco State College. His most recent book,* The Idea of Happiness, *was published in 1967 by Frederick A. Praeger, Inc., of New York.*

INTRODUCTION BY THE EDITORS

According to Professor McGill's report, the contemporary controversy concerning happiness is primarily a continuation of the dispute between Aristotle and Kant. The basic issue concerns whether happiness can and should provide the fundamental moral norm of human action. Aristotle is the classic exponent of the position that happiness does provide such a norm. Kant is the principal upholder of the opposing view with his claim that "the principle of private happiness is the direct opposite of the principle of morality."

In the current dispute, as Dr. McGill indicates, Aristotle's doctrine does not come directly under attack. For English and American philosophers at least, the main proponents of the happiness principle are the utilitarians, Jeremy Bentham, J. S. Mill, and their followers. The main critics of the principle are the so-called formalists, who readily acknowledge their indebtedness to Kant. Thus the first three parts of Dr. McGill's report are devoted to an analysis of the recent literature dealing with the utilitarian version of the happiness principle and the formalist attack upon it. Aristotle's own theory does not explicitly enter the contemporary discussion until we reach the theory of self-realization advanced by certain psychologists and psychotherapists. This is described in the fourth part.

Aristotle's theory remains central, however, to the discussion of happiness. Mill's utilitarian theory is best viewed as a version or variant of the Aristotelian doctrine. In fact, in his book Dr. McGill shows how the entire history of the discussion of happiness is seen most clearly when it is considered in terms of the Aristotelian analysis. Aquinas, for example, provides a variant in which Aristotle's teaching is integrated with Christian supernaturalism. Spinoza's theory merges the position of Aristotle with that of the Stoics. Both the Stoics themselves and Kant can be understood as an attempt to refute Aristotle and to provide a substitute. It is not too much to claim, then, that without an understanding of Aristotle's theory, it is scarcely possible to make good sense of the subject of happiness and the controversy about it.

Aristotle uses only a small number of terms for his analysis of happiness. Of these terms, "happiness" and "good" are the most important; the others are "pleasure," "virtue," "wealth," "honor," and the notion of an order of goods in which some goods serve as means to other goods as ends.

A quick overall view of Aristotle's account of happiness can be gained by considering certain paradoxes about it to which he calls attention. He notes that happiness is something that all men desire, and yet they disagree strongly and widely about what it consists in. Again, happiness involves pleasure, yet it is not identical with pleasure. So too, happiness cannot be attributed with certitude to any man while he still lives, even though it is only through the active life that men can become happy. By overcoming and resolving these apparently conflicting statements, one can grasp what Aristotle understands by happiness.

The first of these paradoxes arises from the special and even peculiar relation in which happiness stands to the good. If by "good" we understand anything that is desirable (that is, an object capable of being desired and of satisfying a desire), then it is clear at once that happiness is unique among goods. Of any good except happiness, it makes perfectly good sense to ask why one wants it. It is easy to imagine situations in which a person might ask himself, or be asked by another, why he wants a certain job, or why he wants an education, or wealth, position, fame, or even virtue or knowledge. But it makes no sense to ask this question of happiness, at least as Aristotle understands it. One cannot conceive of making a sentence of the form "I want happiness because. . . ."

This unique character of happiness as a good is described by Aristotle in terms of its being a last or final end. Happiness is *that for the sake of which* all other good things are desired as means. But to talk of happiness in this way is misleading if it leads one to think of happiness as only one good among other goods, even if it is regarded as the last or highest of goods. "We think it most desirable of all things," Aristotle claims, "without being counted as one good thing among others; if it were so counted it would clearly be made more desirable by the addition of even the least of goods; since the addition would result in a larger amount of good, and of goods the greater is always more desirable" (*Nicomachean Ethics*, 1097b17). But nothing can be added to happiness to make it a greater good, since of itself it "makes life desirable and lacking in nothing" (*ibid.*, 1097b16).

As lacking in nothing, happiness is not one good among others; it is the whole of goods. One "assigns all good things to the happy man," Aristotle says (*ibid.*, 1169b9). Happiness, then, is *the* good for man, conceived as the aggregate of all good things. In short, happiness for Aristotle is the good human life. It justifies all particular goods as constituting that life or contributing to its attainment. Men may differ and disagree about what constitutes it, but there is no doubt that all men do want a good life.

So far, there is nothing normative about the conception of happiness; it is not yet a moral norm. It does not become a norm until its constituents are identified and their relation to one another is specified. These are the questions, of course, that generate disagreement. "Verbally there is very general agreement," Aristotle remarks, "for both the general run of men and people of superior refinement . . . identify living well and doing well with being happy; but with regard to what happiness is they differ, and the many do not give the same account as the wise. For the former think it is some plain and obvious thing, like pleasure, wealth, or honor; they differ, however, from one another—and often even the same man identifies it with different things, with health when he is ill, with wealth when he is poor." (*Ibid.*, 1095a16.)

Such differences reveal the need for a normative conception of happiness. The aggregate of all good things does not by itself suffice to define happiness. Particular goods may conflict with one another: pleasures of food and drink, for example, may have to be subordinated to health. Some measure of wealth is necessary, for, although man may not live by bread alone, he still needs food; yet wealth *by itself* does not constitute happiness. Then, too, there are many different kinds of good. If happiness is to provide a moral norm that will apply to all men, these goods must be exhaustively enumerated and established in an ordered relation to one another, so that one may know which is to be preferred to another when conflict arises.

According to Aristotle, this task is not impossible of accomplishment. Given the kind of being that man is, with his needs and capacities, one can specify the goods that are necessary for their fulfillment. There is no question of enumerating all individually good things; we need know only the general kinds of goods that are necessary for a completely good human life. Collecting together all the particular kinds of goods, we obtain the following enumeration of the goods that Aristotle holds are necessary for happiness: wealth, health, pleasure, friends, good society, honor, virtue, knowledge. Under wealth would be included all the external and economic goods needed for life and the good life; all the remaining goods divide into the goods of the body and goods of the soul. Among the latter, virtue and knowledge provide the means of subordinating the inferior to the superior goods and of enabling one to make the proper choice in case of conflict.

Happiness, so conceived, constitutes a moral norm; it establishes a standard by which men ought to measure and control their actions. Men naturally desire a good human life. But they ought also to do what is necessary to attain it, and Aristotle claims that happiness, as he has analyzed it, lays down what ought to be done. Happiness is thus both natural and moral—natural as being the end that men do in fact desire, and moral as being so constituted that it is violable, so that men may not only misconceive it but fail to do what they ought. Two features, in particular, give it a moral and violable character. One is the fact that it is constituted by a multiplicity of different kinds of goods, all based on the capacities of man as man. The other derives from there being one

right order among these many goods. Aristotle's doctrine of virtue is meant to explain how this order can be established and maintained in the individual human life. One may go wrong with respect to either the enumeration or the order of the goods necessary for happiness. But by aiming at, and achieving, virtue, one may be sure that he has done all that is within man's power for attaining happiness.

One other note still remains to be considered in order to complete our understanding of the Aristotelian definition. This is contained in the observation—often taken as the most paradoxical contention of all— that a man can never be said *to be* happy. As long as he lives, he can only be in the process of *becoming* happy. Yet this conclusion is implicit in the position that happiness consists in the aggregate of all goods properly ordered. Obviously, the totality of goods cannot be possessed by a man simultaneously at any one time in this earthly life; if possible at all, this is possible only in heaven through union with God. Man's temporal life is successive, and the goods constituting happiness can only be acquired in a successive order and not all at once; in fact, the possession of some goods interferes with having others, as intense sensual pleasures prevent rational contemplation. Further, happiness depends, as we have seen, upon certain external goods, and these are notoriously subject to the vicissitudes of fortune. Hence, Aristotle claims, happiness requires a whole life, just as it consists in a whole aggregate of goods: "One swallow does not make a summer, nor does one day; so too one day, or a short time, does not make a man blessed and happy" (*ibid.*, 1098a18).

Collecting the various notes, we can define happiness, as conceived by Aristotle, as activity in accordance with complete virtue in a complete life attended by a sufficiency of the goods of fortune (cf. 1098a17; 1101a15; 1102a5).

We have resolved two of the three paradoxes with which we began. The third one—the paradox about pleasure—still remains. With the distinctions so far made, that is readily resolved.

The argument used to show that happiness cannot be one good among many also serves to disprove the identification of happiness with pleasure. For if "the pleasant life is more desirable with wisdom than without, and if the mixture is better, pleasure is not the good; for the good cannot become more desirable by the addition of anything to it" (ibid., 1172b28). This argument, Aristotle says, shows that pleasure is "one of the goods and no more a good than any other." In this sense, pleasure is to be identified with sensual goods, such as the pleasure of food and drink, and it is one kind of good along with other kinds, such as health, wealth, knowledge, and virtue. Pleasure, as only one object of desire among many, is obviously not all or everything that a man can desire. He may frequently turn his back on sensual pleasures, such as food and drink, for the sake of health, wealth, or any one of many other objects that are judged to be more important.

There is another use of "pleasure," however, in which it names not just one object of desire but the satisfaction that is experienced when the object of any desire is attained. It is not in itself a particular object of desire; it is satisfaction of any desire. Thus, when food and drink are objects of desire, we may experience the sensual pleasures of taste in eating and drinking and also have the nonsensual pleasure that is identical with having satisfied our hunger and thirst. The pleasure of satisfaction is entirely distinct from the pleasure that is the object of desire. In fact, satisfaction by itself cannot ever be an object of desire. It cannot be one object, since it is achieved by fulfilling any desire indiscriminately. Furthermore, if it could be desired as an object distinct from all others, the desire for satisfaction would be condemned paradoxically to endless dissatisfaction. A desire for a drink is readily satisfied by obtaining a drink. But what could satisfy a desire for nothing but satisfaction removed from any other object? Pleasure as satisfaction, Aristotle says, accompanies and completes an activity, it is not an activity in itself; he compares it to the bloom of youth on those in the flower of their age (ibid., 1174b32).

The failure to keep these two senses of pleasure distinct—that is, pleasure-as-an-object-of-desire and pleasure-as-satisfaction-of-desire—makes nonsense of Aristotle's conception of happiness. No doubt, we sometimes use the word "happiness" and its cognates in one or the other of these two senses of pleasure. We speak of "feeling happy" and mean only that we are enjoying a pleasant condition of the body or that we have achieved some satisfaction. No one can ever "feel happy" in Aristotle's sense, since happiness consists in a whole life made perfect by the possession of all good things. The miser and the playboy, as well as the good man, can "feel happy," but only the good man can be happy. But he is happy only after a lifetime spent in desiring and enjoying all good things in due measure and proper order.

The Idea of Happiness

If man's greatest good is happiness, and happiness is attainable, it seems clear that we should do everything in our power to bring it about. Its claims will have priority over all others, and, for this reason, it must be the foundation of morality. A good man is one who works efficiently to attain or further happiness, using his talents and opportunities fully to this main purpose, and if he pursues other goods they must be instrumental or in harmony with the supreme good. Men are bad or wicked, similarly, insofar as they produce suffering when they might have produced happiness. Punishment of wrongdoers must itself aim at happiness, or at a reduction of unhappiness. The ideal of happiness thus provides a remarkable unification of the whole world of desire, purpose, and morality, of education, positive law, and institutional life. Faced with controversial actions, policies, and institutions, and conflicting rules of conduct, we can put them all to the test. They are justified if, and only if, their tendency is to further happiness, or to prevent the opposite.

The main tradition of Western philosophy since Plato and Aristotle has insisted that man's supreme good is happiness and that happiness is attainable.[1] Kant, however, denied both and insisted that the supreme good can only be doing one's duty for duty's sake, i.e., obedience to the moral law out of pure respect for the law alone. This austere doctrine, which belittled human happiness and hopes for happiness, was supported by arguments of great power and appeal. Even when unmistakable logical flaws were exposed in the pattern of Kant's argument, the underlying idea could make its appeal to human conscience all over again, like the giant Antaeus who, when thrown down, drew strength from the earth. The liveliest contemporary opponents of the happiness principle are fundamentally Kantians, and are called "formalists," or "deontologists."

The contemporary formalists contend that rights and obligations cannot be explained in terms of pleasure or happiness, or even "good." What we *ought* to do cannot be reduced to "contribute as much as we can to the greatest good of the greatest number," which is what the utilitarians propose. Nor is it always our duty to produce the most happiness possible, or the least unhappiness, in the Aristotelian sense of "happiness," or in any other sense. It is not even our duty always to produce the most good that we can. For considerations of fairness or justice and solemn commitment have priority. Sometimes it is our duty *not* to produce the greatest happiness or good, in order that justice may prevail.

---

1 For a full analysis, *see* my book *The Idea of Happiness* (New York: Frederick A. Praeger, Inc., 1967).

In the present controversy, the formalists are pitted against all "teleologists," and all teleological ethics, i.e., ethics that explain what is right and obligatory as "producing the most happiness or good, or the least unhappiness or evil," but their chief adversaries are the utilitarians. The utilitarian principle of the greatest good for the greatest number is the very opposite of what the formalists believe. The utilitarians are also criticized by other philosophers who offer a variety of objections, viz., utilitarianism cannot even be stated in a clear intelligible fashion; people are not always seeking pleasure and should not; pleasures cannot really be added up or calculated; and so on, as we shall see. There are also disagreements between rival conceptions of happiness that will be touched on as we proceed.

RECENT ATTACKS ON UTILITARIANISM

Utilitarianism, the theory that the supreme good is the greatest happiness of the greatest number, is at present under sharp attack, but it has many defenders, too. Some of the criticism denies the very significance of the conception. Thus Marcus George Singer argues that expressions like "the sum of pleasure" or "the greatest amount of happiness" are only apparently meaningful. They result from:

> . . . reifying the pleasure or "good," and thinking of it as if it were like money, which can be thought of in abstraction from the people whose money it is, and thus can be said to have an independent existence. It would make sense to speak of the amount of money in the universe. . . . because there is a method of calculating it. But it makes no sense to speak of the amount or sum of good (or pleasure). . . .[2]

The argument is not very convincing, because it assumes that the pleasure of a thousand employees at the announcement of a raise in pay is no greater, not more, not greater in amount, than the pleasure of one of them; and that if you cannot add pleasures as you do money, you cannot add them at all.

Henry Hazlitt also objects to the calculation of the *amount* of pleasure that an act will produce, when *amount* is understood quantitatively. He echoes a timeworn criticism of the utilitarian calculus of pleasures when he says:

> We may say . . . that we prefer to go to the symphony tonight to playing bridge. . . . But we cannot meaningfully say that we prefer going to the symphony tonight 3.72 times as much as playing bridge (or that it would give us 3.72 times as much pleasure).[3]

---

2 *Generalization in Ethics* (New York: Alfred A. Knopf, Inc., 1961), pp. 182–83.
3 *The Foundations of Morality* (Princeton: D. Van Nostrand Co., Inc., 1964), p. 27.

The reason is that pleasure is not quantifiable, as cheese is, and this has to be admitted. But Hazlitt gives another reason, namely, that pleasures are qualitatively different, as Aristotle held, so that you cannot say that the pleasure of swimming is *more* than the pleasure of writing poetry. More *what?* There is no common denominator for these two pleasures. But whether or not pleasures are qualitatively different is itself a debatable question.

If these criticisms are correct, the utilitarians' "hedonic calculus" would appear to be impossible. How can we calculate the amounts of pleasure that will result from alternative acts open to us at a given time and choose the act that will produce the greatest amount? How can we so act as to contribute to the greatest sum of pleasure, which according to Jeremy Bentham and other utilitarians is what we ought to do? And how, then, can the greatest pleasure of the greatest number be man's happiness or highest goal?

The argument is convincing to many. Utilitarians reject it. Since we calculate pleasures every day, it cannot be impossible. Actions can be chosen because they promise more pleasure than any others open to us, even though pleasure is not quantitative. The utilitarian also has another escape hatch. Instead of talking about amounts of pleasure, he can deal with observable degrees of preference, while still maintaining in theory that it is greater pleasure that determines preference. The shift has long since taken place in economics, and the measurement of preferences has an important place in the social sciences. Recently the formal logic of preference has been developed for the first time by Georg Henrik von Wright, in his *The Logic of Preference*.[4] The advantage of treating value judgments, such as judgments about degrees of pleasure, in terms of relative preference is now clearer than ever.

R. M. Hare complains that the happiness of the utilitarians is so indeterminate that we are unable to identify the happy man. To do so, we must begin by imagining ourselves in his shoes, with all his likes and dislikes, and in *his* circumstances. But this is difficult. If I decide a certain mental defective could not be happy, that he misses too much, it may be simply that my imagination has failed. On the other hand, if I decide that a man whose likes and dislikes are exactly opposite to mine is "satisfied," in the sense that he has what he wanted, I will not be willing to say he is "*happy.*"

Happiness, Hare says, is a more complicated matter. We cannot conclude from his external state of life, however glorious, that a person is happy, for suppose "he himself hates every minute of his existence."[5] Nor can we trust reports of states of mind; they can likewise mean many

4 Edinburgh: Edinburgh University Press, 1963.

5 *Freedom and Reason* (London: Oxford University Press, 1963), p. 128.

things. "This explains," Hare says, "why the utilitarians had so little success in their attempts to found an empiricist ethical theory upon the concept of happiness."[6]

Yet the difficulty of spotting the happy man has certainly been exaggerated. We can at least come to know that some people are *happier* than others, from their personal reports, their corroborating behavior, and the advantages of their circumstances. We must not look, of course, for some quality that shines from the happy person. The Finnish philosopher Wright argues that a man's being happy is a relationship in which he stands to the circumstances of his life, not to this or that detail but to "the whole thing," so that we could say, "He likes his life as it is."[7] Of this he is the final judge; no one is in a position to contradict him. He may be insincere in saying "I am happy," but of this, too, he is the final judge. This does not prevent him from being badly mistaken about what future things will make him happy, Wright points out, and here others may instruct him.

If a person is the final judge of how happy he is, then the statistical studies of the variation of happiness with environmental factors, to be reviewed later, are right in starting off with the testimony of the individuals themselves. And if, as Hare emphasizes, reports of happiness, or relative happiness, can mean quite different things, then these studies have done well to check such reports with other testimony and facts about the subject's life. For the present, let us turn to other objections to the ideal of happiness and the ethics that goes with it.

Another author, P. H. Nowell-Smith, objects to morality's being based on any single end.

> Teleologists, in their desire to construct a single all-embracing system of morality, have tried to represent all moral rules as dependent for their validity on their tendency to promote a single end which they call Pleasure, Happiness, The Good Life or, since it is obvious that virtue is not always rewarded in this world, Eternal Bliss. But in so doing, they have distorted the logic of moral words and their conclusions either turn out to be disguised logical truisms or to be false or at least questionable.[8]

We can paint the most beautiful picture of happiness or the eternal life we please, Nowell-Smith says; it does not in the least follow that we *ought* to bring it about. It always "makes sense to ask 'Ought I to try achieve this state?'" Yet if the utilitarian *defines* "what we ought to do" as "what conduces to the greatest pleasure of the greatest number," then

---

6 *Ibid.*, p. 129.
7 *The Varieties of Goodness* (London: Routledge & Kegan Paul, Ltd., 1963), p. 98.
8 *Ethics* (Baltimore: Penguin Books, 1961), p. 220.

106

the one expression could always be substituted for the other in a sentence without changing the meaning of this sentence, and it would not make sense to ask "Ought I to do what conduces to the greatest pleasure of the greatest number?" It would be like asking "Ought I to do what I ought to do?" But the question of whether I ought to promote the greatest pleasure does make sense, Nowell-Smith insists, and he thus concludes that utilitarianism fails, from the beginning, to state its position.

The utilitarian can avoid this criticism in two ways. He need not *define* "ought" in this way, or in any way; or he can retain his definition, not in the sense that permits substitution, but in the sense that a definition is a clarification of the term defined.

Nowell-Smith also complains, as other recent authors have, that reducing morality to the pursuit of a single end, such as pleasure or happiness, leads to conclusions that are plainly false or to empty truisms. No one would claim that a judge in rendering a decision should try to promote the greatest sum of pleasure or happiness: his duty is to render a just decision in the case. Kurt Baier states the objection in general terms:

> We do not have a duty to do good to others or to ourselves, or to others or/and ourselves in a judicious mixture such that it produces the greatest amount of good in the world. We are morally required to do good only to those who are actually in need of our assistance. The view that we always ought to do the optimific act, or whenever we have no more stringent duty to perform, would have the absurd result that we are doing wrong whenever we are relaxing, since on those occasions there will always be opportunities to produce greater good than we can by relaxing.[9]

It would have been wrong, according to Baier, for the Good Samaritan to have refrained from giving help when it was requested, but it does not follow from this that it would be wrong for him, or for us, to refrain from promoting the greatest amount of good.

J. S. Mill, long ago, tried to parry this stroke. There are relatively few occasions, he held, on which we have any chance of promoting the happiness of the wider community; there is time enough for leisure, which is also useful. But if we *know* that we can help a lot of people on a given occasion, would it not be wrong to relax?

Utilitarianism is also said to generate truisms in disguise. Alasdair MacIntyre contends that although hedonists start out with pleasure as a specific goal, they eventually so dilute it, in replying to puritanical objections, that pleasure becomes no different than any other goal.[10] "Con-

9 *The Moral Point of View* (New York: Random House, Inc., 1965), p. 109.
10 *A Short History of Ethics* (New York: The Macmillan Co., 1966).

cepts like 'pleasure' and 'happiness' are stretched and extended in all directions until they are used simply to name whatever men aim at."[11] Thus the claim that all men aim at pleasure comes to mean only "They aim at what they aim at." Unfortunately, pleasure reduced to "what we desire" affords us no standard for choosing whether to cultivate new desires and dispositions, or which to cultivate, and how to compare them with those we now have.

> The injunction "Pursue happiness!" when *happiness* has been given the broad, undifferentiated sense which Bentham and Mill give to it is merely the injunction "Try to achieve what you desire." But as to any question about rival objects of desire, or about alternative and competing desires, this injunction is silent and empty.[12]

Robert B. Braithwaite, the Cambridge philosopher, also complains of the emptiness of any single, final standard for moral conduct. In "Moral Principles and Inductive Policies," he contends that both Mill's happiness and Aristotle's eudaemonia (happiness) are "inscrutable" concepts.[13] "The reason would seem to be," he says, "that, in order to justify all lesser goods, they have to be so comprehensive as to lose all cognitive content. An ascending series of ends each of which is a necessary condition for its *predecessors* in the series soon fades into ineluctable obscurity."[14]

In an ascending series of scientific hypotheses—as when, in explaining the motion of a planet, we go, for example, from Kepler's law of planetary motion to Newton's law of gravitation and then Einstein's general theory of relativity—"the propositions become stronger and stronger so that we are saying more and more. . . ." It is quite different if, in attempting to justify a certain action, we do so in terms of a proximate end, and then try to justify this end by a higher end, and so on. "In ascending the hierarchy of ends the propositions become weaker and weaker and weaker, so that we are saying less and less."[15] Another difference is that in the hierarchy of scientific hypotheses a final hypothesis, a final explanation, would be unthinkable. An empiricist, Braithwaite says, will also avoid finality in the series of ends. Instead of being bullied by a Socrates into giving a final justification of his various particular ends, the empiricist can justify them "by reference to their invariance as means towards any further end."

11 *Ibid.*, p. 236.

12 *Ibid.*

13 *Studies in Philosophy*, ed. J. N. Findlay (London: Oxford University Press, 1966), p. 112.

14 *Ibid.*, pp. 112–13.

15 *Ibid.*, p. 112.

And the empiricist, if he wishes, may perfectly well use traditional teleological language, and speak of pursuing eudaemonia or of pursuing happiness, using these abstract nouns not to denote unique but nebulous concepts but, in a way in which both Aristotle and Mill seem frequently to have used them, as collective names for the Kingdom of all final Ends.[16]

All the actual goods in order of their preference could remain. The empiricist would only insist that the questions whether given behavior subserves an end, and given ends subserve a broader end, be settled by scientific methods that have proved their worth, that is, by empirical methods. Advantages of teleological ethics, both utilitarianism and Aristotle's eudaemonism, could thus be preserved without assuming that happiness is a unitary concept which "justifies all lesser goods."

THE DEFENSE OF UTILITARIANISM

Utilitarianism—the view that the final good is the greatest pleasure of the greatest number, and that we *ought* to do everything in our power to bring it about—is an ethical view. It is typically accompanied by the theory that every man does, as a matter of fact, pursue his own pleasure. Thus Bentham combined the two doctrines, when he said at the beginning of his *An Introduction to the Principles of Morals and Legislation:*

> Nature has placed mankind under the governance of two sovereign masters, *pain* and *pleasure.* . . . On the one hand the standard of right and wrong, on the other the chain of causes and effects, are fastened to their throne. They govern us in all we do, in all we say, in all we think. . . .

Critics have often claimed that there is a conflict between these two doctrines, but they are mistaken. John Hospers points out that though Bentham held that men *do* seek their personal satisfaction or pleasure in what they do, he also insisted that they *ought* to find their personal satisfaction in contributing to the happiness of others, as well as of themselves. What Bentham had in mind was that people " 'can be trained and educated in such a way that they will derive their maximum personal satisfaction out of doing things for others.' "[17] Conscience can be developed in children which makes the thought of theft or murder distinctly unpleasant. And where conscience fails, public opinion and the law come into operation, making crime and selfish conduct personally unat-

<hr>

16 *Ibid.*, pp. 113–14.
17 Hospers, *Human Conduct* (New York: Harcourt, Brace and World, Inc., 1961), p. 145.

tractive, and social conduct personally satisfying. The main problem, as Bentham saw it, was to improve the laws so that they would serve this end more effectively than they did in his time.

Psychological hedonism, according to Hospers, does not mean that men are always selfish. Bentham claimed only that people, whether they are just or vicious, generous or selfish, seek their own personal satisfaction or pleasure. "Why should one refute a view which is so unobjectionable?"[18] If a man gave all he had to the poor, we can scarcely call him selfish because he derived personal satisfaction from the giving.

18 *Ibid.*

When, on the other hand, psychological hedonism is taken to mean that people desire only their own pleasure, it is clearly false. When we want to see a certain production of *Hamlet* or to spend a day in the country with friends, these specific things are what we want, Hospers reminds us, and we seldom actually think of the pleasure they will bring. This is obvious. But it is obvious to the utilitarians, too. They do not claim that people are always calculating future pleasure; their claim is rather something like this: Men seek all sorts of things, from alcohol to mathematical knowledge, but when they sit down in a cool moment to assess the comparative value of such goods, they *tend* to use pleasure and pain as *the* yardstick, and they *should* do this consistently.

Another favorite criticism of utilitarianism misfires for the same reason. It is called "the paradox of hedonism," and is the argument that the more we aim at pleasure and make it our main concern, the less pleasure we get. If we are continually thinking of the pleasure we expect or are getting from the party, the concert, the game of tennis, instead of attending to these things themselves, we shall miss most of the pleasure they afford. This again is pretty obvious, but it fails as a criticism of utilitarianism. For though utilitarians hold that only pleasure is good in itself, they are far from saying that people are always (or should always be) thinking of pleasure. Indeed, when thinking of pleasure interferes with the enjoyment of pleasure, the utilitarian would be the first to insist that we *stop* thinking of it.

One might as well claim that there is a paradox of happiness if it is conceived as a life of virtue. A sure way of missing a life of virtue, it has been maintained, is to be continually thinking of one's virtue instead of the objects that virtue intends, such as helping the poor or defending innocents. Would not such a man be a prig? It is the way we all become Philistines, Max Scheler contended. Virtue is to be "worn" like a garment, not sought. But did Aristotle and the Stoics hold that, because virtue is good in itself, we should always be thinking of it and aiming at it? Aristotle, at least, shows in many passages that courage, temperance, and so on have by their very nature certain specific results in view, and that they are shams if they do not. Although some recent authors have complained that Aristotle's good man shows a self-centered concern for his own virtue, the criticism does not seem to be justified. The germ of wisdom it contains is that the best way to get goods such as pleasure, virtue, or excellence is not to aim at them but at other things that turn out to be the means to them.

Critics never cease to attack the central thesis of utilitarianism, that pleasure alone is intrinsically good, i.e., the only thing that is good in itself. Even some leading utilitarians have felt obliged to renounce this sweeping claim. The first great renegade, Henry Sidgwick (1838–1900), after a long struggle, concluded that other things besides pleasure could be good in themselves. G. E. Moore (1873–1958) insisted that if you add knowledge, beauty, or moral qualities to a world already pleasurable, you would have a world that is certainly better, though it contained no more pleasure. This view that other things besides pleasure are intrinsically valuable is called "ideal utilitarianism," or better, "pluralistic utilitarianism," and is very widely held today. Another defection from utilitarianism came in the nineteenth century, when Mill maintained that pleasures are not qualitatively alike, i.e., differing only in intensity, duration, and number, as utilitarians had ·held. In announcing that he would rather be Socrates dissatisfied than a pig satisfied, he was saying in effect that even a little refined human pleasure was more valuable than a lot of coarse pig pleasure. Mill did not think of this as a betrayal of utilitarianism, but it was: it meant that something besides the greatest amount of pleasure should be our final goal.

In his doughty defense of utilitarianism, J. J. C. Smart does not give an inch to the enemy. Bentham, he says, might also have preferred being Socrates dissatisfied to being a pig satisfied or a contented fool, but he would have done so for an *extrinsic* reason, not an *intrinsic* one. In itself, or intrinsically, the quantitatively greater pleasure of the pig or the fool is preferable, but extrinsically—in view of the consequences—the smaller (or even null) pleasure of Socrates is preferable. We often sacrifice the pleasure of the day, or even undergo torment, for the sake of the future, and this is the choice that the utilitarian can consistently make in this case. For the pleasures of the pig and the fool are not productive of future pleasure, whereas "the discontented philosopher is a useful catalyst in society and . . . the existence of Socrates is responsible for an improvement in the lot of humanity generally."[19]

Smart takes the same hard line in dealing with Bentham's provocative statement that "pushpin is as good as poetry" so long as it is just as pleasurable. Considered by itself, this is true, he says, but we must not forget that poetry is "fecund" of future pleasure, whereas pushpin is not. Poetry is "permanently pleasurable in revival," it is said, increases the awareness of human possibilities, and can spread happiness; pushpin and sunbathing have no such culmination.

A really alarming problem for utilitarianism is presented by the recent discovery, by James Olds and Peter Milner, of centers for pleasure in the brain of the rat. It was demonstrated that when electrodes were attached to these areas of the rats' brains, and so wired that the rats could maintain the current themselves by pressing a bar, they would continue to press it indefinitely, showing no interest in water, food, or sleep, until they were completely exhausted. Now, since pleasure centers have also been discovered in the human brain, the question arises: What could the utilitarian lose by spending his days, or at least his evenings after work, operating the electrodes? How could he lose if he gained a whole world of pleasure, without effort? Smart can answer that these pleasures would not be fecund, and that he would be neglecting his duty to contribute to the happiness of others. But now suppose the situation changed so that these objections would not be valid. Would we then say that the electrode operator was really happy? No, Smart seems to say, for none of us would be willing to change places with him; all of us non-electrode operators would prefer to find our pleasure in real activities in the world.

The argument thus seems to end with an unintentional plug for Aris-

---

19 *An Outline of a System of Utilitarian Ethics* (Melbourne: Melbourne University Press, 1961), p. 8.

totle's eudaemonism, which holds, in effect, that each man enjoys the pleasure of satisfaction which accompanies the activities he values, and that the two are inseparable. Right or wrong, this explains in part the revulsion against the increasing use of psychedelic drugs. It is felt that the joy of workmanship and creation cannot be detached from successful achievement, and that, if it could be, it would be a fool's paradise which, as Smart would say, none of us would knowingly exchange for the real thing, however contented we might become.

Pertinent and illuminating here is Wright's distinction between three main forms of pleasure: passive pleasure, active pleasure, and the pleasure of satisfaction or contentedness. The tendency since Plato to equate all pleasure with passive pleasure, with "sensuous pleasure," as it is called, has muddled philosophical discussion, Wright says.[20] Instances of sensuous pleasure have regularly been used to condemn all pleasure, and the Epicureans have been denounced as licentious although they in fact cared most for friends and conversation.

The tendency to narrow down pleasure to passive, sensuous pleasure had another unfortunate consequence, according to Wright. It led to the bad mistake of taking pleasure to be an object of the mind, like a sensation of pain or an emotion of delight. Here Wright agrees with Gilbert Ryle, who insists that pleasure is not any sort of sensation or emotion, or a process either, but rather a liking or enjoying something.[21] Aristotle had already shown that pleasure cannot be a process, for a process goes slowly or quickly and completes itself toward some end, whereas pleasure is not for the sake of something else, and does not complete itself since it is complete at every moment. "It is not possible to move otherwise than in time," Aristotle adds, "but it *is* possible to be pleased; for that which takes place in a moment is a whole."[22] Ryle's way of putting it is that pleasures are not "clockable." You cannot say exactly where your being *pleased with* begins or ends.

In contrast to "passive pleasure," we have "active pleasure," which comes from doing things one "is *keen on doing, enjoys* doing, or *likes* to do."[23] Wright remarks that though active pleasure seems to be as important for ethics as the pleasure of the senses is, practically no philosopher except Aristotle has given any attention to it. As for the third form of pleasure, the pleasure of satisfaction or contentedness, Wright says it comes from "getting that which we desire or need or want—irrespective of whether the desired thing by itself gives us pleasure."[24]

---

20 *The Varieties of Goodness* (London: Routledge & Kegan Paul, Ltd., 1963), p. 64.
21 "Pleasure," *Dilemmas* (Cambridge: Cambridge University Press, 1954).
22 *Nicomachean Ethics*, 1174a13–b8; *GBWW*, Vol. 9, p. 428b–d.
23 Wright, *op. cit.*, p. 64.
24 *Ibid.*, p. 65.

Corresponding to these "three *forms* of pleasure" are "three types of *ideals of happiness* or of the happy life." Passive pleasure yields what Wright calls *"Epicurean ideals,"* according to which true happiness "derives above all from *having* things which please."[25] The pleasures here are not only sensuous but include the enjoying of friendship, conversation, and beautiful things. But would passive pleasure be enough for happiness? If what a man wants most of all is "a favourable balance of passive pleasure over passive 'unpleasure,' i.e. of states he enjoys over states he dislikes, and if he were successful in this pursuit of his, then the Epicurean recipe of living would, by definition, make him happy. . . ." However, a consideration of human nature suggests "that very few men are such pleasure-lovers that the supreme thing they want for themselves in life is a maximum of passive pleasure."[26] Yet this gives us no ground for denying that if there *are* men who love passive pleasure so much and manage to fill their lives with it, they cannot be genuinely happy. Indeed, "to deny this would be to misunderstand the notions of happiness and the good of man and would be symptomatic, I think, of some 'moralistic perversion.'"[27] Passive pleasure is, after all, indisputably good, and if it is what a man supremely wants and can get, that is the end of the matter.

The pleasure of satisfaction or contentedness corresponds, Wright thinks, to the utilitarian ideal of happiness. "The utilitarians thought of happiness, not so much in terms of passive pleasure, as in terms of satisfaction of desire."[28] Happiness for them was a good ratio between wants and needs and their satisfaction, which we might express by the fraction

$$\frac{\text{satisfaction of desires}}{\text{desires}}$$

Wright points out that one way of gaining happiness is to restrict the number of our desires, thereby eliminating many unsatisfied desires which make for *un*happiness, and he calls this *"the ascetic ideal* of life." This "crippled ideal," he says, involves the logical mistake of assuming that happiness is the *contradictory*, whereas it is really the *contrary*, of unhappiness. If unhappiness were the *contradictory* of happiness, then a man could be happy simply by avoiding unhappiness; but since happiness is in fact the *contrary* of unhappiness, a man could stay clear of unhappiness and yet not be happy. He could be neither happy nor unhappy, like a stone. "The man of *no* wants, if there existed such a creature, would not be unhappy. But it does not follow that he would be happy."[29]

---

25 *Ibid.,* p. 92.
26 *Ibid.,* p. 93.
27 *Ibid.*
28 *Ibid.*
29 *Ibid.,* p. 94.

Wright leaves the impression that this ascetic recipe is the utilitarian ideal of happiness, which is odd, especially in view of Bentham's diatribe against asceticism. One would have thought that utilitarian happiness was to be attained as much, or more, by increasing the number of satisfied desires as by restricting desires; as much by increasing the numerator of the above fraction as by decreasing the denominator. On the other hand, Stoicism seems to fit the ascetic formula exactly. Epictetus, for example, continually advised us that the path to happiness is the elimination of all desires the satisfaction of which is not completely in our power. This meant that happiness was attainable only by the suppression of practically all of our desires, wants, and needs.

It must be admitted, however, that those modern eudaemonists, the self-realization philosophers, have complained of the poverty of the happiness with which the utilitarians were contented. They themselves held that happiness is the complete fulfillment of the individual's potentialities and is therefore a maximal attainment, rather than a prudent surplus of pleasure over pain. Calculation of units of pleasure and pain, even if it was for the happiness of the greatest number, showed a petty shopkeeper's outlook. The insignia of happiness for John Dewey was not at all a good ratio of satisfied to unsatisfied desires, but rather growth and the capacity for growth, an ability to form new desires and interests and to avoid fixation on modes of response no longer appropriate. Satisfaction of a desire was anything but final; if it did not turn into a desire for something further, it turned stale. From Spinoza on, self-realization philosophers have beckoned to an endless climb and quest. They represent the most expansive conception of happiness, the Stoics the most contracted view, while utilitarianism appears to be intermediate.

Wright's third ideal of happiness is based on active pleasure. It

> . . . seeks happiness neither in passive pleasure nor in the satisfaction of desire, but in that which we have called active pleasure, *i.e.* the pleasure of doing that on which we are keen, which for its sake we like *doing*. In the activities we are keen on doing, we aim at technical goodness or perfection. . . . the more talented we are by nature for an art, the more can the development of our skill in it contribute to our happiness.[30]

The fact that we seek out, cultivate, and exercise the arts which yield active pleasure gives this ideal of happiness an advantage over that based on "passive" pleasure. It is less hazardous to let our happiness result from what we *do* and *become* than to let it depend on what we *are* or *get*, which should not suggest, Wright warns, that this life is sure or easy.

Happiness, according to Wright, is not the whole of man's ultimate

---

30 *Ibid.*

good. "Welfare" is the "broader and more basic notion." It has to do with what is beneficial or good *for* the person, and harmful or bad *for* him.[31] Following Plato, Wright suggests that the wider welfare of the person is to be understood as analogous to health, which has both a positive and negative aspect, the latter being "more basic." The latter "consists [of] bodily pain and of pain-like states, which are consequent upon the frustration of needs and wants of a normal life," whereas the former "consists in the presence of feelings of fitness and strength and in similar pleasant (agreeable, joyful) states. In the enjoyment of those states the healthy body and mind can be said to flourish. . . . Of the being, who enjoys this aspect of its welfare, we say that it is happy. Happiness could also be called the flower of welfare."[32]

It is apparent that welfare and happiness, as Wright understands them, are very intimately related, and that welfare is regarded as more fundamental because happiness and life itself depend on the "health" of the organism and person. While Wright separates these two aspects of man's ultimate good, Aristotle combines them in a single pattern of eudaemonia, comprising excellent activities, pleasures appropriate to them, and a variety of instrumental conditions.

THE FORMALIST POSITION AND ITS DIFFICULTIES

N othing can possibly be conceived . . . which can be called good, without qualification, except a good will," Kant wrote in 1785.[33] Happiness itself may arouse pride and presumption and is good only if there is a good will to protect us against such effects. It is not happiness, then, which constitutes the supreme good of man; it is rather the performance of duty, i.e., obedience to the moral law "out of pure respect" for this law. Only in this way can we become *worthy* of happiness. The moral law stated: Act only according to rules which can be consistently universalized, so that all other rational beings could also act according to them. Keeping promises, telling the truth, etc., could be universalized, Kant argued, while breaking promises, lying, etc., even if doing so would save many lives or produce much happiness, could not possibly be universalized and would therefore be always wrong. For a duty makes no sense unless it is equally the duty of all men, regardless of the consequences of the dutiful act. A duty must also be binding on the will of all men, as rational beings; i.e., *as* rational beings they must necessarily assent to it and make it their own. In the same way, as rational beings, we

---

31 *Ibid.*, p. 88.
32 *Ibid.*, pp. 61–62.
33 *Fundamental Principles of the Metaphysic of Morals; GBWW*, Vol. 42, p. 256a.

necessarily adopt the multiplication table, and not for the sake of future happiness or any other extraneous reason, but out of a rational respect, as we might say, for arithmetic. It follows, accordingly, that the moral aim must never be the production of one's own happiness, for tastes differ and my duty would thus be determined by my peculiarities and would not be duty at all. Men necessarily desire their own happiness, Kant holds, whereas duty involves "*constraint* to an end reluctantly adopted."[34]

In recent times, philosophers have been greatly concerned with the problems raised by Kant and by related questions. H. A. Prichard set off a chain reaction by his early article in *Mind*, "Does Moral Philosophy Rest on a Mistake?,"[35] when he raised the question: Why should I keep my promises and fulfill my engagements in those cases where I stand to lose by it—where my happiness is at stake. Prichard argues that in the utilitarian doctrine there is a glaring gap between the happiness of the greatest number and the individual's duty to contribute to it. Suppose a man is told he ought to keep his promise because his doing so will contribute to the general happiness. He can reply in a number of ways, viz.: "Why should I work for the happiness of others? My happiness is my concern." "I concede the general rule, but I stand to lose too much in this particular case. If I repay the debt now I'll be ruined." "I admit that in general keeping promises is essential to the existence of a social order, but this is a special case. If I return Jones's pistol to him now, as I promised, he will probably shoot himself, for he is in a suicidal mood." If duty is based on the happiness principle, it would seem that a man need not keep his promise when it entails too great a personal sacrifice or creates misery instead of happiness, or when he simply does not accept the obligation of promoting the happiness of society. How can a mere factual situation—the possibility of contributing to the future happiness of society—generate an obligation? Does existence, or possible existence, ever imply that anything ought to be done? Moore had already answered this question, in effect, when he argued that the good (which includes happiness) is something that *ought to be*, and that this *ought to be* defines and justifies the *ought to do*, one *ought* thus generating the other. Prichard, however, rejects this remedy since, he says, *ought* refers to actions, never to things or states of affairs.

The notion that we should keep our promises, pay our debts, and tell the truth *for the reason* that it will make people more comfortable and prosperous, or happier, Prichard says, is "plainly at variance with our moral consciousness."[36] Imagine a man saying he is going to keep his promise or pay his debt to you *because*, after considering the matter, he

---

34 *Metaphysical Elements of Ethics; ibid.*, p. 369d.
35 Reprinted in *Moral Obligation: Essays and Lectures* (Oxford: Clarendon Press, 1949).
36 *Ibid.*, p. 5.

is inclined to believe that a better balance of pleasure over pain would result from his doing so than from his refusing! Utilitarianism fails to account for our sense of obligation, Prichard says, and he implies that the Aristotelian theory is not much more successful. According to Aristotle, we should fulfill our engagements because such acts are good in themselves and go to make up happiness. But the difficulty here is that, if we care for our parents because of the intrinsic goodness of the act, we shall not feel that we are obliged to do it, that it is our duty. If, on the other hand, we care for them because we feel obliged, it will not be because of the intrinsic goodness of the act.[37] The fact is, Prichard contends, we are never obliged to do our duty *from a good motive*. The man who pays his debt from a bad motive (e.g., to further his plan to fleece his victim later) has discharged his obligation as much as his neighbor who acted from a noble motive.

W. D. Ross added a further reason why we are never obliged to do our duty from a good motive. It is never my obligation to do something I cannot do, he says, and surely I cannot instantaneously call forth a praiseworthy desire I do not have, which will be effective in causing me to do my duty. The best I can do is to try to discipline myself so that in the future such a praiseworthy desire, e.g., love or sympathy for my creditor, will appear of itself.[38] Although Ross's argument has a plausible ring, it has been frequently questioned. For example, the Cambridge philosopher A. C. Ewing has pointed out that we do blame people for acting from a malicious motive, which seems to imply that they could have altered their motive as well as their action. Moreover, if we assume with Ross that the motive is the cause of the action, it is not clear how the action could be in our control if the motive to it is beyond our control.

According to Prichard, however, the reason for our doing our duty cannot be the good or happy consequences that will ensue. It cannot be anything but the formal structure of our commitment. Promises are things to be kept, contracts to be fulfilled, debts to be paid, by their very nature. The apprehension of obligation "is immediate, in precisely the sense in which a mathematical apprehension [as that $2 + 2 = 4$] is immediate."[39] If we consider the *consequences* of the act, it is only to assure ourselves that it *is* the act which will fulfill our duty, as when we consider whether a check sent to a certain address will get to our creditor in time.

Formalism in ethics gives rise at once to two difficulties. First, since the moral rules prescribed by one society differ, often widely, from those prescribed in another, what is your right or duty in one location may be wrong or wicked in another. Formalism leads to ethical relativism, which

37 *Ibid.*, p. 6.
38 *The Right and the Good* (Oxford: Clarendon Press, 1930), pp. 4–5.
39 Prichard, *op. cit.*, p. 8.

is precisely what, above all, it wished to avoid. Morality depends on where you were born and the rules which were inculcated in you in childhood. The other big problem for formalism is what to do with conflicts of duties within a given society—within a given code. Suppose the time has come for Mr. Smith to pay his debt, but his child has suddenly been struck down by polio and the best care for him will take every cent he can raise for a year to come.

How can Mr. Smith, if he is a formalist, justify his refusal to pay his debt, to honor his solemn promise? Or how, if he is a formalist, will he justify his absolute duty of truth-telling to people who insist that being kind on all occasions is the self-evident and paramount duty? The ethics of happiness has a clear answer: Perform that act which will, or to the best of your knowledge will, produce the greatest possible happiness, or the least unhappiness. The partisan of happiness has an answer because he has the yardstick of happiness. The formalist, it seems, has none.

To take account of the conflict of duties, Ross distinguished between overall obligations and *prima facie* obligations, and he thereby set the stage for the current debate between formalists and utilitarians. A *prima facie* duty is a moral claim on us, which we recognize as obligatory unless it conflicts with a stronger claim, i.e., a more stringent *prima facie* obligation. If a *prima facie* duty is not contradicted in a given situation by a more stringent *prima facie* duty, it is our overall duty or obligation; it is actually incumbent on us to do it. Although these *prima facie* duties are "conditional," Ross says, there is nothing arbitrary about them. We do have *prima facie* duties to tell the truth, to keep our promises or engagements, to make reparations for wrongful harm we have done others, to act with gratitude, to improve the condition of others "in respect of virtue, or of intelligence, or of pleasure," to avoid injuring others, to improve ourselves in virtue or intelligence, and to aim at a redistribution of happiness more in accord with deserts, with justice.[40]

We have an additional duty, whenever there is a conflict of duties, to perform the one that carries the most stringent *prima facie* obligation. Unfortunately, it would be very hard to obey this second-order duty, since Ross gives us no rule for deciding which *prima facie* duties are more stringent. He had no yardstick of his own, and he cannot, in general, use the yardstick of happiness since more happiness for him does not necessarily mean more good.

Increasing the sum of happiness in the world might result in a loss of goodness, said Richard Price in 1758, in his *Review of the Principal Questions and Difficulties in Morals*, for suppose the increase all went to the worst villains. It cannot be our only duty to work for the greatest happiness of the greatest number; a just distribution of happiness is also some-

---

40 Ross, *op. cit.*, p. 21.

thing intrinsically good. Many contemporary philosophers, including Ross, echo Price's conviction. They repeatedly cite examples to show that utilitarianism, by neglecting the *distribution* of happiness, falls into one absurdity after another. If all that counts is the quantity of happiness produced, why should I keep my promises to a person in cases where it will only make him or myself unhappy, or when I can make someone else just as happy or even happier? Why make reparations to the person I have injured, when I am in a position to do more good to someone else? And why not punish an innocent man if doing so, in a particular case, will serve to deter others from crime most effectively and thus redound to the greatest net happiness of society? And why should not a judge impose very unequal penalties for the very same offense if some defendants can be more quickly reformed than others and returned to society as good citizens? Or, as Samuel Butler once put it, why not send all the prospective murderees to jail (if they could be located) instead of the murderers? One procedure would stop murder just as effectively as the other. Suppose, too, that criminals could be reformed by kindness and luxurious surroundings, and all other purposes of punishment could be served equally well by pampering. There would be a clear gain in the general happiness. What would be lost?

In answer, the utilitarians point out that the common rules pertaining to telling the truth, keeping promises, making reparations to injured parties, etc., and legal rules such as equal punishment for equal offenses, represent the accumulated wisdom of the race, and that society itself might not survive if they were not *generally* observed. The short-range gain in happiness by telling a kind lie or by murdering a wicked tyrant, therefore, is usually outweighed by the long-range loss in happiness resulting from the weakening of these precious rules, which suffer attrition with every violation. Generally, then, and unless the overall hedonic gain from infraction is clear and unmistakable, most utilitarians insist that we obey these accepted moral injunctions. Some indeed claim that the way to achieve the greatest happiness (pleasure) of the greatest number is not to attempt to calculate the total gains and losses entailed by a given act but rather to be guided in particular actions by general rules which will, we can be sure, give the best results in most cases. These utilitarians are called "rule utilitarians." The "act utilitarians," on the other hand, emphasize that there are rules and rules, and some embody more prejudice or ignorance than wisdom. They object to consistently obeying any rule that is admittedly only true in *most* cases. Although general rules can be useful, it is the consequences of the act itself that determine its rightness. But whether of one camp or the other, all utilitarians accept general rules (when they do), not because they disclose what is intrinsically right, but because following them has generally had good or happy consequences, or avoided the reverse. Human happiness or good gives them a measure, as we have seen, by which to decide between general rules which often conflict when applied in particular situations.

The formalists, however, show ingenuity in conjuring up instances in which the breaking of a moral rule could hardly be supposed to weaken it; e.g., as when I have made a solemn promise to a dying man in secret which I find inconvenient to keep. Why should I, if I am a utilitarian?

The formalists also enjoy asking the really challenging question: "If there is to be a certain quantity of happiness in the world, is it really a matter of indifference to you, as a utilitarian, how it is distributed?" Price and Kant were greatly impressed with this consideration, and so are contemporary philosophers. John Rawls argues that an increase of general happiness would be desirable only if it were *fair;* i.e., if it did not involve depriving some to give to others.[41] Richard B. Brandt, similarly, insists that utilitarianism be "extended" to include another intrinsic good, in addition to the maximum good or happiness asserted by utilitarianism, namely, "an *equal* distribution of welfare."[42] Although this "extended utilitarianism" is really inconsistent with utilitarianism as usually defined, it is interesting to remember that it was Bentham who had given impetus to egalitarianism in economics. He had argued that "the nearer the actual proportion [in the distribution of wealth] approaches to equality, the greater will be the total mass of happiness."[43] Thus equal distribution was, for Bentham, not something to be added to utilitarianism, but precisely the condition which favored the greatest general happiness.

Another formalist argument against utilitarianism is that to calculate the pleasure–pain consequences of keeping our promises or paying our debts is discordant with our moral consciousness and convictions. Utilitarians answer that they do not claim we should always be carrying out hedonic calculations, but only when they are needed; i.e., when there is reason to suspect that the act in question is an exception to the general rule, or the rules themselves conflict. Utilitarians also point out that reference to moral convictions, which are evaluations, does not refute utilitarianism in the sense that the citing of facts can refute a scientific theory.[44] It is true, as the formalist says, that in practice we often praise actions which have no tendency to produce the greatest happiness, e.g., as when a man returns to a cruel death at the hands of a tyrant only because he had promised him to do so, but the praise *may be* owing to our sentimentality, confusion, or thoughtless rule-worshiping. On the other hand, there are clear cases where an act of great generosity or courage just *happens* to turn out badly for all, but these the utilitarian himself would be

41 "Justice as Fairness," *Philosophical Review*, 67 (1958) 164–94.

42 *Ethical Theory* (Englewood Cliffs, N.J.: Prentice-Hall, Inc., 1959), p. 404.

43 *The Theory of Legislation* (London: Routledge & Kegan Paul, Ltd., 1950), p. 104.

44 Smart, *op. cit.*, pp. 40–41.

eager to praise. He praises them because they are kinds of acts which *usually* have happy consequences, and he wants to encourage acts of this kind.

The present revolt against the happiness principle is often based on the conviction that *fairness* or *justice* is also something good in itself, and that, in fact, the greater happiness must give way if it entails unfairness. We have already touched on the demand for fairness, but now we must mention a special form of it, viz., the demand for fairness in the distribution of benefits and burdens. We all see, for example, that if people enjoy the benefits of an electoral system they ought to assume the burden of voting at elections, for without votes the whole democratic process would collapse. But suppose citizen Jones argues as follows: "My one vote can't affect the outcome in any way at all, and if I stay in the hot city to vote I shall miss my day of relaxation in the country, which I badly need. It is my utilitarian duty to promote what happiness I can and to avoid misery. Therefore I ought to skip voting on this occasion." Jones's conscience now says: "But suppose everyone acted in this way." To this, Jones replies: "I know they won't. The number of people who will vote in this election is calculated in advance. And my staying away will not influence anyone else to do the same, because no one will know that I didn't vote." Conscience: "But will it not have a bad influence on *you?* Will you not, perhaps, be more inclined in the future to excuse yourself from a duty while enjoying the benefits of other people's doing theirs?" Jones: "I don't see why. In the future, as now, I expect to do my duty, and my duty consists in acting for the sake of happiness rather than unhappiness. Abiding by this principle, I shall *usually* do what is conventionally expected of a citizen. But I am not a worshiper of conventions; I usually follow them, because doing so usually produces the best results." Conscience: "Maybe you are right, then."

Although Jones has succeeded in silencing his conscience, the argument is not finished. It may be asked why the people who voted would be indignant if they learned that Jones had excused himself from voting for the reason that, since he knew *they* would vote, *his* vote was unnecessary. They would say: "What right does this fellow have to make an exception of himself? We were all in the same boat. Suppose we had all reasoned this way." They would thus be expressing "the generalization principle," namely: What is right or obligatory for one person must be right or obligatory "for every similar person in similar circumstances," about which Singer has recently written a whole book.[45] Singer acknowledges its obvious resemblance to Kant's categorical imperative: "Act only on that maxim whereby thou canst at the same time will that it should become a universal law."[46] And like Kant's imperative, Singer's generalization prin-

---

45 Singer, op. cit., pp. 37 and *passim*.
46 *Ibid.*, p. 9.

ciple—and what he calls "the generalization argument": If the consequences of doing X would be undesirable, then it would be wrong for
anyone to do X—clearly conflicts with the happiness principle and with
teleological ethics in general. When they are in conflict, considerations of
"fairness" are to outweigh the prospect of happiness.

In our example above, it was wrong of Jones to skip voting for the
sake of a day in the country, since the consequences of everyone's doing
the same would be undesirable. He should have voted, though the result
would have been an overall loss of happiness or good. David Lyons has
shown that cases of this sort arise not only where "the relative distribution
of benefits and burdens" is concerned but also in relation to "impartiality
and discrimination," to the fixing of fair procedures, and to special areas
of social cooperation.[47] In present discussions, the utilitarians are mostly
concerned to show that clear cases of justice are only apparently in conflict with optimum consequences, that when *all* consequences are taken
into account the conflict disappears. Formalists argue the reverse.

Lyons makes the pertinent comment that those who insist on an exact
balance between burdens and benefits are assuming the dictum:

> From each according to his benefits,
> to each according to his burdens.

---

47 *Forms and Limits of Utilitarianism* (Oxford: Clarendon Press, 1965), pp. 161ff.

But an alternative dictum might have just as much justification:

> From each according to his resources,
> to each according to his need.

"No doubt neither constitutes by itself a sufficient criterion. But these suggest the shortsightedness of that form of egalitarianism according to which all persons are to benefit (or share) equally. It would seem that some consideration must be given to burdens and needs."[48] Lyons also analyzes the part played by *ceteris paribus* assumptions in Singer's generalization argument: How often can we know that the relevant factors are equal enough for large numbers of individuals to warrant the generalization?

The campaign of recent formalists is naturally directed against utilitarianism rather than other philosophies of happiness. Aristotelian eudaemonism is not in the direct line of fire, for though happiness here is the supreme good, it contains justice or fairness and other virtues within it as integral parts, and these virtues are good in themselves. It might seem, then, that we ought to be fair and just and keep our engagements, no matter what consequences follow. But Aristotle cannot mean this. He does not say that we should return a sword we have borrowed when

---

48 *Ibid.*, p. 174.

we have promised if, at that time, the owner is in a homicidal state, or that a ruler should stick rigidly to his engagements even if the authority or security of the state is thereby endangered. On the contrary, consequences must be weighed in with the sanctity of engagements and the general virtues. In particular cases, "perception" must often be our guide. The modern self-realization philosophers also wove justice or fairness and optimal consequences into one fabric, so that here, too, any conflict between them became a problem internal to their system.

SOME CONTEMPORARY VERSIONS OF ARISTOTELIANISM

The influence of Aristotle continues strong in English-speaking countries, but his theory of happiness (eudaemonia), taken as a whole, is not much debated. In brief, this theory states that happiness is a full life of self-fulfillment of natural powers in accordance with virtue or excellence, accompanied by pleasure, and provided with sufficient external goods, leisure, and reasonably good fortune. The virtues, both moral and intellectual, are discussed in detail, as are other basic features of the ideal. It is still the most elaborate account of happiness available, and probably the most influential. The theory of self-realization which had its beginning with Spinoza, as we have mentioned, owed a great deal of its substance and inspiration to Aristotle. Two decades ago, when the philosophy of John Dewey was uppermost, self-realization was still the living creed of many philosophers, educators, lawyers, and social scientists. Now, though it lives on in education and other fields, it is no longer a focus of philosophical interest. It is still, however, an important conception. It states that the supreme good or happiness is the full realization of human excellence and of the potentialities of the individual, and that right and obligation are counsels to achievement that entail achievement.

In the meantime, these two ideals of happiness and the good life are enjoying wide recognition in the more practical provinces of psychotherapy and psychology of personality. The theory of positive mental health or happiness, put forward by influential psychotherapists and psychologists, whether it is called "self-actualization," "productiveness," "happiness," or something else, is in the tradition of eudaemonism and self-realization, which it resembles in basic respects.

It is not often that contemporary psychologists in the clinical field hail the supporting views of philosophers, but at least two self-actualization authors do. Erich Fromm and A. H. Maslow both cite the similarity of their views to the eudaemonism of Aristotle and the original self-realization theory of Spinoza. Fromm compares the "productiveness" that is for him the measure of man's happiness with the achievement that plays such an important role in Aristotle's ethics. In Aristotle's view, Fromm says, "one can determine virtue . . . by ascertaining the function of man. Just as in the case of a flute player, a sculptor, or any artist, the good is thought to reside in the specific function which distinguishes these men from others and makes them what they are, the good of man also resides in the specific function which distinguishes him from other species and makes him what he is."[49] Fromm goes on to quote a passage from Aristotle in which he observes how important it is to recognize that happiness is excellence of activity, rather than a virtuous *state*. If happiness were merely the latter, a happy man could spend his life asleep, or "without producing any good result." We must agree with Aristotle that the happy man is one "who by his activity, under the guidance of his reason, brings to life the potentialities specific of man."[50] Fromm also finds his ideal of productiveness anticipated in Spinoza's *Ethics*, where virtue consists in the realization of the natural powers of man and is expansive rather than ascetic.

Fromm also agrees with Plato, Aristotle, and Spinoza on the relation of pleasure to happiness: Pleasure is an accompaniment of natural activities that perfects them and is most valuable when it belongs to our highest nature, i.e., theoretic reason; pleasure is of different kinds and is not to be identified with happiness. In Spinoza's system, Fromm calls attention particularly to the definition of joy, as "a passage from a less to a greater perfection" (or power); the famous last Proposition of the *Ethics*, "Blessedness (or happiness) is not the reward of virtue but virtue itself. . . ."; and the implied doctrine that productive activity is the end of life.

Maslow also finds his key concept of self-actualization anticipated in part by Aristotle and Spinoza. "We may agree with Aristotle," he remarks, "that the good life consisted in living in accordance with the true nature of man. . . ."[51] He insists, with Aristotle and self-realization authors, that cognitive and other higher needs be given due place in psychological explanation, and he decries the neglect of "beauty, art, fun, play, wonder, love, happiness, and other 'useless' reactions," in present-day psychology. "Expressive behavior," which has to do with the arts and enjoyments, is as important as "coping behavior," which is instrumental and adaptive. The organism does more than merely restore equilibria that have been disturbed. Recent developments have shown that it possesses "some sort of positive growth or self-actualization tendency, which is different from its conserving, equilibrating, or homeostatic tendency," and also from coping responses. This self-actualizing tendency has been recognized by

---

49 *Man for Himself* (New York: Rinehart and Co., 1947), p. 91.
50 *Ibid.*, p. 92.
51 *Motivation and Personality* (New York: Harper & Brothers, 1954), p. 341.

Aristotle and many other philosophers. And "among psychiatrists, psychoanalysts, and psychologists it has been found necessary by Goldstein, Rank, Jung, Horney, May, and Rogers."[52]

Among the authors who endorse self-actualization as the natural tendency and ideal norm of personality development or as the furthermost goal of psychotherapy, there are many differences. Kurt Goldstein holds that the *only* drive "is to actualize the individual capacities as fully as possible."[53] In sheer contrast with the holism of Goldstein is the integrative view of G. W. Allport, according to which personality is formed by the integration of simple units, such as reflexes, into ever larger, more complex formations, and there exist many, diverse drives. Yet Goldstein and Allport agree that the hallmark of normality is the growth or actualization of the individual's capacities, and that integration is never and should not be complete, for it is better to be embroiled in conflict than to settle for integration on a lower level.

This last point is particularly emphasized by Nevitt Sanford, who believes that the concern of psychologists—for example, in counseling university students—should not be to see that they avoid conflicts and problems but to see that their natural growth potential toward "expansion and increasing complexity" is not thwarted.[54]

The capacity for continuous "growth," for continuous development of human powers and personal talents, is certainly the crux of self-actualization. Some authors, however, prefer to express the ideal as a tireless urge and readiness to learn—a freedom from learning blocks, from rigidity, oversimplicity, and stereotypes which characterize the "authoritarian personality." Lawrence S. Kubie takes mental health to be a high resistance to stress and "freedom and flexibility to learn through experience, to change and to adapt to changing circumstance,"[55] and Robert W. White likewise ties growth to learning when he says: "It is now generally recognized that emotional disorders can be traced to blocks in the learning process. . . . These blocks are produced by defenses against anxiety," which prevent further learning. "It is implicit in this account that normal growth signifies unblocked learning, a process of *continuous change*."[56] For John Dewey, likewise, uninterrupted "growth," which is the human ideal and moral condition, is defined as the unceasing readiness to learn, the willingness to put our favorite ideas to new tests, no matter how successful or comforting they have been in the past. This

---

52 *Ibid.*, p. 124.

53 *Human Nature in the Light of Psychopathology* (Cambridge: Harvard University Press, 1951), p. 141.

54 "Normative Conceptions in Psychology," *Writers on Ethics*, eds. Joseph Katz *et al.* (New York: D. Van Nostrand Co., Inc., 1962.)

55 *Psychoanalytic Quarterly*, 28 (1954), 172.

56 *Lives in Progress* (New York: The Dryden Press, 1952), p. 328.

untrammeled readiness to learn is, it is generally agreed, nowhere more productive than in the sphere of the emotions and affections. That successful psychoanalysis is primarily a reeducation of the emotions has been emphasized by Franz Alexander, T. M. French, Karen Horney, Fromm, and many others.

The list of doctrines that the self-realization authors agree upon, though with great differences of accent, is fairly long, and they belong also to the tradition of eudaemonism and self-realization. But without going further it is easy to see that self-realization theory is opposed to both utilitarianism and ethical formalism. It rejects hedonism in general, holding that pleasure is the *accompaniment* of self-fulfilling activity, not its goal or *raison d'être*. Nor would it accept general rules as a guide *merely* because of their formal structure, or reject moral rights and duties because they cannot be extended to everyone. Its main concern is the divergent development of individuals in different situations.

Self-actualization authors, indeed, say little about moral rules or obligations. But this does not mean that they are amoral or value-neutral. They take it for granted, as John Dewey often did, that following well-tried moral rules is generally necessary, though not sufficient for growth, achievement, aesthetic enrichment, and other things which make up happiness, individual and social.

One objection to the ideal of self-realization, and to the tradition from which it springs, is always brought up—by philosophers and by some psychologists, too. Thus Marie Jahoda, in her influential *Current Concepts of Positive Mental Health*, complains that "the Growth, Development, Self-Actualization Concept" of positive mental health does not make clear whether the self-actualizing process is supposed to be going on in all organisms or only in healthy ones. She thinks that the ambiguity may be owing to "Aristotelian teleology," and especially to "the notion of realizing one's potentialities."[57]

> The need for making the distinction in a discussion of mental health becomes urgent if one realizes that not only the development of civilization but also self-destruction and crime . . . are among the unique potentialities of the human species.[58]

We have seen Fromm replying to this objection by a quotation from Aristotle. The virtues or excellences of man are determined once we know the functions which distinguish his species from others, and the same is true of human potentialities. The well-functioning flute player is not one who murders the music, nor is a well-functioning man one who destroys himself or makes a career of crime.

---

57 New York: Basic Books, Inc., 1958, p. 31.
58 *Ibid.*

SOME OPINION SURVEYS

The opinion survey provides another approach to gaining an understanding of happiness. Interviews with several thousand people are conducted in which they are asked whether they would describe themselves as "very happy," "pretty happy," or "not too happy." In order to supplement and evaluate the answers they give, they are also asked how much they worry, what they worry about, and to what they attribute their happiness or unhappiness. The answers obtained are then collated and correlated to show the most important sources of happiness, of unhappiness, and of worry in the "very happy" group in comparison with the groups which give themselves a lower happiness rating. The three groups have been compared in many other respects, such as age, economic status, job satisfaction, extent of education, health, self-referral for psychotherapeutic aid, and reaction to international crisis. The interrelations of numerous variables lead to a reassessment of answers and techniques and to a growing understanding of what happiness means in typical American small-town communities.

In a recent study, Gerald Gurin, Joseph Veroff, and Sheila Feld explain how interrelations of numerous answers can furnish corrections or substantiation. The gist of the method is sketched as follows:

> At the simplest level one can ask the respondent[s] to tell you . . . directly what things they are happy about. . . . The other approach is more indirect and analytic. We can get some idea [in an interview] of what it means for persons to say they are "very happy" as contrasted to "not too happy" by relating these responses to their responses to other questions and seeing some of the ways that people in these two extremes differ. Using both approaches, for example, we can indicate that happiness means economic well-being not only by the fact that people tell us that they are happy for such reasons but also by our demonstration that people of higher income express greater happiness. Or, we can indicate that happiness is tied to a happy marital relationship not only because people very often mention marriage as a source of happiness but also because people spontaneously mentioning greater satisfaction from their marriages express greater happiness generally.[59]

Reports on Happiness: A Pilot Study of Behavior Related to Mental Health, by Norman M. Bradburn and David Caplovitz, also follows a complex procedure in evaluating and checking the answers: "very happy," "pretty happy," and "not too happy."[60] These answers were correlated with sex, age, education, income, socioeconomic status, health, etc., and

---

59 *Americans View Their Mental Health: A Nationwide Interview Survey* (New York: Basic Books, Inc., 1960) p. 23.

60 Chicago: Aldine Publishing Co., 1965, p. 8.

with the expression of particular worries, anxieties, cheerful or gloomy outlook, and so on. The economic angle could be examined from a single vantage point, since the four communities studied in Illinois were of comparable size, two suffering from depression and two economically in good shape. The study of psychological correlates of happiness, of positive and negative feelings, of reported illness and symptoms, of marital troubles and the like were considered important. It was easy to see that "happiness is not a simple phenomenon that can be understood in terms of a single dimension, but rather a complex resultant of the satisfactions and dissatisfactions, the gratifying and frustrating emotional experiences that occur in a person's life situation."[61]

The authors of these two volumes are aware of ambiguities and pitfalls that face studies of this kind, and their procedure is tentative and self-correcting. There is reason enough for caution. It might be maintained, for example, that the authors are not dealing with people's happiness, but only with individuals' self-assessment of their happiness. In reporting that they are *very* or *not too* happy they might well be mistaken. In judging how happy they are, men may use a different base line or make a different estimate of the average happiness. But this need not be fatal. Psychologists have studied shifts of base line (adaptation level) and can often control or allow for it. And besides, people's assessments of their happiness are correlated with their more concrete feelings, attitudes, and facts of their lives, and this provides a check and allows for corrections. But in the end, after we have sifted a man's meaning and sincerity in saying he is very happy, it would be absurd, as Wright points out, to question his judgment. Even if we believe he is insincere or mistaken, we can scarcely do without his confirmation. Asking people questions is thus indispensable to a study of their happiness, and though the problems involved are many and serious, they do not seem to be hopeless.

A few results have a bearing on our previous discussion of happiness. The two surveys agree that education and income are both positively strongly correlated with happiness, whereas the correlation with age is *negative;* higher education and income are apparently favorable to happiness, increasing age unfavorable to it. These results are in line with expectations, and high positive correlation of income and education with happiness is assumed by the self-actualization theory discussed in this chapter, and by the tradition to which it belongs.

It was found that, in a group of some 2,500 people interviewed, 46 percent gave children and marriage as the main source of their happiness, 29 percent gave an economic and material source, while all the other sources of happiness mentioned—such as the health of the respondent and family, job, other interpersonal sources (beyond the family), and inde-

---

61 *Ibid.*

pendence—made up the remaining 35 percent.[62] As sources of *un*happiness, on the other hand, only 12 percent mentioned children and family; the largest sources of unhappiness are economic, personal characteristics (and problems), and community, national, and world problems. Very instructive is the authors' comment which follows:

> The answers to these questions give, in a sense, the respondents' explicit definition of happiness and unhappiness. They were combined into categories according to the area of life viewed as the source of happiness or unhappiness—economic and material things, the marriage relationship, the job, one's health or the health of others close to one, and so on.[63]

The measure of happiness here is not the quantity of pleasure, and indeed neither survey talks in terms of pleasure. It is the *kind* of activity preferred which determines the happiness, and this varies within the group. But the 46 percent for whom happiness is mainly activity centering around children and the family also find some happiness in other things and can of course understand that other people should have different preferences.

Of all the results reported in these two surveys, those which relate to the positive and negative components of happiness seem most pertinent to our theme. It is shown in general that happy people worry less and unhappy people more. In fact, 65 percent of the "very happy" claim they never worry, or not much. Yet being worried and being unhappy, though they both spring from frustrating experiences, differ from each other profoundly. Unhappiness reflects "an absence of positive satisfactions in life . . . a lack of positive resources" to cope with reverses, and is associated with a pessimistic outlook; whereas worrying often goes along with positive satisfactions, personal resources, and optimism. A happy man can thus be a frequent worrier.[64]

Another study examined the balance of positive and negative feelings in the composition of happiness. People were asked how often, during the previous week, they had had positive feelings (such as, for example, being "pleased about having accomplished something") and negative feelings (being "very lonely or remote from other people," for example). It was found, as had been expected, that the positive feelings correlated positively with happiness, and the negative feelings correlated negatively with happiness. What was surprising was that the positive and negative feelings do not correlate with each other, one way or the other. In other words, it appeared that more negative feelings (or rather, experiences with negative affect) do not imply fewer positive feelings, nor vice versa. The data of this and other studies show that:

62 Gurin, *op. cit.*, p. 24.
63 *Ibid.*, p. 25.
64 *Ibid.*, pp. 34–35.

. . . forces contributing toward increased negative feelings, such as anxiety, marital tension, and job dissatisfaction, do not produce any concomitant decrease in positive feelings, and those forces which contribute toward the development of positive feelings, such as social interaction and active participation in the environment, do not in any way lessen negative feelings. Thus it is possible for a person who has many negative feelings to be happy, if he also has compensatory positive feelings.[65]

It is not the avoidance of negative feelings that makes for happiness; it is rather the gaining of experiences having positive affect through active participation. "It is the lack of joy in Mudville rather than the presence of sorrow that makes the difference," Bradburn wrote in 1963.

F. Hertzberg and R. M. Hamlin recently reached a somewhat similar conclusion, Bradburn reports. There are people who "find their source of satisfaction in a sense of personal growth, or the satisfaction of self-actualization needs," and there are others who seek theirs in the avoidance of unpleasant experiences. The former are on the "mental health dimension," and with luck can "achieve positive mental health and self-actualization"; the latter live on the "mental illness dimension," and with luck can achieve transitory satisfactions, but are "truly mentally ill."[66]

These findings and interpretations give their support, for all it is worth, to the self-realization theory we have discussed, and to the tradition of Aristotelian eudaemonism from which it derives. This is the expansionist strand in the long quest of the best feasible view of happiness. It is in the spirit of Goethe's Faust of whom the angels said. "He who ever strives cannot be lost," and of Emerson's Everyman, of whom he said: "Each is uneasy until he has produced his private ray into the concave sphere, and beheld his talent also in its last nobility and exaltation." At the opposite extreme is that Stoicism which would sacrifice man's birthright of abundance and adventure for security and tranquillity. This has lost its appeal. The great productive capacity of a few countries has enlightened the rest, and no one any longer dares extol to rising populations the virtues of submission and contentment. On the other hand, the appeal of the eternal supernatural happiness, mentioned at the beginning of this essay, remains unabated, though perhaps with considerable variation in "psychic distance." It is no longer controversial, however, and it is as if the subject had been completed. The conflict between the utilitarians and formalists could go on indefinitely with modest progress in subtlety and precision, though as positions on both sides are more cautiously stated there is a tendency to convergence. The Aristotelian philosophy of happiness could gain by any clarifications reached; it by no means answers all questions about duty versus happiness and has potential to grow.

---

65 Bradburn, op. cit., pp. 56–57.
66 Ibid., p. 58.

BIBLIOGRAPHY

BAIER, KURT. *The Moral Point of View.* New York: Random House, Inc., 1965.

BENTHAM, JEREMY. *The Theory of Legislation.* London: Routledge & Kegan Paul, Ltd., 1950.

BRADBURN, NORMAN M., and CAPLOVITZ, DAVID. *Reports on Happiness: A Pilot Study of Behavior Related to Mental Health.* Chicago: Aldine Publishing Co., 1965.

BRAITHWAITE, R. B. "Moral Principles and Inductive Policies," *Studies in Philosophy,* ed. J. N. FINDLAY. London: Oxford University Press, 1966.

BRANDT, RICHARD B. *Ethical Theory.* Englewood Cliffs, N.J.: Prentice-Hall, Inc., 1959.

EWING, A. C. *Ethics.* London: English Universities Press, 1953.

FROMM, ERICH. *Man for Himself.* New York: Rinehart and Co., 1947.

GOLDSTEIN, KURT. *Human Nature in the Light of Psychopathology.* Cambridge: Harvard University Press, 1951.

GURIN, G., VEROFF, J., and FELD, S. *Americans View Their Mental Health: A Nationwide Interview Survey.* New York: Basic Books, Inc., 1960.

HARE, R. M. *Freedom and Reason.* London: Oxford University Press, 1963.

HAZLITT, HENRY. *The Foundations of Morality.* Princeton: D. Van Nostrand Co., Inc., 1964.

HOSPERS, JOHN. *Human Conduct.* New York: Harcourt, Brace and World, Inc., 1961.

JAHODA, MARIE. *Current Concepts of Positive Mental Health.* New York: Basic Books, Inc., 1958.

KUBIE, LAWRENCE S. *Psychoanalytic Quarterly,* 28 (1954), 172.

LYONS, DAVID. *Forms and Limits of Utilitarianism.* Oxford: Clarendon Press, 1965.

MACINTYRE, ALASDAIR. *A Short History of Ethics.* New York: The Macmillan Co., 1966.

MASLOW, A. H. *Motivation and Personality.* New York: Harper & Brothers, 1954.

MCGILL, V. J. *The Idea of Happiness.* New York: Frederick A. Praeger, Inc., 1967.

NOWELL-SMITH, P. H. *Ethics.* Baltimore: Penguin Books, 1961.

PRICHARD, H. A. "Does Moral Philosophy Rest on a Mistake?," reprinted in *Moral Obligation: Essays and Lectures.* Oxford: Clarendon Press, 1949.

RAWLS, JOHN. "Justice as Fairness," *Philosophical Review,* 67 (1958), 164–94.

ROSS, W. D. *The Right and the Good.* Oxford: Clarendon Press, 1930.

RYLE, GILBERT. "Pleasure," *Dilemmas.* Cambridge: Cambridge University Press, 1954.

SANFORD, NEVITT. "Normative Conceptions in Psychology," *Writers on Ethics,* eds. JOSEPH KATZ *et al.* New York: D. Van Nostrand Co., Inc., 1962.

SINGER, MARCUS GEORGE. *Generalization in Ethics.* New York: Alfred A. Knopf, Inc., 1961.

SMART, J. J. C. *An Outline of a System of Utilitarian Ethics.* Melbourne: Melbourne University Press, 1961.

WHITE, ROBERT W. *Lives in Progress.* New York: The Dryden Press, 1952.

WRIGHT, GEORG HENRIK VON. *The Logic of Preference.* Edinburgh: Edinburgh University Press, 1963.

———. *The Varieties of Goodness.* London: Routledge & Kegan Paul, Ltd., 1963.

NOTE TO THE READER

T he essential documents for understanding the background of the controversy about happiness are included in *Great Books of the Western World.* Aristotle's *Nicomachean Ethics* is in Vol. 9, Kant's *Fundamental Principles of the Metaphysic of Morals* is in Vol. 42, and Mill's essay *Utilitarianism,* in Vol. 43.

Chapter 33 of the *Syntopicon* is devoted to the idea of HAPPINESS, and the reader will find in the *Introduction* and the references a guide to the wealth of material on the subject contained in *Great Books.* Chapter 19 on DUTY and Chapter 97 on VIRTUE and VICE should also be consulted for their bearing on the general discussion of happiness.

The Contemporary
Status
of a Great Idea

ETIENNE
GILSON

Etienne Gilson, one of the most eminent scholars of the twentieth century, was professor of the Collège de France from 1932 until 1951, founder of the Pontifical Institute of Mediaeval Studies at the University of Toronto in 1929 and its director until 1968, member of the French delegation to the San Francisco Conference on the United Nations in 1945, senator of the Fourth French Republic from 1947 to 1948, and is, as a member of the Académie Française since 1946, one of "the forty immortals" of France. Born in Paris on June 13, 1884, Gilson took his baccalaureate at the Sorbonne in 1907 and his doctorate in 1913. He served as a French Army officer during World War I, spending two years as a prisoner of war. In 1919 he became professor at Strasbourg, and in 1921 at the University of Paris. His career of productive scholarship results thus far in a bibliography of books and articles covering seventy pages. During the past academic year Professor Gilson gave a series of lectures on Thomism at the University of California at Berkeley. Some of his best-known books came out of famous lectureships he has held at European and American universities. Among them are The Spirit of Mediaeval Philosophy *(Gifford Lectures at Aberdeen, 1930–31),* The Unity of Philosophical Experience *(William James Lectures at Harvard, 1938),* Being and Some Philosophers *(Powell Lectures at Indiana, 1940),* Painting and Reality *(Mellon Lectures at Washington, 1955). His many studies of mediaeval thinkers have contributed decisively to the contemporary reassessment and reinterpretation of the achievements of the Middle Ages. Master of an elegant and lucid style, in English as well as French, he has written extensively on literature as well as on philosophy and theology. Yet while he is a scholar and an author, Gilson prides himself most on being a Christian philosopher.*

The Idea of God
and the Difficulties
of Atheism

I have often been asked for a demonstration of the existence of God. Let me confess that I have never been able to develop a passionate interest in the question. I am certain that there is a God, but that certainty does not rest on any demonstration of his existence. It seems to me so absolutely certain that a reality transcending both myself and the world actually exists that the prospect of looking for proofs of something I feel so sure of appears to me a waste of time. My certainty, in fact, makes me curious about the reasons atheists have for believing there is no God. To me, the inexistence, or nonexistence, of God is the question. Therefore, I wish to test some of the reasons invoked in favor of atheism. Dogmatic and positive atheism is what I am speaking of—the doctrine which, after mature reflection and serious consideration of the problem, concludes as a rational certainty that nothing answering the word "God" exists in reality. By "nothing" I mean no "being."

I shall begin by defining the notion of which the affirmation will be considered an affirmation of God, and the negation a negation of God. The constituent elements of that notion, its *essentialia* as Christian Wolff would say, are three in number: (1) God must be a transcendent being, that is, a being that exists apart from both myself and the world; (2) he likewise must be a necessary being; (3) he must be the cause of whatever else exists.[1] The reason for setting up these precise requirements is that affirming the existence of anything called God is not necessarily the same as affirming God.

For instance, *New World and Word of God* recently observed that "the first attribute of that God [of the Christians] is not being, it is not all-powerfulness, but rather it is love." The God of the Christians certainly is Love, but for him to be love, he first has to *be*. That is true even of

---

1 M. J. Adler, "God, Religion and Modern Man," a lecture delivered at the Aspen Institute for Humanistic Studies, August 0, 1000. I am indebted to Dr. Adler for his kindness in sending me a copy of that remarkable lecture, the more so as there is nothing in it to which I cannot unreservedly subscribe. Philosophical agreement is too scarce a commodity not to heartily welcome whenever one is lucky enough to find it. For the ensuing remarks, see *Esprit* (October, 1967), pp. 482 and 486.

Christ: if he *is* not, he cannot possibly *be* God. One cannot rightly define Him as the "communication of Himself," as "the gift of oneself," nor define his allpowerfulness as the "communication of being," without first acknowledging that He has some being to communicate, that in short, he *is* being.

It has rightly been observed that there are all sorts of atheism. If there is not exactly a "scientific" atheism—science is not qualified to deal with the notion of God—there is at least an atheism born in the minds of those who are exclusively devoted to scientific problems handled by scientific methods. A purely personal attitude, such positivist atheism is neither demonstrable nor refutable; we are not concerned with it. There is also a practical atheism, perhaps its most widely represented form, inasmuch as religion considers it the most insidious threat within the consciences of the believers themselves—impiety, living as though there were no God. We are not concerned with that form of atheism either. There is also a social and political form of atheism, such as the Marxist atheism of the modern Russian state. We would like to put it aside, for it is neither philosophical nor theological in essence, but we cannot since it constantly intrudes upon the very questions with which we are now concerned.

Thus only one form of atheism is relevant to our discussion, philosophical atheism. It can also be called theological in the sense that the metaphysical notion of God, which is at stake, is the crowning piece of what is called "natural theology"; we shall not concern ourselves with the self-revealed God of religion. To the extent that it claims to be taken seriously, the new "religious atheism" does not make sense. Neither can I find any sense in the notion of a "Christian atheism," in which the notion of Christ would act as a substitute for that of God, for indeed the God of Christ is the Christian God. Should our reflections lead us to the conclusion that atheism does not exist, it should be understood as meaning that atheism does not exist as a philosophical conclusion.

Is God Dead?

The words of Nietzsche, "God is dead," have become a cliché. Yet, when he wrote them in *Thus Spoke Zarathustra*, those words represented only the first half of his message. The other half was: "I am teaching you the superman." To Nietzsche, the first half did not make sense without the second. Zarathustra, leaving the forest where he had visited an old hermit, summed up the interview to himself: "That old saint has not yet learned that God is dead." For Nietzsche, that was only the first of the required conditions under which the reign of man, the lawful successor of God, was about to begin.

The meaning of those words, however, is not quite clear. Literally understood, they signify that a certain being, named God, has finally ceased to exist. Thus understood, the proposition is meaningless,[2] for even the pagan Greeks used to identify the notion of "God" with "immortal being." To say "the immortals," or "the gods," was to say the same thing, just as for us to say "a mortal," or "a man," is still to use two practically synonymous terms. The bond between the notions of divinity and of immortality has become so tight that even to us, the notion that a God should die is absurd. If there ever was a God, there must still be one, for if that being died, he was no God. There is no point in belaboring that truism, except that too many people content themselves with repeating certain slogans without realizing that, in fact, they are devoid of meaning. However, let us admit that Zarathustra was not announcing the final demise of some mortal being wrongly believed to be immortal. His formula then could mean that the belief—widely accepted until recently—that there is a God has finally ceased to be accepted as true. But if that is all it means, the celebrated formula is little more than a banality. What did it really mean to Nietzsche?

ETHICAL ATHEISM

To Nietzsche himself, the notion of the death of God was an essentially ethical notion. In leaving the forest and its hermits, Zarathustra leaves behind saints who, living in solitude as he himself has done, spend their lives in the praise of God. The hermits symbolize the race of those men who renounce the world, abdicate the autonomy of their wills, and submit their minds to the recognition of transcendent values, imposed upon them from on high. Such values are known to us under the names of *good* and *evil*, and codified in what we call ethics. To go beyond good and bad is to overcome those conventional notions of good and bad conduct, as well as of right and wrong ways of thinking.

Generally speaking, the reformation which Nietzsche seeks is the elimination of the Judeo-Christian ideal of humility and its exaltation of meekness, in order to substitute for it a glorification of power, of force, in short an exaltation of all the powers of man at their highest level. What is truly dead, therefore, is the Christian God of traditional ethics. Why does Nietzsche say of that God that he is dead? Because it has become impos-

---

2 In "God, Religion and Modern Man," quoted above, Dr. Adler defines what he calls the existential meaning as simply: "God does not exist." Hence he concludes that "all of our new theologians—our death-of-God theologians—are atheists . . . . They indulge in the most outrageous double-talk in order to try to persuade their readers that, with the death of God, a new theology has come into existence; or what is more absurd, a new era in man's religious life . . . The 'death of God' movement should be described as the death, not of God, but of theology and religion." This perfectly clear-cut statement of the problem is unassailable; one can only wonder if it is not made with an intellectual precision foreign to that class of so-called theologians.

sible even to blaspheme him, since no longer is there anyone to hear our blasphemies. "Formerly, the greatest of all blasphemies was the blasphemy against God, but God is dead and that blasphemy died along with him." From now on, the truly grievous blasphemy is against man; it consists in attributing to the earth less importance than to heaven, in giving less importance to man than to God.

The volcanic thought of Nietzsche defies summary. What he omits is not necessarily foreign to his mind; in this case, however, it can be observed that Nietzsche's negation of God does not apply, explicitly at least, to the physical and metaphysical notion of God as creator of the world and man. Were I asked what he thought of the question, I would not know what to answer. It is even harder for me to imagine what would have become of that notion if Nietzsche had subjected it to his own criticism and replaced it with a new one. He would have objected to the God of the Jews and of the Christians in any case, but what about the gods of the Greeks? Did not their worshipers conceive them as so many supermen, or superworkers, like the Demiurge of the *Timaeus*, a divine author of nature and a quasi creator of the world? For indeed, Plato says, everything is becoming, nothing really is, and everything that becomes must of necessity be produced by some cause, for "without a cause nothing can be produced."

Nietzsche himself was conscious of not having answered that part of the problem, for he was a moralist rather than a metaphysician, and he knew it. Careless readers may fail to observe this important limitation of his point of view, but Nietzsche himself was aware of it. In his own words, "It is theology that has stifled God, just as morality has stifled ethics," but God himself is not putrefying after the manner of a corpse, but he is rather, "like a snake shedding its old skin and putting on a new one. God is shedding his *moral* skin, and you soon will see him back, beyond good and evil." In one of his notes, headed *The refutation of God*, Nietzsche wrote: "In reality, only the *moral* God is refuted."[3]

There thus remains a whole theological field which Nietzsche knew he

---

3 Nietzsche, *Also sprach Zarathustra*, French transl. by G. Bianquis (Paris: Gallimard, 23 ed., 1950), Appendix, § 62, p. 310. By turning Nietzsche's words into a slogan, the mass media have obliterated that important distinction, but Jean Paul Sartre has clearly perceived and vividly illustrated it in his play *The Flies*. In the central scene of the drama Zeus urges Orestes to recognize him as the supreme power that rules the world; Orestes answers that nature indeed stands on the side of God, but if there is a God for nature, there is no God for man because man, unlike nature, is endowed with a will and therefore is free. Aristotle had not foreseen this unexpected application of his own principle that everything caused is caused either by a nature or by a will. To him, even the will is a sort of nature. Not so in the doctrine of Nietzsche; for this reason his ethics does not consist in accepting the values found by reason in nature, but, rather, in overthrowing them. Sartre has correctly understood Nietzsche's brand of atheism: God and nature on one side; man and his will on the other.

had not covered. To most of those who repeat after him that God is dead, the God they have in mind is precisely the metaphysical God, creator of the heaven and earth, preserver of the universe, and, to man, a Providence. Of course, the metaphysical atheists are well aware of some of the consequences of atheism on the level of practical morality, but it is remarkable that a "libertine" used to be considered both an atheist and a rake. "If there is no God," the father of *The Brothers Karamazov* says, "all is permitted!" This explains why the name of libertine used to be given to "one who professed free opinions, especially in religion," and to "one who professed a licentious life."

Nietzsche, however, believed that "unless we ourselves make the death of God a grandiose act of renunciation and a continuous victory over ourselves, we shall have to bear the loss."[4] Once it is agreed that there is no God above man, man himself will have to be God. But man as he now is, rather, as he must now become: the Superman. Along with the new God, Nietzsche intends to retain some religion, to the extent that religion essentially is "a doctrine of the hierarchy," as he says, "of a cosmic scale of power." He continues: "In this century of populism, a noble and well born mind should begin each day *by thinking of the hierarchy,* for that is where his duties lie, along with the subtlest of his misdecisions."[5]

I am not attempting to turn Nietzsche into a defender of the belief in the existence of God. His moral atheism is absolute, violent to the point of being pathological, as it was in fact to become at the end of his life, in his *Ecce Homo;* but his atheism is actually an antichristianism (including an antisemitism); it is a violent denunciation of the Jew Christ, the man of sorrows, and the preacher of an ideal based on the refusal to serve this world, the only world there is. The *non serviam* of Nietzsche is a revindication, to the benefit of man, of the privileges usurped by the God of the Jews and of the Christians. His Superman is man such as he is about to become after having liberated himself from the fetters of conventional religion and morality.

This is going to be an uphill fight for which few men are fit. Nietzsche probably would despise most of those who now pretend to be his disciples. "They overthrow images and statues," Nietzsche says, "and they say there is nothing holy and deserving to be worshipped, because they themselves are incapable of forming for their own use the image of a God, and of creating him."[6] What does the authentic thought of Nietzsche have in

---

4 *Ibid.,* § 61, p. 310. This point has been stressed by Jean Paul Sartre in his book *Existentialism Is a Humanism.* Atheism is the heroic effort of a free will resolved to liberate itself from the fetters of both nature and God.
5 *Ibid.,* § 63, p. 310, and § 72, p. 311.
6 *Ibid.,* § 110, p. 317.

common with the cheap brand of atheism now associated with his name? As he once said: "It has always seemed to me impossible to teach the truth there where a vile way of thinking obtains."[7]

By what sign, you may well ask, will it be known that God is really dead? To this I would answer: by the complete silence and oblivion into which his very name will have sunk. When something is truly dead, nobody will waste his time demonstrating that it has really deceased. Jupiter and Neptune are dead; we would not dream of proving that these myths have lost all conceivable reality, except for their poetic existence in imagination. The dead are soon forgotten. If there really were no God left, nobody would speak of him; such great writers as Nietzsche would not drive themselves crazy fighting the illusion of his existence. People do not simply say: everybody knows there is no God; his nonexistence is not considered a matter settled once and for all, so much so that we now can quietly dismiss it from our minds. But, that is undoubtedly what will happen when God is really dead; his very notion will then become merely an archaeological curiosity.

This has already happened to many now antiquated notions, and the founder of French Positivism, Auguste Comte, thought that all metaphysical notions—that is, all notions that cannot be justified scientifically—would meet the same fate. In his *Discourse on the Positive Spirit*, Comte suggested that all opinions on insoluble problems should be neither refuted nor even denied, but simply neglected, overlooked; they should be allowed by "sound philosophy" to fall into disuse. By sound philosophy, Comte meant a refusal to deal with notions that are pure products of the imagination bearing on objects inaccessible to direct observation. Such notions, Comte would say, are susceptible neither of affirmation nor of negation. "No doubt, nobody has ever logically established the nonexistence of Apollo, of Minerva etc.; nor has the nonexistence of the fairies of the East and of other similar poetic creations ever been demonstrated, but that has not prevented the human mind from irrevocably

---

7 *Ibid.*, § 105, p. 317. I am not denying the atheism of Nietzsche; I only wish to define its nature. If he ever said: "I am the first atheist," which I doubt he did, it was in the same sense that he said: "I am the first immoralist" (*Ecce Homo*, French transl. by Alexandre Vialatte [Paris: Gallimard, 1942], p. 99). In his own language, the "Infamous" is neither religion nor God, it is Christianity, Jesus Christ, and his notion of moral life. For Nietzsche, his cosmic mission was to reveal to the world the pestilential character of Christian ethics, with its deification of weakness and of renunciation. In doing that, Nietzsche has "cut in two the history of mankind" (p. 175); he is "Dionysus in front of the Crucified" (p. 177). Christianity has dethroned the values of life and enthroned the values of death. The result is a "morale," which Nietzsche calls: "an idiosyncrasy of decadents guided by the secret intention, often successful, to revenge himself on life" (p. 174). Immoralism is the very essence of Nietzsche's atheism (p. 172). Plain atheism is only a "natural instinct" with him (p. 42); for him atheism is the natural rebellion against everything that pretends to transcend—except, of course, man himself.

giving up such ancient beliefs, as soon as they ceased to agree with the situation then obtaining."

Comte was quite right. However, even if it would be ridiculous to demonstrate that Napoleon I is dead—a proposition, by the way, that cannot be demonstrated scientifically—it is far from ridiculous to undertake the demonstration of the proposition that there is no God. The mere fact that men still go to the trouble of declaring themselves atheists, and of justifying their disbelief by means of such arguments as the existence of evil, clearly shows that the issue is still a living one. If the death of God means his final death in the minds of men, the persistent vitality of atheism constitutes for atheism its most serious difficulty. God will really be dead when no one will still think of denying his existence. Until then, the death of God remains an unconfirmed rumor.

CASUAL ATHEISM

It is often said, and deplored, that the modern churches have lost the support of the working classes, and it may well be true, but nobody exactly knows the extent or depth of the loss. Looking at facts from without, it rather seems that atheism is invading all social groups.

Cicero asserted, as something self-evident, that philosophers do not believe in the existence of gods. He probably was right, for indeed the gods of the Roman pantheon, which itself included all the other pantheons of the Empire, offered an easy target for philosophical criticism in Cicero's lifetime. No doubt that was the meaning of his remark; philosophers could not be expected to believe in the legends of the Greco-Roman gods. At any rate, if the ancient philosophers were atheists, the cause of the phenomenon was not that they were poor and formed an exploited proletariat.

There were many poor artisans and peasants in the cities and villages of sixteenth- and seventeenth-century Europe; yet the churches were full, and nothing authorizes the supposition that atheism prospered among those needy populations. On the contrary, it was the wealthy classes that were the hotbeds of immorality and incredulity. The French and Italian libertines of the time, the rakes of the English Restoration, the incredibly dissolute life at the court of the Most Christian King of France Louis XIV, clearly show that atheism and immorality prosper in wealth as much as in poverty. But agnosticism and licentiousness are not atheism. The dukes of Vendôme and Nevers, as Saint-Simon describes them in his *Mèmoires*, seem to have been moral wrecks, but whether they died as confirmed atheists is very difficult to say.

La Bruyère, who personally knew the libertines of the royal court, made a remark that is universally applicable when he said that straight atheism, solidly grounded on philosophical reasons, is hard to find. "I

143

would be exceedingly curious to find a man really convinced that there is no God; he at least would be able to tell me the invincible reason that has convinced him of it." Finding none, he added: "The impossibility in which I find myself of proving that there is no God unveils to me his existence."[8]

La Bruyère does not say, "*proves* to me his existence," he only says *unveils*. The absence of any proofs of the nonexistence of God does not amount to a proof of his existence, but that absence invites us to think that some fact or reason—the nature of which remains to be determined —must account for it. Those who say that God does not exist find themselves in exactly the same situation into which they put their opponents. I do not pretend that there are no arguments in favor of their position; I only observe that they do not seem to care to employ any such arguments —if they do, none of them has ever been able to find a conclusive answer to the question.

This is what La Bruyère seems to have had in mind in that passage, perhaps a little flippant in tone but so pertinent, where, after saying that "atheism does not exist," he specifies that atheism does not exist at least as a philosophically justified position; he declares: "The noblemen, more suspect of atheism than the rank and file, are too lazy to make up their minds that God does not exist. Their indolence leaves them cold and indifferent on that capital point, as well as on the nature of their soul and on the importance of a true religion; they neither deny nor concede such things; they do not think of them at all."[9]

This is exactly it: they do not think of such things; let us only add that this atheism, so to speak of inadvertence, is not more proper to the nobility than to the rank and file, since we find it in Friedrich Nietzsche, who did not belong in either class. Let us read more of the *Ecce Homo* passage already quoted: "God, immortality of the soul, redemption, deliverance, so many ideas to which I never devoted any attention or time, not even in my early youth. Perhaps I have never been enough of a child for that? I could not see atheism as a conclusion, or a consequence; with me it is a natural instinct." To Nietzsche a more important question than that of salvation, so dear to the theologians, was that of food, or let us say, of diet. What should one eat in order to be well and strong? After relating a few culinary experiments, some of them unfortunate, Nietzsche dogmatically concludes: "The best all around cooking is that of Piedmont." Food is surely important, but cooking is not a problem comparable in importance to that of the existence of God. That Nietzsche thinks it is, or pretends that it is, shows what little interest he has in the question. He

---

8 La Bruyère, *Les Caractères ou les mœurs de ce siècle*, ed. G. Servois and Alf. Rébelliau (Paris: Hachette, 1901), "Des Esprits forts," p. 480.
9 *Ibid.*, p. 481.

himself admits it: "I am too inquisitive a mind, too sceptical, and too proud to satisfy myself with one of those gross answers that are an insult to a thinker, something like a final and brutal prohibition against proceeding—a positively no thinking."[10]

If such is the spontaneous reaction of a mind like Nietzsche's to the mere mention of the word "God," one can easily imagine how philosophically superficial the atheism of most atheists is. I do not pretend to know the inner thoughts of the majority of those who consider themselves atheists; it only seems to me that La Bruyère's description of atheists tallies remarkably with Nietzsche's own atheistic attitude. An agreement between such different men and mentalities suggests that the type is a fairly common one. Some do not think of the question; others feel indignant at the mere mention of it. By and large, La Bruyère was right; whether or not it be possible to prove that there is no God, no atheists go to the trouble to prove it. If that is insufficient proof of God's existence, it at least suggests that there are no invincible reasons to deny it.

WHAT THE ATHEISTS CALL GOD

O f all the branches of theology, that of atheism has recently become the most confused one. At the same time it has become a major concern not only with the various churches but with the world of journalism as well. Once successfully launched by its author as a kind of challenge, the formula of Nietzsche has become a sort of slogan. The weekly *Time* has given the best proof it could that the question is a live one. For the first time in forty-three years, on April 8, 1966, its cover carried no portrait of any man of the week, no image or picture of any sort, nothing but these three words: *Is God dead?* After vainly searching for months, the editors had given up their quest for "a work of art suggesting a contemporary idea of God," and "came to the conclusion that no appropriate representation could be found." For the first time, the problem of the death of God has filled the space usually devoted to political, business, or entertainment personalities.

One readily believes *Time* when it speaks of the enormous effort required for the preparation of the five pages entitled "Toward a Hidden God." Some readers will regret not being given the complete results of their extensive inquiry, but that would have far exceeded the space available. At any rate, the documents retained by the editors already provide ample matter for reflection.

Let us first observe the survival of the spiritual family already described by La Bruyère, that of the atheists by inattentiveness, or oversight. Some of them are very distinguished persons. For instance Claude Lévy-Strauss,

---

10 Nietzsche, *Ecce Homo*, p. 42.

Professor of Social Anthropology at the Collège de France, calmly declared that he personally has never found himself confronted with the notion of God. A truly astonishing statement, one might think, for an ethnologist who has endured many and severe hardships to observe *in vivo* what little is left of some tribes barely surviving in the forests of the Amazon. Lévy-Strauss considers it perfectly possible that he should spend his whole life in the knowledge that he shall never account for the universe, but since he professes to know nothing of God, not even that he is dead, we cannot expect from him any information on the problem. But there are many other things for which Professor Lévy-Strauss will never account in that very same universe, for instance, the cause of the existence of the very same Amazonian tribes so lovingly studied by him; yet his indifference to the question did not prevent them from existing while he was studying them. From the fact that an eminent professor of ethnology is not interested in the problem of God's existence, it would be a *non sequitur* to conclude that God does not exist. Inattentiveness accounts for such naïve forms of atheism and makes itself felt in the very vagueness of its expression.[11]

This type of atheism has a second characteristic. When it chooses to invoke positive reasons, it starts from a previously given notion of God and, finding it unsatisfactory upon later examination, it then infers that since *that* God is not satisfactory, there can be no God of any kind. In other words, we had formed a certain notion of God; that notion accounted for a number of things, but when we realize that the explanation raises bigger difficulties than those which it explains, we drop it.

That is what happened to Simone de Beauvoir on the day she realized that it was easier for her to think of a creatorless world than of a creator responsible for all the contradictions of the world.[12] The argument would be conclusive if the problem of the existence of a creator of the world depended for its solution on the personal notion that Mme de Beauvoir entertains of his nature. She belongs to a school of thought that forcibly stresses the meaninglessness of reality. No philosopher, of course, has invoked the notion of a creator in order to account for that kind of a universe but, rather, to account for the surprising intelligibility of the one we live in. Leibniz thought that he had found an answer to the question. Thomas Aquinas probably would explain to us why the problem is both unavoidable and insoluble, but that is not our problem. One only asks

---

11 *Time* (April 8, 1966), p. 60, col. 3. Similar to the atheism of inattention is the atheism of distraction, that of the people John Courtney Murray described as being "too damn busy" to find the time to worry about God. All that was already familiar to Moses Maimonides, followed by Thomas Aquinas and renovated by Pascal in his famous notion of "divertissement" (hunting, games, anything that can help man to forget both himself and God).

12 *Ibid.*, p. 60, col. 3.

what weight the personal decision of such and such a professor of philosophy should carry in the discussion of the question. One even wonders what unit of weight the professor can use in deciding that the arguments in favor of a godless universe are more weighty than those against it. The reasons of Leibniz for engaging in the maze of his *Theodicy* are known. He preferred to risk it rather than to admit that there are no intelligible reasons why there should be something rather than nothing. Renouvier preferred to resort to the hypothesis of a finite God rather than to leave that fundamental question unanswered. Still others prefer to leave it at that, which nobody can prevent them from doing, but one hardly needs a Gallup Poll among professors of philosophy in order to determine the correct answer, the more so inasmuch as the professors of philosophy might happen not to be the best possible judges of the question.

Many priests and ministers seem to identify atheism with the abstention from religious practice, which they call an absence of religion. When it is reported that in 1965, 97 percent of the U.S. population has answered that they believed in God, that impressive figure probably means that being asked: *Do you think there is a God?*, 97 percent have put a cross in the *yes* column, and only 3 percent answered *no*. There is no ambiguity in those replies, for although there be many individual differences in the way of affirming God, and of denying him, all those who have answered *yes*, for whatever reason and in whatever sense, certainly intended to distinguish themselves from those who answered *no*. The case is different when it comes to the quality of that belief in God and the inquirer observes that of the 97 percent who said they did believe in God, only 27 percent declared themselves deeply religious.[13] At that point, the inquiry is moving to a different ground. Religion is a moral virtue, and all those who believe in God do not necessarily possess that virtue. Of those who possess it, how many, who do not consider themselves deeply religious, nevertheless are so after the manner of the publican? At any rate, to know whether or not one is deeply religious and to know whether or not one believes there is a God, are two different questions. No religious man, however slightly religious he may be, is an atheist. To Nietzsche, such a man remains one of the many "who do not know that God is dead."

Still another shift takes place when the inquiry gauges the depth of the religious feeling by the frequency of the church attendance. Over 120 million Americans today belong to some particular church, and a recent Gallup Poll reveals that only 44 percent of them attend religious services every week. Many consider themselves as religiously lukewarm because they are seldom seen in a church. But that is something else again. To

---

13 *Ibid.*, p. 61, col. 1.

believe there is a God is not necessarily to profess a particular religion, and
to profess a certain particular religion is not necessarily to practise its cult
with the assiduity which recommends itself. A wide gulf separates the
proposition that there is a God from the decision to worship him, in a
particular way, at certain times, and in certain places. The belief in the
existence of God is common to different religions, although they may
have different modes of worship. The usual ways to pay homage to God
are contingent and human; liturgy can seem to some of us too flashy and
theatrical, while others find it rather mean; in both cases it may be
resented as unbearable. That is the moment when the American girl says,
in the anguish of her heart: "I love God, but I hate the church."[14] For a
believer, that surely is an uncomfortable feeling, but it is not the same as
believing that God is dead.

Professor Novak, of Stanford University, is one of those who complain about their inability to "understand God, and the way in which he
works. If, occasionally, I raise my heart in prayer," this witness continues,
"it is to no God I can see, or hear, or feel. It is to a God in as cold and
obscure a polar night as any unbeliever has ever known." Some churchmen actually betray a similar uncertainty. For instance, the Episcopal
Dean of the National Cathedral of Washington, Francis B. Sayre, confesses himself to be "confused as to what God is" too, but, he adds, "so is
the rest of America."[15]

Rather than indicating atheism, such remarks are confessions of ignorance about the essence of God, and they reveal a soul far advanced on
the path to the only knowledge of God accessible to us in this life. When
the Episcopal Dean of the National Cathedral of Washington modestly
confesses: "I am confused as to what God is," he uses the very words of
Thomas Aquinas in the passage of his question on the *Sentences*, where
he describes the condition of one who, progressing from negation to
negation toward a purer notion of God, ultimately finds himself "in a
certain confusion."[16] In other words, the Dean and the rest of America
should not worry too much about their failure to reach, beyond analogies,
a clear notion of the essence of God. Their "learned ignorance" (*docta*

---

14 *Ibid.*, p. 61, col. 2.
15 *Ibid.*, p. 61, col. 1–2.
16 *Ibid.*, p. 61, col. 2. (Cf. Thomas Aquinas, *In I Sent.*, dist. 8, art. 1, ad 4, ed. Man-
donnet, vol. I, p. 196.) The classical theme of *docta ignorantia* can be misunder-
stood; for instance, as when the Roman seminarian says: "God is all that which I
cannot understand." The categories of the "hard to understand," even of the "incomprehensible," do not suffice to situate God among objects of thought. Naturally,
the fact that painters naïvely represent God as a human being is irrelevant to our
problem (*loc. cit.*, p. 61, col. 2 and 3). What the article calls "the anthropomorphic
God of Raphael" is only that of the paintings of Raphael. Strictly speaking, God
cannot be painted at all.

ignorantia) represents for Aquinas the apex of the knowledge of God accessible to us by purely natural means.

SCIENTIFIC ATHEISM

It has been said that the more active agent of the secularization of modern minds is "science."[17] There is some truth in that statement, but in what sense?

We must first eliminate from the discussion the well-known clashes between religious beliefs and scientific ideas of the world. The conflicts are only too real, but they take place only between science and mythology, and not between science and religion. Mythologies are an inevitable phenomenon. Man does not think without images; even if he thinks of some object whose very nature escapes imagination, he will form some image of it. The Greek and Roman pantheons had to be opposed by the early Christians because they were a worship of "false gods" and prevented the recognition of the "true God," yet even the first Christians never pretended that the false gods of the pagans did not exist; on the contrary, they identified those gods with what they themselves called the devils. At our present distance from the quarrel, we need not take sides. In fact, we could not, even if we wanted to. This much at least can be said, that an element of genuine piety must have been present in the pagan worship of the idols, just as a genuinely religious feeling expressed itself in many of the pagan fables. The Greek philosophers did not wait for Christianity in order to denounce the immorality of the stories which the pagans were telling about their gods, but there still is, and there always will be, a mythological element in our way of imagining a being that by virtue of its very essence is beyond nature and therefore escapes imagination. To substitute science for mythology in our representations of God and of the divine, is to substitute a new mythology for a former one. It's up to the theologians to settle the thorny problem of "the names of God," but the very existence of the problem shows that some mythology is unavoidable, because we cannot name God without imagining him, and we cannot imagine him without more or less mythologizing him.

All that science can do in this respect is to update our mythologies; true religious faith is not concerned with such operations. Whether the created world is that of Homer and of the Babylonian myths, or that of Aristotle, of Galileo, of Descartes, of Newton, of Darwin, or of Einstein, is not a problem for religious belief. Religions have now learned not to tie their own truths to scientific systems, which succeed one another in the

---

17 *Ibid.*, p. 62, col. 3.

world at ever increasing speed. Whatever science says the world is, any believer is willing to accept as the best notion the human mind can now form about the work of God. But God himself remains for us the hidden God, the invisible cause of the visible world, of whom we only know *that* he is, *what* he is not, and *how* the world he has made is related to him.

Much more to the point is the remark, attributed to the Anglican theologian David Jenkins, that the growing prestige of science is obscuring every other mode of knowledge, including even that of religious faith.[18]

For such a devaluation of the spontaneous belief in the existence of God to have taken place, a confusion must have occurred between the very notion of God and the so-called proofs of his existence, for indeed, neither Descartes, nor Leibniz, nor Pascal, nor Kant, nor Bergson has ever found in science any reason to doubt the existence of God. So the true problem must be a different one, and we shall now attempt to define it.

The True Problem

All the questions so far discussed concern our knowledge of God, our way to conceive of him, the theological speculations about his nature, as well as the personal feelings his notion raises in us, but none

---

18 *Ibid.*, p. 62, col. 3–p. 63, col. 1. This remark is true in itself, and it summarizes an immense historical experience. The development of science since the end of the Middle Ages has favored the spreading of what can be called the "scientific spirit," that is to say, a generalized desire to know everything in a scientific way and a general rejection of all problems and solutions incapable of scientific treatment. Such a positivist, or scientific, mentality is a fact. Science is a fecund source of improvements for the material side of human life; metaphysics and theology are not. More important still, science and its methods are chiefly intent on the knowledge of nature and of man only to the extent that he can be handled as one more being of nature. Hence the progressive decay of the classical humanities at the same time as that of metaphysics and theology. Science needs no ontology since it presupposes the very givenness of being. The most dangerous aspect of the present crisis in the churches is that the scientific mentality has now invaded countless minds wholly innocent of scientific knowledge and formation. When those are the minds of churchmen, as often happens, the peril gets worse, and it is at its worst when such churchmen, prompted by a misdirected religious zeal, seek in scientism itself for a remedy to the destructive effects it works on humanism, theology, and religion. This problem has been clearly seen and discussed in *Gaudium et spes*, the Vatican II Pastoral Constitution on the Church in the World of Today, *Foreword*, 3, 5, 7; on the roots and forms of contemporary atheism, 19, especially § 2. Concerning the remedies for atheism, it is remarkable that (21, § 5) the Council mentions only four remedies, none of which is borrowed from philosophy: (1) an adequate presentation of the doctrine (in which, however, metaphysics probably has a part to play); (2) the purity of life of the Church and its members; (3) the testimony of a living and adult faith trained to acknowledge the obstacles and able to overcome them; (4) lastly, "that which most contributes to reveal the presence of God, is the brotherly love of the faithful working together, with a unanimous heart, for the faith of the Gospel and exhibiting themselves as a sign of unity."

of them directly concerns the objective reasons for holding that God is still alive or that he is already dead.

I can think of no better way to deal with the problem than to attempt a philosophical reexamination of what is called, rather improperly, proof by the universal consensus. It is a fact, not that all men agree that there is a God, but that in all countries and, as it seems, at all times, however low their level of culture, all men have heard of some higher being, or power, on which man depends for his safety and prosperity, in short, for his life. Whether they call it God or something else is another question. The ethnologists are right in denouncing the illusion of civilized observers, most of them missionaries, who indiscriminately attribute a notion of God to all populations, civilized or not, with which they establish contact. The Gods of Aristotle, Descartes, and Kant are certainly not known to all peoples. The philosophical notion of a divinity is too highly abstract for minds not yet initiated to logical and scientific modes of thinking; but even the most primitive of populations betray an awareness of the kind of realities (beings, or forces) which they call supernatural. By that word, I merely mean an awareness that what we can see and touch is not the whole of reality, and that the unseen part of reality is more important for us than the one we see. Even in our own days, animism, or "spiritualism" as they say, is a widespread form of worship in some primitive tribes of Africa and the Amazon. At any rate, the peoples of the Western world are more easily observable; and no matter how far back we dig into the past we find some divinities—even, as in the case of Jehovah, that of one (true) God fighting for the complete elimination of the other (false) gods.

THE IDEA OF GOD

Saint Augustine distinguished three different sources of the notion of God: the poets, the City, and the philosophers. Before him, Aristotle had distinguished two such sources, the starry sky and the self-awareness of the soul, thus prefiguring the well-known saying of Kant: the starry sky above me, the moral law within. Self-observation shows the situation in a still simpler light. Western man lives in a society where the notion of God comes to him through family and school; religion is imbedded in the various literatures, and in the many locutions of his language. Why should so many men take pleasure in swearing by a God and a hell in the existence of which they profess not to believe? To know if a human being born and bred in total solitude would form such ideas is a meaningless question, for indeed such a man does not exist, and, if he did, how could we communicate with him? It is certain that as a social animal, man finds the notion of some divine being, and power, present in the society in which he lives, as soon as he is conscious of belonging to it. This need, this germ, even if it is an exceedingly confused feeling, is the origin and

151

substance of the future notion of God in the minds of philosophers as well as of plain believers. Born of rational reflection or of revelation, all further information about the divinity will apply itself to that elementary religious feeling.

These remarks do not imply any particular answer to the question: how do men come by that elementary feeling, or notion, of the divinity? Some of them *assure us* they have seen God, be it only in a cloud, as Moses saw Yahweh; others say that God unexpectedly raised them up to himself, thus revealing to them things they cannot describe and telling them words they are unable to repeat; but most of them simply find in the sight of the universe, as well as within their own souls, visible marks of his existence. It was a trite teaching of the Fathers of the Church and of the scholastic theologians, all of them following the tradition of the Old and New Testaments, that God has left on his work the visible mark of his craftsmanship so that it is inexcusable for us to pretend not to know of his existence. The clearest of those marks is man himself, especially his intellect and will, made by God in his own image and likeness.

Each of these answers is valid in its own way, but all of them raise some difficulties. In the case of the privileged men who claim to have seen God, all we can do is to believe them; but our belief in their revelation is very different from our having been granted that revelation. As to the classical answer, inspired by the Apostle, that men have known God from seeing his creation, it may be true, but it leaves unanswered the main question for a philosopher: How, without some preexisting notion, or feeling, of the divinity, did men form the concept of a cause so utterly different in nature from its observable effects? Euhemerism tells us that the first gods were men divinized by other men, but the difficulty remains. The question indeed is: How do men come by that notion of God, so utterly different from that of man? If I have an idea of God, I understand the proposition of Euhemerus—I can conceive the gods as so many supermen. But the question actually is how and why should I think of a God who is as far from divinity as man is?

We are here reaching a point that I cannot help finding mysterious. A certain notion is found in the minds of many men for which there is no known model in experience. That all peoples have a certain notion of the sun, of the moon, of the earth with its mountains, rivers, forests, and all the animals that live on it, is not mysterious. A notion of the sun is found everywhere because the sun exists for all men to see. The first problem raised by the presence of the notion of God in the mind of man is to know where it comes from, since no man alive has ever seen God, nor even a god. We don't even know what he should be like in order to look like him.

From this point of view the remark of La Bruyère becomes fully intelligible. It was neither a paradox nor an artifice to get rid of a problem. It is a simple truth. The question was: Does that being—of which we have a notion, if not an idea—actually have existence or not? Naturally, when we think of such a being, we conceive him as real. At any rate, we are not aware of making up the notion; we find it there, and though its presence does not prove that an actual being answers the notion in reality the *onus probandi* lies with him who denies it rather than with him who affirms it. The problem of the inexistence of God comes first. How could man have formed the notion of a being not given in sense experience, and not of his own conscious making, if that being does not exist?

The primacy of the notion with respect to the proof is seen in several of the traditional ways of presenting the problem of the existence of God. It almost looks as though no way of posing the problem could successfully avoid inscribing the notion among its data.

First is the concrete meaning of the celebrated doctrine of the innateness of the idea of God. If it is innate, its presence in human minds is thereby accounted for and, by the same token, the actual existence of its object becomes practically certain. In fact, all the defenders of the innateness of the idea of God infer from it that God actually is, or exists. That seems to be the only thing the innateness of the notion of God means to them, for if asked how they understand it, they give very different answers. It may be a kind of reminiscence in the manner of Plato; or it can mean that every man at some time in his life discovers he has a certain notion of God, as if it had always been there. Or else it can mean that since that notion cannot have come to the mind from outside it must have come from within in a way that remains to be defined. The point is that even the demonstrations of the existence of God taken from the physical world presuppose in the mind the presence of a confused notion of divinity. Each one of the five ways of Thomas Aquinas starts from a nominal definition of God; without such a conditional concept of God, the mind would not know what it has found at the end of its demonstration.

Here I would like to add parenthetically that the famous *quinque viae* of St. Thomas[19] are in themselves purely rational and philosophical demonstrations. I mean by that that they could be extracted from the *Summa* and introduced, just as they are, in a treatise of philosophy; but even a philosopher could not ask the question of whether God exists without first having in mind some notion of what he is looking for. Each one of the five ways leads to the existence of a first being in a certain order of reality: motion, efficient causality, possibility and necessity, etc. After concluding that such a prime being exists, Aquinas simply adds: "And all understand that it is God." In other words, all understand at once that the prime immovable mover is the being that they are already used to calling God even before proving his existence. There is therefore a

---

19 Aquinas, *Summa Theologica*, Pt. I, q. 2, art. 3; *GBWW*, Vol. 19, p. 12c.

precognition of God anterior to the proofs. The same is true of the second way: "One must therefore posit a prime efficient cause, which all call God: *quam omnes Deum nominant.*" What can be the origin of that prenotion—from the first education of the child, from the universal consensus in consequence of which practically nobody can spend his life without having heard the word "god"? In his treatise *On Separate Substances*, chapter I, Aquinas goes so far as to speak of an innate knowledge of God, at least in this sense that whenever men have reached the notion of a first principle of all things it was innate in them to call it God. That spontaneous anticipation is not a proof, yet it still plays its part in the interpretation of the proof. Were it not for that anticipation, we would not know that the Prime Being, Mover, Cause, etc., is the very same being which all men agree in calling "God."

From the very outset Aquinas knows that what he is looking for is God, and indeed nothing is more fitting in a Sum of Theology. In his own *Metaphysics,* the philosopher Avicenna never says "God," but always *Primus*, and that too is most fitting, because "God" is a religious rather than a philosophical notion. As soon as we say that the Prime Being is God, we cease talking philosophy and begin to talk theology in the religious sense of the word. To Aquinas the origin of the notion of God was well known; it was God himself revealing to man his own existence. But there can be other sources of our knowledge of God, and the common, spontaneous belief of men in the existence of supernatural beings resembles the revealed knowledge of God in that it is not abstractly speculative, not "philosophical" or "metaphysical." It is not obtained by proceeding one step beyond physics in the scientific investigation of reality and its causes. Just as faith is a revelation from on high, the plain, common notion of God is a reaction of the whole man to the confusedly perceived presence of God in nature and in himself. That is the truth hidden in the well-known notion of an *anima naturaliter Christiana* of Tertullian. One cannot be a Christian by nature, only by Christ, but had Tertullian spoken of an *anima naturaliter religiosa*, he would have been right.

No particular notion of God is here at stake. Even what is considered the most formidable objection to the existence of God, namely, the presence of evil in the world, in no way affects what has just been said about the presence of the idea of God in us. On the contrary, it rather strengthens the significance of that fact. If it is absurd that there should be evil in a God-created universe, the omnipresence of evil, since it is felt and experienced by all men with an overwhelming evidence, should make it impossible for human minds to form a notion of God. Now they do not think of God despite evil, but quite particularly when suffering evil and especially when in fear of death. As Spinoza puts it at the very beginning of his *Tractatus theologico-politicus*, if men always knew with certainty how to run their business, or if they always were favored by fortune, superstition would find no place in their minds. This, Spinoza adds, is the true cause of superstition, despite the claim of others that it arises from the presence of a certain confused notion of the Divinity in the minds of men. Ever since the time of Lucretius, the notion that fear is the very root of religious feeling has been a familiar one, but it certainly looks paradoxical to claim, at one and the same time, the fear of evil as the chief source of man's belief in the existence of God and as an argument against it.

A detailed survey of the history of the problem would, I believe, support that conclusion. One cannot understand otherwise how such a scientific genius as Descartes can have imagined that the presence in us of the notion of God constitutes a solid basis for a proof of his existence. As is well known, Descartes considered that notion an innate idea.[20] Some think, with John Locke, that his position can be refuted simply by establishing that there are no innate ideas.[21] But even if his opponents are right, Descartes still could ask them: if my idea of God is not innate in me, how did I form it? For that is the true meaning of the Cartesian notion of the innateness of the idea of God. The innateness of the notion cannot be distinguished from the power of forming it. Since I find the model of such a notion neither in me nor outside of me, it must have been "put in me by some substance itself actually infinite." Hence the conclusion of the third *Metaphysical Meditation:* "consequently it follows of necessity that God exists." The objection of Locke and the empiricists that the elements of the notion are provided by sense experience does not alter the fact that the notion itself has no model in interior or exterior reality. No infinite object is given in any kind of experience. To say that the elements of the concept of God are so given does not explain the presence in us of the pattern according to which the elements are associated in the mind so as to constitute such a concept. In fact, many successors of Descartes, from Malebranche up to the later school of the so-called ontologists, draw the natural inference: if I think of a being called God, then that being exists. This was what I meant by saying that what stands in need of rational justification is atheism, much more than the spontaneous belief that there is a God.

PROLETARIAN ATHEISM

Karl Marx did not content himself with observing that God does not exist, which is the proper position of speculative, or theoretical, atheism. He decided to suppress God—to eradicate the very notion from

---

20 Descartes, *Meditation III;* GBWW, Vol. 31, pp. 81d–89a.
21 Locke, *Essay I.* iii, 8–16; GBWW, Vol. 35, pp. 114–117a.

men's minds. The poet Heinrich Heine said that Kant was the Robespierre of natural theology. (Robespierre publicly said of King Louis XVI: "We are not here to judge him, but to kill him.") What Heine said of Kant is much more true of Marx—his first intention was indeed to kill God. Because Marx was essentially a revolutionist, his whole doctrine was dominated by the notion of praxis. As with some theologians, thought for him was only legitimate as a means of action. In trying to understand Marx, his justly famous saying should be recalled: "Until now the philosophers have contented themselves with interpreting the world in several different ways. It is now a question of transforming it."[22]

It could therefore be said that the atheism of Marx is no concern of philosophy nor the philosophers. His decision, that there is no God, lies outside, in an order where the philosopher is powerless. One can persecute believers, close the churches, and kill the priests, just as in past centuries one could burn atheists at the stake, but one fails to see what "philosophical" meaning can be attributed to such acts. The very decision to turn philosophy into a praxis is not—if taken in itself—a philosophical decision. If the belief that there is a God is truly necessary for salvation, then it is the duty of the theologians to make men believe there is a God; if it is necessary for the success of the proletarian revolution to suppress the belief of men in the existence of God, then men should be made to disbelieve it. In neither case are philosophers as such concerned with the proceeding.

Why then are we, as philosophers, talking about it? We are talking about Marx for the same reason we are talking about Aquinas. Aquinas says that we should believe there is a God, and having said so he at once proceeds rationally to demonstrate it in five different philosophical ways; so also, having decided to kill God, Marx proceeds at once to the task of proving that, in fact, God has never existed except as a harmful illusion in the minds of men. Thus Marxist atheism is the speculative justification of a politico-practical decision.

The project of examining such a doctrine with a view to refuting it, therefore, does not make sense. One does not dialectically refute a decision of the will. A dialogue, as they call it today, between any form of theism and Marxian atheism is doomed to failure beforehand because the two positions belong to two specifically different orders. In the words of one of its recent exponents, Marxist philosophy is "before everything else a guide for action, an instrument in the hands of the proletariat."[23] Armed

---

22 Marx, "Thèses sur Feuerbach," XI, in F. *Engels et la fin de la philosophie classique* (Paris: Les Revues), p. 145. In view of what follows, note Thesis X: "The basis of ancient materialism was bourgeois society. The basis of the new materialism is human society, or socialized humanity" (p. 145).
23 G. Yakhot, *Qu'est-ce que le matérialisme dialectique?*, translated into French from the Russian (Moscow: Editions du Progrès), p. 46.

with that revolutionary theory, the proletariat becomes a fearless fighter for the realization of Marxist ideals, that is, for the whole of Marxist mankind. "For that reason a momentous historical task devolved upon Marxism from its first appearance—to establish an alliance between Marxist socialist theory and the proletarian movement—an alliance between the spiritual weapon of theory and the material power capable of using that weapon, that is to say, the proletariat, the 'people'."

One sees at once under what conditions that declaration of principles becomes intelligible. First, we are asked to concede their right to speak of spiritual forces in a materialistic doctrine; but that is nothing. The real difficulty is to conceive *theory* as a *weapon;* in other words, to accept as an objective view of reality as it is any doctrine that is expressly conceived in order to transform it. The proper philosophical order would be: first, to see reality as it is, and then, as scientists do with the physical world, to imagine possible and desirable transformations of it by means of engineering. The radical error of Marxism is to justify revolutionary social changes by an erroneous view of the social reality.

For the same reason, I can see no point in attempting to refute the Marxist conception of the history of philosophy that reduces it to a never ending fight between materialism and idealism. That notion is the more surprising since Marxism, which professes to be a straightforward materialism, sees itself as a reinterpretation of Hegelianism, which is the clearest case of idealism one could quote.[24] But perhaps the notion of the opposition between idealism and materialism is not perfectly clear in the minds of our own Marxist contemporaries.

How does contemporary Marxism understand the opposition of materialism and idealism? It is the fundamental problem in philosophy, G. Yakhot says, and it can be asked, with Engels, in the following terms: "Has the world been created by God, or does it exist from all eternity? To this question, the materialists and the idealists give mutually exclusive answers."[25]

Aquinas saw no contradiction between the notion of a world created by God and that of an eternally existing world.[26] Moreover, the question of the eternity of the world has nothing to do with that of its materiality.

---

24 "Hegel founded objective idealism. For him, the absolute Idea, the universal Spirit, was the basis of nature and of society . . . The absolute idea is the Demiurge, the creator of reality, the latter being but the external manifestation of the Idea. You certainly have noticed that, in saying this, Hegel simply restates, under a veiled expression, the religious notion of the creation of the world by God." (Yakhot, *op. cit.*, pp. 35–36.) The author shows (p. 37) how the dialectical method of Hegel, having finally "betrayed itself in favour of his metaphysical system" and thus begotten German imperialism, "nevertheless became one of the speculative sources of Marxism."

25 *Op. cit.*, p. 14.

26 Aquinas, *op. cit.*, Pt. I, q. 46, art. 1–2; GBWW, Vol. 19, pp. 250a–255a.

God could have created a universe of pure immaterial substances, or spirits, like that of Berkeley, and could have created it from all eternity. Or else there might be both matter and spirit in an uncreated and eternal universe like that of Aristotle. There is obviously a great deal of confusion on this point in contemporary Marxism.

The reason for it is that, in the mind of the Marxists, unless matter is eternal, one cannot be sure that there is not a God to create it, and since they are reluctant to think of a material God—a notion familiar to the Stoics, the Epicureans, and even to the Christian Tertullian—the mere notion of God seems to them to entail some sort of idealism, the possibility, that is, of some actually existing immaterial being. "Idealism," Lenin used to say, "has been invented in favor of religion and to defend it."[27] Obstinately confusing the two notions of materialism and of the eternity of the world, Yakhot insists that according to materialism, "matter, nature, have always existed." Aristotle also believed that matter and nature were eternal, but he was no materialist. If nobody has created matter, Yakhot goes on to say, "the evolution of the world does not stand in need of a supreme and divine force. God is superfluous, the world eternally evolves without his intervention. Thus and in this way does materialism lead to the negation of God. It is unavoidably tied up with atheism. The materialist is at the same time an atheist." This obviously is a warring and fighting atheism. Yakhot asks: who profits by the theses of theism and idealism, who "if not the capitalists and the profiteers! By doing so, idealism supports all that which is reactionary and out-of-date, from the profiteers up to religion."[28] Summing up his whole doctrine in a terse formula, Yakhot concludes: "All philosophy expresses the interests of a well-determined class."[29]

Nothing is harder to refute than an evidently false statement. It is a well-known fact that Christianity was originally and for a long time thereafter a religion of a poor and small people. As to the notion that each and every philosophy answers a determined social and economic class, it is so amazingly false that one does not know what to answer. In what sense is the philosophy of Parmenides the expression of a class? For what class did it cease to be true between his own time and that of Hegel? How could one explain that the philosophy of Aristotle, true for him in the Macedonian empire in the fourth century B.C., still was true for a Persian

---

27 Yakhot, *loc. cit.*
28 *Op. cit.*, p. 15. To the ensuing remarks a Marxist would answer that, from the point of view of their influence on speculation, all non-Marxist economic systems are practically identical. All idealisms "invite in some way or other the workers to give up their fight against capitalism and misery." (*Ibid.*) In that sense, one could say that St. Francis of Assisi has served the interests of the capitalists and exploiters of the people. Here too, "Who is not with me is against me."
29 *Op. cit.*, p. 17.

Muslim, Avicenna, in the tenth century, for the Spanish Muslim Averroës in the twelfth century, for the Christian monk Thomas Aquinas in the thirteenth century, and, to make a long story short—even supposing we could put all those men into the same social and economic class—how are we to add to the collection a twentieth-century French philosopher who is as little partial to the capitalist class as Jacques Maritain? Even reducing all the systems to two classes, idealism and materialism, what relation is there between the materialism of the Greek Epicurus—according to whom, the wise man with a little bread, water, and a few friends, is the equal of Jupiter himself—or of the slave Epictetus, on the one side, and that materialism, on the other, of such a modern Jew as Marx, himself living under conditions just as bourgeois as the Russian Lenin?

To sum up, in saying that there is a God, you work for capitalism, whereas in saying that there is no God, you work for the proletariat; the proletariat is the truth, consequently there is no God. The position is perfectly consistent; only it is a position, as they used to say in the old philosophical schools, *extranea philosophiae*—innocent of all philosophical meaning. Until the proletariat becomes the whole of mankind, even for Marxism the death of God remains a mere hope; to non-Marxists, it means nothing.[30]

THE CORE OF THE PROBLEM

The experiment of the Marxist state to eradicate from minds the notion of God—and its failure—is doubly significant. On the one hand, it suggests that belief in the existence of some divine being is a fact of nature—mankind does not seem to be able to subsist without it. Let us repeat that this does not prove the existence of an object answering that spontaneous and natural belief. It may be that man cannot live, and that mankind cannot endure, so to speak biologically, without some belief of that sort, but that still would not prove that the notion of God is more than a necessary illusion. My point is that, even as an illusion, its generality,

---

30 There would be no point in discussing the arguments of the Marxists in favor of their own position. They presuppose an ignorance of the history of philosophy encyclopædic in its dimensions. They regularly mistake the notion that the world is eternal for the different one, that the world is uncreated: "The scientific thesis that the world is eternal definitively overthrows the religious belief in the creation of the world." (Yakhot, *op. cit.* p. 62.) Now Aquinas sees no impossibility in the notion of an eternally created universe. As to the discovery, attributed by the Communist Party to the great Russian scientist Lomonosov, that "in nature nothing is born of nothing, and nothing vanishes without leaving traces of itself" (p. 63), it is at least as old as the verse of the Roman poet Persius, "*gigni de nihilo nihilum, in nihilum nil posse reverti*" (*Sat.* III, 34). The Church, Marxists say, is incapable of refuting these arguments (p. 64). Now it is precisely because nothing can come from nothing that the Church requires an uncreated God as the cause of a created world.

its persistence, its apparent ineradicability are remarkable. No other notion presents the same characteristics; as a simple fact alone that notion is a problem. Philosophical reflection is required in order to solve it.

It is noteworthy, on the other hand, that the spontaneous belief in the existence of God, far from dissolving at once under the scrutiny of reason, offers a remarkable resistance to all efforts to destroy it. A striking confirmation of that truth is found in a letter from Benjamin Constant dated Hardenberg, 11 October, 1811, to his friend Claude Hochet:

> In a few days, hopefully, I shall see written completely my History of Polytheism. The whole plan has been recast as well as more than three quarters of the chapters. I had to do so in order to obtain the order I had in mind, an order which, I think, I have now attained. Another reason was that, as you know, I am no longer that intrepid philosopher, certain that there is nothing after this world, and so well pleased with it that he rejoiced in the thought that there is no other one.
>
> My work is a singular proof of the truth of Bacon's saying, that a little science leads to atheism and more science to religion. It was positively by scrutinizing the facts, by collecting them from all sides, and by stumbling on the countless difficulties they oppose to incredulity, that I finally saw myself forced to regress into religious ideas. I certainly did so in perfect good faith, for each and every backward step cost me a great deal. Even at present all my habits, all my memories still are those of a philosopher, and I am fighting to defend, one after the other, all the positions which religion is reconquering from me. There even is a sacrifice of self-love involved in the process, for I believe it would be hard to find a stricter logic than the one I had used in attacking all the opinions of that kind.
>
> My book had absolutely no other defect than to run counter to all that which, at present, I consider good and true. I certainly would have had a political success. I even could have had still another kind of success, for at the price of a few very slight pushes, I could have made of the book what people now prefer, to wit, a system of atheism for gentlemen, a manifesto against the priests, the whole being combined with the admission that there should be certain fables for the rank and file, an admission that gives satisfaction to political authority as well as to personal vanity.

Up to a point, such personal experiences may well account for the durability of the widespread belief in the actual existence of an object answering the notion of God. Even under heavy social and political pressure some men refuse to give up that notion, sometimes for no reason at all, but also sometimes because reason finds it most acceptable and rationally justified.

From this second point of view—that of its intrinsic rationality—the notion of God constitutes a still more remarkable fact. To state it as succinctly as possible, the mind finds the strange characteristic about the notion of God that its object cannot be thought of as nonexistent. There is only one other notion of which the same thing can be said, namely, being. That similarity, incidentally, accounts for the fact that all the proofs of the existence of God ultimately consist in establishing the necessity of a certain being and its primacy in the various orders of reality. Being is the very name of God when the spontaneous notion is translated into the language of philosophical reflection. At any rate, it looks as absurd to think of a nonexisting God as it is to speak of a nonexisting being. All the rest, including the universe and our very selves, we can imagine as not existing, but the only way to do the same with God is to refuse to take his idea into account. "If God is God," St. Bonaventure says, "God exists." This necessary quality of the relationship between the notion of God and that of actual existence is another fact to be taken into account.

The whole history of the so-called ontological argument, plus that of ontologism, could be quoted in support of this assertion, but since I am here dealing with the notion of God and its intrinsic necessity as an empirical fact, I shall content myself with recalling the testimony of the one or two authorized philosophers and theologians.

To quote St. Anselm in relation to this problem is superfluous, but even though Aquinas does not consider valid the proof of the *Proslogion*,[31] he too upholds the view that, speaking of God as taken in himself, his existence is evident: "*Nam simpliciter quidem Deum esse per se notum est; cum hoc ipsum quod Deus est, sit suum esse.*" ("Absolutely speaking, that God exists is self-evident, since what God is is His own being." *Contra Gentiles* I, 11, 1.)

The Fifth *Metaphysical Meditation* of Descartes contains a perfect formulation of that inseparability of the two notions of God and of actual existence. Confronted with the objection that there is nothing to prevent us from attributing actual existence to God, even though God does not exist, Descartes answers by stressing the uniqueness of the existential implication of the notion of God. From the fact that there can be no mountain without a valley, it does not follow that there are mountains and valleys, whereas, "from the sole fact that I cannot conceive God without existence, it follows that existence is inseparable from Him and, consequently, that He exists." The argument of St. Anselm is justified by Descartes as follows: "While from the fact I cannot conceive God without existence, it follows that existence is inseparable from Him, and hence that He really exists; not that my thought can bring this to pass, or impose any necessity on things, but, on the contrary, because the necessity which lies in the thing itself, i.e. the necessity of the existence of God, determines

---

31 St. Anselm's *Proslogion* is reprinted below in Part Four, p. 316.

me to think in this way."[32] In other words, it may not be necessary that I should ever think of God, but, if I do, I cannot think of him otherwise than as existing in reality. For, Descartes goes on to say, "is there anything more clear and manifest than to think that there is a God, that is to say, a sovereign and perfect being, in whose notion alone necessary or eternal existence is comprised and, consequently, who exists?" The consequence, I repeat, may not be valid, but the fact itself that the notion of God is such, and is the only one to be such, can hardly be denied.

Read in the light of that fact, the long history of the ontological argument ceases to be that of a sophism. However we interpret it, that puzzling notion is there. In short, Ariste says to Theodore in Malebranche's second *Entretien métaphysique:* "You define God as God has defined himself when he said to Moses: *God is He Who Is* (Ex. III, 14)." One can think of this and that being without its existing, one can see its essence without seeing its existence, one can see its idea without seeing it, but "if one thinks of God, he must needs be." Even in the doctrines of such "atheists" as Spinoza and Hegel, the very notion of what they still call God entails that of its existence. Volumes could be written on the history of that notion. They would not be useless, but we are interested here in the notion of God as a given observable fact only.

We will now examine the part played by that notion in the affirmation of the existence of its object, or more what precisely is the fundamental obstacle to its negation.

Is the Nonexistence of God Truly Thinkable?

The preceding considerations invite us to wonder if the nonexistence of God can really be conceived, that is, other than in words only. It is both satisfying and distressing to observe that we are, in a quite unpremeditated way, rediscovering the old tracks left by our great predecessors in similar inquiries. In fact, not seeing how the existence of God can be denied, or at least why it should be denied—and yet that it is denied—we can think of only two explanations. First, those who do so are fools (*insipientes*); second, they deny it in words only without fully realizing the import of their words. The first answer is too blunt for our modern notion of a philosophical discussion, but we still can ask the atheists if they truly realize the meaning of the words they use. When they deny the existence of God, do they really mean it?

THE CAUSE OF THE IDEA

From whatever angle we consider the problem, we are led back to the same question. What is the cause of the idea of God in us and of its exceptional, not to say unique, existential connotations?

---

32 Descartes, *Meditation V; GBWW*, Vol. 31, p. 94b–c.

This question, let us repeat, is quite distinct from that of the nature of a possible demonstration of the existence of God. The so-called physical proofs seem to evade it. They say that our intellect forms that idea on the basis of the data of sense experience, and that we conceive the notion of God *a creatura mundi*. No doubt this is true, but what secret light leads the mind from the sight of the material universe to the notion of an eternal, immaterial, and self-subsisting cause? I look at things, Augustine says, and I ask them: Are you my God? They answer me: We are not thy God; look for him above us. Tell me at least something about him, Augustine insists, and all of them, heaven, sun, moon, stars, answer with a loud voice: He is He Who made us.[33] Well and good, but who or what suggested to Augustine his own questions? Why was he asking for a God, for *his* God?

All the so-called physical proofs of the existence of God will develop from that starting point, but they all raise the same question: How do you know what you are looking for? The real message of Augustine is precisely his acute feeling of the inevitability of the question. However we look at it, the origin of the proof lies in the mind from which the question arises. Where in the mind does it come from if not from some cognition which, while perhaps not a cognition of God himself, is at least a cognition of an object so different from those of sense perception, with characteristics that transcend everything else, an object that can be none other than what we call God? The doctrine of the divine illumination is too well known to need repeating. We also know how the epistemology of Augustine differs from that of Aquinas,[34] and how that difference affects the very structure of their respective proofs of the existence of God. What often escapes notice is how deeply the two epistemologies and two natural theologies agree in spite of their differences; and it is worthwhile observing because their meeting point lies in the most secret mystery of our knowledge of God.

The five ways of Aquinas, precisely because they start from sense experience, constitute five inductive arguments. Now there is something mysterious about all induction. There is nothing mysterious in deduction because its conclusions are already contained in the premises. Incidentally, this accounts for the frequent attempts of theologians, even within the so-called Thomist school, to turn each of the five inductions of the *Summa Theologica* into deductions starting from first principles, such as those of causality, identity, and finally, noncontradiction. Now, of course, all demonstrations must take place in accordance with principles and under their control; however, the last term of these inductions is not a prin-

---

33 Augustine, *Confessions*, X. vi. 9; *GBWW*, Vol. 18, p. 73c–d.
34 *See* my study on *The Christian Philosophy of Saint Augustine* (New York: Random House, 1960), Introduction, chap. ii.

ciple of knowledge but is rather a cause of reality; not a thought, but a being—the Prime Mover, the Necessary One, the Prime Cause, the Prime Being, and the Supreme End. In no one of these cases is the conclusion already given in the premises; on the contrary, it transcends them infinitely. The operation, of course, is the work of the intellect, but the question remains: How, in virtue of what power, does the intellect, starting from sense cognition, reach those lofty conclusions so different from its starting point? This is not a question for Aquinas alone, it was already a question for Aristotle, and it still is a question for all philosophers. Let us call it the mystery of induction. In the many works contained in his *Organon*, Aristotle has said precious little on the subject. Always both glib and scientifically precise in dealing with the deductive operations of the intellect, Aristotle has devoted only twenty lines to the problem of induction—more precisely, to the problem of the inductive process by which, starting from sense perception, we rise from it to the cognition of principles.

Twenty lines are not much on the question of knowing how the intellect reaches the first principles in the light of which it knows all the rest. But there are good reasons for Aristotle's surprising discretion, and we can appreciate them by reading with due care what he says on the question in the *Posterior Analytics*. The first sentence alone would deserve a long, attentive meditation: "It is therefore evident that induction is what makes us know principles, for it is by means of it that sensation causes the universal in us." So the instantaneous operation whereby, given a sense perception, the intellect forms in itself a concept, is already an induction. According to Aristotle, the formation of principles by the intellect is of the same nature. Here is the most mysterious and, to my mind, the most important passage in the whole *Organon:*

> Since, with the exception of intuition, no kind of cognition is more exact than science, it must needs be an intuition that grasps the principles. This follows, not only from the preceding considerations, but also from the fact that the principle of demonstration is not itself a demonstration. So there can be no science of science. If therefore we possess some kind of true knowledge other than science, it is intuition alone that is the principle of the principle itself, and science is to the whole of reality as intuition is to the principle.[35]

The difficulty of the passage is due to its density and also to the fact that, instead of appealing to reason, as does the theory of syllogistic deduction, it appeals to the intuitive power of the intellect. What Aristotle

---

35 Aristotle, *Posterior Analytics II.* xix, 100^b 12–17; *GBWW*, Vol. 8, p. 137.

says here is hard to put into more explicit words, because what he is trying to say is found at the coming together of three converging, yet distinct, philosophical problems: the origin of general ideas or universals, the origin of principles, and the origin of the idea of God.

The problem of universals is, or should be, the *crux philosophorum*. Personally, I confess that it remains a mystery to me despite all that I have read on universals. We all repeat the mediaeval formula: *sensus est particularium, intellectus universalium* (sense knows particulars, the intellect universals). The wise thing to do is to accept it and keep out of trouble. But I find it difficult to believe without adding many qualifications. The objects of sense cognition are particulars, but I do not perceive particulars as such; I only perceive sensible qualities, color for sight, sounds for hearing, etc. It is also true that the objects of intellection are universals, but I cannot think without images, so that sensations leave their mark of origin on every concept. What really happens is that intellectual cognition and sense experience are inextricably blended together. For instance, I say I see a dog, but *dog* is an abstract concept; it represents or signifies a species. Now I do not see or touch any species, whether it is a dog or a man or anything else. I see patches of colors, at most colored patterns, and I *know* that what I see or touch is a certain sort of animal or a man. Perception is intellectual as much as, if not more than, it is sensible. The traditional theory of abstraction invoked in order to account for the fact that the intellect separates, in the particular, the intelligible from the sensible does not go beyond the mere formulation of a fact. Neither Aristotle nor any Aristotelians have said how that metaphysical chemistry operates, or, let us say, how sense and intellect operate in that metaphysical chemistry. If the intelligible that is present in the sensible is not a concept, then what is it? Aristotle boldly declares that it is sensed. I see a dog because, by a sort of rapid induction, I know that the particular sense pattern that I see is caused by an individual belonging to the species of what my intellect knows to be what I call a dog. Not nominalism, not realism, not even the curious hybrid called "moderate realism" has fully been able to account for the mysterious induction that ends with what sensation gives to the intellect—not a mere sensible quality, but the pattern of sensible qualities we call a thing.

What about principles? Aquinas says principles are not innate, but that they are known in the natural light of the intellect in connection with sense knowledge. Again, what the principles say is given in the material objects that make up the substance of reality, yet the principles themselves are immaterial and exist as such only in knowing minds. I perceive beings, not being. I observe agents and patients, and I call the former causes and the latter effects, but I do not observe causality itself. By a bold induction, I can infer that there are no effects without causes—but this is simply to explicate the definition of either *cause* or *effect*. It was Hume, as I seem to remember, who said that this is just about the same thing as saying that there are no husbands without wives. If you corner a metaphysician, he will finally agree that there is something mysterious in our cognition of any principle. No wonder, since we know them in the light of the agent intellect, which, Aquinas says, is the light of which it is said in Scripture *Signatum est super nos lumen vultus tui Domine* (*Psalms*, 4: 6–7), as if to say: "It is by the imprint of the divine light that everything is shown to us."[36] Therefore, even in the natural light of the intellect, there is some trace of the mystery that surrounds the divinity.

I also mentioned the notion of God in the human mind, and, on that point, it should suffice to recall some of our preceding remarks on the distinction between the Prime Being whose existence philosophy proves, on the one hand, and the God of sacred theology, on the other. But let us bypass that incidental difficulty in order to consider the very operation by which, in philosophy, the intellect affirms the existence of a first cause of the universe. It is of exactly the same nature as that by which it forms the notion of its own principles of knowledge, particularly of its own first principle—being, which is but another name for God. That operation again is an induction, and there is a marked tendency among philosophers to reduce the terms or steps of that induction to the smallest possible number, so that it becomes in the final analysis a kind of immediate inference. The relative implies the absolute: motion implies immobility; finitude implies infinity; caused causality implies uncaused causality; etc. All the five ways end with that sort of "passing to the limit" under the form of an "impossibility to go on to infinity." But is that impossibility owing to the nature of the intellect or to the nature of reality? Its intervention in the proof led Kant to say that all the proofs of the existence of God imply some hidden recourse to the ontological argument. The remark is correct in the sense that even in the concluding phase of the so-called physical proofs, there is no difference between affirming the necessity of positing an absolute and of affirming its existence. There always is something not quite satisfactory in an induction when its last term can only be inferred without actually being perceived. Behind all the demonstrations of the existence of God, there lurks old man Parmenides. For being is, and if God is being, God is. That is something we feel sure of prior to any demonstration of any sort, and is not that certitude the moving force that drives us on in our quest till we reach an absolutely first term which, as such, necessarily is and—since its being is necessary—is God? To put it even more simply, since we ask *Utrum Deus sit* (whether God exists), the notion of God is already here, and the notion of him is that of a necessary being.

---

36 Aquinas, *op. cit.*, Pt. I, q. 84, art. 5; *GBWW*, Vol. 19, p. 447b.

THE DIFFICULTIES OF ATHEISM

Atheists like to denounce the shortcomings of the proofs of God's existence, and many of the proofs are inadequate, but some of them appear convincing to trained metaphysical minds, while there has never been a convincing metaphysical proof that there is no God.

I am not claiming that there are no professed atheists—men who remain persuaded, after mature reflection, that no reality answers the word "God." My point is, first, that anybody can quote half a dozen or more classical proofs of the existence of God even if he does not subscribe to them; on the other hand, proofs of the nonexistence of God are scarce. My next point is that such proofs consist in showing that the proofs of the existence of God are not conclusive—a different proposition than the nonexistence of God. Third, the very fact that the nonexistence of God requires proof is corroboration of the reality of what I have called the spontaneous and naïve belief in the existence of God. The violent campaigns conducted by the atheistic governments against religion would not be necessary were it not so certain that the people, left to themselves, would go on believing that there is a God and in worshiping him. Besides, why look at governments when the case of private individuals is so clear? Men never consider what they significantly call "losing their faith" a happy event. There is no apparent reason why this should be so. To have rid oneself of what one has come to consider an error, or a mere prejudice, should be a cause instead for celebration. Literature, however, abounds in depressing descriptions of how thinkers and writers have lost their faith. A case little known outside the circle of specialists in French literature is that of the poet Stéphane Mallarmé. Though chary of confidences on such questions, Mallarmé wrote to his friend Henry Cazalis that he was just emerging from an exhausting crisis in the course of which he had finally overcome—not without tremendous efforts—"that old plumage," God. Why should there be such resistance to an idea of something that does not exist?

To us philosophers, perhaps the most instructive of such cases is that of Immanuel Kant. For Kant remains an outstanding example of what he himself considered the first virtue in a philosopher—seriousness, the habit of never playing with ideas but of treating them seriously. Kant could not stand cheating in philosophy, and this makes the more remarkable his attitude toward our problem. Having asked in the *Critique of Pure Reason* if speculative reason is qualified to establish the existence of a being, which is doubly impossible for sense experience, Kant answered his own question in the negative, but he did so with regret and not without adding qualifications to his answer.

The modern successors to Kant have stressed the negative part of his doctrine, stated in the conclusion of his *Critique of Pure Reason*, that no metaphysical knowledge is possible. Accordingly, the existence of God is among the many propositions that must be considered indemonstrable, but it is only one of them. What is truly remarkable in Kant's case is that after reaching that conclusion he continued to feel absolutely certain of the existence of God. Indeed, in his *Critique of Practical Reason* Kant went out of his way to demonstrate that that indemonstrable conclusion remained a truth nonetheless. It is true, one remembers, as a postulate, because otherwise the necessary character of moral duty, which to Kant is a fact, would be impossible.

I do not think that Kant was contradicting himself. On the contrary, I wish to stress the obstinacy with which he insists that the conclusions of the second *Critique* leave intact the conclusions of the first one. Why should Kant still feel sure that there is a God after demonstrating that it is impossible for speculative reason to prove it? From this point of view, the central chapter of the *Critique of Practical Reason* is I,2,7: "How is it possible to conceive an extension of pure reason from the point of view of practice without, at the same time, extending its knowledge from the point of view of speculation?" Indeed, how can such a trick be performed successfully? However I arrive at it, the certitude acquired by practical reason is, by definition, a rational certitude. Rational faith, as Kant calls it, cannot extend our knowledge in the speculative order even though reason —as is the case with moral duty—is bound to bow to it. In short, the certitude that there is a God both precedes and survives intact the demonstration that it cannot be demonstrated. More brilliant homage was never paid to the rational indestructibility of a notion whose intrinsic certitude remains unaffected by the demonstration of its indemonstrability.[37] That indestructibility of the notion of God in the human mind is the heaviest stumbling block in the path to atheism. It should help us to realize that logic, dialectic, and physics cannot have the last word, because they do not have the first one. It is natural that man should look for a rational justification of his spontaneous belief that there is a God, but because belief comes first, that belief is independent of such justifications; it is their cause rather than their effect.

THE FIRST WORD

It might seem to follow that there can be no atheists, but I do not mean that. I mean that even when atheism is real, it is a negation implying the presence in the mind of the very notion it denies, a negation fighting, more or less successfully, against a natural tendency of reason to affirm it.

To reject that affirmation as metaphysical is a great naïveté. Of course it is metaphysical to say there is a God, but it is equally metaphysical to say there is no God. "To believe that there is a God," Charles Péguy wrote,

---

37 Kant, *Critique of Practical Reason*; GBWW, Vol. 42, p. 349b–353a.

"is a metaphysical, a religious operation; to believe that there are several gods implies as many such operations as there are gods, and to believe that there is neither one God nor several is to perform as many negative operations, both metaphysical and religious, as it would require positive operations to affirm them." Péguy concludes in the language of the Schoolmen "that atheism is a philosophy, a metaphysics; that it perhaps is a religion, even a superstition; and that it can become what is the most wretched thing in the world, a system or, rather, and to speak more exactly, that there can be several atheisms and many of those things at one and the same time; nay, that atheism is indeed all those things by the same title and neither more nor less than so many theisms and so many deisms, so many monotheisms and so many polytheisms, and mythologies, and pantheisms; that it too is a mythology, like the others and, like the others, is a language; and that, if it comes down to the fact that there must needs be languages, there are more intelligent ones."[38]

In short, an inverted metaphysical position remains metaphysical. Neither would it help atheism to object, in the manner of Kant, that we know the notion of God for what it is, namely a transcendental "illusion" of reason. Even if that were true, one still would ask why, once denounced as an illusion, that ancient notion should not at once vanish from human minds? For millennia it was believed that the sun moved around the earth; it still looks that way to our eyes, but we know it is not so, and we have ceased to believe it. It also was believed that the universe consisted of solid concentric spheres; but since Galileo demonstrated that that is not true, the notion of heavenly spheres has vanished from our minds. The other notion, that those spheres are animated, or at least moved, by movers of their own, is now nothing more than a historical curiosity for us. Perhaps some of us still have a poetic hankering for it, but that is all; we may wish it were true, we no longer believe that it is. One of the convictions most solidly implanted in people's minds used to be that the animal species had always been such as we see them. When Boucher de Perthes exhibited fossils for the first time, he was cruelly ridiculed, yet it was the French Academy of Sciences that was making itself ridiculous; the old belief in the immutability of the animal kingdom is now dead, and we feel no temptation to revive it. Why then should not the old belief in God also be likewise dead, now that we know that it is an illusion? Indeed, why did Professor Kant continue to believe in it, even to the

---

38 Charles Péguy, "De la situation faite au parti intellectuel," in *Œuvres en prose (1898–1908)* (Paris: La Pléiade), pp. 1072–73. In the preceding pages (1071–72) Péguy had insisted that "metaphysical negations are metaphysical operations by the same title as metaphysical affirmations." The "negative affirmations," as he aptly calls them, are "inverted metaphysical affirmations," often more precarious than are pure metaphysical affirmations. Péguy remarks in the same vein concerning the belief in an eternal life: to refuse to believe it is just as metaphysical an operation as to believe it (p. 1073).

point of demonstrating its necessity in a new way after he himself had established it was an illusion?

The difference of the notion of God from the others is that, in all the other cases, what was at stake was some illusion of imagination, while what is at stake in the case of the notion of God is, in Kant's own words, an illusion of reason. An amazing notion indeed, but one which we should nevertheless subscribe to if the illusory character of the belief in God were really demonstrated. As a matter of fact, Kant did not even attempt to demonstrate it. All he did was to ask himself: Is the certitude of that notion of the same nature as that of the scientific notions that constitute the science of Newton? The answer, of course, has to be negative; but this simply means that as soon as you stop asking metaphysical questions, you cease getting metaphysical answers. If it is asked why we should go on asking metaphysical questions, the answer is because thought is by its very essence metaphysical. To think is to think being and about being. If being is an illusion, transcendental or not, then thinking itself is an illusion; at least knowing is an illusion and we should quit worrying about all problems related to it. Science would then remain possible, but the very notion of science itself would lose its intelligibility.

This takes us back to the remark that all proofs of the existence of God are essentially metaphysical, and that the proofs are all related to the essentially metaphysical notion of being, conceived as transcending species, genus, and any conceivable particular determinations, but as including them at the same time as it transcends them. The considerable task of analyzing the metaphysical notion of being is not my concern now. My present point is that anyone losing sight of that notion, because he substitutes physical being for it, by the same token loses sight of the idea of God. As he ceases to see the notion, it is no wonder that its object ceases to exist for him.

By a strange coincidence, that very peripety marked the personal evolution of Kant himself. When one says that Kant proved that the notion of God is a transcendental illusion, we should ask, which Kant, and at what time of his life? In 1764, answering a question asked by the Academy of Berlin, Kant wrote his *Inquiry Into the Distinctness of the Principles of Natural Theology and Morals*. He then found himself at grips with the problem of what it is possible to know about God. Realizing the immensity of the task to examine all that all philosophers had said on the question, Kant contented himself with observing that "the capital notion that presents itself to the metaphysician here is the absolute necessity that there actually be some being." In addition, he said, "To grasp it, one first should ask *whether it is possible that there should be absolutely nothing?* For he who asks the question is bound to realize that where no *existence* is given, there remains nothing to be *thought* nor, generally speaking, any possibility of any kind, so that he must only look for what is to be found at the origin of all possibility. That reflection will broaden itself and thus establish the determined concept of the absolutely necessary being."

It is to be regretted that Kant reached that point but then seemed to lose courage and did not proceed along that metaphysical way. It is true that that was the Wolffian way of possibility, which ultimately proves to be a metaphysical blind alley. In a realistic epistemology, the question: *Could there be nothing?* does not arise, because in fact there is something, and if it were possible that nothing should be, there would be nothing. Not only would there be no thought, as Kant says, but Kant himself would not be there to ask the question. Because something is, then, there is necessary being, for actual reality is necessary by right. The only question still to be asked about it is: In all that necessary being, what has a right to be called God? A thought that moves within being also moves within actual existence from the very first moment of its inquiry; similarly, it moves within necessity, proceeding as it does from conditioned necessities to absolute necessity. The question then cannot possibly be whether or not there is a God, for that is beyond doubt; the question is what, or who, is our God?

The idea that the contemporary position on the question is new is an illusion. There is nothing new about materialism. Augustine himself had first been a materialist, and today he might well be a Marxist; but if he were, he would again ask matter, along with all the goods it contains—including the social and economic—Are you my God? And with a loud voice they still would answer: We are not thy God. Augustine then would perhaps ask Kant: Is the voice of duty my God? But moral conscience too would answer with a loud voice: I am not thy God; for indeed in what light do I see what is right and just, and how is it that every man, consulting his own reason, spontaneously agrees with other men as to what is true and false, morally right and wrong? If there is anything above man, Augustine asked, shall not we agree that it is God? Yes, Comte says, and that is Humanity; and yes again, Nietzsche agrees, the Superman is God. But humanity and superman do not take us far beyond man, and so our end is in our beginning. If God is a strictly transcendent being, even the false gods we are being offered are witness to the true one. True atheists are not scarce; they do not exist, because true atheism—that is, a complete and final absence of the notion of God—is not only difficult, it is impossible. What indeed exists is an immense crowd of people who do not think of God, and perhaps a still larger crowd of worshipers of false gods, but that is something different from consciously accepting the world and man, without any further explanation, as self-sufficient cause and end. There is indeed ample justification for doubt, hesitations, and uncertainties in man's seeking for the true God, but the very possibility of such a quest presupposes—no, it implies—that the problem of the existence of God remains for the human mind a philosophical inevitability.

RECENT BOOKS AND
ARTICLES

BADO, WALTER, S. J. "What Is God? An Essay on Learned Ignorance," in *The Modern Schoolman*, XLII (November, 1964), 3–32.

BARTH, KARL. *Anselm: Fides Quaerens Intellectum. (Faith in Search of Understanding.)* English Translation by I. W. ROBERTSON. New York: Meridian Books, 1962 (paperback).

BORNE, E. *Atheism.* New York: Hawthorn Books, 1961.

CHRISTIAN, W. A. *Meaning and Truth in Religion.* Princeton: Princeton University Press, 1964.

COLLINS, JAMES. *God in Modern Philosophy.* Chicago: Henry Regnery Co., 1959.

———. "Philosophy and Religion," in *The Great Ideas Today 1962*, ed. by ROBERT M. HUTCHINS and MORTIMER J. ADLER. Chicago: Encyclopædia Britannica, Inc., 1962, pp. 314–72.

Commonweal. "God: Commonweal Papers (1)." LXXXV (February 10, 1967).

Continuum. Issue devoted to the contemporary experience of God. V (Winter, 1967).

DANIÉLOU, J. *God and the Ways of Knowing.* New York: Meridian Books, 1957.

DIRSCHERL, D. (ed.). *Speaking of God.* Milwaukee: Bruce Publishing Co., 1967.

FABRO, CORNELIO. *God in Exile: A Study of the Internal Dynamic of Modern Atheism from Its Roots in the Cartesian Cogito to the Present Day.* Westminster, Md.: Newman Press, 1968.

FERRÉ, FREDERICK. *Basic Modern Philosophy of Religion.* New York: Charles Scribner's Sons, 1967 (paperback).

FLEW, ANTONY. *God and Philosophy.* New York: Harcourt, Brace and World, 1966.

FLEW, ANTONY, and MACINTYRE, ALASDAIR (eds.). *New Essays in Philosophical Theology.* New York: The Macmillan Co., 1955, 1964 (paperback).

GILSON, ETIENNE. *A Gilson Reader.* Selected Writings of Etienne Gilson, ed. by ANTON C. PEGIS. Chapter 12, "God and Christian Philosophy," pp. 192–209. Garden City: Hanover House, 1957.

HARTSHORNE, C. *Anselm's Discovery: A Reexamination of the Ontological Proof for God's Existence.* LaSalle, Ill.: Open Court Publishing Co., 1966 (paperback).

———. *A Natural Theology for Our Time.* LaSalle, Ill.: Open Court Publishing Co., 1967.

HICK, J. H., and McGILL, A. C. (eds.). *The Many-faced Argument: Recent Studies on the Ontological Argument for the Existence of God.* New York: The Macmillan Co., 1967 (paperback).

JOHNSON, O. A. "God and St. Anselm," in *The Journal of Religion*, XLV (October, 1965), 326–34.

LACROIX, J. *The Meaning of Modern Atheism.* New York: The Macmillan Co., 1965.

LeFEVRE, PERRY. *Philosophical Resources for Christian Thought.* New York: Abingdon Press, 1968.

LUBAC, H. DE. *Discovery of God.* New York: P. J. Kenedy and Sons, 1960.

MATSON, W. I. *The Existence of God.* Ithaca: Cornell University Press, 1965.

MURRAY, J. C. *The Problem of God.* New Haven: Yale University Press, 1964.

NEVILLE, ROBERT C. *God the Creator: On the Transcendence and Presence of God.* Chicago: University of Chicago Press, 1968.

NOGAR, RAYMOND J., O. P. "The God of Disorder," in *Continuum*, IV (Spring, 1966), 102–13.

PHILLIPS, D. Z. (ed.). *Religion and Understanding.* New York: The Macmillan Co., 1967.

PLANTINGA, A. *God and Other Minds: A Study of the Rational Justification of Belief in God.* Ithaca: Cornell University Press, 1967.

———. (ed.). *The Ontological Argument: From St. Anselm to Contemporary Philosophers.* Garden City: Doubleday Anchor Books, 1965 (paperback).

SIX, J. E. *L'athéisme dans la vie et la culture contemporaines.* 2 vols. Paris: Desles, 1967–68.

SMART, N. *Philosophers and Religious Truth.* London: SCM Press, Ltd., 1964 (paperback).

SMITH, JOHN E. *Experience and God.* New York: Oxford University Press, 1968.

———. *Reason and God: Encounters of Philosophy and Religion.* New Haven: Yale University Press, 1967 (paperback).

STEARNS, J. BRENTON. "On the Impossibility of God's Knowing That He Does Not Exist," in *The Journal of Religion*, XLVI (January, 1966), 1–8.

VALECKY, L. C. "Flew on Aquinas," in *Philosophy*, XLIII (July, 1968), 213–30.

The Review of a
Great Book

The Canterbury Tales

Mark Van Doren

This discussion of Chaucer's *Canterbury Tales,* which constitutes the first
of what the editors of *The Great Ideas Today* intend as a series of contemporary readings by eminent persons of works included in *Great Books of
the Western World,* was the last extended piece of prose undertaken by Mark
Van Doren, who finished it shortly before his death on December 10, 1972.
Readers of *The Great Ideas Today* will recall Mr. Van Doren as a contributor
to the volumes published in 1961 and 1969; in the latter, at the request of the
editors, he offered a list of books which he thought might survive as great
works of the twentieth century in literature—a selection difficult to make,
he said, and one that, as he did not say, only an experienced and accomplished reader could with any credibility have made at all. In asking Mr. Van
Doren to commence this series, the editors gave him his choice among a
number of titles, from which he selected *The Canterbury Tales.* The sadness
with which we record his subsequent death is tempered for us, so far as
possible, by the fact that he lived to complete the task, and by our belief that
the result is a fresh and perceptive study, at once lucid and loving, of one of
the great poems of the world.

Geoffrey Chaucer, who wrote *The Canterbury Tales* in England at the end of the fourteenth century, was then and is now one of the most lovable poets in the world, and this in spite of the fact that the substance of his tales is bitter quite as often as it is sweet, and in spite of the further fact that his language, his English, has grown difficult with time. To hear his verse as he expected it to be heard—as he himself read it in the English court, for he wrote before the invention of printing—requires now a student's knowledge of Middle English, a language that is ours and yet not ours, for many things about it both look and sound strange. Even then, however, the words that Chaucer so cunningly put together, no matter how imperfectly we say them to ourselves, caress us as we read, make love to our hearts and minds, and find their way into our memories where they manage to remain. But even if we have to read him in modernized form we still can be convinced that the charm his contemporaries praised him for is real. He is so good a poet, so great a poet, that he survives translation; and his substance is so rich and rare—so familiar too, as coming from the most companionable of poets—that he is never truly alien to us.

He was born a few years after 1340 and lived in London until 1400, when he died famous as the author of *The Canterbury Tales*, of *Troilus and Criseyde*,* and of other works that need not concern us here, though many of them are beautiful too, and *Troilus and Criseyde*, the longest of his poems, is sometimes called his masterpiece. Of Chaucer's life nothing whatever is known that throws any light upon his poetry. He moved through the London of his day as anonymously as Shakespeare did two centuries later—as anonymously, that is, in his capacity as genius. The

---

* *Troilus and Cressida; GBWW*, Vol. 22, pp. 1–155.

only records of him are of the offices he held and of the public work he did. He was a soldier, an ambassador of minor rank, a traveler on the Continent with special commissions to perform; and latterly he was such things as comptroller of the customs and subsidy of wools for the port of London, justice of the peace for Kent, and clerk of the king's works for royal properties in or near London. About his wife, Philippa, nothing much is known beyond her name and, though he may have had a daughter and a son, it is not certain that this was so. For years he enjoyed the favor of John of Gaunt, and he was never out of favor with any of the three kings he served: Edward III, Richard II, and Henry IV.

All of which adds up to so little that the modesty with which he introduces himself in *The Canterbury Tales*—he is there, even if only as a figure of fiction—has led us all to assume that he was mild of manner, quiet of voice, and unimposing in his person, though none of these assumptions is warranted by any evidence. The only thing of which we have a right to be sure is that he was born old—born, that is to say, always to be wise beyond his years, and always to be possessed of the comic genius that comes with wisdom of the ripest, finest sort, the wisdom that sees far and remembers everything, and is so intimate with feeling as to be full of it after all.

His English has been a problem for readers of him ever since the century that followed upon his death. Edmund Spenser in 1596 could hail Chaucer as a "well of English undefyled," but Spenser was a lover of the antique both in language and in thought, and even then he lamented the ravages that "wicked Time" had inflicted upon the fair body of Chaucer's poems, which he feared were already "quite devourd and brought to nought." It is a fear that anyone at any time may feel in the face of evidence that obsolescence is working to obliterate precious things, literary or not—morals, for example, and good manners.

Dryden in 1700 found the language of Chaucer so unfamiliar in its forms that he thought it necessary to modernize certain of *The Canterbury Tales* for inclusion in his *Fables*. By this time even the memory of how Chaucer's English was pronounced had been lost, so that Dryden could say that his verse was no longer harmonious, though "they who lived with him, and some time after him, thought it musical," a judgment which Dryden only partially accepted, granting that

> there is the rude sweetness of a Scotch tune in it, which is natural and pleasing, though not perfect. 'Tis true, I cannot go so far as he who published the last edition of him; for he would make us believe the fault is in our ears, and that there were really ten syllables in a verse where we find but nine: but this opinion is not worth confuting; 'tis so gross and obvious an error, that common sense . . . must convince the reader that equality of numbers . . . was either not known, or not always practised, in Chaucer's age.

176

. . . We can only say, that he lived in the infancy of our poetry, and that nothing is brought to perfection at the first.

Whereas we now know that Chaucer was one of the most musical of poets, and a master of English verse. What Dryden did not believe was that the letter *e,* now mute at the end of many words and elsewhere too, was sounded in Chaucer's time, so that *longe,* for example, like *bookes* and *goode,* to take three instances quite at random, had two syllables instead of one, at least in positions where the *e* was not elided. And this makes all the difference. It creates what Matthew Arnold called "Chaucer's divine liquidness of diction, his divine fluidity of movement," virtues of which Arnold found it "difficult to speak temperately," so entranced he was with the lovely sound of Chaucer's lines. The sweetness of Chaucer's verse, in other words, was not rude but real. Dryden, whose praise of Chaucer laid the foundation for his reputation as we know it, was wrong about him only in this one respect, and we cannot hold it against him in view of the fact that he went ahead anyway to discover the great poet whom his own generosity still helps us to appreciate.

Meanwhile, let us remember that the music of Chaucer's verse is something like the music of Mozart—high and fine, and yet so powerful that it never breaks: a golden wire that stretches between heaven and earth, sounding incessantly its own note, its own idea. We shall have no occasion to meet him as a lyric poet, but he is superb in that role—indeed, in his "Balade" from *The Legend of Good Women,* supreme:

> *Hyd, Absolon, thy gilte tresses clere;*
> *Ester, ley thou thy meknesse al adoun;*
> *Hyd, Jonathas, al thy frendly manere;*
> *Penelope and Marcia Catoun,*
> *Mak of youre wyfhood no comparisoun*
> *Hyde ye youre beautes, Ysoude and Eleyne;*
> *Alceste is here, that al that may desteyne.*
>
> *Thy faire body, lat it not appere,*
> *Lavyne: and thou, Lucresse of Rome toun,*
> *And Polyxene, that boughte love so dere,*
> *Ek Cleopatre, with al thy passioun,*
> *Hide ye youre trouth in love and your renoun;*
> *And thou, Tysbe, that hast for love swich peyne:*
> *Alceste is here, that al may desteyne.*
>
> *Herro, Dido, Laodomya, all in-fere,*
> *Ek Phillis, hangyne for thy Demophoun,*
> *And Canace, espied by thy chere,*
> *Ysiphile, betrayed with Jasoun*

> *Mak of youre trouthe in love no bost ne soun;*
> *Nor Ypermystre or Adriane, ne pleyne:*
> *Alceste is here, that al that may disteyne.**

Nothing is said here except that Alcestis bedims all other good women with whom she may be compared. Nothing except just *that,* and it is everything, as the sound of the words keeps on saying, as the movement of the lines, so urgent, so exigent, keeps pressing us to believe and feel. *Rome* has two syllables, surely, and *espied* and *betrayed* both have three. The long *i* is pronounced *ee,* and the long *a* is like the *a* in *father.* Still more could be said about the difference between Chaucer's voice and ours, but let it suffice to suggest that the reader is free to find what music he will in this imperishable song. The music is there, waiting for him to realize its triumphant, almost tearful perfection.

But our subject is story, not style, and so we come at last to *The Canterbury Tales,* which Chaucer himself came to last, for he died writing them, or perhaps only arranging and ordering them, some of them from manuscripts of an earlier day. Perhaps the work was finished after all; perhaps Chaucer wanted it to strike us as incomplete, which on the whole it does. The effect might have been intentional; he hated prolixity except when it served his comic purpose, and he was too sensible a man to suppose that completeness itself is a virtue; for him, indeed, there could be an art of incompleteness, a trick of leaving things undone that would only bore us if they *were* done. In any event, and however he regarded them, the tales were his crowning achievement, and the one for which he will always be best known. *Troilus and Criseyde* had been matchless in its kind, and it continues to be admired by all who read it to its profoundly moving end. *The Canterbury Tales,* however, are more than admired; they are loved as folklore is loved, they live on with a certain casual air that seems to say they may pass for anonymous for all the author cares. They give us the impression of having been easy to write. A false impression, doubtless, but the fact that we have it is somehow connected with the truth.

Chaucer was one of those happy authors who discover before they die what they always should have been doing. Cervantes, who in *Don Quixote* made the same discovery, had previously been a competent student of the conventions, and as such had written romances that we might find admirable if we ever read them. The vein he opened with *Don Quixote,* however, was bright with his own life's blood, and the result was one of the immortal books—real and romantic both, as life itself is. So Chaucer, serving his apprenticeship as the author of dream poems, abstractions, and al-

---

* Glossary: *Hyd,* hide; *gilte,* golden; *clere,* clear, bright, splendid; *desteyne,* bedim; *Ek,* also; *swich,* such; *peyne,* toil, distress; *in-fere,* together; *espied,* disclosed; *chere,* appearance; *bost,* boast; *soun,* sound, boast; *pleyne,* complain, lament.

legories such as the age can be said to have demanded, did fine work which yet now counts for little, or relatively little, alongside the plain surface of *The Canterbury Tales,* the familiar look and feel of their images and figures, the casual, conversational tone they take with us their readers, the amateur effect they manage to provide without appearing to have striven for it. Not that the years of preparation were wasted, either for Chaucer or for Cervantes. Plainness and lifelikeness come late, not early, as simplicity does. And both Chaucer and Cervantes brought with them to their final work a certain courtliness, a cushion of "gentilesse," to use Chaucer's own term, which kept the realism of their masterpieces from being too brutal and flat, as realism in shallower imaginations may all too easily be.

The Canterbury Tales were easy to write, then, in the special sense that they were not written against the grain. Nevertheless, they were work, and if Chaucer was glad to do it, and did it with all of his old energy, we should not fail to recognize how busy the man's mind was as he proceeded, how actively it ranged over an immense territory that lay open for exploration. Chaucer was among other things a great reader; it is clear that he loved books, just as it is clear that he delighted in telling us about them, as if they were good friends he was proud to say he knew. He read, one can imagine, incessantly—until, he suggests in one of his autobiographical poems, he was "dumb" and "dazed"—and he seemed to remember every word on every page. In order to write *The Canterbury Tales* he had to find plots for them, to translate or adapt these plots, and then to conceal the signs of his having done so, for the tales must seem to be his own, as of course in the last analysis they are. But he had to find them somewhere first; they had to be in books, as Shakespeare's plots did also; neither poet was ready to write until he had before him the substance of his action, and people bearing names—historical, fictitious, dramatic, it mattered not which—who acted out the parts, and even spoke some of the lines, though Chaucer was to give them better lines, the lines that we ourselves remember.

The last thing he expected to be praised for was the thing we sometimes call originality, meaning by the word a cleverness in making up stories out of nothing. For him there had to be something, and it had better be something old, that more than one mind had handled, though if only one had, and it was Boccaccio's, so much the better, for in Boccaccio he recognized a master whom it was a pleasure to rewrite, making as free as he liked with the materials being borrowed—the original materials, which now are his because he made them his, and in doing so managed to be original in the richest sense of the word. But the author he used did not have to be as famous or as great as Boccaccio; he could be anybody, and sometimes he has been hard for the scholars to dig out of the record; but there he almost invariably is. Most of Chaucer's *Tales,* that is to say, have their sources, and in due course these will be mentioned.

179

Chaucer's hunger for stories was something he shared with the writers of his time; they all were cormorants, diving and devouring discernible creatures in the human sea. In this respect they were like writers at any time: like the Greek poets who ransacked myth and legend for the stuff of their tragedies, like the Elizabethan playwrights who plundered both ancient and modern literature for plots, like the makers of movie and television scripts who proceed in the same fashion, searching in every known corner for stories to retell. Perhaps the medieval poets had one special advantage: the diversity of their field, the range of it, the color, the richness of texture. Chaucer at any rate made the most of this advantage. His mind was naturally skeptical; he never seemed to know just what he should believe; but his skepticism was of that delightful sort which permitted him to believe everything—not nothing, but everything, on the chance that it might be true. Such skepticism—such loving skepticism—is what underlies, we must suppose, the account of the fairies that occurs in the first twenty-five lines of *The Wife of Bath's Tale*. Chaucer was at home in mythology; in the lore of chivalry; in popular folklore; in the legends of Arthur and his knights; in the literature of astronomy, astrology, and alchemy; in the lives of the saints and the degrees of power among the clergy; in the biographies of heroes; in the fineries of privilege and rank—for the English court in his time was the most luxurious in Europe; in the arts of costume and display; in the involutions of allegory as all contemporary poetry practiced it; in the spectacles of injustice, real or alleged, of which the time was full—injustice, without which fiction cannot flourish; in the backyard domain of the *fabliaux,* those dirty stories that everybody seems to have relished; in the deep wells of proverb and allusion that sent up buckets of wisdom and dishes of wit whenever anybody plumbed them.

The England of Chaucer's century had only four million people in it, and half of those died in the plagues that came again and again, but who feels this while reading *The Canterbury Tales*? Their world is densely populated, and every possible idea seems to exist in it. It is the world of the Middle Ages, which was so far from ignorant that it could invent the university and build the cathedrals we never cease to wonder at. It was sophisticated to the hilt; it thought of itself as old, not young, as corrupt, not innocent, as luxurious, not barren, as rich, not poor, though plenty of people were poor as plenty of people still are. It was this world that Chaucer knew so well—knew at first hand, but also knew from books, whose pages he once said were as delicious to his taste as the breath of a May morning; and who does not remember how Chaucer, like all of his countrymen for that matter, adored the darling month of May that took so long to come?

It was this world that he played upon in his *Canterbury Tales* like an instrument with strings, like an organ with many pipes. It was this world that he knew so well he often refused to describe it, for he thought his readers knew it too; he is constantly dismissing details as of no importance in comparison with his main theme, and he does so as if he were not aware that he is using a rhetorical figure familiar to everybody in his audience; but he knows they know he is aware, and he smiles a certain secret smile that we associate with his very name. Not so secret either, perhaps. "There is a sort of penumbra of playfulness round everything he ever said or sang," says G. K. Chesterton, who is one of his best critics, "a halo of humor" that we never miss if we read him well. At the same time there is the music in him of hidden tears, a piercing music that never lets us forget the power of his pity, the seriousness of his soul as he contemplates reality.

The reality of his times was terrible, and he could never have doubted that it was. The Black Death, the Hundred Years' War, the peasant rebellions that burned sections of London and beheaded archbishops, the ghastly executions, the beggars in the streets, the famines in the fields—Chaucer may not speak of these things, but he could not have been indifferent to them, and if nothing else his silence may be taken as meaning much; it has been remarked that throughout his part of the Hundred Years' War he never wrote one patriotic line; and if he was neither a Lollard nor a Wycliffite—that is to say, a social and theological liberal—at least his Plowman in *The Prologue* to the tales is given an almost ideal character, as distinguished from the contempt with which it was fashionable to treat the lower orders.

The Prologue

The Prologue is justly one of the most famous poems in English. It sets the company of pilgrims in motion toward Canterbury, on an April morning as they leave the Tabard Inn on horseback with Harry Bailey, their host, directing the order in which they shall ride, and in which they shall tell the tales—two for each of them on the way, and two others for each of them coming back—that are Chaucer's principal business; he too is of the company, and will take his turn with most of the others. Not all of the twenty-nine will have tales to tell, and the riders for that matter never return to London, for the action stops at Canterbury; one hundred and sixteen stories would have been a staggering number in any case, and surely Chaucer never intended that there should be so many—told, incidently to a music of hooves and bridles and jingling ornaments, and with the company strung out so far along the road that no one voice could have reached every ear. Chaucer, to tell the truth, does not let us think of things like this as he starts to describe his pilgrims and goes on with such spirit that his people come alive before us and remain long after in our minds; he has the supreme gift that every storyteller would have if he only could, the gift of being able to bring the reader in and make him feel that he is there.

The pilgrimage was to the shrine of Saint Thomas à Becket, who was murdered at the altar in the cathedral of Canterbury in 1170, and who had become a figure of holiness for countless of the faithful who still journeyed there in Chaucer's century. The motive for such a journey varied with the persons who took it: some were devout, some were merely on a vacation, and for some it might have been hard to assign any motive at all; but all who went did have a common purpose which it was not necessary to discuss, so that with Chaucer's pilgrims there was no talk of anything but what passed through their minds as they rode more or less harmoniously along. "The time chosen," wrote William Blake of the painting he made of the pilgrims and advertised in a catalogue in 1809,

> *is early morning, before sunrise, when the jolly company are just quitting the Tabarde Inn. . . . The Landscape is an eastward view of the country . . . as it may be supposed to have appeared in Chaucer's time. . . . The characters of Chaucer's Pilgrims are the characters which compose all ages and nations: as one age falls, another rises, different to mortal sight, but to immortals only the same; for we see the same characters repeated again and again, in animals, vegetables, minerals, and in men; nothing new occurs in identical existence; Accident ever varies, Substance can never suffer change nor decay.*

"The Canterbury Pilgrims," engraving by William Blake, 1810; in the British Museum

This is a rather grand way of saying that Chaucer's pilgrims are presented to us both as typical and as individual—a necessary ingredient in any narrative that hopes to be memorable. The secret of fiction, if there is only one, consists in the author's firm understanding that any person is at least three things simultaneously: a member of the human race, a member of a group within the race—a class, a type, a profession, a sex, a youth, an elder, a nondescript—and simply himself. How well Chaucer understood this was noted by Dryden in the preface to his *Fables*:

> *He must have been a man of a most wonderful comprehensive nature, because, as it has been truly observed of him, he has taken into the compass of his* Canterbury Tales *the various manners and humours (as we now call them) of the whole English nation in his age. Not a single character has escaped him. All his pilgrims are severally distinguished from each other; and not only in their inclinations, but in their very physiognomies and persons. . . . The matter and manner of their tales, and of their telling, are so suited to their different educations, humours, and callings, that each of them would be improper in any other mouth. Even the grave and serious characters are distinguished by their several sorts of gravity: their discourses are such as belong to their age, their calling, and their breeding; such as are becoming of them, and of them only. Some of his persons are vicious, and some virtuous; some are unlearn'd, or (as Chaucer calls them) lewd, and some are learn'd. Even the ribaldry of the low characters is different: the Reeve, the Miller, and the Cook, are several men, and distinguished from each other as much as the mincing Lady-Prioress and the broad-speaking gap-toothed Wife of Bath. But enough of this; there is such a variety of game springing up before me that I am distracted in my choice, and know not which to follow. 'Tis sufficient to say, according to the proverb, that here is God's plenty. We have our forefathers and great-granddames all before us, as they were in Chaucer's days: their general characters are still remaining in mankind, and even in England, though they are called by other names than those of Monks and Friars, and Canons, and Lady Abbesses, and Nuns; for mankind is ever the same, and nothing lost out of Nature, though everything is altered.*

Better things than that have never been said about Chaucer; with those words he was welcomed into the circle of the great. Even Matthew Arnold, who in 1880 denied that Chaucer *was* one of "the great classics," was forced by Dryden's eloquence to agree with him as far as he went. "Chaucer's power of fascination," said Arnold,

> *is enduring; his poetical importance does not need the assistance of the historic estimate; it is real. He is a genuine source of joy and*

strength, which is flowing still for us and will flow always. He will be read, as time goes on, far more generally than he is read now. His language is a cause of difficulty for us; but so also, and I think in quite as great a degree, is the language of Burns. In Chaucer's case, as in that of Burns, it is a difficulty to be unhesitatingly accepted and overcome.

If we ask ourselves wherein consists the immense superiority of Chaucer's poetry over the romance-poetry—why it is that in passing from this to Chaucer we suddenly feel ourselves to be in another world, we shall find that his superiority is both in the substance of his poetry and in the style of his poetry. His superiority in substance is given by his large, free, simple, clear yet kindly view of human life—so unlike the total want, in the romance-poets, of all intelligent command of it. Chaucer has not their helplessness; he has gained the power to survey the world from a central, a truly human point of view. We have only to call to mind the Prologue to The Canterbury Tales. *The right comment upon it is Dryden's. . . . It is by a large, free, sound representation of things that poetry, this high criticism of life, has truth of substance; and Chaucer's poetry has truth of substance.**

The Prologue is more than a series of portraits; there is so much life in the manner of its painting that it may be taken as the first unit of a narrative: the first chapter of a novel or the first scene of a play, it scarcely matters which. The opening lines can remind us now of the miracle that spring once was anywhere in the temperate zone; it is still a miracle, but it has become a muted one, what with our heated houses, our plowed and salted highways, our conveyances which themselves are heated so that many of us seldom have the sense of really being out of doors. In Chaucer's time, as for that matter in Shakespeare's and in Dryden's, and on for nearly two centuries after that, winter was an ordeal from which mankind emerged in April and May with song and thanksgiving for gentle winds and the voices of returning birds; life was literally beginning again. So Chaucer's pilgrims gaily begin their trip, and the host manages, at least at first, to maintain pleasant relations among them all. Harry Bailey, who as it happens tells no tale, is far from being the least important of the pilgrims. He has a lively sense of who his people are and of how they ought to be addressed. The entire work would be weaker without him.

So would it be without the clergy who are so numerous among the troupe. It takes a certain effort of the imagination to recall that England was once a Catholic country, with priests and monks, with friars and canons, with abbeys and cathedrals everywhere at hand. It has been Protestant so long that one can be startled by realizing that it was Catholic for even

---

* *The Study of Poetry; GGB,* Vol. 5, pp. 29–30.

longer. So too with the professions and the trades, and the relations between husbands and wives. Everything was different, as Dryden says, yet
everything was the same. All of which means that Chaucer had the richest
of opportunities before him: the opportunity of dealing with both eternity
and time, with both the representative and the unique in human behavior. Not that he needs to be understood as ever saying such a thing to
himself; he was more modest than that. But he did, we can be sure, feel
somewhat free at last to talk his own language and think his own thought,
to feel as Geoffrey Chaucer felt, and say so in the liveliest language he
could command.

The whole of *The Canterbury Tales* is a story that could be summarized without retelling the tales themselves; the links between the tales,
the conversations, the quarrels, the compliments, the oaths, the asides are
actually so interesting that some commentators have advocated the radical
procedure of ignoring the tales and concentrating on their framework.
But it is simply not true, as Chesterton asserts, that the tales are inferior
in interest to their tellers. The tales are still the thing, as the following
pages hope to show.

The Knight's Tale

The evening before the pilgrims set forth, their host, the big man with the
merry voice and the protuberant eyes, got their assent to a plan he had
for their comfort and amusement on the way. He proposed that each of
them tell two tales going and two returning, and they voted their agreement. Now in the morning, at the first watering place where they stop to
refresh the throats of their horses, he suggests that they draw cuts to see
which of them shall tell the first tale.

> *And, to make short the matter, as it was,*
> *Whether by chance or whatsoever cause,*
> *The truth is, that the cut fell to the knight.*

Chaucer is doubtless hinting here that the host made sure the Knight
would be first. For knights were still first in everything, despite the decay
of chivalry which many men deplored, and the host might have been uncomfortable with any different result. At any rate the Knight, being the
perfect gentleman described in *The Prologue,* the worthy man who loves
truth and honor, freedom and courtesy, beyond all other things, is willing
to keep his promise of the night before, and so with the briefest of pre-
ambles begins the tale of Palamon and Arcita.

It is a proper tale for him to tell, since the very stuff of it is love and
honor, and the style of it has the dignity and splendor that we soon learn
to associate with Chaucer's own knight, a most excellent man who also

possesses a sense of humor. The story given him to tell had probably been written by Chaucer several years before under the title "Palamon and Arcite," though if this is true nothing is known of any changes made in it now. It had been taken from Boccaccio's epic poem *Il Teseida,* which Chaucer translated so freely that only a few hundred of its lines are traceable to the original; the rest is adaptation, or else it is Chaucer's own. He also made use of the Roman poets Statius and Ovid, of the philosopher Boethius, and of the *Roman de la Rose,* which for

every fourteenth-century poet was a gold mine of materials. Dryden modernized Chaucer's reworking of these sources in his *Fables,* where it occupies first place.

The story of Palamon and Arcita as Chaucer's knight tells it is grave and painful, with an unhappy ending for one of its heroes which only philosophy can render endurable—the philosophy, that is to say, of Boethius, a sixth-century Roman scholar and Christian martyr who wrote his *Consolation of Philosophy* in prison while awaiting execution at the order of the emperor Theodoric. It is a stoic philosophy, counseling men to accept whatever fate offers them no matter how unjust it may seem. Boethius was widely read in the Middle Ages, and Chaucer turned to his doctrine in many of his own works. In *The Knight's Tale* its chief exponent is Theseüs, duke of Athens, who is called upon to preside over the destinies of two Theban knights, cousins by birth, whom he has taken captive and now at the beginning of the tale holds in prison without ransom till they die. Year after year they suffer confinement in a tower that overlooks the garden where Emily, sister of Hippolyta the wife of Theseüs, sometimes walks; and one day Palamon, seeing her there, falls in love with her beauty; but so does Arcita, even more deeply if that is possible, and hence a rivalry springs up between the noble cousins, a rivalry that will have the most tragic consequences.

Both knights are made free of the tower, Arcita by exile and Palamon by escape, but both are unhappier away from the vision of Emily than they were before. By chance they encounter each other in a grove and renew their rivalry to the point of deciding upon a duel, for which they duly arm themselves and come at last to blows, fighting, says Chaucer, up to their ankles in blood. It chances that Theseüs, walking nearby with Hippolyta and Emily, arrives upon the scene and commands them to meet in more formal fashion on a day he will appoint. The day of the tournament dawns; each cousin with the hundred knights he has been supplied with as seconds prays to his chosen deity—Palamon to Venus and Arcita to Mars—and the contest begins.

It is won by Arcita, whom Theseüs judges to be the victor; but Arcita, riding in triumph and looking up at Emily, soon he thinks to be his bride because he has won her in fair fight, is thrown from his horse when the horse shies, and is injured so terribly that he has no chance of living. His death, and the ceremonial burning of his body, Chaucer treats with a fine eloquence such as he can always summon when he cares to, just as he gives Palamon and Arcita, when they are praying to their deities, the full benefit of a rhetoric he has studied to make magnificent if the occasion demands magnificence. The sage and serious Theseüs, through whom we hear the voice of Boethius speaking as if no centuries intervened, may remind us of the Theseus who was duke of Athens in Shakespeare's *A Midsummer-Night's Dream,** and who in that play also had Hippolyta to wife.

All the while, however, what has been called the elvish disposition of Chaucer is delightfully in evidence—rarely, to be sure, yet unmistakably. Chaucer could never contemplate extravagance of thought or feeling without wincing and grinning a little. So here, where much of the action borders upon the preposterous, and where what Arnold called romance-poetry might be at home, Chaucer refuses to suppress his own intelligence, and lets us know this, as it were, between the lines. His two heroes are breathless in adoration of Emily, but Chaucer can say:

> *Her yellow hair was braided in one tress*
> *Behind her back, a full yard long, I guess.*

And he can wake her on the morning of the tournament that will decide her future with a line that has become famous wherever Chaucer is known:

> *Up rose the sun and up rose Emily.*

If that is not irreverent, two lines about the death of Arcita surely are:

> *His spirit changed hous, and wente ther,*
> *As I cam never, I can nat tellen wher.†*

Yet not so surely either, for the sequel is a description of Arcita's burial pyre that is authentically Homeric in its full-throated grandeur. And the mingling of sorrow and joy in the wedding of Palamon and Emily is ordered by a poet who wholly understands such things.

---

* *GBWW,* Vol. 26, pp. 352–75.
† Cf. *GBWW,* Vol. 22, p. 206.

The Miller's Tale

It used to be considered a grotesque accident, an editorial blunder, that *The Knight's Tale,* so stately and superb, is followed in the manuscripts by a tale so different from it, so grossly and shockingly different, as to jolt the reader into an amazed attention. The Miller, who in *The Prologue* has been called "a stout churl," chunky and broad, with a red beard as wide as a spade, with a wart on his nose from which rose a tuft of hairs as red as the bristles of a sow's ears, with huge black nostrils and a mouth like a furnace door, with a habit of ribald speech, and with a bagpipe in his possession which he has blown to bring the party out of town—this fellow, hearing the host ask the Monk for a tale to follow that of the Knight, puts in drunkenly, for he is pale with liquor and sits unsteadily on his horse, that he wants to be next; he has a good lively tale, he says, of a carpenter who had a wife, and a clerk made a fool of him; at which the Reeve, himself a carpenter, calls out that the Miller must shut up, for wives should not be traduced; but the Miller, unstoppable, proceeds to tell his tale of two young men in the town of Oxford who become rivals for the pretty young wife of a wealthy old carpenter.

In other words, here is the situation in *The Knight's Tale* all over again on another level, and doubtless a lower one, though as the tale continues we forget about levels and thoroughly enjoy a brilliant and beautiful *fabliau*—meaning, a dirty story and a funny one, such as medieval courts loved to laugh at between romances of courtly love, themselves also concerned with adultery, but high-toned adultery, and the language was elevated. Not so in the *fabliaux*, of which *The Miller's Tale* is one of the best-known examples. It is rank with reality, and candid in every word, and funny in the heartless way of stories that have no other end than laughter in view. Perhaps we should feel pity for the witless old carpenter here who is made a cuckold without even knowing he is, but pity is alien to farce, and this is farce at its finest.

The two rivals for the favors of his wife are Nicholas, a poor but clever clerk, or scholar as he is sometimes called, and Absalom, a parish clerk who is something of a dandy, though for all the beauty of his curly golden hair and his somewhat mincing ways he has no chance against Nicholas because Nicholas lives in the carpenter's house, and because he has already handled Alison, the young wife, in such a bold, surprising way that when the time comes she will be all his for the asking. She has a body as slim and small as a weasel's, wears bright clothes, and is lickerish of eye,

She sings like a swallow, dances like a kid, and is as skittish as a colt. In other words she is irresistible, and neither young man can wait for the moment he has imagined. The moment will give him less pleasure than he plans, but that is a part of the joke on everybody that this hilarious story was framed to tell. Only Alison escapes without humiliation or pain. The three men bring their troubles on themselves, in a double plot which deserves all the praise it has been given for the ingenuity of its contrivance.

For there are two *fabliaux* here, joined so neatly that one word—"Water!"—can signal the climax for both. At the same instant that the carpenter, aloft in his tub which he has tied to the ceiling in anticipation of a latter-day Noah's flood, hears Nicholas crying for relief of his back-side, which Absalom has burned in revenge for Alison's insulting kiss, he cuts the rope that holds him there and falls and breaks his arm; nor can he get any sympathy from those who listen to his explanation of what he has been doing, for he sounds as crazy as Nicholas says he is—Nicholas, who has persuaded him to take refuge in the tub so that Alison might be enjoyed without interruption; but Absalom does interrupt them twice.

Any summary of the action tends to be longer than the tale itself. Chaucer, who sometimes loved to be long, here chose to be short, and the result is one of his masterpieces. Indeed, it is one of *the* masterpieces, for very few tales have ever been told with such spirit or with such aptness and beauty of detail. Furthermore, the Miller's telling of it gives *him* a satisfaction that he must have thirsted for as he listened to all the fancy business of Palamon and Arcita and Emily—all that talk of love without anybody doing anything about it, all that yearning and mooning and philosophizing to what end? So the Miller must have wondered, boozily, while the Knight held everyone else's attention but after a while lost his. This would have been why he was so insistent upon being second: he would show life as it really is, he would make them all sit up and listen. No courtly love now; back to the barnyard be it.

The Reeve's Tale

Probably the Miller does not know that the Reeve has at one time learned the carpenter's trade—he is now steward of an estate in Norfolk, hence his title—and therefore might be offended by a tale told at the expense of another carpenter, and an old one too. Not that the Reeve is ancient, but *The Prologue* has described him as lean and long-legged and saturnine of countenance, which perhaps is the reason that he always rides hindmost of the troupe and has little to say at any time. Now he refuses to laugh with the rest of the company at the tale the Miller has told, and even breaks into speech about millers in general as men given to ribaldry and abusive talk. It is therefore natural that the host should ask him for a

tale, suspecting him of knowing one about a miller; and sure enough he does, and instantly complies, remarking before he begins:

> *This drunken miller has related here*
> *How was beguiled and fooled a carpenter—*
> *Perchance in scorn of me, for I am one.*
> *So, by your leave, I'll him requite anon;*
> *All in his own boor's language will I speak.*
> *I only pray to God his neck may break.*

His neck, that is to say, rather than merely his arm. The morale of the expedition would seem already to have suffered damage. More damage is to come, but more good feeling too; the unity of the group will never be destroyed.

The Reeve's Tale is another *fabliau,* and a bitterer one as befits the character of the teller; he admits to being an old man who has put love behind him yet recollects the language of it, so that now he can relate how a miller was once repaid for his dishonesty to two students of Cambridge by their making free with his wife and daughter in his own bedroom. It is not known in what form Chaucer read either this *fabliau* or that of the Miller; such stories circulated widely, and everybody knew them; they survive today in many places, often to the private delight of scholars. At any rate Chaucer did know these two, along with two others still to be considered; and it is clear that he enjoyed them, just as it is clear that he knew how to make us do so.

The Reeve's Tale is not merry like the Miller's, but it gets to its point with a like celerity. This miller of Trumpington is not only a snob but a thief, and there is a connection between the two faults: he cheats customers of their grain so that he can become richer and rise high enough in the world to marry his daughter well; the fact that her mother, the miller's wife, is herself the daughter of the village parson, and therefore illegitimate, seems not to trouble him. The two students he has robbed of some of their corn have little more than revenge in mind when they climb in bed with the wife and daughter, just as the Reeve when he tells his tale may have uppermost in his mind the desire to get even with the Miller. Yet there is one touch near the end that renders the whole more human than farce by definition is permitted to be. It is the dialogue between the daughter and Alain the student when he prepares to leave her:

> *Alain grew weary in the grey dawning,*
> *For he had laboured hard through all the night;*
> *And said: "Farewell, now, Maudy, sweet delight!*
> *The day is come, I may no longer bide;*
> *But evermore, whether I walk or ride,*
> *I am your own clerk, so may I have weal."*
> *"Now, sweetheart," said she, "go and fare you well!*

But ere you go, there's one thing I must tell.
When you go walking homeward past the mill,
Right at the entrance, just the door behind,
You shall a loaf of half a bushel find
That was baked up of your own flour, a deal
Of which I helped my father for to steal.
And, darling, may God save you now and keep!"
And with that word she almost had to weep.

That is poetry, and that is Chaucer almost at his best. The daughter is presumably less marriageable now, but she has so lost her heart to Alain that her father and his affairs have ceased to be of consequence to her. Her father may think she has lost everything, but she has the memory of this night.

The Cook's Tale

A third *fabliau* follows, but in so unfinished a state that Chaucer can be supposed to have decided that two were enough, at least just here; though there are other possible reasons why *The Cook's Tale* is merely a fragment. It is a lively beginning, and we shall always wonder about the middle and the end. The irresponsible apprentice, Perkin, gives promise of being a rogue whose fortunes we might be more than willing to follow, though the pilgrim who presents him to us is far from attractive; nobody forgets the running sore on his shin.

The Tale of the Man of Law

In the prologue to his tale the Man of Law complains that a poet named Chaucer has got ahead of him and written most of the stories he might have told, so that he is reduced to telling one in prose—though he then proceeds in verse, and elaborate verse at that, since he uses a seven-line stanza. Our Chaucer, who of course has written the rather condescending words spoken of himself by the Man of Law, is dismissed as a vulgar versifier although a crafty rhymester; he enjoyed such sly pleasantries at his own expense, but in this case he may have had some practical or professional reason for listing numerous works of his own, including the *Legend of Good Women*. The Man of Law gives him credit for only one thing: he never has told stories of incestuous loves, as for example between father and daughter. This has a bearing on the Man of Law's own avoidance of that theme as he writes the life of Constance. Not that Constance has ever been involved in such a relationship, but heroines like her, and there were many of them in the literature of the Middle Ages, sometimes were so cursed. The type as such was an innocent, long-suffering woman

193

falsely accused of hideous deeds and persecuted by her stepmother, her mother-in-law, her father, or someone else close to her, until after long and painful trials she rejoined her family and witnessed the punishment of her enemies. Chaucer took his plot from Nicholas Trivet's prose *Chronicle,* a French work of the early fourteenth century, and perhaps also from the *Confessio Amantis,* a long poem by his contemporary, John Gower.

The story can be recounted briefly. Constance, daughter of the emperor of Rome, goes to marry the sultan of Syria, but at her wedding feast sees all of the guests massacred by order of the sultan's mother because the sultan has become a Christian. As the only survivor she is placed in a ship and sent to sea, where she wanders for years before landing in England on the shores of Northumberland; she eventually marries King Alla—after being cleared of the charge of murdering Dame Hermengild, her savior and dearest friend—and has a male child by him; but the king's mother, who hates her because she is a Christian, intercepts letters between her and Alla and substitutes forgeries that order her banishment by boat; once more she is put to sea, this time with her young son, and it is five years before she reaches Rome again and through a series of miraculous meetings is reunited not only with Alla but with her father, the emperor.

None of this sounds probable, but Chaucer never raises the question, and so the vessel of his verse moves musically on and takes us willingly with it. The terse, tart language of the *fabliaux* is not heard here; his chronicle of Constance returns us to the style that we shall encounter many a time hereafter, especially in *The Clerk's Tale,* where it is even more magical than it is in these stanzas that all but hypnotize us as we read. Yet it does not tire, nor at his best is Chaucer ever tiresome, no matter how long his subject, no matter how strange to us it is. His mind is eternally fresh; he himself seems never to tire; eagerly, confidently, he continues to explore his theme, which it never occurs to him that we shall be less delighted by than he is. There is no more precious gift than this. Shakespeare has it, Cervantes has it, Homer has it, but few others.

Constance herself might be thought to be tiresome after, say, Alison of *The Miller's Tale,* she is so perfect in resignation, so uncomplaining under persecution that continues for years. Yet she is anything but dull, she is never inane; and this is partly because she does not contemplate her own virtue, which indeed she does not seem to know she has, but also because the poet who gives her to us loves her as comic geniuses always love their characters, without sentiment or self-deception. There is no surface comedy in *The Man of Law's Tale,* only an intelligence that never abdicates, a sense of proportion that leaves the outline clear and keen, that keeps the essence of Constance—her patience—steadily before us.

How are we to believe that she could drift on the sea in an open boat for three years, and then again for five? Once more it is pertinent to say that Chaucer does not prompt us to ask the question. To ask it would be to doubt her perfection, and that has already been established. Her perfection is itself a work of art, a sculpture, a strain of music that carries on and on like a single note played forever on some unearthly violin. It is powerful, it is moving, as the fidelity of Shakespeare's later heroines is— Imogen, Hermione, Marina, Miranda—because it is conceived with purity and executed with passion. The final reward for the reader is the eloquence with which Constance after long silence can cry out, as here when she sets sail with her child in the belief that Alla's letter of banishment is genuine. She is addressing the Virgin—"O thou bright Maid, Mary"—in full recognition that there is no comparison between Mary's woe and her own, and yet she calls as one distressed mother to another:

> *"Thou sawest them slay Thy Son before Thine eyes;*
> *And yet lives now my little child, I say!*
> *O Lady bright, to Whom affliction cries,*
> *Thou glory of womanhood, O Thou fair May,*
> *Haven of refuge, bright star of the day,*
> *Pity my child, Who of Thy gentleness*
> *Hast pity on mankind in all distress!*

> *"O little child, alas! What is your guilt,*
> *Who never wrought the smallest sin? Ah me,*
> *Why will your too hard father have you killed?*
> *Have mercy, O dear constable!" cried she,*
> *"And let my little child bide, safe from sea;*
> *And if you dare not save him, lest they blame,*
> *Then kiss him once in his dear father's name!"*

The Tale of the Wife of Bath

Then, however, comes a different kind of woman altogether: in the flesh, as we have seen her in the general *Prologue* to all the tales; in direct address, as we hear her now in her own prologue; and finally in her tale, which is briefer than her prologue because her prologue is about herself, and nothing interests her more than the person, the absolutely astonishing person, she knows very well she is.

The general *Prologue* is known for few things better than for its portrait of her—a housewife from near Bath, somewhat hard of hearing, with teeth set wide apart (a sign of amorousness, she thinks), with a bold, red face and doubtless a vigorous voice; wearing scarlet hose and sharp spurs, around her ample hips an extra skirt, and on her head, which is well swathed with a wimple, a hat "as broad as is a buckler or a targe" (a shield). On Sundays she wears a towering headdress that weighs all of ten pounds, and she will never let any other woman get ahead of her with an offering at church: a sign, some have said, of sinful pride. She has known

many men, both as a girl and later as a wife, for she has been married five times. She has also made numerous pilgrimages: to Italy, to France, to Spain, to Germany, and three times to Jerusalem. She is a great cloth-maker; she laughs a lot as she talks; and she knows everything there is to know about love.

We learn this much from Chaucer in 32 lines, and from the 828 lines of her own prologue we naturally learn volumes more, almost forgetting that Chaucer wrote this too, so close it brings us to the speaker. The Wife of Bath is one of those creations that really are creations, for we cannot see how they are put together, nor can we imagine them as ever having been made merely with words. Here at any rate she is, sitting easily on her nag, dominating the company while she tells them things they wouldn't have supposed anyone could say. She is as far from Constance as any woman could be: she is rank, she is gross, she is willing to call things by their commonest names, she is frank, she is cynical, she is wonderful to see and hear. Her first three husbands were old and rich, and she does not hesitate to say that she wore them out in bed. As for that activity, she refuses to believe that God frowns upon it; otherwise, why did He supply us with organs of generation? It has been the very center of her life, the thing she lived for and the thing she now treasures in her memory.

> *But Lord Christ! When I do remember me*
> *Upon my youth and on my jollity,*
> *It tickles me about my heart's deep root.*
> *To this day does my heart sing in salute*
> *That I have had my world in my own time.*

Her fourth husband, a reveller, was unfaithful to his vows; he kept a paramour. The Wife got even for this by studying all sorts of ways to make him jealous; she took no lover, but she made him think she did, and that was all she wanted; she got him to frying in his own grease.

Well, he died, and then there was Jenkin, once a student at Oxford and still no more than half her age: twenty years against her forty. She married him for love, not money, and was foolish enough to make over all her land to him. They were insatiable lovers, but he developed the unfortunate habit of reading aloud to her books that denounced and defamed all women, from Eve on down. He kept this up until one day she grabbed the book from which he was reading and tore three pages out of

196

it. He retaliated by striking her on the head and knocking her down—the cause of her deafness, she believes—but then he knelt to ask her forgiveness, and in due course she had the upper hand of him; sovereignty, not to speak of house and land, was henceforth hers, not his. The solution was therefore perfect:

> *After that day we never had debate.*

The only trouble was, Jenkin died too, and now the Wife does not deny that she would be willing to wed a sixth husband if one appeared.

The tale she tells, after a passage of words between the Summoner and the Friar—each has at least one story in mind that will discredit the other's profession, but the host will have none of that now, he is all impatience to hear the Wife's tale—contains a theme consistent with the burden of her prologue. It is the theme of sovereignty in love and marriage, and she has no doubt as to which of the sexes deserves to possess that prize. Her tale has its origin in a body of story, amounting almost to a literature in itself, about a "loathly lady" who turns out to be beautiful after all. Chaucer sets it in King Arthur's time, and assigns to one of King Arthur's knights the traditional role of the man who discovers what it is that women most desire.

The knight in question has ravished a maid and is condemned to death for the crime, but at the last moment, at the request of the queen, is given a year of grace in which to find out what it is that women want more than any other thing. He sets out hopefully, but has no luck until he meets with a hideous old hag who promises him, if he will do whatever she asks of him, to supply him with an answer that will save his life. She whispers it in his ear; they go to court together; he repeats the answer:

> *"Women desire to have the sovereignty*
> *As well upon their husband as their love,*
> *And to have mastery their man above."*

No listener denying this, the knight is saved, only to be told now what it is that the hag has in mind for him to do. It is to marry her. Disgusted, he refuses; then, reminded of his vow, he consents, but once in bed with her cannot bear to kiss her as she desires; won by arguments to the effect that beauty is more than skin deep, he finally gives in to her, only to realize that he holds in his arms a damsel supremely fair; and they live happily ever after. The moral is clearly to the Wife of Bath's liking, and no more is said upon the subject.

Dryden's modernization of this tale in his *Fables* begins with a spirit and a grace that he maintains throughout. Perhaps this is the place to show what Chaucer could become in his skillful hands, in his melodious voice. Few translations have ever been more successful than these opening lines of the Wife's tale, amplified to be sure, but nevertheless bewitching in their way:

197

In days of old, when Arthur fill'd the throne,
Whose acts and fame to foreign lands were blown,
The king of elfs and little fairy queen
Gambol'd on heaths, and danc'd on ev'ry green;
And where the jolly troop had led the round,
The grass unbidden rose, and mark'd the ground:
Nor darkling did they dance; the silver light
Of Phoebe serv'd to guide their steps aright,
And, with their tripping pleas'd, prolong'd the night.
Her beams they follow'd, where at full she play'd,
Nor longer than she shed her horns they stay'd,
From thence with airy flight to foreign lands convey'd.
Above the rest our Britain held they dear;
More solemnly they kept their sabbaths here,
And made more spacious rings, and revel'd half the year.
  I speak of ancient times, for now the swain
Returning late may pass the woods in vain,
And never hope to see the nightly train;
In vain the dairy now with mints is dress'd,
The dairymaid expects no fairy guest,
To skim the bowls, and after pay the feast.
She sighs, and shakes her empty shoes in vain,
No silver penny to reward her pain:
For priests with pray'rs, and other godly gear,
Have made the merry goblins disappear;
And where they play'd their merry pranks before,
Have sprinkled holy water on the floor;
And friars that thro' the wealthy regions run,
Thick as the motes that twinkle in the sun,
Resort to farmers rich, and bless their halls,
And exorcise the beds, and cross the walls:
This makes the fairy choirs forsake the place,
When once 'tis hallow'd with the rites of grace.
But in the walks where wicked elves have been,
The learning of the parish now is seen,
The midnight parson, posting o'er the green,
With gown tuck'd up, to wakes, for Sunday next
With humming ale encouraging his text;
Nor wants the holy leer to country girl betwixt.
From fiends and imps he sets the village free,
There haunts not any incubus but he.
The maids and women need no danger fear
To walk by night, and sanctity so near:
For by some haycock, or some shady thorn,
He bids his beads both evensong and morn.

The Friar's Tale and the Summoner's Tale

The Friar and the Summoner, both of whom have been sharply drawn in the general *Prologue* as rogues—and even that is a mild term for them, for Chaucer has spared no effort to make them thoroughly loathsome, the Friar as a cynical travesty upon the original image of the friar, the Summoner as a sneak, an informer, and a pimp, with a hideous complexion in the bargain—now tell their tales, each at the expense of the other, the Friar making it clear that the summoner of his tale is indistinguishable from the devil, and the Summoner bringing the friar of his tale to an ignominious and humiliating defeat. Both tales are unsavory, so that our escape from them into the world of *The Clerk's Tale* is a profound and blessed relief.

The Clerk's Tale

The Clerk of Oxford, who in the general *Prologue* has been said to be as lean as his horse, a sober and scholarly young man not yet provided with a benefice (a living within the Church), more content with his twenty books bound in black and red than he would be with rich robes and gaiety, supposing those things to be available, hopeful only for an opportunity to keep on learning and to teach his Aristotle—this model person, notable for the few words he speaks, and those always sensible, is suddenly asked by the host for a "merry" tale. With great courtesy he declines, explaining that he prefers to entertain the audience, if it will be kind enough to listen, with a tale he learned in Padua, from a learned clerk named Francis Petrarch. He would have added, had he known it, that Petrarch had learned it from Boccaccio, for it is in his *Decameron*. Chaucer's text follows the Latin of Petrarch and the French of an anonymous prose translation of Petrarch—follows them faithfully, except for alterations and additions which make *The Clerk's Tale* one of the most beautiful poems in the world, and one of the most moving. Even the prose of Petrarch is moving—so much so that once a friend to whom its author showed it broke down in tears and had to have the rest of it read aloud to him.

There is a strange power in the story, no matter how it is told, that suggests a folklore, fairy-tale origin, and presumes in Walter the husband and Griselda the wife a supernatural dimension. Both of them are so difficult to believe that they *must* be true, according to the logic that rules the world of popular story; both are monsters perhaps, yet how wonderful it would be if all people existed with their intensity, and acted with their undivided purpose, their unrelenting purity of conviction.

The Wife of Bath, listening as the Clerk recites the tale, undoubtedly says to herself that he is somehow commenting upon the thesis she had developed both in her prologue and in her tale—the thesis that women should be sovereign—and there can scarcely be a question that the Clerk does so intend, and Chaucer for him; if there is a Marriage Group within *The Canterbury Tales,* as much of the criticism maintains, then here we are at the heart of it: the Clerk is presenting a sovereign husband for the Wife to consider, and if the Wife is thinking that she had never contemplated *this* much sovereignty in even the most powerful imaginable woman, then that is the kind of drama that Chaucer may have hoped to develop in the interstices of his work, in the spaces between his tales.

And the tale is told in stanzas like those of *The Man of Law's Tale* and of *Troilus and Criseyde*—that is to say, in stanzas that weep with a sense of their own beauty, that break their own hearts even before they break yours. Again it is true that Chaucer writes without evident humor, though the comic genius he cannot help being proves its presence by the startling reality of these preposterous events: the marriage of Walter, marquis of Saluzzo, to the penniless girl, Griselda, and the series of tests he subsequently makes of her patience and obedience—the taking of her children from her, the having her suppose that they are killed, the announcement after twelve years that she is to be put away in favor of another wife, her submission to this even to the point of returning to the palace as a servant in rags who will wait on her successor, the arrival of the new child-wife with her brother, and the disclosure to Griselda that they are her own children, who all the while have been safe in Bologna.

Many readers have found the sadness unbearable, or else the madness of Walter, if it is madness, unforgivable. Why should a man need so much proof of something that needs no proof? For the sweetness of Griselda is there all the time for us to feel as if we ourselves were the beneficiaries of it; it is created in the very music of the stanzas that describe her, and that tell how she was taken from the house of her old father, Janicula, directly to the palace and established in a luxury that she would never have demanded had she been given ten thousand wishes.

Strangely enough, the sympathy of Chaucer for his heroine—the pity so eloquent, in spite of its never being directly expressed, that it pierces our sides with a like pity—is communicated to us through an intensification of Walter's cruelty, and of the pressures that consequently bear down upon Griselda, rather than upon any effort to relieve the picture of her suffering. It is almost as if Chaucer himself wanted to hurt her more. Whereas he is preparing for the recognition and reconciliation scene that is comparable with any similar scene in Shakespeare's last plays, which is all that needs to be said in praise of it.

> *O young, O dear, O tender children mine*

That one line, spoken by Griselda before she swoons with joy, in the only outburst she permits herself throughout her lengthy trial, is ample evidence of the strength and the sweetness that had grown in Chaucer himself through every moment of his career.

The Merchant's Tale

But so had the strength and the bitterness, testimony to which we turn a single page and find in the savage tale of January and May, the old man and the young wife he never should have married, any more than the old carpenter in *The Miller's Tale* should have married Alison. The depth of Chaucer shows finally in his variety, and impresses us nowhere so much as in the juxtaposition of tales as different from each other as these two. Both have roots in the past of human story, countless analogues to them having been discovered by scholars in the literature of many countries. In the case of *The Merchant's Tale* the root runs back and down to tales of adultery in a fruit tree, usually on the part of a young wife and her young lover, though the special emphasis here on the unloveliness of the old husband is not a necessary ingredient of the fiction. Chaucer's interest was chiefly, it would seem, in January, the meagerness of whose spirit matches the ugliness of his beard and body. He deserves whatever punishment May inflicts upon him for his total inadequacy as a mate. His cynicism precedes hers, and presumably causes it.

And the reader can wonder just what prompted the Merchant, as soon as the Clerk finished his tale, to speak up about his own wife of no more than two months, who is so little like Griselda that it isn't funny. Is she anything like May? Probably not, for she is a shrew, and cruel, yet something drives the Merchant with his forked beard and his Flemish beaver hat to tell this tale which nothing except its cleverness redeems.

The Squire's Tale

And no sooner is that done than the host, who has nothing good to say about his own wife, calls upon the Squire to tell a tale of love, possibly in the hope that the handsome young bachelor, son of that fine gentleman the Knight, will turn the tide of melancholy and bitterness that has flooded in without anyone's particularly desiring it. The Squire, an active youth of twenty or so, a warrior who also likes to play the flute and dance, and who is as fresh as the month of May even though love keeps him awake

all night, who wears dashing clothes and sits well on his horse, obliges with a tale that does indeed brighten the sky: a romantic tale with magic in it. It has never actually suffered by being incomplete, for it breaks off without warning at the beginning of the third part; if anything it benefits by this, sparkling all the more brilliantly as it resembles a diamond that accident has divided. Spenser was moved to continue the tale in his *Faerie Queene,* and Milton, musing in "Il Penseroso" upon the power of old stories to beautify imagination's world, immortalized it in seven lines:

> *Or call up him that left half told*
> *The story of Cambuscan bold,*
> *Of Camball, and of Algarsife,*
> *And who had Canace to wife,*
> *That owned the virtuous ring and glass,*
> *And of the wondrous horse of brass*
> *On which the Tartar king did ride.**

The tale itself is so charming that we can wonder why Chaucer was content to abandon it—unless, to be sure, death cut it off with much else that is missing from the entire work, or unless the poet tired of it, or unless he preferred the truncated form we have. The scene is the court of Cambinskan, a Tartar king whose name may be a corruption of Genghis Khan. It is related that Cambinskan (or Cambuscan, as Milton spelled it) had three children by his queen, Elpheta: two sons, Algarsyf and Cambalo, and a daughter, Canace. Into his palace one day, while a feast was going on, there rode a strange knight astride a steed of brass, holding in his hand a mirror of glass, wearing on his thumb a golden ring, and dangling at his side a naked sword. He explained to Cambinskan that the king of Araby and Ind had sent these gifts by him, and he recited their several virtues: the steed of brass could bear the Tartar king anywhere in the universe he desired to go and could then, at the twisting of a pin, bring him back and set him down unharmed; the mirror could reflect any adversity or treachery that was about to be, and thus forewarn the person who gazed into it; the ring, worn on Canace's thumb, for it was sent specifically to her, could make her understand the language of any bird beneath the heaven; the sword, capable of cutting through the thickest armor, could both kill and cure, for if laid flat against a wound it would heal the wound.

This is familiar stuff of romance—we at once remember the Green Knight who invaded King Arthur's court and astonished all the warriors and ladies there; and indeed every detail of the story is more or less commonplace in tales of the mysterious East. So also with the remarkable things that Canace, wearing the magic ring, hears a peregrine falcon saying in a dead tree far overhead, weeping as she speaks and tearing at her

---

* Cf. *GBWW*, Vol. 32, p. 23.

flesh with her own beak until there is danger of her falling from her perch and dying. What she discloses is that her falcon lover has left her for a kite flying elsewhere in the sky; so now she is "love-lorn without remedy," and does not know what to do except hurt herself as she continues doing. Shortly after this the fragment ends, having contributed to the spectrum of the tales a brilliant patch of color and sound.

The Franklin's Tale

The Franklin, having listened to the Squire, laments aloud the looseness of his own son's life, wasted as it is on dice and other such follies; he is nothing like this excellent young Squire, who though handsome and gay is still courteous and modest, and in no sense a wastrel. The host, impatient for the moment with talk about courtesy, a virtue which perhaps is often overpraised in his opinion, brusquely bids the Franklin get on with his tale without more ado, and the Franklin does so. A franklin was a freeholder or country gentleman, and this specimen of the class represents it at its best; he is, according to the general *Prologue*, white-bearded and ruddy-faced; he loves food and drink, being "Epicurus' very son": he is noted for his hospitality and for the generosity of his table, which is always set; he is fond of partridges; he has a fishpond full of bream and pike; and he requires of his cook that highly seasoned sauces be always available; he has been a sheriff, and he presides at county sessions.

The tale Chaucer gives him to tell is once again from Boccaccio: not this time from the *Decameron,* though it is there too, but from *Il Filocolo.* It is clear that Boccaccio was Chaucer's favorite source for plots, and no wonder, for Boccaccio was an extraordinarily fertile and fascinating story-teller. In this case he was supplemented for Chaucer by Geoffrey of Monmouth's *History of the Kings of England* and a Breton lay which has not been identified, though it is the only source the Franklin says he knows. If there is a Marriage Group among the tales, this can be considered the maturest member of it, though not necessarily the most moving one: that would be either the tale of Griselda or *The Wife of Bath's Tale,* and the first of those would certainly be preferred by most readers. The controversy about whether husband or wife should have the sovereignty in marriage is settled and dismissed as soon as Arviragus and Dorigen decide on matrimony. He volunteers the promise

> *That never in his life, by day or night,*
> *Would he assume a right of mastery*
> *Against her will, nor show her jealousy,*
> *But would obey and do her will in all*
> *As any lover of his lady shall;*
> *Save that the name and show of sovereignty,*
> *Those would he have, lest he shame his degree.*

In another kind of story Arviragus would prove unable to keep his promise; with the best will in the world he would sooner or later become possessive and jealous. But this is not that kind of story, and so not only Arviragus maintains his nobility of mind but Dorigen also never wavers from the position she outlines in an answering speech:

> *She thanked him, and with a great humbleness*
> *She said: "Since, sir, of your own nobleness*
> *You proffer me to have so loose a rein*
> *Would God there never come between us twain,*
> *For any guilt of mine, a war or strife.*
> *Sir, I will be your humble, faithful wife,*
> *Take this as truth till heart break in my breast."*
> *Thus were they both in quiet and in rest.*

So for a year or more their lives pass smoothly and blissfully; then Arviragus, being a knight, crosses the Channel from Brittany where they live to serve awhile at King Arthur's court; and Dorigen misses him so dreadfully that she does nothing but grieve in solitude and brood among other things over the terrible black rocks that line the cliffs of her native peninsula, hating them for their hardness and blackness, and fearing them for the damage they may do to the vessel that will bring Arviragus home. Her friends eventually prevail upon her to be social again, and once at a dance she is told by a squire named Aurelius, a man she has been aware of for two years but has not especially noticed, that he is sick with love for her and will doubtless die unless she gives him herself in the time-honored manner of courtly lovers.

Because she is unable to return his devotion, her only response is playful: she will accept him as her lover provided he causes the black rocks along the coast to disappear. She assumes that this will leave her safe, but Aurelius has a brother who knows a magician in Orleans; the magician is consulted, and for a thousand pounds he offers to remove the rocks. He does so by deep devices and optical illusions which Chaucer does not claim to comprehend, and the rocks do cease to be there. Dorigen, confronted with this fact, is desperate to the point of planning suicide when Arviragus returns from England and she cannot refrain from telling him what has happened. He at once decides that she must carry out her part of the bargain, since truthfulness is the better part of love; and she endeavors to do so, only to be told by Aurelius that the nobility of Arviragus is such that

> *I would myself far rather suffer woe*
> *Than break apart the love between you two.*

So now the only question is how Aurelius shall pay the magician his thousand pounds. He takes half the sum in earnest of the remainder he will get by begging if necessary; but now it is the magician's turn to be magnanimous; he cancels the debt, and the tale is ended. Presumably the rocks reappear, for the magician has not undertaken to remove them for longer than a week. And the Franklin has only one thing to add:

> *Masters, this question would I ask you now:*
> *Which was most generous, do you think, and how?*

The question is not answered by anyone, nor is it a very interesting question, since the virtues of these persons have a certain synthetic quality and therefore are not of the stuff great fiction is made of. In Chaucer's best tales the people are free of Chaucer; they do not take their places in a pattern, a symmetry, that he has arranged; they are free because they are truly created, and the good in them is seldom a thing that they intend, nor is the evil a thing that they either acknowledge or enjoy. *The Franklin's Tale* is expertly told, and it is justly admired, but it has neither tears nor laughter in it, none of the unpremeditated passion, none of the unrehearsed intensity that can make the strongest of us helpless all at once.

The Physician's Tale

The Doctor of Physic, whose portrait in the general *Prologue* is singularly dull, manages to make the tale he takes from Livy's *History of Rome* and from the *Roman de la Rose,* the tale of Appius and Virginius, quite as unimpressive as he himself is. It is at least a grisly fable—Virginius beheads his beautiful young daughter, Virginia, to save her from the corrupt judge, Appius, who has suborned witnesses to swear that the girl is actually his own daughter—but the force of it is lessened by the determination of Virginius to tell Virginia what he is going to do. She pleads for a little time to lament her death as Jephthah's daughter did in the Book of Judges, but Virginius proceeds to strike off her head and carry it by the hair to Appius in court. The conclusion is just enough: Appius, seized by a crowd sympathetic to Virginius, is thrust into a cell where he kills himself, and the false witnesses are hanged.

The story as it stands is probably too short; at any rate it is barren of the interest it ought to have. The host is excited by it and cries out in wrath against so vile a judge as Appius, but he is not listened to. Then, as if he needed relief from pain, he calls upon the Pardoner to tell "some pleasant tale or jest." The other pilgrims say no, for then the Pardoner will be ribald. They would rather have from him "some moral thing." Which he agrees to supply, but first he must think and drink.

The Pardoner's Tale

His tale is both a sermon and a story, the two of them embedded in a confession so outrageous that the pilgrims who listen—and all of them must be supposed to listen, for the speaker has an eloquence from which no one can turn away, even for all the rottenness in it—are silent until the end, when the furious host, moved to obscenity by what he has heard, is so insulting to the Pardoner that no more is spoken by him that day. The whole episode, in the light of the Pardoner's portrait in the general *Prologue,* where Chaucer tells us that he has long, stringy yellow hair, a voice that bleats like a goat, shiny eyes like those of a rabbit, and a perfectly smooth face—no possibility of a beard

("I think he was a gelding or a mare"), though he can sing merrily and loud and talk forever until stopped—is one of the richest things in any literature, one of the most astonishing and memorable. The spectacle of this rogue haranguing a company of strangers with proofs of his own viciousness—he begins by saying he is vicious and rejoices in it—has no parallel in fiction. He is a mountebank, a hypocrite, a liar, and a thief—he hints once that he is also a lecher, though we can doubt that—and he carries a wallet full of religious relics that he offers for sale along with spurious pardons said to come direct from Rome. And just to make sure that all of his talents are appreciated, he preaches a sermon, a specimen sermon, on his favorite text: *Radix malorum est cupiditas,* which we know best in English as "The love of money is the root of all evil."

He preaches against other things than avarice—drunkenness, gambling, gluttony, lust—but avarice is the sin he bears down on. Why? Because he thereby satisfies his own greed for money: the more people he convinces that they should give away their money, the more he gets. He is quite frank about this, and sometimes funny in his frankness, though most of the time he is merely shocking. We never hear what the religious pilgrims think of his exhibition—the Prioress, the Parson in particular—but we do observe at least one reaction to what he has said when at the close we observe that the Knight, gentleman that he is, hushes the host as the host curses the Pardoner, and insists that they kiss each other before they go on, which then they do. There is no better Christian in the company than he who told the tale of Palamon and Arcita.

It is *The Pardoner's Tale,* however, that gives the episode its ultimate distinction. It has been said that no better short story exists, and this could very well be true. What it accomplishes it accomplishes with a celerity that takes the breath. The plague has come to Flanders, and among the wretched people still alive are three young men in a tavern, carousing there as if there were no woe in the world.

> *And as they sat they heard a small bell clink*
> *Before a corpse being carried to his grave.*

Upon asking who has died they learn that he was sitting and drinking in this very place last night when a stranger called Death came by with a spear and clove his heart in two. This stranger Death has been busy everywhere of late; in one village nearby no living souls are left. The three roisterers drunkenly declare war on Death and go forth to find him. They meet an old man near the village whose inhabitants are dead and ask him why he is all wrapped up except for his face. The ancient says it is because he can find no man who will "give his youth in barter for my age," and so he must keep his old age until God chooses to relieve him of it.

> *"Not even Death, alas! my life will take;*
> *Thus restless I my wretched way must make,*
> *And on the ground, which is my mother's gate,*
> *I knock with my staff early, aye, and late,*
> *And cry: 'O my dear mother, let me in!*
> *Lo, how I'm wasted, flesh and blood and skin!*
> *Alas! When shall my bones come to their rest?' "*

The roisterers rudely insist that he tell them where Death is, and he at last does so. Death is up this crooked road, at the foot of an oak tree. They run there, and find not Death but eight bushels of gold florins, which to be sure will be Death to them, but at the moment they do not know this.

They gloat over their treasure for a while; then one of them, realizing that they will attract too much notice if they carry it away now, calls for a drawing of straws to determine which one of them shall go into town for bread and wine to sustain them all until dark. The youngest of them, sent by lot, is no sooner on his way than one of his elders proposes to the other that they murder him on his return so that each of them will have a half instead of a third of the shining treasure. The young one, alone in town, conceives meanwhile a plan whereby he can come into possession of all the treasure. He buys poison, telling the merchant it is for rats, and on the way back to his companions with the bread and wine, puts enough of the poison into two of the bottles to dispose of his friends for good. The three of them are soon victims of that stranger Death whom they had vowed to eliminate.

The tale has a power which defies analysis, especially as Chaucer tells it; for of course he is only retelling it. The old man whose face we never really see, Death whom we only hear about, and the plague that rages even while we read—all three of these, to name no other thing in this country where everything is terrible, take on an almost otherworldly force that is only in part explained by the circumstance that the tale in its outline is one of the most widely distributed narratives ever known. The telling here is by a master, and the sign of his mastery is a terror we feel without being able to assign a cause for it. The irony in the three murders, yes, and the presence of the plague, of course; but some darkness that overhangs this world and renders every inhabitant of it hoarse—that is the element of mystery, the contribution of genius, which we can only recognize before going on.

The Shipman's Tale

The Shipman, represented in the general *Prologue* as a prosperous sea captain who at times can be a bit of a pirate, making the masters of vessels he captures walk the plank, has not too nice a conscience to keep him from telling with relish a *fabliau* tale, known also to Boccaccio in the *Decameron,* of a merchant's wife who cashes in on her sexual charm, to the tune of a hundred marks, first with a monk who makes free with women whenever he pleases, and second with her own husband, elaborately deceived by both churchman and spouse, with no one caring because no money is actually lost. It is a tale of cleverness, cleverly told, and nothing more. The monk in it is like the Monk who goes among the pilgrims: an "outrider," a buyer of supplies for his monastery, a man whose religious function is practical, not spiritual, a lover of hunting, of expensive clothes, of fine horses, of rich food—his specialty is roast swan—and of soft boots; he is bald as glass and his bulging eyes gleam like fire beneath a pot. Perhaps the Shipman thinks all monks are like this one, or may as well be for all he cares.

The Prioress's Tale

The portrait of the Prioress in the general *Prologue* is probably the most famous portrait in that famous gallery. She is smiling, modest, and quiet; she is known as Madam Eglantine, and the French she speaks is not of Paris but of an English nunnery; her table manners are exquisite, and in general her deportment is courtly; sensitive to the pain of others, she will weep if she sees a mouse caught in a trap; she keeps little dogs whom she feeds roasted meat, mild, and fine white bread; she has blue eyes, a small mouth, and a fair, broad forehead; she wears coral beads for ornament, and a gold brooch on which is written *Amor vincit omnia,* "Love conquers all."

This delicate lady tells without hesitation a tale she may have known by heart, and tells it in Chaucerian stanzas that have the quality with which the tale of Constance and the tale of Griselda have already made our ears familiar. The accent of her speech is childlike, perhaps, in its extreme simplicity, but this seems to go with her character as we know it, and possibly excuses a certain obtuseness in her view of the material her

narrative treats. For her tale is of a murder supposedly committed in some Asian city by Jews, and the details of the murder are not nice; neither are the details of the murderers' punishment later on—their bodies are drawn by wild horses and then hanged. But first the crime itself: it is a ritual murder by Jews who cannot bear to hear a seven-year-old Christian choir-boy singing the *Alma redemptoris* antiphon as he walks along the street. They waylay him, cut his throat, and dispose of his body in a privy. However, he refuses to die, or at any rate to stop singing; his voice is heard, he is looked for and found, and even as he is being buried he continues with the miraculous help of the Virgin to sing his song in praise of her.

All this is far from agreeable to contemplate, but the Prioress does not shudder as she proceeds. She seems to take for granted that the myth of the ritual murder is verifiable history, though it is not. And while it might be asking too much of her that she be a critical historian of popular beliefs, yet we remember her daintiness at table and her little dogs of which she is so fond, and we conclude, as perhaps Chaucer did, that the love she celebrated on her brooch was a limited thing. Of course she had never seen a Jew, since Jews had been expelled from England in 1290 and were not readmitted until the seventeenth century, so that Shakespeare never saw one either. In the reign of Richard I, late in the twelfth century, all the Jews of York had either killed themselves and their families or had been massacred by the citizens of York in the royal castle. It is a terrible story, and we do not know what Chaucer thought about it, or of course what the Prioress did. It does appear, however, that Chaucer, whose portrait of the Prioress is gently satirical, may be suggesting that a lady who takes such tender care of her pet animals—in violation, too, of the rules of her Order—might have winced a little more at the spectacle she spreads before us here. Not that her tale is undeserving of its reputation. It is beautifully told, and Matthew Arnold selected one of its lines,

> *O martir, souded to virginitee*

as being by itself "enough to show the charm of Chaucer's verse."* It is perhaps an untranslatable line, but that does not greatly matter. The important thing is how the story moves, is the power of the mother's agony to pierce us once again and the steadfastness of the child that refuses to be silent until he has no further reason not to. And all the while, music as of a mass is sounding.

Chaucer's Tale of Sir Thopas

We may have forgotten that Chaucer himself is one of the pilgrims, so seldom has he mentioned himself. Then suddenly, after the Prioress is

---

* *The Study of Poetry; GGB,* Vol. 5, p. 30.

finished, and after a period of sober silence has passed in contemplation of the miracle she celebrated, the host, ready as always for a change of tone and pace, glances over at Chaucer and says: "What man are you?"

> *"You look as if you tried to find a hare,*
> *For always on the ground I see you stare.*
> *Come near me then, and look up merrily.*
> *Now make way, sirs, and let this man have place;*
>
> . . . .
>
> *Why, he seems absent, by his countenance,*
> *And gossips with no one for dalliance.*
> *Since other folk have spoken, it's your turn;*
> *Tell us a mirthful tale, and that anon."*

Chaucer replies that he has no tale, only a long rhyme he learned long ago; and the host says, "That is good."

But the host doesn't find it very good, for after Chaucer has recited thirty-one stanzas and begun another, he breaks in abruptly, beseeching Chaucer to be done with doggerel, for that is what he thinks of Sir Thopas. He is right; the tale is doggerel; but he does not appreciate it as a parody of many a popular romance that was no sillier than it is. It describes a Flemish knight who dresses himself, goes forth on a grey stallion, is challenged by a giant, and returns to prepare himself for mortal combat —which we never behold because it is then that the host interrupts him. The poem is a piece of literary satire, and very amusing of its kind; but the host is not literary, and neither are the pilgrims, judging by the fact that none of them protests and asks for more. Sir Thopas is a homespun knight who has never seen the inside of a real castle; nor has his poet, who can write:

> *They brought him, first, the sweet, sweet wine,*
> *And mead within a maselyn,*
> *And royal spicery*
> *Of gingerbread that was full fine,*
> *Cumin and licorice, I opine,*
> *And sugar so dainty.*

And what does he draw over his white skin, what garments of finest linen, clean and sheer?

> *His breeches and a shirt.*

Chaucer's Tale of Melibeus

Why not, says the host, a tale in prose that wouldn't waste your time and ours, as this rhyme has? Preferably one with doctrine in it, "good and plain." Chaucer with alacrity says that he does have "a moral tale, right

212

virtuous," with many proverbs in it for good measure. And so we get his excellent version of the tale of the rich man Melibeus and his wife, Prudence, which an Italian judge had written in Latin in the thirteenth century and a Dominican friar had freely translated into French in Chaucer's own century. Chaucer is more faithful to the French text he translates than the friar was to the work of the judge, but even then it is plain how fine a craftsman in prose he was. As for the doctrine, it is unimpeachably wise. Melibeus, injured by three old enemies who in his absence enter his house and beat his wife and grievously wound his daughter, Sophie, does not know how to retaliate; but his wife does—with forgiveness. After long argument he gives in to Prudence, and all parties live in peace thereafter.

The Monk's Tale

The host, after exclaiming that his wife is no such woman as Prudence was, for she is violent and vindictive, turns suddenly to the Monk, tells him to be of good cheer, and remarks that he does not look like a man of religion, a denizen of cloisters. He does not look like a celibate person, and he probably isn't one, the host hints, or at any rate he shouldn't be; he should be a "hen-hopper," and fill the world with his husky, healthy kind. All the vitality of the world seems to have settled in monks, says the host; laymen are feckless and feeble.

Nothing is said about the way the Monk takes all this—the host himself says he isn't serious. And it does appear to be true that the Monk is a conspicuously burly, vital character. Yet all he says is that he intends to keep his promise by telling not one tale but several: of persons who have "stood in great prosperity" but then have fallen into misery and ended their lives wretchedly. In other words, the "falls of princes" will be his theme, as it was the theme of Boccaccio in his *Falls of Illustrious Men* and of other writers whose conception of tragedy, the conception current in medieval times, was that it was nothing but reversal and disaster. The Monk goes on then to rehearse the melancholy fortunes of seventeen persons, from Lucifer to Ugolino, who went from high to low and became legendary in the process.

The Nun's Priest's Tale

"Hold!" cries the Knight. "Good sir, no more of this." Enough of heaviness; now let there be light and life again. The host, agreeing, demands from the nun's priest a tale that will make all their hearts glad; and the priest says he will try.

All readers of Chaucer know that he succeeded, *The Nun's Priest's Tale* is often said to be the high point of all the tales, and certainly it gladdens the heart. Chaucer, for whom it was probably a late work, was never in better form, never in more perfect possession of the comic genius that was his most precious gift. He was never lighter in his touch, never happier in the play of his mind. His scene is a barnyard, but it might just as easily be the world, with a handsome cock and seven hens playing parts that could also be the parts of a human husband and seven wives, so indistinguishable are the species here, and so profound the vanity of Chanticleer. So profound also the practicality of Pertelote his favorite hen, the female who takes no stock in dreams, and who has no sympathy for any male, even her wedded one, if he gives way to fear. But on the fine morning when the story opens, Chanticleer has had in fact a very terrible dream, and it distresses him that Pertelote is not impressed by it. He has dreamed that a strange beast, like a dog yet not a dog, appeared in the barnyard— only appeared there, but that is enough to terrify the cock. Was it a fox? Neither of them says so, but we can suppose they think it.

Pertelote doesn't even believe the beast was there. It was only a dream, an illusion, caused no doubt by vapors, bad secretions, and perhaps plain bile. The cure is a laxative; Chanticleer in her opinion needs to be cleaned out. Which outrages him, for he believes in the efficacy of dreams as fore-tellers of things to come, and to convince her of this he tells her a hair-raising tale of a murdered man who told his friend in a dream where his body would be the next morning: at the gate of the city, in a dung cart. So it was, and the murderers were hanged. He tells other tales, and he reminds her of Daniel, of Joseph, of Croesus who dreamed that he would hang and did, of Pharoah's butler and baker, of Andromache who dreamed of Hector's death which happened the next day.

None of this seems to carry weight with his pretty wife, who is in fact so pretty that he ceases to care about anything except feathering her, which he does twenty times before prime; and is so happy in consequence that he carelessly falls victim to the flattery of a fox (the one he has dreamed of, naturally) that praises his singing, which the fox says is quite the equal of his father's. Will Chanticleer sing for the fox, closing his eyes as his father did and rising on tiptoe and stretching his neck for the max-imum result? Chanticleer does all this, only to be grabbed by the neck and carried away—with all the inhabitants of the barnyard shrieking and whooping in pursuit. It looks bad for Chanticleer, but he thinks of some-thing that saves him. He says to the fox, who now has reached the edge of the woods, that this would be the moment to pause and shout triumphant insults to his pursuers. The fox opens his mouth to do so; Chanticleer flies into a tree; and the tale is done.

The action in it is minor in terms of the space it occupies; most of the tale is talk—digression, if one pleases, but Chaucer is never so happy as when he is digressing, or never so charming. It is his intellect at play, and since his intellect was fine and tireless he is never tedious when he indulges it. On the contrary, he is most alive then, as we his readers are then most alert. "Sir," cries the host when the priest has finished, "for your tale, may blessings on you fall!"

The Second Nun's Tale

Chaucer prefaces this life of Saint Cecilia with a statement in four stanzas of his reason for writing it. He has written it, or rather translated it, to save himself from idleness. It is hard to believe that he was ever idle, or even tempted to be, but confessions to that effect were conventional in the poetry of his time; and so for that matter were saints' lives, of which medieval readers seem never to have tired. Chaucer used the famous *Golden Legend* as his source, and other narratives too; he was seldom content with one original when others were available; he loved to rummage among books for material to reshape. His Saint Cecilia, written in his favorite stanza, tells of a martyrdom in Rome of the third century: Cecilia prefers death by beheading to the sin of sacrifice to the pagan gods. The beheading is botched, so that she suffers long enough to know and even to rejoice that she suffers. A bloody tale it is, encompassing not only Cecilia's death but that of her husband, a Roman whom she has converted, and two other men as well. In later centuries Cecilia became the patron saint of music, celebrated in annual odes; but that was after Chaucer's time.

The Canon's Yeoman's Tale

As the tales approach their end, Chaucer grows more and more interested in the dramatic interludes—if dramatic is the word—that usher the speakers in and out. At this point the most elaborate of them all takes place. At Boughton-under-Blean the company is overtaken by a man in black and his yeoman, or servant, both of whom ride sweaty horses because they have hastened to come where they now are. The man himself, a cleric of some sort, cuts a poor figure in his shabby clothes, and the yeoman is even less impressive. The host, wondering who they are and why they are so excited, learns first from the canon—for that is what his garments show him to be—and then from the yeoman that the two of them have of late

215

been desperate for diversion, and seeing the pilgrims on the road have spurred their horses to catch up. The yeoman, however, goes further than that. Something moves him all at once to blurt out the truth about his master. His master is an alchemist, which is to say, a charlatan, a fraud, and the yeoman is now so disgusted with his performances that he has decided to desert him for good. The canon, listening to this, endeavors to hush his betrayer, but then, the yeoman persisting in his course, mounts his horse and flees away "for very grief and shame."

The tale the yeoman now tells is of the career he has shared with a man who may once have believed that he could convert baser metals into gold but who has latterly been reduced to swindling the credulous and the greedy with mock demonstrations of his skill. Even at that he makes a poor living, and it could still be that alchemy for him is a true science, though the yeoman doubts it, and so do we. The canon himself, of course, is already out of sight for good, so we shall never learn the truth from him. Chaucer, whose interest in the pseudosciences of astrology and alchemy, both popular in his age, was always lively and healthily skeptical, had studied them enough so that in the present case he documents his tale with an immense amount of lore collected by him from numerous sources. His curiosity, never at rest, was seldom busier than it is here.

The Manciple's Tale

The Manciple, by virtue of his office a buyer of supplies for a college, a monastery, one of the inns of court, or some other such institution, precedes the telling of his tale by teasing the Cook because he is drunk, but upon being reprimanded by the host for this, although the host has been doing precisely the same thing, makes amends by giving the Cook still more wine to drink before he begins his tale of Phoebus and his white crow. It seems that Phoebus Apollo once chose to dwell on earth as a mortal man, and to marry a mortal woman with whom he was very much in love. His being a deity in disguise did not provide him with the wisdom to comprehend that no wife ever should be watched lest she be unfaithful. If she is by nature faithful, Chaucer explains, she needs no watching; and if she is by nature false, then no amount of watching will work—she will deceive you whether or no. Apollo's wife, being by nature false, was entertaining a lover one day as the white crow of the house looked on. When Apollo returned home, the

216

crow informed upon his mistress; whereupon Apollo shot her dead with an arrow; but then, reasoning that the crow's being an informer was worse than her being an adulteress had been, he plucked out all the crow's white feathers, replaced them with black ones, and deprived him of his gifts of speech and song, so that he became what all crows after him in the world have been.

The Parson's Tale

The sun is now low in the sky, and the day's end is near. The host, aware of this perhaps because of a touch of chill in the air, a presentiment of shadow, looks over at the Parson and asks him for something jolly—"a fable now, by Cock's dear bones." But the Parson, whom the general *Prologue* has represented as perfect in his calling—sober, responsible, faithful, self-sacrificing, generous, kind, a true shepherd of his flock, in every part of him so good that nobody has ever forgotten this portrait of him, nobody has ever ceased to be moved merely by the recollection of its musical sweet tone, its reverent eloquence—the Parson declines the invitation. If the company, he says, wishes to hear something in which "the moral virtues will appear,"

> *"But if you wish the truth made plain and straight,*
> *A pleasant tale in prose I will relate*
> *To weave our feast together at the end*
> *May Jesus, of His grace, the wit me send*
> *To show you, as we journey this last stage,*
> *The way of that most perfect pilgrimage*
> *To heavenly Jerusalem on high."*

The host, accepting the gentle rebuke, replies:

> *"Say what you wish, and we will gladly hear."*

And adds for only the Parson to hear:

> *"But pray make haste, the sun will soon be down;*
> . . . .
> *And to do well God send to you His grace!"*

The reader is advised to pay particularly close attention to all of the words the Parson has just spoken. For all we know he is willing to agree that stories may contain much truth, though ever since Plato there have been those who doubted that they contain enough, or even any at all; but for the Parson it is better to make the truth "plain and straight," without any admixture of make-believe. So, while he hopes his tale will strike its hearers as a pleasant one, he will tell it in prose; and he will endeavor through it to gather up whatever threads have been left hanging by those who preceded him—whatever meanings, whatever morals, have been left unstated. He will weave all these together at the end of a pilgrimage that he would like his companions to consider as a rehearsal for the perfect one they will sooner or later be making, not to Canterbury, not to any earthly town, but to heaven itself, to "Jerusalem on high."

What follows is not a tale at all, is not a narrative in any sense with which we now are familiar, though if the silence of the pilgrims is any indication of the view they take of its content, it could well be that to the last of them they are interested and respectful. The Miller, the Wife of Bath (yes, that old rip), the Reeve, the lusty Squire, the Monk with his bulging eyes, the wanton Friar, the well-fed Franklin, the delicate Prioress, the loathsome Summoner, and the impossible Pardoner, to name only a few of the listeners, would appear to have been as receptive an audience as the Clerk, the Knight, and the Plowman who had told no tale but who knew how to live in peace and perfect charity, and who loved God most of all but next loved his neighbor even as himself.

Are we to suppose that Chaucer is only pretending that none of this motley crew on horseback protested against the sermon they were offered in place of the jolly fable the host had begun by asking for? At least we hear no protest, and so must assume that the skill of the Parson's rhetoric, the beauty of his poem in prose, the suspense he manages to build up as he discusses penitence and describes the seven deadly sins, and discourses upon contrition and confession, adds up to a masterpiece in its own right, a triumph of language and thought that moves under its own power and establishes its own harmony with the mood Chaucer has chosen to create at the close of his *Canterbury Tales* and indeed of his entire career as a poet and storyteller.

No greater mistake could be made than to suppose that he was merely stuffing into the manuscript at this point a pious nothing that he himself did not take seriously. He was unmistakably serious—as serious as the Parson himself—and we do him no service by denying it. *The Parson's Tale* is sometimes dismissed as dull, but in fact it is exciting. It has a wonderful eloquence which is Chaucer's as well as St. Raymund of Pennaforte's, and as well as that of Guilieumus Peraldus, for Chaucer was putting into English the Latin and the French of those two worthies. *The Canterbury Tales* have been called unfinished; it would be better, as some critics have suggested, to call them incomplete, which manifestly they are in many places; but surely this is the finish that Chaucer was aiming at.

As he looked back over the world of his tales and the people in them, what did he see? His eyes were not our eyes, and so we cannot be certain of what they saw, or at any rate of how they assessed it. The stately Thesëus and the two noble kinsmen Palamon and Arcita; the beautiful lady they both loved and fought to possess; the carpenter's young wife Alison whom two less noble youths found equally attractive; the miller's wife and

daughter whom the Cambridge students made merry with at night; Constance and Griselda whose patience under suffering was almost supernatural and yet we believe it in each case and are powerfully moved; hideous old January and his girl-wife May; Arviragus and Dorigen, those paragons of wedded faith; the three roisterers who almost at the same moment encountered Death; Chanticleer and Pertelote and the fox who was not so canny after all—what do these persons mean, severally or collectively? Do *The Canterbury Tales* have a moral—a single moral—that is plain and straight?

The question is actually embarrassing, so alien it is to the habits and minds most readers, perhaps all readers, have today. And so we tend to dodge it, saying it is not being asked of us. Of whom then *is* it being asked? Of Chaucer, that companionable man with the sophisticated intelligence, the skeptical temper, who makes us so much at home with him as he tells of things both near and far, both ugly and beautiful, both tender and cruel? Is Chaucer probing his own conscience, is he trying to decide whether or not it was well that he wrote what he did write when other things had been possible? And above all, is he asking himself what final difference his stories make? Do they have anything you could call a character? Are they unified in their force, or are they meaninglessly various, are they experiments rather than solutions? Are they, in a word, so many acts of vanity of which in his prime Chaucer might have been proud but for which in these last days of his life, when the sun is low in the sky and will never for him be high again, he should be contrite?

His answer has disturbed and distressed such of his readers as cannot believe he was serious when, rather suddenly they suppose, he added to *The Parson's Tale* an Envoy, a retraction. For in this last utterance he apologizes to Our Lord Jesus Christ because he has written the masterpieces for which posterity adores him. Not just some of the masterpieces but all of them, which he goes ahead and lists, including the Book of Troilus and "The Tales of Canterbury, those that tend toward sin," and certain further writings by him which have not survived save in this mention of their names. Only his pious works, "the translation of Boethius's *de Consolatione,* and other books of legends of saints, and homilies, and of morality and devotion," are recorded here in gratitude, as worthy and not requiring forgiveness.

How is such a statement to be taken? Shall we believe Chaucer, and if we do, what shall we understand him to be saying? That all was vanity, that nothing in these pages means enough? Or shall we regard it as a perfunctory gesture, enjoined by a priest who had charge of him in his last helpless moments? This has been alleged by certain of his readers who allow that he could be serious but doubt that in his right mind he could ever have been as serious as the Envoy on the face of it bids us believe he was. On the other hand, the Envoy does not have the sound of something a man is being forced to say. It seems to be Chaucer's own voice that we hear. And if it is, why on earth is he renouncing his life's work? What should we make of this?

Perhaps we should make of it what we make of Don Quixote's saying to the Bachelor Sampson, when Sampson tries to arouse him from thoughts of death by speaking of new adventures he might undertake: "No more of that, I beseech you. . . . Pray, gentlemen, let us be serious. There's no trifling at a time like this; I must take care of my soul."* Or if such a precedent proves nothing, since Don Quixote may have been mad—was all but universally said to be mad by those who met him, though others who knew him well could doubt that he was—then there are other cases, such as Tolstoy's, who repudiated *Anna Karenina, War and Peace,* and all the rest of his fiction except the tales for children and peasants. Or if Tolstoy proves nothing either, since in his last years he too was strange to say the least, there is Shakespeare, who retired from the stage at forty-eight though he had just written *The Tempest*† and still had four more years to live: four years during which he made no provision for the printing of his plays.

What we should make of such occurrences is the acknowledgement that to any poet as to any man may come a moment when it seems necessary to take into account something greater than any work he happens to have done. And if we acknowledge this, we may be able to perceive how it is—how in so many striking cases it has been—that those whose work is of the highest order, far from being anxious to secure its place, are in the end least concerned about such matters, because they are most capable of seeing beyond them and most interested in coming to terms with what they see. Chaucer himself indicates as much when he tells us in the last sentence we have from him that his renunciation is "so that I may be one of those, at the day of doom, that shall be saved." We must believe he means this, as we must believe that in meaning it he is not diminished but enhanced. For it is only the greatest artists who know how to mean such things. Only those who had everything are willing to be left with nothing in the end. Nothing, that is, except their souls—except their souls, as Hamlet might have said.

---

* Cf. *GBWW*, Vol. 29, p. 427
† *GBWW*, Vol. 27, pp. 524–48.

BIBLIOGRAPHY

The best edition of Chaucer in one volume is *The Works of Geoffrey Chaucer,* edited by F. N. ROBINSON. 1933. 2d ed. Boston: Houghton Mifflin Co., 1957.

Chaucer's Poetry: An Anthology for the Modern Reader, selected and edited by E. T. DONALDSON, is a copious selection with excellent commentaries on all the poems. The text is slightly modernized. New York: Ronald Press Co., 1958.

For scholars, but for readers too, a work of endless interest is *The Text of the Canterbury Tales: Studied on the Basis of all Known Manuscripts,* by JOHN M. MANLY and EDITH RICKERT. 8 vols. 1940. Chicago: University of Chicago Press. This is the nearest that anyone may now come to seeing how *The Canterbury Tales* looked on the page before the invention of printing. The 83 surviving manuscripts, many of them incomplete, are thoroughly described, dated, analyzed, collated, and compared.

A highly readable prose translation of *The Canterbury Tales* is by R. M. LUMIANSKY. New York: Simon & Schuster, 1948.

For anyone interested in the sources of Chaucer's tales, the indispensable work is *Sources and Analogues of Chaucer's Canterbury Tales,* by many hands but collected and edited by W. F. BRYAN and GERMAINE DEMPSTER. 1941. Reprint ed. New York: Humanities Press, 1958.

Of the numerous collections of commentaries on Chaucer, two are especially rewarding:

> *Chaucer Criticism,* vol. 1, *The Canterbury Tales,* edited by RICHARD J. SCHOECK and JEROME TAYLOR. Notre Dame, Ind.: University of Notre Dame Press, 1960.

> *Discussions of the Canterbury Tales,* edited by CHARLES A. OWEN, JR. Boston: D. C. Heath & Co., 1961.

Of the many critical works by individual authors on Chaucer and *The Canterbury Tales,* these are especially recommended:

> *Medieval English Literature,* by W. P. KER. 1912. Rev. ed. London and New York: Oxford University Press, 1969. The final chapter is on Chaucer, but the entire work is illuminating and wise.

> *The Poetry of Chaucer,* by ROBERT KILBURN ROOT. 1900. Rev. ed. Gloucester, Mass.: Peter Smith, 1957.

> *Chaucer and His Poetry,* by GEORGE LYMAN KITTREDGE. Originally published 1915. Cambridge, Mass.: Harvard University Press, 1970.

> *Some New Light on Chaucer,* by JOHN MATTHEWS MANLY. 1926. Reprint. Gloucester, Mass.: Peter Smith, 1959.

> *The Poet Chaucer,* by NEVILL COGHILL. 1949. 2d ed. New York: Oxford University Press, 1967.

> *Chaucer,* by G. K. CHESTERTON. Originally published 1932. New York: Greenwood Press, 1969. The best of them all, because the most like Chaucer.

On Chaucer's times:

> *The Fourteenth Century: 1307–1399.* The Oxford History of England, vol. 5. By MAY McKISACK. New York: Oxford University Press, 1959.

> *Chaucer and His England,* by G. G. COULTON. 1908. 8th ed. London: Methuen & Co., 1963.

> *Chaucer's World.* Compiled by EDITH RICKERT. Edited by CLAIR C. OLSON and MARTIN M. CROW. New York: Columbia University Press, 1948.

> *Geoffrey Chaucer of England,* by MARCHETTE CHUTE. New York: E. P. Dutton & Co., 1946.

Illustration note: The eleven portraits of the Canterbury Pilgrims accompanying this article are from the Ellesmere Manuscript (ca. 1410) of Chaucer's *Canterbury Tales.* This exceptional manuscript (EL 26c 9), now in the Henry E. Huntington Library, San Marino, California, is distinguished by the complete set of illustrations portraying each of the twenty-three Canterbury storytellers. These paintings and the decorated margins are considered the handsomest example of Middle English manuscript illumination. The style of the work suggests that perhaps three or four different artists produced the portraits, yet each portrait closely reflects Chaucer's description in *The Prologue.* Of particular interest is the portrait of Chaucer, which appears on page 225 of this article.

NOTE TO THE READER

The Canterbury Tales is, as its name indicates, a collection of stories; but it is also a poem, or perhaps a collection of poems, which in Chaucer's time meant the same thing. Thus, the reader will find most of the relevant material in the great books cited and discussed in Chapter 69 of the *Syntopicon*, which is concerned with poetry. See especially Topic 4*b*, which deals with tragedy and comedy; Topic 5*a*, which considers the aims of poets (among them Chaucer) to instruct as well as delight; Topics 7*a*, 7*b*, and 7*c*, in which the poetic elements of narrative, plot, and diction are separately considered (there are a number of citations to Chaucer himself in connection with the last of these); and Topic 8*b*, where rules as to poetic language and standards of style are taken up, with numerous references to *The Canterbury Tales.*

Volume 5 of *GGB* contains discussions of poetry and poets by various writers, among them Dr. Johnson, Schiller, Shelley, Arnold, Whitman, and T. S. Eliot. Arnold's comments on Chaucer may be found in his essay "The Study of Poetry," which appears in this volume.

The 1960s witnessed a revival of interest in the idea of rhetoric. It is an idea with a long and sometimes glorious past, as is indicated by its appearance among the 102 ideas into which the *Syntopicon* is divided, but a long time had elapsed since it had excited any intellectual or academic interest. Then in 1958 a two-volume work in French appeared, written by Ch. Perelman and L. Olbrechts-Tyteca and entitled *The New Rhetoric: A Treatise on Argumentation.* More than any single item, this work aroused a renewed interest in the idea, as is attested by the articles, books, journals, and conferences that have been devoted to the book and its thesis.

Chaim Perelman, who is most closely associated with the new rhetoric, is a Professor of Philosophy at the Free University of Brussels and a director of the Center for the Philosophy of Law and the National Center for Logical Research. Born in Warsaw in 1912, he went to Belgium in 1925, where he took a doctorate in law as well as in philosophy at the Free University of Brussels. After war service in Belgium, where he was a leader of the Resistance movement, he returned to the university as Professor of Logic, Ethics, and Metaphysics and began a remarkably productive career. The bibliography of his writings includes some 150 titles, four of which are books translated into English. His work has been widely translated, and he has received honorary degrees from the University of Florence and the Hebrew University of Jerusalem. He is well known in North America, having served as visiting Professor at Pennsylvania State University, the State University of New York at Buffalo, and McGill University.

Chaim Perelman

The New Rhetoric:
A Theory of Practical Reasoning

The Loss of a Humanistic Tradition.—The last two years of secondary education in Belgium used to be called traditionally "Poetry" and "Rhetoric." I still remember that, over forty years ago, I had to study the "Elements of Rhetoric" for a final high-school examination, and I learned more or less by heart the contents of a small manual, the first part of which concerned the syllogism and the second the figures of style. Later, in the university, I took a course of logic which covered, among other things, the analysis of the syllogism. I then learned that logic is a formal discipline that studies the structure of hypothetico-deductive reasoning. Since then I have often wondered what link a professor of rhetoric could possibly discover between the syllogism and the figures of style with their exotic names that are so difficult to remember.

Lack of clarity concerning the idea of rhetoric is also apparent in the article on the subject in the *Encyclopædia Britannica,* where rhetoric is defined as "the use of language as an art based on a body of organized knowledge." But what does this mean? The technique or art of language in general, or only that of literary prose as distinct from poetry? Must rhetoric be conceived of as the art of oratory—that is, as the art of public speaking? The author of the article notes that for Aristotle rhetoric is the art of persuasion. We are further told that the orator's purpose, according to Cicero's definition, is to instruct, to move, and to please. Quintilian sums up this view in his lapidary style as *ars bene dicendi,* the art of speaking well. This phrase can refer either to the efficacy, or the morality, or the beauty of a speech, this ambiguity being both an advantage and a drawback.

For those of us who have been educated in a time when rhetoric has ceased to play an essential part in education, the idea of rhetoric has been definitely associated with the "flowers of rhetoric"—the name used for the figures of style with their learned and incomprehensible names.

Translated from the French by E. Griffin-Collart and O. Bird.

This tradition is represented by two French authors, César Chesneau, sieur Dumarsais, and Pierre Fontanier, who provided the basic texts for teaching what was taken for rhetoric in the eighteenth and nineteenth centuries. The work of Dumarsais, which first appeared in 1730 and enjoyed an enormous success, is entitled *Concerning tropes or the different ways in which one word can be taken in a language*.[1] Fontanier's book, reprinted in 1968 under the title *The figures of discourse,* unites in one volume two works, which appeared respectively in 1821 and 1827, under the titles *A classical manual for the study of tropes* and *Figures other than tropes*.[2]

These works are the outcome of what might be called the stylistic tradition of rhetoric, which was started by Omer Talon, the friend of Petrus Ramus, in his two books on rhetoric published in 1572. The extraordinary influence of Ramus hindered, and to a large extent actually destroyed, the tradition of classical rhetoric that had been developed over the course of twenty centuries and with which are associated the names of such writers as Aristotle, Cicero, Quintilian, and St. Augustine.

For the ancients, rhetoric was the theory of persuasive discourse and included five parts: *inventio, dispositio, elocutio, memoria,* and *actio.* The first part dealt with the art of finding the materials of discourse, especially arguments, by using common or specific *loci*—the *topoi* studied in works which, following Aristotle's example, were called *Topics.** The second part gave advice on the purposive arrangement or order of discourse, the *method,* as the Renaissance humanists called it. The third part dealt mainly with style, the choice of terms and phrases; the fourth with the art of memorizing the speech; while the fifth concerned the art of delivering it.

Ramus also worked for the reform of logic and dialectic along the lines laid down by Rodolphus Agricola in his *De inventione dialectica* (1479) and by the humanists who followed him in seeking to break away from scholastic formalism by restoring the union of eloquence and philosophy advocated by Cicero. This reform consisted essentially in rejecting the classical opposition between science and opinion that had led Aristotle to draw a distinction between analytical and dialectical reasoning—the former dealing with necessary reasonings, the latter with probable ones. Analytical reasoning is the concern of Aristotle's *Analytics,*† dialectical reasoning that of the *Topics, On Sophistical Refutations,* and the *Rhetoric.*‡

Against this distinction, this is what Ramus has to say in his *Dialectic:*

> *Aristotle, or more precisely the exponents of Aristotle's theories, thought that there are two arts of discussion and reasoning, one applying to science and called Logic, the other dealing with opinion and called Dialectic. In this—with all due respect to such great masters—they were greatly mistaken. Indeed these two names, Dia-*

lectic and Logic, generally mean the very same thing, like the words dialegesthai and logizesthai from which they are derived and descended, that is, dispute or reason. . . . Furthermore, although things known are either necessary and scientific, or contingent and a matter of opinion, just as our sight can perceive all colors, both unchanging and changeable, in the same way the art of knowing, that is Dialectic or Logic, is one and the same doctrine of reasoning well about anything whatsoever. . . .[3]

As a result of this rejection, Ramus unites in his *Dialectic* what Aristotle had separated. He divides his work into two parts, one concerning invention, the other judgment. Further, he includes in dialectic parts that were formerly regarded as belonging to rhetoric: the theory of invention or *loci* and that of disposition, called *method*. Memory is considered as merely a reflection of these first two parts, and rhetoric—the "art of speaking well," of "eloquent and ornate language"—includes the study of tropes, of figures of style, and of oratorical delivery, all of which are considered as of lesser importance.

Thus was born the tradition of modern rhetoric, better called stylistic, as the study of techniques of unusual expression. For Fontanier, as we have seen, rhetoric is reduced to the study of figures of style, which he defines as "the more or less remarkable traits and forms, the phrases with a more or less happy turn, by which the expression of ideas, thoughts, and feelings removes the discourse more or less far away from what would have been its simple, common expression."[4]

Rhetoric, on this conception, is essentially an art of expression and, more especially, of literary conventionalized expression; it is an art of style. So it is still regarded by Jean Paulhan in his book *Les fleurs de Tarbes ou la terreur dans les lettres* (1941, but published first as articles in 1936).

The same view of rhetoric was taken in Italy during the Renaissance, despite the success of humanism. Inspired by the Ciceronian ideal of the union of philosophy with eloquence, humanists such as Lorenzo Valla sought to unite dialectic and rhetoric. But they gave definite primacy to rhetoric, thus expressing their revolt against scholastic formalism.

This humanistic tradition continued for over a century and finally produced in the *De principiis* by Mario Nizolio (1553) its most significant work from a philosophical point of view. Less than ten years later, however, in 1562, Francesco Patrizi published in his *Rhetoric* the most violent attack upon this discipline, to which he denied any philosophical interest whatsoever. Giambattista Vico's reaction came late and produced no immediate result. Rhetoric became a wholly formal discipline—any living

* *GBWW*, Vol. 8, pp. 139–223.
† *GBWW*, Vol. 8, pp. 37–137.
‡ *GBWW*, Vol. 8, pp. 139–253; Vol. 9, pp. 585–675.

ideas that it contained being included in Aesthetics.

Germany is one country where classical rhetoric has continued to be carefully studied, especially by scholars such as Friedrich Blass, Wilhelm Kroll, and Friedrich Solmsen, who devoted most of their lives to this study. Yet, even so, rhetoric has been regarded only as the theory of literary prose. Heinrich Lausberg has produced a most remarkable work, which is the best tool in existence for the study of rhetorical terminology and the structure of discourse, and yet in the author's own eyes it is only a contribution to the study of literary language and tradition.[5]

The old tradition of rhetoric has been kept longest in Great Britain— it is still very much alive among Scots jurists—thanks to the importance of psychology in the empiricism of Bacon, Locke, and Hume, and to the influence of the Scottish philosophy of common sense. This tradition, in which the theory of invention is reduced to a minimum and interest is focused on the persuasive aspect of discourse, is represented by such original works as George Campbell's *The Philosophy of Rhetoric* (1776) and Richard Whately's *Elements of Rhetoric* (1828). In this work, Whately, who was a logician, deals with argumentative composition in general and the art of establishing the truth of a proposition so as to convince others, rhetoric being reduced to "a purely managerial or supervisory science."[6] His disciple, the future Cardinal John Henry Newman, applied Whately's ideas to the problems of faith in his *Grammar of Assent* (1870). This outlook still consists in seeing in rhetoric only a theory of expression. It was the view adopted by Ivor Armstrong Richards in his *Principles of Literary Criticism* (published in 1924) and in his *Philosophy of Rhetoric* (1936).

While in Europe rhetoric has been reduced to stylistics and literary criticism, becoming merely a part of the study of literature insofar as it was taught at all, in the United States the appearance of a speech profession brought about a unique development.

Samuel Silas Curry, in a book entitled *The Province of Expression* (1891), was the first to emphasize spoken discourse and its delivery, rather than the composition of literary prose, and to claim autonomy for speech as opposed to written composition. "Expression," as he understood it, did not mean the way in which ideas and feelings are expressed in a literary form, but instead the manner in which they are communicated by means of an art of "delivery." Concern for this element, apparently one of lesser importance, clearly reveals a renewed interest in the audience, and this interest helped to promote the creation of a new "speech profession," separate from the teaching of English and of English literature. Under the influence of William James, James Albert Winans published a volume entitled *Public Speaking* (1915) that firmly established a union between professors of speech and those of psychology. With the cooperation of specialists in ancient and medieval rhetoric, such as

228

Charles S. Baldwin, Harry Caplan, Lane Cooper, Everett Lee Hunt, and Richard McKeon, the whole tradition of classical rhetoric has been re-traced. This study has been continued and further developed in the works of Wilbur Samuel Howell, Donald C. Bryant, Karl R. Wallace, Walter J. Ong, Lloyd F. Bitzer, Douglas Ehninger, and Marie K. Hochmuth. The work of these scholars—the titles of which can be found in the Bibliography that has been regularly published by the *Quarterly Journal of Speech* since 1915—constitutes a unique achievement which is as yet too little known outside the United States.[7]

An ornamental or a practical art?

There is nothing of philosophical interest in a rhetoric that has turned into an art of expression, whether literary or verbal.[8] Hence it is not surprising that the term is missing entirely from both André Lalande's *Vocabulaire technique et critique de la philosophie* and the recent American *Encyclopedia of Philosophy* (1967). In the Western tradition, "Rhetoric" has frequently been identified with verbalism and an empty, unnatural, stilted mode of expression. Rhetoric then becomes the symbol of the most outdated elements in the education of the old regime, the elements that were the most formal, most useless, and most opposed to the needs of an equalitarian, progressive democracy.

This view of rhetoric as declamation—ostentatious and artificial discourse is not a new one. The same view was taken of the rhetoric of the Roman Empire. Once serious matters, both political and judiciary, had been withdrawn from its influence, rhetoric became perforce limited to school exercises, to set speeches treating either a theme of the past or an imaginary situation, but, in any case, one without any real bearing. Serious people, especially the Stoics, made fun of it. Thus Epictetus declares: "But this faculty of speaking and of ornamenting words, if there is indeed any such peculiar faculty, what else does it do, when there happens to be discourse about a thing, than to ornament the words and arrange them as hairdressers do the hair?"*

Aristotle would have disagreed with this conception of rhetoric as an ornamental art bearing the same relation to prose as poetics does to verse. For Aristotle, rhetoric is a practical discipline that aims, not at producing a work of art, but at exerting through speech a persuasive action on an audience. Unfortunately, however, those responsible for the confusion between the two have been able to appeal to Aristotle's own authority because of the misleading analysis he gave of the epideictic or ceremonial form of oratory.

---

* *Discourses* II. 23; *GBWW*, Vol. 12, pp. 170–71.

In his *Rhetoric* Aristotle distinguishes three genres of oratory: deliberative, forensic, and ceremonial. "Political speaking," he writes, "urges us either to do or not to do something: one of these two courses is always taken by private counsellors, as well as by men who address public assemblies. Forensic speaking either attacks or defends somebody: one or other of these two things must always be done by the parties in a case. The ceremonial oratory of display either praises or censures somebody." But whereas the audience is supposed to act as a judge and make a decision concerning either the future (deliberative genre) or the past (forensic genre), in the case of an epideictic discourse the task of the audience consists in judging, not about the matter of discourse, but about the orator's skill.* In political and forensic discourse the subject of the discourse is itself under discussion, and the orator aims at persuading the audience to take part in deciding the matter, but in epideictic discourse the subject—such as, for example, the praise of soldiers who have died for their country—is not at all a matter of debate. Such set speeches were often delivered before large assemblies, as at the Olympic Games, where competition between orators provided a welcome complement to the athletic contests. On such occasions, the only decision that the audience was called upon to make concerned the talent of the orator, by awarding the crown to the victor.

One might well ask how an oratorical genre can be defined by its literary imitation. We know that Cicero, after having lost the suit, rewrote his *Pro Milone* and published it as a literary work. He hoped that by artistically improving the speech, which had failed to convince Milo's judges, he might gain the approbation of lovers of literature. Are those who read this speech long after its practical bearing has disappeared any more than spectators? In that case, all discourses automatically become literature once they cease to exert a persuasive effect, and there is no particular reason to distinguish different genres of oratory. Yet it can be maintained, on the contrary, that the epideictic genre is not only important but essential from an educational point of view, since it too has an effective and distinctive part to play—that, namely, of bringing about a consensus in the minds of the audience regarding the values that are celebrated in the speech.

The moralists rightly satirize the view of epideictic oratory as spectacle. La Bruyère writes derisively of those who "are so deeply moved and touched by Theodorus's sermon that they resolve in their hearts that it is even more beautiful than the last one he preached." And Bossuet, fearful lest the real point of a sermon be missed, exclaims: "You should now be convinced that preachers of the Gospel do not ascend into pulpits to utter empty speeches to be listened to for amusement."[9]

Bossuet here is following St. Augustine's precepts concerning sacred discourse as set forth in the fourth book of his work *On Christian Doc-*

trine. The orator is not content if his listener merely accepts the truth of his words and praises his eloquence, because he wants his full assent:

> *If the truths taught are such that to believe or to know them is enough, to give one's assent implies nothing more than to confess that they are true. When, however, the truth taught is one that must be carried into practice, and that is taught for the very purpose of being practised, it is useless to be persuaded of the truth of what is said, it is useless to be pleased with the manner in which it is said, if it be not so learnt as to be practised. The eloquent divine, then, when he is urging a practical truth, must not only teach so as to give instruction, and please so as to keep up the attention, but he must also sway the mind so as to subdue the will.*

The listener will be persuaded, Augustine also claims,

> *if he be drawn by your promises, and awed by your threats; if he reject what you condemn, and embrace what you commend; if he grieve when you heap up objects for grief, and rejoice when you point out an object for joy; if he pity those whom you present to him as objects of pity, and shrink from those whom you set before him as men to be feared and shunned.*†

The orator's aim in the epideictic genre is not just to gain a passive adherence from his audience but to provoke the action wished for or, at least, to awaken a disposition so to act. This is achieved by forming a community of minds, which Kenneth Burke, who is well aware of the importance of this genre, calls *identification.* As he writes, rhetoric "is rooted in an essential function of language itself, a function that is wholly realistic and is continually born anew; the use of language as a symbolic means of inducing cooperation in beings that by nature respond to symbols."[10] In fact, any persuasive discourse seeks to have an effect on an audience, although the audience may consist of only one person and the discourse be an inward deliberation.

The distinction of the different genres of oratory is highly artificial, as the study of a speech shows. Mark Antony's famous speech in Shakespeare's *Julius Caesar*‡ opens with a funeral eulogy, a typical case of epideictic discourse, and ends by provoking a riot that is clearly political. Its goal is to intensify an adherence to values, to create a disposition to act, and finally to bring people to act. Seen in such perspective, rhetoric becomes a subject of great philosophical interest.

---

* *Rhetoric* I. 1358b 1–13; *GBWW*, Vol. 9, p. 598.
† *On Christian Doctrine* IV. 13, 12; *GBWW*, Vol. 18, p. 684.
‡ Act III, scene ii; *GBWW*, Vol. 26, pp. 584c ff.

Thinking about values

In 1945, when I published my first study of justice,[11] I was completely ignorant of the importance of rhetoric. This study, undertaken in the spirit of logical empiricism, succeeded in showing that *formal justice* is a principle of action, according to which beings of one and the same essential category must be treated in the same way.[12] The application of this principle to actual situations, however, requires criteria to indicate which categories are relevant and how their members should be treated, and such decisions involve a recourse to judgments of value. But on positivistic methods I could not see how such judgments could have any foundation or justification. Indeed, as I entirely accepted the principle that one cannot draw an "ought" from an "is"—a judgment of value from a judgment of fact—I was led inevitably to the conclusion that if justice consists in the systematic implementation of certain value judgments, it does not rest on any rational foundation: "As for the value that is the foundation of the normative system, we cannot subject it to any rational criterion: it is utterly arbitrary and logically indeterminate. . . . The idea of value is, in effect, incompatible both with formal necessity and with experiential universality. There is no value which is not logically arbitrary." [13]

I was deeply dissatisfied with this conclusion, however interesting the analysis, since the philosophical inquiry, carried on within the limits of logical empiricism, could not provide an ideal of practical reason, that is, the establishment of rules and models for reasonable action. By admitting the soundness of Hume's analysis, I found myself in a situation similar to Kant's. If Hume is right in maintaining that empiricism cannot provide a basis for either science or morals, must we not then look to other than empirical methods to justify them? Similarly, if experience and calculation, combined according to the precepts of logical empiricism, leave no place for practical reason and do not enable us to justify our decisions and choices, must we not seek other techniques of reasoning for that purpose? In other words, is there a logic of value judgments that makes it possible for us to reason about values instead of making them depend solely on irrational choices, based on interest, passion, prejudice, and myth? Recent history has shown abundantly the sad excesses to which such an attitude can lead.

Critical investigation of the philosophical literature yielded no satisfactory results. The French logician Edmond Goblot, in his work *La logique des jugements de valeur*,[14] restricted his analysis to derived or instrumental value judgments, that is, to those judgments that use values as a means to already accepted ends, or as obstacles to their attainment. The ends themselves, however, could not be subjected to deliberation unless they were transformed into instrumental values, but such a transformation only pushes further back the problem of ultimate ends.

We thus seem to be faced with two extreme attitudes, neither of which is acceptable: subjectivism, which, as far as values are concerned, leads to skepticism for lack of an intersubjective criterion; or an absolutism founded on intuitionism. In the latter case, judgments of value are assimilated to judgments of a reality that is *sui generis*. In other words, must we choose between A. J. Ayer's view in *Language, Truth, and Logic* and G. E. Moore's view in *Principia Ethica*? Both seem to give a distorted notion of the actual process of deliberation that leads to decision making in practical fields such as politics, law, and morals.

Then too, I agreed with the criticisms made by various types of existentialism against both positivist empiricism and rationalistic idealism, but I could find no satisfaction in their justification of action by purely subjective projects or commitments.

I could see but one way to solve the dilemma to which most currents of contemporary philosophy had led. Instead of working out *a priori* possible structures for a logic of value judgments, might we not do better to follow the method adopted by the German logician Gottlob Frege, who, to cast new light on logic, decided to analyze the reasoning used by mathematicians? Could we not undertake, in the same way, an extensive inquiry into the manner in which the most diverse authors in all fields do in fact reason about values? By analyzing political discourse, the reasons given by judges, the reasoning of moralists, the daily discussions carried on in deliberating about making a choice or reaching a decision or nominating a person, we might be able to trace the actual logic of value judgments which seems continually to elude the grasp of specialists in the theory of knowledge.

For almost ten years Mme L. Olbrechts-Tyteca and I conducted such an inquiry and analysis. We obtained results that neither of us had ever expected. Without either knowing or wishing it, we had rediscovered a part of Aristotelian logic that had been long forgotten or, at any rate, ignored and despised. It was the part dealing with dialectical reasoning, as distinguished from demonstrative reasoning—called by Aristotle *analytics*—which is analyzed at length in the *Rhetoric, Topics,* and *On Sophistical Refutations.* We called this new, or revived, branch of study, devoted to the analysis of informal reasoning, *The New Rhetoric.*[15]

Argumentation and demonstration

The new rhetoric is a theory of argumentation. But the specific part that is played by argumentation could not be fully understood until the modern theory of demonstration—to which it is complementary—had been developed. In its contemporary form, demonstration is a calculation made in accordance with rules that have been laid down beforehand. No recourse is allowed to evidence or to any intuition other than that of the

233

senses. The only requirement is the ability to distinguish signs and to perform operations according to rules. A demonstration is regarded as correct or incorrect according as it conforms, or fails to conform, to the rules. A conclusion is held to be demonstrated if it can be reached by means of a series of correct operations starting from premises accepted as axioms. Whether these axioms be considered as evident, necessary, true, or hypothetical, the relation between them and the demonstrated theorems remains unchanged. To pass from a correct inference to the truth or to the computable probability of the conclusion, one must admit both the truth of the premises and the coherence of the axiomatic system.

The acceptance of these assumptions compels us to abandon pure formalism and to accept certain conventions and to admit the reality of certain models or structures. According to the classical theory of demonstration, which is rejected by formalism, the validity of the deductive method was guaranteed by intuition or evidence—by the natural light of reason. But if we reject such a foundation, we are not compelled to accept formalism. It is still insufficient, since we need good reasons to accept the premises from which we start, and these reasons can be good only for a mind capable of judging them. However, once we have accepted the framework of a formal system and know that it is free from ambiguity, then the demonstrations that can be made within it are compelling and impersonal; in fact, their validity is capable of being controlled mechanically. It is this specific character of formal demonstration that distinguishes it from dialectical reasoning founded on opinion and concerned with contingent realities. Ramus failed to see this distinction and confused the two by using a faulty analogy with the sight of moving and unmoving colors.[16] It is sometimes possible, by resorting to prior arrangements and conventions, to transform an argument into a demonstration of a more or less probabilistic character. It remains true, nonetheless, that we must distinguish carefully between the two types of reasoning if we want to understand properly how they are related.

An argumentation is always addressed by a person called the orator—whether by speech or in writing—to an audience of listeners or readers. It aims at obtaining or reinforcing the adherence of the audience to some thesis, assent to which is hoped for. The new rhetoric, like the old, seeks to persuade or convince, to obtain an adherence which may be *theoretical* to start with, although it may eventually be manifested through a disposition to act, or *practical,* as provoking either immediate action, the making of a decision, or a commitment to act.

Thus argumentation, unlike demonstration, presupposes a meeting of minds: the will on the part of the orator to persuade and not to compel or command, and a disposition on the part of the audience to listen. Such mutual goodwill must not only be general but must also apply to the particular question at issue; it must not be forgotten that all argumentation aims somehow at modifying an existing state of affairs. This is why every society possesses institutions to further discussion between competent persons and to prevent others. Not everybody can start debating about anything whatever, no matter where. To be a man people listen to is a precious quality and is still more necessary as a preliminary condition for an efficacious argumentation.

In some cases there are detailed rules drawn up for establishing this contact before a question can be debated. The main purpose of procedure in civil and criminal law is to ensure a balanced unfolding of the judicial debate. Even in matters where there are no explicit rules for discussion, there are still customs and habits that cannot be disregarded without sufficient reason.

Argumentation also presupposes a means of communicating, a common language. The use of it in a given situation, however, may admit of variation according to the position of the interlocutors. Sometimes only certain persons are entitled to ask questions or to conduct the debate.

From these specifications it is apparent that the new rhetoric cannot tolerate the more or less conventional, and even arbitrary, limitations traditionally imposed upon classical rhetoric. For Aristotle, the similarity between rhetoric and dialectic was all-important.* According to him, they differ only in that dialectic provides us with techniques of discussion for a common search for truth, while rhetoric teaches how to conduct a debate in which various points of view are expressed and the decision is left up to the audience. This distinction shows why dialectic has been traditionally considered as a serious matter by philosophers, whereas rhetoric has been regarded with contempt. Truth, it was held, presided over a dialectical discussion, and the interlocutors had to reach agreement about it by themselves, whereas rhetoric taught only how to present a point of view—that is to say, a partial aspect of the question—and the decision of the issue was left up to a third person.†

It should be noted, however, that for Plato dialectic alone does not attain to metaphysical truth. The latter requires an intuition for which dialectic can only pave the way by eliminating untenable hypotheses.‡ However, truth is the keynote for dialectic, which seeks to get as close to the truth as possible through the discursive method. The rhetorician, on the other hand, is described as trying to outdo his rivals in debate, and, if his judges are gross and ignorant, the triumph of the orator who shows the greatest skill in flattery will by no means always be the victory of the best cause. Plato emphasizes this point strongly in the *Gorgias,* where he shows that the demagogue, to achieve victory, will not hesitate to use techniques unworthy of a philosopher. This criticism gains justi-

---

* See *Rhetoric* I. 1354a 1 6, 1355a 35–37, 1355b 8–10, 1356a 30–35, 1356b 35, 1356b 37–38; *GBWW*, Vol. 9, pp. 593–96.
† Plato, *Republic* I. 348a–b; *GBWW*, Vol. 7, p. 306.
‡ *Republic* 511; *GBWW*, Vol. 7, p. 387. *Seventh Letter* 344b; *GBWW*, Vol. 7, p. 810.

fication from Aristotle's observation, based evidently on Athenian practice, that it belongs to rhetoric "to deal with such matters as we deliberate upon without arts or systems to guide us, in the hearing of persons who cannot take in at a glance a complicated argument, or follow a long chain of reasoning."*

For the new rhetoric, however, argumentation has a wider scope as nonformal reasoning that aims at obtaining or reinforcing the adherence of an audience. It is manifest in discussion as well as in debate, and it matters not whether the aim be the search for truth or the triumph of a cause, and the audience may have any degree of competence. The reason that rhetoric has been deemed unworthy of the philosopher's efforts is not because dialectic employs a technique of questions and answers while rhetoric proceeds by speeches from opposing sides.† It is not this but rather the idea of the unicity of truth that has disqualified rhetoric in the Western philosophical tradition. Thus Descartes declares: "Whenever two men come to opposite decisions about the same matter one of them at least must certainly be in the wrong, and apparently there is not even one of them who knows; for if the reasoning of the second was sound and clear he would be able so to lay it before the other as finally to succeed in convincing *his* understanding also."‡ Both Descartes and Plato hold this idea because of their rejection of opinion, which is variable, and their adoption of an ideal of science based on the model of geometry and mathematical reasoning—the very model according to which the world was supposed to have been created. *Dum Deus calculat, fit mundus* [While God calculates, the world is created] is the conviction not only of Leibniz but of all rationalists.

Things are very different within a tradition that follows a juridical, rather than a mathematical, model. Thus in the tradition of the Talmud, for example, it is accepted that opposed positions can be equally reasonable; one of them does not have to be right. Indeed, "in the Talmud two schools of biblical interpretation are in constant opposition, the school of Hillel and that of Shammai. Rabbi Abba relates that, bothered by these contradictory interpretations of the sacred text, Rabbi Samuel addresses himself to heaven in order to know who speaks the truth. A voice from above answers him that these two theses both expressed the word of the Living God."[17]

So too, for Plato, the subject of discussion is always one for which men possess no techniques for reaching agreement immediately:

> *Suppose for example that you and I, my good friend [Socrates remarks to Euthyphro], differ about a number; do differences of this sort make us enemies and set us at variance with one another? Do we not go at once to arithmetic, and put an end to them by a sum? . . . Or suppose that we differ about magnitudes, do we not*

*quickly end the differences by measuring? . . . And we end a con-
troversy about heavy and light by resorting to a weighing machine?
. . . But what differences are there which cannot be thus decided,
and which therefore make us angry and set us at enmity with one
another? I dare say the answer does not occur to you at the moment,
and therefore I will suggest that these enmities arise when the
matters of difference are the just and unjust, good and evil, honour-
able and dishonourable.§*

When agreement can easily be reached by means of calculation, measuring, or weighing, when a result can be either demonstrated or verified,
nobody would think of resorting to dialectical discussion. The latter
concerns only what cannot be so decided and, especially, disagreements
about values. In fact, in matters of opinion, it is often the case that neither
rhetoric nor dialectic can reconcile all the positions that are taken.

Such is exactly how matters stand in philosophy. The philosopher's
appeal to reason gives no guarantee whatever that everyone will agree
with his point of view. Different philosophies present different points of
view, and it is significant that a historian of pre-Socratic philosophy has
been able to show that the different points of view can be regarded as
antilogies or discourses on opposite sides, in that an antithesis is opposed
in each case to a thesis.[18] One might even wonder with Alexandre Kojève,
the late expert in Hegelian philosophy, whether Hegelian dialectic did not
have its origin, not in Platonic dialectic, but rather in the development of
philosophical systems that can be opposed as thesis to antithesis, followed
by a synthesis of the two. The process is similar to a lawsuit in which the
judge identifies the elements he regards as valid in the claims of the opposed parties. For Kant as well as for Hegel, opinions are supposed to be
excluded from philosophy, which aims at rationality. But to explain the
divergencies that are systematically encountered in the history of philosophy, we need only call these opinions the natural illusions of reason as
submitted to the tribunal of critical reason (as in Kant) or successive
moments in the progress of reason toward Absolute Spirit (as in Hegel).

To reconcile philosophic claims to rationality with the plurality of
philosophic systems, we must recognize that the appeal to reason must
be identified not as an appeal to a single truth but instead as an appeal
for the adherence of an audience, which can be thought of, after the manner of Kant's categorical imperative, as encompassing all reasonable and

---

* *Rhetoric* I. 1357a 1–4; *GBWW*, Vol. 9, p. 596.
† Plato, *Cratylus* 390c; *GBWW*, Vol. 7, pp. 88–89. *Theaetetus* 167d; *GBWW*, Vol. 7, p. 526.
‡ *Rules for the Direction of the Mind; GBWW*, Vol. 31, p. 2.
§ *Euthyphro* 7; *GBWW*, Vol. 7, pp. 193–94.

competent men. The characteristic aspect of philosophical controversy and of the history of philosophy can only be understood if the appeal to reason is conceived as an appeal to an ideal audience—which I call the universal audience—whether embodied in God,* in all reasonable and competent men, in the man deliberating or in an elite.[19] Instead of identifying philosophy with a science, which, on the positivist ideal, could make only analytical judgments, both indisputable and empty, we would do better to abandon the ideal of an apodictic philosophy. We would then have to admit that in the discharge of his specific task, the philosopher has at his disposal only an argumentation that he can endeavor to make as reasonable and systematic as possible without ever being able to make it absolutely compelling or a demonstrative proof. Besides, it is highly unlikely that any reasoning from which we could draw reasons for acting could be conducted under the sign of truth, for these reasons must enable us to justify our actions and decisions. Thus, indirectly, the analysis of philosophical reasoning brings us back to views that are familiar in existentialism.

Audiences display an infinite variety in both extension and competence: in extent, from the audience consisting of a single subject engaged in inward deliberation up to the universal audience; and in competence, from those who know only *loci* up to the specialists who have acquired their knowledge only through a long and painstaking preparation. By thus generalizing the idea of the audience, we can ward off Plato's attack against the rhetoricians for showing greater concern for success than for the truth. To this criticism we can reply that the techniques suited for persuading a crowd in a public place would not be convincing to a better educated and more critical audience, and that the worth of an argumentation is not measured solely by its efficacy but also by the quality of the audience at which it is aimed. Consequently, the idea of a rational argumentation cannot be defined *in abstracto,* since it depends on the historically grounded conception of the universal audience.

The part played by the audience in rhetoric is crucially important, because all argumentation, in aiming to persuade, must be adapted to the audience and, hence, based on beliefs accepted by the audience with such conviction that the rest of the discourse can be securely based upon it. Where this is not the case, one must reinforce adherence to these starting points by means of all available rhetorical techniques before attempting to join the controverted points to them. Indeed, the orator who builds his discourse on premises not accepted by the audience commits a classical fallacy in argumentation—a *petitio principii.* This is not a mistake in formal logic, since formally any proposition implies itself, but it is a mistake in argumentation, because the orator begs the question by presupposing the existence of an adherence that does not exist and to the obtaining of which his efforts should be directed.

The basis of agreement

The objects of agreement on which the orator can build his argument are various. On the one hand, there are facts, truths, and presumptions; on the other, values, hierarchies, and *loci* of the preferable.[20]

Facts and truths can be characterized as objects that are already agreed to by the universal audience, and, hence, there is no need to increase the intensity of adherence to them. If we presuppose the coherence of reality and of our truths taken as a whole, there cannot be any conflict between facts or truths on which we would be called to make a decision. What happens when such a conflict seems to occur is that the incompatible element loses its status and becomes either an illusory fact or an apparent truth, unless we can eliminate the incompatibility by showing that the two apparently incompatible truths apply to different fields. We shall return to this argumentative method later when dealing with the dissociation of ideas.

Presumptions are opinions which need not be proved, although adherence to them can be either reinforced, if necessary, or suppressed by proving the opposite. Legal procedure makes abundant use of presumptions, for which it has worked out refined definitions and elaborate rules for their use.

Values are appealed to in order to influence our choices of action. They supply reasons for preferring one type of behavior to another, although not all would necessarily accept them as good reasons. Indeed, most values are particular in that they are accepted only by a particular group. The values that are called universal can be regarded in so many different ways that their universality is better considered as only an aspiration for agreement, since it disappears as soon as one tries to apply one such value to a concrete situation. For argumentation, it is useful to distinguish concrete values, such as one's country, from abstract values, such as justice and truth. It is characteristic of values that they can become the center of conflict without thereby ceasing to be values. This fact explains how real sacrifice is possible, the object renounced being by no means a mere appearance. For this reason, the effort to reinforce adherence to values is never superfluous. Such an effort is undertaken in epideictic discourse, and, in general, all education also endeavors to make certain values preferred to others.

After values, we find that accepted hierarchies play a part in argumentation. Such, for example, are the superiority of men over animals and of adults over children. We also find double hierarchies as in the case in which we rank behavior in accordance with an accepted ranking of the agents. For this reason, such a statement as "You are behaving like

---

* Plato, *Phaedrus* 273c; *GBWW*, Vol. 7, p. 138.

a beast" is pejorative, whereas an exhortation to "act like a man" calls for more laudable behavior.

Among all the *loci* studied by Aristotle in his *Topics,* we shall consider only those examined in the third book, which we shall call *loci of the preferable.* They are very general propositions, which can serve, at need, to justify values or hierarchies, but which also have as a special characteristic the ability to evaluate complementary aspects of reality. To *loci of quantity,* such as "That which is more lasting is worth more than that which is less so" or "A thing useful for a large number of persons is worth more than one useful for a smaller number," we can oppose *loci of quality,* which set value upon the unique, the irremediable, the opportune, the rare—that is, to what is exceptional instead of to what is normal. By the use of these *loci,* it is possible to describe the difference between the classical and the romantic spirit.[21]

While it establishes a framework for all nonformal reasoning, whatever its nature, its subject, or audience, the new rhetoric does not pretend to supply a list of all the *loci* and common opinions which can serve as starting points for argumentation. It is sufficient to stress that, in all cases, the orator must know the opinion of his audience on all the questions he intends to deal with, the type of arguments and reasons which seem relevant with regard to both subject and audience, what they are likely to consider as a strong or weak argument, and what might arouse them, as well as what would leave them indifferent.

Quintilian, in his *Institutes of Oratory,* points out the advantage of a public-school education for future orators: it puts them on a par and in fellowship with their audience. This advice is sound as regards argumentation on matters requiring no special knowledge. Otherwise, however, it is indispensable for holding an audience to have had a preliminary initiation into the body of ideas to be discussed.

In discussion with a single person or a small group, the establishment of a starting point is very different from before a large group. The particular opinions and convictions needed may have already been expressed previously, and the orator has no reason to believe that his interlocutors have changed their minds. Or he can use the technique of question and answer to set the premises of his argument on firm ground. Socrates proceeded in this way, taking the interlocutor's assent as a sign of the truth of the accepted thesis. Thus Socrates says to Callicles in the *Gorgias:*

> *If you agree with me in an argument about any point, that point will have been sufficiently tested by us, and will not require to be submitted to any further test. For you could not have agreed with me, either from lack of knowledge or from superfluity of modesty, nor yet from a desire to deceive me, for you are my friend, as you tell me yourself. And therefore when you and I are agreed, the result will be the attainment of perfect truth.**

240

It is obvious that such a dialogue is out of the question when one is addressing a numerous assembly. In this case, the discourse must take as premises the presumptions that the orator has learned the audience will accept.[22]

Creating "presence"

What an audience accepts forms a body of opinion, convictions, and commitments that is both vast and indeterminate. From this body the orator must select certain elements on which he focuses attention by endowing them, as it were, with a "presence." This does not mean that the elements left out are entirely ignored, but they are pushed into the background. Such a choice implicitly sets a value on some aspects of reality rather than others. Recall the lovely Chinese story told by Meng-Tseu: "A king sees an ox on its way to sacrifice. He is moved to pity for it and orders that a sheep be used in its place. He confesses he did so because he could see the ox, but not the sheep."[23]

Things present, things near to us in space and time, act directly on our sensibility. The orator's endeavors often consist, however, in bringing to mind things that are not immediately present. Bacon was well aware of this function of eloquence:

> *The affection beholdeth merely the present; reason beholdeth the future and sum of time. And therefore the present filling the imagination more, reason is commonly vanquished; but after that force of eloquence and persuasion hath made things future and remote appear as present, then upon the revolt of the imagination reason prevaileth.*†

To make "things future and remote appear as present," that is, to create presence, calls for special efforts of presentation. For this purpose all kinds of literary techniques and a number of rhetorical figures have been developed. *Hypotyposis* or *demonstratio,* for example, is defined as a figure "which sets things out in such a way that the matter seems to unfold, and the thing to happen, before our very eyes."[24] Obviously, such a figure is highly important as a persuasive factor. In fact, if their argumentative role is disregarded, the study of figures is a useless pastime, a search for strange names for rather farfetched and affected turns of speech. Other figures, such as *repetition, anaphora, amplification, congerie, metabolè, pseudo direct discourse, enallage,* are all various means of increasing the feeling of presence in the audience.[25]

---

* Plato, *Gorgias* 487 d–e; *GBWW*, Vol. 7, p. 273.
† *Advancement of Learning*, Bk. II, xviii, 4; *GBWW*, Vol. 30, p. 67.

In his description of facts, truths, and values, the orator must employ language that takes into account the classifications and valuations implicit in the audience's acceptance of them. For placing his discourse at the level of generality that he considers best adapted to his purpose and his audience, he has at hand a whole arsenal of linguistic categories—substantives, adjectives, verbs, adverbs—and a vocabulary and phrasing that enable him, under the guise of a descriptive narrative, to stress the main elements and indicate which are merely secondary.

In the selection of data and the interpretation and presentation of them, the orator is subject to the accusation of partiality. Indeed, there is no proof that his presentation has not been distorted by a tendentious vision of things. Hence, in law, the legal counsel must reply to the attorney general, while the judge forms an opinion and renders his decision only after hearing both parties. Although his judgment may appear more balanced, it cannot achieve perfect objectivity—which can only be an ideal. Even with the elimination of tendentious views and of errors, one does not thereby reach a perfectly just decision. So too in scientific or technical discourse, where the orator's freedom of choice is less because he cannot depart, without special reason, from the accepted terminology, value judgments are implicit, and their justification resides in the theories, classifications, and methodology that gave birth to the technical terminology. The idea that science consists of nothing but a body of timeless, objective truths has been increasingly challenged in recent years.[26]

The structure of argument

Nonformal argument consists, not of a chain of ideas of which some are derived from others according to accepted rules of inference, but rather of a web formed from all the arguments and all the reasons that combine to achieve the desired result. The purpose of the discourse in general is to bring the audience to the conclusions offered by the orator, starting from premises that they already accept—which is the case unless the orator has been guilty of a *petitio principii*. The argumentative process consists in establishing a link by which acceptance, or adherence, is passed from one element to another, and this end can be reached either by leaving the various elements of the discourse unchanged and associated as they are or by making a dissociation of ideas.

We shall now consider the various types of association and of dissociation that the orator has at his command. To simplify classification, we have grouped the processes of association into three classes: quasi-logical arguments, arguments based upon the structure of the real, and arguments that start from particular cases that are then either generalized or transposed from one sphere of reality to another.[27]

Quasi-logical arguments

These arguments are similar to the formal structures of logic and mathematics. In fact, men apparently first came to an understanding of purely formal proof by submitting quasi-logical arguments, such as many of the _loci_ listed in Aristotle's _Topics,_ to an analysis that yielded precision and formalization. There is a difference of paramount importance between an argument and a formal proof. Instead of using a natural language in which the same word can be used with different meanings, a logical calculus employs an artificial language so constructed that one sign can have only one meaning. In logic, the principle of identity designates a tautology, an indisputable but empty truth, whatever its formulation. But this is not the case in ordinary language. When I say "Business is business," or "Boys will be boys," or "War is war," those hearing the words give preference, not to the univocity of the statement, but to its significant character. They will never take the statements as tautologies, which would make them meaningless, but will look for different plausible interpretations of the same term that will render the whole statement both meaningful and acceptable. Similarly, when faced with a statement that is formally a contradiction—"When two persons do the same thing it is not the same thing," or "We step and we do not step into the same river,"—we look for an interpretation that eliminates the incoherence.

To understand an orator, we must make the effort required to render his discourse coherent and meaningful. This effort requires goodwill and respect for the person who speaks and for what he says. The techniques of formalization make calculation possible, and, as a result, the correctness of the reasoning is capable of mechanical control. This result is not obtained without a certain linguistic rigidity. The language of mathematics is not used for poetry any more than it is used for diplomacy.

Because of its adaptability, ordinary language can always avoid purely formal contradictions. Yet it is not free from incompatibilities, as, for instance, when two norms are recommended which cannot both apply to the same situation. Thus, telling a child not to lie and to obey his parents lays one open to ridicule if the child asks, "What must I do if my father orders me to lie?" When such an antinomy occurs, one seeks for qualifications or amendments—and recommends the primacy of one norm over the other or points out that there are exceptions to the rule. Theoretically, the most elegant way of eliminating an incompatibility is to have recourse to a dissociation of concepts—but of this, more later. Incompatibility is an important element in Socratic irony. By exposing the incompatibility of the answers given to his insidious questions, Socrates compels his interlocutor to abandon certain commonly accepted opinions.

Definitions play a very different role in argumentation from the one they have in a formal system. There they are mostly abbreviations. But in

243

argumentation they determine the choice of one particular meaning over others—sometimes by establishing a relation between an old term and a new one. Definition is regarded as a rhetorical figure—the oratorical definition—when it aims, not at clarifying the meaning of an idea, but at stressing aspects that will produce the persuasive effect that is sought. It is a figure relating to choice: the selection of facts brought to the fore in the definition is unusual because the *definiens* is not serving the purpose of giving the meaning of a term.[28]

Analysis that aims at dividing a concept into all its parts and interpretation that aims at elucidating a text without bringing anything new to it are also quasi-logical arguments and call to mind the principle of identity. This method can give way to figures of speech called *aggregation* and *interpretation* when they serve some purpose other than clarification and tend to reinforce the feeling of presence.[29]

These few examples make it clear that expressions are called figures of style when they display a fixed structure that is easily recognizable and are used for a purpose different from their normal one—this new purpose being mainly one of persuasion. If the figure is so closely interwoven into the argumentation that it appears to be an expression suited to the occasion, it is regarded as an argumentative figure, and its unusual character will often escape notice.

Some reasoning processes—unlike definition or analysis, which aim at complete identification—are content with a partial reduction, that is, with an identification of the main elements. We have an example of this in the rule of justice that equals should be treated equally. If the agents and situations were identical, the application of the rule would take the form of an exact demonstration. As this is never the case, however, a decision will have to be taken about whether the differences are to be disregarded. This is why the recourse to precedent in legal matters is not a completely impersonal procedure but always requires the intervention of a judge.

Arguments of reciprocity are those that claim the same treatment for the antecedent as for the consequent of a relation—buyers-sellers, spectators-actors, etc. These arguments presuppose that the relation is symmetrical. Unseasonable use of them is apt to have comic results, such as the following story, known to have made Kant laugh:

> *At Surat an Englishman is pouring out a bottle of ale which is foaming freely. He asks an Indian who is amazed at the sight what it is that he finds so strange. "What bothers me," replies the native, "isn't what is coming out of the bottle, but how you got it in there in the first place."*

Other quasi-logical arguments take the transitivity of a relation for granted, even though it is only probable: "My friends' friends are my friends." Still other arguments apply to all kinds of other relations such as that between part and whole or between parts, relations of division, comparison, probability. They are clearly distinct from exact demonstration, since, in each case, complementary, nonformal hypotheses are necessary to render the argument compelling.[30]

Appeal to the real

Arguments based on the structure of reality can be divided into two groups according as they establish associations of succession or of coexistence.

Among relations of succession, that of causality plays an essential role. Thus we may be attempting to find the causes of an effect, the means to an end, the consequences of a fact, or to judge an action or a rule by the consequences that it has. This last process might be called the pragmatic argument, since it is typical of utilitarianism in morals and of pragmaticism in general.*

Arguments establishing relations of coexistence are based on the link that unites a person to his actions. When generalized, this argument establishes the relation between the essence and the act, a relation of paramount importance in the social sciences. From this model have come the classification of periods in history (Antiquity, the Middle Ages), all literary classifications (classicism, romanticism), styles (Gothic, baroque), economic or political systems (feudalism, capitalism, fascism), and institutions (marriage, the church).[31] Rhetoric, conceived as the theory of argumentation, provides a guidance for the understanding both of the manner in which these categories were constituted and of the reasons for doing so. It helps us grasp the advantages and the disadvantages of using them and provides an insight into the value judgments that were present, explicitly or implicitly, when they took shape. The specificity of the social sciences can be best understood by considering the methodological reasons justifying the constitution of their categories—Max Weber's *Idealtypus*.

Thanks to the relations of coexistence, we are also able to gain an understanding of the argument from authority in all its shapes as well as an appreciation of the persuasive role of *ethos* in argumentation, since the discourse can be regarded as an act on the orator's part.[32]

Establishing the real

Arguments attempting to establish the structure of reality are first arguments by example, illustration, and model; second, arguments by analogy.

The example leads to the formulation of a rule through generalization

---

* See J. S. Mill, *Utilitarianism; GBWW*, Vol. 43, pp. 443 ff.

from a particular case or through putting a new case on the same footing as an older one. Illustration aims at achieving presence for a rule by illustrating it with a concrete case. The argument from a model justifies an action by showing that it conforms to a model. One should also mention the argument from an antimodel; for example, the drunken Helot to whom the Spartans referred as a foil to show their sons how they should not behave.

In the various religions, God and all divine or quasi-divine persons are obviously preeminent models for their believers. Christian morality can be defined as the imitation of Christ, whereas Buddhist morality consists in imitating Buddha. The models that a culture proposes to its members for imitation provide a convenient way of characterizing it.[33]

The argument from analogy is extremely important in nonformal reasoning. Starting from a relation between two terms A and B, which we call the *theme* since it provides the proper subject matter of the discourse, we can by analogy present its structure or establish its value by relating it to the terms C and D, which constitute the *phoros* of the analogy, so that A is to B as C is to D. Analogy, which derives its name from the Greek word for proportion, is nevertheless different from mathematical proportion. In the latter the characteristic relation of equality is symmetrical, whereas the *phoros* called upon to clarify the structure or establish the value of the *theme* must, as a rule, be better known than the *theme*. When Heraclitus says that in the eyes of God man is as childish as a child is in the eyes of an adult, it is impossible to change the *phoros* for the *theme*, and vice versa, unless the audience is one that knows the relationship between God and man better than that between a child and an adult. It is also worth noting that when *man* is identified with *adult*, the analogy reduces to three terms, the middle one being repeated twice: C is to B as B is to A. This technique of argumentation is typical of Plato, Plotinus, and all those who establish hierarchies within reality.

Within the natural sciences the use of analogy is mainly heuristic, and the intent is ultimately to eliminate the analogy and replace it with a formula of a mathematical type. Things are different, however, in the social sciences and in philosophy, where the whole body of facts under study only offers reasons for or against a particular analogical vision of things.[34] This is one of the differences to which Wilhelm Dilthey refers when he claims that the natural sciences aim at explaining whereas the human sciences seek for understanding.

The metaphor is the figure of style corresponding to the argument from analogy. It consists of a condensed analogy in which one term of the *theme* is associated with one term of the *phoros*. Thus "the morning of life" is a metaphor that summarizes the analogy: Morning is to day what youth is to life. Of course, in the case of a good many metaphors, the reconstruction of the complete analogy is neither easy nor unambiguous. When Berkeley, in his *Dialogues*,[35] speaks of "an ocean of false learning," there are various ways to supply the missing terms of the analogy, each one of which stresses a different relation unexpressed in the metaphor.

The use of analogies and metaphors best reveals the creative and literary aspects of argumentation. For some audiences their use should be avoided as much as possible, whereas for others the lack of them may make the discourse appear too technical and too difficult to follow. Specialists tend to hold analogies in suspicion and use them only to initiate students into their discipline. Scientific popularization makes extensive use of analogy, and only from time to time will the audience be reminded of the danger of identification of *theme* and *phoros*.[36]

The dissociation of ideas

Besides argumentative associations, we must also make room for the dissociation of ideas, the study of which is too often neglected by the rhetorical tradition. Dissociation is the classical solution for incompatibilities that call for an alteration of conventional ways of thinking. Philosophers, by using dissociation, often depart from common sense and form a vision of reality that is free from the contradictions of opinion.[37] The whole of the great metaphysical tradition, from Parmenides to our own day, displays a succession of dissociations where, in each case, reality is opposed to appearance.

Normally, reality is perceived through appearances that are taken as signs referring to it. When, however, appearances are incompatible—an oar in water looks broken but feels straight to the touch—we must admit, if we are to have a coherent picture of reality, that some appearances are illusory and may lead us to error regarding the real. One is thus brought to the construction of a conception of reality that at the same time is capable of being used as a criterion for judging appearances. Whatever is conformable to it is given value, whereas whatever is opposed is denied value and is considered a mere appearance.

Any idea can be subjected to a similar dissociation. To real justice we can oppose apparent justice and with real democracy contrast apparent democracy, or formal or nominal democracy, or quasi democracy, or even "democracy" (in quotes). What is thus referred to as apparent is usually what the audience would normally call justice, democracy, etc. It only becomes apparent after the criterion of real justice or real democracy has been applied to it and reveals the error concealed under the name. The dissociation results in a depreciation of what had until then been an accepted value and in its replacement by another conception to which is accorded the original value. To effect such a depreciation, one will need a conception that can be shown to be valuable, relevant, as well as incompatible with the common use of the same notion.

We may call "philosophical pairs" all sets of notions that are formed

247

on the model of the "appearance-reality" pair. The use of such pairs makes clear how philosophical ideas are developed and also shows how they cannot be dissociated from the process of giving or denying value that is typical of all ontologies. One thus comes to see the importance of argumentative devices in the development of thought, and especially of philosophy.[38]

Interaction of arguments

An argumentation is ordinarily a spoken or written discourse, of variable length, that combines a great number of arguments with the aim of winning the adherence of an audience to one or more theses. These arguments interact within the minds of the audience, reinforcing or weakening each other. They also interact with the arguments of the opponents as well as with those that arise spontaneously in the minds of the audience. This situation gives rise to a number of theoretical questions.

Are there limits, for example, to the number of arguments that can be usefully accumulated? Does the choice of arguments and the scope of the argumentation raise special problems? What is a weak or an irrelevant argument? What is the effect of a weak argument on the whole argumentation? Are there any criteria for assessing the strength or relevance of an argument? Are such matters relative to the audience, or can they be determined objectively?

We have no general answer to such questions. The answer seems to depend on the field of study and on the philosophy that controls its organization. In any case, they are questions that have seldom been raised and that never have received a satisfactory answer. Before any satisfactory answer can be given, it will be necessary to make many detailed studies in the various disciplines, taking account of the most varied audiences.

Once our arguments have been formulated, does it make any difference what order they are presented in? Should one start, or finish, with strong arguments, or do both by putting the weaker arguments in the middle— the so-called Nestorian order? This way of presenting the problem implies that the force of an argument is independent of its place in the discourse. Yet, in fact, the opposite seems to be true, for what appears as a weak argument to one audience often appears as a strong argument to another, depending on whether the presuppositions rejected by one audience are accepted by the other. Should we present our arguments then in the order that lends them the greatest force? If so, there should be a special technique devoted to the organization of a discourse.

Such a technique would have to point out that an exordium is all-important in some cases, while in others it is entirely superfluous. Sometimes the objections of one's opponent ought to be anticipated beforehand

and refuted, whereas in other cases it is better to let the objections arise spontaneously lest one appear to be tearing down straw men.[39]

In all such matters it seems unlikely that any hard-and-fast rules can be laid down, since one must take account of the particular character of the audience, of its evolution during the debate, and of the fact that habits and procedures that prove good in one sphere are no good in another. A general rhetoric cannot be fixed by precepts and rules laid down once for all. But it must be able to adapt itself to the most varied circumstances, matters, and audiences.

Reason and rhetoric

The birth of a new period of culture is marked by an eruption of original ideas and a neglect of methodological concerns and of academic classifications and divisions. Ideas are used with various meanings that the future will distinguish and disentangle. The fundamental ideas of Greek philosophy offer a good example of this process. One of the richest and most confused of all is that expressed by the term *logos,* which means among other things: word, reason, discourse, reasoning, calculation, and all that was later to become the subject of logic and the expression of reason. Reason was opposed to desire and the passions, being regarded as the faculty that ought to govern human behavior in the name of truth and wisdom. The operation of *logos* takes effect either through long speeches or through questions and answers, thus giving rise to the distinction noted above between rhetoric and dialectic, even before logic was established as an autonomous discipline.

Aristotle's discovery of the syllogism and his development of the theory of demonstrative science raised the problem of the relation of syllogistic —the first formal logic—with dialectic and rhetoric. Can any and every form of reasoning be expressed syllogistically? Aristotle is often thought to have aimed at such a result, at least for deductive reasoning, since he was well aware that inductive reasoning and argument by example are entirely different from deduction. He knew too that the dialectical reasoning characteristic of discussion, and essentially critical in purpose, differed widely from demonstrative reasoning deducing from principles the conclusions of a science. Yet he was content to locate the difference in the kind of premises used in the two cases. In analytical, or demonstrative, reasoning, the premises, according to Aristotle, are true and ultimate, or else derived from such premises, whereas in dialectical reasoning the premises consist of generally accepted opinions. The nature of reasoning in both cases was held to be the same, consisting in drawing conclusions from propositions posited as premises *

---

* *Topics* I. 100a 25–32; *GBWW*, Vol. 8, p. 143.

Rhetoric, on the other hand, was supposed to use syllogisms in a peculiar way, by leaving some premises unexpressed and so transforming them into enthymemes. The orator, as Aristotle saw, could not be said to use regular syllogisms; hence, his reasoning was said to consist of abbreviated syllogisms and of arguments from example, corresponding to induction.

What are we to think of this reduction to two forms of reasoning of all the wide variety of arguments that men use in their discussions and in pleading a cause or justifying an action? Yet, since the time of Aristotle, logic has confined its study to deductive and inductive reasoning, as though any argument differing from these was due to the variety of its content and not to its form. As a result, an argument that cannot be reduced to canonical form is regarded as logically valueless. What then about reasoning from analogy? What about the *a fortiori* argument? Must we, in using such arguments, always be able to introduce a fictive unexpressed major premise, so as to make them conform to the syllogism?

It can be shown that the practical reasoning involved in choice or decision making can always be expressed in the form of theoretical reasoning by introducing additional premises. But what is gained by such a move? The reasoning by which new premises are introduced is merely concealed, and resort to these premises appears entirely arbitrary, although in reality it too is the outcome of a decision that can be justified only in an argumentative, and not in a demonstrative, manner.[40]

At first sight, it appears that the main difference between rhetoric and dialectic, according to Aristotle, is that the latter employs impersonal techniques of reasoning, whereas rhetoric relies on the orator's *ethos* (or character) and on the manner in which he appeals to the passions of his audience (or *pathos*).*[41] For Aristotle, however, the *logos* or use of reasoning is the main thing, and he criticizes those authors before him, who laid the emphasis upon oratorical devices designed to arouse the passions. Thus he writes:

> *If the rules for trials which are now laid down in some states—especially in well-governed states—were applied everywhere, such people would have nothing to say. All men, no doubt, think that the laws should prescribe such rules, but some, as in the court of Areopagus, give practical effect to their thoughts and forbid talk about non-essentials. This is sound law and custom. It is not right to pervert the judge by moving him to anger or envy or pity—one might as well warp a carpenter's rule before using it.*

For this reason, after a long discussion devoted to the role of passion in oratorical art, he concludes:

250

> *As a matter of fact, it [rhetoric] is a branch of dialectic and similar to it, as we said at the outset.†*

To sum up, it appears that Aristotle's conception, which is essentially empirical and based on the analysis of the material he had at his disposal, distinguishes dialectic from rhetoric only by the type of audience and, especially, by the nature of the questions examined in practice. His precepts are easy to understand when we keep in mind that he was thinking primarily of the debates held before assemblies of citizens gathered together either to deliberate on political or legal matters or to celebrate some public ceremony. There is no reason, however, why we should not also consider theoretical and, especially, philosophical questions expounded in unbroken discourse. In this case, the techniques Aristotle would have presumably recommended would be those he himself used in his own work, following the golden rule that he laid down in his *Nicomachean Ethics,* that the method used for the examination and exposition of each particular subject must be appropriate to the matter, whatever its manner of presentation.‡

After Aristotle, dialectic became identified with logic as a technique of reasoning, due to the influence of the Stoics. As a result, rhetoric came to be regarded as concerned only with the irrational parts of our being, whether will, the passions, imagination, or the faculty for aesthetic pleasure. Those who, like Seneca and Epictetus, believed that the philosopher's role was to bring man to submit to reason were opposed to rhetoric, even when they used it, in the name of philosophy. Those like Cicero, on the other hand, who thought that in order to induce man to submit to reason one had to have recourse to rhetoric, recommended the union of philosophy and eloquence. The thinkers of the Renaissance followed suit, such as Valla, and Bacon too, who expected rhetoric to act on the imagination to secure the triumph of reason.

The more rationalist thinkers, like Ramus, as we have already noted, considered rhetoric as merely an ornament and insisted on a separation of form and content, the latter alone being thought worthy of a philosopher's attention. Descartes adopted the same conception and reinforced it. He regarded the geometrical method as the only method fit for the sciences as well as for philosophy and opposed rhetoric as exerting an action upon the will contrary to reason—thus adopting the position of the Stoics but with a different methodological justification. But to make room for eloquence within this scheme, we need only deny that reason possesses a monopoly of the approved way of influencing the will. Thus, Pascal, while professing a rationalism in a Cartesian manner, does not

---

* *Rhetoric* I. 1356a 5–18; *GBWW*, Vol. 9, p. 595.
† *Rhetoric* I. 1354a 19–27, 1356a 30–31; *GBWW*, Vol. 9, pp. 593, 595–96.
‡ *Ethics* I. 1094b 12–27; *GBWW*, Vol. 9, pp. 339–40.

hesitate to declare that the truths that are most significant for him—that is, the truths of faith—have to be received by the heart before they can be accepted by reason:

> *We all know that opinions are admitted into the soul through two entrances, which are its chief powers, understanding and will. The more natural entrance is the understanding, for we should never agree to anything but demonstrated truths, but the more usual entrance, although against nature, is the will; for all men whatsoever are almost always led into belief not because a thing is proved but because it is pleasing. This way is low, unworthy, and foreign to our nature. Therefore everybody disavows it. Each of us professes to give his belief and even his love only where he knows it is deserved.*
>
> *I am not speaking here of divine truths, which I am far from bringing under the art of persuasion, for they are infinitely above nature. God alone can put them into the soul, and in whatever way He pleases. I know He has willed they should enter into the mind from the heart and not into the heart from the mind, that He might make humble that proud power of reason. . . .**

To persuade about divine matters, grace is necessary; it will make us love that which religion orders us to love. Yet it is also Pascal's intention to conduce to this result by his eloquence, although he has to admit that he can lay down the precepts of this eloquence only in a very general way:

> *It is apparent that, no matter what we wish to persuade of, we must consider the person concerned, whose mind and heart we must know, what principles he admits, what things he loves, and then observe in the thing in question what relations it has to these admitted principles or to these objects of delight. So that the art of persuasion consists as much in knowing how to please as in knowing how to convince, so much more do men follow caprice than reason.*
>
> *Now of these two, the art of convincing and the art of pleasing, I shall confine myself here to the rules of the first, and to them only in the case where the principles have been granted and are held to unwaveringly; otherwise I do not know whether there would be an art for adjusting the proofs to the inconstancy of our caprices.*
>
> *But the art of pleasing is incomparably more difficult, more subtle, more useful, and more wonderful, and therefore if I do not deal with it, it is because I am not able. Indeed I feel myself*

so unequal to its regulation that I believe it to be a thing impossible.

Not that I do not believe there are as certain rules for pleasing as for demonstrating, and that whoever should be able perfectly to know and to practise them would be as certain to succeed in making himself loved by kings and by every kind of person as in demonstrating the elements of geometry to those who have imagination enough to grasp the hypotheses. But I consider, and it is perhaps my weakness that leads me to think so, that it is impossible to lay hold of the rules.†

Pascal's reaction here with regard to formal rules of rhetoric already heralds romanticism with its reverence for the great orator's genius. But before romanticism held sway, associationist psychology developed in eighteenth-century England. According to the thinkers of this school, feeling, not reason, determines man's behavior, and books on rhetoric were written based on this psychology. The best known of these is Campbell's *The Philosophy of Rhetoric,* noted above.[42] Fifty years later, Whately, following Bacon's lead, defined the subject of logic and of rhetoric as follows:

I remarked in treating of that Science [Logic], that Reasoning may be considered as applicable to two purposes, which I ventured to designate respectively by the terms "Inferring" and "Proving," i.e., the ascertainment of the truth by investigation and the establishment of it to the satisfaction of another; and I there remarked that Bacon, in his Organon, *has laid down rules for the conduct of the former of these processes, and that the latter belongs to the province of Rhetoric; and it was added, that to infer, is to be regarded as the proper office of the Philosopher, or the Judge;—to prove, of the Advocate.*[43]

This conception, while stressing the social importance of rhetoric, makes it a negligible factor for the philosopher. This tendency increases under the influence of Kant and of the German idealists, who boasted of removing all matters of opinion from philosophy, for which only apodictic truths are of any importance.

The relation between the idea that we form of reason and the role assigned to rhetoric is of sufficient importance to deserve studies of all the great thinkers who have said anything about the matter—studies similar to those of Bacon by Prof. Karl Wallace and of Ramus by Prof.

---

* *On Geometrical Demonstration; CPWW, Vol. 88, p. 110.*
† Ibid., p. 441.

Walter J. Ong.[44] In what follows, I would like to sketch how the positivist climate of logical empiricism makes possible a new, or renovated, conception of rhetoric.

Within the perspective of neopositivism, the rational is restricted to what experience and formal logic enable us to verify and demonstrate. As a result, the vast sphere of all that is concerned with action—except for the choice of the most adequate means to reach a designated end—is turned over to the irrational. The very idea of a reasonable decision has no meaning and cannot even be defined satisfactorily with respect to the *whole* action in which it occurs. Logical empiricism has at its disposal no technique of justification except one founded on the theory of probability. But why should one prefer one action to another? Only because it is more efficacious? How can one choose between the various ends that one can aim at? If quantitative measures are the only ones that can be taken into account, the only reasonable decision would seem to be one that is in conformity with utilitarian calculations. If so, all ends would be reduced to a single one of pleasure or utility, and all conflicts of values would be dismissed as based on futile ideologies.

Now if one is not prepared to accept such a limitation to a monism of values in the world of action and would reject such a reduction on the ground that the irreducibility of many values is the basis of our freedom and of our spiritual life; if one considers how justification takes place in the most varied spheres—in politics, morals, law, the social sciences, and, above all, in philosophy—it seems obvious that our intellectual tools cannot all be reduced to formal logic, even when that is enlarged by a theory for the control of induction and the choice of the most efficacious techniques. In this situation, we are compelled to develop a theory of argumentation as an indispensable tool for practical reason.

In such a theory, as we have seen, argumentation is made relative to the adherence of minds, that is, to an audience, whether an individual deliberating or mankind as addressed by the philosopher in his appeal to reason. Whately's distinction between logic, as supplying rules of reasoning for the judge, and rhetoric, providing precepts for the counsel, falls to the ground as being without foundation. Indeed, the counsel's speech that aims at convincing the judge cannot rest on any different kind of reasoning than that which the judge uses himself. The judge, having heard both parties, will be better informed and able to compare the arguments on both sides, but his judgment will contain a justification in no way different in kind from that of the counsel's argumentation. Indeed, the ideal counsel's speech is precisely one that provides the judge with all the information that he needs to state the grounds for his decision.

If rhetoric is regarded as complementary to formal logic and argumentation as complementary to demonstrative proof, it becomes of paramount importance in philosophy, since no philosophic discourse can develop without resorting to it. This became clear when, under the influence of logical empiricism, all philosophy that could not be reduced to calculation was considered as nonsense and of no worth. Philosophy, as a consequence, lost its status in contemporary culture. This situation can be changed only by developing a philosophy and a methodology of the reasonable. For if the rational is restricted to the field of calculation, measuring, and weighing, the reasonable is left with the vast field of all that is not amenable to quantitative and formal techniques. This field, which Plato and Aristotle began to explore by means of dialectical and rhetorical devices, lies open for investigation by the new rhetoric.

Further developments

I introduced the new rhetoric to the public for the first time over twenty years ago, in a lecture delivered in 1949 at the Institut des Hautes Etudes de Belgique.[45] In the course of the same year, the Centre National de Recherches de Logique was founded with the collaboration of the professors of logic in the Belgian universities. In 1953 this group organized an international colloquium on the theory of proof, in which the use and method of proof was studied in the deductive sciences, in the natural sciences, in law, and in philosophy—that is, in the fields where recourse to reasoning is essential.[46] On that occasion Prof. Gilbert Ryle presented his famous paper entitled "Proofs in Philosophy," which claims that there are no proofs in philosophy: "Philosophers do not provide proofs any more than tennis players score goals. Tennis players do not try in vain to score goals. Nor do philosophers try in vain to provide proofs; they are not inefficient or tentative provers. Goals do not belong to tennis, nor proofs to philosophy."[47]

What, then, is philosophical reasoning? What are "philosophical arguments"? According to Ryle, "they are operations not *with* premises and conclusions, but operations *upon* operations with premises and conclusions. In proving something, we are putting propositions through inference-hoops. In some philosophical arguments, we are matching the hoops through which certain batches of propositions will go against a worded recipe declaring what hoops they should go through. Proving is a one-level business; philosophical arguing is, anyhow sometimes, an interlevel business."[48]

If the notion of proof is restricted to the operation of drawing valid inferences, it is undeniable that philosophers and jurists only rarely prove what they assert. Their reasoning, however, does aim at justifying the points that they make, and such reasoning provides an example of the argumentation with which the new rhetoric is concerned.[49]

The part played by argumentation in philosophy has given rise to numerous discussions and to increasing interest, as is shown by the special issue of the *Revue Internationale de Philosophie* of 1961 devoted to the subject, by the colloquium on philosophical argumentation held in Mexico City in 1963,[50] by the collection of studies published by Maurice Natanson and Henry W. Johnstone, Jr., entitled *Philosophy, Rhetoric and Argumentation*,[51] and by the special number of *The Monist* in 1964 on the same subject.

Professor Johnstone has for many years been particularly interested in this topic and has published a book and many papers on it.[52] To further the study of the relation between philosophy and rhetoric, he organized with Prof. Robert T. Oliver, then head of the Speech Department at Pennsylvania State University, a colloquium in which philosophers and members of the speech profession met in equal numbers to discuss the question. The interest aroused by this initiative led to the founding in 1968 of a journal called *Philosophy and Rhetoric*, edited jointly by Professor Johnstone and Prof. Carroll C. Arnold.

That so much attention should be focused on argumentation in philosophical thought cannot be understood unless one appreciates the paramount importance of practical reason—that is, of finding "good reasons" to justify a decision. In 1954 I drew attention to the role of decision in the theory of knowledge,[53] and Gidon Gottlieb further developed it, with particular attention to law, in his book *The Logic of Choice*.[54]

Argumentation concerning decision, choice, and action in general is closely connected with the idea of justification, which also is an important element in the idea of justice. I have attempted to show that the traditional view is mistaken in claiming that justification is like demonstration but based on normative principles.[55] In fact, justification never directly concerns a proposition but looks instead to an attitude, a decision, or an action. "Justifying a proposition" actually consists in justifying one's adherence to it, whether it is a statement capable of verification or an unverifiable norm. A question of justification ordinarily arises only in a situation that has given rise to criticism: no one is called upon to justify behavior that is beyond reproach. Such criticism, however, would be meaningless unless some accepted norm, end, or value had been infringed upon or violated. A decision or an action is criticized on the ground that it is immoral, illegal, unreasonable, or inefficient—that is, it fails to respect certain accepted rules or values. It always occurs within a social context; it is always "situated." Criticism and justification are two forms of argumentation that call for the giving of reasons for or against, and it is these reasons that ultimately enable us to call the action or decision reasonable or unreasonable.

In 1967 a colloquium was held on the subject of demonstration, verification, justification, organized jointly by the Institut International de Philosophie and the Centre National de Recherches de Logique.[56] At that meeting I emphasized the central role of justification in philosophy. Among other things, it enables us to understand the part played by the principle of induction in scientific methodology. Prof. A. J. Ayer claimed that the principle of induction cannot be based on probability theory;[57] yet it did seem possible to give good reasons for using induction as a heuristic principle.[58] But this is only a particular case of the use of justification in philosophy. It is essential wherever practical reason is involved.

In morals, for example, reasoning is neither deductive nor inductive, but justificative. Lucien Lévy-Bruhl, in his famous book *La Morale et la science des moeurs* (1903), criticized the deductive character of much traditional moral philosophy and proposed the conception of the science of morals that made it a sociological discipline, inductive in character. Yet in morals absolute preeminence cannot be given either to principles—which would make morals a deductive discipline—or to the particular case—which would make it an inductive discipline. Instead, judgments regarding particulars are compared with principles, and preference is given to one or the other according to a decision that is reached by resorting to the techniques of justification and argumentation.[59]

The idea of natural law is also misconceived when it is posed in ontological terms. Are there rules of natural law that can be known objectively? Or is positive law entirely arbitrary as embodying the lawmaker's sovereign will? A satisfactory positive answer cannot be given to either question. We know that it is imperative for a lawmaker not to make unreasonable laws; yet we know too that there is no one single manner, objectively given, for making just and reasonable laws. Natural law is better considered as a body of general principles or *loci*, consisting of ideas such as "the nature of things," "the rule of law," and of rules such as "No one is expected to perform impossibilities," "Both sides should be heard"—all of which are capable of being applied in different ways. It is the task of the legislator or judge to decide which of the not unreasonable solutions should become a rule of positive law. Such a view, according to Michel Villey, corresponds to the idea of natural law found in Aristotle and St. Thomas Aquinas—what he calls the classical natural law.[60]

For government to be considered legitimate, to have authority, there must be some way of justifying it. Without some reasonable argumentation for it, political power would be based solely on force. If it is to obtain respect, and not only obedience, and gain the citizens' acceptance, it must have some justification other than force. All political philosophy, in fact, aims at criticizing and justifying claims to the legitimate exercise of power.[61]

Argumentation establishes a link between political philosophy and law and shows that the legislator's activity is not merely an expression of unenlightened will. From lack of such a theory, Hume and Kelsen were right in making a sharp distinction between what is and what ought to be and claiming that no inference can be made from one to the other.

Things take a different outlook, however, when one recognizes the importance of argumentation in supplying good reasons for establishing and interpreting norms. Kelsen's pure theory of the law then loses the main part of its logical justification.[62] The same befalls Alf Ross's realist theory of the law, as has been shown in the remarkable essay by Prof. Stig Jørgensen.[63]

The new rhetoric has also been used to throw new light upon the educator's task, on the analysis of political propaganda, on the process of literary creation, as well as on the reasoning of the historian.[64] But it is in the field of law that it has made the largest impact.[65] Recent studies and colloquia devoted to the logic of law testify to the keen interest that the subject has aroused, especially among French-speaking jurists.[66] The faculty of law at Brussels has just inaugurated a new series of lectures, entitled "Logic and Argumentation."[67]

Lawyers and philosophers working in collaboration have shown that the theory of argumentation can greatly illuminate the nature of legal reasoning. The judge is obliged by law to pass sentence on a case that comes before him. Thus Article 4 of the Code Napoléon declares: "The judge who, under pretext of the silence, the obscurity, or the incompleteness of the law, refuses to pass sentence is liable to prosecution for the denial of justice." He may not limit himself to declaring that there is an antinomy or lacuna in the legal system that he has to apply. He cannot, like the mathematician or formal logician, point out that the system is incoherent or incomplete. He must himself solve the antinomy or fill in the lacuna. Ordinary logic by itself would suffice to show the existence of either an antinomy or a lacuna, but it cannot get him out of the resulting dilemma: only legal logic based on argumentation can accomplish that.

To conclude this general, but far from exhaustive, survey, it is necessary to stress again the import that the new rhetoric is having for philosophy and the study of its history. Twenty years ago, for example, the *Topics* and *Rhetoric* of Aristotle were completely ignored by philosophers, whereas today they are receiving much attention.[68] Renewed interest in this hitherto ignored side of Aristotle has thrown new light upon his entire metaphysics[69] and attached new importance to his notion of *phronesis* or prudence.[70] Renewed attention is being given to the classical rhetoric of Cicero,[71] and we are now gaining a better understanding of the historical development of rhetoric and logic during the Middle Ages and the Renaissance.[72]

It is possible too that the new rhetoric may provoke a reconsideration of the Hegelian conception of dialectic with its thesis and antithesis culminating in a synthesis, which might be compared to a reasonable judge who retains the valid part from antilogies. This new rhetorical perspective may also help us to a better understanding of the American pragmatists, especially of C. S. Peirce, who, in his approximation to Hegel's objective logic, aimed at developing a *rhetorica speculativa*.[73]

For these inquiries to be pursued, however, the theory of argumentation must awaken the interest of philosophers and not merely that of lawyers and members of the speech profession. In a synoptic study of the subject, Professor Johnstone deplores the fact that the theory of argumentation is still little known in the United States, although it is now well known in Europe.[74] Attention has been focused on the problems raised by the use of practical reason, and the field has been explored and mapped by theoreticians and practitioners of the law. There is much that philosophers could learn from this work if they would cease confining their methodological inquiries to what can be accomplished by formal logic and the analysis of language.[75] A more dynamic approach to the problems of language would also reveal the extent to which language, far from being only an instrument for communication, is also a tool for action and is well adapted to such a purpose.[76] It may even prove possible to achieve a synthesis of the different and seemingly opposed tendencies of contemporary philosophy, such as existentialism, pragmaticism, analytical philosophy, and perhaps even a new version of Hegelian and Marxist dialectic.[77]

1 Dumarsais, *Des tropes ou des différents sens dans lesquels on peut prendre un même mot dans une même langue* (1818; reprint ed., Geneva: Slatkine Reprints, 1967).

2 Pierre Fontanier, *Les figures du discours*, ed. Gérard Genette (Paris: Flammarion, 1968).

3 Petrus Ramus, *Dialectic*, 1576 edition, pp. 3–4; also in the critical edition of *Dialectique*, 1555, ed. Michel Dassonville (Geneva: Librairie Droz, 1964), p. 62. Cf. Walter J. Ong, *Ramus: Method, and the Decay of Dialogue* (Cambridge, Mass.: Harvard University Press, 1958).

4 Fontanier, *Les figures du discours*, p. 64. *See also* J. Dubois, F. Edeline, J. M. Klinkenberg, P. Minguet, F. Pire, and H. Trinon, *Rhétorique générale* (Paris: Larousse, 1970).

5 Heinrich Lausberg, *Handbuch der literarischen Rhetorik*, 2 vols. (Munich: M. Hueber, 1960).

6 Douglas Ehninger, ed., Whately's *Elements of Rhetoric* (Carbondale: Southern Illinois University Press, 1963), p. xxvii.

7 Robert T. Oliver and Marvin G. Bauer, eds., *Re-establishing the Speech Profession: The First Fifty Years* (New York: Speech Association of the Eastern States, 1959). *See also* Frederick W. Haberman and James W. Cleary, eds., *Rhetoric and Public Address: A Bibliography, 1947–1961* (Madison: University of Wisconsin Press, 1964). Prof. Carroll C. Arnold of Pennsylvania State University has graciously supplied me the following information: "The statement about the bibliography in *Quarterly Journal of Speech* is not quite correct. The 'Bibliography of Rhetoric and Public Address' first appeared in the *Quarterly Journal of Speech* in 1947 and was published there annually to 1951. From 1952 through 1969, the bibliography was annually published in *Speech Monographs*. As it happens, the bibliography will cease to be published in *Monographs* and, beginning with this year, 1970, will be published in a *Bibliographical Annual*, published by the Speech Association of America. As far as I know, this bibliography remains the only multilingual listing of works (admittedly incomplete) on rhetoric published in the United States."

8 *See* Vasile Florescu, "Retorica si reabilitarea ei in filozofia contemporanea" [Rhetoric and its rehabilitation in contemporary philosophy] in *Studii de istorie a filozofiei universale*, published by the Institute of Philosophy of the Academy of the Socialist Republic of Rumania (Bucharest, 1969), pp. 9–82.

9 Ch. Perelman and L. Olbrechts-Tyteca, *The New Rhetoric*, trans. John Wilkinson and Purcell Weaver (Notre Dame, Ind.: University of Notre Dame Press, 1969), p. 50. French edition: *La nouvelle rhétorique* (Paris: Presses universitaires de France, 1958).

10 Kenneth Burke, *A Rhetoric of Motives* (New York: Prentice-Hall, 1950), p. 43.

11 Ch. Perelman, *The Idea of Justice and the Problem of Argument*, trans. John Petrie (New York: Humanities Press, 1963), pp. 1–60.

12 Ibid., p. 16.

13 Ibid., pp. 56–57.

14 Edmond Goblot, *La logique des jugements de valeur* (Paris: Colin, 1927).

15 Perelman and Olbrechts-Tyteca, *The New Rhetoric*. *See also* Olbrechts-Tyteca, "Rencontre avec la rhétorique," in *La théorie de l'argumentation*, Centre Nationale de Recherches de Logique (Louvain: Editions Nauwelaerts, 1963), 1, pp. 3–18 (reproduces nos. 21–24 of *Logique et Analyse*).

16 This identification is faulty, as dialectical reasoning can no more than commonplaces (*topoi*) be reduced to formal calculation. Cf. Otto Bird, "The Tradition of the Logical Topics: Aristotle to Ockham," *Journal of the History of Ideas* 23 (1962): 307–23.

17 *Babylonian Talmud, Seder Mo'ed* 2, 'Erubin 136 (ed. Epstein). Cf. Ch. Perelman, "What the Philosopher May Learn from the Study of Law," *Natural Law Forum* 11 (1966): 3–4; idem, "Désaccord et rationalité des décisions," in *Droit, morale et philosophie* (Paris: Librairie générale de droit et de jurisprudence, 1968), pp. 103–10.

18 *See* Clémence Ramnoux, "Le développement antilogique des écoles grecques avant Socrate," in *La dialectique* (Paris: Presses universitaires de France, 1969), pp. 40–47.

19 Perelman and Olbrechts-Tyteca, *The New Rhetoric*, §§ 6–9.

20 Ibid., §§ 15–27.

21 Ch. Perelman and L. Olbrechts-Tyteca, "Classicisme et Romantisme dans l'argumentation," *Revue Internationale de Philosophie*, 1958, pp. 47–57.

22 Perelman and Olbrechts-Tyteca, *The New Rhetoric*, p. 104.

23 Ibid., p. 116.

24 *Rhetorica ad Herennium* 4. 68.

25 Perelman and Olbrechts-Tyteca, *The New Rhetoric*, § 42.

26 To mention only a few works besides Thomas Kuhn's *The Structure of Scientific Revolutions* (Chicago, Ill.: University of Chicago Press, 1962), there is Michael Polanyi's fascinating work significantly entitled *Personal Knowledge* (London: Routledge & Kegan Paul, 1958). The social, persuasive, nay, the rhetorical aspect, of scientific methodology was stressed by the physicist John Ziman in his brilliant book *Public Knowledge* (London: Cambridge University Press, 1968). The latter is dedicated to the late Norwood Russell Hanson, whose *Patterns of Discovery* (London: Cambridge University Press, 1958), and *The Concept of the Positron* (London: Cambridge University Press, 1963), gave much weight to the new ideas.

27 Perelman and Olbrechts-Tyteca, *The New Rhetoric*, §§ 45–88.

28 Ibid., pp. 172–73.

29 Ibid., p. 176.

30 Ibid., §§ 45–59.

31 Ch. Perelman, ed., *Les catégories en histoire* (Brussels: Editions de l'Institut de Sociologie, 1969).

32 Perelman and Olbrechts-Tyteca, *The New Rhetoric*, §§ 60–74.

33 Ibid., §§ 78–81.

34 Ch. Perelman, "Analogie et métaphore en science, poésie, et philosophie," *Revue Internationale de Philosophie*, 1969, pp. 3–15; *see also* Hans Blumenberg, *Paradigmen zu einer Metaphorologie* (Bonn: H. Bouvier, 1960), and Enzo Melandri, *La linea e il circolo: Studio logico-filosofico sull'analogia* (Bologna: Il Mulino, 1968).

35 George Berkeley, *Works*, 2 vols. (London, 1843), 2:259.

36 Perelman and Olbrechts-Tyteca, *The New Rhetoric*, §§ 82–88.

37 Ch. Perelman, "Le réel commun et le réel philosophique," in *Etudes sur l'histoire de la philosophie, en hommage à Martial Guéroult* (Paris: Fischbacher, 1964) pp 127–38.

38 Perelman and Olbrechts-Tyteca, *The New Rhetoric*, §§ 89–92.

39 Ibid., §§ 97–105.

40 Ch. Perelman, "Le raisonnement pratique," in *Contemporary Philosophy*, ed. Raymond Klibansky (Florence: La Nuova Italia, 1968–), 1:168–76.

41 *See* Paul I. Rosenthal, "The Concept of Ethos and the Structure of Persuasion," *Speech Monographs*, 1966, pp. 114–26.

42 Cf. V. M. Bevilacqua, "Philosophical Origins of George Campbell's Philosophy of Rhetoric," *Speech Monographs*, 1965, pp. 1–12; and Lloyd F. Bitzer, "Hume's Philosophy in George Campbell's Philosophy of Rhetoric," *Philosophy and Rhetoric*, 1969, pp. 139–66.

43 Whately, *Elements of Rhetoric* (1828), pp. 6–7.

44 Karl Wallace, *Francis Bacon on Communication and Rhetoric* (Chapel Hill: University of North Carolina Press, 1943); and Ong, *Ramus: Method, and the Decay of Dialogue*.

45 It was published in 1950 in the *Revue Philosophique de la France et de l'Etranger* under the title "Logique et Rhétorique," 75th year, pp. 1–35, and reprinted in Ch. Perelman and L. Olbrechts-Tyteca, *Rhétorique et philosophie* (Paris: Presses universitaires de France, 1952), pp. 1–48.

46 The *Proceedings* appeared in the *Revue Internationale de Philosophie*, 1954, 27–28.

47 Gilbert Ryle, "Proofs in Philosophy," *Revue Internationale de Philosophie*, 1954, p. 150.

48 Ibid., p. 156.

49 See in this respect Perelman and Olbrechts-Tyteca, *Rhétorique et philosophie*, especially "La quête du rationnel," and "De la preuve en philosophie." The latter was published in English in the *Hibbert Journal* 52 (1954): 354–59. The same theme was dealt with more fully in the articles "Self-evidence and Proof," published in Perelman,

The Idea of Justice and the Problem of Argument, pp. 109–24; and "Self-evidence in Metaphysics," *International Philosophical Quarterly*, 1964, pp. 1–19.

50 Reports published in the *Symposium Sobre la Argumentación Filosofica*, Mexico, 1963.

51 Maurice Natanson and Henry W. Johnstone, Jr., eds., *Philosophy, Rhetoric and Argumentation* (University Park: Pennsylvania State University Press, 1965). *See also* Stanislaw Kaminski, "Argumentacja filozoficzna w ujeciu analytikow" [The philosophic argumentation in the conception of the analysts] in *Rozprawy Filozoficzne* (Toruń Poland: TNT, 1969), pp. 127–42.

52 Henry W. Johnstone, Jr., *Philosophy and Argument* (University Park: Pennsylvania State University Press, 1959); idem, "Philosophy and Argumentum ad Hominem," *Journal of Philosophy* 49 (1952): 489–98; idem, "The Methods of Philosophical Polemic," *Methodos* 5 (1953): 131–40; idem, "New Outlooks on Controversy," *Review of Metaphysics* 12 (1958): 57–67; idem, "Can Philosophical Arguments Be Valid," *Bucknell Review* 11 (1963): 89–98; idem, "Self-refutation and Validity," *The Monist*, 1964, pp. 467–85.

53 Perelman, *The Idea of Justice and the Problem of Argument*, pp. 88–97.

54 Gidon Gottlieb, *The Logic of Choice* (London: George Allen & Unwin, 1968).

55 See Ch. Perelman, "Jugements de valeur, justification et argumentation," *Revue Internationale de Philosophie*, 1961, 11, 327–35; reprinted in Perelman, *Justice et raison* (Brussels: Presses universitaires de Bruxelles, 1963). Also in Perelman, *Justice* (New York: Random House, 1967), chap. 4.

56 *Entretiens de Liège* (Louvain: Nauwelaerts, 1968).

57 A. J. Ayer, "Induction and the Calculus of Probabilities," in *Entretiens de Liège*, pp. 95–108.

58 Cf. Ch. Perelman, "Synthèse finale," in *Entretiens de Liège*, pp. 338–40.

59 See "Jugement moral et principes moraux," and "Scepticisme moral et philosophie morale," in Perelman, *Droit, morale et philosophie*.

60 Michel Villey, *Leçons d'histoire de la philosophie du droit* (Paris: Dalloz, 1957), and, especially, "Questions de logique juridique dans l'histoire de la philosophie du droit," in *Etudes de Logique Juridique* 2, Centre National de Recherches de Logique (Brussels: Bruylant, 1967), pp. 3–22.

61 Ch. Perelman, "Autorité, idéologie et violence," in *Annales de l'Institut de Philosophie de l'Université Libre de Bruxelles* (Brussels: Editions de l'Institut de Sociologie, 1969), pp. 9–20.

62 Ch. Perelman, "La théorie pure du droit et l'argumentation," in *Law, State, and International Legal Order: Essays in Honor of Hans Kelsen*, ed. Salo Engel and Rudolf A. Métall (Knoxville: University of Tennessee Press, 1964), pp. 225–32.

63 "Argumentation and Decision," in *Festkrift Alf Ross*, ed. Mogens Blegvad, Max Sørenson, and Isi Foighel (Copenhagen: Juristforbundets Förlaget, 1969), pp. 261–84 (with numerous bibliographical notes).

64 Max Loreau, "Rhetoric as the Logic of the Behavioral Sciences," trans. Lloyd I. Watkins and Paul D. Brandes, *Quarterly Journal of Speech*, 1965, pp. 455–63; Otto Pöggeler, "Dialektik und Topik," in *Hermeneutik und Dialektik*, ed. J. C. B. Mohr (Tübingen, Germany, 1970), 2:273–310. Cf. "Education et rhétorique," in Perelman, *Justice et raison*, pp. 104–17; and B. Gillemain, "Raison et rhétorique, les techniques de l'argumentation et la pédagogie," *Revue de l'Enseignement Philosophique*, 1960, (3), 1961, (2); Paolo Facchi, ed., *La propaganda politica in Italia* (Bologna: Società editrice il Mulino, 1960). Also, Renato Barilli, *Poetica e retorica* (Milan, 1969); Ch. Perelman, ed., *Raisonnement et démarches de l'historien*, 2d ed. (Brussels: Editions de l'Institut de Sociologie, 1965); and Giulio Preti, *Retorica e logica* (Turin: G. Einaudi, 1968).

65 Edgar Bodenheimer, "A Neglected Theory of Legal Reasoning," *Journal of Legal Education*, 1969, pp. 373–402.

A. H. Campbell, "On Forgetting One's Law," *The Journal of the Society of Public Teachers of Law*, London, 1963.

George G. Christie, "Objectivity in the Law," *Yale Law Journal*, 1963, pp. 1311–50.

Per Olaf Ekelöf, "Topik und jura," in *Universitetet och forskningen* [University and science], ed. Birger Lindskog (Uppsala, 1968), pp. 207–24. The author also refers to Stephen E. Toulmin's *The Uses of Argument* (London: Cambridge University Press, 1958), in which Toulmin develops a theory of topics without referring to rhetoric or even to the idea of an audience.

Alessandro Giuliani, *Il concetto di prova: Contributo alla logica giuridica* (Milan: A. Giuffrè, 1961); idem, "L'élément juridique dans la logique médiévale," in *La théorie de l'argumentation* (*see* note 15), pp. 540–90; idem, "Influence of Rhetoric on the Law of Evidence and Pleading," *The Juridical Review*, 1969; idem, "La logique juridique comme théorie de la controverse," *Archives de Philosophie du Droit*, 1966, pp. 87–113; idem, *La controversia, Contributo alla logica giuridica* (Pavia, Italy: Pubblicazioni della Università di Pavia, 1966).

Graham Hughes, "Rules, Policy and Decision-Making," in *Law, Reason, and Justice: Essays in Legal Philosophy,* ed. Graham Hughes (New York: New York University Press, 1969), pp. 101–35.

Luis Recaséns-Siches, *La lógica de los problemas humanos* (Mexico: Dianoia, 1964), pp. 3–34. "The Logic of the Reasonable as Differentiated from the Logic of the Rational," in *Essays in Jurisprudence in Honor of Roscoe Pound,* ed. Ralph A. Newman (Indianapolis, Ind.: Bobbs-Merrill Co., 1962).

Julius Stone, *Legal System and Lawyers' Reasonings* (London: Stevens & Sons, 1964), pp. 325–37.

Ilmar Tammelo, "The Law of Nations and the Rhetorical Tradition of Legal Reasoning," in *Indian Yearbook of International Affairs* (Madras: Diocesan Press, 1964), pp. 227–58.

Renato Treves, "Metaphysics and Methodology in the Philosophy of Law," in Hughes, *Law, Reason, and Justice,* pp. 235–54.

Theodor Viehweg, *Topik und Jurisprudenz* (Munich: Beck-Verlag, 1963), and his introduction to the German edition of my studies on justice, *Die Gerechtigkeit* (Munich: Beck-Verlag, 1967).

Franz Wieacker, "Zur praktischen Leistung der Rechtsdogmatik," in Mohr, *Hermeneutik und Dialektik,* 2:311–36.

George Wróblewski, "Legal Reasonings in Legal Interpretation," in *Etudes de Logique Juridique* 3 (Brussels: Bruylant, 1969), pp. 3–31.

66 *See* the volume of the *Archives de Philosophie du Droit* of 1961 devoted to the logic of law; the colloquium of Toulouse on legal logic, *Annales de la Faculté de Droit de Toulouse,* 1967, fasc. I; that of the *Instituts d'Etudes Judiciaires de Paris,* 1967, of which the Proceedings appeared under the title *La logique judiciaire* (Paris: Presses universitaires de France, 1969). The next Congress of the International Association for Legal Philosophy, which will be held in Brussels in 1971, will deal with the same theme.

67 *See* Ch. Perelman, "Droit, logique et argumentation," *Revue de l'Université de Bruxelles,* 1968, pp. 387–98. The works produced by the legal section of the Centre National de Recherches de Logique have undeniably brought a remarkable contribution to a renewed outlook of the whole subject (*see* A. Bayart, "Le Centre National Belge de Recherches de Logique," *Archives de Philosophie du Droit,* 1968, pp. 171–80; and Paul Foriers, "L'état des recherches de logique juridique en Belgique," in *Etudes de Logique Juridique* 2, pp. 23–42). Besides numerous articles written by members and of which several appeared in the *Journal des Tribunaux,* Brussels, the Center has published, since 1961, three large volumes, respectively entitled *Le fait et le droit* (Brussels: Bruylant, 1961), *Les antinomies en droit* (Brussels: Bruylant, 1965), and *Le problème des lacunes en droit* (Brussels: Bruylant, 1968).

68 We will mention, in this respect, W. A. de Pater's thesis *Les topiques d'Aristote et la dialectique platonicienne,* Etudes Thomistiques, vol. 10 (Fribourg: Editions St. Paul, 1965), as well as the fact that the 3rd Symposium Aristotelicum of Oxford has been entirely devoted to the *Topics* (G. E. L. Owen, ed., *Aristotle on Dialectic* [Oxford: Clarendon Press, 1968]).

69 Pierre Aubenque, *Le problème de l'être chez Aristote* (Paris: Presses universitaires de France, 1962).

70 Pierre Aubenque, *La prudence chez Aristote* (Paris: Presses universitaires de France, 1963).

71 Alain Michel published, in 1960, an essay on the philosophical foundations of the art of persuasion entitled *Rhétorique et philosophie chez Cicéron* (Paris: Presses universitaires de France), while Renato Barilli devoted an important, lively chapter to Cicero in his *Poetica e retorica* (*see* note 64).

72 We have already mentioned Alessandro Giuliani, whose works cover the period stretching from Aristotle to the Scottish philosophy, without neglecting medieval logic, and shed new light on the history of legal logic. Mention must also be made of G. Chevrier's suggestive study "Sur l'art de l'argumentation chez quelques romanistes médiévaux au XIIe et au XIIIe siècle," *Archives de Philosophie du Droit*, 1966, pp. 115–48. Finally let us recall the well-known works of Eugenio Garin and of his disciples, which have drawn attention again to the Italian philosophy of the Renaissance and to fifteenth- and sixteenth-century humanism, in which discussions concerning the relations between philosophy, dialectic, and rhetoric occupied a central place: Garin, *Medioevo e Rinascimento* (Bari, Italy: Laterza, 1961); and Garin, Paolo Rossi, and Cesare Vasoli, eds., *Testi umanistici su la retorica* (Rome: Fratelli Bocca, 1953). Besides Garin's own writings, we must mention those of Paolo Rossi: "La celebrazione della retorica e la polemica antimetafisica nel *De principiis* di Mario Nizolio," in *La crisi dell'uso dogmatico delle ragione*, ed. Antonio Banfi (Milan, 1953), pp. 99–221; and Cesare Vasoli, *La dialettica e la retorica dell'umanesimo* (Milan: Feltrinelli, 1968).

73 C. S. Peirce, *Collected Papers*, 6 vols., ed. Charles Hartshorne and Paul Weiss (Cambridge, Mass.: Harvard University Press, 1931–35), 1:444.

74 Klibansky, *Contemporary Philosophy* (*see* note 40), 1:177–84.

75 *See* my article "What the Philosopher May Learn from the Study of Law," *Natural Law Forum* 11 (1966): 1–12, reproduced as an appendix to the volume *Justice*.

76 Cf. Ch. Perelman and L. Olbrechts-Tyteca, "Les notions et l'argumentation," *Archivio di filosofia*, Rome, 1955, pp. 249–69; idem, "De la temporalité comme caractère de l'argumentation," *Archivio di Filosofia*, 1958, pp. 115–33. L. Olbrechts-Tyteca, "Les définitions des statisticiens," *Logique et Analyse* 3 (1960): 49–69. Ch. Perelman, "Avoir un sens et donner un sens," in *Thinking and Meaning*, Entretiens d'Oxford, in *Logique et Analyse*, 1962, pp. 235–39.

77 Ch. Perelman, "The Dialectical Method and the Part Played by the Interlocutor in the Dialogue," in Perelman, *The Idea of Justice and the Problem of Argument*, pp. 161–67; idem, "Dialectique et Dialogue," in *Hermeneutik und Dialektik* (*see* note 64), 2:77–84.

NOTE TO THE READER

Professor Perelman notes that the new rhetoric combines elements that were treated separately by Aristotle as belonging to dialectic and rhetoric. Both ideas, it should be remembered, merit entire chapters in the *Syntopicon,* Chapter 18 being devoted to DIALECTIC and Chapter 81 to RHETORIC. In these chapters the reader will find abundant material on the classical tradition of these arts.

In *The Praise of Folly* by Erasmus, printed below in Part Four, the reader will find a minor masterpiece that reflects and commemorates an earlier revival of rhetoric, that which occurred at the time of the Renaissance.

The new rhetoric is not only an art, but, as is indicated by the subtitle Professor Perelman has given his essay, it is also a theory of practical reasoning. Further consideration of this subject, from another approach, is given above, in Part Two, in Professor Letwin's account of recent work in the social sciences.

THE GREAT BOOKS LIBRARY

MARK
VAN DOREN

Mark Van Doren was born in Hope, Illinois, in 1894. He received his M.A. from the University of Illinois in 1915; his first critical work, Thoreau, *appeared the following year. He took his Ph.D. at Columbia University in 1920, and began his distinguished, thirty-nine-year career as Professor of English there. Simultaneously, he was literary editor of* The Nation *(1924–28) and its film critic (1935–38). He is one of the founders of the Great Books movement, having helped to originate the famous Humanities course at Columbia in the 1920's, and acting for many years as a supporter of and lecturer at St. John's College; his views on* Liberal Education *were published in 1943. His first book of poems,* Spring Thunder, *appeared in 1924; a collection culled from numerous volumes won the Pulitzer Prize for Poetry in 1939. Subsequent volumes of verse included* Selected Poems *(1954),* Collected and New Poems *(1963),* The Narrative Poems of Mark Van Doren *(1964), and the latest of some sixty books,* That Shining Place *(1969). He has written novels—*The Transients *(1935) and* Windless Cabins *(1940)—and a large number of short stories; many of these were gathered in* Collected Stories *(1962),* Collected Stories Volume II *(1965), and* Collected Stories Volume III *(1968). He is also a playwright:* The Last Days of Lincoln *was published in 1962, and* Three Plays *appeared in 1966. He has written studies of* The Poetry of John Dryden *(1920),* Shakespeare *(1939),* Hawthorne *(1949), and a critique of ten great poems,* The Noble Voice *(1946). Occasional criticism was collected in* The Private Reader *(1942) and* The Happy Critic *(1961). He served on the advisory board of editors of* Great Books of the Western World.

266

Great Books of the Twentieth Century in Literature

The latest work of literature in *Great Books of the Western World* was Dostoevsky's *The Brothers Karamazov* (1880). On the assumption that a modern *Great Books* may some day exist, and if so that it will embrace the period, roughly a hundred years, between 1880 and whatever date at which the twentieth century shall by that time have arrived, what works of literature should be included in it? I have been asked to speculate concerning this, and in the following pages I shall do so in the spirit of one who guesses rather than knows. For there is no science of the future, and it is with the future reputations of modern authors that I shall be concerned. Nothing whatever can be known about such things. The mortality of reputations, literary or otherwise, is notoriously high; many a book considered by its contemporaries to be a classic has been ruthlessly beached upon the shores of time. And so it could be with some, or even many, of the books that I shall name. All I can do is use the judgment available to me.

The word *literature*, I must furthermore confess, embarrasses me at the very beginning. How does it happen that the word has come to mean only one kind of book out of the many kinds there are? And worse yet, how does it happen that this kind has been distinguished by the qualifying term *imaginative?* History, philosophy, and science are imaginative too; or if not, they are nothing. The best word would be *poetry;* but that too has lost most of its traditional content. In essence it meant *story:* the lives of invented individuals; or if not wholly invented, then individuals reshaped to suit the poet's purpose. Story is not history, though the two are related; it is not philosophy, though if philosophy is totally absent from it we cannot believe it; it is not science or mathematics, though if the elegances of those are missing in it we shall yawn. Story, then, is story; or as Aristotle put it, poetry is poetry. And Aristotle's three kinds of poetry are still the only kinds there are: epic, dramatic, and lyric. Modern epic poetry is represented by the novel; dramatic poetry by the drama; and lyric poetry by the song and the short story. Even lyric poetry, when it is powerful, has epic and drama at its roots: as song, it implies story; as short story, it implies still more story than it states. I trust it is clear that I have accepted Aristotle's refusal to identify poetry with verse.* When either verse or prose is powerful, poetry is present. It is the power that matters.

---

* *On Poetics*, 1451b4; *GBWW*, Vol. 9, p. 686a.

For practical purposes I shall assume that the modern *Great Books* which may some day exist will have room for as many as ten volumes of literature—I return to the term, again with the desire to be practical, and with the certainty that I shall be understood. And I shall assume that the ten volumes will be generous in size, for I intend to pack a great deal into each one. If in some cases this is too much, the editor can decide what must be trimmed; I shall not be the editor, God forbid. I am not deciding, I am suggesting. I am guessing what books of recent or present time will live. Or perhaps I am only saying what books I hope will live for the simple reason that I especially like and respect them. Here then are the ten volumes.

I. MARK TWAIN AND SHOLOM ALEICHEM

I put these men together, as others have, because they are both masters of humor, and also because each of them masterfully renders a place and its people. In Mark Twain's case the place is Middle America, and the people speak a special English proper to that place. In Sholom Aleichem's case the place is the Pale of Settlement in Eastern Europe, and the people speak Yiddish. It is perhaps only a coincidence that each author's name is a pseudonym: Mark Twain for Samuel Langhorne Clemens (1835–1910) and Sholom Aleichem for Solomon Rabinowitz (1859–1916). The pseudonyms, as a matter of fact, in both cases are pertinent to the material with which the authors deal. "Mark Twain" was a term used by Mississippi River pilots, and "Sholom Aleichem" is still the most familiar Hebrew greeting—so familiar, so casual, that instead of meaning "Peace be unto you," it can mean on occasion simply "hello." Mark Twain was born on the Mississippi River but wrote about it years after he had moved away; he died in New York. Sholom Aleichem was born near Kiev (Yehupetz in his stories); lived in Russian cities before he emigrated, toward the end of his life, to the United States; and died in New York (the Bronx). The imagination of each man, wherever he lived and wrote, was most richly at home in a region he knew to the bottom and deeply loved. Mark Twain never forgot the Mississippi; and Sholom Aleichem, who for decades had entertained and moved the entire Yiddish-speaking world, asked that only these words be put on his tombstone: "Let me be buried among the poor, that their graves may shine on mine, and mine on theirs." The resemblances are innumerable. A further one is that the regions rendered, the places immortalized, have now ceased to be. Mark Twain's Middle America, lazy and remote, mysteriously out of the world, is not there any more; and the Kasrilevkas of Sholom Aleichem, the villages into which his poor beloved Jews were huddled, have been utterly depopulated by Hitler.

Not that the successful rendering of a place is in itself sufficient proof of literary greatness. We must be on guard against the tendency, everywhere noticeable in our time, to assume that the sole duty of a novel, or of any story, is to be true to life as it is lived somewhere outside the story. Its first and last duty is to be true to itself and to human life as every human being knows it; so that the final test of any fiction is its power to convince and move those readers who have no firsthand knowledge of the place where its action is set. Such readers may end up by adopting the place as their very own, and even by feeling homesick because they cannot be literally there. But that is not the same thing as recognizing a patch of earth with which one is already familiar. Poetry, in other words, is not identical with history, as Aristotle explained centuries ago.* Whereas, to our loss, we now tend, as I have said, to identify the two. And yet, as I have also suggested, there is a connection between them. A story has to take place somewhere, and this had better be a place of whose reality we are convinced. Stories without roots in the known earth have little or no chance to survive; the penalty they pay is a thinness, a meaningless abstraction. Whereas the London of Dickens, the Moscow of Tolstoy, the Spain of Cervantes—well, how could we do without those, even though what happens in them is ultimately more important than they are in themselves? To be universal we must begin by being local, and the locality, as I have said, had better be one of whose existence we have no doubt. So poetry must have history in it, as for that matter history must have story in it: must move, must be narrative, must have a beginning, middle, and end as the raw material of the past perhaps has not. But this merely reminds us that the writing of history is an art; so is the writing of fiction, but it cannot do without reference to recognizable reality.

The reality of Mark Twain's two masterpieces, *Life on the Mississippi* (1883) and *The Adventures of Huckleberry Finn* (1884), is a dream reality, I grant; but I do not doubt the reality of such dreams as these. I would include in Volume I the first twenty chapters of *Life on the Mississippi*, written nearly a decade before the huge book to which they serve as introduction, and of course *Huckleberry Finn* entire. The earlier work, someone may object, is autobiography rather than fiction, but I choose to call it fiction, since the river becomes alive in it as only things created do. The fact that Mark Twain was a river pilot in his youth has nothing to do with the final effect, which is of a river, vast and wild beyond imagination, that winds with tortuous force between banks it cuts away, then builds again, as the ocean does its shores. Beyond these banks people live, but not as the river lives, nor as the men who navigate it. Mr. Bixby, the veteran pilot who initiates Mark Twain into the mysteries of points and shoals, is a hero worthy of Homer, except that he is absolutely American too, and his vernacular authenticates itself with every amazing revelation

* *Ibid.*

he makes: of the size of the river, of its Protean character, and of the unlikely objects—trees, barns, houses—that float down it like chips in a gutter. The revelations are both magnificent and amusing, for on its grand scale this is a very funny book; the fun, however, being always subdued to the overarching wonder of the element whose vagaries the youthful pilot has set himself to learn. There is a glory in all this that only poetry can achieve; and so I call it poetry, or fiction if you prefer.

Huckleberry Finn is no less centered on this same river, which slides through its pages as if nothing on either shore—no village, no house, no person—counts in eternity as it surely does. There are plenty of people off there, and a goodly number of them have roles in the story before it is finished; but the river is the chief person of the book, unless Huck is— Huck, who lies in the bottom of his little boat and looks at the sky and congratulates himself because at last he has escaped from the respectable world where he will never be at home. He is Mark Twain, if you please, remembering his youth and getting even with the Establishment that wants him to forget it. For he was never wholly comfortable in the world he spent the second half of his life in. Indeed, this is understatement, for he never left off castigating that world, even though the fame and riches it bestowed upon him pleased him. Doubtless he was never more happy than he was as he wrote this book and listened to the priceless dialogues between Huck Finn and black Jim who went with him most of the way. Not only was the river out of this world as any river, independent of its banks, knows how to be, but Huckleberry Finn, thumbing his nose at authority, was also out of any world whose problems are too numerous to endure.

Sholom Aleichem's body of work came into being by the accident that a few sketches he contributed to a newspaper in Kiev were immediately and widely successful; more were called for; and the rest of his life was spent in trying to meet the demand, not merely in Russia but around the world. His fame in 1916, when he died still working, was something not to be measured. More than 150,000 persons lined the streets of New York on the day of his funeral, to which deputations came from both nearby and distant cities and towns. The reason was that his stories—hundreds of them—had spoken for an entire people, and the characters in them had become household possessions, as they still are and will continue to be. He himself had started life in a Kasrilevka; and though the rest of his days were to pass elsewhere, he never forgot his origins. He never lost the accent of the "little people," the obscure, put-upon people whose life was saved from being miserable by the fact of their living it together, with laughter, with shouting, with whispering, with prayers, with curses, with love, with tears. The world he renders is everywhere warm, is frequently ridiculous, is frank in expressing itself, is schooled in the disciplines of want and courage, of no hope and of hope. All that the people of the

Pale really had was themselves and their Bible, plus a deep sense of their ancient beginnings in a world far away from here.

Of these people Sholom Aleichem was a faultless historian. Yet he was more than that, too. He was their poet, their secular psalmist; he was somebody who understood them even better than they understood themselves. And it is here that he emerges as a universal figure. For it is not necessary to be a Jew in order to feel the force of his tales. Doubtless Jews feel it most directly and keenly, but he reaches everyone who has a heart and mind. His Tevye the dairyman is one of the finest creations in modern fiction; and then there are dozens of others who are not the least like Tevye. They may be found in the following stories that I would include in Volume I:

> *The Town of the Little People*
> *The Inheritors*
> *Tevye Wins a Fortune*
> *A Page from the Song of Songs*
> *Two Dead Men*
> *The Clock That Struck Thirteen*
> *Home for Passover*
> *The Enchanted Tailor*
> *A Yom Kippur Scandal*
> *In Haste*
> *Eternal Life*
> *Hannukah Money*
> *Tit for Tat*
> *Modern Children*
> *The Convoy*
> *The Fiddle*
> *The Day Before Yom Kippur*
> *Three Little Heads*
> *A Country Passover*
> *The Lottery Ticket*
> *Hodel*

II. IBSEN, SHAW, AND CHEKHOV

It would be unthinkable, for me at any rate, to begin this volume of plays with any others than Ibsen's. The only question is, which ones? For this dour, embattled Norwegian (1828–1906) tried his hand at many types of drama: tried, and nearly always succeeded. In verse, in prose, in tragedy, in comedy, he had done massive work; and by the time of his death he was acknowledged master of the European theater. Playfulness, perhaps, was the only thing his genius lacked. In retrospect he seems a grim figure, even a scowling one, with eyes set firmly in search of signif icant themes. And that is the only figure which many see when they hear his name. But this, I am confident, is only because they have not been reading him: have not been in contact with his unparalleled intensity. For he is unfailingly intense; and since he is a highly skillful playwright, he therefore is unfailingly effective. There is a darkness in his plays, indicative of the cold country where he was born and died—though he lived in voluntary exile from it for twenty-seven years. But the intensity is never absent, nor the attention to dramatic detail which distinguishes him among the playwrights of the world.

I have selected *A Doll's House* (1879), *Hedda Gabler* (1890), and *John Gabriel Borkman* (1896). It has been painful to leave certain of the others out, but of these I am sure. *A Doll's House* is well-nigh perfect in its rendering of the young wife Nora who leaves her husband and shuts the door behind her—a famous door that nobody forgets. Nora's husband, Torvald Helmer, is perfect too in his less admirable way; he has thought to make a child of Nora, and he thinks he has succeeded until the dramatic moment when she tells him she must go forth into the real world and find out for herself what it is like. *Hedda Gabler* is no less successful in the handling of its heroine, but she is far from being another Nora, with sweetness in her as well as strength. In Hedda there is nothing but a cold, contemptuous strength, an unexplainable unrest, a cruelty of heart which makes us fear her at the same time that it fascinates us. She is a Medea of the North, with no children to kill but with two men to hurt—her husband and the author whose manuscript she burns—before she ends the play by shooting herself: good riddance to all-but-divine rubbish. *John Gabriel Borkman*, whose hero, a disgraced banker, at first is only heard, not seen, as he walks overhead and broods upon the good he had intended to do with the money he embezzled, is powerful not only because of him but also because of his wife Gunhild and her twin sister, whose mutual loathing at the start is like something out of Greek tragedy. A Greek tragedy the whole play is: dark and bitter, yet beautiful too in the way it works itself out.

It has been equally difficult to choose among the fifty-odd plays of Bernard Shaw (1856–1950), that inexhaustible fountain of comedy who when he stopped bubbling at the age of ninety-four had established a reputation quite as firm as Ibsen's. If he had any hero among his contemporaries it was Ibsen; not that he was anything like Ibsen save in his insistence upon candor as he anatomized the society of his time. He always met resistance and always overcame it—in his case, as he once modestly remarked, by being "unbearably brilliant." His high spirits, his impudence on occasion, his absolute fearlessness, and his genius for dialectic—his complete understanding of whatever it is that makes good talk—these were his comic weapons, and they never failed him. He is the master of comedy in modern times, and that alone would explain his presence here. As for his dialectic, the distinction of it lies in his power to comprehend those persons in his plays who think differently from him; he gives them ample chance to refute him and even to ridicule him, though he never abandons the position he assigns to some character who more or less represents his own thinking. He had stout convictions, but so do all of his people, every one of whom he seems to like at the same time that he finds him—or her—absurd. His plays have sometimes been dismissed as nothing but talk—the essence, as it happens, of the comic spirit. Tragedy is action, comedy is talk. And there is always something more to say.

It has been difficult to choose, but here are my choices:

> *Caesar and Cleopatra*
> *Man and Superman*
> *Major Barbara*
> *Heartbreak House*
> *Saint Joan*

Caesar and Cleopatra (1898) conveys among other things the conviction of Shaw that Julius Caesar was one of the great men of all time, and therefore superior, Shaw thought, to the figure Shakespeare gave him to cut in the great play that bears his name. Shaw's Caesar is witty—of course—and strong-willed: two qualities with which he endows all of his heroes. The story is of how Caesar came to Egypt before Antony did and found another Cleopatra than Shakespeare's. *Man and Superman* (1903) has in John Tanner a man who preaches, somewhat in Ibsen's vein, a doctrine of the "life force"—Ibsen, in his gloomy vein, was for ever praising life and light—but John Tanner is Shaw's own man: opinionated, headstrong, eloquent, yet wittily aware of his own absurdity if someone like Ann, whom he loves in spite of his resolution never to yield his freedom to any woman, has the audacity to point it out. This may still be Shaw's masterpiece, despite all the fine work that followed it. It is endlessly engaging. *Major Barbara* (1905) contains in Andrew Undershaft a further vehicle for Shaw's conviction that strength of intellect and will is everything. Undershaft, a munitions-maker, justifies his trade on the ground that it may help men to shoot and kill such abominations as poverty, which he thinks the Salvation Army, in the person of Barbara, sentimentally encourages rather than cures. The dialectic is between these two, and again the adversaries are generously matched. *Heartbreak House* (1919), written in the shadow cast by World War I, is subtitled by Shaw "A Fantasia in the Russian Manner on English Themes." The reference is surely to Chekhov (1860–1904), of whom more later; but Chekhov nowhere has a character as positive in force as Captain Shotover, another of Shaw's frank heroes whose conversation is perpetually salted with surprises. But the fabric of the play symbolically expresses a society which has seen its own fabric shattered by falling bombs. *Saint Joan*

(1923) is Shaw's only tragedy, if indeed it is a tragedy; and doubtless it is, since the death of Joan at the end is truly painful. But even here the razors of Shaw's dialectic go on flashing, for the heart of the play is the series of conversations between Joan of Arc and the authorities—religious, secular—who either try to tell her how she can be saved or else explain to her why she has to die. Once more we have a conflict of wills, and once more the balance is even; for the death of Joan does not absolve those who burned her, even though they had the best of reasons. They represented authority, and authority makes sense, as over and over Joan is told. So, however, does a conscience like this girl's: there is the irreducible difference.

Of Chekhov's plays it would be a temptation to say, as many have done, that their chief value is as a record, or perhaps a revelation, of the decay into which Russian society had fallen by the close of the nineteenth century. And it is true that the prevailing mood in these plays is despair, or if not precisely that, then a sort of witless wonderment as to what life has come to mean. The people are restless; they feel that they are caged; no prospect is satisfactory; they want to be somewhere else; they remember better times than these, and they dream of better times to come; they are absentminded; they are bored. So the temptation is to say: Ah, that is how it was then and there; now we know what Russia was like before the Revolution. Once more we are faced by the question of poetry and history, of the root and the flower. And we cannot dismiss the reality that surrounds Chekhov's scenes. But we must remember that if the only merit of these scenes is their truth to a perishable moment in time, then the chances of their surviving into future ages are bound to be slight, since that moment will surely be forgotten. Was Falstaff, a decayed knight, true to his type in fourteenth-century England? The absurdity of the question is its own answer.

If I did not believe that Chekhov's plays would survive, these three would not be included here:

> *Uncle Vanya*
> *The Three Sisters*
> *The Cherry Orchard*

Sonia and her Uncle Vanya (1897), left at the end in the same predicament that they were in before the pompous Professor Serebryakoff came to muddle their existence, see only monotony ahead of them, only a dreary round of days. "What can we do?" asks Sonia. "We must live out our lives. . . . You have never known what it is to be happy, but wait, Uncle Vanya, wait! We shall rest. We shall rest. We shall rest." This is not the speech of a woman who typifies something; it is the speech of a woman indeed, and she could have existed in any play at any time. The delicate compassion of Chekhov transcends time and place. So does it in *The Three Sisters* (1901), whose heroines are stifled in the atmosphere they must breathe; they dream of Moscow, where they fancy life would be perfect, but they will never get there. Which does not mean at all that the only aim of Chekhov is to expose the limitations of provincial towns. It is, I think, to give us Olga, Masha, and Irina, along with their brother Andrei, exactly as they are: alike, yet different, and all of them unhappy as people anywhere, given the present situation, might reasonably be. *The Cherry Orchard* (1903) could seem to be the best case for proving, if proof was desired, the documentary nature of Chekhov's dramas. The irresponsible Liuboff Andreievna and her still more irresponsible brother Gaieff, who imagines he is playing billiards when he is supposed to be thinking seriously about the future of the estate—his mind is never where *he* is—are so vivid before us that we can have the illusion of being on-lookers at a certain moment when the history of Russia opens itself for our inspection. Yet the vividness is the answer. These people are not copied from anything. They hold their places in the long line—but not too long—of persons that drama has managed to make live and keep on living.

III. LYRIC POETRY

G*reat Books of the Western World* made no attempt to represent the lyric poetry of Europe. The reason is that lyric poetry suffers more than any other kind from translation. The language of lyric is a highly specialized thing, so fine in its effects that only a comparable genius in another tongue can be trusted to carry it over without fatal loss. Rilke's German, Mallarmé's French, Lorca's and Neruda's Spanish, to cite no further instances, have so far failed to find the comparable English, so that readers of existing translations, some of which are of course better than others, still have to believe rather than know how good the originals are. We are left, then, with six poets of England, Ireland, and the United States who in my opinion cannot be ignored. The lyric poetry of the period under review has substance and beauty, and I cannot imagine a corpus of modern literature that would leave it out.

Emily Dickinson.—She was at her best during the American Civil War, but Emily Dickinson (1830–1886) became known only at the end of her century, and it was not until the present century that she came to be recognized as one of the world's great poets. It was in this century too that publication of her work became complete. Only a handful of poems escaped into print while she lived as a recluse in Amherst, Massachusetts; when she died she asked that all her manuscripts be burned; this was not done, but their publication was gradual, volume by volume, until now the total number of her poems in print is 1,775—an astonishing number, and it suggests that she had no other life than poetry, plus of course the precious things—friends, animals, the weather, love, death, God—that the poetry was about. In brief, it was about nothing less than the whole world, which she knew as only genius knows it. Her style is terse to the limit; she lights landscapes, actual or imagined, temporal or eternal, as lightning does. I suggest these poems of hers for the volume:

> *Success is counted sweetest*
> *A wounded deer leaps highest*
> *The heart asks pleasure first*
> *The soul selects her own society*
> *To fight aloud is very brave*
> *I taste a liquor never brewed*
> *I like to see it lap the miles*
> *Hope is a subtle glutton*
> *I felt a cleavage in my mind*
> *At half-past three a single bird*
> *A bird came down the walk*
> *Presentiment*
> *A narrow fellow in the grass*
> *I'll tell you how the sun rose*
> *Elysium is as far as to*
> *If you were coming in the fall*
> *She rose to his requirement*
> *The way I read a letter's this*
> *I died for beauty*
> *I've seen a dying eye*
> *Because I could not stop for Death*
> *After a hundred years*
> *I felt a funeral in my brain*
> *I heard a fly buzz when I died*
> *The difference between despair*
> *She dealt her pretty words like blades*
> *I should not dare to be so sad*
> *I had not minded walls*
> *After great pain a formal feeling comes*
> *I got so I could hear his name*
> *Summer has two beginnings*

Thomas Hardy.—He left behind him in his *Collected Poems* a body of work which in my view far outshines his novels and even his vast drama *The Dynasts*. Hardy (1840–1928) is one of the great English poets, though it takes patience to find him at his best in the huge bulk of the *Collected Poems*. His theory of life was bleak, but his account of it in song and story —he is rich in examples of both—is warm and wonderful. He is most at home in mist and gloom, and then, lo, in brilliant sun. His verse is crabbed and peculiar; but once we are accustomed to his voice it is something we want to keep on hearing. For this volume I nominate the following poems:

Hap
Nature's Questioning
Drummer Hodge
On an Invitation to the United States
God-forgotten
The Darkling Thrush
Let Me Enjoy
The Homecoming
The Roman Road
The Pine Planters
The Convergence of the Twain
The Discovery
The Moth-Signal
Near Lanivet, 1872
The Blinded Bird
The Oxen
Old Furniture
Logs on the Hearth
The Head Above the Fog
Weathers
The Garden Seat
"A man was Drawing near to Me"
"If it's ever Spring again"
The Fallow Deer at the Lonely House
After a Romantic Day
The Whitewashed Wall
Epitaph
An Ancient to Ancients
The Sheep Fair
Nobody Comes
The Shiver
Afterwards

William Butler Yeats.—I can imagine no person who would challenge the right of Yeats (1865–1939) to a high place in this volume. Perhaps the highest; yet, who knows? It is sufficient to say that from his early years in Ireland to his death at 74 he was a poet of commanding importance in the mind of the world. He began with song, he went on in middle life to matters more metaphysical, and then in his old age he returned to song—not with a lilt as in the old days but with a dagger: the dagger of wit. He was a superbly accomplished craftsman at the same time that he reached deeply into the mysteries of existence. He is the most quoted of modern poets in English, and with good reason; he thought priceless thoughts, and for each one of them he found the proper dress. Here are the poems of his that belong, I think, without question:

To an Isle in the Water
Down by the Salley Gardens
The Lake Isle of Innisfree
When You are Old
The Lamentation of the Old Pensioner
The Ballad of Father Gilligan
The Everlasting Voices
The Lover tells of the Rose in his Heart
The Song of Wandering Ængus
To his Heart, bidding it have no Fear
He wishes for the Cloths of Heaven
The Fiddler of Dooney
The Folly of Being Comforted
Never Give all the Heart
O Do Not Love Too Long
His Dream
A Woman Homer Sung
Brown Penny
To a Friend whose Work has come to Nothing
The Cold Heaven
That the Night Come
A Coat
The Wild Swans at Coole
The Cat and the Moon
Easter 1916
The Second Coming
A Prayer for my Daughter
Sailing to Byzantium
Leda and the Swan
Among School Children
For Anne Gregory
Byzantium
Crazy Jane talks with the Bishop
Under Ben Bulben

Edwin Arlington Robinson.—Time has not tarnished the reputation of E. A. Robinson (1869–1935). It was a reputation for wisdom, wit, and singularly delicate feeling which· nevertheless delivered its discoveries coolly, with impeccable phrasing. My list of his poems is not long, partly because two of them are longer themselves than might seem to justify my calling them lyrics. Yet "Ben Jonson Entertains a Man from Stratford," possibly Robinson's most famous poem, is one protracted note of extraordinary music; and "Isaac and Archibald" sings likewise to itself. I am certain that this poet will live.

Miniver Cheevy

Mark Van Doren

Old King Cole
Luke Havergal
John Evereldown
The House on the Hill
Mr. Flood's Party
Isaac and Archibald
The Sheaves
New England
The Dark Hills
Variations of Greek Themes
Ben Jonson Entertains a Man from Stratford

Robert Frost.—He wanted his epitaph to be: "I had a lover's quarrel with the world." When Frost (1874–1963) died at 89 he was a man who still puzzled a country that knew him as a familiar figure and thought it loved him as a sage. It did love him, but he was always surprising and disturbing it, or at any rate being quizzical when it thought he should be sober. Robert Frost was never to be caught out or pinned down. New England to the bone, though he was New England only by adoption, he insisted to the end on saying his own say, singing his own song. He had in abundance that most priceless gift for a poet, humor; nor did this mean that he wasn't serious; only, when was he more serious and when was he less? Meanwhile he had published poems which no one has been able to forget; and that is the main thing. They will outlast any of the numerous legends about the man. He remains a poet of world importance, a man speaking with a distinctive voice and saying things of the profoundest kind.

Into My own
Mowing
Revelation
The Tuft of Flowers
Mending Wall
The Death of the Hired Man
The Mountain
Home Burial
After Apple-Picking
The Wood-pile
The Road Not Taken
An Old Man's Winter Night
The Telephone
Hyla Brook
The Oven Bird
Birches
The Cow in Apple-Time
The Hill Wife
Two Witches

Fire and Ice
Nothing Gold can Stay
The Runaway
Stopping by Woods on a Snowy Evening
To Earthward
The Lockless Door
Spring Pools
Once by the Pacific
Bereft
The Flood
Acquainted with the Night
A Drumlin Woodchuck
Desert Places
Neither Out Far nor in Deep
The Silken Tent
The Gift Outright
A Cabin in the Clearing
One More Brevity

T. S. Eliot.—Here is a modern poet in the special and restricted sense which we have in mind when we say "modern art," and mean by that a kind of art that self-consciously breaks with the past. Eliot (1888–1965) was so respectful of the past, so drenched in tradition, that he felt free to continue it in his own brilliant fashion; he never thought of himself, nor should we think of him, as one who ran wild without knowledge of where he was running. His attempt in fact was to restore the greatest tradition of all, the tradition that forces poetry in any age to face the spirit of that age and reflect it without loss or blur. That he succeeded with our age is attested by his great fame; for his vogue, if vogue it was, has never diminished. If at first he sounded strange, and seemed to be in love with disorder, the reason was the view he took of a fragmented culture, a wasteland of poorly remembered things. As soon as this was understood, he ceased to be altogether strange; though the uncanny perfection of his verse will remain strange in the way that perfection always does. His subject matter, satirical in the beginning, slowly moved toward a high seriousness; he became a powerful religious poet. Yet his mind never ceased to play, nor do his final poems truly contradict the poems by which he originally got to be known. He is a haunting figure, destined to last.

The Love Song of J. Alfred Prufrock
Rhapsody on a Windy Night
Morning at the Window
Mr. Appollinax
The Hippopotamus
Sweeney Among the Nightingales

The Waste Land
The Hollow Men
Ash-Wednesday
Journey of the Magi
A Song for Simeon
Marina
Eyes that last I saw in tears
The wind sprang up at four o'clock
Choruses from "The Rock"
Four Quartets

IV. THE SHORT STORY

If *Great Books of the Western World* did not represent what we now call the short story—or the tale, for we use that term for longer stories that are still not novels—the reason clearly was that no corpus of such things existed. It is the nineteenth and twentieth centuries that have supplied the corpus, brilliantly and in abundance. Scattered back over previous periods we encounter tales, to be sure, by Cervantes for example, but these do not bulk significantly, for the form had not been found. The form of the short story or tale may be difficult to describe, but no modern reader is without knowledge that it exists. The product is lyric, not epic; there is no sweep of action, but rather an intense concentration upon one moment, or a series of moments, during which illumination comes. More action may be implied—much action in some cases—but it is not stated. The body of stories that has resulted within the past century is beautiful and important, and it is inconceivable that it should go unrepresented here. The choice has been the problem—of stories, and of authors. I have chosen eleven authors.

Guy de Maupassant.—From the publication of his famous story "Boule de suif" on to the end of a blazing career in France, Maupassant (1850–1893) enjoyed an eminence that has never since been questioned. His people are of many kinds: peasants, priests, soldiers, merchants, clerks, prostitutes—every kind, it would seem. But all of them are driven, as their creator also is while he works out the ironies of their lives; for irony is his matter, as intensity is his manner. The following stories will at least suggest his range:

Boule de suif
Martin's Girl
The Necklace
Yvette
A Piece of String
The Stor of a Farm Girl
Hautot Senior and Hautot Junior
The Farmer's Wife

The Olive Grove
A Country Excursion
The Legacy
Miss Harriet

Anton Chekhov.—At about the same time in Russia another master was making himself known. The plays of Chekhov (1860–1904) are few, but his short stories are all but innumerable. Himself a physician by training, he probed the souls of people, many of them frustrated and harassed but some of them happy, with a skill that has few parallels anywhere. Like Maupassant, he worked with lightning speed: no word is wasted, just as no soul is spared his merciless yet merciful scrutiny. I have selected these stories:

Easter Eve
Agafya
The Witch
Volodya
A Father
The Name-Day Party
Gusev
In Exile
The Grasshopper
A Woman's Kingdom
The Man in a Case
The Darling

Henry James.—This man's massive output preponderantly takes the form of novels, but his so-called tales—longer than most short stories, yet shorter at any rate than his own extended narratives—are in my opinion his finest work. Their settings are usually English or European, though James (1843–1916) was American by birth; he lived in England from 1876 until his death. I have selected the following tales:

Daisy Miller
The Turn of the Screw
The Beast in the Jungle

The first of these has for its heroine an American girl, beautiful, innocent, and willful, who goes through Europe without any other thought than that she should behave there as she had behaved at home in Schenectady: her own mistress, free to see whom she pleases and to say whatever is in her mind. Her death from Roman fever is no punishment for this; rather, it is the accidental consequence of a rash visit one night to the Colosseum with a beautiful young man of Rome against whom she has been warned. "Daisy Miller" (1878) lingers in our minds for the lightness of her step and the freedom of her spirit; she was one of James's first

Americans whom he showed against the background of an older world. Not that this is history; it is poetry, or it would not be here.

"The Turn of the Screw" (1898) is James's most famous tale, and one of the best tales in the world. It is a study of evil in the form of a ghost story—a ghost story unless the governess who tells it has imagined it all. Opinions differ as to this; but the evil, whether outside the governess's mind or in it, is real enough for horror of immense dimensions. The pupils of the governess, Miles and Flora, have undoubtedly been corrupted, but by whom? Peter Quint and the former governess, Miss Jessel? The present governess? James does not say, nor would he ever say when asked, just as he refused to name the evil. The great distinction of the tale lies in the very fact that definition is absent; though the thing to be defined is weirdly and profoundly there.

"The Beast in the Jungle" (1903) might seem insubstantial, since nothing happens in it: nothing at any rate of the sort that John Marcher, the protagonist, has spent his life expecting. Something vivid, something terrible, certainly. But at the end he realizes that "he had been the man of his time, *the* man, to whom nothing on earth was to have happened." That is the fate, as it is the sorrow of Mary Bartram whose love he might have returned instead of wasting his days in a jungle of his own mind's making.

Rudyard Kipling.—Kipling (1865–1936) was universally beloved in his time, and the passage of more time has not diminished the force of his best tales, which might be these:

> *The Phantom Rickshaw*
> *The Strange Ride of Morrowbie Jukes*
> *The Man Who Would Be King*
> *"They"*
> *Without Benefit of Clergy*
> *The Mark of the Beast*
> *Rikki-Tikki-Tavi*

All of these except "They" take place in India, where Kipling's imagination was most at home. In "They" there are some children—or are they imaginary?—who may remind us of James's Miles and Flora, but only insofar as their existence is debatable, or rather, the nature of their existence. The Indian stories, now cruel, now tender, reveal a mastery of detail such as only Kipling could achieve. Not that detail is everything in art; understanding is essential too; but Kipling had that, as he had humor and sympathy.

Sir Arthur Conan Doyle.—The character created by this man has no equal for fame in any other character created during the century now past. Sherlock Holmes is familiar around the world. his face, his cap, his pipe, his self-assurance, his apparently unlimited knowledge, and his genius at what he called "deduction." Doyle's success with him, sensational in its time, remains sensational; what we call the detective story, though it had practitioners before Doyle (1859–1930), truly came into being when Holmes and Dr. Watson started talking in the rooms on Baker Street where anything could happen, did happen, and went on happening through endless adventures. England was a web of which this was the twitching center; word traveled here of distant trouble, and in an instant, or at any rate by the next express, Holmes was off to solve and rectify it. With difficulty I have made the following selection; with difficulty, for I like them all:

> *The Red-headed League*
> *The Boscombe Valley Mystery*
> *The Five Orange Pips*
> *The Adventure of the Speckled Band*
> *The Adventure of the Copper Beeches*
> *The Yellow Face*
> *The Musgrave Ritual*
> *The Adventure of the Empty House*
> *The Adventure of the Dancing Men*
> *The Adventure of the Solitary Cyclist*

H. G. Wells.—Before he became a novelist, a historian, and a critic of society, Wells (1866–1946) wrote what has come to be known as science fiction; and in this mode he has never been surpassed. Of his scientific years—but they are more than that, for the imagination in them is serious and civil—"The Time Machine" (1895) may well be the best, though other readers will have other favorites. A machine has been invented which will move backward and forward through time, and in it we travel forward until we are in the year 802, 701. The world then is both different and the same: the same to the extent that it has two sets of inhabitants, the Eloi and the Morlocks, who correspond to the consumers and producers of today; but different to the extent that both sets have degenerated in ways that any reader may see. How prophetic "The Time Machine" may be it will take millennia to tell; yet all of Wells's scientific romances have been prophetic, and this one may be so too.

Joseph Conrad.—Born Józef Teodor Konrad Korzeniowski, Conrad, much of whose life (1857–1924) was spent at sea, became a British subject in 1886 and put the Polish language behind him. His novels are celebrated, but his shorter narratives are no less so. I have chosen among them:

> *Youth*
> *The Secret Sharer*
> *To-morrow*
> *Typhoon*

The first of these has for its chief character an ill-fated but indomitable ship; the second has two chief characters, a young merchant captain and a refugee officer whom he hides in his cabin; the third takes place on land, but a whiff of sea air still blows through it; and the fourth—in my opinion Conrad's masterpiece—takes a ship and its Captain MacWhirr through the terrors of a storm such as never, I think, has had its peer in the pages of any book. The steadfastness of MacWhirr, his incapacity to admit defeat, is rendered with a perfection such as manifests itself in all of Conrad's novels and tales. Steadfastness, fidelity, inarticulate courage—these were the virtues Conrad most admired, and he has no equal in their subtle delineation.

Isak Dinesen.—She was a Danish aristocrat—the Baroness Karen Blixen of Rungstedlund (1885–1962)—who loved Shakespeare and learned to write English; under her pseudonym she became famous in 1934 as the author of *Seven Gothic Tales*. Other volumes followed, all of which had the same quality: stories in her hands became myths, even when the setting was contemporary. She had a magic way of endowing people with powers —beauty, clairvoyance, passion—undreamed of by the realists who surrounded her. Her world is cool, strangely lighted, and somehow perfect. It is a world that time will be helpless to alter. Her position is secure. I have chosen these tales:

> *The Deluge at Norderney*
> *The Supper at Elsinore*
> *The Young Man with the Carnation*
> *Sorrow-Acre*
> *The Sailor-boy's Tale*
> *Peter and Rosa*

Ernest Hemingway.—His world was about as far away from Isak Dinesen's as the imagination can stretch. Not only his world, but the voice in which he reported it. Hemingway (1899–1961) was tight-lipped by comparison, and so were his characters. They implied more than they ever said; and the difference made him famous; younger writers imitated his laconic vein, though most of them failed to put the depth into silence that he did. He was committed to death as a subject, and suffering, and blood; with interludes in which his people, still laconic, nevertheless alluded to such a world—flowing, bright-colored, and beautiful—as Isak Dinesen had always at her command. On the whole, however, bullfights, prizefights, deep-sea fishing, big-animal slaughter, and murder were his meat, served with the sauce of understatement. Of the following stories the last is the best, and indeed it is his masterpiece, partly because the old man in it has a richer mixture of feelings than anyone else in all of Hemingway's work.

> *Indian Camp*

The Undefeated
The Killers
Fifty Grand
An Alpine Idyll
The Short Happy Life of Francis Macomber
The Snows of Kilimanjaro
The Old Man and the Sea

Ring W. Lardner.—When asked what his middle initial stood for, he said "Worm." Lardner (1885–1933) was sardonic to the limit, and diabolically skillful in the art of making stupid or brutal people reveal themselves in speech. It was not that he thought there were only people like that in the world; clearly he believed in wisdom and goodness; but his genius was satire, and he worked at it full time. His gallery of mean and shallow persons has no modern parallel that I know. Readers will visit it for a long time in search of mankind, so to speak, in reverse. He is Swift without parable, he is Timon of Athens without glory. And he is funny as often as he is terrible.

The Maysville Minstrel
I Can't Breathe
Haircut
Champion
A Day With Conrad Green
Old Folks' Christmas
Alibi Ike
The Golden Honeymoon
Some Like Them Cold

James Thurber.—In "The Secret Life of Walter Mitty," he may have made one of the few modern contributions to the world's folklore; for this little man who has daydreams of being big has become famous everywhere that words go, and countless people know his name without ever having heard of Thurber (1894–1961)—the kind of consummation that any author devoutly (and perhaps secretly) wishes. Thurber for two generations of readers has represented modern humor at its highest and best, and his output before he died was so copious that many volumes were needed to contain it. But the three following stories are a sufficient indication of his quality, which was pure and fine, and very funny.

The Night the Bed Fell
The Secret Life of Walter Mitty
The Catbird Seat

It might be objected that the first of these, which is hardly less famous than "Walter Mitty," is autobiography rather than fiction. Certainly it is both; but in any case I could not leave it out.

V. JAMES JOYCE

Joyce (1882–1941) is a literature in himself, and all of his books would belong here were there space enough in a single volume. His genius is such, and his reputation is such, that students of him spend their lives inside his work alone, as if there were no other work in the modern world, no other author worthy of attention. Their devotion is excessive, and yet it is comprehensible. Once he fixes your attention, it is hard to look away. I must be content, however, with the following selection, and even that is long:

> The Dead, from Dubliners
> A Portrait of the Artist as a Young Man
> Ulysses

One of the fascinating things about Joyce is his own fascination with language. I do not mean by this merely that he studied many languages other than English and used them more and more steadily from book to book. In college in Dublin he is known to have studied Latin, French, and Italian, and even Norwegian so that he might read Ibsen in the original, for Ibsen was one of his literary heroes. I mean rather, and especially, that language as such—English as such—was the very medium of his imagination, which loved words inordinately, obsessively, and played with them as if they alone were the substance of literature. They are not the substance of literature, nor is it true that Joyce thought so, since his own books have much to say—or, since they are narratives, tell. But his final work, Finnegans Wake (1939), is so tortuous with its puns and double meanings, so imbedded in what seems a quagmire, a quicksand, of reference and cross-reference, that only scholars in Joyce have a right to say that they can read it at all. It was the end product of an evolution that conceivably could be called tragic, since it culminated in a book from which most readers are shut out. Ulysses (1922) before it had seemed difficult, and it still is difficult for all the familiarity we now have with its contents; but the difficulty of Ulysses is less in its language, though that is there too, than in its arrangement, than in the order of its parts. Dubliners (1914), at the commencement of this fabulous career, was lucid as any finely written book can be lucid. Yet even Dubliners took ten years to get published, and then not in Dublin; for it was considered an insult to Joyce's native city, concerning whose people its stories maintain a detachment so icy as to seem cruel, though the cruelty is now no longer apparent—certainly not in the great short story "The Dead," the last in the book. Indeed there is warmth and depth in "The Dead," though there is no sentiment, a thing foreign to Joyce. The discovery that Gabriel Conroy accidentally makes of a young man in his wife's past, a young man who had died for her in a distant part of Ireland, is deeply touching as Joyce discloses it and immediately after muffles the pain of it in a superb passage describing the snow that begins "falling faintly through the universe and faintly falling, like the descent of their last end, upon all the living and the dead."

The absence of sentiment in Joyce has much to do with another fascinating fact about him, namely, that although Dublin is the scene of all his fiction, and the center of all his thought, he was unable to live there after 1904; the rest of his life was spent in Switzerland, Italy, and France; he was self-exiled as Ibsen was, and possibly for the same reason—a sense of confinement, a fear of being smothered by what each of them felt to be a national sentiment, an organized conspiracy against candor and right judgment. However that was, Joyce at any rate devoted the whole of his art in absentia to the streets and pubs of Dublin, no inch or corner of which he seems to have been able to forget. It was not nostalgia; it was simply that his imagination had all it needed in the region he knew best. And if the tissue of language in which he wrapped this region became ever thicker and richer—well, distance may have had something to do with that, and a consequent sense of Dublin as existing both in and out of place and time: eternally there, a city abstract as well as concrete.

A Portrait of the Artist as a Young Man (1916) is generally understood to have Joyce's own youth in Dublin as its moving subject. Its hero, Stephen Dedalus, in other words, is Joyce himself, with whatever differences art may account for, and doubtless there are many of those. One important difference is that Dedalus was not about to leave Ireland; he is still there in *Ulysses*, where he is one of the two leading characters, the other being Leopold Bloom, who was to have appeared in *Dubliners* except that the story Joyce planned for him was not written then; it was saved for his masterpiece. The story of Dedalus in the *Portrait* is the story of a gifted young man who learns what it is that he no longer believes, and what it is therefore that he must cast out of his mind if he should ever be the artist he hopes to be. The story, then, is the story of how the author became an author: a familiar theme in modern fiction, and one that we shall find again in Proust. What Dedalus rejects is the religion that has been taught him, and the national sentiment. "Look here," he says at the end, "I will not serve that in which I no longer believe, whether it call itself my home, my fatherland, or my church: and I will try to express myself in some mode of life or art as freely as I can and as wholly as I can, using for my defense the only arms I allow myself to use, silence, exile, and cunning." This was Joyce's own program, as the sequel showed; nor was the final entry in Stephen's diary irrelevant to that program: "So be it. Welcome, O life! I go to encounter for the millionth time the reality of experience and to forge in the smithy of my soul the uncreated conscience of my race."

"The uncreated conscience of my race"—a deeply interesting phrase in view of the Dublin, and the Ireland, we find laid open to our gaze in *Ulysses*, whose world is as far removed from the glory of Homer as the world of T. S. Eliot's *Waste Land* was removed from the time when Shakespeare wrote the beautiful unearthly lines that now and then drift into the text as if to underscore the fall from grace that twentieth-century man has committed. The point in either case, if the word "conscience" be remembered, was that the modern world was degenerate without knowing it was; was even, in fact, proud of its ignorance of all that it once had been. The title *Ulysses* is of crucial importance; the parallel with Homer* is always present. Stephen Dedalus, still an unformed youth, stumbling through Dublin with no sense of direction, is searching for his spiritual father, and finds him, more or less, in Leopold Bloom, the central character of the novel. Bloom, a Dublin Jew, has come to little or nothing in his own life, and Molly his wife is about as far from Penelope as a woman could be—her reverie at the close, a single sentence forty-six pages long, is quite as obscene as the censors thought, who for decades prevented the book from being sold above the counter—but Bloom has a rich inner life which he keeps wholly to himself, so that only the reader knows it. He has a scientific imagination; he remembers all the things he has ever read, and he is well-read; he is decent and sensitive; he would be a hero if he could. The scene in which he takes Stephen home with him at the end of the twenty-four hours which the entire action of the book covers is in some sense an unsatisfactory scene, and intentionally so; there is nothing like the recognition of Odysseus by Telemachus;† the climax is anticlimax at the best. Yet it is a kind of climax, the one, Joyce seems to be suggesting, that Dublin now deserves, just as Molly's reverie is all that Bloom, poor good fellow, has the potency to inspire.

Of course I have mentioned only three persons in a book that seems to contain thousands, so rich it is in character and event, so noisy with talk, so overlaid with meanings new and old. A behemoth among modern novels, it rages with energy throughout, and is brilliant everywhere. To read it is a discipline, but the discipline is something that any successful reader must consider to have been worth acquiring. Most of the world's fiction since its day has been formed or influenced by it. It is a monument that time will not overturn; or so I guess.

I. MARCEL PROUST

R*emembrance of Things Past*, that endless novel—but endlessly absorbing, too—in which Proust (1871–1922) recaptured his life, appeared between 1913 and 1927 in seven parts:

The Odyssey; GBWW, Vol. 4.

Ibid., Book 16; *GBWW*, Vol. 4, p. 274a.

Swann's Way
Within a Budding Grove
The Guermantes Way
Cities of the Plain
The Captive
The Sweet Cheat Gone
The Past Recaptured

Doubtless not all of its thousands of pages can be crammed into the present volume, but it would be wonderful if they could, for the work, however long drawn out, is still one piece, and I can merely recommend that as much of it as possible, beginning with the beginning, be included. If it has to be cut off after *The Guermantes Way*, so be it. But what a pity to lose *Cities of the Plain*, and the next two parts dealing with Albertine, and the final part that draws so many threads together.

I shall discuss it all, for I do not know how to separate its themes that are one theme, any more than Proust knew how to hurry his novel toward its end. Asthmatic since childhood, he sealed himself at last into a cork-lined room and did nothing but write in a race with death; the last three parts appeared posthumously in France, when the fame of the work was already firmly established; yet he never skimped his task, he continued at the leisurely, looping pace he had started with. The pace is leisurely without ever seeming slow, or, at any rate, dull. The analysis of action and motive, the description of landscapes and rooms, the carrying out of every impression and thought to the finest end—these ought to make for tedium, but strangely they do not, in spite too of sentences so long that sometimes they run for pages. The reason is the author's saturation with his subject, which infects us so that we are with him wherever he is, wanting to know what he wants to know; for the story is of how he gradually learns the truth about a number of things—the truth from other points of view in the beginning, then finally, or more or less finally from his own. More or less, because the relativity of truth is constantly announcing itself in this novel that seems to occupy all space, all time.

I remarked of Joyce's *Ulysses* and indeed of all the works of Joyce that their central subject was the preparation of the author for becoming the author he was; and I said that this would also be true of *Remembrance of Things Past*. It is still more true. The narrator of *Remembrance of Things Past*, a boy named Marcel who grows older with every volume and who writes the entire work in the first person, has ambitions to be a writer; it is assumed by his family and friends that that is what he will become; and he does, he tells us, from the moment when as a man he tastes a little cake, a madeleine soaked in tea, such as he had loved when he was a child—tastes the cake, and there by some miracle his own past lies around him like a living thing. So he starts to put it down in words, goes on; branches out into further landscapes that are folded within these

290

like Chinese boxes; remembers persons, places, things; peers at them passionately in order to make sure that he understands their relations to one
another; thence on and on to what of course could never be an end, except
that one is satisfactorily present in a final sentence which shows him still
wanting to live long enough—naturally he did not—to understand absolutely everything.

The narrator is named Marcel, and much of what he remembers is
what Marcel Proust remembered. Yet the novel is so much more than
this that it lives in its own right as a work of the imagination. It finally
makes no difference which Marcel is telling us these things, the author
himself or a person he has invented. I for one, notwithstanding the parallels that scholars in the subject keep finding between persons inside and
outside *Remembrance of Things Past*—so-and-so is identified as so-and-so—
prefer to take the whole thing as a glorious fiction, illuminated by laws
of its own making and true as poetry is true. In other words, I insist on
believing that it is the Marcel of the book, not the Marcel whose last
name was Proust, who tells what he remembers. And what he remembers!
The list of persons whom *we* shall remember is long and long, beginning
with Marcel's mother and grandmother in the country house at Combray,
and Françoise, the old servant whom Marcel will never be able to do
without, either at Combray or later on in Paris, when he will live in a
house connected with the great house of the Duc de Guermantes and the
Duchess—live there with Albertine as his prisoner. But this is to anticipate, as it also is to make any mention of the fabulous Guermantes, although they are neighbors of Marcel's family in the country too, and
never indeed are out of Marcel's mind; as M. Charles Swann is not, a
friend of his parents who made a disastrous marriage with the courtesan
Odette—disastrous, yet he survived it, and in fact their daughter, Gilberte,
was the first girl whom Marcel loved, long before he met Albertine at
Balbec, the seaside resort on the coast of Normandy where she and the
girls who were her friends came and went from sight like little waves from
the deep, and she herself was to obsess Marcel through most of the years
of his life, though he was finally to banish her from his bed and she was
to die of an accident in Balbec.

I realize suddenly how hopeless it is to attempt a synopsis of this book,
whose component parts weave in and out of our attention, entangled from
beginning to end in a tissue which holds them all and never lets any one
of them fly off by itself. I know I am suggesting confusion; but there is no
confusion. Every detail, of person or of place, is clear as dreams are clear,
even though, as is true in dreams, emphasis and meaning are constantly
in process of change: of change into still greater clarity, for many things
that Marcel begins by thinking of as fixed are by no means fixed, and
characters will shift and recombine as the bits of colored glass do in a
kaleidoscope, or as details in a magic-lantern picture are clarified when

the focus is perfected. The focus here is always being altered as Marcel learns more and more; as for instance in the case of the Baron de Charlus, another friend of Marcel's family who never disappears out of the work, though he grows more and more monstrous as the work proceeds. He is the arch-homosexual of a book that contains many of his tribe, not only in the section called *Cities of the Plain* (the French title is *Sodome et Gomorrhe*) but everywhere else as well. The jealousy that devours Swann is not only of the men who may be Odette's lovers but of the women who perhaps have been, or for that matter still are. And the jealousy that consumes Marcel—for the novel is among other things a study of this universal passion in all of its phases—has the same base: a suspicion, which time makes a certainty, that Albertine's girl friends are Lesbian friends.

But I still have only begun to name the persons who throng this book. Bloch, Marcel's friend. Bergotte, the novelist. The Marquis de Norpois. The Marquise de Villeparisis. The composer Vinteuil and his daughter (also a Lesbian). The Verdurins, who maintain a salon which they think is the last word in elegance, but they are absurdly ignorant of who anyone is. Robert de Saint-Loup, who deserves a paragraph to himself. Elstir, the painter. The Prince and Princesse des Laumes. The Princesse de Parme. The actress Berma. And there are hundreds more, for all of France seems to be here; not only the Faubourg Saint-Germain where the nobility have fabulous parties in fabulous houses, but seaside inns as well, and apartments of the middle class, and at the bottom of the scale the terrible room where Charlus, far gone in his vice, hires young men to flog him with a cat-o'-nine-tails studded with nails. These young men have no idea who the Baron is; and neither in the last analysis does Marcel think *he* does, for he refrains from judging his old friend, as indeed he exercises a similar restraint throughout his unending memoir. It is as if he thought of himself as a historian merely; such and such things happened, and he slowly became aware of what they meant.

Remembrance of Things Past is not the history of France between 188 and 1920, though the Dreyfus case is at one point much in evidence, and World War I is important in the closing part. Nor is it sociology, though the wealthy and functionless nobility of the Faubourg might seem at moments to be the object of a student's scrutiny. No, it is fiction; which is to say that it is poetry. Seldom has any poem contained so much, or been so memorable. If portions of it seem evanescent and trivial, if the dukes and duchesses have their preposterous side as well as their overwhelming reality in Marcel's dream, then we can say, as I have said in another place, that *Remembrance of Things Past* lacks the solidity of Homer's and Tolstoy's poetry, where the whole world is somehow present and looks exactly like what it is. This world is a special one, even a decayed one, and doubtless that is a limitation. Nothing like it, neverth less, has come to view in modern literature, and it would be as wrong to leave it out of the present set as it would be to leave out *Ulysses,* or certain other large works still to come; or as it would have been to leave out *Huckleberry Finn*, the stories of Sholom Aleichem, and the plays of Ibsen and Shaw.

VII. THOMAS MANN

Mann's *Joseph and His Brothers* (1933–44) is not as long as *Remembrance of Things Past*, but it is long, and Proust's title would be a perfect fit for it if its own title were not the simple one it doubtless ought to bear. It is concerned with time—centuries of it in this case—and it has a comic overcast comparable with that which I might have noted, and did not, in *Remembrance of Things Past*. The events in it are serious events, but the view taken of them is so long a view that any suggestion of tragedy dissipates in the perspective Mann (1875–1955) establishes. The end of course is happy—Joseph is reunited with his father, Jacob— but that is not what I mean. I have in mind rather the great stretch of time that takes the edge of crisis off things and renders them equal, so that no one thing is more crucial than any other. The comic spirit— man's profoundest invention—has never been more at home than it has been in the modern novel, as the masterpieces of Joyce, Proust, and Mann alone would attest. The emphasis in those masterpieces is upon perspectives that shift even as we watch them, so that judgments we have been tempted to pass have to be reconsidered; the truth is richer than at first it seemed to be, and its outlines more multiple. The spirit of comedy likes to view things from all angles, and insists upon suspended judgment. That is why it takes its time; why it is willing to be long; and why on the way it delights in the kind of conversation that dissolves barriers even while it illuminates the field of vision.

Joseph and His Brothers is forty-five times as long as the portion of *Genesis* where we first find the story.* *Genesis*, we may be inclined to suppose, did its job perfectly; and so it did, for the story of Joseph there is one of the finest in the world. Why then did Mann retell it as he did? The answer is that he wanted to write a novel, not a fable or a tale, and that he hoped to exhaust all of the possible meanings the Bible left unexplored. The Bible was interested, there as elsewhere, only in what Mann calls "the facts," and it knew how to put those down so that they would stay put, as certainly they have. Mann, respecting his original so much that he never departed from it in any essential, went on to fill in the interstices between the doings, the gaps where there was no psychology; for in the Bible there is no psychology, no discussion of reasons why things are done; the people do them and that is that. It is possible that

---

* *Genesis*, 37:39–50.

in the very longest run this is still the best way to proceed, since there are fashions in psychology, and what is said about motives in one age may be unintelligible in another. In the case of the Joseph story, however, we may congratulate ourselves upon having both things: the tale and the novel. For *Joseph and His Brothers* was not intended as a substitute for the biblical narrative which its author constantly refers to. It was intended as an elaboration of it in terms, among other things, of time. It was intended as a celebration of the immemorial quality, the ageless truth, that, if we only know how to look for it, we can find in any ancient tale that has come down to us.

Mann commences not with Joseph but with the deep well of time down which we can peer and see his forefathers, all of whom look like him and like one another, though there are differences too, since men are both the same and other: the same in that they are men, and other in that they are individuals, are unique. Yet comedy is less interested in the uniqueness than in the sameness. The same things happen over and over in human time; the actors in tales are barely distinguishable from one another, given enough of that human time; and comedy rubs its hands over this, because the last thing it cherishes is novelty. It rejoices because there is nothing new under the sun; because fathers and sons have forever been what they are today; and because, when a father has a favorite son, and says so, he is committing an error so ancient that nobody can remember when the consequences were not thus and so. Error is possibly the wrong word here; the partiality of Jacob for his brilliant and beautiful boy Joseph was something we might have felt had we been he. Which is precisely the point, and which has nothing to do with the consequences of whatever it was if it wasn't error. Comedy passes no judgments in such cases; it simply remembers and nods its head.

Abraham, Isaac, and Jacob in his early days are figures, then, in the deep well of time at the edge of which Mann stands at the beginning of his epic, looking down and down. Soon enough, however, Joseph rises out of the well and takes over: Joseph, and his brothers who hate him because their common father so obviously adores him and favors him. Joseph even adores himself; he takes it for granted that any boy as bright as he must be lovable, as indeed he is. His vanity is something that Mann handles with great delicacy and skill. It is not a vice, not a sin; it is entirely natural. But so is the hatred of the brothers, and soon enough there is the selling of Joseph into captivity, and his disappearance from the family view for all the years that it takes him to get to Egypt and to become indispensable there; for his brightness and his beauty never fail him, and though he begins by being Potiphar's Hebrew slave he ends by being in effect his master, whom neither Potiphar nor his wife can live without.

It is this section that Mann most lavishly embroiders. The court of

Pharaoh, the household of Potiphar, the whole splendor of Egypt unroll before us in a profusion that we cannot help finding wonderful. To old Jacob back in Israel, grieving for his son whom he considers dead, all this would not be beautiful; or if it were, the beauty would have about it the terrible aspect that things Egyptian had for every Jew, and that they would continue to have after Moses in later times. Egypt for Israel was a corrupt place, worshiping death and defiling life; it was incapable of simplicity, it was unable to conceive the mightiness of an altogether invisible God. But Joseph enjoyed himself there, rose in rank and privilege, learned the secrets of the place, and one day found himself beloved by the wife of Potiphar. He did not return this love, yet it somehow pleased him. As for Potiphar's wife, it meant nothing but agony until she could revenge herself by getting Joseph thrown into jail—where, ironically, his fortunes really began to rise. Before long he is for all practical purposes a prince of Egypt, who eventually marries an Egyptian girl and so seems to cast off all ties to his own race. Yet not so; for there is the famine, and there is the coming of his brothers by whom he is recognized and with whom he is reconciled, and at last there is the swift journey to the Land of Goshen in a magnificent chariot from which Joseph alights to greet his father, come all the way from Israel in a wagon with his family and herds about him. It was a great meeting, and of course Mann makes the most of it, though he does not neglect to have Jacob before he dies predict that Joseph will never have a prime place among the patriarchs of his race. His contribution to that race has been the saving of it, yet the salvation was not spiritual, and so he will not be mentioned in times to come in the same breath with Abraham and Isaac; Jacob does not add his own name, but the Bible does. Abraham, Isaac, and Jacob: those were the First Fathers, and Joseph was never of their company.

If Mann's Joseph did not fully understand this, though in filial piety he accepted it, the reason had something to do with the fact of his being the hero of a comedy. All heroes, whether of comedy or of tragedy, lack self-knowledge at some point. However brilliant they may be, they still cannot see themselves as others see them, or as God does. So Joseph, for all his cleverness, cannot see that there is something much greater than cleverness: simplicity of soul and grandeur of heart. Mann's recognition of this in the case of Joseph is by no means inconsistent with his adoration of Joseph, an adoration we also feel. Nevertheless, Joseph has his limits; and it is Mann's comedy that reveals them. The achievement is classic in our time. Mann left other novels of true distinction behind him, and there may be those who would prefer to find one of them here. But *Joseph and His Brothers*, if only because it is a masterpiece of comedy— I hope it is clear how seriously I take the term—belongs, I think, where I have placed it.

VIII. WILLIAM FAULKNER

O nce again the question of poetry and history raises its head. Does Faulkner's distinction lie in the report his novels made of life in northern Mississippi, or does it lie in the use he made—as a poet—of that life as he knew it, remembered it, and understood it? Certainly he knew it; he lived there; and he did unquestionably make use of it, for it supplies his landscape and his atmosphere, not to speak of his people, who may or may not be portraits of particular persons but who have the air of belonging in a world outside his fiction to which he can go whenever he pleases for individuals as well as types. Once again, however, it is the inside world that finally matters: the created world which has a consistency, a hue, that only imagination can explain. The world of William Faulkner (1897–1962), one of the richest worlds in modern fiction, is a world transformed; it is not copied, it is not drawn from what we are in the habit of calling life. It has its own life, and the source of it is Faulkner's genius. Otherwise he would not be here.

Of his many books I have chosen these:

Sartoris
The Sound and the Fury
As I Lay Dying
"Barn Burning"
"A Rose for Emily"

Sartoris (1929), the opening novel in the long series dealing with life in and around the fictitious town of Jefferson, Mississippi—Faulkner lived in Oxford—introduces the two families that always will figure in the series: the Sartorises and the Snopeses, who represent respectively the top and the bottom of Jefferson society. The Sartorises are the aristocracy, the Snopeses the scum. Colonel Sartoris, who had a career in the Confederate Army and who subsequently built a fine house for himself outside of town, is the progenitor of the clan as we encounter it, though in *Sartoris* it is only the ghost of his importance that makes itself felt; he had been murdered, as Faulkner's own great-grandfather, Colonel William C. Falkner, had been. Now Bayard Sartoris, an old banker who will die in this book, represents the family, along with young Bayard who has just returned from being an aviator in World War I, and along with Miss Jenny, the ancient sister of Colonel Sartoris, whose tart tongue has much to tell us about the wildness of the tribe—the wildness yet the beauty too, for this is the only family, except for the de Spains, the Sutpens, the Compsons, the Benbows, and the Griersons, that holds on to the decent, gracious traditions of a past now threatened by the Snopeses. A Snopes, who has worked his way out of Frenchman's Bend, a filthy, degenerate village not far out from Jefferson, is working in the bank, of all places; and he is writing anonymous letters to Narcissa Benbow which disgust and terrify her. Narcissa is to fall in love with young Bayard Sartoris and marry him; but wildness in him, after his return to find his first wife dead, has taken the form of racing a car madly about the neighborhood in the hope that he may kill himself: a consummation he achieves at the end, not in his car but in a plane, and this is a fitting death because another thing that haunts him is the death of his twin brother John in France, an aerial death he fancies he might have prevented. There is much more than this in the book. There is the love, for instance, of Horace Benbow for his sister Narcissa, a love that hovers on the edge of incest, like the love of Quentin Compson for his sister Candace in *The Sound and the Fury*.

The Sound and the Fury, also published in 1929—Faulkner, once he conceived the series, rushed to realize it—is perhaps more powerful than *Sartoris* because it is more concentrated; but the concentration is so intense, and the torment of its people so terrible, that Faulkner scrambled his time-scheme in an effort to make all the events seem simultaneous. The result has puzzled and confused many readers, though the passion in these people is authentic passion, and the book has found an audience that justly admires it. The invention of Faulkner is most impressive, as is the capacity to identify himself, then us, with the suffering of the Compsons. His plot is rich with complications that remind us of Dostoevsky; his eloquence is likewise comparable with that of the Russian master. If it is true, as has been said, that he caught fire midway of *Sartoris* and burned steadily thereafter with a purpose that did not rest until the entire series was finished—if indeed it was finished by anything other than his death—then we have the spectacle of an artist profoundly involved with his material, and an artist, furthermore, who gave it the kind of devotion for which there is no other word than love. By which I do not mean sentiment, for a certain humor in him kept sentiment down. In *The Sound and the Fury*, for instance, Jason Compson reveals himself as more a Snopes than a Compson, let alone a Sartoris. He is one of the meanest characters in fiction and as such stands in cold contrast to the Compsons around him: people with hearts and minds, people with the power, whatever their weaknesses and errors, to touch us deeply, to speak with voices that have music in them, as of course Jason's voice has not.

Within a year (1930) Faulkner had published *As I Lay Dying*, which some students of him consider his masterpiece, though if it is a masterpiece it is a minor one, since the subject matter is slight. Perhaps that very slightness is what recommends it to readers who feel that other novels by Faulkner are thickets of conversation and event through which they must fight in order to reach open air once more. Read with the care he deserves, Faulkner does not justify such a feeling any more than Dostoevsky does, though it is true that his fare can be at moments all but unbearably rich. In *As I Lay Dying*, however, we have nothing but a backcountry family on its way to bury Addie Bundren, wife and mother, in Jefferson where she had always wanted to lie. The father and the children—grown sons and daughters—are of an irreducible simplicity. One of them is making a coffin even before the poor woman who is to occupy it has drawn her last breath. The others, including Dewey Dell, who is pregnant out of wedlock and looks forward to finding some medicine in Jefferson that will make all well again, manifest their simplicity in monologues which give Faulkner full rein with the humor he has in ripe abundance. The story is of the trip to Jefferson in a mule wagon with Addie and her coffin properly displayed. The only trouble is that there has been a heavy rain, so that as they ford a swollen river the mules are drowned and the wagon turns over; but it is righted, coffin and all, and at last the burial takes place—in good time, too, for days have passed since the little procession started, and people along the way are offended by what they smell. It is an idyll for all of this, a perfect rendering—wry, ridiculous, charming, moving—of one far-off moment in Faulkner time.

Faulkner's short stories fill in the crevices between the novels; it is as if he could not bear the thought of incompletion. "Barn Burning," one of the best, brings a Snopes and a de Spain together. This Snopes, certainly one of the worst, a savage, cold, terrible man, is given to burning the barns, or threatening to burn them, of landowners to whom he is bound as a sharecropper; any insult from the landowner, real or imagined, brings swift retribution by night. In the present case Snopes is angered by the de Spains: by the lady because she is outraged over his defilement of her house—he has walked through cow dung and he grinds the residue into her finest rug; and by de Spain himself who gets a judgment against him in court. The story is told from the point of view of Snopes's young son, a boy who cannot bear to accompany his father any longer with kerosene and kindling. He is forced to do so this night, but afterward, when his father has been shot, he walks away as if he were going on forever out of a world whose ugliness he has ceased to be able to tolerate. "A Rose for Emily" deals with a Grierson, Miss Emily, who poisons the man she loves and shuts herself up in her house for forty years with his skeleton on her bed. A grim tale, yet even then a grace note to Faulkner's incomparable saga.

IX. KAFKA, CAMUS, AND ORWELL

I put these three together because of one thing they did in common: they wrote parables. Not Utopias, not satires, though sometimes they are credited with that intention, but parables—stories with something abstract in them, something of the universal under the guise of here and now. Our age has produced many such works, for it is an age even more nervous about the future than appalled by the present; it is an unhappy age, as perhaps all ages have been, but with the difference that commentary grows ever sharper and sharper, and the reference to conceivable perfection—only, alas, conceivable—grows more and more pointed. These three men are not alike, either in subject matter or in power; yet neither are they absolutely unlike, for each of them in his way is writing fairy tales of the mind: a valuable thing to do, now or at any time. And all of them have done it with a distinction that will not be forgotten.

The chief of them for me is Franz Kafka (1883–1924), whose two posthumous novels, *The Trial* and *The Castle*, were to have been burned by his friend Max Brod, as Emily Dickinson's poems were to have been burned by her sister Lavinia; but Brod, to our good fortune, saved them and published them. They are among the most brilliant and fascinating works of the present century, and commentary upon them has been various as well as endless. They are often taken to be satires on contemporary society, but I take them to be something deeper and higher than that. For me they are theological in their bearing: *The Trial*, I think, deals with damnation and *The Castle* with election; or, if you prefer, one is a parable of guilt and the other is a parable of grace. This may sound strange in view of the fact that Kafka was a Jew of Prague (he wrote in German), but it is relevant to know that he had read the Danish philosopher Kierkegaard, and almost knew by heart his *Fear and Trembling*. In any case he penetrated to the center of Calvinist dogma, where he discovered things that most people today are ignorant of—and that, incidentally, is one of the things his books mean.

The hero of *The Trial*, called Joseph K., is arrested one morning for reasons he does not know and never will find out. He is not only arrested; he is interrogated; he himself interrogates the court that has condemned him; and finally he is executed, still ignorant of the cause. There is no cause except that he has been picked out of thousands to be damned— something that is plain to us but is not so plain to him. The women of the novel find him attractive, as they find any condemned man attractive, and in our minds too he takes on a certain distinction because of the mystery that attends his fate. Mystery is the word. Why does God hate this man and love that other? Naturally there is no answer, any more than there is an answer to the famous question, as old as the world, What does he see in her, or she in him? Love, like the absence of love, is not to be explained, though the heroes of these two novels break their very brains in search of reasons why they should be treated as they are. For the hero of *The Castle* has been offered grace, again without discernible cause, but he does not know how to accept the gift, and eventually it seems to be withdrawn, though of this we cannot be sure because the novel does not end.

The courts that condemn Joseph K. are unimaginably complex and impenetrable, so that some commentators have assumed that Kafka intended satire upon the law's delays. Not so, I believe. The parallel is inevitable; and hence the parable. But the gist of the matter is unearthly, not earthly. Joseph K. is damned for all eternity, not because he has broken any law, but simply because it suits the universe to damn him. So with K. in *The Castle*, who comes to a snowbound village at the foot of a hill on which a mysterious building stands, expecting to be admitted because he bears a letter inviting him there to be a land surveyor. But he never finds anybody who knows about the letter, and every attempt he makes to communicate with the Castle ends in frustration—the telephone does nothing but buzz, and the offices up there are too busy with documents to consider his case. The only official whose name he ever hears, Klamm, is so far from being available that K. can imagine he doesn't even exist, in spite of evidence—Frieda, Klamm's former mistress—that he does. The people down in the village cannot understand the aggressive eagerness of K. to gain admittance and be recognized. They belong to the Castle even though they live downhill from it, as Piccarda in the *Divine Comedy* says she belongs in Paradise even though she does not inhabit its inmost circle.* The villagers suggest that if K. could relax he might eventually understand that he is already in and of the Castle, but this is something he cannot do. He remains bewildered by the barriers between him and Klamm, somewhat as visitors to modern business offices are thwarted by telephone operators who say their bosses are in conference, or by receptionists whose desks cannot be passed. So *The Castle* has often been taken to be a satire on bureaucracy and paper work, but again it is vastly more than that. Our paper work provides its symbol, but its essence is something more ethereal altogether, just as its moral, supposing it has one, is simpler than a child could say: When grace is given us we should know how to accept it and should not ask for proof that as a gift it is genuine.

In one sense I am misleading about Kafka: my exegesis of him sounds too solemn. His nimble style—short, plain words that run on and on till the reader, enchanted, is out of breath—and his charming invention—delicious details, always so logical and at the same time so surprising—these are primary virtues in one who would write, as I am certain he did, of supernatural things. Then add to all this that he is often amusing; he is said to have laughed uncontrollably when he read the manuscripts aloud. Amusing, yet, under the aspect of eternity, terrible. Eternity is real in these parables, even though we are not permitted to inhabit it. We merely note that those who stray from it into time—into the ordinary world where we ourselves live—soon become weary, and find it hard to breathe. They are God's fish out of water. And who could suggest this

---

* *Paradise* III; *GBWW*, Vol. 21, p. 109d.

but Kafka? It is my way at last of saying that in his two priceless narratives he came as near as mortal man can come to stating the truth about the moral universe. At any rate, we have from him a pair of classics of the highest and purest order.

The Plague, to which some readers may prefer *The Stranger* or *The Fall,* also by Albert Camus (1913–1960), is a parable in a special and perhaps a limited sense. Published in France in 1947, it is ostensibly an account of something that happened in the African city of Oran, namely, the coming of the plague and the long quarantine of the city in consequence, but who has ever doubted that it is really about the German occupation of France, and particularly of Paris, during the painful years between 1940 and 1945? The model for it is surely Defoe's masterpiece of reporting, *A Journal of the Plague Year,* which seems for all the world to be the account of an eyewitness, though Defoe was only five years old when the plague devastated London. This was a good model for Camus to take, because he must have wished to be as plain, and to sound as unimpassioned, as it was possible for him to be, considering how hard he had taken the occupation of his own beloved city. The parallel is all the deadlier for this calm in the narrator's voice. The details of the plague at Oran are wonderfully conceived and placed. It is a permanent work, and its final paragraph, speculating about the possible return of the plague at some future time, cannot be lost on any reader.

Animal Farm, by George Orwell (1903–1950), which preceded *The Plague* by two years (1945), is of a different order altogether. It reads like a children's story, which certainly it is not; or if it is, it is for children much older than their years. I might have chosen his *Nineteen Eighty-Four,* a savage Utopia in reverse, a Swiftian prophecy so bitter that it is all but unbearable, but the year 1984 will soon be here, and what of the prophecy then? True even now, one might declare, but I prefer to represent this mordant critic of the modern world by a book that so far as I can see need never seem out of date. It is a tale of some pigs who suddenly were seized with the desire to form a perfect society. They did so, and then the society, perhaps like all such things, let corruption in. The corruption in this case consisted of letting human beings in, with the result that before too long the men could not be told from the pigs, nor the pigs from the men. A summary all too brief, but it may suffice to show Orwell's intention. His fable, or if you please his parable, continues to the end to read like a children's story: a bedtime one, perhaps, to be read in the last evening of the world.

X. ALEXANDR SOLZHENITSYN

R ussian fiction since 1917 has not been notable for any qualities that would remind us of the great novelists—Gogol, Turgenev, Goncharov, Dostoevsky, Tolstoy—of the nineteenth century. Not, that is, until now, when Solzhenitsyn's *The First Circle* has stolen its way out of Russia and been recognized as the masterpiece of horror—and of beauty, too—which I agree with others that it is. I know I am taking a risk when I select for this hypothetical set of great modern works so recent a one as *The First Circle*, but it is a risk I do not hesitate to take, for two readings of it have convinced me that Solzhenitsyn belongs with the masters who preceded him so long ago, when literature in Russia, whatever difficulties beset it, still was not forced to consider itself an arm of government, a celebration of things as they are. No reader of him will doubt that he deals with things as they are, but neither will any reader be surprised to learn that what he has written could not be published in his own country. The wonder is that he could write it at all, and then get it somehow into the hands of the rest of the world.

Once again, and for the last time, I have to remind myself of the difference between poetry and history. *The First Circle* is history to the extent that it satisfies our curiosity concerning one phase of life in Russia under Stalin. The time it covers is four days in 1949, and the scene is a prison on the edge of Moscow where several hundred scientists are confined while they work on projects assigned to them by the authorities above. They are all political prisoners, and most of them—like Solzhenitsyn himself as it happens—had served terms in Siberian labor camps before they were sent here to work in relative comfort; but only relative, since they still were prisoners of an absolutist government and scarcely needed reminding that they had not escaped from hell; they had merely been moved up to its first circle, as the pagan philosophers in Dante had been sent to spend eternity in Limbo*; and they could always be sent down again, as in fact the hero of the novel, Nerzhin, finally is, for no other reason than that he refuses a new assignment. He will never see the bright world again, nor be again with his wife, Nadya, its chief ornament for him as he is for her.

To speak thus of Nerzhin and Nadya, whom we see only once together during a thirty-minute visit she is permitted to pay him—they may not touch each other, nor say what they really mean except with their eyes—is all at once to make it clear that *The First Circle* is poetry: is story, with a hero and a heroine. Before Nerzhin was told that the visit would be paid, he had been tempted to make an assignation with a girl, Simochka, in the Acoustics Laboratory where he works, but now the sight of Nadya sweeps all such desire away, and when the time comes he tells Simochka so. Were there nothing else in the book, this love story would distinguish *The First Circle* among the novels of the world.

But there is much else—so much more that the range of it can merely

---

* *Hell* IV; *GBWW*, Vol. 21, p. 5d.

be suggested here. There is the prison itself, with dozens of men in it whom we come to know intimately as we hear them talk and watch them work. And the central man among them is Nerzhin, whose integrity—of which he never boasts, for it is something he scarcely knows—provides one of the most moving spectacles I have ever encountered. It is this that I had in mind when I spoke of beauty: the human spirit of Nerzhin, doomed though he may be, is a star in the gloom of a prison so dreadful that the mind reels considering it, a star whose light no cruelty or stupidity can extinguish. The specific nature of this cruelty we discover from what happens to a man on the outside, Volodin, whose story begins and ends the book; and his story has a crucial relation to the story of the prisoners, notably Rubin, who will identify in the Acoustics Laboratory the voice of Volodin as that of the man who had tried to telephone a warning to Professor Dobroumov not to put himself in danger from the secret police. The telephone call had been taped, and it is Rubin—Nerzhin's friend—who makes the identification. The consequences for Volodin are too terrible to print, but that is not my present point, which is rather that Solzhenitsyn's art has thus placed the prison itself in a perspective where we shall always see it. Volodin, a hitherto happy denizen of the bright world, is the focus through which we suddenly peer into the grim interior of a circle, a cavern, a pit, where excellent men who cannot be aware of what they are doing do inhuman things.

Even then I have not exhausted the contents of this long and powerful work. To do so might require as much space as the work itself occupies. But that is true of any masterpiece. I am content to call it that, and to put it last, if only in point of time, among its peers.

BIBLIOGRAPHY

CAMUS, ALBERT. *The Plague.* Translated by STUART GILBERT. New York: Random House, Inc., 1966 (paperback).

CHEKHOV, ANTON. *The Major Plays.* Translated by ANN DUNNIGAN. New York: New American Library, Inc., 1964 (paperback).

———. *Selected Tales of Chekhov.* Translated by CONSTANCE GARNETT. 2 vols. New York: Barnes & Noble, Inc., 1963.

CONRAD, JOSEPH [JÓZEF TEODOR KONRAD KORZENIOWSKI]. *The Shorter Tales of Joseph Conrad.* New York: Doubleday, Doran & Co., Inc., 1924.

DICKINSON, EMILY. *The Complete Poems of Emily Dickinson,* ed. THOMAS H. JOHNSON. Boston: Little, Brown & Co., 1960.

DOYLE, ARTHUR CONAN. *The Complete Sherlock Holmes,* ed. CHRISTOPHER MORLEY. New York: Doubleday & Co., Inc., 1953.

ELIOT, T. S. *The Complete Poems and Plays, 1909–1950.* New York: Harcourt, Brace & Co., Inc., 1952.

FAULKNER, WILLIAM. *As I Lay Dying.* New York: The Modern Library, Inc., 1967.

———. *The Collected Stories of William Faulkner.* New York: Random House, Inc., 1950.

———. *The Faulkner Reader.* New York: The Modern Library, Inc., 1959.

———. *Sartoris.* New York: New American Library, Inc., 1957.

———. *The Sound and the Fury.* New York: The Modern Library, Inc., 1967.

FROST, ROBERT. *Complete Poems of Robert Frost, 1949.* New York: Henry Holt & Co., Inc., 1949.

———. *In the Clearing.* New York: Holt, Rinehart & Winston, Inc., 1962.

HARDY, THOMAS. *Collected Poems of Thomas Hardy.* New York: The Macmillan Co., 1926.

HEMINGWAY, ERNEST. *The Old Man and the Sea.* New York: Charles Scribner's Sons, 1954.

———. *The Short Stories of Ernest Hemingway.* New York: Charles Scribner's Sons, 1956.

IBSEN, HENRIK. *Last Plays of Henrik Ibsen.* Translated by WILLIAM ARCHER. New York: Hill & Wang, Inc., 1959 (paperback).

———. *Three Plays of Ibsen.* New York: Dell Publishing Co., 1960 (paperback).

ISAK DINESEN [KAREN BLIXEN]. *Seven Gothic Tales.* New York: The Modern Library, Inc., 1961.

———. *Winter's Tales.* New York: Vintage Books, Inc., 1961.

JAMES, HENRY. *The Turn of the Screw and Other Short Novels.* New American Library, Inc., 1962 (paperback).

JOYCE, JAMES. *Dubliners,* ed. ROBERT SCHOLES and RICHARD ELLMANN. New York: The Viking Press, Inc., 1967.

———. *A Portrait of the Artist as a Young Man.* New York: The Viking Press, Inc., 1967.

———. *Ulysses.* New York: Vintage Books, Inc., 1961 (paperback).

KAFKA, FRANZ. *The Castle.* New York: Alfred A. Knopf, Inc., 1954.

———. *The Trial.* New York: Alfred A. Knopf, Inc., 1957.

KIPLING, RUDYARD. *Kipling: A Selection of His Stories and Poems.* Vol. 2. New York: Doubleday & Co., 1956.

LARDNER, RING. *The Collected Short Stories of Ring Lardner.* New York: The Modern Library, Inc., 1941.

MANN, THOMAS. *Joseph and His Brothers.* New York: Alfred A. Knopf, Inc., 1948.

MARK TWAIN [SAMUEL LANGHORNE CLEMENS]. *The Adventures of Huckleberry Finn.* Indianapolis: Bobbs-Merrill Co., Inc., 1967.

———. *Life on the Mississippi.* New York: Harper & Row, Inc., 1965.

MAUPASSANT, GUY DE. *Complete Short Stories.* New York: Garden City Books, Inc., 1955.

ORWELL, GEORGE. *Animal Farm.* New York: New American Library, Inc., 1956.

PROUST, MARCEL. *Remembrance of Things Past.* New York: Random House, Inc., 1941. (Also available in seven volumes from The Modern Library, Inc.)

ROBINSON, EDWIN ARLINGTON. *Collected Poems.* New York: The Macmillan Co., 1948.

SHAW, GEORGE BERNARD. *Caesar and Cleopatra.* Baltimore: Penguin Books, Inc., 1964.

———. *Heartbreak House.* Baltimore: Penguin Books, Inc., 1964.

———. *Major Barbara.* Baltimore: Penguin Books, Inc., 1965.

———. *Man and Superman.* Baltimore: Penguin Books, Inc., 1957.

———. *Saint Joan.* Baltimore: Penguin Books, Inc., 1962.

SHOLOM ALEICHEM [SOLOMON RABINOWITZ]. *Selected Stories of Sholom Aleichem,* ed. ALFRED KAZIN. New York: The Modern Library, Inc., 1956.

SOLZHENITSYN, ALEXANDR I. *The First Circle.* New York: Harper & Row, Inc., 1968.

THURBER, JAMES. *The Thurber Carnival.* New York: Dell Publishing Co., 1964 (paperback).

WELLS, H. G. *The Time Machine and The War of the Worlds.* New York: Heritage Press, 1964.

YEATS, WILLIAM BUTLER. *The Collected Poems of W. B. Yeats.* New York: The Macmillan Co., 1956.

The Year's Developments
in the
Arts and Sciences

A Symposium

on

Contemporary Poetry

CONTENTS

LOUIS SIMPSON

Mr. Simpson was born in 1923 in Jamaica, West Indies. He was educated in Jamaica and at Columbia University in New York, where he received his B.S. in 1948, his M.A. in 1950, and his Ph.D. in 1959. After serving as a rifleman during World War II, he became an editor for the Bobbs-Merrill Publishing Company, a position he held until 1955. He then taught at The New School for Social Research, Columbia University, and the University of California at Berkeley. He is now Professor of English at the State University of New York at Stony Brook. A prolific author, his books have included a novel, Riverside Drive *(1963);* An Introduction to Poetry *(1967);* James Hogg: A Critical Study *(1962); and five volumes of poetry:* The Arrivistes *(1949),* Good News of Death and Other Poems *(1955),* A Dream of Governors *(1959),* At the End of the Open Road *(1963), and* Selected Poems *(1965). He has also published poems, criticism, and stories in many magazines:* Harper's Magazine, The London Magazine, The Critical Quarterly, The New Statesman, The Sixties, The Nation, *and* The American Scholar. *His awards include the Prix de Rome, 1957–58; a Guggenheim Fellowship in 1962–63; and the Pulitzer Prize for Poetry in 1964. He is married and has three children.*

308

The New American Poetry

It is not possible to discuss poetry without talking about the ideas that poets have, nor can we find a poet of any importance who has not had, at one time or another, a set of ideas. Tendencies, movements, schools—these are the manifestations of ideas. Some people think that poetry should not be discussed in this manner; poetry is something that simply happens. But booksellers have more copies than they can move of books by poets with talent and no principles. Their works, like the Junes in which they were written, soon wither. As a Frenchman said, when we have done something foolish we say that it came from the heart. Poetry, however, comes out of intelligence and ideas about the writing of poetry, and these of course include the poet's feelings.

In the 1940's three reputations overshadowed the writing of verse in America: W. B. Yeats, T. S. Eliot, W. H. Auden. Each spoke for an era: Yeats for romanticism and symbolism; Eliot for the imagist movement, the Depression, and a turning toward dogma (for Eliot it was Christian dogma, for others Marxism); Auden for technical ingenuity and an agile curiosity turning in several directions—Marx, Freud, Kierkegaard, Christianity. Through the 1940's it was Auden who still influenced younger poets most clearly; in retrospect the poets of the time—Delmore Schwartz and Karl Shapiro come to mind—were imitating Auden more than they knew, together with imitations of Eliot and Yeats, and sometimes of Rilke. (It is odd to think of Rilke as a model in those years, for in his self-searching and his belief in angels Rilke was far removed from Marxist determinism and fashionable references to psychoanalysis.)

At the beginning of the 1950's Dylan Thomas burst on the American scene, bringing with him a new concept—at least it seemed new at the time—of poetry as the spoken rather than the written word. This example was to have a powerful effect some years later when the Beats and other poets began performing in public. This is anticipating, however, for in his poems Thomas was working in the old symbolist techniques; there was nothing in his concept of the poem itself that was new, only in the manner of delivery.

From the end of the war until the mid-1950's there was a dearth of new ideas about poetry in America. Older poets—Robert Frost, Wallace Stevens, E. E. Cummings, Marianne Moore, William Carlos Williams, and Ezra Pound—were writing, but Pound, *"il miglior fabbro,"* was a patient in St. Elizabeth's Hospital, and the others, however fine their works might be, did not strike the young as teachers. Each older poet would come out of obscurity to be given a prize and have his vogue. So it was with Stevens after 1954 when the *Collected Poems* won the National Book Award. But the older poets were distant planets, each whirling in a separate volume. The influential ideas about poetry came from the New Critics and in the postwar years there was seen a phenomenon, poetry imitating criticism.

The New Critics—R. P. Blackmur, Cleanth Brooks, John Crowe Ransom, Allen Tate, Robert Penn Warren, and their men in the universities—regarded the poem as an object for rigorous, empirical, objective analysis (textual criticism). The poem was treated "primarily as poetry and not another thing," without reference to the author's life or intention (the intentional fallacy), to history, to genre, or to the effect of the work on the reader's feelings (the affective fallacy). Young poets hastened to oblige the critics by writing poems that would be suitable for this kind of analysis. Above all, personality was to be omitted, except under a mask, and the speaking voice was ironic. Discipline of this kind produced two brilliant poets: Robert Lowell (*Lord Weary's Castle*, 1946) and Richard Wilbur (*The Beautiful Changes, and Other Poems*, 1947). They were like Browning and Tennyson. Lowell was full of obscure references; he wrote couplets or alternate rhymes that pounded like a jackhammer; his subject was violence and guilt:

> Is there no way to cast my hook
> Out of this dynamited brook?
> —"The Drunken Fisherman"

Wilbur wrote in elegant, mellifluous stanzas; his poems were a dance of similes and play of ideas:

> Mind in the purest play is like some bat
> That beats about in caverns all alone . . .
> —"Mind"

In 1957 an anthology, *New Poets of England and America*, presented a number of poets who had much in common with Lowell and Wilbur.

W. S. Merwin, Anthony Hecht, Howard Nemerov—in different tones each was producing a kind of verse that was guarded, indirect, self-deprecatory, and usually written in rhymed stanzas. Perhaps the most representative poet in the anthology was Nemerov, who wrote of a vacuum cleaner:

> The house is so quiet now
> The vacuum cleaner sulks in the corner closet,
> Its bag limp as a stopped lung, its mouth
> Grinning into the floor, maybe at my
> Slovenly life, my dog-dead youth.
>
> —"The Vacuum"

Poetry such as this was too domestic. However, something new might be observed in the poetry of W. D. Snodgrass. His poems in the anthology, later to be published in a first book, *Heart's Needle*, spoke of personal matters, though in conventional stanzas. His subject was divorce and visiting hours, the last frontier for an American turning toward suburbia:

> If I loved you, they said, I'd leave
> and find my own affairs.
> Well, once again this April, we've
> come around to the bears;
>
> punished and cared for, behind bars,
> the coons on bread and water
> stretch thin black fingers after ours.
> And you are still my daughter.
>
> —"Heart's Needle"

This signaled a change toward a more direct kind of writing, and the change was coming from other directions at the same time. Let us step back to Pound, doing penance in St. Elizabeth's. Pound had been the most useful disseminator of ideas about writing in English in this century, but Pound's poems had no influence while the New Criticism predominated. The "open," discursive writing of the *Cantos* did not please the taste nurtured on Yeats, Eliot, and Auden. These men were "makers" of finished poems; Pound was a bard, a prophet, and his poems were never finished. The *Cantos* frequently were dismissed as incoherent rambling that contained, by accident, lyrical passages. Nor did Williams, with his flat, prosey lines and "American speech rhythms," excite readers accustomed to the regular accents of Yeats, Eliot's music, and Auden's jazzy stanzas. But an underground of new poets had been springing up, who took Pound and Williams as masters. These poets—Charles Olson, Robert Duncan, and Robert Creeley, with the addition of Denise Levertov and disciples—developed a school of "Projective Verse." According to Olson, their theorist, Projective Verse was to be "composition by field."

311

He defined a basis for structure of the poem in terms of its *kinetics*—"the poem itself must, at all points, be a high energy-construct" and, "at all points, an energy-discharge." "Form," Olson said, "is never more than an extension of content" and "One perception must immediately and directly lead to a further perception." He distinguished between breathing and hearing, as these relate to the line: "the line comes (I swear it) from the breath, from the breathing of the man who writes, at the moment that he writes. . . ."

The poems of Olson's followers were harvested in an anthology, *The New American Poetry* (1960). Several of these poets were Westerners, and perhaps the most outstanding, Robert Duncan and Gary Snyder, wrote of Oregon and California—unlike the poets of the 1957 anthology who were attached to the East Coast. The "New American" poets wrote lines according to Olson's system of breathing (I find Olson's theories hard to explain, as I am sure he must find them himself). These poets were rhapsodic; at times they seemed, as has been said of Pound, to be translating at sight from an unknown poem:

> *The Thundermakers descend,*
> damerging a nuve. A nerb.
> The present dented of the U
> nighted stayd. States. The heavy clod?
> Cloud. Invades the brain. What
> if lilacs last in *this* dooryard bloomd?
> —Robert Duncan, "A Poem Beginning with a Line by Pindar"

Snyder was best when he detailed his logging-camp and hiking experiences:

> Stone-flake and salmon.
> The pure, sweet, straight-splitting
> with a ping
> Red cedar of the thick coast valleys
> Shake-blanks on the mashed ferns
> the charred logs . . .
> —"Burning"

Another group of new poets was represented in the 1960 anthology: the Beats (from "beat up" or "beatific"—no one knows what the word means exactly, probably a little of both). The most notable of the Beats was Allen Ginsberg, whose debt was to Williams rather than to Pound. Listing common things in the American grain, he wrote about supermarkets and bus terminals. Ginsberg's long loose lines were not in the manner of Williams, who was always tightly controlled; in rhythm the model was Whitman. What was original, however, was Ginsberg's temperament; he had a talent for hysteria. He spoke or rather ululated for the middle-class children who had grown up after World War II in an affluent society and who suffered from acute neuroses. The Beats were creating a subculture with their own heroes and saints—smokers of marijuana, motorcyclists, and jazz musicians who spoke familiarly of Buddha:

> I saw the best minds of my generation destroyed by madness,
>   starving hysterical naked,
> dragging themselves through the negro streets at dawn looking
>   for an angry fix,
> angelheaded hipsters burning for the ancient heavenly connection to
>   the starry dynamo in the machinery of night . . . .
>
> —Allen Ginsberg, "Howl"

This opening was as famous for a while as Eliot's "April is the cruelest month," and a later generation ("generations," like art movements, are coming faster and faster) that calls itself not Beat but hippie counts Ginsberg, along with Tim Leary and the man who plays the sitar, among the gurus. To the flower-children, Ginsberg, like Whitman, is a "good gray poet," and at the present moment Ginsberg is the most famous poet in America.

With Snodgrass' *Heart's Needle*, the poems of Duncan and Snyder, and Ginsberg's "Howl," though they arrived from different directions— Snodgrass from the New Criticism, Duncan and Snyder from the ideas of Pound and Williams as interpreted by Olson, and Ginsberg from bohemia, with some credit to Williams—we begin to see an idea held in common, a turning away from the New Critics' idea of the poem-as-object, a construction, and a turning toward poetry of direct, personal utterance. Irony was being replaced by sincerity. Lowell took the step in 1959 with *Life Studies;* with his defection from the teachings of Brooks and Warren one could see the handwriting on the wall. The new sincerity produced, in the manner of Lowell, so-called confessional verse— Anne Sexton (*To Bedlam and Part Way Back*) and Sylvia Plath (*Ariel*)— and in the coffeehouses an outpouring of monologues in the manner of Ginsberg.

Most Beat or "confessional" poetry seems as short-lived as the topics it deals with: drug-using, personal "hang-ups," news items. But this might also be said of poetry of every kind, in every period; there is nothing less durable than a mediocre sonnet; and it is possible that poems by Ginsberg and Plath will still be alive some years from now. The New Critics tipped the balance too far toward a mechanical idea of poemmaking; in reaction the Beats have swung toward poetry as hallucination. Confessional poetry, however, with its frequent reliance on shock, becomes a mere mannerism as does every form of writing that is used automatically. The following statement by Joseph Conrad, in *A Personal*

313

Record, indicates just where the poetry of Ginsberg, Lowell, and their imitators of one kind and another begins to fail:

> In order to move others deeply we must deliberately allow ourselves to be carried away beyond the bounds of our normal sensibility— innocently enough, perhaps, and of necessity, like an actor who raises his voice on the stage above the pitch of natural conversation —but still we have to do that. And surely this is no great sin. But the danger lies in the writer becoming the victim of his own exaggeration, losing the exact notion of sincerity, and in the end coming to despise truth itself as something too cold, too blunt for his purpose— as, in fact, not good enough for his insistent emotion. From laughter and tears the descent is easy to snivelling and giggles.

"The exact notion of sincerity"—this phrase may serve as an introduction to another kind of new poetry rising in the 1960's. The poets of whom I wish to speak—sometimes called the "Sixties poets" because Robert Bly, their chief spokesman, edits a magazine in Minnesota called *The Sixties*—differ from poets such as Nemerov, products of the New Criticism, in that they wish to speak with a personal voice; and differ also from the Beat and confessional poets in that they wish to speak truly about visible things. The poems of James Wright, Robert Bly, Donald Hall, John Haines, Galway Kinnell, William Stafford, David Ray, and others are a continuation of the "modernist" experiments of Pound and the surrealists.

The "Sixties poets" import models from Germany, Scandinavia, Spain, and South America. There is even an American way of writing a Chinese poem. As I describe it, this movement may not seem new, but actually it is in the sense that it is continuing an experimental movement that was never fulfilled in America. During the 1930's and 1940's poetry in America and Britain turned its back on the modernism of 1910, as well as on the experimentalism of the young Pound, Stevens, Cummings, and Williams.

Due to the New Criticism, poetry in the United States became a formalistic imitation of metaphysical verse or, under the influence of Auden, a retailing of journalistic ideas. Modernism in English stopped before it had barely started, and the age that in other countries saw such poets as Pablo Neruda develop to their full stature, in the United States produced poetry of a conventional kind. It would be interesting to account for this retraction of the spirit; I think it was caused by the Depression, in the imagination of poets as well as in economics, but I must leave this for someone else to explore. The poetry I am now describing is a renewal of the aborted modernism of the generation of 1910. There is not a great difference between some of the poetry of James Wright and this translation by Pound, in *Cathay* (1915):

314

Louis Simpson

"Separation on the River Kiang"
Ko-jin goes west from Ko-kaku-ro,
The smoke-flowers are blurred over the river.
His lone sail blots the far sky.
And now I see only the river,
    The long Kiang, reaching heaven.

Here is the naming of objects, then the imaginative leap from object to heaven, or to the interior world of the psyche, that is characteristic of Wright:

Close by a big river, I am alive in my own country,
I am home again.
Yes: I lived here, and here, and my name,
That I carved young, with a girl's is healed over, now,
And lies sleeping beneath the inward sky
Of a tree's skin . . .
                     —James Wright, "Rip"

A movement from the outward, objective world toward the inner world of the psyche—this is practically imagism, as Pound described it. In an imagist poem, Pound said, "one is trying to record the precise instant when a thing outward and objective transforms itself, or darts into a thing inward and subjective."

The "Sixties poets" are rooted in American landscapes, somewhat to the bewilderment of New York reviewers who cannot believe that anyone takes nature seriously. It is evident, from the rise of poets such as these, that American poetry is not confined, as English poetry has been, by the taste of a single literary capital. Minnesota and Seattle are as good places for poetry as New York, and in some ways more stimulating.

It may be their preoccupation with nature that has made the "Sixties poets" so concerned with protesting against that most unnatural enterprise, the war in Vietnam. Other poets have written against the war, but the Sixties Press has published the most original and interesting poems on this subject, in an anthology of poems together with statements "by General Araki, Abraham Lincoln . . . Adolf Hitler . . . Lyndon B. Johnson," under the title *A Poetry Reading Against the Vietnam War* (1966, 1967). The poems in this collection are not propaganda; they express an urgent, individual involvement; at the same time, the quality of the writing is high. Here is William Stafford's "At the Bomb Testing Site":

At noon in the desert a panting lizard
waited for history, its elbows tense,
watching the curve of a particular road
as if something might happen.

It was looking at something farther off
than people could see, an important scene
acted in stone for little selves
at the flute end of consequences.

There was just a continent without much on it
under a sky that never cared less.
Ready for a change, the elbows waited.
The hands gripped hard on the desert.

In speaking of groups as I have done, I am not forgetting that every
true poet is *essentially* different from other poets. Yet poets are not
autonomous; they need other people and other people's ideas. It is true
that a poet usually finds out about poetry by himself and begins his work
in solitude, thinking that no one else is doing the same sort of thing. But
then he discovers that other poets have been moving along the same line,
for all are subject to history and the ideas of their time. For a while these
people agree; they write letters to one another and meet and discuss
ideas; they may publish a magazine, issue manifestos, and make anthologies. Then the group splits apart, each one going his own way.
But their criticism of one another has had far-reaching consequences.
So it was with Pound. But for the thinking he did in conjunction with
T. E. Hulme, Ford Madox Ford, and Eliot, Pound would not have developed into a major poet. So it was with the "Oxford poets" of the
thirties: Auden, Spender, MacNeice, and C. Day Lewis; their poems
shared the same symbols: pylons and locomotives; they spoke of the same
characters: Homer Lane, Marx, and Freud. And so it is today. I believe
that Denise Levertov no longer considers herself a follower of Olson;
Ginsberg wishes no longer to be called Beat; and James Dickey is now
loath to be associated with Bly; but at crucial moments these poets
shared certain ideas with other poets, and the moments determined the
kind of poetry they would go on to write.

Still, in making divisions as I have done, I have passed over some
poets of considerable achievement such as James Dickey, David Ignatow,
Thomas McGrath, and George Hitchcock, editor of the magazine *Kayak*
in San Francisco. I feel less uneasiness when I consider that I have not
mentioned the work of New York poets such as Frank O'Hara and John
Ashbery who frequented literary circles and art galleries. They were
chic; their verse did not rise above a surrealism without depth or aim.
And there are always the poets that one forgets simply because they
have not written poems of any importance, however active they may
be on reading circuits.

What do we want in poetry? We want the world transformed. We want
songs and stories, and now and then, but not too often, we want to be
persuaded. We want images and rhythms that are natural, yet unexpected.
We want ideas realized in images, and images that start ideas. No one

has ever been able to say what poetry is, but everyone, it seems, is able to recognize it sooner or later. In this age as in every other, a few poets have imposed themselves; they have imagination and a voice; they have created poems that cannot be argued with. Such a man was Theodore Roethke, whose *Collected Poems* appearing posthumously in 1966 showed for the first time the full range of his talent. Though he was in touch with current practice, Roethke did not have at his disposal the chorus of reviewers that Lowell commanded. Roethke wrote his poems in solitude, and in his last poems was extending the reaches of poetry in free-flowing lines that dredged up images from nature and his psyche:

> I have come here without courting silence,
> Blessed by the lips of a low wind,
> To a rich desolation of wind and water,
> To a landlocked bay, where salt water is freshened
> By small streams running down under fallen fir trees.
> —"The Long Waters"

Poetry such as Roethke's is not limited by traditional form nor by psychoneurosis but springs from deep sources of pleasure.

No one can predict the future of poetry, but I think that the trend toward free forms and personal expression will continue for some time, and so will the writing of political verse. I do not mean occasional verse or propaganda, but verse in which the poet is aware of his time and place and the issues at stake. Political verse is written by the poet who has a habit of thinking of other men; it is an angle of vision, perhaps only a tone of voice. In general, we can hope for a more inclusive kind of poetry. In the 1940's and 1950's an American poet was likely to conceive of poetry as a perfect thing from which "rough," factual, shocking material was excluded. To write a poem was to whittle down one's perceptions to a defensible core. But there is an opposite kind of poetry, involving suffering and humor; a poetry less perfect, but more humane and important. This is the kind of poetry that we are beginning to write.

JAMES DICKEY

Mr. Dickey was born in Atlanta, Georgia, on February 2, 1923.
He was educated at Clemson College and Vanderbilt University,
where he received his B.A. and M.A. degrees. Mr. Dickey has
been a star college athlete, a night fighter pilot with over one
hundred missions in World War II and Korea, a hunter and
woodsman, and a successful advertising executive in New York
and Atlanta. He has taught at Rice University and the University
of Florida and was Poet in Residence at Reed College during
1963–64 and the University of Wisconsin in 1965. The recipient
of numerous awards, he won the National Book Award in 1966 for
his collection of poems entitled Buckdancer's Choice; a Guggenheim fellowship in 1962–63; the Longview Award for 1959; the
Vachel Lindsay Award for 1959; and the Union League Civic and
Arts Foundation Prize in 1958. In 1966–68 he was Consultant in
Poetry to the Library of Congress. A frequent contributor to such
magazines as The Atlantic Monthly, Harper's Magazine, Commentary, The New Yorker, Poetry, and Partisan Review, he has
also published two books of criticism—The Suspect in Poetry
(1964) and Babel to Byzantium (1968). He has written six volumes
of poetry: Into the Stone (1960), Drowning with Others (1962),
Helmets (1964), Two Poems of the Air (1964), Buckdancer's
Choice (1965), and Poems 1957–1967 (1967). He lives in Leesburg,
Virginia, with his wife and two sons.

The Self as Agent

Every poem written—and particularly those which make use of a figure designated in the poem as "I"—is both an exploration and an invention of identity. Because the poem is not the actual world of tactile sensations and relations, but must be represented as such by the agreed-upon meanings and the privately symbolic values of words, the person who is so identified often bears only a questionable and fugitive resemblance to the poet who sits outside the poem, not so much putting his I-figure through an action but attempting to find out what the I-figure will do, under these circumstances as they develop and round themselves out. The poem is admittedly a fiction; its properties are all fictional even if they are based on fact, and its devices are those of consciously manipulated artifice. The poem is created by what is said in it, and the *persona* of the I-figure is correspondingly conditioned far more by the demands of the poem as a formal linguistic structure than by those of the literal incident upon which it may be based. Therefore the notion of a poem-self identifiable with the author's real one, and consistent from poem to poem, is a misreading of the possibilities of poetic composition.

What is the motive on the part of the poet, in this regard? Why does he assign to "himself," as he appears in his own poems, such and such traits, such and such actions? In other words, why does he make himself act the way he does in his poems? This question could of course be answered in the most obvious way, by saying that there is bound to be some degree of wish-fulfillment present in the poet's practice, and undoubtedly there would be truth in the assertion. But more important than that, the I-figure's actions and meanings, and indeed his very being, are determined by the poet's rational or instinctive grasp of the dramatic possibilities in

319

the scene or situation into which he has placed himself as one of the elements. To put it another way, he sees the creative possibilities of the lie. He comes to understand that he is not after the "truth" at all but something that he considers better. He understands that he is not trying to tell the truth but to *make* it, so that the vision of the poem will impose itself on the reader as more memorable and value-laden than the actuality it is taken from. In the work of many a poet, therefore, the most significant creation of the poet is his fictional self. The identity that is created by the devices and procedures of the poem has made him into an agent fitted more or less well, more or less perfectly, to the realm of the poem. The personality that the I-figure has therein may never recur, and the external poet, the writing poet, is under no obligation to make him do so. Likewise the *author's* personality as it changes from poem to poem is not itself assignable to any single poem. A certain Protean quality is one of the poet's most valuable assets. Therefore he is almost invariably embarrassed at the question he is bound to be asked about his poems: "Did you really *do* that?" He can only ask in turn: "Did *who* do it?"

From poem to poem the invented self is metamorphosed into whatever it is to become in the poem. Though language itself is the condition that makes the poem possible, there are a great number of other factors that make this particular *use* of language possible and, with luck, desirable. To use an analogy, the poem is a kind of local weather, and what creates it is the light that words in certain conjunctions play upon each other. It is a place of delicate shades as well as of sudden blindnesses, and, while it is in the process of being made, it is impossible for its creator to tell what the total light of the completed poem will be like. But no matter whatever else it may be likened to, the poem is a realm that is being created around the I-figure as he is being created within it. The poet knows that his figure will be taken for him; he knows that "this is supposed to be me," but the conditions by which he is limited and delimited in the poem are, in fact, nothing like the same ones that shape his actual life. During the writing of the poem, the poet comes to feel that he is releasing into its proper field of response a portion of himself that he has never really understood.

As for the I-figure himself, he is at first nebulous, ectoplasmic, wavering in and out of several different kinds of possible identity. He is a stranger in a half-chaotic place that may with fortune and time become familiar. Though by the time the poem is completed he may have become solid, dominant, and even godlike, he is tentative indeed at the beginning of the poet's labors. The poet in his turn exercises an expectant vigilance, always ready to do what the agent-self inside the poem requests him to; he will do what he can to make his agent act, if not convincingly, then at least dramatically, tellingly, memorably. The questions he must answer in this respect come to the poet in forms not so much like "What did I do then?" but rather "What might I have done?" or "What would it be interesting for me to do, given the situation as I am giving it?" Or perhaps, if the poet is prone to speak in this way, "What can I make my agent do that will truly *find* the poem: that will focus it on or around a human action and deliver a sense of finality and consequence, and maybe even that aura of strangeness that Bacon said every 'excellent beauty' must possess?"

As we know, it is part of the way in which the human being makes identifications to take the *persona* of the poem for the poet himself: to make him personally accountable not only for the poem's form and its insights but for the events which the poem describes, translated back into the world of real human beings and non-mental objects. Who does not, for example, identify Prufrock as Eliot? It is hard not to do this, even when the I-figure is designated in the title or by other means as a *persona*, as in Browning's "The Bishop Orders His Tomb at Saint Praxed's Church." In reflecting on such matters, one realizes the implications, both artistic and personal, that reside in Proust's injunction to Gide to the effect that one can "say anything, so long as one doesn't say 'I.'"

II

What does the poet begin with in attempting to create a personage in a poem who will bear the name "I"? With an individual in a time and at a place, or reflecting in a kind of timeless and placeless mental limbo. The poet usually gives him some overt or implied reason for speaking, and for reacting in a certain way to the events in which he finds himself or those that he thinks about. What he reacts to, for example, may be a condition or a person he knows well, or one he knows to some degree, or it may be something that acts upon him with the wonderful or uncertain or dreadful shock of newness. Now the poet believes that he understands his *persona* only to the extent that he understands himself. But that is not quite the case. For some unfathomable reason, the poet may find his "self" acting in quite an inexplicable way, often doing things that the poet never knew either of them knew. So the poem becomes not so much a matter of the poet's employing a familiar kind of understanding but rather a matter of aesthetic and personal curiosity: the placing of a part of himself into certain conditions to see what will come of it in terms of the kind of interaction between personality and situation he has envisioned from the beginning. He must of course then empathize, he must think himself into the character, but he must realize that his character also possesses the power to think itself into him and to some extent to dictate what he writes. For the poet's part, one of the most interesting things to note is that the poet is just as likely to attribute to his character traits that are diametrically opposed to those that the poet displays during his day-to-day existence. For this reason as well as for others, it is possible for psychologists to make a very great deal out of poems, as Ernest Jones does with *Hamlet*, to take one of the most obvious cases. But the poem, though it may be useful or instructive in this way, does not exist exclusively or even primarily for this reason, as we know. It is not because of its psychologically revelatory qualities that the poem interests us; it is its capacity to release to us—and release us to—insights that we otherwise assuredly would not have, giving these by means of the peculiar and inimitable formal devices of a practiced art.

As a poet, I have done a good deal of speculating on the kinds of ways certain poets might be presumed to make themselves think, act, and speak in their poems. And in my own work I have wrestled with the problem in my own way. For example, should the poet cause his I-figure to speak in a manner in which he might be expected to speak, but which *feels* wrong to the poet? And are the advantages and perils of first-person narration the same for poems as they are for novels and stories? Some of the best of our fiction writers—Henry James comes to mind—have called the first-person device a limited and even "barbarous" method. But for poetry as well as for fiction it has one quite simply incomparable characteristic, and that is credibility. When the poet says "I" to us—or, as Whitman does, "I was the man, I suffer'd, I was there"—we must either believe him completely or tell him in effect that he's a damned liar if his poem betrays him, by reason of one kind of failure or another, into presenting himself as a character in whom we either cannot or do not wish to believe. Because of its seeming verisimilitude, some recent writers have so overused the first person that they are designated—and rightly—as "confessional." And, though all poetry is in a sense confessional, no really good poetry is ever completely so, for "confessing" means "telling the truth and nothing but the truth," and, setting aside the question of whether that is really possible to any creature lower than the angels, it is evident that for any imaginative poet there are too many good opportunities outside of and beyond the mere facts to pass up; in most instances these are the opportunities that, when utilized and realized in the poem, make it more telling dramatically—and "truthful" as well. What the poet wishes to discover or invent is a way of depicting an action in a manner that will give at the same time the illusion of a truth-beyond truth and the sense of a unique imaginative vision. The real poet invariably opts for the truth of the poem as against the truth of fact, the truth of truth.

And so the poet is aware, more than he is aware of anything else, of the expressive possibilities of his use of himself: that agent in the poem whom he calls "I." He feels a strange freedom and a new set of restrictions when he realizes that he can call into play—can energize—any aspect of himself he wishes to, even if he doesn't yet know what it is to be: any self that

322

the poem calls for. He exults in his "negative capability" and can, as Keats says, take as much delight in creating an Iago as an Imogen. His personality is fluid and becomes what it is most poetically profitable for it to become, in the specific poem in which it comes to exist. Poems are points in time when the I-figure congeals and takes on a definite identity and ascertainable qualities, and the poet is able to appear, for the space of the poem, as a coherent and stabilizing part of the presentation, observing, acting, and serving as a nucleus of the unities and means and revelations of the poem, a kind of living focal point—or perhaps it would be better to say that he finds himself *living* the focal point. The better the poet is—Shakespeare, Browning—the more mercurial he will be, and, paradoxically, the more convincing each of his *personae* will be, for he can commit himself to each independently and, as it were, completely. The better the poet is, the more personalities he will have, and the more surely he will find the right forms to give each of them its being, its time and place, and its voice. A true poet can write with utter convincingness about "his" career as a sex murderer, and then in the next poem with equal conviction about tenderness and children and self-sacrifice. As Keats says, it is simply that the poet "has no personality." I would say, rather, that he has a personality large enough to encompass and explore each of the separate, sometimes related, sometimes unrelated, personalities that inhabit him, as they inhabit us all. He is capable of inventing or of bringing to light out of himself a very large number of I-figures to serve in different poems, none of them obligated to act in conformity with the others.

To speak personally, this has always seemed to me to constitute the chief glory and excitement of writing poetry: that the activity gives the poet a chance to confront and dramatize parts of himself that otherwise would not have surfaced. The poem is a window opening not on truth but on possibility: on the possibility for dramatic expression that may well come to *be* what we think of as truth, but not truth suffering the deadening inertia of what we regard as "actuality," but flowing with energy, meaning, and human feeling. I am quite sure that I myself, for example, owe to the activity of writing poetry my growing conviction that truth is not at all a passive entity, merely lying around somewhere waiting to be found out. I conceive it as something that changes in accordance with the way in which it is seen and more especially with the way it is communicated. And if the poem in which the poet's I-figure serves as an agent concretizes and conveys this sensation of emotional truth, a humanly dramatic and formally satisfying truth, then the literal truth has given birth to a thing more lasting than itself, and by which it will inevitably come to be remembered and judged.

It has always seemed to me that Plato's "The poets lie too much" should be construed as an insult of quite another kind than Plato intended.

To be most genuinely damaging to the poets, the philosopher might better have said, "Our poets do not lie creatively enough; I prefer the real world untouched by their fabrications based upon it." For it is within the authentic magic of fabrication (a making-up as a making) that the I-figure moves, for as he receives his kind of reality—both an imposed and a *discovered* reality—from the poet and from language, so his being, his memorability, and his *effect* increase, and his place in his only world is more nearly assured.

The reader, on the other hand, knows that the thing he is dealing with is a *poem*, and not a news bulletin; therefore he can enjoy the luxury of submitting to it; that is, of abandoning his preconceptions about reality and entering into the poem's, for whatever there might be in it for him.

It is quite possible that I am oversimplifying, and drawing the lines too sharply. If the personality and being of the I-figure and the poet himself were *entirely* separate from each other, it would be much easier to discuss the two. But, of course, that is not—and could not be—the case. What happens is that the poet comes on a part of himself inadvertently; he surprises this part and then uses it, and, as he uses it, he more fully discovers it. For instance, suppose that one imagined himself as questioning Wordsworth about the composition of "Tintern Abbey." And suppose the poet answered, as he might well have done, "Yes, I *did* once find myself in just such a situation, and I did, as I recollect (in tranquillity!), feel very much as the poem says I did." And yet the point to note here is that the emotion could not possibly have presented itself, at the time of which it speaks, in the particular images and rhythms of the completed poem; these were factors that were added and worked in later, much after the fact, in an attempt to give the incident some kind of objectifying scheme of reference: to present it by means of a linguistic construction which could, by virtue of the fact that men may communicate verbally in several ways including the poetic, make the experience in at least some ways generally available. Put another way, Wordsworth might conclude of the devices and form of his poem, "They *might be said* to convey something like what I think I remember about that day, and how I felt about it, now that I have thought of it in this way."

Let me take a more recent example—Bernard Spencer's "Ill":

> Expectant at the country gate the lantern. On the night
> Its silks of light strained. Lighted upper window.
> "Is it you who sent for me?" The two go in
> To where the woman lies ill, upstairs, out of sight.
>
> I hear sky softly smother to earth in rain,
> As I sit by the controls and the car's burning dials.
> And always the main-road traffic searching, searching
>   the horizons.
> Then those sounds knifed by the woman's Ah! of pain.

324

Who dreamed this; the dark folding murderer's hands
  round the lamps?
The rain blowing growth to rot? Lives passed beneath a
  ritual
That tears men's ghosts and bodies; the few healers
With their weak charms, moving here and there among
  the lamps?

Now one cannot say with certainty whether Spencer ever *did* anything like this or not, though such is the persuasiveness of the poem that one is more likely than not to believe he did. But what is certain is that he reinvented himself in order to write the poem. He put himself in a car in the dark outside a country house, and he gave this figure of himself a way of thinking, a set of images and rhythms, and above all a way of speaking that he believed were right to body forth the scene in his particular way of being a poet. We are in the poem because he is, at a definite place and time, and we experience the invisible doctor and sick woman through his reactions. What he thinks and feels are what a reflective and imaginative mind has *found* to say about the incident between the time it happened or was invented and the time the poem was completed.

The I-figure does not live in the real world of fact but in a kind of magical abstraction, an emotion- and thought-charged personal version of it. Rather than in a place where objects and people have the taciturn and indisputable tangibility, the stolid solidity, of fact, the poetic agent inhabits a realm more rich and strange and a good deal "thicker" than reality, for it gathers to itself all the analogies and associations—either obvious or farfetched—that the poetic mind as it ranges through the time and space of its existence can bring to the subject. Constrained only by the laws imposed on him by the situation of any and all types, from the most matter-of-fact sort of reporting to the wildest phantasmagoria, he can be whatever his poem needs him to be. It is by virtue of his having his existence in just such a specialized kind of linguistic fiction that the I-figure—and in another way the poet—becomes what he is: a man subject to the permutations and combinations of words, to the vicissitudes of denotation and connotation. Both are creatures trapped by grammar, and also at the mercy of its expressive possibilities and those of all the particulars and means of the poem. The poet is also a man who has a new or insufficiently known part of himself released by these means. He is set free, for he is more inclusive than before; he is greater than he was.

STEPHEN SPENDER

Stephen Spender, who contributed the essay on literature in The
Great Ideas Today 1965, *is a well-known writer and poet. Spender
first published his poetry and criticism in the early 1930's, and as
a translator, editor, lecturer, poet, and critic, he has continued to
enhance our enjoyment of literature. He was born in London in
1909 and received his education at University College, Oxford.
Graduating in 1930, he initially achieved recognition as a member
of the group of young Oxford poets noted for including social
and political commentary in their verse. Prior to World War II
he coedited the influential literary journal* Horizon. *After the war
he served as counselor in the section of Letters in UNESCO and,
in 1953, was one of the founders of* Encounter *magazine. He has
lectured at many universities, and was appointed Visiting Professor of English at Northwestern University in 1963. Among his
many books are:* Collected Poems, 1928–1953 *(1955); an autobiography,* World Within World *(1951); and collections of critical
essays:* The Creative Element *(1953),* The Making of a Poem
(1955), and The Struggle of the Modern *(1963). His most recent
books are* Selected Poems *(1964) and* The Magic Flute *(1966). He
gave the A. W. Mellon Lectures in Washington in 1968. To honor
his contributions to English letters, Spender was made a Com-
mander of the British Empire in 1962.*

The Vital Self and
Secondary Means

The ways in which poets think about their own and others' poetry are inevitably complex and confusing. We know that poetry is a vocation, and yet it is not a spiritual calling like religion, with values not of this world. Poetry is not a profession; yet being a poet and living on the by-products of poetry—such as lecturing and teaching—has become one, just as the owner of a coal mine might live on the by-products of coal and make no profit from the coal itself. To all intents and purposes, poetry cannot be taught, and yet a person with poetic talent has to learn to write poetry.

It is a cliché to say that poets are born and not made, and a nuisance to say it when it is used to argue that what X writes must be poetry because he is a "poet." All the same, I feel certain that what makes a poem poetry is some primary quality of sensibility—more than sensibility, of being—which only the true poet is gifted to make the language of the poem realize. The fact that this primary quality is *sine qua non* makes nonsense of all poetic movements, schools, promotion programs, and awards, and even of most critics' judgments of contemporary poetry. For this reason, we feel an immediate sympathy when Robert Graves says that a poem has to be addressed to the Muse. Graves may talk nonsense when he lays down the law in favor of Muse-poetry and against Apollonian poetry; yet we know that what he has said is important in that it means poetry must be to or for or about something else than a

327

fashion, a movement, a gang, an award, or just the poem itself. In the same way, when A. E. Housman declares, echoing Wordsworth and the Romantics, that Dryden and Pope wrote not poetry but versified prose, we answer the charge not by defending a rationalist poetry of meaning, but by pointing out that the path of tough-minded intellectual argumentation did lead Dryden and Pope to write lines which we recognize as poetry with the same tingling response as we recognize Shakespeare, or Blake, or Wordsworth himself for that matter.

It seems almost a sign of a major contemporary poet that he is extremely uncertain about his own poetry, or—putting it more subtly—uncertain as to whether he has ever written poetry. A poet's critical statements about writing tend to be those of a technician, a craftsman, and a critic of other men's works; thus they produce often an impression of confidence, of dogmatism even. A poet writing about his craft is naturally concerned with what I call secondary matters. The primary matter of whether it is poetry at all is the one he can least deal with, because in the last analysis what makes poetry poetry is indefinable. In their public statements modern poets lead us up to the point beyond which there is the indefinable, "language rich and strange," the sensation that makes the hair at the back of the neck bristle. This is what Pope and Dryden sometimes have in common with Shakespeare and Blake.

When a poet writes of poetry as an intellectual game, we cannot be sure that he means quite what he says. I suspect that this is how he talks to a poetry-reading public. But when he is discussing poetry with a fellow poet, he is likely to single out a line and say "that is poetry." Eliot used to say that sometimes when writing he felt an excitement which gave him confidence. Then, at a certain interval after finishing a poem, he might read it with an excitement which corresponded to that he had when writing it. But later, he would feel quite remote from the lines he had written with passionate certainty.

Rilke endured ten years in which he was unable to write poetry. Yet without building up a poet's silence as a variety of his expression, one may feel that this interval was devoted to poetry through being devoted to waiting. It shows Rilke knew that the routine part of poetry is secondary to the most important thing which is a kind of attention, a waiting for the poetry as for a visitation. And if one hears that William Carlos Williams wrote a few lines every day, this does not contradict Rilke's ten years' silence, for one immediately supposes that Williams' attention was keeping himself in a state of athletic technical preparedness for the poetry, when it came.

The experience of poets seems to show then that although discipline, technique, routine, skill are of course necessary, just obeying the rules does not, in itself, result in poetry. Very little critical attention seems to have been given to the interesting question of what made poets like

Wordsworth and Tennyson dry up. The usual answers all really amount to saying that the poets grew old and weary and disillusioned and therefore prosaic and dull in their poetry. It seems to me possible that one contributing factor for the dullness of the later Wordsworth and Tennyson is that they got too skilled at writing their kind of verse, so that there was no struggle with form and words. There was too little of "the fascination of what's difficult." The goals of their technique were too easily achieved.

I do not altogether believe that form and technique are absolutely inseparable. I think that in some of the most interesting poetry there is, moving within the form, the struggle of the expression to find that form.

One reason for thinking this is that great poetry is the expression of sensibility which is unique. Form, the formal, is a mold for which there is precedent, just as technique, as such, observes rule. Therefore the unique state of sensibility must always struggle with form, be a bit outside the technique. In the great passages of *The Prelude*, or for that matter in *The Lotus Eaters*, there is the feeling of an exhilaration in the one, of lassitude in the other, which breaks through or weighs down the form. Poetry can be great while still leaving the reader with a feeling that form and content are not a perfect fit.

What I am saying has some bearing on the argument that poetry is an intellectual game with language like a crossword puzzle. Eliot and Auden have both at times supported this argument, but I am not convinced they quite meant what they said. That poetry is an intelligent pastime, not serious, is a good thing to say to people whose unseriousness consists in taking things too seriously—solemnly: questioners at poetry readings who ask poets to support and inspire social causes become "unacknowledged legislators of mankind," who think that a poet should provide the answer to the great human problems.

However, the idea of poetry as a game of form and words could only mean two things. First, that the feeling, idea, subject, or content, which makes the poet write the poem, is important only in that it gives him the opportunity of playing such a verbal game, according to rules provided, or which he may invent. This would be to abolish the distinction which is widely (and rightly, I think) held to exist between "occasional" poetry and poetry. The distinction may indeed be slighter than the common reader thinks, but still I believe it exists, and that Eliot was trying at the deepest level of his activity to "say something" in *Four Quartets*, and that, for him, poetry was the best way of saying it. For a poet who has something not just the poem itself to communicate, poetry is simply the best possible way of saying it. There is also, of course, the game of saying it as well as possible and according to set rules. The answer to the "only an intellectual game" theory is that saying things, whether in prose or poetry, can be both serious as well as amusing. Poetry, if you like, is serious (as something said) and amusing (as verbal play) at the same time. Probably the writer of the *Book of Revelations* enjoyed working out his apocalyptic imagery. But this does not mean that he was not serious about what he had to say.

Second, the "poetry is only a game" theory can be taken to mean that a poet cannot be single-mindedly thinking of a feeling or an idea which he expresses in the poem, because he has also to think of a rhyme or the stanza form. Balzac uses this as an argument against poetry in his introduction to Stendhal's *Chartreuse de Parme*. But if you think that poetry is the best way of saying certain things, this idea falls to the ground unless it were argued—as I do not think it can be—that saying anything—whether in poetry or prose—becomes a divided and compromised aim if part of your attention is directed to the way of saying it—as it surely must be if it is to be said truly and well.

The "poetry is only a game" theory plays into the hands of the people it is directed against, those who think that poetry to be "sincere" and "serious" must be rhymeless free verse, or even must—as Karl Shapiro at one time was arguing—be prose poems. It lends itself to false dichotomies such as those alternatives set forth by Louis Simpson in an interesting article, "Dead Horses and Live Issues" (*The Nation*, April 24, 1967), between "New Critics" poets and their self-expressionistic opposites. The first (now superseded) kind of poet stands for:

> the poem treated as an object complete in itself; impersonality, a distance between the poet and the poem, use of a persona, irony, et cetera

His opposite, now in the ascendancy, can be defined by what he does not, rather than what he does, want to write:

> They don't want to write Low Tide verse—about finding a dead fish at low tide; or the poem about the statues in the Villa Medici; or the well-rhymed poem about picking up the kid's busted tricycle and thinking of the death of Patroclus. In fact, they don't want to write any kind of rhymed poem . . . They don't want to write the so-called 'well-made' poem that lends itself to the little knives and formaldehyde of a graduate school.

Simpson also tells us:

> The change can be measured by comparing the reputation of W. H. Auden today with what it was twenty years ago. Auden was nothing if not rational. Reading an Auden poem today is a chilling experience. Talk about snows of yesteryear!

But Simpson notes wisely:

> schools of poetry are a contradiction in terms and cannot last. For poets, who really are, want poems above everything else and will

330

recognize good work and condemn bad, even if the praise and condemnation are not in accordance with their own aesthetic, political
or other interests.

The attitudes of the "New Critic" poets, or ex-poets, and of the now
fashionable poets who are "anti" them are not Simpson's own, it seems.
He is merely reporting them. Both sets of attitudes seem significant to
me in a rather negative way, in that they make me think of contemporary
poetry as a kind of squalid playground in which gangs of ambitious
nonentities claiming to belong to "schools" are squabbling about the
rules of the game—whether poems should rhyme or not, whether some
member on his side should cultivate an air of ironic detachment or one of
psychedelically "turned on" sincerity. It seems an incredibly petty
community, this which measures by its modishness the reputation of
Auden. And in case the reader of this essay suspects me of some personal
bitterness, I should make a distinction between the feelings of disappointment one may have which are the almost inevitable accompaniment of
practicing an art before critics and public, and the feeling that the conditions in which that art exists are narrowing, petty, and soiling. What is
really discouraging about the life of writers, which literature, after all, is
rooted in, is that it was and remains for most of those participating "Grub
Street." A literary rabble, whether composed of New Critical lecturers in
English departments of a New University or of psychedelic beatniks,
is shameful, because it introduces into art politics and the competitiveness
of the marketplace—or, of the examination room.

When poets start worrying about publicity and rewards, there is the
danger of dragging poetry down to the level of other things that are
produced by routines and can be priced and ranked.

Some reader may protest that competitiveness and fashion are less
dangerous to poetry than a false piety which accepts everything called
poetry and makes few distinctions. It is better to attack what is good
unfairly than to allow what is bad to pass as good. I would accept this.
So be it. Poetry has to be controversial; poets have to make a living,
usually in other ways than by writing poetry; there has to be some kind
of patronage, whether by universities offering jobs, or foundations making
awards; the very fact that poetry is a mysterious vocation makes poets
unsure of themselves and therefore vain, anxious to promote themselves
and their friends, do down their rivals. We do have to live in Grub Street.

The important thing, however, is that the distinction between what
is primary as a state of being, of sensibility, to be communicated in poetry
and what is secondary as means, technique, conditions of work, promotion, publishing, awards, jobs, should not be lost. It is difficult to discuss
what is primary—what makes a poet a poet and a poem a poem—because it is indefinable and can only be indicated. as when we say that a
poem has a certain tone, or that it produces on us a physical sensation.

I hesitate to say what I fear both the academics and the psychedelics will find unacceptable: that I believe poetry, in common with all the arts, to be a language for another pre-verbal language of feeling, experiences recollected, and sensibility—a language of the "soul" so immediate and intimate to the essential nature of the artist that music, rhythm, and imagery are like membranes, skin of an eardrum, which while drummed upon with sound are a medium of communication for a meaning which is beyond the sound.

Paul Gauguin, discussing the origin of a painting, writes:

> Where does the execution of a picture start, where does it end? At the moment when intense feelings are fused in the depths of one's being, that the work then, suddenly created, brutally if you wish, but great and superhuman in appearance. Cold and rational calculations have nothing to do with this eruption, for who knows when, in the depths of his being, the work was begun, perhaps unconsciously?

And the famous passage from Proust's *Time Regained* with which Randall Jarrell so effectively concludes his essay, "The Obscurity of the Poet," extends the conception of art as language for another language beyond art, to something within the conditions of life itself which seems outside life:

> All that we can say is that everything is arranged in this life as though we entered it carrying the burden of obligations contracted in a former life; there is no reason inherent in the conditions of life on this earth that can make us consider ourselves obliged to do good, to be fastidious, to be polite even, nor make the talented artist consider himself obliged to begin over again a score of times a piece of work the admiration aroused by which will matter little to his body devoured by worms, like the patch of yellow wall painted with so much knowledge and skill by an artist who must for ever remain unknown and is barely identified under the name Vermeer. All these obligations which have not their sanction in our present life seem to belong to a different world, founded upon kindness, scrupulosity, self-sacrifice, a world entirely different from this, which we leave in order to be born into this world, before perhaps returning to the other to live once again beneath the sway of those unknown laws which we have obeyed because we bore their precepts in our hearts, knowing not whose hand had traced them there—those laws to which every profound work of the intellect brings us nearer and which are invisible only—and still!—to fools.

The primary then is the feeling, the impulse, the sense even of a task, a vocation, "invisible only to fools." This is the source of the qualities, the attributes, which we call great or minor, good or less good (just as we might define a shade of a color), when they are realized through the poet and all the means he employs—means that begin with his intelligence and physical vitality and end with technique, paper and ink, or a listening audience. I do not want to lose sight of the fact that the secondary qualities are extremely important. We are quite right to keep them in the forefront of critical discussion. For they are what can be most usefully analyzed, yet they are secondary qualities.

The most important thing is the quality of being of the poet, and this can only be realized by means which are to him the right and inevitable ones and which cannot be dictated by anyone else. For this reason I feel a certain dismay when I read that the young poets "don't want to write any kind of rhymed poem" or a remark of Auden's which appeared recently in *The Times Literary Supplement* that today poetry can only be written in a "drab" style. Remarks of this kind can only mean that those who make them are talking about what they themselves can write or want to write; and that they are adding to this that they do not think that anything else in any other manner should be written. The manner and means used at a particular moment are held up as the example of the form within which the primary impulse should express itself. This seems to me wrong. The primary impulse of a poet has to discover its own means, which may not be those of other poets, and to state that only certain means can be used is an attempt to dictate the quality of the impulse. The tyranny of a freedom which is held to be only capable of expression in a modish way can be just as inhibiting as the tyranny of an established academic style. The fallacy of academicism here becomes identical with the fallacy of a movement which is opposed to the academic. In both cases the fallacy is to think that at a certain time and place poetry can only be written according to a fixed formula or a fixed refusal to accept any rule. In the one case past conventions are set up as dogma, in the other case, the zeitgeist.

My argument is that poets are judged on two levels. First—and most important—the level of what they are as sensibility, consciousness, with qualities realized in the poetry, and capable of being analyzed; second, as employers of means. In means I include love of words and ability to play the games of language, without which none, whatever his qualities of soul, can write poetry. Technical skill is means. But also a program, such as refusing to write in rhyme, or even belonging to a poetic clique, or even having a job at a university, or taking drugs, must be counted as means, since all these contribute to a style.

I insist then on the importance of what a poet is. Ultimate judgment relates to the quality of his being, though I would certainly agree that the most useful and practical criticism relates to his way of doing it.

If one keeps the two things—primary essence and means—in mind, it is possible, I think, to feel critical of some of the attitudes of recent schools of poets reported in Simpson's essay—which I take to be representative. Discussing the young poets who "don't want to write any kind of rhymed poem," Simpson tells us that "There is an accelerating movement away from rationalistic verse toward poetry that releases the unconscious, the irrational, or, if your mind runs that way, magic. Surrealism was buried by critics of the thirties and forties as somehow irrelevant; today it is one of the most commonly used techniques of verse." My objection to this—which probably puts me in the rank of those who think of surrealism as "somehow irrelevant"—is that these poets seem to count on there being a shared subconscious which is readily accessible to a great many poets. For it is confusing to describe surrealism as "a technique," unless one considers being "turned on" as a technique. To my mind the confusion is like describing falling in love, writing poetry for the Muse, dreaming, or getting drunk as a technique. Surely these are states of mind induced in order that the poet may then write poetry which requires technique. Technique is conscious or it is nonexistent. In fact, what was so dull about surrealist poetry written in the late twenties and thirties (and which surely none can bear to read now) is precisely that "turning on," the surrealist trance of disassociation from rational meaning, was mistaken for technique.

The more important part of my objection arises from my conviction that poetry puts the reader in touch with the quality of a poet's awareness and sensibility deriving from his unique self, and that this quality cannot be the same in all poets. The overall term "the subconscious" suggests that all poets have the same inner life and that "surrealist technique" is a way of tapping this so that it pours out in an uninterrupted, undifferentiated flow. A good deal of poetry now being written does seem to presuppose that there are poets who do think this. And, of course, if you regard the basic self within the subconscious as the same in all poets—in the way that gas under the ground tapped by pipes is the same—then the question of secondary means of literary technique becomes irrelevant. To rhyme or bother about meter would merely interrupt the flow, once the "technique" had been found for tapping such a flow.

It seems to me that there are two ideas which ought to be resisted. The first is the idea that poetry is an intellectual game with words. This implies that the experience, sensation, impulse in life, from which the poem originates is simply the occasion for a form of words, and that after the language has been found nothing remains except the verbal play. This is better, of course, than thinking that poetry is self-expression, but still it is not true. It is an idea put forward to ward off the vulgar like the "mask" or artificial "personae" that poets used to go in for in the 1890's.

While I was writing the preceding page of this essay, by one of those coincidences that are happy, I opened a magazine and my eye happened to fall on a quotation from Wallace Stevens' letters: "With a true poet his

334

poetry is the same thing as his vital self. It is not possible for anyone else to touch it." This answers the "word game" theory of poetry. It also answers the theory that poetry is an untapping of the unconscious mind turned on by "surrealist techniques." Of course, poets write out of dreams, trance, the subconscious. But the point at which the subconscious becomes potential poetry is that at which it becomes differentiated as the individual life of the poet, with his "vital self." It may be said that no one would dispute this. But the surrealists did—or some of them did—defend surrealism on political grounds as the communism of the spirit precisely because it was pre-individual, everyone's subconscious. And current ideas of poetry as something that can be "turned on," by drugs, or by the projective verse writers' methods ("a system of breathing and using the typewriter that will enable anyone to write poetry naturally, without thinking . . ."—Louis Simpson) also postulate technique as invocation, something of the order of table-rapping.

Thinking along these lines affects my attitude to current poetry. I do not dismiss poetry which is either academic or anti-academic. I think that both the academic and the anti-academic are means of communication. What matters is that they should in each case be justified as means in their performance and in their communication of a "vital self" beyond the means employed, which must realize itself in the words, but which is not just the words but is experience and being communicated *through* the words.

The Year's Developments
in the Arts and Sciences

Music, Painting, and Sculpture
ROY McMULLEN

ROY McMULLEN

Roy McMullen was born in Gays Mills, Wisconsin, on May 9, 1911. He received his B.A. from the University of Oregon in 1935 and his M.A. in English Literature from the University of California at Berkeley in 1941 and was a teaching fellow at the latter institution from 1939 to 1941. He served as a glider pilot and intelligence officer in England and France during World War II, and after the war he joined the staff of the New York Herald Tribune *in Paris, where he still lives. Since 1963, he has been a consultant on the fine arts for the* Encyclopædia Britannica. *He has been a contributing editor of* Art News *and the European editor of the combined magazines* High Fidelity *and* Musical America, *and he has written on music, literature, and the visual arts for the* Herald Tribune, House Beautiful, Réalités, Connaissance des Arts, *and* Horizon. *He is the author of a forthcoming book on Marc Chagall.*

Music, Painting, and Sculpture

The Thomist philosopher and historian Étienne Gilson, in a recent and rather ruthless little book disarmingly entitled *The Arts of the Beautiful*, remarks that "one can seldom be completely wrong when speaking about art, for the truth about art is so manifold that it would be sheer bad luck to miss the target completely." I hope he is right, for the present article will be defensible neither as an exhaustive survey nor as a definitive evaluation (we are too close to my examples for that). It will indeed be merely a kind of "speaking about art." More specifically, it will try to show that the great ideas of the Western tradition are thoroughly relevant to what has been happening during the last few years in modern music, painting, and sculpture; and I know that to some readers such an aim will seem predestined to miss the target completely.

Both conservatives and avant-gardists may object that what is characteristic of twentieth-century art is precisely the fact that it has broken with, and frequently thumbs its nose at, the Western tradition. I would agree, if by "tradition" we mean—sticking to my three arts—such formal, stylistic, and referential phenomena as the key system in music, optical naturalism in painting, and the heroic human image in sculpture. The great ideas—as listed in the *Syntopicon* of *Great Books of the Western World*—constitute a tradition in a deeper sense—so much deeper that "tradition" may not be the right word. These ideas are not styles, procedures, and opinions; they are terms, topics, and problems about which Western man has been talking for more than two thousand years. As such, it seems to me obvious that they can still be relevant to art, even though the continuity (by which we usually, if unconsciously, mean the Renaissance continuity) of artists' attitudes toward many of them has been broken.

There exists, however, a far more troublesome objection to my undertaking. In one of its forms it is stated by Gilson, in the book from which I have just quoted. Art, he declares flatly, "is *not* a kind of knowledge . . . not a manner of knowing"; it belongs in "the order of making." Then, almost as if he were objecting specifically to the present article, he goes on to say:

> . . . I do not think I am betraying the real intentions of most of those who write about art, by saying that their chief concern is to turn it into something that can be talked about. In order to succeed, they have to interpret an act of production as if it were an act of expression and of communication.

Susan Sontag, in her *Against Interpretation, and Other Essays*, takes practically the same position when she refers to the critical search for meaning as a "revenge of the intellect upon art." In *Sign, Image, Symbol*, edited by Gyorgy Kepes, the American abstractionist Ad Reinhardt publishes some maxims which include:

> Messages in art are not messages.
> Explanation in art is no explanation.
> Knowledge in art is not knowledge.
> Learning in art is not learning.

A few years ago, in his *The Tradition of the New*, Harold Rosenberg reported the typical New York painter as saying, "Art is not, not not not not. . . ."

Such remarks are of course just the most recent manifestations of a current of opinion which has been flowing, largely through France and Germany, ever since the eighteenth century, when aesthetics as a distinct discipline was born—or christened, anyway. Sixty years ago, it was already fashionable to maintain that a work of art does not mean but simply is. Debussy, asked by an earnest conductor how the soloist should "interpret" the principal theme of *Prélude à l'après-midi d'un faune*, said it was merely about "a shepherd playing the flute, his hind end in the grass." In 1854, Gérard de Nerval announced that his half-mad poems "would lose their charm in being explained." In 1836, Théophile Gautier gave currency to the notion of art for art's sake. In 1790, Kant, in the midst of complaining about the loud singing of hymns by his neighbors, affirmed that music "speaks by means of mere sensations without concepts, and so does not . . . leave behind it any food for reflection" (Vol. 42, p. 535d). He did grant that painting "can penetrate . . . into the region of ideas" (p. 537a), but I imagine he would have promptly withdrawn that concession if he had foreseen the twentieth century's nonfigurative trends.

There have always been, to be sure, other opinions. Skimming through aesthetic history, we are reminded that the ancient Greeks and Romans derived a surprising amount of intellectual comfort from the cruder forms of the theory of art as imitation. In the Middle Ages, allegorical meanings were discovered in just about everything. Renaissance theorists often went in for mystical analyses of proportions. While Kant was writing, neoclassicism and rationalism were occupying other, and usually less acute, minds. In 1793, the painter Jacques Louis David issued a most unphilosophical philosophical manifesto (cited by Lionello Venturi in his *History of Art Criticism*):

> The artist must . . . be a philosopher. Socrates, able sculptor; J. J. Rousseau, good musician; the immortal Poussin, tracing on canvas the most sublime lessons of philosophy—these are so many witnesses who prove that the genius of the arts must have no other guide than the torch of reason.

In the nineteenth century, idealism and then empathy found favor. In our own era, Freudian and Marxist interpretations have been widely used. Modern scientific and philosophical modes of thought have been applied to symbolism, with impressive results in books like Susanne Langer's *Philosophy in a New Key* and *Feeling and Form*. Since World War II, information theory has interested a number of writers on art.

Yet I can think of no formal aesthetic theory that might serve as solid protection from the slings and arrows of Reinhardt, Gilson, Miss Sontag, and their historical allies, including Kant, although Gilson denounces him as a philistine. The plain fact is that music, painting, and sculpture as such—in their "pure" states, that is—are not at all "a manner of knowing." *As such*, they do indeed, as Kant says, speak "by means of mere sensations," and so they cannot be said to actually communicate concepts. In the chaos of our routine consciousness, even the most effective sonata, picture, or statue intervenes at first as a mere sharpening of emotional focus and perhaps a vague awareness of order, followed by a posthypnotic feeling of having been unusually attentive, unusually alive, for a few moments. All this may be very agreeable. But how can we talk about ideas of any sort, let alone the great occidental ones, in such a context?

Common sense, it seems to me, supplies the only possible answers. In the first place, no sensible critic today would try to construct a complete replica in conceptual language of a musical composition, a painting, or a statue. That sort of enterprise went out of fashion, I should guess, about when the last heroic-biography interpretation of Beethoven's *Eroica* was given up (the position of the "Funeral March" made the protagonist die too soon anyway). In the second place, art is by no means the only much-discussed human experience which cannot really be translated into conceptual language. A theory like that of Gilson, which—at least in the passage I have quoted—seems to tell us to be silent about the unutterable in a painting by Victor Vasarely or an opera by Gunther Schuller (I am about to mention both), should also stop all the talk about sex and weather. After all, the most industrious critic of sex cannot ever have experienced more than half of what he is talking about, unless he happens to be a new Tiresias (*GIT*, 1966, p. 355); and since we are always in weather, recapturing it in words is rather like trying to recall one melody while hearing another. Yet we do talk intelligibly to each other about sex and the weather. Obviously—as Gilson concedes in passing, and as indeed his book itself demonstrates—an experience which is not as such "a manner of knowing" can become a subject or an object of knowledge. Kant was right in saying that music speaks "without concepts," but wrong in concluding that it "does not . . . leave behind it any food for reflection."

Also, a plain fact is nearly always overlooked in abstruse arguments of the sort I have got myself into. It is simply that music, painting, and sculpture *as such*—in their isolated purity—are just philosophical fictions. The realm of "mere sensations" in which Kant puts them is only a convenience for discussion, since during our experience of them we cannot escape from our human realm of conceptual language. Indeed, without concepts there could be no music, painting, and sculpture; a Percheron cannot react to, or even recognize, Rosa Bonheur's "Horse Fair" "as such." (Hence, although saying so here is uneconomical, I find a semantic confusion in all accounts of the aesthetic activity of animals: their "art" is not ours.) One can be, and certainly should be, against judgments and literary paraphrases which shut off, and eventually become substitutes for, a full sensuous appreciation of the aural and visual arts. One can insist, again, that these arts do not *communicate* concepts. One can argue that the relevant ideas can only be very general and, so to speak, open-ended (which is exactly what the great ideas are). But finally one cannot be against interpreting these arts in words. Man's mind, being human, refuses to function in any other fashion.

THE HOW AND THE WHAT

Although there are many ways in which the great occidental ideas can be relevant—always and inevitably with the help of words—to current music, painting, and sculpture, two broad categories of "how" can be made out. In the first, the words are chosen by the artist and integrated with the work; operas and songs are the most common examples, but one can also cite paintings and pieces of sculpture that refer to literature or bear titles which are not just tags—which are as much a part of the work as a libretto is of an opera. In the second category, which of course often overlaps with the first, the artist leaves the choice of interpretative words pretty much up to his listeners or viewers, although he may, especially if he is a composer, supply explanatory notes written by himself or by an authorized critic. Here the common examples are nondescriptive instrumental music and abstract painting or sculpture.

Perhaps we can never be sure of having got a particular work tied to the most relevant great idea. All good art is open to more than one interpretation, and masterpieces are open to many. But the truth is that we still know very little about the psychology of art, and I would not dismiss the possibility (although it could reopen the whole argument about communicating concepts) that aural and visual works can function as fairly exact analogies, or sensuous metaphors, for verbal thinking. If we accept the notion of psychosomatic illness, why should we reject the notion of psychosomatic, or somatopsychic, art? Personally, I find that certain pieces of modern music in particular may be experienced as if they were working models of general ideas (it helps, I grant, to have read the program notes). How such models may operate is described by Erwin Panofsky in his fascinating essay *Gothic Architecture and Scholasticism* (the italics are his):

> Modern Gestalt psychology, in contrast to the doctrine of the nineteenth century and very much in harmony with that of the thirteenth, "refuses to reserve the capacity of synthesis to the higher faculties of the human mind" and stresses "the formative powers of the sensory processes." Perception itself is now credited—and I quote—with a kind of "intelligence" that "organizes the sensory material under the pattern of simple, 'good' Gestalten" in an *"effort of the organism to assimilate stimuli to its own organization"*;[1] all of which is the modern way of expressing precisely what Thomas Aquinas meant when he wrote: "the senses delight in things duly proportioned *as in something akin to them; for, the sense, too, is a kind of reason as is every cognitive power."*

I am not positive that Thomas Aquinas meant precisely all of that (*see* Vol. 19, p. 26b). But at least the passage does illustrate my belief that the great ideas of the Western tradition can be relevant to twentieth-century art. In fact, in this particular context every reference to the *Great Books* listed in the *Syntopicon* under the term SENSE is to the point.

We can now move on, without feeling too heretical, into more specific illustrations. These will be drawn from the productions of several recent seasons, partly to compensate for the omission of my subject from previous volumes of this series and also because my three arts do not have publication dates like those of literature—a picture or a song may be in existence for quite a while before one gets a chance to see or hear it. And that last fact reminds me to remind the reader that these illustrations are being supplied by an appreciator who has been living in and working out of Paris for a number of years. I do not think that this

1 R. Arnheim, "Gestalt and Art," *Journal of Aesthetics and Art Criticism*, 1943, pp. 71 ff.; *idem*, "Perceptual Abstraction and Art," *Psychological Review*, LIV (1947), 66 ff., especially p. 79 (Note by Professor Panofsky).

has much affected my awareness of artistic trends, since they are all thoroughly international today. But it has certainly affected my acquaintance with particular works. Even with the help of discs, the radio, television, color prints, and specialized publications, a critic of music, painting, and sculpture has to go to things in order to be informed, and there are always limits on how far and when he can go. He is thus apt to be rather provincial in comparison with literary critics, who can be snugly cosmopolitan in their armchairs.

WORDS, MUSIC, AND COMMITMENT

To turn from Thomas Aquinas to tenors and prima donnas may seem more than a bit absurd. There is, I know, a widespread and already venerable opinion that opera is the fool among the arts. Even among addicts there is little disposition to take a libretto seriously, and among nonaddicts there is general agreement with Dr. Johnson's scorn for the whole enterprise as "an exotick and irrational entertainment." Hardly anyone assumes that an operatic composer can have the sort of active commitment to general ideas which is taken for granted whenever a man of letters is discussed.

Yet the evidence of such commitment has never been scarce. If you want to know how a sensitive mind at the close of the Age of Enlightenment thought and felt about liberty, listen to the *"O welche Lust"* chorus of the prisoners in Beethoven's *Fidelio.* In Wagner's *Tristan und Isolde* you can hear an effective, if not quite orthodox, introduction to Schopenhauer's thoughts on will, along with some clear anticipation of Freud's speculations about Eros and death (Vol. 54, pp. 790a–791d). The music of Verdi was so closely associated with the Risorgimento that the slogan *"Viva Verdi"* became the recognized equivalent of *"Viva Vittorio Emanuele Re D'Italia."* At least one nineteenth-century opera—nowadays no longer heard in its entirety—can be called a national liberator, for the Belgian revolt of 1830 began after a performance of Auber's *La Muette de Portici.* And certainly, to cite two classics of our own era, one cannot call Berg's *Wozzeck* and Schoenberg's *Moses und Aron* intellectually frivolous. The first plunges deep into the nature of man and of evil; and the second is a musical inquiry into problems of religion, true knowledge, and artistic communication.

During recent seasons, no new opera has been comparable in terms of musical quality to the masterpieces I have just mentioned, and none to my knowledge has provoked a war of independence. However, two works thoroughly committed to serious ideas—and highly praised by critics from all over the world—had their first performances last year in West Germany. One was Hans Werner Henze's *The Bassarids,* which was presented at the Salzburg festival. The other was Gunther Schuller's

344

The Visitation, which had its premiere at the Hamburg State Opera (by the time these words are in print it will have been heard, if present plans go through, at the new Metropolitan in New York's Lincoln Center).

Henze merits attention for several reasons. At forty-one he has emerged as beyond question the most lavishly gifted composer of the postwar German renaissance. In fact, he is the first German composer since Richard Strauss to have a truly wide—rapidly becoming worldwide—audience. But at the same time, perhaps because of his talent and his success, he has become a rather troubling example of the young musician of the twentieth century trying to find a free, personal style in the midst of both modern and traditional academic schools.

He began his career under the influence of the scholarly, conservative Paul Hindemith and especially of Igor Stravinsky, who at that time was still neoclassical in outlook. Then the Young Turks of German music discovered the twelve-tone series of Arnold Schoenberg, whose works had been banned as decadent and Jewish by the Nazis. In 1952, Henze brought forth a completely serial opera, *Boulevard Solitude*, which told in terms of today's Left-Bank Paris the Manon Lescaut story; and his success was such that he was promptly hailed as the leader of the German, even the European, avant-garde. But then, in 1953, he suddenly committed what many of the more extreme modernists still feel was an act of desertion: he moved to the island of Ischia (eventually to Naples) and fell in love with Italian melody. He began to fear that the more strict kinds of serialism would, in his own words, "lead music into the grayness of dry algebra and destroy the ability to represent the most simple of authentic musical events."

His next opera, *König Hirsch*, and his *Five Neapolitan Songs* revealed a rejection of orthodox avant-gardism; and his work since then has been what he calls "freely invented music." If you are unsympathetic, you can dismiss it as fluent eclecticism. If you like it—and it is very hard to dislike —you can describe it as a sensuous, translucent synthesis of everything from a bit of jazz to Italian opera, Wagner, and even Massenet, strung between the poles of Schoenbergian counterpoint and Stravinskyan neoclassicism.

His other operas, besides *The Bassarids*, are *Der Prinz von Homburg*, a moody work based on Kleist's play; *Elegy for Young Lovers*, with a text by Chester Kallman and the poet W. H. Auden (the librettists for Stravinsky's *The Rake's Progress*); and the comic *Der junge Lord*, for which the young poet Ingeborg Bachmann did the libretto. He has also composed five symphonies, the cantata *Novae de Infinito Laudes*, several ballets, and a long string of minor works. Available on records are *Five Neapolitan Songs*, sung by Dietrich Fischer-Dieskau; excerpts from *Elegy for Young Lovers*, with the same singer; and the five symphonies, with Henze himself conducting the Berlin Philharmonic. The *Fourth Symphony* is also the second-act finale of *König Hirsch*.[2]

The libretto for *The Bassarids*, again by Auden and Kallman, is simply *The Bacchantes* of Euripides (Vol. 5, p. 340) brought up to date— or rather, given all sorts of dates. The principal characters and the plot of the play are kept: the puritanical young Theban king, Pentheus, who is determined to stamp out the worship of "this new god Dionysus" (p. 341d), is tricked by the god himself into attending an orgy of the Bacchantes, or Bassarids, and is torn member from member by the possessed women, who are led by Agave, daughter of Cadmus and mother of Pentheus. Old Cadmus, however, is the only personage in Greek robes. Pentheus is dressed as a medieval ruler, Dionysus appears first as a Valentino-type sheik and then as Beau Brummel, blind Teiresias is an English clergyman in dark glasses, and Agave wears an elaborate nineteenth-century gown. The run-of-the-mill Bassarids are beatniks and Bardots who are equipped with flashlights for their insane hunt for their victim. The settings mix classical Greek with Baroque and modern, and include television antennas.

The music—with the exception of a comic intermezzo which is painfully uncomic—is by far the most dramatically pointed and emotionally stirring that Henze has so far written. He is much kinder to voices than most of today's avant-gardists are, and he provides his cast with some beautifully traditional arias and fine choral numbers. But the orchestral part is the important thing, so much so that at times, in principle although not in the actual sound, a return to Wagnerian music drama is implied. The entire opera is a mammoth four-movement symphony which runs without a break for two and a half hours. This abstract structure may have been suggested to Henze by the example of Berg's *Wozzeck*, which is based very precisely on instrumental forms, and it can be regarded as simply a kind of scaffolding—helpful to the composer during the organizing of his material, but of no concern to the listener. In fact, however, it is capable of becoming, at least after a few hearings, a working model of the ideas in the libretto, for the two themes of the traditional symphony can represent the fundamental conflict between Pentheus and Dionysus. I do not mean to suggest that these themes are all-important in the work, nor that Henze is old-fashioned. He is very good at handling the complex rhythms and patterns of timbres favored by post-World War II modernists. But he is clearly doing some thinking as well as some music-making in *The Bassarids*.

What the thinking is about is arguable, of course, but not very much

---

2 Readers interested in the recordings mentioned in this article should consult their local dealers. Discs are often released under different labels in different countries and some may have to be imported.

The orchestral part is still often the important thing, so much so that at times a return to Wagnerian music drama is implied

so. In the opera as in Euripides' play there is a struggle between mind and sense, between man and the animal in him, between the rational and the irrational. The irrational wins, partly because the rational overestimates its own power and underestimates that of the enemy, and partly because that is how things are: the gods are jealous and vengeful. Possibly Henze was unconsciously attracted to the subject for personal reasons; in his art he has experienced a struggle between the temptations of sensuality and those of the puritanical rationalism in the dodecaphonic system. And, at the terrible level of national history, he knows from having grown up under Hitler that a whole people can indeed be hypnotized and possessed by the irrational.

Schuller, who is a year older than Henze and was something of a boy prodigy, has back of him an astonishing amount and variety of musical experience. He was a boy soprano in his native New York, and then a boy flutist. At fourteen he picked up the French horn and two years later began a professional career with that instrument which took him from the Ballet Theatre to the Cincinnati Symphony and then back to New York, where he remained with the Metropolitan Opera Orchestra until 1959. He has taught both privately and at the Manhattan School of Music and at Yale. Last year he was appointed president of the New England Conservatory of Music. His interests include folk music, the Ars Nova of the fourteenth century, jazz, and the most recent avant-garde developments. His *Horn Technique* wa published by the Oxford University

347

Press in 1962. He has been a writer, radio commentator, conductor, and the organizer of the concert series called "Twentieth-Century Innovations." He is an admirer of Duke Ellington, Count Basie, Dizzy Gillespie, Charlie Parker, Thelonious Monk, John Lewis and the Modern Jazz Quartet, and he has coined the phrase "third stream" to describe a kind of music that combines the subtlety, spontaneity, and rhythms of jazz with the dynamics and structures of the modern twelve-tone classical system.

His more than fifty compositions include concertos, symphonies, songs, jazz pieces, and a good many fantasies in which he exhibits his interest in unusual tone colors. The range of his eclecticism can be heard in the delightful *Seven Studies on Themes of Paul Klee*, composed eight years ago but just recently given a fine recording by the Boston Symphony under the direction of Erich Leinsdorf. One of the Klee pictures is evoked with the microtonal effects of Arabic music. The other studies are serial but are full of delicate blends of jazz and traditional timbres. Particularly successful is the one based on the painter's famous "Twittering-machine," now in the New York Museum of Modern Art.

In view of all this, the raw vigor of *The Visitation* may have surprised some listeners. The three-act libretto, written by Schuller himself, is based on Franz Kafka's novel *The Trial;* you might say that it is intended to focus for present-day Americans the Kafka nightmare of unmotivated injustice and human isolation. The place is an ordinary city somewhere in the United States. The baritone protagonist is a young colored man named Carter Jones, whom Schuller describes as "the type of Negro whose personal and racial characteristics have become undefined because of attempts over the years to adapt himself to the dominating social order. He simply wants to lead a decent life in an indecent society." Jones, like the central character in the Kafka story, is accused of a vague crime by vague accusers. He is taken to a cotton warehouse by a group of white men, who subject him to a sort of trial and then beat him. He loses his apartment and his job, and appeals in vain for the help of friends, lawyers, and a preacher. At the end the gang of white men murder him with a shovel and bury him.

The music is as raw and violent as the libretto, and quite naturally of the "third-stream" kind. In fact, the idea for the libretto appears to have occurred to Schuller not only because of his deep sympathy for the civil-rights struggle of American Negroes but also because he had been asked to compose a twelve-tone jazz opera for Rolf Liebermann, the director of the Hamburg Opera and himself the composer of a third-stream *Concerto for Jazz Band and Symphony Orchestra* (recorded several years ago by the Chicago Symphony under Fritz Reiner). The use of Negro music—mostly from a jazz septet improvising in the midst of the full orchestra—suggested that the opera itself ought to deal with the problem of the relations between whites and Negroes. Schuller

348

added some Negro spirituals and reinforced the orchestral interpretation of white violence with taped crowd noises emerging from loudspeakers in the back of the theater. Helped by many theatrically effective vocal numbers, the whole mixture not only miraculously held together but became a complex *musical* statement about problems of justice which have been the concern of Western thinkers ever since at least Plato's day. I wonder if Dr. Johnson, who in his Tory fashion was a stout believer in inalienable rights, might not have changed his mind about opera if he could have seen *The Visitation*. He once startled "some very grave men at Oxford" (Vol. 44, p. 363b) by proposing a toast "to the next insurrection of the Negroes in the West Indies."

An oratorio is a kind of opera without scenery, costumes, or acting, and the traditional musical setting of the Passion of Christ is a kind of oratorio. Hence this seems the place to mention the *Passion and Death of Jesus Christ According to St. Luke*, by the Polish composer Krzysztof Penderecki. The work was a sensational success in performances in Cracow, Warsaw, and Venice last year, and was recorded by the Cracow Philharmonic Orchestra and an excellent group of Polish singers under the direction of Henryk Czyz.

The surge forward in Polish art since the relaxation of political control in 1956 has been as striking in music as in painting and the movies. Several Polish composers—notably Witold Lutoslawski and Tadeus Baird—have acquired international reputations during the last five or six years, and their styles have suggested that musical innovation was about to stop being a monopoly of the non Communist world. Penderecki, who is still only thirty-four and whose first important opus dates only from 1958, is the latest and by far the most spectacular of these new men. He has attracted attention by composing for such unconventional "instruments" as typewriters, files, saws, and sirens, and by insisting on unusual techniques in general; a violinist, for example, may be instructed (by means of a new system of symbols instead of standard notation) to play on the tailpiece or behind the bridge, to use the wood instead of the hair of the bow, or simply to treat his instrument as a small drum. The result is often an extreme form of what Schoenberg called *Klangfarbenmelodie*, "tone-color melody," in which a single note is made expressive merely by changes in timbre. In *Threnody for the Victims of Hiroshima*, composed in 1960 and now also available on discs, such techniques led to a work of rare emotional concentration—a long, almost intolerably restrained orchestral sob broken by ominous clucking and clicking and the sound of something falling through a vast psychic space. The composer maintains, however, that his break with the past is largely technical; and the eclecticism in his *St. Luke Passion* shows that he means what he says.

The new work is manifestly by the same Penderecki who wrote the *Threnody*. Long, swaying, fluttering passages in the orchestra may blend

349

imperceptibly with the singing voices, or be broken by a dramatic crash, or turn into a thin whistle and then the shouts and hisses of the crowd mocking Jesus. Quarter tones add subtlety to the parts for soprano and strings. The basic structure is atonal and serial, and the melodic line leaps and dives sometimes in the post-World War II manner. But there is a lot of traditionalism mixed in with the modernism (in addition to the fact that the Passion form itself takes us back a couple of centuries). The basic phrase in the series is *b*-flat, *a,c,b;* and since in the German nomenclature our *b*-flat is *b* and our *b* is *h*, the theme of the whole work is *b-a-c-h*—used by Bach himself in *The Art of Fugue* and by many later composers as a tribute to the author of the sublime *St. Matthew Passion.* Penderecki adds Gregorian elements and some reminiscences of medieval mysteries and occasionally allows his music to become definitely tonal. The text, in Latin, includes not only the Gospel narrative but also the *Stabat Mater*, some Psalms, and material from the Roman Breviary for Good Friday.

Some of the effects are a trifle obvious, and some are to my mind too operatic for the sacred subject matter. Also, with the passage of time, the mixture of traditional and modern elements may begin to sound like a weakness rather than the strength it now seems to be. But there can be no denying that this *St. Luke Passion* is religious music on the old, grand scale, informed by profound feeling and thought. Moreover, it is a great deal more than just the music of a Western cult. Penderecki has said, and he makes the listener feel, that the work is simultaneously about the sufferings of Christ and the sufferings of modern man, at Auschwitz and many other places. It is a meditation on an eternally contemporary tragedy.

The Venice festival, which offered the musical tourist a chance to hear the *St. Luke Passion,* a thoroughly Roman Catholic work by a composer from a Communist nation, also offered a thoroughly Communist work by a composer from a Roman Catholic nation: Luigi Nono's *A floresta é jovem e chea de vida* ("The forest is young and full of life"). This piece was not a success, but it is worth mentioning because of its connection with the question of an artist's commitment to the great ideas of the occident.

Nono, who was born in Venice in 1924, emerged in avant-garde circles in 1950 as a serialist who was at once strict and poetic (he later married Schoenberg's daughter). His Italian background quickly asserted itself, however, and much of his music is in one way or another vocal; I say "one way or another" because he has experimented with magnetic tape and with the range of sound effects possible between electronic music and the electronically transformed human voice. Among his noteworthy works are *Polifonica-Monodia-Ritmica* and *Incontri*, both recorded, the opera *Intolleranza 1960*, which created a scandal at its premiere in Venice, and complex settings of poetic texts by Federico García Lorca, Paul Éluard, Cesare Pavese, Antonio Machado, and Giuseppe Ungaretti. I want to stress that I consider him a composer with a very original talent, a lot of artistic courage, and a rare kind of integrity. Nevertheless, *A floresta é jovem e chea de vida* is an embarrassing affair—in no less than six languages.

The title is from a remark by a rebel in Angola. About half of the text is derived from an article in *Fortune,* by Herman Kahn, about escalation and the cold war. There are also quotations from Fidel Castro, Patrice Lumumba, Vietnamese and Venezuelan Communists, an anonymous Berkeley student ("Is this all we can do?"), two Italian workers, and an anonymous anti-automation worker in Detroit ("If the struggle does not begin here in the coal mines in the auto steel electrical industries there shall be no freedom"). Some of this material is delivered from tape through loudspeakers, fortissimo; some is chanted, sung, or shouted by four live singers. The accompaniment is provided by taped sound, a clarinet electronically amplified, and a row of large, limber sheets of metal—similar to those which have long been rattled in theater wings to create thunder. The conclusion of the text, in Italian, is to the effect that the United States is an international murderer and liar. But the actual effect of the whole piece on the listener is boredom, relieved only a little by some interest in the unusual equipment and, if the listener is not a Communist, by some irritation or amusement at the extreme intellectual Left's ability to be just as bombastic and hammy as the extreme nonintellectual Right.

I am sure that Nono was absolutely sincere when he undertook this work and that he is capable of composing convincing music on his big themes of justice and peace. But here he is obviously not evoking ideas for their own sakes; he is simply trying to use them for propaganda. He also appears to have forgotten the plain fact that music is by its very nature positive and general in its effects rather than negative and specific: it was almost certain to sound hollow and ludicrous when required to say something against automation and the United States. Nono can of course dismiss these comments as mere evidence of American prejudice. I think he would be wiser, however, to ask himself if he is serving his own cause effectively by writing ineffective music.

We all know songs whose lyrics are so familiar that to hear the tune is to seem to hear the words. The German composer Giselher Klebe does a nice variation on this phenomenon in his *Missa Miserere nobis,* which was written three years ago but has only recently come my way. The familiar Latin words of the Mass are written into the score, but instead of being sung they are "recited" by eighteen wind instruments. The mysterious, rather mystical effect is heightened by contrapuntal means and especially by a careful choice of tone colors: *"Kyrie eleison"*

ABOVE, VLADIMIR USSACHEVSKY IN ROOM 317, ELECTRONIC MUSIC CENTER. RIGHT, N.Y.C. PRO MUSICA ENSEMBLE

Music, since it is a time art, is particularly suited to experimenting with the many aspects of change. It has undergone transformations ranging from the audio to the visual, and in many cases the change has obliterated the visual aspect of a musical production

is recited by the flutes, oboes, and clarinets; the brass section comes in with *"Gloria in excelsis Deo"*; the trombone chants *"Credo in unum Deum."* The *b-a-c-h* phrase used by Penderecki occurs again here, in *"Dona nobis pacem."* The whole work might indeed have been accepted by Thomas Aquinas as a sensuous model of ideas.

Klebe, who was born in 1925 in Mannheim, deserves to be better known beyond the Rhine than he now is. He is the author of several ballets and operas and like Schuller has done an interpretation of Klee's "Twittering-machine." His music for Goethe's *Roman Elegies* (the poems are simply recited) has been recorded.

CHANGE AND CHANCE

So far, as the reader has probably noticed, I have been taking the easy way toward what Gilson calls turning art into "something that can be talked about." The operation becomes more difficult when we do not have the help of words supplied, or implied, by the artists themselves—when we leave the category of vocal music, for instance, and start trying to talk about purely instrumental, or "absolute," music. But even here the great ideas can be shown to be relevant. The trick is to concentrate on ideas which are sufficiently general to go well with **abstract works.**

An interesting example is the idea of change. All of modern art, when compared with traditional nineteenth-century European art, can of course be thought of as a sensuous working model of this idea. Twentieth-century musicians, painters, and sculptors allow us to hear and see, to feel in our nervous systems, the accelerating process of Western history; they affirm with Heraclitus that reality is a flux—that we never step in the same water twice in the stream of time. They thus disagree with Socrates, who was impatient enough with the notions of Heraclitus to remark that a "man of sense" will not believe "that all things leak like a pot, or imagine that the world is a man who has a running at the nose" (Vol. 7, p. 114a). Music, since it is a time art, is particularly suited to experimenting with the many aspects of the concept of change, plus the related idea of chance.

Here it is necessary to review some twentieth-century artistic history in order to appreciate what has been happening during the last few years. If we are willing to ignore temporarily, merely for the sake of the argument, a large number of emotional factors, it is possible to see in the twelve-tone system developed by Schoenberg around 1923 an attempt to construct a musical model of being and becoming. If it were not for the date, one could imagine that he had been reading the *Syntopicon* (Vol. 2, p. 198a):

> For the ancients, the basic contrast between being and becoming (or between the permanent and the changing) is a contrast between the intelligible and the sensible. This is most sharply expressed in Plato's distinction between the sensible realm of material things and the intelligible realm of ideas.

Being, or the permanent, is well represented in the Schoenbergian system by the series itself, which is an arrangement (it *can* be thought of as a "theme," but the word has to be shorn of any suggestion of a melody), for a given composition, of all the twelve notes of the system; this arrangement is repeated over and over again throughout the given composition without any alteration of the intervals between the notes. However, becoming, or the changing, is also represented in the system: the series may be used horizontally (as a melody, that is) or vertically (in chords); it may occur, at any of the twelve possible pitch levels, forward, backward, upside-down, and backward upside-down—in a total of forty-eight forms. And the analogy with Plato's distinction is reasonably close, for in practice the initial series—the model of the idea of being, or the permanent—is for the average listener pretty much a purely intellectual construction; what he actually hears is the continuous variation—the working model of the idea of becoming, or the changing.

Toward the close of the 1940's, serial composers on both sides of the Atlantic were seized by what might be called, to keep our Platonic analogy alive, a rage for pure being. They began to employ rows not only of tones, as Schoenberg had done, but also of tone colors, time values, intensities, and instrumental attacks. The rage went a little too far for many tastes; there was some talk of "totalitarian" trends in musical circles, and within a few years a number of lyrical spirits—Henze, for example—seceded from the avant-garde. But the idea that music can be an aspect of the "permanent" in reality, much as mathematics can be, is still attractive to many cool, modern minds.

The American composer Milton Babbitt, now fifty-one and Professor of Music at Princeton, is generally credited with having written the first "totally organized" serial composition, although at the time—1948—his revolutionary accomplishment did not attract much attention in the wide world. Babbitt is an expert mathematician as well as an expert Schoenbergian, and his music is notable for the elegance of its detail. Among the works which date back to his heroic 1948–51 period, and which are all available on discs, are *Composition for Four Instruments, Composition for Viola and Piano, Composition for Twelve Instruments* (the austerely abstract titles are characteristic), and the song cycle *Du*. Among his more recent things are a large orchestral piece, *Relata*, and *Philomel*, for soprano and magnetic tape. Refinement and order are apparent everywhere, and in the best pieces there is a quality that suggests intellectual processes crystallized into sound. Is it all a little too cerebral and cold? Perhaps it is, but Babbitt thinks that people will discover an emotional content in his work when they come to know his new musical language. "If," he has said, "you get a telegram in Swahili telling you your dearest friend has dropped dead, how can you have an emotional reaction?"[3] While he is waiting for the ordinary public to learn his language, he is happy to remain one among the growing number of American composers who regard the university rather than the commercial concert hall as their natural habitat. The university provides him with the equipment for electronic music, to which he has been led logically by his rationalist approach to composing (I shall have occasion to mention him again in this connection). He has also made it clear that the campus suits his uncompromisingly intellectual attitude toward his art:

> There must be a verbal responsibility and a verbal discourse about music today. There must be a dissemination of ideas. I would rather be known as an academic composer as opposed to a commercial composer. . . . The milieu of the professional world, of the performer, the orchestra manager, the artist's representative is inappropriate to me. There is no communication between us. We are in the university because it is the only place where we can function.[4]

3 *High Fidelity*, October, 1966, p. 107.
4 *The New York Times Magazine*, September 11 1966, p. 55.

The dangers in such an attitude are evident. But so long as the world of commercial concerts continues to be more interested in money and star performers than in new music, it can scarcely complain of being ignored by living composers.

In France the move into totally organized serial music was made by Pierre Boulez, in 1951 with *Polyphonie X*. He later withdrew this fiendishly difficult work from public performance, and he has since turned away from its strict serialism toward much more free and personal methods of composition. But I think it is still fair to say that he belongs among those modernists who think of a piece of music as more a kind of permanent intelligible structure than a kind of perpetual sensuous change. His most recent work, written for a chamber orchestra and entitled *Éclat*, does indeed begin as if it were sort of improvising itself and might finally decide to be just a model of the following lines in Plato's *Theaetetus* (Vol. 7, p. 517d):

> I am about to speak of a high argument, in which all things are said to be relative; . . . there is no single thing or quality, but out of motion and change and admixture all things are becoming relatively to one another, which "becoming" is by us incorrectly called being, but is really becoming, for nothing ever is, but all things are becoming.

The rhythm, as always in the work of Boulez, is extremely free: now slow, now rapid, sometimes suspended. The tone colors change constantly. But gradually all of these musical atoms are pulled together, there is something like a condensation and then a small explosion— an *éclat*—at the last minute, and the listener is aware that the process of becoming has brought a definite form into being.

Boulez, who at forty-two has lost none of his energy and his famous bad temper, is having so much success as a conductor these days (of *Parsifal* at Bayreuth, among other exploits) that the general public may be apt to forget his services to the cause of contemporary music as composer, animator, teacher, and writer. Among his recorded works are *Le Soleil des eaux* and *Le Marteau sans Maître*, both for voice and orchestra; *Structures*, for two pianos; and the early *Sonatine*, for flute and piano. Also noteworthy are *Visage nuptial* and *Pli selon pli*, both for voice and orchestra, and *Doubles*, for orchestra. He has recently resigned as the organizer and director of "Domaine musical," the principal avant-garde concert series in Paris. His pupils are now taking their places as part of the second European postwar generation of composers. He is the author of numerous essays (a collection of them has been published under the title *Relevés d'apprenti*) and of a book, *Penser la musique aujourd'hui*, which is both a blast in favor of the independence of the modern composer and a study of modern techniques of composition. Like Babbitt, he is an expert mathematician who believes firmly that music is a science as well as an art; but, again like Babbitt, he sees no conflict between creative imagination and rational technique. On the last page of his book he writes: "Technique is not really a dead weight that one must drag around. . . . It is the exciting mirror which the imagination forges for itself and in which are reflected the imagination's discoveries."

Here I should like to point out that the reader can disagree with my opinions about specific works without worrying me. He can declare, for example, that all he can hear in a piece by Boulez is the buzz of a perpetual "becoming" which never gets around to becoming an intelligible "being"—a form that sticks in the mind. The model of "being," he can maintain, exists merely in the paper score and never becomes audible. None of this, I repeat, would worry me, for it would not destroy my argument that the great ideas are in one way or another relevant to contemporary art. However, I should be surprised if the reader were to disagree with my opinion that the great idea of *chance* is specifically relevant to what has been happening lately in modern art, particularly in music. During many centuries Western composers felt that their discipline had nothing to do with the fortuitous, the contingent, the casual, the incidental, the adventitious, the merely accidental. They accepted, probably without being aware that they were doing so, the contention of Plotinus, among many other thinkers, that "chance . . . has no means of producing, has no being at all" (Vol. 17, p. 347d). Today the attitude of many musicians on this question has undergone a radical and very conscious shift.

Actually, the shift has been under way since the beginnings of modern art. It is implicit in the strange last poem of Stéphane Mallarmé, "*Un Coup de Dés jamais n'abolira le Hasard*" ("A Cast of the Dice Will Never Abolish Chance"). In 1913, Guillaume Apollinaire wrote down scraps of his friends' café conversation, tested a few by singing them, and then assembled them into poems. There is an element of chance in the "ready-made" sculpture of Marcel Duchamp, in many of the stunts of the Dadaists, and in the automatic writing and the assemblage of "found objects" practiced by the Surrealists. The idea has been mixed up with ideas about the modern artist's creative liberty and irrational spontaneity, and also with the theories—not always interpreted correctly by artists and critics—of probability and indeterminacy developed by modern scientists. Another part of the mixture has come from very ancient notions about the influence of the fickle goddess Fortune on human life.

Much of all this went unnoticed by the general public until the 1950's. Then, in a number of artistic fields, the idea of chance, along with a lot of related ideas, suddenly became prominent. There was the Action painting of Jackson Pollock and other artists of the New York Abstract-Expressionist school; although it was rarely an actual result of chance, it often seemed to be, and in art seeming is important. A little later came the paintings and "objects" of Robert Rauschenberg, in which Action painting was combined with the apparent nihilism of Duchamp and the Dadaists in such a fashion as to confuse dramatically the old distinction between the necessity, or order, of art and the chaos of "life" and "reality." The so-called Theater of the Absurd, represented chiefly in the work of Samuel Beckett and Eugène Ionesco, added a philosophical tinge to the new climate; and then came the partly theatrical, partly "environmental" Happening (the term is said to have been coined by the American painter Allan Kaprow), in which much is left to chance and improvisation. A wildly improbable and unmotivated kind of farce began to appear in American novels. Music was a little slow to reflect the trend but has since more than made up for its tardiness.

How are we to explain the scope of this cultural phenomenon, which has disconcerted many quite sophisticated modern critics in about the way Pentheus was upset by the new cult of Dionysus? The absurdity of a world war, which had much to do with the original Dadaist satirical use of chance, can scarcely explain the popularity of chance today. Professor Wylie Sypher sees an attempt to explore some age-old problems of art criticism:

> Far from being anarchy, the new painting and the new music intently study the emergence of form from the formless, of necessity from accident, of music from noise, of purpose from purposelessness, of art from the random.[5]

Calvin Tomkins also sees some intellectualism but stresses the link with the pre-1914 attitude of Duchamp:

> A good deal of the new art both in this country and in Europe seems to make its appeal less to the eye than to the mind, and if the intellectual level of this appeal is rarely exalted, it is more often than not carried out in a spirit of mockery, iconoclasm, or sheer bumptiousness not far removed from the hilarity that Duchamp aimed at.[6]

Boulez takes rather the Tomkins line, but with a burst of disapproval:

> We have learned, from Nietzsche, that God is dead, and then, from Dada, that Art is dead; we know it very properly; there is no need to return to the days before the Flood and attempt—at whatever cost—to supply us with pedantic demonstrations which were once brilliant.[7]

---

5 *Book Week*, May 9, 1965, p. 14.
6 *The New Yorker*, February 6, 1965, p. 38. The article is reprinted in Tomkins' book *The Bride and the Bachelors* (New York: The Viking Press, Inc., 1965).
7 *Penser la musique aujourd'hui* (Geneva: Éditions Gonthier S. A., 1964), p. 21.

There is much to be said for all three points of view, according to the critics who are required to report on avant-garde festivals.

Last year, during the festival at the Maeght Foundation in St. Paul de Vence, France, I happened to be present during the composition of some of the new "music of chance," which was destined for a performance by Merce Cunningham and his dance company. The composer was John Cage, and his method was to switch a small radio set rapidly from one European station to another and record on tape snatches of classical music, jazz, popular songs, news broadcasts, and loud squeals and squawks. A few hours later I heard the complete composition via four loudspeakers and did not like it. On another evening, the music for the ballet consisted of Cage telling pointless stories in a thunderous voice over the four speakers. I did not like that either. However, some months earlier I had heard some of the same composer's *Sonatas and Interludes for Prepared Piano*, written between 1946 and 1948, and had found them full of a genuine, if slightly askew, charm.

Such experiences bracket reasonably well, I think, the actual achievement of Cage, who is partly a professional clown, partly a man of slender but highly original musical talent, and entirely an avant-garde intellectual. He is rather surprisingly a pupil of Schoenberg, and also of the American composer Henry Cowell, who extended and refined the invention of piano "tone clusters" (obtained by hitting the keys with fists and forearms) and added such now-common tricks as plucking the strings by hand. The "prepared" piano is a further extension of such unorthodox techniques: Cage modifies the timbres and pitches of the instrument, in ways for which the listener is totally unprepared, by the addition of hairpins, bolts, coins, rubber bands, erasers, ashtrays, and other small objects to the strings. But this innovation has become a minor thing, one gathers, from the point of view of Cage the clown and Cage the intellectual. His compositions (several of them have been recorded) have become in recent years more and more just demonstrations of his notion that music can be created from a chance mixture of noises and silences. This notion is linked to a notion that art is anything that happens in a situation in which we expect art: hence if we happen to be waiting for music in a concert hall and somebody toots an automobile horn outside, the toot becomes music. In fact, the silence that follows the toot also becomes music. Such doctrines have made Cage at fifty-five the acknowledged leader not only of one group of today's musical extremists but also of many other artists—particularly in painting, sculpture, and the theater—who are committed to the partly Dadaist, partly serious enterprise of exploring the zone between form and formlessness, between the necessary and the accidental.

The ambiguity in this enterprise is such that our usual artistic criteria quickly become irrelevant. And Cage himself is hard to judge. His

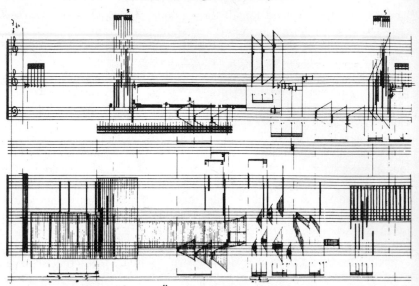

FRAGMENT FROM A PAGE OF BÜLENT AREL'S STEREO ELECTRONIC MUSIC NO. 1, *which shows some aspects of the changes performed in the transcription of music when it comes to an electronic composition*

musical talent and musical experience make you slow to think he is not in earnest, and his clowning makes you wonder if he is not just trying to pull your leg—in which case you are presumably required to exhibit an avant-garde sense of humor and a camp taste. I shall simply report, therefore, that for me at least his theory does not work; at St. Paul de Vence last year, the audience, myself included, was certainly in a situation in which art was expected, but the jumble of radio broadcasts nevertheless turned out to be non-music. The explanation seems to me quite obvious: it is simply that Cage overlooks the fact that art contributes to the creation of what he calls an artistic situation. That first toot of an automobile horn outside a concert hall may indeed, for a split second, have the vividness and form of music because the audience inside was expecting music. But with the second toot the psychological situation changes; the audience is no longer expecting music from that outside source, and so chance noises remain just chance noises. The sort of objection I am making can be raised against nearly all of the recent neo-Dada, neo-Duchamp experiments. One ready-made object in a sculpture show may seem to be a piece of sculpture, but a large number of such objects will kill the sculpture-show type of expectation (for all visitors who are not determined avant-gardists) and will therefore be non-sculpture.

Must we conclude that Plotinus was right, at least so far as art is concerned, in maintaining that chance "has no means of producing"?

The answer will of course depend on what we mean by "chance." My feeling is that the word is being used a bit loosely and too often in art criticism these days for all sorts of randomness and spontaneity; and so I propose to continue the discussion under the heading of other ideas—without, however, excluding chance altogether.

ITINERARIES FOR SUPPOSEDLY FREE WILLS

I have suggested (not too heavily, I hope, for after all music is music before it is something that can be talked about) that the serial system as conceived by Schoenberg can be thought of as a model for both being and becoming, for both the permanent and the changing. By emphasizing the series itself, composers eventually arrived at the sort of totally organized, mathematically impeccable music which can be thought of as pure, frozen "being"—and which has the defect, for many people, of being very hard to follow by ear. I now want to talk about what emerged when composers put the emphasis on the variations of the initial series of notes. The result was a kind of music which seems to be perpetually "becoming," and which is usually referred to as "aleatory" or "aleatoric."

The adjective is now too well established to be avoided, but it is not very satisfactory. "Aleatory," from the Latin *aleatorius*, "of a gambler," and ultimately from *alea*, a dice game, is defined in my Webster as "de-

SEGMENT FROM "THE FLOW OF (i), 1965" BY KENNETH GABURO

The composition consists of electromechanical operations on a synthesized and prerecorded phoneme, (i). The vertical axis indicates the frequency, the horizontal axis indicates time. The segment shown does not indicate the actual complex wave forms nor does it show timbre quality

pending on an uncertain event or contingency as to both profit and loss" and also as "relating to good or especially bad luck." Most of the aleatory music being produced today has nothing to do with luck and is equally remote from the kind of blind chance Cage is interested in. It is rather a return to the ancient idea of associating the performer, and hence to a degree the listener, with the composer in the process of making music. It is not quite the same thing as improvisation, but it is a reminder that improvisation was for centuries and until quite recently a great and exciting part of our musical tradition. The fact is that before about 1800 a composition was never played or sung exactly as written; the performer was expected to add ornaments and indulge in a good deal of very personal interpretation. The prelude and the toccata were once thoroughly "aleatory" forms. In the seventeenth and eighteenth centuries, harpsichord accompaniments were nearly always partly invented by the players. So, of course, were cadenzas, as recently as the Brahms *Violin Concerto*.

Modern aleatory music differs from the older sort in having its "improvisations" built into the composition and, so to speak, forced upon the performers. It is thus a model of the great Western ideas of free will and necessity—of man moving by choice into a predestined pattern. And since those are rather big words, I had better add right away that often, especially in works for small instrumental groups, the procedure yields nothing more philosophical than the effect of a solemn jam session by a very cool jazz outfit, with perhaps an ultrasophisticated rhythm section. The random elements float, as it were, inside serial or post-serial forms. In a typical piece, half a dozen musicians may be obliged to follow exactly the rise and fall of the notes in the score, but will be required to improvise such elements as loudness or softness and the duration of a sound or a silence. Thus much of the emotional drive in the music, like that in jazz numbers and flamenco songs, may depend upon the ability of the performers to sense each other's moods and pick up cues rapidly—as, in non-musical life, one free will has to operate within limits set by other free wills. In works for large orchestras, most of the randomness must of course come from the conductor and be a choice of rehearsal material.

Karlheinz Stockhausen's *Klavierstück XI* (Piano Piece XI), which was composed in 1956 but not performed until the next year, is generally listed as the first example of modern aleatory music, although the idea was already in the air in both France and Germany. The score of *Klavierstück XI* is a single large sheet on which are arranged the nineteen "sequences" of the piece, each marked with its own tempo and other indications of the usual kind for the interpreter. The pianist begins with whatever sequence his eye falls on and plays it without paying attention to the indicated nuances. He then selects another sequence at random, but this time he is not permitted to *ad lib* the tempo and intensity; he must follow the instructions marked on the *first* sequence played. In his third random selection, he follows the markings on the second, and so on through the nineteen sequences, if he plays them all. He may stop when he wishes, or when he has played any sequence twice. Other combinations of nuances and notes—other itineraries through the composition—are possible; in fact, although certain elements recur, one might play *Klavierstück XI* every evening during an entire festival without its ever sounding like a repetition.

Since that pioneer work, Stockhausen has continued to explore the possibilities in freedom of interpretation. His *Plus Minus*, which I heard last year, is practically little more than fourteen pages of notes and symbols—of raw musical material waiting for performers to become the author's co-composers. These were two pianists and two percussionists last year (apparently almost any number can play), and they were obviously well supplied with free will. The percussionists spent part of their time scratching a large pane of glass and pouring water out of casseroles into three yellow basins. One would hit the glass now and then with the small leafy branch of a tree. Meanwhile, one of the pianists might blow a small whistle for a long while and then get up and bang the lid of his "prepared" instrument. The second pianist had little to do besides scraping a stick slowly along one string and getting up to start a tape machine.

As this account may have suggested, Stockhausen has been affected —too much for his own good, in my opinion—by some of Cage's ideas. At thirty-nine he still seems far more interested in experimentation than in actual composition. But that he has had many bright ideas of his own cannot be denied. One of them led to the remarkable *Gruppen für drei Orchester*, in which three masses of instrumentalists, led by three conductors, surround the audience and engage in an elaborate game of confrontation, absorption, and counterpoint. He has done valuable research in the electronic studios attached to the Cologne Radio. Among his recorded works are *Zeitmasse, Zyklus*, and *Refrain*. The last-named is a particularly subtle mixture of silences—perhaps the most eloquent kind of musical "becoming"—and the timbres of pianos, wood blocks, celesta, ancient cymbals, vibraphone, cowbells, and glockenspiel.

The American composer Earle Brown, born in 1926, perhaps ought to be ranked ahead of Stockhausen as a pioneer in aleatoric music. He also has been influenced to some extent by Cage, but not—at least not in the pieces I have been able to hear in Europe—in the direction of blind-chance mixtures of noise. In fact, although he has done a good deal of work with tape music, his sensitive handling of more or less conventional musical sounds reminds me now and then of Debussy—an aleatoric Debussy, of course. Available on records are his *Music for Violin, Cello and Piano, Music for Cello and Piano*, and *Hodograph*. Performed recently in Paris was his *Calder-Piece*, for four percussionists; the reason for the title is that a large, heavy, red-orange and rather sluggish "mobile," created by Alexander Calder for this specific composition, stands in the middle of the concert stage and acts as "orchestra conductor": the performers, that is, vary the tempo, the intensities, and the sequence of parts of the work according to the speed and positions of the gadget's revolving forms. Given a stiff breeze, the music might therefore be called partly a product of chance. But during the performance I saw and heard there was not even a draft from the air conditioning, and so the drummers had to push and beat the mobile into action (and then duck and sidestep to avoid being hit as the thing gathered speed). My conclusion was that the piece was a demonstration of free human wills starting a chain reaction—or possibly a model of Duchamp's notion that one person's chance is not the same as another person's chance. Anyway, the timbres and rhythms were constantly interesting, and the whole business had a fine quality of tension and risk.

THE LISTENING EYE AND THE SEEING EAR

A leatory music raises a thorny little question about which both modernist critics and modernist composers are usually prudently silent. We can get at it by assuming that we hear a piece of this music only once and that we have no program notes to tell us that it is aleatoric. Will it *sound* aleatoric? I am afraid I must admit, on the basis of personal experience and with a bow toward Gilson and Kant, that it will not, at least not to any striking degree. There may be an effect of spontaneity, of on-the-spot creation, but we cannot really know that this is not the result of markings in the score; after all, that kind of effect can be heard in the music of Mozart, Rossini, and dozens of other pre-modern composers. We must hear, as a minimal requirement, two performances, preferably not very widely separated in our memories, if the piece is to become for our unaided ears even a ghost of a sensuous working model of the great ideas of chance and of freedom of the human will; and of course the opportunities to do so are rare in concerts and nonexistent, so far as I know, on records.

In the concert hall, however, the eye can usually save the situation for an ear deaf to concepts; in addition to reading the program notes we can watch the performers exchanging cues and doing other things which reveal that the music is the result partly of randomness and partly of freely chosen itineraries through the written composition. This simple fact, I suspect, is the principal reason for something that might have surprised Schoenberg: from an emphasis on the "becoming" aspect of serialism and then on chance and will, composers have gone on to an emphasis on the visual aspects of performance. That there are other reasons for the evolution can be granted; it is not confined to aleatoric music, it is perhaps related to a long-term trend which began with the mane-tossing Romantic virtuoso, and it has parallels in other modern arts. But it is particularly noticeable among composers of the random sort, as I may have suggested in my accounts of Brown's *Calder-Piece* and Stockhausen's *Plus Minus*. Other examples are at hand, for most of the avant-garde evenings I have experienced during the past year have included at least one number which crossed the border that used to separate concerts from theatrical, vaudeville, and sporting events.

Mauricio Kagel's *Match* is fairly typical of the trend. The contest referred to in the title is between two cellists, who are given a percussionist for referee. Following a "score" which is actually a collection of stage instructions, the cellists hurl glissandi and pizzicati at each other, laugh insultingly, and occasionally pretend to doze in boredom. Meanwhile, the "referee" indulges in virtuoso passages on his large battery of percussion instruments, throws dice on the xylophone, gives confusing orders to the cellists, and finally blows a whistle to stop the match. At the performance I saw/heard in Venice, the cellists used a large assortment of Italian gestures to add an extra dimension to the foolery.

Kagel, who was born in Buenos Aires in 1931, has had a varied career as conductor, professor, composer, and avant-gardist in Argentina, Europe, and the United States. Since 1957, his headquarters has been Cologne, where he has been the principal member of the group of experimenters around Stockhausen. Among his recorded works are the aleatoric *String Sextet* and *Transición II* for piano, percussion instruments, and two tapes.

Concerning *Match*, he has said that his intention was to persuade the listener to ignore, little by little, the sounds and noises being produced and to notice only the behavior of the musicians. He succeeded perfectly with me; I have at this moment no memory at all of having heard something during the Venice performance. Why should a composer have an intention so oddly destructive of the conventional point to his activity? I can only guess. Perhaps Kagel merely wished to transpose to the level of farce Keats's line about the sweetness of unheard music; if so, he succeeded again with me, for I did find the performance amusing in a nonsensical way. He may have wished to experiment, as artists have been doing throughout the twentieth century, with the notion of the power of absence in art, another notion which dates back at least to Mallarmé. Or perhaps *Match* is simply a working model of Aristotle's observation that "the greater stimulus tends to expel the less" (Vol. 8, p. 685d). As such it is undeniably efficient.

Luciano Berio's *Circles*, for voice, harp, and two percussion complexes, is an entirely different matter, although in the seven years since its creation it has become something of a minor classic in the theatrical-concert genre to which *Match* belongs. It has been described as follows in a program note by the composer:

Circles is based on three poems by e. e. cummings: numbers 25 ("stinging gold swarms . . ."), 76 ("riverly is a flower . . .") and 221 ("n[o]w the how dis[appeared] cleverly world . . .") of the *Collected Poems*. The order of the poems in the composition is 25-76-221-76-25; poems 76 and 25 thus appear twice, at different moments in the musical development. My aim was not to compose a series of vocal pieces with instrumental accompaniment, but rather to work the three poems into a single form, in which not only the different levels of meaning, but also the vocal action and the instrumental action (in the widest sense of the term) would be strictly conditioned, even in a concrete way, by the phonetic qualities. The harp and the percussion instruments, that is, develop or provoke certain specific characteristics of the vocal action, and vice versa. The *theatrical* aspect of the execution is inherent in the structure of the work, which is essentially a structure of actions. If it were still possible to make such a distinction, I would say that *Circles* is to be listened to as theater and to be seen as music.

Mezzo-soprano Cathy Berberian, harpist Francis Pierre, and percussionist Jean-Pierre Droulet have performed the work frequently in both Europe and America in recent years, in my experience with the assistance of percussionist Jean-Claude Casadesus, and they have become expert at conditioning each other's "actions" on the stage. Miss Berberian recites, whispers, shouts, and sings (the range of her voice is extraordinary) the poetry.

A held vowel may be developed in the plunks and liquid siftings of the harp; a held consonant may merge with the brittle rattle of a small drum. Some of the "structure of actions" is reduced to her gestures; some of it seems to drift and tick spontaneously out of the instruments as she circles slowly among them.

Berio, who was born in Italy in 1925, is today almost as well known in the United States as in Europe, having taught at the Berkshire Music Festival, Mills College, Harvard, and the Juilliard School of Music in New York, in addition to acting as a musical director and advisor. In 1954, he became a director of the Studio di Fonologia Musicale of the Italian national radio network and thus had an opportunity to develop his interest in the analysis of pure sound. Among today's modernists, he is notable for his ability to produce music which is at once very advanced and very direct in its appeal to ears and emotions.

His recorded works include *Circles, Serenata I, Differences, Sequenza* (with the brilliant flutist Severino Gazzelloni), and *Visage.* In the recorded version of *Circles,* the invisible Miss Berberian naturally loses much of her theatrical impact, but not quite as much as one might think, for the microphone adds emphasis to the way the instruments "develop or provoke certain specific characteristics of the vocal action, and vice versa."

MATHEMATICS AND THE ELECTRONIC FUTURE

Whereas the struggle with the manifold aspects of the ideas of change, being, becoming, chance, and freedom has led some modern composers into the realms of the concert-drama, the concert-vaudeville, and the concert-game, it has led others deep into the realm of higher mathematics (from which they sometimes emerge again in the realm of games). Music has of course been associated with mathematics since ancient times, and not merely for technical reasons. In his eloquent passages on the nature of the universe, Plotinus makes almost no emotional distinction between the two disciplines (Vol. 17, p. 76a):

> For who that truly perceives the harmony of the Intellectual Realm could fail, if he has any bent towards music, to answer to the harmony in sensible sounds? What geometrician or arithmetician could fail to take pleasure in the symmetries, correspondences and principles of order observed in visible things?

Today, however, partly with the help of computers, composers have become so involved in such problems as those of probability and of continuous and discrete quantities that a more relevant comment from the *Great Books* might be Fourier's "mathematical analysis has outrun observation" (Vol. 45, p. 183a).

Such analysis has certainly outrun hearing for most concert-goers, myself included; it has become, to borrow Babbitt's word, Swahili to the general. Also, even for adepts it is often more a matter of avant-garde composers' techniques than one of significant form. Can we therefore safely ignore it, on the grounds that anyway the proof of a musical mathematical proposition is in the listening? I suppose we can, just as we can, and usually do, ignore the recipe for an interesting dish. But doing so here would deprive me of another opportunity to suggest that Kant was mistaken in thinking that music provides no food for reflection.

Iannis Xenakis is one of the most enthusiastically mathematical and also one of the most musically gifted of the new European calculating composers. He has had a curiously unconventional career, even for an avant-gardist. At Athens, where he was born in 1922, he studied mathematics and eventually obtained a diploma from the Polytechnic School. He then went to Paris, where he studied architecture with Le Corbusier and music with Arthur Honegger, Darius Milhaud, and Olivier Messiaen. For twelve years he was an assistant to Le Corbusier; he participated in the creation of such monuments of modern architecture as the Dominican monastery of La Tourette, France, and the public buildings at Chandigarh, India. He himself conceived the Philips Pavilion for the Brussels World's Fair of 1958 and composed for his building a piece of tape music: *Interlude Sonore*. By that time he was also the author of several works for orchestra, of which *Metastasis* and *Pithoprakta* have been recorded. Among his instrumental pieces since then are *Nomos x*, *Strategie*, and *Eonta*. He has taught composition at the Centre d'Humanisme Musical in Aix-en-Provence and at the Berkshire Festival in Massachusetts. He has just created in Paris a group of experts to study mathematically the nature of musical phenomena everywhere in the world; among the other members of the group are several professors of aesthetics, psychology, and mathematics; the scientific adviser of IBM-France; and the anthropologist and structuralist Claude Lévi-Strauss. I mention these facts because Xenakis has sometimes been unfairly suspected of adding mathematics to his music just for fun and mystification.

His arguments can be followed up to a certain point even by non-mathematicians. He maintains that the destruction of the tonal system has left the art of music in dire peril of falling to pieces, that Schoenbergian serialism or some other sort of linear polyphony is bound to be too complex to be followed by the mind and ear, and that aleatoric music is largely an unsuccessful attempt by composers to turn their problem over to performers. He believes that we must forget our old-fashioned notions of notes, scales, chords, and all that and think instead of a music formed of clouds of small sounds—clouds which he compares to the sound of hail or rain on a roof and to the sound of thousands of grasshoppers. The task of the composer, then, is to shape these clouds of buzzing indeterminacy into something that makes sense to our minds, ears, and emotions. How is he to go about this task? In much the same way, according to Xenakis, that a statistician goes about making sense of a crowd of unpredictable individuals, and a physicist goes about making sense of particles: by the use, that is, of mathematical equations—in particular those that deal with probability.

Here I begin to have trouble. Are the equations merely the composer's tools for shaping a cloud of sound? No, evidently they are meant to be somehow a part of the finished composition. Are they to be regarded as substitutes for the traditional structures of Western music or for those that can emerge from Schoenbergian serialism? No, they are not quite that, for they are too complex to make sense to an unaided ear: some have to be worked out on electronic computers. How, then, are we to appreciate the music?

My personal method is to assume that Xenakis is actually two artists in one. He is an anti-academic composer who insists on the importance of sheer sound and on the magic that lies beyond technique—on what he calls "meta-music." As such he is in the line of Hector Berlioz, Debussy, Edgard Varèse, and Messiaen. But he is also a composer who sets algebra to music in the way other composers set words; he is a creator of songs and chamber operas with mathematical poems and librettos. As such he can be fully understood, I think, only after some study and with the

When the ordinary public learns the new musical languages, the concert halls as we know them now will have a hauntingly lonely look

help of pretty elaborate program notes. As such, however, he is squarely in an ancient tradition of his native Greece; he is a modern descendant of Aristotle's "so-called Pythagoreans," who ". . . in numbers . . . seemed to see many resemblances to the things that exist and come into being" and who "supposed . . . the whole heaven to be a musical scale and a number" (Vol. 8, pp. 503d–504a).

The Xenakis who is the meta-musical continuator of Varèse and Messiaen has composed some of the most exciting sound patterns to be heard in today's concert halls. I particularly recommend *Eonta* (it has recently been recorded), in which a vast sound-cloud rises from practically all of the strings of a piano and encounters an adamantine cloud emanating from two trumpets and three trombones (this brass section was doubled for a recent Paris performance). The composer translates the title as "beings" and likes to have it printed in the syllabic Cretan-Mycenaean script used in the Linear B texts discovered at Knossos. He suggests that the piece should be listened to with the eyes closed.

Xenakis the Pythagorean sometimes offers clues to listeners who feel up to following what I think of as his hidden librettos. In *Pithoprakta*, he has explained, the densities of the clouds of stringed-instrument sound were calculated with the help of the well-known distribution law of S. D. Poisson, and "the slopes of the glissandi" were worked out according to a formula of K. F. Gauss, J. C. Maxwell, and Ludwig Boltzmann. The solo cello piece *Nomos x* is described as "symbolic music" with a structure which "is outside of time and is based on the theory of groups." The work is therefore dedicated "to the imperishable achievements of Aristoxenus of Tarentum, musician, philosopher, mathematician and founder of the theory of music; to the mathematician Évariste Galois, founder of the theory of groups; and to Felix Klein, his worthy successor."

Mathematical music might be expected to lead naturally to electronic music, in which the composer has full control over the "performance" and "interpretation" of a composition and need not worry about the ability of a musician's fingers to follow the Poisson distribution law. That it has not done so to any great degree can be attributed, I suppose, to a lingering sentiment for the looks of the old instruments (their sounds are easily duplicated electronically), to the scarcity of fully equipped recording centers, and of course to our interest in human singers and instrumentalists —listening to loudspeakers in a concert hall can be a melancholy experience. How long will these and other restraints continue to work? For a good many years, I would guess; and the guess does not greatly depress me, in view of the poor quality of most of the electronic music I have heard. However, an excellent piece is produced now and then, and there are some records on the market which suggest what the electronic future may be like when and if it arrives. Several years ago the Paris research studio set up by the French national radio network produced Boulez's *Étude II*, Xenakis's *Diamorphoses*, and some interesting things by Pierre Schaeffer, the inventor of *musique concrète*. From the studio of the Cologne Radio has come Stockhausen's *Gesang der Jünglinge*. The Columbia-Princeton Electronic Music Center has given us Vladimir Ussachevsky's *Creation—Prologue*, Ilhan Mimaroglu's *Bowery Bum* and *Le Tombeau d'Edgar Poe*, Otto Luening's *Gargoyles*, and Babbitt's *Composition for Synthesizer*. From the University of Illinois have come Kenneth Gaburo's *Lemon Drops* and *For Harry*. The discs have appeared under various commercial labels.

*posed to what we see in
s picture, some compos-
prefer to have no com-
nication with the profes-
nal world, the performer,
 orchestra manager, and
ose to function in the
university campus*

IN OPPOSITION TO BISHOP BERKELEY

S everal of the great Western ideas which I have been attaching to
  modern music can be attached also to modern painting and sculpture,
and I have already attempted some of the attaching—in talking about
Cage, for instance. However, they are peculiarly relevant to music because music is a time art. It is so in many ways. It has a clock time for
performance and a felt time for listening (five minutes of Nono are
longer than five of Berio). It has tempo, of course, and beaten time. It has
an arrival time for each of our ears, a fact of which we have been reminded by stereo records. It has, for most people, rather more of historical time than other arts have: it preserves associations. All of this
complex temporality encourages composers to construct models of
change, being, becoming, and chance.

Painters and sculptors do not have this sort of encouragement; they
have to appeal to the philosophical imagination by means of works
whose primary mode of existence is that of things—things in the sense
in which the stone Dr. Johnson kicked was a thing. It seems fair to recognize this situation, and it seems doubly fair when we notice that many
modern painters and sculptors, unlike their illusionist nineteenth-century
predecessors, are inclined to stress their arts' primary mode of existence.

They are inclined, for instance, to demonstrate in favor of the reality
of matter—that "unknown *somewhat*" which aroused the scorn of Bishop
Berkeley and of which he said: ". . . I do not find that there is any kind
of effect or impression made on my mind different from what is excited
by the term *nothing*" (Vol. 35, p. 428b–c). One can wonder if he would
have said that after seeing some of the art shows of the 1960's. Perhaps he
would have, for of course today's painters and sculptors do not actually
refute his argument. Their method is simply to make us vividly conscious
of what we commonly assume to be matter. They repeat, according to
their temperaments and their opportunities, Dr. Johnson's historic Har-
wich kick and confident "I refute it *thus*" (Vol. 44, p. 134d).

Here, and in the rest of this essay, the method I have been using for
speaking about music had better be modified. I can perhaps do more
with the relevance of the great ideas to the visual arts by saying a bit
more about general trends, at the cost—my space being limited—of
saying less about each artist and very little about specific works. The
latter are available everywhere, at least in reproduction, whereas pieces
of contemporary music are not.

Let me back up for some perspective on the idea of matter. If a viewer
of the "Mona Lisa" shifts his attention from the smile, a first consequence
is likely to be some fresh awareness of Leonardo's paint as paint. If a
listener ceases to concentrate on the recurrence of a theme in a Beethoven
symphony, or on the tonal axis, he is likely to have a parallel experience;

he may hear Beethoven's characteristic sound as just sound. A museum visitor who goes through a room of Greek sculpture in reverse chronological order will find his awareness of stone as stone increasing as he moves toward the earlier and less realistic pieces. An admirer of old houses may tell you that when a beam is not carved into decoration, but is merely structural, the appeal of the wood as wood is stronger. Shakespeare's "Sa, sa, sa, sa" (Vol. 27, p. 275c) sticks oddly in my mind partly, I suppose, because it is not dissolved in the semantical; it is the very breath of Lear. In sum, we can guess that the mere existence of twentieth-century abstract painting and sculpture, atonal music, functional architecture, and obscure poetry has produced in us a quickened and more sensuous consciousness of the basic materials that go into works of art of any kind. Such "materialism" in today's painting and sculpture is partly just a psychological by-product of modern ideas of form, reality, and aesthetic ambiguity. Many of the artists involved are only inadvertently kicking at Berkeley's argument.

There is, however, nothing very inadvertent in the materialism advocated by the sculptors in metal who have been flourishing in Europe and the United States since World War II. Among these, one of the finest, and the most aggressively matter-minded, was the American David Smith, who died two years ago—at the age of only fifty-nine and at the height of his imaginative powers. He was of course much else besides a materialist. He had begun working in welded metals as early as 1933, and was influenced by the abstract Constructivism developed during and just after World War I by the Russians Vladimir Tatlin, Naum Gabo, and Antoine Pevsner. He was something of a Surrealist, a critic of society, and a homespun humorist. He was an ardent symbolist who gave his creations such titles as "Cathedral," "The Rape," "Tanktotem," and "Portals." The pieces finished just before his death show him preoccupied with architectonic qualities and with a very personal, almost Mannerist animation of space; blocks, cylinders, and beams of steel are assembled so as to leave each element off-center and apparently ready to contradict its structural function. But in everything he did there is the same vigorous emphasis on the need to face up to the reality of raw matter. "Possibly," he once said, "steel is so beautiful because of all the movement associated with it, its strength and functions. Yet it is also brutal; the rapist, the murderer and death-dealing giants are also its offspring."

There is nothing very inadvertent either in the kicks aimed in the general direction of Berkeley by Jasper Johns, who at thirty-seven is now established as the old master of the New York avant-garde. He too is much more than a materialist; he is one of the less tiresome strategists in the neo-Dada game of trying to confuse art with non-art, he has a classical knack for composition, and on the few occasions when he has made the attempt he has demonstrated that Pop need not be a soggy art of agreeing with the values of an other-directed consumer society. But his matter is particularly striking. In his recent pictures, certain patches of paint call attention to themselves as examples of the traditional well-done morsel, while others have the impasto and brush tracks of Abstract Expressionism. To these techniques he adds assemblage and collage: the paint serves as a background for such objects as beer cans, a coat-hanger, a broom, a kitchen chair, wooden letters, a ruler, a door, and a silk-screen reproduction of a scrap of a newspaper.

In France, the undisputed champion among the materialists is still Jean Dubuffet, although at sixty-six he has begun to show an interest in pattern as well as stuff and texture. During the past twenty years, he has "painted" with mud, tar, asphalt, manure, butterfly wings, putty, clinkers, and old sponges; and even in his more conventional moods he has used varnishes and enamels to produce the crackles which most painters spend their lives trying to prevent. He has frequently increased the impact of his matter by drawing in the manners of children and cavemen, and also by issuing truculent statements. In an introduction for a Paris show a few years ago, he wrote:

> I wish to call attention to the fact that my pictures represent soil. . . . Many people will without doubt recognize this right away, but one cannot take too many precautions in order to be understood, especially in these times of infatuation with abstraction. Nothing here of that sort. Nothing but pieces of soil . . .

The critic Peter Selz quotes him as saying:

> I see no great difference (metaphysically, that is) between the pastes I spread and a cat, a trout or a bull. My paste is a being as these are. Less circumscribed, to be sure, and more emulsified; its ordinance is stranger, much stranger certainly; I mean, foreign to us, humans, who are so very circumscribed, so far from being formless (or, at least, think ourselves to be).[8]

I am not sure of the proper label for the philosophical tendency here being adumbrated, but I am pretty sure Bishop Berkeley would have disapproved of the implications.

In any event, the eminent art theorist and psychologist Rudolf Arnheim disapproves. In one of his recently collected essays, he cites Dubuffet and then comments:

> Here the realistic tendency reveals itself as the relinquishment of the active grasp of meaning that characterizes man's relationship to reality when he is in full possession of his mental powers. . . . The painter cultivates his pastes and fluids as a gardener cultivates the

---

8 *The Work of Jean Dubuffet* (New York: Museum of Modern Art, 1962), p. 63.

soil; he becomes a breeder and trainer. He no longer produces images but matter. And the matter he is creating with the refined chemicals of a late civilization is the world before the Creation, the attractive infinity and variety of the chaos. It is the escape from the duty of man—the final refuge and the final refreshment . . . Perhaps, then, we are witnessing the last twitches of an exhausted civilization . . .[9]

Just about the only reason for hope he can find in the situation is the possibility that we are nearing "the nadir we must touch in order to rise again." This view seems to me too apocalyptic and too much the kind of outraged response the foxy Dubuffet is often trying to provoke in conservative viewers. But Arnheim does touch here on an important tendency in modern art—a cycle which can be seen accomplishing itself in the work of Dubuffet and to some extent in that of Johns. Raw matter is used to shatter old-fashioned "form" and illusionist "realism" in the name of a more real "realism." This new realism turns into abstractionism, and then the raw matter becomes so real that a new kind of form and figuration seems called for if the whole business is not to skid out of the domain of art altogether.

It may seem that no amount of form and figuration can keep us from being too strongly aware of asphalt and butterfly wings as just asphalt and butterfly wings—as non-art, that is. But on this point, Gilson, in a book earlier than the one I have already cited, has some illuminating comment:

> Everything hangs on what Focillon has so admirably called the "formal vocation" of each and every kind of material . . . Anything can be used by the artist, but the choice that he freely makes of a certain material will determine to a large extent the nature of his future work. To be sure, the painter is the sole judge of the possibilities latent in the material he has decided to use. Still, when all is said and done, the formal vocation of a painting material has both its possibilities and its limits. This is the moment the causality attributable to their matter becomes a determining factor in the genesis of the works of art.[10]

The problem, then, is simply to discover the formal vocation of asphalt and butterfly wings, or of thick impasto, or of iron and steel. What kinds of forms do these kinds of matter "want" to become? From the point of view of the practical artist—and of the practical critic—the question can often be partly answered by a process of elimination: a block of steel, for example, being hard to work, does not have much of a vocation for becoming a realistic nymph; if it is forced to do so, the result may seem more a tour de force than a work of art. There is an implication here

---

9 *Towards a Psychology of Art* (London: Faber & Faber, Ltd., 1967), pp. 190–91.
10 *Painting and Reality* (New York: Meridian Books, Inc., 1959), p. 72.

that within very wide limits each kind of artistic matter is already a kind of form, waiting for the artist to impose on it another stage of individuation. And with this implication we approach a long chain of philosophical speculation which began with Aristotle (see *Syntopicon, GBWW*, Vol. 3, p. 69a–b).

SPACE, PLACE, EXTENSION, THE VOID, AND MAN

Everybody agrees that a fresh emphasis on space is as important as the emphasis on matter in the general ambiguity of modern painting and sculpture. Yet the notion of "real" space remains, in the words of William James, "a very incomplete and vague conception in all minds" (Vol. 53, p. 626b). So does our notion of the relations of consciousness to space—"the problem," to quote James again, "known in the history of philosophy as the *question of the seat of the soul*" (p. 139a). About all I can say, then, is that in the next few pages I should like to call attention very incompletely and vaguely to the "real" space in current art objects and at the same time talk at greater length about the question of the seat of the soul in the twentieth century. In other words, I shall be talking mostly about the sort of space in which people feel assured or uneasy, purposeful or disoriented, expansive or constricted, significant or insignificant. Painting and sculpture are of course not the only expressions of this kind of psychic space; obviously, architecture may suggest it, and so may other arts, in particular music and the novel. We may feel it in the sciences, particularly in modern physics and psychology. But painters and sculptors have an advantage over musicians, novelists, and scientists in being able to depict space, and an advantage over architects in not having to worry about practical questions.

These speculations need to be qualified by an admission that aesthetic space, and perhaps the scientific sort as well, is largely conventional. A void is a void, a not-something defined by an arrangement of something. Appreciation of such an arrangement is learned with considerable difficulty. Observations of the behavior of infants, and studies of the congenitally blind who have suddenly been able to see, suggest that our "natural" vision of space is comparable to the misty confusion of silhouettes we make out when we concentrate on a distant scene. Even for adults with years of practice, the ability to *realize* a void is likely to be more limited than we normally suppose, as many would-be pilots discover when they take their first depth-perception tests. Perhaps Berkeley went a little further than the facts warranted, but he was on the right track in suggesting that we learn to perceive "distance or outness" by means of "a connexion taught us by experience . . . after the same manner that words of any language suggest the ideas they are made to stand for"

(Vol. 35, p. 420d). It would seem to follow that an art critic, in spite of the warnings of Gilson and Kant, has a bit of the same right to speak of the different expressions of space in different eras that a literary critic has to speak of the different conceptions to be found in poetry and the novel. Space "language" is vague, but legible.

On this basis I shall risk a pair of generalizations. From the Renaissance until the twentieth century a very important (although not the only) trend in all the major Western arts was toward a psychic space which was anthropocentric, fully "realized," rational, static, and framed. In the modern era, a very important (although not the only) trend has been toward a psychic space which is incompletely "realized," nonrational, dynamic, and unframed. I should say that in the old aesthetic space at its best and most typical, the average person has a vivid sense of exactly who, what, and where he is and hence feels reassured, at home, reasonable, and rather weighty. In modern aesthetic space at its best and most typical, the average person is apt to have a vivid sense of having emerged somehow into the open and hence feels a bit lost, or perhaps serene, or excited by the unknown, and in any event rather immaterial—in more than one sense.

It seems to me that the rejection by Copernicus in 1543 of the notion that everything revolved around the earth has inspired a certain amount of over-think about the way our ancestors felt about themselves. This frequently takes the form of elaborating on the assumption that man—Western man, that is—suddenly discovered the humiliating truth that he was a mere speck in space, and a peripheral speck at that. Now of course one can find some literary evidence that supports this assumption; man is said to be a reed, a mere fly in the eyes of the gods, the weakest of the animals, and so forth. But most of this is in a tradition that goes back a long way before 1543. And if we turn to the visual arts, we get a strikingly different impression. The great majority of pictures and pieces of sculpture produced between 1543 and late Romanticism suggest that man was not feeling at all diminished and peripheral, that in fact he was feeling more important than at any other period in his history. His psychic space was decidedly anthropocentric—a void around a portrait or a statue of himself.

It was also, particularly in painting, a remarkable example of what artistic conventions can do—probably the most remarkable in the history of world art. The cave artists of Altamira and Lascaux were good at verisimilitude in general (although their skill has been exaggerated by our surprise at their ability to paint at all), and excellent at expressiveness, but they fumbled the problem of realizing space. The Egyptians devised conventions which are so crude we are obliged to assume a temperamental or religious repugnance for foreshortening. Chinese landscapists, especially those of the Sung dynasty, were fascinated by deep space, but their methods of realizing it were usually no more exact than a high point of view, a screen of foliage, and mist in the distance. In short, the importance of the discovery of the laws of mathematical perspective in Italy in the fifteenth century cannot be overstated. For the first time anywhere, man had a way of measuring and *realizing* voids in his imagination, right down to the last corner. At last he had before him a picture-universe that was consistent and subtle enough to fix the position and distance of objects, and hence the situation of the self in psychic space. In early-Renaissance examples of perspective, and in the treatises which often accompanied them, one can still catch a faint residue of a scientific, philosophical, and mystical exaltation which was once quite as strong as the aesthetic interest.

This space is rational in an expressive as well as a mathematical way; it makes the viewer feel that the world is an order. It achieves this effect, however, usually by being a framed illusion which suggests the theater, and nearly always by being static: it rests on the assumption that an implication of the passage of time—of movement by the viewer or the represented figures and objects—is incompatible with a full and exact experience of space. To come suddenly upon a picture by a great space-realizer like Piero della Francesca is to feel as if a clock has been stopped and you have been ordered not to budge. How, he seems to be asking, can you realize exactly where you are if you and the things you see are in motion? The question cannot be asked in the same fashion by a sculptor, of course, but in a lot of pre-1900 statues there is an effect of frozen, rather than potential, movement which is the equivalent of the characteristic perspective stillness in pre-1900 painting.

Last year in Paris, there were opportunities to see the work of four twentieth-century masters—Pablo Picasso, Mark Tobey, Willem de Kooning, and Alexander Calder—who have contributed greatly to the creation of the modern psychic space which has replaced the one I have just been discussing. None of the four is exactly news, but not to mention them in the present context would be both unjust and misleading.

Picasso's Cubism is usually, and of course correctly, described as the decisive blow against the types of figurative forms which became dominant in painting after the Renaissance. But it was just as decisive for the voids for which the old forms had served as points of reference. It thawed the frozen world of mathematical perspective into fragments and facets which could be spread out on the flat canvas; it forced the viewer to shift his angle of vision constantly and to contemplate a temporal series of episodes within a single pictorial area. To be sure, one can feel that the price paid for this dynamism was high; Cubist and much of post-Cubist pictorial space is relatively nonrational, thoroughly disrespectful of the human image, and very incompletely realized—in it you cannot know exactly where you are. But one can scarcely feel that the price was too high: a sensitive viewer is apt to be more liberated and challenged than "lost" in this space. And for such a viewer there is historical drama in the thought that the chief inventor of this space—the man who has done more than any single artist has ever done to change our notions of art—is at the age of eighty-six still painting and still having one-man shows.

Cubist space, however, still recalls the Renaissance frames; it still, that is, has structures arranged so as to imply an awareness of the limits of a picture. Tobey, who is nine years younger than Picasso, went on to destroy that awareness. In his most characteristic paintings, an overall— or rather, allover—pattern of strangely organic microscopic elements extends the void as far as the imagination can see (hence these paintings are often quite small, there being no point in enlarging a sample of the infinitely large). The microscopic elements vibrate slightly before our intent eyes, but there is none of the Cubist implication of a point of view in motion, and therefore no implication of a chronological order. Following a distinction made by Locke (Vol. 35, p. 159b–d), we might say that Tobey's space is a sensuous model of the idea of duration and that Picasso's Cubist space is a model of the idea of time. However, I should add that for Tobey the idea of space is more a religious than a philosophical idea. On the occasion of a Paris retrospective show a few years ago he remarked:

> The dimension that counts for the creative person is the space he creates within himself. This inner space is closer to the infinite than the other, and it is the privilege of a balanced mind to be as aware of inner space as he is of outer space . . .

A number of comments might be made on the attitude this implies, but they might take us out of the great ideas of the Occident and into those of the Orient.

De Kooning, who was born in 1904, represents another generation of space-artists. In his work, as in that of many of his fellow New York Abstract Expressionists, the few traces of mathematical and rational space which can be found in Cubist fragments and facets are obliterated by the furious brushwork of the artist in action, and the resulting picture space is as subjective as the spaces we create in the air when speaking with gestures. It is also unusually aggressive. Whereas the space of Tobey always seems far away, that of de Kooning (his pictures tend to be large) seems close enough to envelop the viewer.

Calder, who will soon be seventy, has been amusing and charming the modern world for such a long while that we may be in danger of overlooking his genius and assuming that his mobiles and stabiles are just natural products of the period. In a way they are. The mobiles in particular (they were invented as far back as 1932 and were named by Duchamp) can be regarded as working models of half of what I have been talking about in this article; they evoke almost as well as music does the ideas of change, becoming, and chance, and they create space which is completely unframed, incompletely realized, completely dynamic, and full of a delicately calculated unreasonableness.

Two British artists, the sculptor (if that is the word) Anthony Caro and the painter Francis Bacon, have recently made brilliant demonstrations of how relevant the idea of space is to contemporary art. And each of them has raised again the old question of how relevant the idea of man is—the humanist's idea of man, that is.

Caro was the young-sculptor-of-the-year in 1966 on both sides of the Atlantic, with important works on view at the Venice Biennale and the London sculpture triennial and a small stream of articles about himself in the art-conscious American press. I call him "young," for although he is now forty-three his present mature and very successful style is only seven years old.

Before 1960, he was a figurative artist working in bronze, partly under the influence of the British master Henry Moore. Then he went to the United States, met David Smith and other abstract artists, recalled that he had a degree in engineering from Cambridge, and returned to England to start a new career in welded iron, aluminum, and steel. The style he developed is a kind of Constructivism which is so abstract, so austere, and apparently so elementary it has been variously labeled as "minimal," or "ABC," or "primary" sculpture. It is certainly about as far from old-fashioned heroic statuary as one can get. A characteristic work may consist of a few metal rods, beams, and plates distributed seemingly at random on the ground and covered with bright paint. The viewer is apt to conclude at first glance that there is little matter and no form. But if he lingers near the contraption he may find himself walking around and through it, squinting from different angles from one element to another, and getting involved generally; and he may then discover that the "matter" is mostly a zone of unframed, nonrational, and dynamic space which is constantly emerging from formlessness into different forms as he attempts to "realize" it—to get his bearings. He may discover, that is, that he is somewhat in the role of a modern musician choosing itineraries through an aleatoric composition.

Bacon, who had an impressive show in Paris last year, is of course an entirely different sort of artist. He was born in 1910 and therefore belongs to the generation of British painters who were influenced by Expressionism, Surrealism, and the violent distortions of the human figure produced by Picasso in the 1930's. Since World War II, he has also been influenced by photographs: not the artistic kind but such things as candid (preferably blurred) news shots of people in the midst of gestures and grimaces, and the famous studies of motion made by Eadweard Muybridge in the nineteenth century. He has combined these influences with a personal vision of humanity which is one of the most genuinely alarming in contemporary art, and also with a talent for creating an immediate emotional impact—for what he calls, citing Paul Valéry, "giving the sensation without the boredom aroused by the fact of the transmission."

In most of his paintings, a single personage, sometimes naked, always hysterical, is caught in a smudged, twisting movement that makes the flesh look wounded and rotten. A reptilian mouth may be open in a nightmarish scream. The colors—mauve, green, brown, red—are applied with savagely bad taste, and usually some lines and scribbles are added in a partly transparent dead white. The space, however, is more disturbing than anything else. Occasionally it is designed to induce agoraphobia, but more often, breaking the general modern rule, it is an airless box. Frequently the personage is enclosed in what appears to be a glass cage inside the airless box.

Are Caro and Bacon furthering what conservative critics have called the dehumanization of art? I do not think so. Caro's sculpture is of course not of the sort he calls "people substitutes," but it calls strongly for the participation of actively curious people: it comes close to being do-it-yourself art. And Bacon's paintings do not exclude man at all; they simply suggest that he is still unredeemed.

Toward the close of the chapter on the idea of space, the editor of the *Syntopicon* observes (Vol. 3, p. 817d):

> Whatever may be thought of the ether as a physical hypothesis, the problem still remains whether action can take place at a distance through a void or must employ what Faraday calls "*physical* lines of force" through filled space.

Takis, a forty-two-year-old Greek sculptor (again that may be the wrong word) who shows his work regularly in Paris, has been wrestling in his own fashion with this problem. His ambition, in his own words, is "to get away from art and nearer to invisible forces." For the past seven years, his invisible force—actually his sculptural material—has been electromagnetism, which he uses to suspend or agitate needles and other objects magically in midair. He is happy to be able to avoid in this way what he calls "the dead iron of falsely modern sculptors." His trouble has been that the distance across which his action takes place is relatively short and that the "real" space in his works tends to be overly occupied by equipment which looks suspiciously like dead iron and which distracts the imagination's attention from the invisible sculpture. Last year, being Greek, he arrived at a Pythagorean remedy: most of the pieces on exhibit emitted a musical sound when the action at a distance was taking place. One might have, and perhaps should have, visited the show blindfolded.

FROM OBJECT TO FORM TO OBJECT

In his memoirs, Wassily Kandinsky describes one of the germinal accidents of the modern period, an incident comparable to the laboratory chances from which modern science has occasionally profited. The time was apparently the very end of the nineteenth century, some ten years before the first abstraction, and the place was the painter's studio in Munich. He had been working outdoors and had returned at dusk, his mind "entirely plunged" in the day's accomplishment. Suddenly he noticed, leaning against the wall, a picture which was "unutterably beautiful, completely irradiated with an interior light," but in which the depicted object was unrecognizable. A second look revealed that the marvel was merely one of his own figurative works, and by the next morning the magic had faded:

> Even when I turned it on its side, I re-found *the object* each time, and also the blue light of the dusk was lacking. I then realized definitely that objects were injurious to my painting . . .

The anecdote is often stopped at this point, at least in the versions by admirers of abstract art. Kandinsky, however, in his intelligent, earnest, rather humorless way, continues:

> A frightening abyss opened beneath my feet, while at the same time an imposing responsibility was offered to me and all sorts of questions arose, of which the most important by far was: What should replace the object?[11]

What indeed except *form?* (*See* Vol. 2, p. 527c–d.) That answer is of course almost as hard to think about as Kandinsky's abyss, but abstract painters and their friendly critics have on the whole held to it throughout the twentieth century. Partisans of the geometrical sorts of abstractionism, which are sometimes more difficult to explain than the lyrical and expressionist sorts, have even on occasion let it be understood that the form of a painting might somehow be a visual metaphor for Form in the Platonic sense (Vol. 7, p. 382a–c, among many other passages). This argument appears to be based on a deep misunderstanding of what Plato was talking about, but I mention it to show the level at which discussion has been conducted.

During the last few years, however, with the return to favor of Mondrian's type of geometrical abstractionism under such labels as Hard-Edge and Structural (one must never concede that what one is doing has been done before), a tendency has appeared to drop the notion of form and to defend a painting as being itself an "object." The up-to-date answer,

---

11 Michel Seuphor, *L'Art abstrait* (Paris: Maeght, 1950), p. 18.

that is, to Kandinsky's anguished question is that his represented object should be replaced by a cool refusal to imagine *any* kind of referent in a work of visual art. This answer, in various degrees of explicitness, has been common for some time among far-out sculptors and neo-Dadaist or Pop practitioners of solid collage, but finding it in a realm where one used to come and go talking of Plato still seems a little odd.

Frank Stella, who at thirty-two has become one of the leaders of the new geometrical school in the United States, can serve as one of several possible representatives of the current I have in mind. Referring to his elegantly simple diagonals, chevrons, and triangles, he has said:

> I always get into arguments with people who want to retain the old values in painting—the humanistic values that they always find on the canvas. If you pin them down, they always end up asserting that there is something there besides the paint on the canvas. My painting is based on the fact that only what can be seen there *is* there. It really is an object. Any painting is an object and anyone who gets involved in this finally has to face up to the objectness of whatever it is that he's doing. He is making a thing. All that should be taken for granted. If the painting were lean enough, accurate enough or right enough, you would just be able to look at it.[12]

This can be regarded, if one wishes to be a philosophical troublemaker, as the ultimate and logical consequence of the doctrine that the non-literary arts can speak to us only by means of sensations and cannot leave behind them any food for reflection. Or perhaps it should be regarded as merely a heretical offshoot of that doctrine, as a kind of Gnostic reductionism stemming from the true faith. In any event, I am tempted to reply as the American critic John Canaday has in a similar context:

> The weakness in the argument that art is a purely visual experience is, simply, that art is *not* a purely visual experience.[13]

In fact, to pick up the argument with which I began this article, scarcely anything is a purely visual experience. We are incorrigible animists, conceptualists, symbolists, and devotees of the pathetic fallacy. Baudelaire's *Correspondances* is a factual as well as poetic statement of the situation in which our possession of a reflective language puts us:

> La Nature est un temple où de vivant piliers
> Laissent parfois sortir de confuses paroles;
> L'homme y passe à travers des forêts de symboles
> Qui l'observent avec des regards familiers.[14]

---

12 *Art News*, September, 1966, p. 58.

13 *The New York Times*, International Edition, February 27–28, 1965, p. 5.

14 Nature is a temple in which living pillars/Sometimes allow confused words to slip out;/In it man passes through forests of symbols/Which watch him with familiar glances.

"SCULPTURE SPATIO-DINAMIQUE" BY NICOLAS SCHÖFFER

"EXPOSURE," BY BRIDGET RILEY,
EMULSION ON CANVAS, 1966

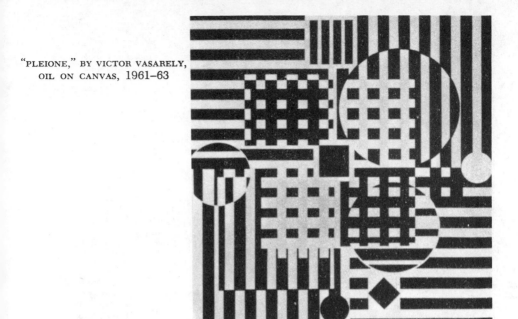

"PLEIONE," BY VICTOR VASARELY, OIL ON CANVAS, 1961–63

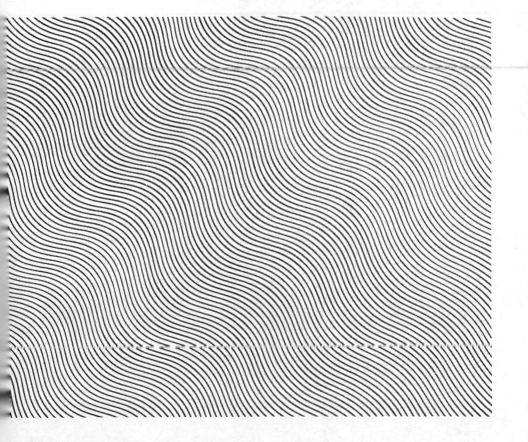

"GREEN WHITE," BY ELLSWORTH KELLY,
OIL ON CANVAS, 1967

"DOUBLE SIGNAL (RED AND AMBER)," BY TAKIS,
1966

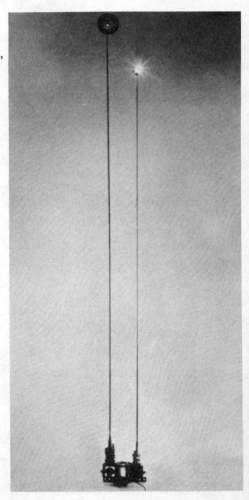

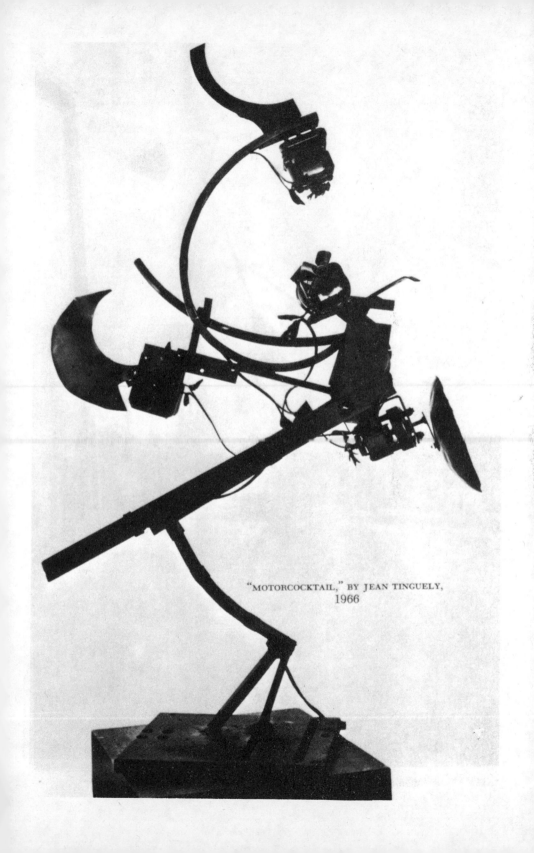

"MOTORCOCKTAIL," BY JEAN TINGUELY, 1966

"SPIRALE," BY ALEXANDER CALDER, 1962

At UNESCO in Paris, near the Conference building

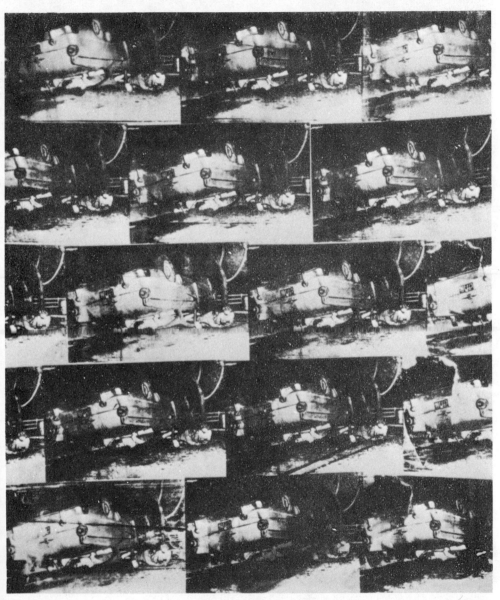

"ORANGE DISASTER," BY ANDY WARHOL, SILKSCREEN ON CANVAS, 1963

"THE BILLBOARD," BY GEORGE SEGAL, PLASTER, WOOD, METAL, AND ROPE, 1966

"MAGNIFYING GLASS,"
BY ROY LICHTENSTEIN,
OIL ON CANVAS, 1963

"TARGETS," BY JASPER JOHNS,
ENCAUSTIC AND COLLAGE
ON CANVAS, 1966

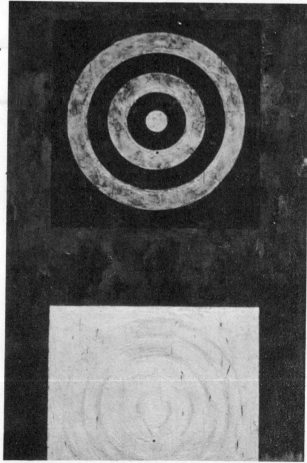

"U.N. PAINTING," BY LARRY RIVERS, OIL ON CANVAS

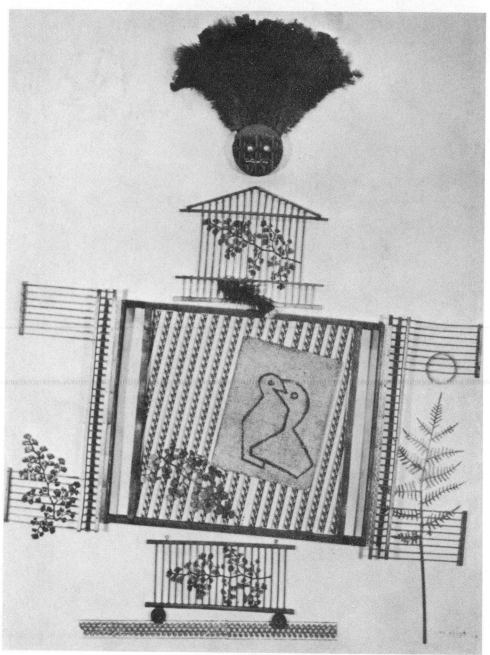

"HARPE EOLIENNE," BY MAX ERNST, MIXED MEDIA, 1963

"WOMAN WITH A HAT," BY
WILLEM DE KOONING, OIL ON
PAPER, 1966

"BATEAU DE PÊCHE," BY JEAN DUBUFFET,
GOUACHE, 1964

"LES NANAS," BY NIKI DE SAINT-PHALLE,
GROUP VIEW, 1965

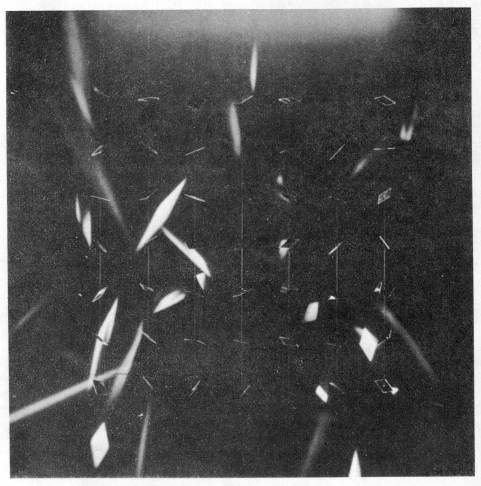

"CONTINUEL-MOBILE, CONTINUEL-LUMIÈRE" BY JULIO LE PARC

"THE BRIDE STRIPPED BARE BY HER BACHELORS, EVEN" BY MARCEL DUCHAMP

"CONVOLUTE," BY MARK TOBEY, TEMPERA, 1966

"TROPHY FOR MERCE CUNNINGHAM," BY ROBERT RAUSCHENBERG, COMBINE PAINTING,
1959

"THE PARTY," BY MARISOL, MIXED MEDIA AND MIRROR, 1965–66

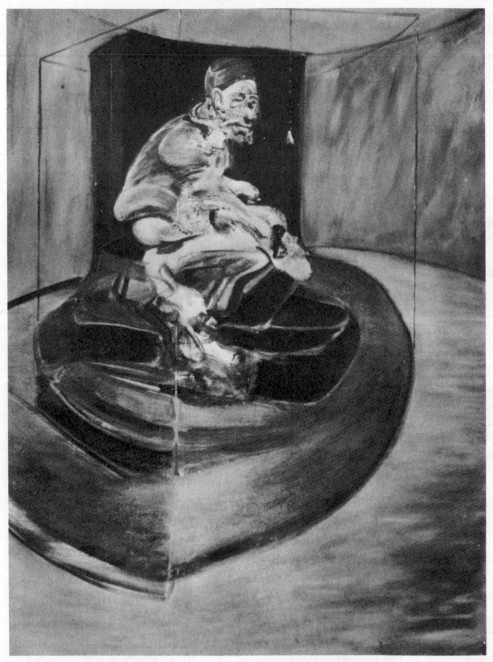

"STUDY FROM INNOCENT X 1962," BY FRANCIS BACON, OIL ON CANVAS

"TÊTE D'HOMME," BY PABLO PICASSO, OIL
ON CANVAS, 1964–65

"THREE PIECE RECLINING FIGURE," BY
HENRY MOORE, BRONZE, 1961–62

"CUBI X," BY DAVID SMITH,
STAINLESS STEEL, 1963

"9 BOULES," BY POL BURY, WOOD

"RAINFALL," BY ANTHONY CARO, PAINTED STEEL, 1964

"MOULTONVILLE III," BY FRANK STELLA, FLUORESCENT ALKYD AND
EPOXY PAINT ON CANVAS, 1966

And since nature usually fails to create "objects" that persuade us that "only what can be seen there *is* there," I am inclined to think the operation impossible for a painter. He must eliminate every trace of individual brushwork, for instance, since otherwise we are apt to find his personality in the "object." He must avoid, of course, any shapes that might be taken to be analogical or symbolic. He must simplify into nothing the relations of part to part and of the parts to the whole, for otherwise we are apt to see an order in the picture and to start talking of Plato again. He must avoid any hint of a conventional frame, for otherwise he may set off those aesthetic responses which have been conditioned by traditional art. Now Stella is evidently aware of these difficulties. He works, to use the current okay term, in a very "minimal" fashion; he is quite clearly trying to paint what Hazlitt said somebody said Turner painted, *"pictures of nothing, and very like."* But for me at least he does not succeed; for me there is "something there besides the paint on the canvas." There is, to begin with, an obvious statement to the effect that in a painting one ought *not* to see something besides the paint on the canvas, and here I am not just reaching for a paradox: such a pictorial statement by a talented young man in the richest country in the world in the second half of the twentieth century offers plenty of what Kant called "food for reflection." It implies an almost total rejection of what Stella calls "the old values . . . the humanistic values," not only in art but in our culture generally.

It seems to me, therefore, that what he is really attempting to say in his unconvincing theorizing about "objects" and "things" is that his work cannot be judged by the old criteria for painting. This is certainly true. It is true, however, not only of Stella's work but also of the work of other geometrical abstractionists—of that of Ellsworth Kelly, for instance, who is a more direct heir of Mondrian. It is true of Mondrian's work, the success of which can be accounted for neither by old-fashioned aesthetic theory nor by Mondrian's own somewhat foggy metaphysics. The plain fact is that we do not know enough about perception to explain abstract and other kinds of "minimal" or "structural" art; we do not know why, in the words of Thomas Aquinas, "a form existing in the senses is somewhat a principle of knowledge" (Vol. 20, p. 1034a). More investigations in the line of those described by Arnheim in his collected essays are needed: more inquiries into such visual phenomena as "fields," "figure and ground," and elementary "images of significant life situations." Such inquiries might help us to discover in the diagonals and triangles of Stella certain values which, perhaps unconsciously, he is trying to substitute for those bad old humanistic ones.

ASSORTED OBJECTS AND IDEAS IN MOVEMENT

During the past two years, there have been large exhibitions of optical, or Op, art and of kinetic art in—among other places—Paris, New York, Boston, Berkeley, San Francisco, Venice, London, Brussels, Glasgow, and Tel Aviv. Here, then, is one of the liveliest aesthetic trends in the world today. I say "one" because I am going to speak about the whole thing under the general label "kinetic." My authority for doing so comes from an excellent recent book (in a magazine format) on the subject: entitled *Kinetic Art*, it consists of four scholarly essays by Stephen Bann, Reg Gadney, Frank Popper, and Philip Steadman. At the start of his essay, Popper explains his intentions, and incidentally describes the whole trend very neatly:

> I personally am prepared to use the expression "kinetic art" for works ranging from abstract illusionist pictures whose repetitive patterns are designed principally to create illusory movement to the most complex electronic three-dimensional constructions, which are dominated by mechanical movement. . . . I shall divide the field into three main areas: kinetic works in "virtual" movement, three-dimensional works in "actual" movement and two-dimensional works in "actual" movement. The first category must also be divided into works whose movement is purely illusory and works whose virtual movement is engendered by movements of the spectator, by his active intervention or manipulation. The three-dimensional works must be divided into those which, in their similarity to machines, appear to be predictable, and those which have been called "mobiles" and are propelled by air currents. In addition, the question of randomness and predictability will arise in relation to two-dimensional works in actual movement—projections or reflections of moving forms upon screens or walls.

All of these categories were in existence long before the twentieth century. "Actual" movement was represented by theatrical machines, mechanical toys, marionettes, human automatons, and more or less successful color-organs. "Virtual" movement was represented by illusory effects on facades, tricks with mathematical perspective, eye-dazzling drawings, and paintings distributed on blades so as to change as the viewer changed his position. However, with a few exceptions (the color-organ is one), these things were not intended as works of art; they were meant to amuse, or to demonstrate optical theories. Also, they usually referred to movements and structures to be found in nature, or in man. Today's kinetic works, although frequently playful, are intended as art and are nearly always abstract. Their twentieth-century ancestors were created by Calder, the Constructivists, the Cubists, the Dadaists, and Mondrian.

Three of the best artists in the category of actual movement (all of them occasionally turn to the virtual kind) are the Belgian Pol Bury, forty-five; the Hungarian Nicolas Schöffer, fifty-five; and the Swiss Jean Tinguely, forty-two. One of the best in mixtures of the actual and the virtual is the Argentine Julio Le Parc, thirty-nine. Two of the best in the virtual category are the British Bridget Riley, thirty-five; and the Hungarian Victor Vasarely, fifty-nine. Miss Riley works in London, the others in Paris.

Bury, who at the moment is my favorite among the kinetic three-dimensionalists, continues into abstractionism the ancient tradition of the makers of human automatons. He conceals small electric motors and discs behind his tableaux and inside his usually wooden pieces of sculpture, hooks the discs by means of string and wire to the filaments, spheres, and rods visible on the surfaces of the works, and runs each apparatus at a speed so slow as to be almost imperceptible. The results are models of the movement of the life force at the levels of the virile reflex, of the heliotrope turning toward the sun, of something unnameable in the ocean. In spite of his interest in mechanical principles, Bury is clearly a vitalist in the line of Aristotle. Some of his machines, if you watch them through their cycles of rest, slow stir, and rest again, can also be taken as models of Freud's conjecture that instinct is "the manifestation of inertia in organic life" (Vol. 54, p. 651d).

Schöffer, whose work seems to me intellectually interesting and emotionally rather unsatisfying, is a craftsman and visionary whose eyes are fixed on the distant day when ultramodern art and ultramodern science will merge, he hopes, to form a new philosophy, even a new religion. In the introduction to one of his several exhibitions last year he wrote:

> It is more than probable that our notions of duration, beginning, end, limit or threshold are to be revised. It is more than probable that the universe as man imagines it is only one part of an ensemble, much more vast, of macro-systems and micro-systems possessing different time structures and even timeless ones, animated by a sort of respiratory movement with an infinitely variable rhythm, nourishing each other mutually, having certainly neither beginning nor end—in short, an ensemble whose complexity would be far beyond us, prisoners that we are of our narrow space-time carapace. Our only chance is our intelligence. . . . At this point we must return to *art*, the only human action that goes beyond us and guides us at the same time, the *only one that gives to man, by the intermediary of man, a substance superior to man.*

He began as a neo-Constructivist, creating dynamic and incompletely realized space by means of open, right-angled structures of brass and aluminum. He then added transparent or translucent plexiglass and colored light patterns moving in cycles at variable, sometimes random speeds. More recently he has been experimenting with what he calls "chronodynamism" and "micro-time" by means of flashes of colored light which are rotated mechanically and speeded up by means of mirrors: the idea is to saturate with signals the moment between the emission of a signal of motion and the moment we perceive it. This should help to crack our space-time carapace.

Tinguely has become an international celebrity in the years since 1960, when one of his machines committed suicide at the New York Museum of Modern Art, and so there is not much to say about him that has not been said in dozens of media, including television. Two points about his recent work, however, seem to me worth some emphasis. First, although the machines are just as futile as they used to be, they do not look quite as crazy; they do not wave as much junk in the air, they run better, and most of those I have seen have been painted. Second, this new—and very relative—sober look brings out strongly the fact that Tinguely, in addition to being a satirist and a Swiss toymaker of genius, is that rare thing, a purely conceptual visual artist. His zany "sculpture" cannot be appreciated at all in terms of volume, mass, structures, texture, and form. Once you get past a simple description, you can talk about it only in terms of ideas— ideas about the state of art, about technological progress, about alienation, about the death of our civilization, and of course about farce. Here, I submit, is at least one case in which no critic can be, in Miss Sontag's slogan phrase, "against interpretation."

With Le Parc, who won a grand prize at the Venice Biennale last year, we may be entering an age of absolute innocence, absolute democracy, and absolute anonymity in art. His attitude toward his work can be summarized by quoting from a manifesto of the Paris Groupe de Recherche d'Art Visuel, of which he is a cofounder:

> Although our experiments may still have the traditional appearance of paintings, sculpture and bas-reliefs, we do not situate plastic reality in the realization of a work or in emotion, but in the constant relation existing between the plastic object and the human eye. . . . Making the plastic object move will modify the preceding data by the addition of time. However, we do not envisage movement as soliciting an emotional response or as a demonstration, but as a new visual proposition.[15]

That seems clear enough: lots of phenomenology, and no ontology at all. In carrying out this program, Le Parc resorts principally to brightly polished metal, fashioning it into boxes of shifting patterns of light and shade, into distortion mirrors, and very often into strips which are suspended so as to flutter like silver leaves in an aseptic autumn breeze. His works are cool, mildly amusing, and sometimes beautiful, and anybody can enjoy them: I have seen a cat doing so, apparently in exactly the same way

---

15 Bann *et al.*, *Kinetic Art* (St. Albans, England: Motion Books, 1966), p. 52.

that I was. They are, however, open to some serious objections. One responds to them more physiologically than imaginatively. As art they are only a jot above sunlight on water; they do not involve that transfer from one substance to another—that implied metaphor—which contributes to the pleasure in conventional painting and sculpture.

Miss Riley's carefully calculated and drawn waves of virtual movement do involve that sort of implied metaphor, since they are quite conventional pictures. Moreover, she has anticipated the kind of criticism I have just directed at Le Parc and has replied to it in words as well as pictures:

> . . . I have always believed that perception is the medium through which states of being are directly experienced. (Everyone knows, by now, that neuro-physiological and psychological responses are inseparable). . . . The basis of my paintings is this: that in each of them a particular situation is stated. Certain elements within that situation remain constant. Others precipitate the destruction of themselves by themselves. Recurrently, as a result of the cyclic movement of repose, disturbance and repose, the original situation is re-stated.[16]

Here we are back again with Thomas Aquinas' belief that "sense is a sort of reason" (Vol. 19, p. 26b), and so I will say nothing about "neuro-physiological and psychological responses" except that Miss Riley provokes both kinds with unusual intensity. She is one of the few kinetic artists to manage, without the use of actual movement, to introduce enough time in a work for the production of simple musical effects—cycles of "repose, disturbance and repose."

Movement in the work of Vasarely is entirely of the virtual kind, and in the great majority of his paintings it is little more than a shimmer around a zone of color or within a superimposed pattern. The fact is that this cool, fastidious artist is in many ways closer to the first generation of geometrical abstractionists, and through them to traditional painting, than he might like to admit. There is, however, something in nearly all of his recent pictures which in the future, perhaps the distant future of Schöffer's micro-systems and macro-systems, could become more revolutionary than the dazzle of an optical mixture of shapes. We can get at what I mean by noticing that whereas a painting by Van Gogh has a seamless, organic unity, a painting by Vasarely has an assembled, rational unity: a Van Gogh is a sensuous model of the idea of the One; a Vasarely is a model of the idea of the Many. In other words, Vasarely's pictorial "language," unlike that of Van Gogh or of any other artist I can think of at the moment, is noncontinuous both within itself and with any given picture; it consists

---

16 *Art News*, October, 1965, pp. 32–33.

of small colored elements, usually circles and squares, which are without distinctive matter and brushwork and which can be extracted from a particular work and used in a different combination. And my point is that such elements are exactly the sort of code desired by some of our new artistically inclined electronic computers, which will probably never be able to learn to paint in the unique, private, organic language of Van Gogh. We can dismiss as irrelevant the fact that Vasarely did not intend his discrete language for computer use when, several years ago, he invented it. In cultural history, the machines come when we call them, even though we do so unwittingly.

CONCERNING THE HISTORY OF ART

When a critic begins to prophesy, he can assume that his article has reached its natural end. Let me wind up with a comment on some remarks by the American art historian James S. Ackerman, in a paper published in another anthology edited by Gyorgy Kepes. After insisting that the theory of an evolutionary "process" which is often used in political history is "sheer mysticism in the history of the arts," Ackerman says:

> But allowing, for the sake of discussion, that the chronological se-
> quence established by archaeological method justifies a metaphor of
> process, we observe that it is also necessary to suppose that the
> process obeys some purposeful and orderly pattern. If it were
> meaningless flux and change, we could not pretend to make sense
> of it. That the pattern of so-called development is purely meta-
> phorical is demonstrated by our inability to project it into the future.
> An economist can predict with some confidence the effects of a
> change in the monetary structure, but we have no idea where Ab-
> stract Expressionism is "going." We can only construct chronological
> charts and assess the art of the past by hindsight. This method
> provides us with an index showing which works of art were most
> influential. If it stopped there it would be unassailable, but in-
> evitably the influential becomes the important. . . . So it appears
> that the patterns of development that we construct are unrelated,
> and may even be antagonistic, to the distinction of quality.[17]

The remedy for this evil, Ackerman suggests, is to concentrate on the uniqueness of each work of art and to study the intentions of an artist living in a particular place and period. He adds that the ultimate justification for the use of such a remedy is the fact that "we are committed to a conviction as to the positive value of individuality."

17 *The Visual Arts Today* (Middletown, Conn.: Wesleyan University Press, 1960), pp. 262–63.

Roy McMullen

I mention these opinions with no intention of agreeing or disagreeing with them, for to do either would take us beyond the scope of this essay. What I wish to point out is that the great ideas of the Western tradition are relevant not only to modern art but also to modern thinking about art in general. In the course of less than a dozen sentences, Ackerman takes firm positions on a dozen important matters which have been the subjects of debate among powerful minds for hundreds of years. He is of course aware that he is doing so, and he may be right in each instance. But it can do us no harm to remind ourselves that Plato, Aristotle, Augustine, Aquinas, Kant, Hegel, Marx, Tolstoy, Bacon, and Hobbes, among others, might have disagreed.

BLIOGRAPHY

HEIM, RUDOLF, *Towards a Psychology of rt.* London: Faber & Faber, Ltd., 1967.

N, STEPHEN, GADNEY, REG, POPPER, RANK, and STEADMAN, PHILIP. *Kinetic Art.* t. Albans, England: Motion Books, 1966.

LEZ, PIERRE. *Penser la musique aujourd'-ui.* Geneva: Éditions Gonthier S. A., 1964.
-. *Relevés d'apprenti.* Paris: Éditions du uil, 1966.

ON, ÉTIENNE. *Painting and Reality.* New rk: Meridian Books, Inc., 1959.
- *The Arts of the Beautiful.* New York: harles Scribner's Sons, 1965.

ES, GYORGY (ed.). *Sign, Image, Symbol.* ew York: G. Braziller, 1966.
- *The Visual Arts Today.* Middletown, nn.: Wesleyan University Press, 1960.

GER, SUSANNE K. *Feeling and Form.* New rk: Charles Scribner's Sons, 1953.
-. *Philosophy in a New Key.* Cambridge, ass.: Harvard University Press, 1942.

PANOFSKY, ERWIN. *Gothic Architecture and Scholasticism.* New York: Meridian Books, Inc., 1957.

ROSENBERG, HAROLD. *The Tradition of the New.* New York: (Evergreen ed.) Grove Press, Inc., 1961.

SELZ, PETER. *The Work of Jean Dubuffet.* New York: Museum of Modern Art, 1962.

SEUPHOR, MICHEL. *L'Art abstrait.* Paris: Maeght, 1950.

SONTAG, SUSAN. *Against Interpretation, and Other Essays.* New York: Farrar, Straus & Giroux, Inc., 1966.

TOMKINS, CALVIN. *The Bride and the Bachelors: The Heretical Courtship in Modern Art.* New York: The Viking Press, Inc., 1965.

VENTURI, LIONELLO. *History of Art Criticism.* Translated by CHARLES MARRIOTT. New York: E. P. Dutton & Co., Inc., 1964.

413

LEONARD COTTRELL

Leonard Cottrell, born in 1913 at Tettenhall, near Wolverhampton, England, is the author of twenty-seven books, principally on archaeology, history, and travel. Educated at King Edward's Grammar School, Birmingham, he first moved, through journalism, to the British Broadcasting Corporation which he joined in 1942 as a writer-director of documentary programs. During the Second World War he was a BBC war correspondent and afterwards traveled extensively, covering about one million miles and reporting from twenty-five countries. An amateur archaeologist from the age of nine, he wrote his first archaeological book, The Lost Pharaohs, *in 1950, basing it largely on his own studies of Egypt and the information he had received from Egyptologists who believed that a need existed for an introduction to Egyptology written mainly with a lay public in mind. The popularity of this and his later books, including his best-selling* Bull of Minos *(1953), persuaded him, in 1959, to resign from the British Broadcasting Corporation and concentrate entirely on authorship. The subjects of his numerous books range from ancient Egypt to Roman Britain, including* Life Under the Pharaohs *(1955),* The Great Invasion *(1958),* Hannibal, Enemy of Rome *(1961),* The Horizon Book of Lost Worlds *(1962), and* The Lion Gate *(1963). He edited* The Concise Encyclopedia of Archaeology *(1960) and also contributes to learned periodicals and the BBC Third Programme. He is married to Diana Bonakis, a poet, and lives in the Cotswold Hills, in Gloucestershire, England. At present he is working on a biography of the distinguished Egyptologist Sir Flinders Petrie.*

Archaeology

As Dr. Galliani observed in the time of Louis XIV, "Man is the only animal who takes an interest in things which don't concern him." His body is physically weak compared with many other animals, but his mind—"looking before and after"—can assess his situation and carry over into the next generation part of the knowledge acquired by his forefathers: how to make and maintain fire, how to fashion tools and weapons, where the best hunting grounds were, and how to appease the gods. For many thousands of years, down to about 3200 B.C., this information could be transmitted only by speech; and even after this approximate date, the art of writing and record-keeping was known only in a few favored lands.

The purpose of this essay is (a) to show how archaeology, especially in Europe and the Middle East, has developed from treasure-hunting into a reliable adjunct of written history; (b) to show how its scope has been vastly enlarged to extend far beyond the "historical horizon" when written records began; and (c) to demonstrate some of the newer techniques that, during the past fifty years, have extracted from the earth more information about, for example, the ancient Egyptians, the Greeks, and the Romans than, in many cases, they possessed themselves.

There was a time, not very long ago, when the past revealed through archaeology and that depicted from documents touched at very few points; a time when the late Sir Arthur Evans, discoverer of Europe's oldest civilization, wrote to his friend, the scholar Edward A. Freeman: ". . . . There is [at Oxford] going to be established a Professorship of Archaeology, and I have been strongly advised to stand. I do not think I shall unless I see any real prospect of getting it. To begin with, it is to be called the Professorship of Classical Archaeology . . . To confine a Professorship of Archaeology to classical times seems to me as reasonable as to create a chair of 'Insular Geography' or 'Mezozoic Geology' . . . ."

Freeman, in a sympathetic reply, advised Evans to apply, though warning him that "they will have some narrow Balliol fool, suspending all sound learning at the end of his crooked nose, to represent self-satisfied ignorance against you, but I would go in just to tell them a thing or two."

So Evans, at that time a young, unknown scholar, did apply for the post, "told them a thing or two," and, of course, was turned down, losing the chair to Percy Gardner, a "classical" archaeologist more acceptable to the authorities at Victorian Oxford.

I mention this story because it illustrates the dichotomy which once separated archaeology from history. Later the pendulum, as usual, swung too far in the opposite direction, so that an Oxford literary don, irritated by what seemed to him the arrogance of some archaeological colleagues, wrote:

> But 'tis not verse, and 'tis not prose,
> But pottery alone
> Which tells us all that Man has been
> And all that may be known. . .

There has always been rivalry between the historian, who relies mainly on what men have written, and the archaeologist, who reaches beyond the horizon represented by literary records and oral tradition by interpreting the things men made and left behind. By comparison with the historian, the archaeologist is a newcomer on the scene, and it is only within the past century and a half that the study of objects, from Paleolithic flint axes to ancient Egyptian temples, has been accepted as having any scientific value. Gibbon, making the Grand Tour of Europe, saw and admired Roman buildings, but he could have written *The Decline and Fall of the Roman Empire* without any reference to the visible remains of the Roman epoch. In his day, the archaeologist was called an antiquarian, and while historians of Britain, for instance, were happy to make use of the writings of John Leland and Sir William Dugdale, these assiduous researchers were looked upon mainly as archivists.

When it came to the Roman period, evidences of which were scattered widely throughout Great Britain, the historians depended mainly on the scanty references in the works of Tacitus, Suetonius, and others, eked out by the observations of the Venerable Bede and the wild fabrications of Geoffrey of Monmouth. In fact, until the middle of the nineteenth century the "antiquarian"—predecessor of the modern, scientific archaeologist— was usually regarded as a romantic, a collector of "curios," a fantasist whose world merged with that of the poet.

> What song the Sirens sang, or what name Achilles assumed when he hid himself among women, though puzzling questions, are not beyond all conjecture. What time the persons of these ossuaries entered the famous nations of the dead, and slept with princes and counsellors, might admit a wide solution. But who were the proprietaries of these bones, or what bodies these ashes made up, were a question above antiquarianism, . . . Had they made as good provision for their names as they have done for their relics, they had not so grossly erred in the art of perpetuation. But to subsist in bones, and be but pyramidally extant, is a fallacy in duration.[1]

---

1 *Urn-Burial*; *GGB*, Vol. 10, p. 576.

So wrote the Norwich physician Sir Thomas Browne in the seventeenth century, reflecting sonorously on some "Urnes lately found in Norfolk." Archaeologists today do not write such stately prose—more is the pity— but one cannot blame them. For, in our day, archaeology has progressed beyond mere antiquarianism. Speculation is now confined within rigid limits. Today any competent first-year student, digging up those "Urnes" in a Norfolk field, would be able to date them—Neolithic, Bronze Age, Iron Age—by relating them to other burials of similar type, not only in Britain but in Europe, and slot them neatly into his card-index file. The same would apply to an American, French, German, Russian, Chinese student, whether working in his own country or abroad. For now there are accepted rules where once was only speculation.

There is, however, a new development which has little to do with advances in archaeological technique, or with the uneasy rapprochement between "literary" history and that revealed by excavation; and that is the increasing interest, on the part of millions of men and women throughout the civilized world, in the origins of civilization. At a time when the advance of science has opened vast new prospects of man's future, when Freud and his followers have given us fresh and at times terrifying insights into the springs of human conduct, when the physicist and the chemist have revealed possibilities of modifying not only our physical environment but our very natures, more and more people are looking backward in time, seeking an answer to the old question, "How did it all begin?"

This curiosity reveals itself at several levels. On the one hand, the unearthing of a small Mithraic temple in the heart of London produced queues of sightseers in numbers that would have flattered a Hollywood star at a premiere. On the other hand, we see distinguished poets, dramatists, composers, novelists, and painters producing new works of art based on the same myths that inspired Homer, Aeschylus, Virgil, Chaucer, Shakespeare, Milton, Goethe, and Freud. Cecil Day Lewis, Louis MacNeice, Robert Graves, and others return repeatedly to the legends that originated during the childhood of mankind. Michael Tippett writes an opera called "King Priam." Giraudoux rewrites the Amphytrion legend. Henry Miller is excited by Mycenae—and so is Alan Ginsberg. Even as uncompromisingly modern a poet as Christopher Logue is compelled to attempt a new translation of part of *The Iliad*.

Admittedly, artists have been drinking from these primal springs of inspiration since long before archaeological research added a new dimension. But this increasing awareness of our past, the gradual closing of the gap between legend, written history, and archaeologically revealed fact has intensified our experience of life. More than at any time in the past, man is a creature "looking before and after."

Archaeology itself is nothing more or less than exploration, "anthropology in the past" as the late Dr. Margaret Murray described it. Man is insatiably curious about his past. As far back as the seventh century B.C., the Pharaohs ruling from Sais reverently studied and copied the monuments of ancestors who had died two thousand years earlier. Medieval and Renaissance popes collected Greek and Roman antiquities. In 1646 an Oxford professor named John Greaves, commissioned by Archbishop Laud to study and report on the Egyptian pyramids, which he did very expertly, published his conclusions in a work called *Pyramidographia*. Andrea Palladio revived Roman architecture and was responsible for spawning neo-Roman mansions all over Europe. In the eighteenth century, the brothers Adam induced British fox-hunting squires to tear down their ancestral homes and replace them with new ones in the most refined ancient Greek taste. And Napoleon Bonaparte, after his abortive expedition to Egypt, stimulated an interest in ancient Egypt which led to the decipherment of the hieroglyphs and the birth of Egyptology.

Formerly, this curiosity about the past was confined mainly to an educated minority, but nowadays, thanks to the growth of education and the worldwide reporting of archaeological discoveries, this interest has spread to vast numbers of people. Fear of the future may also play its part, but there is no doubt that archaeological technique is advancing more rapidly than at any time in the past, and that more and more people are interested in the results. But to explain the full extent and scope of the new techniques and discoveries it is necessary to show how archaeology has developed from mere treasure-hunting to something approaching a scientific discipline.

The first phase, that of mere treasure-hunting, has already been touched upon. It occurred at several levels, from the Egyptian *fellah* plundering the tombs of his ancestors to the European dilettante searching for Greek or Roman statuary to add to his collection. Both were basically treasure-hunters in that neither was seeking for knowledge but only for objects of value. However, not all antiquarians were indifferent to the light that their discoveries could throw upon man's history. A few recognized this and even anticipated modern archaeological techniques. One such pioneer was Thomas Jefferson.

In 1784 Jefferson excavated an Indian burial mound near the Rivanna River in Virginia. His motive was to test the truth of a statement that such mounds were the tombs of warriors who had been buried in a standing position. His account shows that he conducted the excavation in a systematic and scientific manner. "Appearances certainly indicate," he wrote, "that it has derived both origin and growth from the accustomary collection of bones, and the deposition of them together; that the first collection had been deposited on the common surface of the earth, a few stones put over it, and then a covering of earth, that the second had been

DR. KATHLEEN KENYON AND DR. A. D. TUSHINGHAM DISCUSSING THE STRATIFICA-
TION OF THE JERICHO TELL

laid on this, had covered more or less of it in proportion to the number of bones, and was then also covered with earth, and so on."

He found no evidence that any of the bodies had been buried in an upright position, but that some were of infants, that the stones composing the layers had been brought from the river and from a cliff some distance away, and he described the position of the mound in relation to the surrounding landscape. The fact that he troubled to record this information at all proves that his attitude was that of a true archaeologist, even if an amateur one. By contrast, a century and more after his time, hundreds of British burial mounds, some dating from the Iron Age and the Bronze Age, were carelessly dug out, their contents scattered or lost, and no record kept. There were exceptions, e.g., the great General Pitt-Rivers who excavated burial mounds on his estate with meticulous care and was perhaps the first to recognize the importance of the *stratigraphic* method which is basic to modern archaeological excavation. The essence of this method is to cut careful sections through the soil, to observe and record—by photography or drawing—each successive layer of occupation, noting the objects found in it, however small or apparently insignificant, and to publish one's findings for the benefit of other scholars. In this way it is possible to establish the relative date of each layer, since, on an undisturbed site, the lowest will be the oldest, the topmost the most recent. Thus the site of an ancient settlement or city—especially one occupied continuously for long periods—may show that it was first occupied by people at a Stone Age level of development. A layer of burnt debris may indicate a sacking by invaders. A stratum devoid of pottery or other artifacts indicates a period during which the site was deserted. Higher up

419

DR. L. S. B. LEAKEY (KNEELING) EXAMINES THE STRATIFICATION OF THE OLDUVAI GORGE IN TANZANIA. IN THIS GORGE, HE DISCOVERED THE TWO-MILLION-YEAR-OLD SKULL OF THE SPECIES OF EARLY MAN WHOM HE NAMED *Homo habilis, man with ability*

one may find a different kind of pottery and tools, perhaps including metal objects, suggesting reoccupation by people at a higher level of culture, and so on.

All this information was available to earlier generations of excavators, had they been sufficiently interested to study it, but until little more than a century ago it was ignored. The only recognized historical method was that based on written records in a known language, usually Greek or Latin, and the only buildings that could be accurately dated were those that happened to be inscribed in one of these languages. When Herodotus visited Egypt in the fifth century B.C., he saw that three-thousand-year-old civilization still in being; he admired the monuments and recognized that they were very ancient. But, being unable to read the hieroglyphs, he relied for his information—apart from his own keen observation—on the stories he was told by the priests, which were often garbled and inaccurate. And when the ancient Egyptian language ceased to be spoken or written, all that could be known of Egypt for some fifteen hundred years was what Herodotus and other Greek or Roman writers had recorded. The ancient Egyptians themselves could not speak to us directly until Jean François Champollion and Thomas Young deciphered the hieroglyphs in the second decade of the nineteenth century.

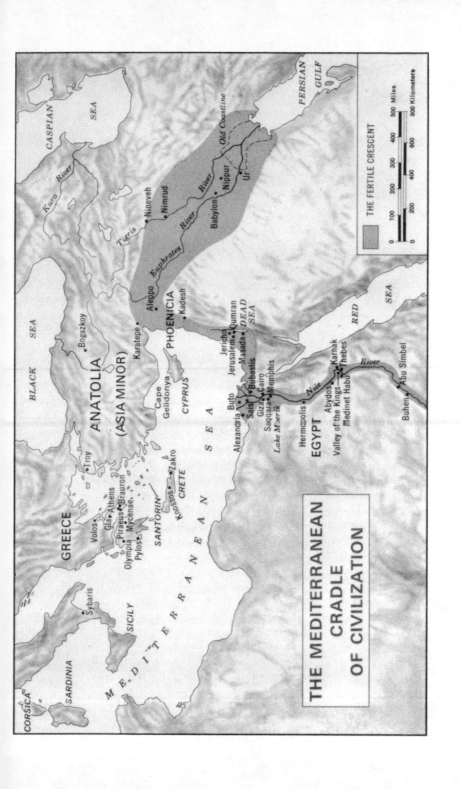

THE MEDITERRANEAN
CRADLE
OF CIVILIZATION

THE FERTILE CRESCENT

0   100   200   300   400   500 Miles
0   200   400   600   800 Kilometers

A MODERN EGYPTIAN SEATED ON THE GRAFFITI-COVERED SUMMIT OF THE GREAT
PYRAMID AT GIZA

EGYPT

Egypt had been a happy hunting ground of treasure-seekers, antiquity-dealers, and amateur archaeologists since the seventeenth century, and in this sense archaeology may be said to have begun there. Though the monuments, covered with inscriptions, remained dumb, they were still magnificent in themselves. The pyramids, being the most accessible, were most widely reported on. Herodotus, writing in the fifth century B.C., left a description which has influenced European writers for nearly twenty-five centuries, and the vast majority of those writers never visited Egypt. Sir Thomas Browne's phrase "pyramidally extant" comes to mind. Thomas Fuller (1608–61) writes: "The pyramids themselves, doting with age, have forgotten the names of their founders"; Shakespeare and Milton also mentioned them.

European explorers who began trickling into Egypt throughout the seventeenth and eighteenth centuries usually carried Herodotus, Strabo, and Pliny in their baggage, since these were generally the latest guides available. Their attitude ranged from the reverential to the derogatory. For instance, a George Sandys, arriving on the pyramid plateau in the year 1610, sweating in his doublet and hose, surveyed the monuments with an appraising but critical eye: "Full West of the City, close upon those Desarts, aloft on a rocky level adjoyning the valley, stand those three Pyramids, the barbarous monuments of prodigality and vainglory, so universally celebrated. . . ."

422

Unlike Herodotus, who had contented himself with an external view, Sandys and his companions essayed the difficult and dangerous descent into the interior, though not without taking due precautions.

> We approached the entrance, seeming as heretofore to have been closed up, or so intended. Into this our Janisarries discharged their Harquebuses, lest some should have skult within to have done us a mischief; and they guarded the entrance as we entered, for fear of the wild Arabs. . . . Our guide, a Moor, went foremost; everyone of us with lights in our hands. A most dreadful passage, and no less cumbersome, not above a yard in breadth and four feet in height. . . . So, alwaies stopping, and sometimes creeping, by reason of the rubbidge, we descended one hundred feet. . . . Here we passed through a long entry, which led directly forward, so low, that it took from us even that uneasie benefit of stooping. Which brought us into a little room with a compact roof, more long than broad, of polisht marble; whose grave-like smell, half full of rubbidge, forced our quick return . . .

Under such conditions, it is not surprising that Sandys was not able to take precise measurements, but he kept his eyes open, as did his successor, Greaves, who in the year 1646 "twice went to Grand Cairo from Alexandria to view them; carrying with me a radius ten feet long most accurately divided, besides some other instruments, for the fuller discovery of the truth." Although Greaves also carried Herodotus and other ancient writers in his baggage, one senses in his book *Pyramidographia* a flavor of the more detailed, scientific approach that distinguishes modern archaeology from mere curiosity. Of the Grand Gallery within the Great Pyramid, he writes:

> . . . A very stately piece of work, and not inferiour, either in respect of curiosity of Art, or richness of materials, to the most sumptuous and magnificent of buildings . . . At the end of it, on the right hand, is the well mentioned by Pliny; the which is circular, and not square, as the Arabian writers describe . . . By my measure sounding it with a line it contains twenty feet in depth. The reason of the difference between Pliny's observation and mine, I suppose to be this, that since his time it hath been almost dammed up, and choaked with rubbidge.

Throughout the eighteenth century a number of daring travelers attempted to explore Egypt; they had to be daring since the menace of the "wild Arabs" remained potent. Muslim fanaticism made Egypt much more dangerous to Europeans than it had been in the days of Herodotus or Pliny, especially if the visitors ventured upriver to Thebes. Robbery with violence, and even murder, were not uncommon, especially among the notorious villagers of El Gournah who had made their homes in some

423

PORTION OF EBONY CARRIAGE INLAID WITH GOLD PICTURE-WRITING

TOMB-RELIEF SHOWING THE BLESSING OF RAMSES II

Ancient hieroglyphics played a greater role in Egyptian art than the role of the modern caption. The characters in the pictograph (top) can stand as individual symbols. In the relief (above), the symbols for "purity" and "life" represent the holy water with which the gods bless the pharaoh. The pillar (right) shows a god and king of nearly equal size exchanging the breath of life in an environment of hieroglyphics. On the papyrus (below) the written language is used as a communications tool. Its holy function (above) and the significance of the individual characters (top and right) have been replaced by a system of quick notation on a less permanent material and for a mathematical end.

SESOSTRIS I
AND THE GOD PTAH

THE RHIND
MATHEMATICAL PAPYRUS

of the ancient Egyptian tombs. One English traveler, W. G. Browne, wrote in 1792:

> They are indeed a ferocious clan, differing in person from other Egyptians. Spears twelve feet long are sudden and deadly weapons in their hands. . . . In the temple of Medinet Habu we observed a large quantity of blood and were told that the Gournese had there murdered a Greek, a traveller passing from Assuan to Cairo, who had strayed thither out of mere curiosity.

Some of these visitors, not all of whom went out of mere curiosity, left descriptions which not only confirmed the descriptions of the ancient writers but also added fresh information. But the event that did more than anything to stimulate interest in ancient Egypt was Napoleon's abortive invasion of 1798. Bonaparte took with him a number of French *savants*, one of whom, Dominique Vivant Denon, was a scholar, a writer, and an artist. His book *Travels in Upper and Lower Egypt*, published in 1802 with its accurate observations, drawings, and plans executed under conditions that would have defeated most men, began a process that was eventually to transform Egyptology from a search for treasure to a quest for archaeological information. The discovery by the French expedition of the Rosetta Stone with its bilingual inscription led directly to the decipherment of the hieroglyphs and thus to a knowledge of ancient Egyptian history, culture, and manners which had been inaccessible for more than fifteen centuries.

In Egypt French scholarship was at first dominant, for Bonaparte's short-lived expedition left its mark. The first director of the Egyptian *Service des Antiquités* was the Frenchman Auguste Mariette (1821–1881). He founded the *Service*, the director of which was until quite recent times usually a Frenchman. The last was M. Drioton. Since his retirement the post has been held by Egyptians. It was Mariette who founded the first Egyptian national collection of Egyptian antiquities, the nucleus of the marvelous display of treasures now housed in the archaeological museum in Cairo, the finest in the world. The purpose of the *Service* was not only to collect objects but to preserve sites and control future excavations. This tradition has been carried on to the present day. Anyone wishing to excavate in Egypt has to obtain a concession from the government, and the *Service* does its best to control indiscriminate digging by local inhabitants, not an easy task. For this purpose it maintains resident inspectors at the principal sites.

Shortly after Mariette was born, his fellow-countryman Champollion found the clue to the decipherment of Egyptian writing, based partly on the bilingual inscription—in Greek and ancient Egyptian—on the famous Rosetta Stone discovered by French troops and later annexed by the British. Other scholars, notably the Englishman Thomas Young, also

CRETAN TRIBUTE-BEARERS

PRISONERS FROM THE SYRIAN WARS

EVIDENCE OF EGYPTIAN CONTACT WITH OTHER CULTURES

BOUND CAPTIVES DRIVEN BEFORE THE CHARIOT OF RAMSES II

PHILISTINES LED BY AN EGYPTIAN

FAIENCE TILES FROM THE PALACE OF RAMSES III

made important contributions. Thanks to these pioneers and their successors, the long-dead language has been resuscitated so that inscription in tombs, on temple walls, and on papyrus scrolls—unintelligible for nearly sixteen centuries—can be read and understood. Another "dead" language, apart from Greek and Latin, could now be read; the philologist now became the ally of the archaeologist.

There is one point which I must try to make clear at this juncture. For reasons of simplicity I am obliged to take each country in turn and trace the growth and fruition of scientific archaeology in that region. But in fact the process was not as simple as that. There was a kind of cross-fertilization. The archaeologists of these different areas did not work in isolation but influenced each other directly or indirectly. What Sir Flinders Petrie and others did and learned in Egyptian excavation had its effect on the work of, say, Sir Arthur Evans in Crete and Sir Leonard Woolley in Mesopotamia. And Petrie's system of "sequence dating," which he developed while working in Egypt, was subsequently adopted by scholars in many parts of the world.

Even more significant, a discovery made in one region might well affect the interpretation of objects found in others. For instance, when Evans found, in the palace of Knossos in Crete, objects which had been imported from Egypt, he was able to fix an approximate date for the layers in which these things were found, since Egyptian artifacts could be fairly accurately dated, whereas, until Evans carried out his excavations at Knossos, Cretan or "Minoan" objects could not. Again, when Evans found at Knossos wall-frescoes depicting men wearing a certain type of costume it was possible to identify these hitherto unknown Cretan people with those whom the ancient Egyptians called the "Keftiu," because portraits of men wearing identical costume had been found in certain Egyptian tombs of the Eighteenth Dynasty. One could cite many other examples of this cross-fertilization.

There is an expression in common use in Britain today among town-planning authorities. It is "in-filling." It is not used in connection with the planning of a new town, but if an old village, say, has vacant plots between existing cottages the local authority will sometimes permit new houses to be built in these gaps. This is known as "in-filling." This phrase could be used to describe much of the archaeological effort of the nineteenth century, particularly the first half. It filled in gaps in our knowledge of the ancient world, but it did little to extend that knowledge. Herodotus had described the pyramids: Greaves, Giovanni Belzoni, Vyse, and their successors examined them in greater detail. Herodotus visited and described the Serapeum, the sacred mausoleum of the Apis Bulls at Saqqara: Mariette rediscovered and excavated it. Strabo had seen the Valley of the Kings, the royal mausoleums of the Pharaohs at Thebes in Upper Egypt: Belzoni and others excavated there, confirmed some of

Strabo's observations, and added some of their own. All this was "infilling," but it did not add greatly to our knowledge. That came with the progress of scientific archaeology in the late nineteenth and the twentieth centuries.

Let us take for example Herodotus. He had the enviable opportunity—in the fifth century B.C.—of studying ancient Egyptian civilization while it was still in being, even if moribund. What he says about ancient Egypt in his *Histories* is of considerable value, but modern archaeological research has proved that he was wrong in a number of ways. He is usually to be trusted when he is describing the life he saw around him. He is less reliable when he deals with Egyptian history because then he had to rely on the testimony of his informants, usually Egyptian priests who had only retained a garbled version of what had happened some thousand or two thousand years before their time.

With one or two exceptions, Herodotus is wrong about the names and reign-dates of the principal Egyptian Pharaohs. He knows about Cheops, Chephren, and Mycerinus, builders of the first, second, and third pyramids at Giza. But he shows no interest in Saqqara where an even older pyramid exists, that of King Zoser (*c.* 2800 B.C.). He knows nothing of the Pharaoh Amenemhat—at least by name—although he describes the so-called Labyrinth near Lake Moeris which probably formed part of that king's palace and temple, or of the mighty Pharaohs who reigned from Thebes more than fifteen hundred years after the Great Pyramid was built by Cheops (Khufu).

He tells stories about a certain monarch, called by him Rhampsinitus, one of which contains echoes of tomb-robbing, a long-established profession in ancient Egypt. Rhampsinitus is obviously a corruption of Ramses, a name borne by many Pharaohs of the New Kingdom including the great Ramses II and III. He also mentions one Sesostris, which is the Greek form of Senusret; several Pharaohs of the Middle Kingdom bore that name, but Herodotus has not the slightest conception of chronological sequence. It was as if a foreign visitor to England, knowing nothing of English history, had had to rely on informants too ignorant or indifferent to tell him the truth. Such a visitor would have heard of King Henry VIII and William the Conqueror but would have had no idea when they lived. But if their monuments had survived he would be capable of ascribing the Tower of London to Henry VIII (although it was begun by William) and the Palace of Hampton Court to William although it was built in the reign of Henry VIII.

The "father of history" is much more reliable when he is dealing with Egyptian history nearer his own epoch. He scores when describing things and events which he has seen with his own eyes, and such passages are the most valuable parts of his report. Modern Egyptologists, being able to read the hieroglyphs, can work out a chronological table of Egyptian

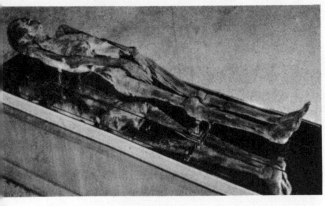

kings from about 3200 B.C. down to the coming of the Romans. Herodotus could not do this, but he can tell us a great deal about Egyptian life and customs current in his time, which still have relevance to modern archaeological discoveries.

> The cats on their decease are taken to the city of Bubastis, where they are embalmed, after which they are buried in certain sacred repositories. The dogs are interred in the cities to which they belong, . . . The same practice obtains with respect to the ichneumons; the hawks and shrew-mice, on the contrary, are conveyed to the city of Buto for burial, and the ibises to Hermopolis.[2]

All this is doubtless true, but it gives a false impression of Egypt in her days of highest glory. By the fifth century B.C. Egyptian religion had degenerated, and the cult of animal-worship had assumed an importance far greater than that which existed in, say, the fifteenth century B.C. On the other hand, his description of the embalmment process was probably as true for the fifteenth century B.C. as for the fifth century.

> The mode of embalming, according to the most perfect process, is the following:—They take first a crooked piece of iron, and with it draw out the brain through the nostrils, thus getting rid of a portion, while the skull is cleared of the rest by rinsing with drugs; next they make a cut along the flank with a sharp Ethiopian stone, and take out the whole contents of the abdomen, . . . After this they fill the cavity with the purest bruised myrrh, with cassia, and every other sort of spicery except frankincense, and sew up the opening. Then the body is placed in natrum for seventy days, and covered entirely over. After the expiration of that space of time, . . . the body is washed, and wrapped round, from head to foot, with bandages of fine linen cloth . . . and in this state it is given back to the relations, who enclose it in a wooden case which they have had made for the purpose, shaped into the figure of a man.[3]

2 *The History* II. 67; *GBWW*, Vol. 6, p. 63a.
3 *Ibid.* II. 86; pp. 65d–66a.

Yet this, too, is "in-filling." Archaeologists confirmed, by examining mummies, that what Herodotus had observed was true. But what was the reason for this elaborate cult of the dead? Why did the ancient Egyptians place such importance on the preservation of the body and its protection within strongly built tombs? Herodotus does not tell us, but the modern archaeologist can, since he is able to read the hieroglyphic inscriptions and is not dependent on priestly hearsay. Again, in the nineteenth century, few scholars, apart from Sir Flinders Petrie, had asked themselves where the ancestors of these highly civilized people came from, and whether theirs was an indigenous culture or one which owed something to foreign influence.

The mention of Petrie brings us to one of those examples of cross-fertilization of which I wrote earlier. What Petrie did in Egypt, and the method of excavation and recording that he evolved, owed something to what European prehistorians had been doing in quite a different archaeological context. In Egypt, for more than a century before Petrie arrived in the eighties of the last century, archaeology had been little more than treasure-hunting. It had long been known that the ancient Egyptians had buried rich and valuable objects with their dead, and the motive of most, if not all, excavators, had been to find valuable or interesting objects for display in museums or private collections, without much regard for their date or the light they might throw on the civilization which had produced them. But in Europe a discipline had developed concerned with a period of man's development compared with which the Pharaohs were of yesterday. The study of prehistory owed nothing to written records or legends. It was allied to geology and natural history, both of which had been anticipated by Greek philosophers. For instance, Xenophanes of Colophon, in the sixth century B.C., observed fossilized remains of seashells in the Sicilian mountains, and the imprints of fishes and seaweed in a quarry near Syracuse. From these he argued that the earth had undergone great changes in its structure.

By the second half of the nineteenth century archaeology had divided its efforts. Some—the prehistorians, in alliance with the geologists and the paleontologists—searched for evidences of man's remote past. Others, sticking to the humanist tradition, continued to enlarge their view of the civilized communities, such as that of Egypt. Yet the two disciplines interacted strongly. For instance, treasure-hunting and the search for ancient works of art hardly entered the world of the prehistorian, occupied as he was with such things as stone axes, arrowheads, scrapers, and awls, or fragments of inscribed reindeer antlers and bone. Such things had little intrinsic value, but they told him a great deal about how primitive man evolved. It occurred to some nineteenth-century archaeologists that the same methods could be applied with advantage to sites falling within the historical period, provided one regarded *every* object as important, not only the lofty temple and richly furnished tomb, but also the primitive stone quern and the mat-lined storage pit.

It was mainly Petrie, in Egypt, who first applied this method, although one must give credit to General Pitt-Rivers in England who was a pioneer of careful excavation, stratigraphic survey, and scrupulous recording. Although Petrie began his work in Egypt and continued it in Palestine, his methods, especially his above-mentioned "sequence dating," became common practice wherever serious excavation was contemplated. It is not too farfetched to say that just as Egypt was the birthplace of civilization (along with Sumeria) so it was also the birthplace of modern scientific archaeological method.

Petrie began by surveying the Giza group of pyramids, including the Great Pyramid, and published the first scientific survey of these wonderful monuments using precise measuring instruments. This was in 1880, when he was still a young man. Later he went on to excavate other known historical sites, particularly those of the pyramid period, the Old Kingdom as it is called. Although he discovered lovely and valuable things, such as

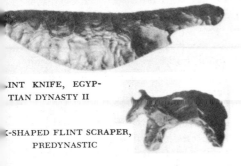

INT KNIFE, EGYP-
TIAN DYNASTY II

-SHAPED FLINT SCRAPER,
PREDYNASTIC

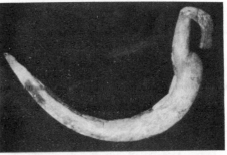

WOODEN SICKLE WITH AN INSET FLINT CUT-
TING EDGE, EGYPTIAN DYNASTY I

gyptian tool-makers gradually refined their craft. After mastering the use of nt, they could control the tool's shape and xture. With new materials, Egyptians were le to fashion tools with more specialized nctions.

COPPER CHISELS, BODKINS, AND NEEDLES
FROM THE TOMB OF ZER AT SAQQARA, EGYP-
TIAN DYNASTY I OR II

FLINT KNIFE, EGYPTIAN DYNASTY I OR II

FLINT KNIFE, EGYPTIAN DYNASTY I OR II

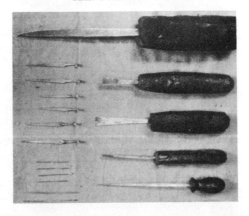

the famous Illahun Treasure, part of which is now in the Metropolitan Museum of Art, New York, his indifference to the more obvious glamour of archaeology is shown by one simple fact. His autobiography, *Seventy Years in Archaeology* (1931), contains only a passing reference to the discovery by Howard Carter and Lord Carnarvon of the tomb of Tutankhamen, the only intact tomb of a Pharaoh ever found, crammed with objects of gold, alabaster, precious woods, and semiprecious stones. It astonished the world, but not, apparently, Petrie. Yet within his own scheme of thinking he was right. The fabulous treasure of King Tutankhamen revealed hardly anything which Egyptologists did not already know from inscriptions and tomb-paintings.

By contrast, Petrie pushed back the frontier of ancient Egyptian history by more than two thousand years, without the aid of any written records save for a few inscriptions on pottery jars. And his grasp of typology enabled him, merely by studying the evolution in style of simple artifacts such as pottery, to establish their relative date. At Abydos he pieced together the shattered remnants of the tombs of kings who had preceded the great pyramid-builders by some five hundred years. Later at Al Badari, Nagada, Amrata, Gerzea, and other sites he traced the ancestors of the civilized Egyptians—primitive agriculturalists using stone tools who, some five thousand years B.C., had been attracted to the Nile Valley by its fecundity and abundance of wild game. These were the people of whom Herodotus, Strabo, and Pliny knew nothing, and who lived long before the Egyptians invented writing and could leave the written inscriptions which Champollion and others deciphered.

I stress these facts because it is too commonly imagined in these days that the revolution in archaeological technique, which we shall be discussing later, has been brought about mainly by sophisticated developments such as radiocarbon dating, aerial photography, electrical resistivity tests, and other products of technology. These have undoubtedly made an important contribution, but the basic improvement on the older, haphazard methods still rests on the stratigraphic system, the study and analysis of fragmented pottery, and other intrinsically worthless objects ignored by earlier excavators, and above all by a revolution in thinking. Men and women still hoped to find treasure in the earth and still do. But after Petrie, and the many students who copied his methods, archaeology was never the same again.

In 1892 he was appointed first Professor of Egyptology at University College, London, a chair founded for him specially by Miss Amelia Edwards who recognized his genius. From that year onward he divided his time between excavating in Egypt and Palestine and teaching in London. Such was the power of his personality, although he was an indifferent lecturer, that he recruited numerous disciples who were prepared to work with him for a mere pittance. Some of these men—and one

Egyptian Tomb Artifacts

15TH CENTURY B.C. WALL PAINTING FROM THEBES SHOWING A DECOY DUCK AND A DOMESTICATED HUNTING CAT

A MASTABA TOMB AT SAQQARA, SHOWING THE RAMP LEADING TO THE SARCOPHAGUS

MASTABA TOMB RELIEFS SHOWING ORE-SMELTING AND COLLAR-FASHIONING. DWARVES ARE PICTURED IN THE LOWER RIGHT CORNER

As well as showing something of the nature of Egyptian life, the tombs have helped modern men to understand the way Egyptians thought. In the hunting scene (above), the painter shows not just what the eye can see, but all that exists in the environment; we see the fish below the water and we see the social hierarchy in the relative sizes of the family members. The toilet articles (below) make clear the emphasis Egyptians placed on appearance during life and afterward. In order to provide him with grain and with family, the effigy of Nebiempet (lower right) was placed in the tomb of her father.

EGYPTIAN JEWELRY AND TOILET ARTICLES FROM A TOMB OF DYNASTY XII

THE TOMB OF NANUPKAN AT GIZA. HIS DAUGHTER IS DEPICTED GRINDING GRAIN. V-VI DYNASTY

woman, the late Dr. Margaret Murray—rose to high eminence in the world of archaeology. Petrie died in Jerusalem in 1942 at the age of eighty-nine and is buried on the Mount of Olives.

Although Petrie may be regarded as the father of modern scientific Egyptology, it would be misleading to isolate him and ignore the contributions made by other scholars. Among these are the Americans George Reisner, whose work on the Great Pyramid and on the evolution of the Egyptian tomb puts him high in the ranks of great Egyptologists, and James Breasted, whose *History of Egypt* (1905) and *Ancient Records of Egypt* (1906) are now standard works on the subject. Among scores of other names of European scholars who have made great contributions to the science of Egyptology one might mention the following: Sir Gaston Maspero, successor to Mariette as director of the Antiquities Service, whose activity, learning, and industry were enormous; his colleague Georges Daressy, who worked at Medinet Habu and who helped Maspero clear the great find of Twenty-first Dynasty mummies; the German scholar Adolf Erman, whose studies led to a completely new conception of the nature of the Egyptian language, and his fellow-countrymen Georg Ebers and Ludwig Borchardt. Some of these scholars concentrated on excavation and the interpretation of finds; others were more interested in the written records and the process of decipherment. Of the latter, perhaps the greatest was Sir Alan Gardiner, who devoted a long lifetime to the study and interpretation of Egyptian documents, and whose *Egyptian Grammar* (3rd rev. ed., 1957) is now a standard work throughout the world. Truly Egyptology is an international science.

Coming to more recent times, one notes a change, almost a revolution, in Egyptology. After the establishment of the Egyptian Republic, following the deposition of King Faruk, an Egyptian was made director of the *Service*, and throughout the country posts formerly held by foreigners have been occupied by Egyptian nationals. There has been an emphasis on Egyptian archaeologists, some of whom, notably Dr. Labib Habachi and the late Mohammad Zakaria Goneim, to name only two, have made important discoveries. To Goneim, who was at various times Chief Inspector of antiquities at Luxor and later at Saqqara, we owe the discovery of a hitherto unknown pyramid and a hitherto unknown king, Sekhemkhet ("powerful of body"). To mislay a pyramid may seem rather careless, but what Goneim found was not a complete building, of course, but the underground chambers and the uncompleted lower courses of a building which had been begun by Sekhemkhet during his lifetime and then abandoned, after which the desert sand covered them up.

The writer was fortunate enough to be present, as Goneim's guest, during a part of two seasons' excavations on the pyramid plateau at Saqqara (about twelve miles south of Cairo) where stands the oldest pyra-

mid in the world, that of King Zoser (*c.* 2800 B.C.) and a number of what
are called "mastaba"-tombs, great mud-brick structures built by kings
of the First to the end of the Second Dynasties, roughly between 3200
B.C. and 2800 B.C., the predecessors of Zoser, whose structure is the
oldest large stone building in the world. Goneim was for a time Chief
Inspector of antiquities at Saqqara under the *Service des Antiquités*; he
lived on the spot and spent much time studying it. The site is dominated
by Zoser's "Step Pyramid" and its ancillary buildings which surround a
great rectangular enclosure bordered by a wall. One day Goneim thought
he noticed, outlined in the desert sand, a similar enclosure at a spot a
few hundred yards south of Zoser's pyramid complex; at certain times of
the day, when the sun is low in the sky, one can sometimes detect the
outline of buried buildings. He was also intrigued by discovering, in
this place, masses of fine stone chippings such as were thrown out by
the workmen who excavated underground chambers five thousand years
ago. Such evidence had been found on other sites. There was also the
fact that though Zoser was known to have had successors (he was the
first Pharaoh of the Third Dynasty), none of their monuments had been
found.

From a close study of Zoser's pyramid enclosure, Goneim estimated
where the buried foundations of the unknown pyramid would lie, and
where the entrance to the underground galleries would be. He dug beneath the sand and was soon rewarded by finding a superb wall, of the

435

EXCAVATIONS AT THE ZOSER STEP PYRAMID AT SAQQARA

typical "paneled-facade" pattern characteristic of the Second and Third Dynasties, faced with fine white limestone and looking as fresh and new as it was when the workmen left it some five thousand years ago. The upper part was unfinished, confirming Goneim's theory that a pyramid and its ancillary buildings had been begun and abandoned.

Some little distance to the south of the wall he noticed a slight depression in the sand in a position at which the entrance to the buried pyramid should be, if such a building had existed. Again he dug, and again he was successful. Soon there appeared a deep rock-cut shaft with a sloping floor leading down into the rock beneath the desert surface. Following the line of this descending passage, the archaeologist came upon the lower courses of a step pyramid of a type similar to Zoser's, built of relatively small stones, since at this period the ancient Egyptians had not learned to use the huge monumental blocks which are such as impressive feature of Khufu's Great Pyramid, built about a century later. The rock-cut approach plunged deep beneath the unfinished pyramid, ending in a rough-hewn, unfinished chamber some ninety feet below the surface, in which lay a fine alabaster sarcophagus without a lid, but sealed at one end by a sliding panel.

This discovery aroused great hopes that the sarcophagus might contain the body of the king who had reigned some fourteen hundred years before Tutankhamen and whose name, identified on clay jar-sealings, was Sekhemkhet, the successor of Zoser. The sliding panel was sealed, and there were what appeared to be the remains of a funerary wreath on top of the alabaster chest. But when, in the presence of President Nasser, the panel was lifted, the sarcophagus proved to be empty; nor had it ever contained a body, as there was no trace of the resinous material which the Egyptians used during the funeral libations. Despite this intense disappointment, Goneim's achievement, based on a very limited financial grant, was a notable one, and a testimony to the skill of the new generation of Egyptian Egyptologists. Much was learned from the construction of the maze of underground galleries, stacked with beautifully fashioned stone jars in enormous quantity to contain the food-offerings needed by the Pharaoh in the afterlife. Goneim's theory was that work on the pyramid ceased after the king's death, which must have been early in his reign. He also suggested that this was only a dummy tomb intended to deceive the tomb-robbers and that the real tomb of Sekhemkhet may still await discovery somewhere under the huge pyramid enclosure. He also gained an unexpected bonus; on the floor of the steeply descending entrance corridor lay some exquisite golden bracelets of the Third Dynasty, probably intended for a princess, together with a pair of eyebrow-tweezers in gold and silver alloy of the same date, about 2750 B.C. These were probably left by some early tomb-robber during a hurried flight.

A limited number of European and American archaeologists are still

VIEW OF THE WESTERN CEMETERY OF MASTABA TOMBS AT GIZA, AS SEEN FROM
THE SUMMIT OF THE GREAT PYRAMID

permitted to work in Egypt, though far less than was the case before the advent of the new regime. Among these is Charles Nims of the University of Chicago, who presides over Chicago House, the University's head-quarters at Luxor, in Upper Egypt. Dr. Nims and his devoted staff, mainly Americans, have for many years been making accurate facsimiles of the painted bas-reliefs in the great temple of Ramses III at Medinet Habu. This work of copying is immensely important, since the temple, like other Egyptian monuments, is decaying, and through Dr. Nims's work a perfect record will be made in full color, so that future Egyptologists will be able to study these valuable inscriptions even if the originals are destroyed.

Another very important investigation is being carried out by Brian Emery of University College, London. Digging on the northern side of the ancient cemetery at Saqqara, he unearthed a series of magnificent mastaba-tombs associated with the Pharaohs of the First and Second Dynasties (*c.* 3200–2800 B.C.). Petrie had discovered at Abydos tombs or cenotaphs associated with the same monarchs, the founding fathers of Egyptian civilization, and it is still not finally established whether the Saqqara monuments were intended to contain the bodies of these kings, or their true tombs were those which Petrie investigated at Abydos. It was common at this period for the Pharaohs to have two or sometimes even three sepulchral monuments. But Emery has proved that as early as 3200 B.C., the conjectural date of the first Pharaoh to rule over a united Egypt, Egyptian civilization had already reached a very advanced stage in art and craftsmanship, such as required an anterior period of development stretching back at least another five centuries.

In more recent years Emery has directed his efforts to finding, if possible, the tomb of the great Vizier (Prime Minister) Imhotep, chief minister to the Pharaoh Zoser and architect of the oldest stone building in the world, the Step Pyramid. In later years Imhotep was deified. He was associated with the invention of writing and with medicine, which led the Greeks to identify him with Asclepius. His tomb, which must have been magnificent, has never been found, but it may still exist, buried under the drifting sand which shrouds thousands of ancient Egyptian sepulchers at Saqqara.

Emery's hopes rose when he stumbled on an enormous underground labyrinth dating mainly from Ptolemaic times (*c.* 323–30 B.C.), extending over several miles. Within these dark decaying corridors, hewn out of the rock beneath the desert, were recesses containing the bodies of over one hundred thousand mummified ibises, the sacred bird which Herodotus mentions in his description of Egypt.[4] The ibis was sacred to Thoth, god of writing, which suggests an association with Imhotep. Although as

4 *Ibid.* II. 75–76; p. 64b–c.

of now Emery has still not located the tomb, he appears confident that it exists somewhere in that bewildering maze of galleries. Given the fate of other ancient Egyptian tombs, it is highly doubtful that it will be found intact.

Emery has made other notable contributions to Egyptology. When the building of the new High Dam above Aswan threatened the whole of ancient Nubia (which lay to the south) Emery carried out important investigations in the area, especially at Buhen, where there existed substantial remains of a Pharaonic fortress, parts of which date from before 2500 B.C. Buhen was one of a string of castles built by the Pharaohs of the Old and Middle Kingdoms to protect their vital trade routes into Central Africa. In size and strength the fortifications at Buhen could stand comparison with Carcassonne, which it resembles also in its massive curtain-walls, pierced by arrow-slits, its projecting bastions and towers, and its strategic siting—all evidences of military sophistication quite comparable with the finest achievements of the European Middle Ages. Yet Buhen was built more than three thousand years before Carcassonne.

Unhappily, this ancient Egyptian fortress, together with many others, will all be swept away by the rising waters as they pile up behind the new High Dam, turning ancient Nubia into a gargantuan lake some three hundred miles long. Fortunately, some of the more durable monuments have been saved. Buhen was built of mud-brick, whereas Abu Simbel, the temple created by Ramses II and carved from the cliffs overlooking the Nile, was of stone. At great expense in time, money, and engineering skill, the temple, and that of Ramses' lovely queen Nefertiti (Nefertari), with their sculptured reliefs, have been sliced out of the mountainside and reerected at a level above that of the rising waters.

But much as one admires the Abu Simbel temples and their dramatic site, they belong to a period of which a large number of other and better monuments survive and are reasonably safe. One would rather have saved Buhen.

Coming to relatively recent times, one of the most interesting and important sites recently excavated was Qasir Ibrim in Nubia. This had been a Roman fortress of which substantial parts remain, and subsequently it was occupied in Christian, Islamic, and Bosnian times. In December, 1963, J. Martin Plumley of Cambridge, England, with his staff, began excavations there which continued until 1967. The writer, returning from a visit to Abu Simbel, happened to call at the site in 1963, not long after Plumley had made his most astonishing discovery; astonishing because the site, a tangle of ruined houses on a rocky bluff overlooking the Nile, unoccupied for centuries, seemed to offer little hope of any interesting archaeological find. But there was, beside the scanty Pharaonic and substantial Roman remains, the foundations of a

Christian church, and here Plumley concentrated his efforts. Under the church he found two crypts, in one of which lay the undisturbed burial of a bishop, the body being fully clad and wearing a vestment. Around the neck of the body had been suspended a wrought-iron cross together with a linen handkerchief, and secreted among the vestments were two paper scrolls.

These, when unrolled, proved to be the consecration deeds of the deceased, giving the date of his consecration which was A.D. 1372. One scroll was written in Coptic, the other in Arabic. As a contrast, illustrating how the medieval occupants of the fortress utilized very ancient material, Plumley found in this same Christian crypt a carved stela dating from the time of the Pharaoh Amenophis I, showing the King and his mother worshiping the god Horus. This stela was at least twenty-eight hundred years older than the Christian burial. Qasir Ibrim had been a fortress in Pharaonic times, had been utilized by the Romans when they occupied Egypt, and subsequently had become a citadel of Christianity and the see of a bishop. What makes this discovery even more important is the fact that Christian bishops were ruling from this place some seven hundred years after the Muslim conquest of Egypt. A Christian minority speaking the Coptic language (which directly descended from ancient Egyptian) continued to survive, as it does to this day.

THE BIBLE LANDS

We move now to what the Victorians called the "Bible Lands," that is, modern Jordan, Syria, Israel, and Lebanon. The most noteworthy archaeological find there, as everyone now knows, has been the Dead Sea Scrolls. The first discovery was made accidentally by a Bedouin shepherd guarding his flock of goats on the rocky uplands above the Dead Sea in Jordan. Scrambling up the rocks in pursuit of a straying goat, he observed a cave in the cliff-face high above him. Being unable to reach it, he threw in a stone and was astonished to hear it shatter some hidden object. When, eventually, he and his companions succeeded in entering the cave, they came upon the remains of a large pottery jar containing a scroll inscribed in Hebrew writing. Subsequently other caves were explored and more scrolls came to light. When archaeologists got to hear of this discovery, the whole area was combed, and eventually it was realized that these documents had been produced by a Jewish sect called the Essenes whose monastery at Qumran had been their refuge after the sack of Jerusalem by the Emperor Titus.

It now appears certain that, knowing their refuge would be discovered and attacked, the Essenes hid their sacred writings in caves which remained undetected for some two thousand years. The interest of the scrolls lies in the fact that they contain the earliest known versions of

440

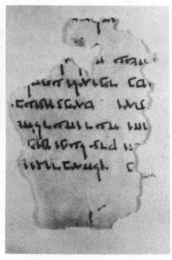

THIS BUNDLE OF LEGAL DOCUMENTS, WHICH DATE FROM 88 TO 135 A.D., WAS FOUND IN A CLIFFSIDE CAVE NEAR THE DEAD SEA. REFUGEES FROM PRINCE BAR KOCHBA'S JEWISH UPRISING DIED IN THE CAVE, LEAVING THESE LETTERS AND THEIR LIVING EQUIPMENT, WHICH WERE DISCOVERED IN 1961

certain Old Testament scriptures, and that some of their prophetic writing appears to anticipate the teachings of Jesus Christ. The matter is highly controversial, and while some authorities seem to regard the scrolls as evidence that the basic precepts of Christianity were known before the birth of Christ (and possibly that He studied under the Essenes), others take the contrary view.

Another dramatic excavation, this time in Israel, in 1965, was that of the mountain fortress of Herod at Masada, on an almost impregnable high point above the Dead Sea. Here another fanatical sect resisted the Romans after the fall of Jerusalem, finally committing mass suicide when the legionaries breached their walls and stormed the citadel. The operation was described by the Jewish historian Josephus; and when the Israeli archaeologist Y. Yadin investigated the site, aided by hundreds of volunteer helpers from all over the world, he found clear evidence that Josephus had been right. The Roman siege-works, including their camps, the walls they built to prevent the defenders escaping, and the mighty ramp on which they mounted their siege engines for the ultimate assault, can still be seen, exactly as Josephus described them; another example of the verification of literary history by archaeology.

But this too was "in-filling"—spectacular and imaginative in its conception, but in fact telling us little about man's history that we did not already know. Far more important archaeologically is the revelation, mainly over the past twenty to thirty years, that what used to be called loosely the "Bible Lands" were among the places where civilization began on earth. And here it is helpful to look back over the past century and to note how, just as in Egypt, men began by examining or looking for remains of known historical monuments—in this case towns and

441

sites mentioned in the Bible—and then were drawn by their discoveries to investigate sites which illustrate what the late Gordon Childe called the "Neolithic Revolution." This was the period, thousands of years before the birth of Egyptian civilization, when in a few favored places man took the momentous step which was ultimately to lead to a settled communal life and the beginning of civilization—the period when, having learned how to grow crops from wild grasses and to domesticate animals, he ceased to be a wandering hunter.

One can trace Palestinian archaeology back to 1865, when the Palestine Exploration Fund was founded for "the accurate and systematic investigation of the archaeology, the topography, the geology and physical geography, the manners and customs of the Holy Land, for Biblical illustration." The last three words sum up the motive. As Kathleen Kenyon remarks in her *Archaeology in the Holy Land* (1960), "It would be true to say that early in the nineteenth century the Jews were the one nation in the ancient Near East with which the European was familiar . . . the Land of the Bible was a potential source of interest exceeding the still rather shadowy empires of Assur-bani-pal and Sargon or Thothmes and Rameses." It is not surprising, therefore, that the foundation of the Palestine Exploration Fund preceded that of the Egypt Exploration Fund. What these early excavators were looking for was something to confirm their Chirstian faith; if they could prove the historical reality of towns and cities mentioned in the Bible, this would help strengthen their beliefs and perhaps help stem the tide of skepticism aroused by the publication of Darwin's theory of evolution.

WHILE DIGGING BENEATH THE FOUNDATIONS OF AN ANCIENT SYNAGOGUE IN MASADA, ISRAEL, YIGAEL YADIN AND HIS TEAM OF ARCHAEOLOGISTS DISCOVERED PORTIONS OF TWO BIBLICAL PARCHMENT SCROLLS. THEY ARE PORTIONS OF THE BOOKS OF DEUTERONOMY AND EZEKIEL

What they were *not* looking for in Palestine and Syria were relics of Stone Age Man. And yet, at the same period, in France, Britain, and other countries of Western Europe, scholars were assiduously searching in the gravels of Norfolk and in the cave-shelters of the Dordogne Valley for Paleolithic (Old Stone Age) relics such as flint axes, awls, scrapers, and spearheads dating from a period immensely more remote than that of the Bible, or even of Zoser's Step Pyramid. They even classified such implements. Those made by chipping pieces of flint were Paleolithic or Old Stone Age; those bearing a polished surface and evidencing a more sophisticated craftsmanship were called Neolithic (New Stone Age). But what these early investigators in Europe at first failed to recognize was that this change marked something much more revolutionary than a mere improvement in tools and weapons; it often marked a complete change in a way of life, from the nomadic hunter, perpetually wandering in search of wild game, to the settled pastoralist and agriculturalist.

Those who went out to Jericho in 1868 and conducted deep and extensive excavations came away satisfied that the double walls they had found at a certain level were those which Joshua had successfully assaulted at a date which they conjectured was around 1400 B.C. (much too early, as it subsequently turned out). But digging much deeper into the great mound or "tell" on which ancient Jericho stood, they came upon stone implements produced by men who had lived there many thousands of years before Joshua was born. Some of these implements John Garstang identified as Mesolithic, an intermediate period between the Paleolithic and Neolithic phases. It was all very puzzling.

Clarification came when later excavators, particularly Kathleen Kenyon and her Anglo-American team, reexamined Jericho at a time when dating could be much more precise. Similar finds were made at other sites; some were "tells" marking the sites of cities known in later Biblical times. Others were unnamed and unknown. Childe, who was primarily a European archaeologist interested in the origins of European civilization, was drawn irresistibly to the lands of the eastern Mediterranean as his curious, questing mind sought for beginnings. Eventually he reached the conclusion that his Neolithic Revolution, when men first learned to be farmers, had its origin in the so-called Fertile Crescent which runs from the Nile Valley in the west to the Tigris-Euphrates valleys in the east by way of the Palestinian coastal strip and the fertile land which stretched from the mountains of Asia Minor to the fringes of the Arabian desert.

Among the archaeologists who have done some of the most important work on this remote period is Miss Kenyon, and the site to which she gave the closest attention was Jericho. It is represented by a mound of about ten acres in extent, is about seventy feet high, and owes its existence to a perennial spring which wells out of the ground nearby and is

THIS IS A VIEW OF THE JERICHO TELL FROM THE NORTH

REMAINS OF A PLATTER OF JOINTS OF MUT-
TON WITH A SHEEP'S HEAD

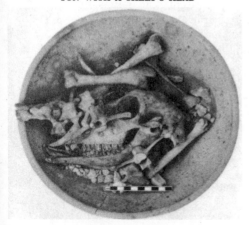

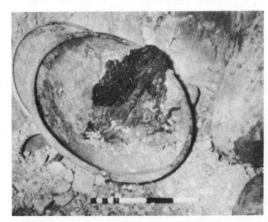

THIS SLAB OF MEAT IS ONE OF THE
OLDEST SURVIVING PIECES OF FOOD

REED AND RUSH MAT FLOOR-COVERINGS FROM NEOLITHIC HOUSES IN THE JERICHO TELL

PLASTERED NEOLITHIC POR-
TRAIT-SKULL AFTER CONSER-
VATION WORK

Kathleen Kenyon and her team of archaeologists have been excavating Jericho for several years. They have learned about cultures which lived on that site in pre-Biblical and pre-Iron Age times. The portrait-skull (left) was made long before Egyptians practised mummification, but it was made with the same idea of preserving the dead man's identity. The archaeologists know what the people ate and what sorts of houses they lived in. Knowing these things we can now calculate their local crops and their involvement in animal husbandry. Study of stratification has yielded a history of invasions and reconstruction periods on the site.

SQUARE-SHAFT TYPE TOMB OF THE INTERMEDIATE
EARLY BRONZE-MIDDLE BRONZE PERIOD, CONTAIN-
ING A SKELETON, JAVELIN, DAGGER, AND POTS

probably fed from some underground river. From her investigations Miss Kenyon has now proved that Jericho has been occupied for at least eight thousand years and is probably the oldest inhabited city on earth. By comparison, the great cities of Egypt did not come into existence until after about 2800 B.C. But there is an important difference. By 3200 B.C. Egypt was a united kingdom under one ruler, whereas Jericho, and other Levantine cities like it, were isolated settlements. We can say, therefore, that whereas the groundwork of civilization—the establishment of small settled communities dependent on agriculture and stock-rearing rather than hunting—began in the middle part of the Fertile Crescent somewhere between 10000 and 5000 B.C., true civilization developed at the tips of the Crescent, along the Nile Valley and the Tigris-Euphrates valleys. The reason was that only these great river valleys could support a large population of agriculturalists, the rivers providing a swift and easy means of communication throughout the entire land. The same development occurred somewhat later along the Indus Valley and its tributaries in India. These civilized communities were produced at a time when man, having at last freed himself from the necessity of following wild game, and having cultivated cereals from wild grasses and domesticated some of the animals he formerly used to hunt, could build permanent houses, found cities, and cultivate the land and also his mind.

Some of these men, able now to live off the labor of others, had leisure to think and invent. Man's artistic instincts, no longer confined to incising patterns on bones and painting ritualistic scenes on cave walls, were free to create temples and palaces of well-hewn stone, particularly when the discovery of metals enabled him to fashion fine cutting tools of bronze, an alloy of tin and copper. Thus another group of specialists came into being, the workers in metal who jealously guarded their craft. Stone tools, however, continued to be used for long periods, as metal was rare and expensive until the coming of iron. It also meant that relatively small numbers of warrior-aristocrats, who alone could afford bronze weapons, could dominate large subject populations.

Herodotus was familiar with the great and ancient civilizations of Egypt and Mesopotamia, but he had no idea how they came into being. Only archaeology, which can penetrate far beyond the "historical horizon" represented by written records, can tell us that. Moving now to Mesopotamia, we find in Herodotus a magnificent description of Babylon as it existed in his day.

> The city stands on a broad plain, and is an exact square, a hundred and twenty furlongs in length each way, so that the entire circuit is four hundred and eighty furlongs. While such is its size, in magnificence there is no other city that approaches to it. It is surrounded, in the first place, by a broad and deep moat, full of water, behind which rises a wall fifty royal cubits in width, and two hundred in

height. . . . On the top, along the edges of the wall, they constructed
buildings of a single chamber facing one another, leaving between
them room for a four-horse chariot to turn. In the circuit of the wall
are a hundred gates, all of brass, with brazen lintels and side-posts.
. . . The houses are mostly three and four stories high; the streets all
run in straight lines, . . .[5]

Herodotus, who visited Babylon when it was under Persian rule, also
described "the sacred precinct of Jupiter Belus" with its "tower of solid
masonry, a furlong in length and breadth," built in eight stages with a
path leading round the tower to a spacious temple at the top, the "Tower
of Babel" of the Old Testament. He also mentioned the palace of the
Babylonian kings which was described in greater detail by Diodorus
Siculus (*c.* 40 B.C.), who wrote of the "hanging gardens" of Queen Semir-
amis. Once it became practicable for Western travelers to travel to the
Middle East—which had been virtually barred to Europeans since the
end of the Crusades—a few venturesome spirits made the journey. They
had been stirred by the accounts of Herodotus and other pagan writers,
and equally by the fact that they were exploring the "lands of the Bible."
If the ruins of Babylon still existed, then why not Nineveh, Nimrud, and
Ur of the Chaldees?

But so far the main impetus driving men toward archaeological exploration was literary, when it was not mere lust for plunder. When the
pioneer Claudius Rich arrived at Babylon in 1811, accompanied by his
young wife, he wrote:

> I thought that I should have distinguished some traces, however
> imperfect, of the many principal structures. . . . I imagined I should
> have said "here were the walls and such must have been the extent
> of the area. There stood the palace, and this most assuredly was the
> tower of Belus." I was completely deceived; instead of a few isolated
> mounds I found the whole country covered with vestiges of
> buildings.

But instead of sentimentalizing over the ruins, Rich measured and drew
what he could of them and published his findings for the benefit of future archaeologists. His *Memoirs on the Ruins of Babylon*, originally
published in Vienna, is illustrated by careful drawings, maps, and plans.
Throughout the first half of the nineteenth century Mesopotamia drew
increasing numbers of investigators, though not all were as scrupulous
as Rich.

Some modern archaeologists deplore the activities of these pioneers,
and wish that the sites could have been left undisturbed until today,
when modern techniques would have extracted more information from

---

5 *Ibid.* I. 178–80; p. 40b–d.

A VIEW OF THE EXCAVATED ISHTAR GATE, LOOKING SOUTH FROM PROCESSION STREET. ALTHOUGH THE SCALE IS GREATER, THE BRICKWORK IS SIMILAR TO THAT USED TODAY

THIS LION WAS RECONSTRUCTED BY GERMAN ARCHAE-OLOGISTS FROM REMAINS FOUND ON THE ISHTAR GATE. IT AND THE FIGURE BELOW WERE MADE OF GLAZED CERAMIC TILE. WHILE THE LION SHOWS CAREFUL ANATOMICAL OBSERVATION, THE MYTHO-LOGICAL FIGURE UNITES CHARACTERISTICS OF BIRD, REPTILE, AND MAMMAL

DURING UR'S FOURTH MILLENNIUM, MEN WORSHIPPED THIS SNAKE-HEADED MOTHER AND CHILD

THIS STELE BEARS THE CODE OF HAM-
MURABI AND A BAS-RELIEF OF THE
KING BEFORE THE SUN GOD SHAMASH

THIS BRONZE HEAD OF THE
MESOPOTAMIAN KING SARGON
IS OVER 4000 YEARS OLD

THESE ANATOLIAN BRONZE BULL STAT-
UETTES WERE MOUNTED ON STAKES
TO SERVE AS GRAVE ORNAMENTS

"PEACE" SIDE OF MOSAIC STANDARD FROM UR
SHOWING GIFT-BEARERS AT BANQUET. OBVERSE
SIDE SHOWS A BATTLE

them. However, leaving known sites untouched would not necessarily have preserved them, as can be shown from several examples. One is the work of Sir Henry Layard at Nineveh. In the 1840's he excavated and removed to England the superb sculptured Assyrian winged lions and bas-reliefs which once adorned the palace of Sennacherib—works of art which, had they been discovered by the Arabs, would undoubtedly have been destroyed, since to the fanatical Muslims of that period any "graven image" was an abomination. Nowadays, under the enlightened administration of the government of Iraq, they would have been safe; but not in 1849. Similar statues and reliefs, excavated by the Frenchman Émile Botta, are preserved in the Louvre and some enrich American museums. To Layard the lure of Nineveh lay not only in thè splendid sculpture which he discovered but in the fact that he was seeing, for the first time, representations of the dreaded Assyrians in the "bloody city" which Nahum had execrated.

> Thy shepherds slumber, O king of Assyria; thy nobles shall dwell in the dust; thy people is scattered upon the mountains and no man gathereth them. (3:18)

This was another example of "Biblical archaeology," the same impetus which had led Garstang to investigate Jericho, and many other explorers to dig in the Middle East in the nineteenth century. But just as in Egypt and the Levant, what had begun with the investigation of sites known from literary sources developed, during the twentieth century, into a probing deep beyond the "historical horizon" to the discovery of a civilization far older than Assyria or Babylon. This was Sumeria, the Biblical "Land of Shinar" lying along the lower Euphrates. The account of its discovery reads like a good detective story.

By 1849, when Layard unearthed the palace of Sennacherib at Nineveh, Sir Henry Rawlinson and other scholars had begun to decipher the so-called Babylonian cuneiform writing which was found inscribed on baked-clay tablets at several sites. When Layard discovered part of the royal Assyrian library consisting of over twenty-six thousand tablets, a new stimulus was given to the task of decipherment. Before very long this writing system, which had been the *lingua franca* of Western Asia for more than two thousand years, yielded up its secrets. The effect upon Mesopotamian archaeology—and later that of Asia Minor—was immense. The Assyrian inscriptions found at Nineveh and dating from the eighth century B.C. could now be read in association with the scenes depicted, and many Biblical correlations were found, e.g., the siege of Lachish mentioned in the Second Book of Kings was actually depicted in one of the reliefs found in Sennacherib's palace.

But this was only a beginning. Soon it was realized that much of the Assyrian library consisted of copies of much earlier documents that originated in Sumeria, in lower Mesopotamia, and fresh expeditions went forth to explore this land, and this time, thanks to the decipherment of the cuneiform system, what had been mere mounds of crumbling mud-brick could be identified as named cities. Such names as Erech, Akkad, Calneh, and Ur of the Chaldees stepped out of the Book of Genesis and became real. A number of American expeditions share the honor of these discoveries, especially at Nippur, where an enormous cache of tablets was found, first by H. V. Hilprecht and later by successive American scholars. Eventually it was realized that long before the rise of Babylon and Assyria there had existed in the lower parts of the Tigris and Euphrates valleys a powerful and advanced civilization which was in being before 3000 B.C., more than twenty-five hundred years before Nebuchadnezzar reigned from Babylon. This Sumerian civilization could rival Egypt in antiquity, and the art of writing began there at about the same time that the hieroglyphic system was invented in Egypt; in fact, it is now generally accepted that the Egyptian system owed something to the Sumerian. One of the fascinating problems exercising the minds of modern Egyptologists is the extent to which Egyptian civilization owed its origin to immigrants from lower Mesopotamia.

There are some remarkable resemblances between the two cultures, e.g., in the "paneled-facade" type of architecture which is found in both early Egypt and Sumeria, and the resemblance between certain hieroglyphic signs and those used by the early Sumerian scribes. Emery, whose investigation of the First and Second Dynasty mastaba-tombs of Egypt has already been touched on, firmly believes that the foundation of Egyptian civilization about 3200 B.C. owes its origin to the invasion of a "master race" which brought with them some of the crafts and skills developed by the Sumerians; he does not, however, necessarily imply that these invaders came from Sumeria; they might have come from some intermediate place which has yet to be discovered, perhaps bordering the Arabian coast of the Red Sea or the Gulf of Aden. This, of course, remains a theory, and not all scholars support Emery. The generally accepted view is that, although there may have been foreign influences at work, there was no mass invasion, but that the ancient Egyptians created their own unique civilization. Emery's intriguing theory is well set out in his book *Archaic Egypt* (1962).

One of the most remarkable discoveries made in Sumeria was at Ur of the Chaldees, Abraham's birthplace. In the twenties Sir Leonard Woolley came upon rich tombs of important personages, possibly kings and queens, who had been buried accompanied by a holocaust of human victims. Thanks to improvements in technique, this excavation was carried out with the scrupulous care which characterized all Woolley's work, and he showed great ingenuity in preserving the fragile objects, such as a gold-plated harp carried by one of the immolated attendants. The instrument had almost perished save for its golden ornaments and inlays of semiprecious stones. But its imprint remained in the earth so that Sir Leonard and his staff were able to reconstruct it on a new wooden frame. A generation earlier archaeologists would have been unable to preserve it.

The Ur tombs dated from between 2700 and 2500 B.C., but within the broadening prospect of Mesopotamian archaeology this date is comparatively recent. For by this time, the twenties and thirties, archaeologists had begun to recognize a pattern of emergent civilization over the whole of the Fertile Crescent. Like Petrie in Egypt, they were more and more concerned with tracing the origin of these early cultures. The mounds or "tells" of Mesopotamia, signifying human occupation over vast periods of time, were no longer puzzling, unidentifiable heaps of mud-brick as they had appeared to Rich. The new generation of investigators—the French at Kish, the Americans at Nippur and elsewhere, the Germans at Warka, the British at Ur—knew how to recognize and record each successive occupation-layer down to the virgin soil.

Various cultures were discovered and named after the type-site where characteristic pottery had first been found; the *Al Ubaid*, the *Jamdat Nasr*, the *Uruk* cultures are three examples. To take but one sample, Woolley excavated at Al Ubaid near Ur a mound at the base of which he found evidence of the very first settlement: remains of the simple reed huts on one of the fertile islands which were emerging, some six thousand or more years ago, as the delta began to dry up. For during the past six millennia the silting up of the mouths of the rivers has caused the Persian Gulf to recede, leaving dry land behind.

Many similar sites have been found since, extending from Iraq through the Levant up as far as Asia Minor. Some of these settlements had been occupied for brief periods and then deserted. Some had been occupied, abandoned, and then reoccupied. Others, like Jericho, had developed over many centuries into large towns with substantial fortifications, streets, temples, and houses. But deep down, at the base of the mounds on which they stood, lay the simple stone tools of the first Neolithic settlers. A number of the Biblical cities besides Jericho had owed their origins to such primitive settlements six or seven thousand years ago.

Sumerian literature, as revealed in the tablets, ranged from historical chronicles to law codes, "wisdom literature" (like the Proverbs), and personal letters. One amusing example of the wisdom literature reads:

> You can have a King, and you can have a Lord
> But the man to fear is the tax-collector. . . .

And here are a few others picked at random from many:

> Friendship lasts a day
> Kinship endures for ever.

452

And:

> Who has not supported a wife or child,
> His nose has not borne a leash. . . .

There is also strong evidence, from certain Sumerian poems, that the story of the Deluge originated in Sumeria. One poem, which probably dates from before 2700 B.C., bears such a strong resemblance to that of Noah's Ark as to make it tolerably certain that the Genesis version derives ultimately from Sumeria, where disastrous floods were a frequent occurrence.

> I watched the appearance of the weather. . . .
> Consternation over Adad reaches the heavens,
> Turning to blackness all that had been light.
> The wide land was shattered like (a pot)!
> For one day the south storm (blew)
> Gathering speed as it blew . . .
> Overtaking the people like a battle.
> No-one can see his fellow,
> Nor can people be recognised from heaven . . .
> Six days and six nights
> Blows the flood wind, as the south storm sweeps the land.
> When the seventh day arrived. . . .
> The sea grew quiet, the tempest was still, the flood ceased.
> I looked at the weather; stillness had set in . . .
> And all of mankind had returned to clay.
> The landscape was as level as a flat roof. . . .

The author of the poem, who has taken refuge in a ship, accompanied by "the seed of all living things," opens a hatch. Light falls on his face.

> Bowing low, I sat down and wept,
> Tears running down my face. . . .
> On Mount Nisir the ship came to a halt,
> Allowing no motion. . . .
> I sent forth and set free a dove.
> The dove went forth, but came back;
> There was no resting-place for it and she turned round. . . .
> Then I set forth and set free a raven.
> The raven went forth, and, seeing that the waters had diminished,
> He eats, circles, caws, and turns not round.
> Then I let our (all) to the four winds
> And offered a sacrifice. . . .[6]

It is customary to write of the "Flood-myth," but there was nothing mythical about the Sumerian floods. Digging under the deeper levels at Ur of the Chaldees, Woolley revealed thick layers of sediment containing no trace of human occupation, though the levels above and below

---

6 S. N. Kramer, History Begins at Sumer (New York, Doubleday, 1959).

THE CUNEIFORM TABLET ON THE LEFT IS FROM UR. IT DEALS WITH THE DISPOSAL
OF DEAD CATTLE TURNED IN BY SHEPHERDS 4000 YEARS AGO. THE TABLET ON THE
RIGHT BEARS THE LAW CODE OF ESHNUNNA

did contain such evidence. It is said to have been Lady Woolley who, coming upon her husband and a group of puzzled archaeologists contemplating one of these blank layers, casually remarked "But of course; that was the Flood," and walked away.

In fact, we now know that ancient Sumeria was devastated by several great floods at various times, as is shown by layers of clean sediment at different levels. One of these catastrophic deluges must have formed the basis of the story in Genesis, incorporated by the Hebrews in their own literature. Certainly such an event is far more likely to have taken place in low-lying Sumeria, on the banks of a great flooding river, than in mountainous Palestine. It has been suggested that the story had been learned by the Hebrews during their captivity in Babylon, but it could equally well have been a folk-tradition absorbed by the Israelites during the long years of wandering, long before they settled in Palestine.

The rich and abundant store of baked-clay tablets excavated by the American archaeologists at Nippur, Shurrupak, and elsewhere has by no means been exhausted, and thousands of tablets still await interpretation. Samuel Kramer may well be right when he entitles one of his books *History Begins at Sumer.* For though the Assyrians and the Babylonians of later times utilized the language which the Sumerians invented, and carefully preserved Sumerian literary texts, there is no doubt the earliest written records of man's achievements in civilization originated in Lower Mesopotamia, and were closely followed by those of the Nile Valley.

THE HITTITES

The cuneiform writing system was used throughout Western Asia, especially for diplomatic correspondence between rulers, and has therefore thrown light on the history of other countries far remote from Sumeria. One of these was the Hittite empire, the capital of which was Hattusas, on the high central tableland of Anatolia, where the German archaeologist Hugo Winckler discovered thousands of tablets, some written in Babylonian cuneiform and others in a script which was at first called Arwazan, from the name Arwaza which occurred in it, the only word which could at first be deciphered. But German scholarship eventually interpreted the language, which turned out to be that of the Hittites. Arwaza was merely one of their provinces.

The Hebrews knew the Hittites; one has only to recall Uriah the Hittite, whose wife Bathsheba King David coveted, and the "Sons of Heth" who sold Abraham a burial place at Machpelah near Hebron. The puzzling fact, however, was that there were also references in Egyptian inscriptions and letters to a people called the "Kheta" and the "Land of Khatti," formidable foes of Egypt at the height of her power, which was between 1500 and 1250 B.C., more than two centuries before the Hittites of King David's time, who appeared to be only a minor tribe occupying part of Syria. Were the "Kheta" and the Hittites the same people? And if so, what had been their homeland, since so powerful a race as to have challenged Egypt must have had territory and a capital city? Apart from the Bible and the Egyptian inscriptions (if indeed these did refer to the Hittites) and certain Assyrian texts, there are no literary allusions to them; by Greco-Roman times they had been entirely forgotten. Here again archaeology came to the rescue.

Long before Winckler found the tablets at Bogazköy, certain stones inscribed in an unknown form of writing had been noted at Hamath and Aleppo, two places in Syria. Again, in Asia Minor explorers had described huge sculptured reliefs depicting men, and apparently gods and goddesses, carved in rocky clefts on the mountainsides, and these were usually accompanied by inscriptions in the same unknown writing system. Up to 1897 no tablets had been found, apart from a letter from the Hittite king Suppiluliumas (Suppililiumas) found in the Foreign Office files of the Pharaoh Akhenaten in Egypt, congratulating that king on his accession, which was in 1370 B.C. A British scholar, Archibald Sayce, put forward the bold theory that these inscriptions were in the Hittite language, and that their homeland had been in Anatolia.

Attention was focused on one particular site, Bogazköy, where on a high buttress of rock between two fast-flowing rivers stood the substantial remains of an ancient city girdled by walls fourteen feet thick and pierced at intervals by mighty gates guarded by sculptured figures of

IN 1925 B.C., BILALAMA RULED ESHNUNNA AND DIRECTED THE BUILDING OF HIS
TOMB. HE SPECIFIED THAT EVERY BRICK IN THE STRUCTURE SHOULD BEAR A HIERO-
GLYPHIC LEGEND IDENTIFYING HIM AND THE PURPOSE OF THE BRICK, SO THAT
SHOULD THE BRICKS BE REUSED HIS IDENTITY WOULD NOT BE LOST

lions and men. No one knew how old it was or who had built it, but
from the style of the art it certainly was not medieval. When, in 1906,
Winckler and his staff unearthed ten thousand baked-clay tablets from
the foundations of a building within the walls that was apparently either
a temple or palace-temple, the mystery was solved. Some of the tablets
were in "Arwazan" which could not, at that time, be read, but others
were in the familiar Babylonian cuneiform script deciphered by Rawlinson, the same type of writing found in the royal library at Nineveh.
These tablets proved beyond any doubt that this was Hattusas, the capital of the Hittite empire, and from correspondence with Egypt found in
these documents it was now positive that the "Kheta" were the Hittites.
Among the documents were letters from an Egyptian queen, the widow of
Tutankhamen (Tutankhamun), and a copy of the treaty of nonaggression
between the Pharaoh Ramses II and the Hittite monarch Muwatallis,
almost word for word as it appears at Karnak in Egypt.

The documents were fascinating. Among them were chronicles describing how the early Hittite kings conquered Asia Minor and then
began to push southward into Syria and beyond. One chronicle refers
to a King Labarnas who lived about 1600 B.C. of whom it was written:

> Formerly Labarnas was king; and then his sons, his brothers, his
> connexions by marriage and his blood-relations were united. And the
> land was small; but wherever he marched to battle, he subdued the
> lands of his enemies with his might. He destroyed the lands and
> made them powerless, and he made the seas his frontiers. And when
> he returned from battle, his sons went each to every part of the
> land. . . . and the great cities of the land were assigned to them.

456

Another chronicle tells of a family quarrel in which the ailing King Labarnas, who had appointed his nephew as his successor, disowns him, much to the anger of the young man's mother. The king's nephew was also named Labarnas.

> Behold I have fallen sick. The young Labarnas I had proclaimed to you (saying) "he shall sit upon the throne"; I, the king, called him my son, embraced him, exalted him, and cared for him continually. But he showed himself a youth not fit to be seen; he shed no tears, he showed no pity, he was cold and heartless. I, the king, summoned him to my couch (and said) "Well, no one will (in future) bring up the child of his sister as his foster-son. The word of the king he has not laid to heart, but the word of his mother, that serpent, he has laid to heart. . . . Enough! He is my son no more." Then his mother bellowed like an ox: "They have torn asunder the womb in my living body! They have ruined him, and you will kill him!" But have I, the king, done him any evil? Behold I have given my son Labarnas a house; I have given him [arable land] in plenty [sheep in] plenty I have given him. Let him now eat and drink. [So long as he is good] he may come up to the city; but if he come forward(?) [as a trouble-maker], . . . then he shall not come up, but shall remain [in his house].[7]

The clash with Egypt came when, in the thirteenth century B.C., Muwatallis, with his allied armies drawn from many countries, threatened Egypt's empire in Syria-Palestine. The two armies met at Kadesh on the Orontes River, in a battle which Ramses II commemorated vaingloriously on his temple walls at Medinet Habu and at Abu Simbel, depicting himself as the hero of an Egyptian victory. In fact, it was an indecisive struggle in which neither side gained a permanent advantage. Afterwards both kings agreed to respect one another's territorial rights and the treaty was the result.

Until comparatively recent times, the other form of writing, the so-called Hittite hieroglyphs carved on the Hamath and Aleppo stelae and on the rocks of Anatolia, defied decipherment. This was because until 1947 no bilingual inscription had been found. But in that year a most remarkable discovery was made at a place called Karatepe—a true "lost city" set in remote and beautiful surroundings in what the ancients called Cilicia, about fifty miles north of the "corner" at which the southern coast of Turkey, running east to west, joins the north to south line of the Syrian coast. Here stood a wooded hill called by the local inhabitants "The Black Mound," and so thinly populated is the country that probably no one save an occasional charcoal-burner ever visited it. As Seton Lloyd writes in his book *Early Anatolia* (1956):

---

7 O. R. Gurney, *The Hittites* (Baltimore, Penguin Books, 1952).

Few, in fact could have suspected that, in times almost beyond the horizon of historical memory, a king had chosen it as his place of residence, and that, beneath the brambles and scrub-oak, the symbols of his authority still lay buried among the ruins of his castle. Yet such was indeed the case. . . . here, before the excavators' eyes, were carefully worded sentences which he had composed himself in two languages and crudely drawn images of a world in which he lived. Among these tumbled galleries of small stone pictures, his people were also to be seen, a graceless folk with sloping foreheads and receding chins, such as are known to have inhabited large areas of Anatolia at this time [about 800 B.C., a thousand years after the historical Hittites had established themselves in Anatolia].[8]

Yet the ancient hieroglyphic script had survived down to that time; on each side of the gate chambers was an identical inscription, one in Hittite hieroglyphs and the other in Phoenician, a known language. Although grammarians had already mastered the basic structure of this language, they could now grasp the meaning of individual words. As a result of this discovery, the Hittite hieroglyphic inscriptions in Asia Minor, and scattered throughout the museums of the world, are beginning to speak. It appears that whereas the Hittites used the well-known and familiar cuneiform for their official correspondence and records, they needed a more monumental script for their public monuments, as did the ancient Egyptians. Most of these inscriptions are short, and refer to kings and queens, gods and goddesses. The basis of the language is Hittite cuneiform, with two hundred signs, of which fifty-six are phonetic and the rest are ideograms; the syllables begin with a consonant and end with a vowel, but whereas the value of the consonants is fixed, the vowel-sounds are variable. This adds to the difficulties of the philologists, but at least there *are* vowel-sounds, none of which exist in the ancient Egyptian script. Certain syntactical devices also occur, for the proper rendering of the grammatical structure of a sentence.

It would appear that after the seventh century B.C. the Hittite hieroglyphic system passed out of use. In any case, the inhabitants of Karatepe were not true Hittites in the older sense, though they had inherited the language and script. According to the inscriptions, they called themselves the Danuna, who could possibly be the Dananians, a tribe listed by Ramses III as a member of the alliance of "Sea Peoples" who invaded his kingdom in the twelfth century B.C. They may also possibly be identified with Homer's "Danaoi," though this is by no means a certain identification.

One cannot leave Turkey without a brief mention of Çatal Hüyük, which has more archaeological implications than any Hittite site. The

---

8 Seton Lloyd, *Early Anatolia* (Baltimore, Penguin Books, 1956).

Hittites belonged in the main to a Bronze Age culture which goes back no earlier than 1800 B.C., or at the earliest 2000 B.C. Çatal Hüyük, discovered in 1961, excavations having continued for five years, is practically unique; a large palace with shrines adorned with vividly painted frescoes, and of elaborate construction, dating from before 6000 B.C. Discovered by James Mellaart, it is a true city, built of walls of unhewn stone (bronze cutting tools not having been invented), and the walls are adorned with lively painted frescoes, depicting, among other scenes, hunting pictures in a lively style, with figures of animals, notably red bulls, pursued with arrows by conventionally drawn huntsmen. These drawings belong to a period before men had begun to grow food crops in abundance, and are reminiscent of the cave-paintings at Lascaux in France and Altamira in Spain. In some of the paintings the male figures, mostly bearded and wearing loincloths and leopard skin, appear to be teasing the animals (as in the Minoan bull-sport) rather than hunting them in earnest. They are depicted, says Mellaart, "with a lively sense of fun and character."

Çatal Hüyük is one of the most significant sites in the world, if only because it proves that even in Neolithic times, long before the discovery of metals, three or more thousand years before the first cities were founded in Egypt and Mesopotamia, some Stone Age men lived a civic existence and built elaborate temples and palaces. Not all lived by scratching a mere existence with stone tools and in reed huts beside some oasis or river. One looks forward to more news from Çatal Hüyük and perhaps the discovery of other Neolithic settlements of comparable sophistication.

The ancestry of urban life may go back much further in time than we have been led to think. Çatal Hüyük also illustrates the early development of religion. It is certainly not the earliest manifestation, since the impulse goes far back in time, even to the primitive cave dwellers of twenty thousand years ago who painted magical scenes of hunting rites on their walls (e.g., at Altamira and Lascaux), but at Çatal Hüyük Mellaart found what must be the oldest *built* temple so far discovered. In one chamber were remains which enable us to reconstruct a ritual in which a robed priestess reverently places a human skull, in a basket, in front of a huge figure of a bull's head, painted and incorporating horns projecting from a plastered wall.[9]

"The funerary buildings and fittings," writes Mellaart in his comment on the site, "are all accounted for in the excavation. Rarely has so little been left to the imagination in an archaeological reconstruction of such a remote period."

---

9 *See* illustration by Alan Scott, *Illustrated London News*, May 9, 1964, pp. 728–29.

The cult of the bull occurs in Crete some three to four thousand years later, and one wonders if it was transported there by invaders or immigrants from Asia Minor, which is the natural land-bridge between Asia and Europe. But before we consider Crete and all it implies as the site of the oldest civilization in Europe, it may be as well to consider the steps which led to this discovery which is continuing to astonish us by fresh revelations.

Throughout the nineteenth century in Europe curiosity about the remote past was increasing. On the one hand, there were the discoveries of Paleolithic (Old Stone Age) man, in France, Spain, and elsewhere— remains going back twenty thousand years and more. On the other hand, the civilized history of the continent seemed to be tied irrevocably to literary evidence. Apart from uncovering Etruscan remains in Italy, archaeologists were content to examine sites and cities associated with the writings of Plutarch, Tacitus, Suetonius, Pausanias, Pliny, and other Greek or Roman observers. Archaeology was still the handmaid of literary history, and in Egypt and the Middle East the decipherment of the Egyptian and Babylonian writing systems, while it helped to interpret the physical remains, only reinforced the archaeologists' dependence on written records. In a sense the triumphs of Champollion, Georg Grotefend, Rawlinson, and others in the field of linguistics arrested the development of pure archaeology, which relies for its evidence solely on physical remains without any literary context.

In Greece, for instance, where the surviving monuments of the "classical" period were often inscribed, and could be accurately related to written history, no one seriously considered that Greek history extended any further back than the date of the first recorded Olympic Games, in the eighth century B.C. Before that time, the stories recorded in the works of Homer, Aeschylus, Euripides, Sophocles, etc., of the "Seven against Thebes," of Agamemnon and Clytemnestra, Menelaus and Helen, Orestes, Iphigenia, Oedipus, and the rest, were regarded as purely mythical. Even the Trojan War, despite its careful description by Homer, was placed in the same category.

In 1846 the historian George Grote could express this opinion, which was generally accepted at the time:

> I begin the real history of Greece with the first recorded Olympiad, or 776 B.C. . . . For the truth is that historical records properly so-called do not begin until after that date. Nor will any man, who candidly considers the extreme paucity of attested facts for two centuries after 776 B.C., be astonished to learn that the state of Greece in 900, 1,000, 1,100, 1,200, 1,300, 1,400 B.C. etc., . . . cannot be described to him with anything like decent evidence . . .

THE GOLDEN "CUP OF NESTOR"

THE GOLD FUNERARY MASK, FROM
THE MYCENAEAN GRAVE SHAFTS,
WHICH IS NAMED FOR AGAMEMNON

THE BRONZE STATUE OF POSEIDON

N estor's cup and Agamemnon's mask were found in the royal graves of Mycenae by Schliemann and those who followed him. They have since been dated approximately 1500 B.C., or nearly 800 years before George Grote's "beginning of recorded time."

The times which I thus set apart from the region of history are discernible only through a different atmosphere—that of poetry and legend. To confound together these disparate matters is, in my judgement, essentially unphilosophical.

That well-known passage was published more than twenty years after the partial decipherment of the Egyptian hieroglyphs had reopened the scroll of ancient Egyptian history, and more than twenty years after Rawlinson, Grotefend, and others had begun to rediscover the world of Assyria, Babylon, and Sumeria. In Egypt and Western Asia, a prospect had opened which extended back to the second millennium B.C., and future researches would carry the story back for another thousand years at least. Yet to Grote it seemed inconceivable that Greece—the birthplace of western civilization—could have had a history of comparable antiquity.

It is paradoxical that the man whose researches eventually demolished Grote's belief and opened a new and unfinished chapter in Greek archae-

461

ology was himself a literalist, in that he believed in the literal truth of Homer's poems. Heinrich Schliemann, born in 1822, was a self-made businessman with little formal education, who did not become an excavator until late in life. Although professional scholars tended to scoff at him, Schliemann—unimpressed by or unaware of what Grote had written—was naive enough to take the Greek myths literally. Homer had written about "windy Troy," of Argos "home of lovely women," and Mycenae "rich in gold." The Greeks of classical times had believed in the truth of these stories, but the classical scholars of the early nineteenth century regarded them, as Grote did, as fairy tales. Yet when Schliemann and his young Greek wife dug the site of Troy, he found the remains of seven superimposed cities, one of which he decided was Priam's Troy. And when, near the lowest level of the mound, he discovered treasure of gold, silver, and bronze, he pronounced this to be that of King Priam, leader of the Trojans against the Greeks. Some of the golden diadems, Schliemann suggested, could have belonged to Helen.

Moving to Greece, he dug at Mycenae, just within the Lion Gate where the Greek travel writer Pausanias, in the second century A.D., claimed to have seen the tombs of Agamemnon and his followers. He unearthed seven shaft graves, containing bodies of men and women bedecked with gold and surrounded by rich funerary equipment. Unlike Petrie, Schliemann was a treasure-seeker, and he relied implicitly on written tradition. He was not a scientific, careful excavator and destroyed much archaeological evidence in his efforts to find valuable objects. Nonetheless, he shook the skepticism of classical scholars because some of the things he discovered, such as the "boar's tusk helmet," the "cup of Nestor" with figures of feeding doves, and representations of the great body-shields carried by some of the Homeric heroes, were very much as the poet had described them. Schliemann was confident that he had unearthed the tombs of Agamemnon, Clytemnestra, and their followers. Later, at Tiryns, he excavated another palace associated with Heracles in Greek myth. And though his assistant, Wilhelm Dörpfeld, a younger man, induced him to use more accurate, painstaking methods, relying as Petrie did on the study and recording of commonplace objects, the mighty lines of Homer still sang in his brain, and he remained more or less convinced to the end of his life that the remains he had unearthed must belong to the period of the Trojan War, which was usually reckoned at about 1190 B.C. In this he was supported by a number of classicists including Gladstone, the British prime minister. In fact, Gladstone wrote a preface to Schliemann's book *Ilios* (1881).

The close of the nineteenth century and the beginning of the twentieth were distinguished by what many consider the greatest single discovery made in Europe. It was also the most romantic, since, like Schliemann's excavations at Troy and Mycenae, it proved that there was a kernel of truth in the stories which classical historians such as Grote had dismissed as mere legends. This was the discovery by Arthur (later Sir Arthur) Evans of remains of a high civilization which had flourished on the island of Crete, a civilization the roots of which went down to below 3000 B.C. and which, between about 2500 and 1400 B.C., was equal to those of ancient Egypt and Mesopotamia; in some ways it was superior. Moreover, like those civilizations, it was literate.

In fact, it was Evans' belief that the civilization Schliemann had first discovered on the Greek mainland and had called "Mycenaean" (after the type-site where these artifacts were first found) must have had a writing system, that led him to Crete. By the end of the nineteenth century, many more Mycenaean sites had been unearthed in Greece, and their characteristic pottery and other manufactured products had been discovered over a wide area, including Egypt, Western Asia, and the Greek islands. Some historians preferred to call this the "Aegean" civilization.

Evans resembled Schliemann only in the fact that both were rich men, but whereas the German archaeologist was a businessman who turned to archaeology late in life, Evans was a scholar from a family of scholars. After Harrow and Oxford, he became for a time an effective war correspondent in the Balkans, where he sided vigorously with the insurgents, and later became curator of the Ashmolean Museum in Oxford, a post which gave him ample opportunities for travel and research.

He was a keen numismatist, with almost microscopic eyesight, although he was short-sighted. His ability to recognize the most minute details of coins, and his acute sense of artistic style, especially in objects of antiquity, were tremendous assets. He examined the objects which Schliemann had found at Troy and Mycenae but believed, on stylistic grounds alone, that these could be much older than the traditional date of the Trojan War. He was fascinated by Mycenaean art and argued that so highly developed a civilization, with well-organized and wide trading connections, could hardly have been without a writing system. The first evidence that led him to a firm conclusion was found on certain tiny "bead-seals" that he discovered on the tray of an antiquity-dealer in Athens.

Evans thought that he could detect, on these very small objects, tiny marks which might represent some form of writing. On learning that the seals came from Crete, he went there with his friend John Myres, and during their exploration of the remotest parts of this lovely mountainous island found many more examples. Though less of a romantic than Schliemann, Evans felt the powerful lure of Crete, home of Minos, scene of the Theseus-Ariadne legend—described, among others, by Plutarch—birthplace of Zeus, king of the Gods, and familiar to Homer, who had written:

463

A MAN ONCE MADE HIS MARK BY THE DESIGN HE PRESSED INTO WET CLAY

SEAL-STONE DESIGNERS PROGRESSED TO GEOMETRIC FORMS. THE SIDE VIEW OF THE STONE (LEFT) SHOWS THE HOLE BY WHICH THE STONE WAS HUNG ABOUT A MAN'S NECK

FROM GEOMETRIC SHAPES, THE BEAD-STONES PROGRESSED TO REPRESENTATIONS OF LIVING THINGS. THIS CYLINDER SEAL SHOWS AN ELEPHANT, A RHINOCEROS, AND A CROCODILE. THE PICTURE IS MADE BY ROLLING THE SEAL (LEFT) IN WET CLAY

MYTH BECAME INTEGRATED INTO THE ART OF THE SEALS. SUN GOD SHAMASH HOLDS THE SAW WHICH CUTS DECISIONS. BEFORE HIM A WORSHIPPER OFFERS A SACRIFICIAL KID. ISHTAR, IN THE GUISE OF WAR-GODDESS, STANDS WITH ONE FOOT ON A LION, HOLDING A MACE AND A SWORD

FINALLY, THE SEALS BORE THE WEARER'S NAME; IN THIS CASE HE WAS "LUGAL-LAM THE SCRIBE." THE HEROES GILGAMESH AND ENKIDU ARE SHOWN FIGHTING A BULL AND A LION

There is a fair and fruitful island in mid-ocean called Crete; it is thickly peopled and there are ninety cities in it: . . . There is a great town there, Cnossus, where Minos reigned who every nine years had a conference with Jove himself.[10]

And Thucydides had also written about King Minos:

. . . the first person known to us by tradition as having established a navy is Minos. He made himself master of what is now called the Hellenic sea, and ruled over the Cyclades, into most of which he sent the first colonies, expelling the Carians and appointing his own sons governors; and thus did his best to put down piracy in those waters, a necessary step to secure the revenues for his own use.[11]

The story of how Evans, with other archaeologists such as the Italian F. Halbherr, the Americans Harriet Boyd and Richard Seager, and the French at Mallia, revealed a great civilization even older than Mycenae is well-known. Here it is only necessary to recall the principal events in order to provide a background to the extraordinary advances in pre-Hellenic archaeology that have been made in recent years. Evans dug at Knossos, in a huge mound that had already attracted the attention of a local amateur (appropriately named Minos) who had unearthed a number of giant *pithoi*—pottery storage-jars. Within weeks Evans found what he had hoped to find, large numbers of clay tablets inscribed with an unknown writing system, part of the palace archives. He was not able to decipher these, though he recognized that they were lists, and that two languages were involved using the same basic characters. He called these "Linear A" and "Linear B."

But as he extended his excavations at Knossos, his discovery of Europe's oldest writing system became only one of a bewildering and exciting series of revelations. The mound proved to contain a palace of enormous size and complexity. Evans, who had the resources, the skill, and the patience needed for the task, set about excavating this building, using the stratigraphic method and keeping careful records. He made mistakes and was perhaps a little over-zealous in some of his restorations. But unlike Petrie, he wished not only to extract every available piece of information from the site but also to preserve and restore it as far as was possible, and this involved a monumental effort and great expense. He devoted thirty years of his life to the work and is believed to have spent about £250,000 of his personal fortune.

Rapidly following his lead, archaeologists of several nations—Italian, French, American, Greek—excavated other Cretan sites at Mallia, Phaistos, Azia, Triada, Gournia, and elsewhere. From their researches, and

---

10 *The Odyssey* XIX. 170; *GBWW*, Vol. 4, pp. 290d–291a.
11 *The Peloponnesian War* I. 4; *GBWW*, Vol. 6, p. 350a.

PART OF THE WEST MAGAZINES OF THE EXCAVATED PALACE OF KNOSSOS

those of their more recent successors, a civilization was revealed which Evans called "Minoan" after King Minos. At first he believed that the objects he was finding were Mycenaean because there were strong similarities. But as he gradually dug deeper and deeper into the great mound of Kephala, the site of ancient Knossos, he found indisputable evidence that a high culture had existed in Crete more than a thousand years before 1500 B.C.—the approximate date of the Mycenaean shaft graves as now established. In fact, the islanders, whose ancestors probably came from western Asia more than four thousand years B.C., had begun to establish their civilization in about 3000 B.C. at roughly the same time as Egypt was first united under the founding Pharaohs of the First Dynasty. The resemblance between Minoan and Mycenaean culture, in pottery, tools and weapons, architecture, dress, ornament, and art appeared to be due to the Mycenaeans, a warrior caste with a rudimentary culture, copying and adapting the achievements of the older civilization.

The first European civilization had been traced back to its Cretan

466

THE RESTORED THRONE ROOM OF THE
PALACE OF MINOS AT KNOSSOS

CRETAN BATHROOM OF THE "QUEEN'S
MEGARON" AT KNOSSOS

THIS MINOAN DAGGER-BLADE IS ENGRAVED WITH
A DESIGN OF FIGHTING BULLS

THIS BEAUTIFUL OCTOPUS VASE WAS MADE BY
AN EARLY CRETAN. HE MAY HAVE BEEN INFLU-
ENCED BY THE SNAKE CULT WHICH EXISTED THEN

homeland. Its isolation, surrounded, as Homer says, by the "deep, dark sea," preserved it from invasion and spoliation. Nearly all this valuable information was obtained, not by consulting written records, which were sparse and inaccurate, but by a scrupulous examination of Cretan artifacts. For Evans never succeeded in deciphering "Linear A" or "Linear B," though he recognized that the tablets were inventories of some kind. The Minoans had trade and cultural connections with Egypt, and the presence of datable Egyptian objects, e.g., statuettes bearing the names of Pharaohs, enabled Evans to establish reasonably firm dates for the levels at which these foreign objects were found. In fact, he was able to draw up a chronology of comparative development based on these objects, which, lacking a known writing system, were all he had to work with. And in Egypt datable tomb-paintings and inscriptions were found depicting men wearing the Cretan costume shown on the wall-frescoes at Knossos.

Yet Minoan culture owed very little to Egypt. There are few resemblances between Cretan and Egyptian art; the Minoans worshiped different gods from those of Egypt, the principal deity being a Mother-Goddess or Snake-Goddess whose effigy was found on miniature seals and in shrines. Moreover, whereas the ancient Egyptians delighted in engraving their temples with written inscriptions, the Minoans did not. Even their tombs were uninscribed, and the mysterious "Linear B," which Evans unavailingly strove to decipher, appeared to be confined to the clerkly productions of the office storekeepers.

There was much academic discussion and argument, sometimes bitter and violent. For instance, for a long time Evans appears to have believed that the Minoans colonized the mainland, and that such sites as Mycenae and Tiryns were offshoots of Cretan culture. His principal opponent, Professor Alan Wace, contested this and averred that the Mycenaean states were always independent, although they imitated Minoan art and may have employed Cretan craftsmen to make their tools and weapons.

Evans depended partly on the legend of King Minos and Prince Theseus of Athens, whose story is told by Plutarch[12] and others. According to this story, Athens was once a tributary state of Crete and had to send a yearly tribute of youths and maidens to be sacrificed to the Minotaur, the Bull-monster—progeny of Queen Pasiphae and a bull—whom Minos kept in a Labyrinth beneath the palace. Support for this belief was provided by certain wall-frescoes at Knossos showing young male and female athletes somersaulting over the back of a charging bull. Also, the Cretan name for the Double Axe, a religious emblem sacred to the Mother-Goddess, was *labrys*, which suggests that this is how the word Labyrinth originated.

---

12 *The Lives; GBWW*, Vol. 14, pp. 1 ff.

Eventually Wace proved his theory to the satisfaction of most scholars, though Evans remained unconvinced to the end of his long life. Wace also argued that the language spoken by the Mycenaeans was an archaic form of Greek and that this would eventually be proved when the tablets were deciphered. This turned out to be a true prophecy when a young British architect named Michael Ventris, who had spent some seventeen years at decipherment, succeeded in 1953 and announced that in his opinion "Linear B" was a primitive form of Greek. To date "Linear A" has not been deciphered. Ventris' system was an almost mathematical analysis of the various signs in the script which he set out in a "grid system," trying to establish possible consistencies in grammar which might afford a clue to the construction of the unknown language. Possibly a computer, programmed with this material, might have produced a result quicker than Ventris did. If such methods had been available to Ventris, I am sure he would have used them. But could any mechanical device have combined Ventris' mathematical ingenuity, historical imagination, and intuitive feeling for the civilizations of Mycenae and Crete? I doubt it.

When Professor Carl Blegen, of the University of Cincinnati, excavated the splendid palace of Nestor at Pylos in the Peloponnese he discovered a rich collection of "Linear B" tablets dating from about 1200 B.C., roughly the time when the mainland Mycenaean centers were being destroyed by the invading Dorians, the precursors of the "classical" Greeks. Examined and classified by Emmett L. Bennett, Jr., these tablets provided Ventris with additional material which enabled him to check his original decipherment based on the tablets that Evans had found at Knossos. Throughout the learned world, in America, France, Britain, Germany, Italy, and Scandinavia, scholars had been wrestling with "Linear B" for more than fifty years. Yet nearly all laid down their pens and saluted the young Englishman when; in 1953, very modestly, he announced in a BBC talk that he believed the language to be an archaic form of Greek, and Homeric Greek at that. At first, he hardly dared to believe that he had "cracked" the script, without the aid of a bilingual clue such as had aided Champollion in Egypt and Rawlinson in Mesopotamia.

After exhaustive analysis and criticism, most scholars now agree with Ventris. It is now generally accepted that the language written by the scribes of Knossos some three thousand years ago was akin to the tongue of Homer. Wace's theory that the Mycenaeans were a Greek-speaking people has been vindicated. In recent years, other examples of "Linear B" have turned up on the mainland, at Mycenae itself, for instance, but only "Linear B." No examples of "Linear A" have been found except in Crete, and some scholars believe that "Linear A" was the language spoken by the Minoans, whereas, when the Mycenaeans, as is now believed, conquered and occupied Crete and took over the Minoan empire, they used the Minoan writing system to write in their own language.

The tablets, as Evans had suspected, turned out to be mere inventories; scholars who had hoped to find "Linear B" transcriptions of the Greek myths, and descriptions of Greek history in preclassical times, were disappointed. The kings and queens of Mycenae and Crete remain silent to this day. All we have, at the present time, are numerous lists of arms and equipment, chariots, swords, women, slaves; accounts of land allocations to kings and to the temples of deities; references to military and naval dispositions at Pylos at the time when the city was threatened by the invading Dorians; and a number of Greek proper names, some of which include gods and goddesses familiar from classical times. But it is odd to find the name Hector, for instance, applied to a mere servant.

In Egypt, the Pharaohs boast at length about their achievements. So do the Assyrians in their inscriptions found at Nineveh and elsewhere. The Hittites of Anatolia have left us chronicles, diplomatic correspondence, poetry, and religious and secular literature of considerable power. But the Mycenaeans and the Minoans keep silence. Only in Homer do we hear faint echoes of that long-vanished world. And although modern archaeology can tell us much about the economy of a Mycenaean state, the weapons and tools they used, the crops they raised, the goods they made and exported, we know hardly any more than Chaucer, Dante, and Shakespeare did concerning what they thought and felt.

However, there have been important developments in the field of Greek philology. We have seen how Schliemann and others were impressed by the apparent resemblances between the heroic world described by Homer and the objects found in the Mycenaean shaft graves—the boar's tusk helmet, the great body-shield covering the warrior from neck to ankle (which is also found represented in Crete), the Homeric *megaron* or hall with its pillared porch, and so on. The difficulty is that Homer, if he existed, lived in the ninth or eighth century B.C., long after the glories of Mycenaean civilization had vanished; when warriors no longer fought in chariots and carried large body-shields as described by the poet; when the dead were cremated, not interred in richly furnished tombs such as Schliemann found; when weapons were of iron, not bronze. How, then, could the Ionian poet and his successors have known about this vanished world?

One solution to this problem which is gaining increasing support is that put forward by Denys Page, notably in his book *History and the Homeric Iliad* (1955). Briefly, the theory is that the Homeric bards and their successors had inherited a mass of oral literature passed on from generation to generation, which preserved, in certain formulaic phrases, memories of a world that had once existed, but that Homer himself had never seen. Over many centuries, descriptions of arming, fighting, sailing ships, fashioning weapons, etc., had been reduced to a standard conventionalized form that was passed on unchanged, or little changed, by generations of bards. When, in the eighth century B.C., the Homeric poems were first written down, these formulaic phrases were retained and subsequently repeated, with little or no alteration, despite the fact that the world of which they are the reflection ceased to exist when the Dorians entered Greece between 1200 and 1100 B.C. This is a kind of "literary archaeology" in which the linguist is concerned not with buried objects but with archaic patterns of thought and behavior. But one must admit that not all archaeologists or linguists take this view. One of the difficulties is the discrepancy between the world revealed by Homer, which was a relatively simple society, and the world of the "Linear B" tablets, which suggests a highly bureaucratic society similar to those of Egypt and Mesopotamia, in which a multitude of scribes and officials administered the economy, levying taxes, making allocations of land, and keeping precise records. There is nothing remotely heroic about the tablets, and it has been pointed out, notably by J. H. Finley, that the Mycenaean world which they partially illustrate is not at all like that described by Homer. Finley, therefore, suggests that "Homer's world" probably dates from an intermediate period between the fall of the Mycenaean states and the flowering of Greek "classical" culture.

And yet there remain, obstinately, the objects which Schliemann found at Mycenae which are now known definitely to date from about 1500 B.C.; and Carl Blegen, who conducted the most recent reexamination of Troy in the thirties and fifties, has demonstrated, to most people's satisfaction, that Priam's Troy was destroyed in about 1250 B.C., not in the latter part of the twelfth century B.C. as had formerly been believed. Incidentally, Blegen also established that the oldest part of Troy dates from the Neolithic period, before 3000 B.C., and that the so-called Treasure of Priam, which Schliemann found in one of the lowest of the superimposed cities, dates from the Early Bronze Age, at least one thousand years before the Trojan War. On the whole, I find Page's theory more convincing, and so do many others.

Blegen's excavation of Pylos ranks among the most exciting ever conducted in Greece. Pylos is associated in Homer with the "sage Nestor," that garrulous old man who was always telling Agamemnon and Odysseus how much better wars were fought in the good old days. On this elevated position, near the coast of the western Peloponnese, Blegen excavated the remains of two Mycenaean palaces, the larger of which is better preserved than Mycenae, though it does not command so glorious a site. But it includes the full ground plan of the *megaron* with annex, porch, and great hall, in which the circular hearth still stands intact, and there is even the pedestal for the throne on which the king sat. Not far away is a well-preserved bathroom with bath, of the type in which Telemachus, son of Odysseus, was bathed by Nestor's daughter, as described in the *Odyssey*. And it was in the archives of this palace that Blegen found the rich store of "Linear B" tablets which enabled Ventris to complete his historic decipherment.

The late John Papademetriou, who died from a heart attack brought on by over-exertion in the cause of archaeology, had a notable triumph at Brauron in Attica, where he unearthed the long-lost temple of Artemis mentioned by Euripides,[13] and the sacred spring beneath the mud in which he found thousands of delicate feminine ornaments—bronze mirrors, gold and bronze brooches, etc.—cast into the water by women who had come to Brauron to make offerings to the goddess. Flooding had preserved these things of beauty and high antiquity. At Mycenae in 1951, Papademetriou and other Greek archaeologists, including G. E. Mylonas, unearthed a second Mycenaean grave-circle containing shaft graves, even older than the one which Schliemann had discovered seventy-five years earlier. Many of the tombs were intact, and contained gold face-masks, rich jewelry, and arms in gold, silver, and bronze. They are now on view in the Archaeological Museum in Athens.

Also in the display there is another remarkable find, this time from the classical period, which owes its preservation partly to Papademetriou. A few years ago, workmen widening a road in the Piraeus, the port of Athens, came upon a bronze rod sticking out of the earth. The foreman informed the Greek Antiquities Service, of which Papademetriou was then head, and a team of archaeologists under his direction took over the excavation. The bronze rod turned out to be part of a Greek statue of the fifth century B.C. Near it, perfectly preserved, lay three other bronze statues, all products of the finest period of classical Greek art. These had evidently reposed in a Roman warehouse near the port, preparatory to being shipped to Rome. But for some fortunate reason they never left Greece. One wonders if other works of art, perhaps an unknown Phidias or Praxiteles, still lie beneath the earth or the sea, awaiting discovery.

Thanks to the efforts of archaeologists from all over the world, including Greeks, more and more treasures are being retrieved from the soil of Greece and its islands. For unlike Egypt, where with a few exceptions excavation is mainly conducted by Egyptian nationals, Greece has always thrown her arms wide open to scholars of other countries—the Germans at Olympia, the French at Delphi, the British at Knossos, and the Americans at a number of sites. One of the most remarkable feats of reconstruction has been the *stoa* or gallery of Attalus, overlooking the ancient agora of Athens, a two-story building restored by the patient efforts of American scholars. Thanks to this restoration, it is now possible to see at least part of the agora as it was in the second century B.C.

---

13 *Iphigenia Among the Tauri* 1463; GBWW, Vol. 5, p. 424a.

In Crete there has been much activity and not a little controversy. The distinguished philologist Leonard Palmer of Oxford aroused some argument when he contested Evans' belief that the Cretan palace of Knossos finally fell in about 1400 B.C., after which date Minoan civilization ceased to exist. Palmer, who holds a minority view so far as this subject is concerned, suggests that Evans was mistaken in his dating of the tablets found at Knossos, and that these *could* date from nearer 1200 B.C., approximately the time when Pylos fell to the Dorians. He believes that the Pylian and Knossian tablets are practically contemporary. Supposing Palmer's theory to be correct, Knossos did not become merely the home of "squatters" (Evans' word) after 1400 B.C. but continued to be occupied by kings down to the end of the second millennium B.C. In this case, arguing on literary evidence alone, King Idomeneus of Crete, who led a contingent of soldiers to support Agamemnon in the Trojan War, was a monarch of some importance and not a mere minor ruler governing a city that had long ceased to embody the power and wealth of Minoan civilization.

However, although Palmer's theory, well argued in his book *Mycenaeans and Minoans* (1961), has been widely publicized in the lay press, it has very few supporters among professional archaeologists. On purely linguistic grounds, Palmer's theory is a tempting one, since it would explain the fact that the Pylos tablets and those found at Knossos appear very similar, despite Evans' dating which would separate them by about two hundred years. But John Boardman, who was for a time Palmer's collaborator, has found no archaeological evidence which substantially shakes Evans' dating, and his view, that the Knossian tablets date from about 1400 B.C., and not 1200 B.C., is accepted by the majority of archaeologists specializing in Greek prehistory.

In Crete and the Aegean generally, important discoveries have been made during the past decade or two. Recently a fourth Minoan palace has been discovered at Zakro in Crete which has yielded rich finds. Even more fascinating is the theory, recently revived, that Crete was the lost continent of Atlantis. Plato tells the story in one of his Dialogues, the *Timaeus* and a fragment of the *Critias*,[14] of how there once existed, far out in the Atlantic, a vast continent, as large as Asia and Africa united, where justice reigned under the aegis of the god Poseidon. It had splendid buildings of hewn stone, a fine harbor, and its ships ranged far and wide. One of its sports was the hunting of wild bulls. Seeking to control the world, it came into conflict with Athens but was defeated by that city more than nine thousand years before the time of Plato. The story, which, according to Plato, was told to the lawgiver Solon by Egyptian priests when he visited Egypt, goes on to describe how Atlantis sank

---

14 *Timaeus* 25; *GBWW*, Vol. 7, p. 446a. *Critias*; pp. 478 ff.

beneath the sea in a day and a night, and how an Athenian army was destroyed.

This could be a mere fable and probably is. But there is a volcanic island called Santorin, formerly named Thera, which lies about seventy miles from Crete and which literally "blew its top" about 1500 B.C. Geologists have calculated that the volcanic force that caused the central part of the island to explode was several times greater than that which destroyed Krakatoa in the eighties of the last century. In the latter eruption, the cloud of volcanic ash was so great that it orbited the world for several years. It caused tidal waves one hundred feet high, devastating the coasts of Java and Sumatra, sweeping away trains and railroad tracks, and hurling a large steamer several miles inland. The tidal waves caused by the eruption of Thera must have been even greater, and could account for the sudden destruction of the Cretan coastal sites and the end of Minoan civilization.

But that is only one part of the story. If it could be proved that Thera was once part of the Minoan empire, belief in the association of Crete with Atlantis would be strengthened. Proof was recently provided when Spyridon Marinatos, now head of the Greek Antiquities Service, identified a Minoan palace on Santorin (that is, on what is left of it) buried under volcanic ash. One theory recently promulgated is that Crete and Thera were both part of the Minoan empire, that the sudden destruction of Thera may be reflected in the Atlantis story, and that although Crete itself was not destroyed, the effect of the catastrophe, in the form of tidal waves, clouds of volcanic ash, and earth tremors, could account for the sudden ending of Minoan civilization. The Mycenaeans, profiting from this, could have moved in and taken over the island some time later.

Those, like Angelos Galanopoulos, a geologist, who agree with the identification of Crete with Atlantis, have put forward some ingenious arguments in support of their belief. For instance, there is the difficulty of equating the certainly mythical date, nine thousand years before Solon, with the geologically established fact that Thera erupted at some time between 1550 and 1400 B.C. Solon, poet and statesman, first achieves prominence in about 612 B.C. Taking the year 600 B.C. as our rough guideline, the destruction of Thera would have occurred about nine hundred, not nine thousand, years before his time. He got the story from the Egyptian priests, who could well have heard of the destruction of this once great civilization of Minoan Crete. Could the priests, or Solon, have made a mistake in their calculations and, in effect, dropped a nought? Galanopoulos thinks so. Applying the same criterion of measurement, Atlantis might be made to appear ten times larger than it was. Therefore, since no such island continent could possibly be accommodated in the Aegean, and since in Solon's time Crete was well known and not in the least mysterious, the belief may have grown up that the "lost continent" had been far out in the Atlantic, into which few Greek navigators had ever ventured, and was as big as Africa and Asia combined.

Personally, I share Marinatos' skepticism regarding the Atlantis myth. It seems more than probable that Plato invented the story to illustrate a point of philosophy. But there can be no possible doubt that Thera (or Santorin) did erupt in the fifteenth century B.C. or thereabouts, that the effects of this eruption can still be seen—since Santorin is now a mere circle of narrow islands surrounding a deep submarine crater—and that they would certainly be felt in Crete in the form of tidal waves, showers of volcanic ash, earth tremors, etc. Therefore, it seems highly likely that it was this, and not armed invasion, which brought the Minoan civilization to an end. It also seems more than probable that at some later date Mycenaean invaders from the mainland exploited the situation by occupying at least part of the island and ruling from Knossos. They would have brought with them their Greek language and adapted the Minoan writing system (Linear A) to write it.

Returning to the mainland, we must mention other important discoveries that have been made there, e.g., at Lerna and Dendra, where Mycenaean *tholos* (beehive-shaped) tombs have recently been found, some intact or partially intact, containing grave-goods which gave further proof of the richness of Mycenaean civilization. There have also been important discoveries at Gla in Boeotia, at Volos in Thessaly (ancient Iolkos from which the "Argo" sailed), and elsewhere, which throw light on the obscure fall of the Mycenaean civilization between the end of the thirteenth and the beginning of the eleventh century B.C. Marks of fire and destruction at Iolkos, Pylos, Gla, and Thessaly support the ancient belief that the Mycenaean civilization was destroyed by newcomers whom one is tempted to equate with the Dorians, the ancestors of the "classical" Greeks.

An odd exception to this general rule was noted by Papademetriou at the Mycenaean citadel near Brauron in Attica. Here, and here alone, there seems to have been no conquest, no evidence of sacking and burning. Occupation—judging from pottery and other artifacts—appears to have ceased peacefully in about 1300 B.C. This, Papademetriou suggested, might confirm the tradition that the hero Theseus, who may have been a Mycenaean king, persuaded the inhabitants of a number of cities voluntarily to abandon them and found a new capital at Athens. This is slender evidence on which to base a final judgment, but the work of Schliemann at Mycenae and Evans at Knossos has provided such convincing proof of what used to be regarded as legend that it would be unwise to dismiss Papademetriou's theory out of hand.

In this essay, I have deliberately stressed Mycenaean-Minoan archaeology because it is in this field that, for me at any rate, the contribution of the pure archaeologist has the greatest value. Not because the My-

475

cenaean world is necessarily more important than that of classical times, but because the latter has the advantage of reliable documentation.

It is now becoming more and more widely accepted that the ancestors of the Mycenaeans in Greece were of Asiatic origin, as is suggested by the legends preserved in classical times. Here again, myth, history, and archaeology seem to mingle. We read that Cadmus, founder of Thebes in Greece, came from Egypt. Europa, who gave her name to the European continent, was a daughter of Agenor, king of Tyre in Phoenicia. Zeus appeared to her in the form of a bull and carried her off to Crete, where she bore him a son called Minos. Archaeologists such as Evans have pointed out resemblances between the artifacts of Crete and those of western Asia. In Homer's *Odyssey*,[15] Menelaus, having recovered Helen after the sack of Troy, takes her to Egypt and brings back rich furnishings for his palace which he displays to Telemachus. And some scholars, e.g., Marinatos, strongly suggest that the gold in the Mycenaean shaft graves came from Egypt, and that the Mycenaeans may have even borrowed their burial customs from those of the Pharaohs. This theory, however, is not universally accepted.

What does seem reasonably certain is that the old-fashioned concept of the "bronze-clad Achaeans" as blonde invaders from northern Europe is no longer valid. The weight of archaeological evidence suggests an Asiatic origin not only for the indigenous inhabitants of Greece but also for the Mycenaeans and the Minoans themselves. In this case perhaps the clue to the decipherment of "Linear A" may come from western Asia.

One's approach to archaeology, as to history, must in the final analysis be subjective. Personal interest, preference, and choice are bound to color it. In this contribution I have tried to cover as wide a field as possible within the permitted space, but, as will now have become obvious, the writer's personal predilections have governed the shape and content, even though these will not be shared by all readers. It would have been easy to compile a dull but reasonably comprehensive catalog of all the most significant discoveries made in the Mediterranean area during the past ten or twenty years and to classify them. I have deliberately left out many discoveries made accidentally, such as that of the mummy of a young girl of remarkable beauty found in a Roman sarcophagus when a bulldozer unearthed it near the Via Cassia in Rome in 1964. The body was so perfectly preserved that it was possible to take fingerprints, though heaven knows why! This was a purely accidental find and has nothing to do with pure archaeology. The same is true of the discovery, also made by a bulldozer, of 7,350 square feet of splendid Roman mosaic floors which came to light in 1963 at Lucus Feroniae, twenty miles from Rome.

---

15 *The Odyssey* IV. 120; *GBWW*, Vol. 4, p. 200b.

Leonard Cottrell

NEW TECHNIQUES

Italian archaeologists have been among the foremost in using the latest scientific techniques, even though they did not invent them. Some of these, e.g., aerial photography and earth resistivity tests, were pioneered in Britain. Others, such as "radiocarbon dating," had their origin in America at a time when the United States dominated the world of nuclear physics. This method is based on the fact that any piece of organic material, e.g., a fragment of wood or other vegetable matter, absorbs radiation throughout its life and once "dead" gives out radiation at a known rate. By the use of accurate measuring instruments, it is theoretically possible to establish the amount of radioactivity remaining, and

THIS AERIAL PHOTOGRAPH OF FYFIELD DOWNS, WILTSHIRE, SHOWS RIDGES LYING BENEATH THE PRESENT TOPSOIL. THESE RIDGES WERE THE LAND DIVISIONS FOR CELTIC FARMERS OF THE LATE BRONZE AGE

thus to find out the approximate age of the specimen. The marginal error may be as great as plus or minus 350 years.

Aerial photography was pioneered in Great Britain by John St. Joseph of Cambridge. Shortly after World War I, experience gained in aerial reconnaissance was applied to the discovery of archaeological sites. In Britain particularly, where the temperate climate and abundant vegetation encourage the rapid accumulation of soil and plant life above buried cities, sites invisible from the ground appear clearly in aerial photographs. The reasons for this are that (*a*) in certain lights, e.g., after sunrise and before sunset, slight excrescences in the soil are revealed by shadows; and (*b*) where a Roman road or the foundations of buildings have been buried under soil, grass or crops growing above such remains will be of a different shade of green. Though this variation may be invisible to the naked eye, it can be detected on a photograph.

Another technological device used by the Italians, and throughout Western Europe, is the magnetometer which measures the resistance of earth to the passage of electricity. This method, too, has been used by British archaeologists for a number of years, both on domestic and foreign sites. It enables the investigator to plot the course of buried walls or filled-in ditches, since these offer more electrical resistance than undisturbed soil. This method is particularly useful when lack of time, money, or other restrictions prevent wholesale excavation. This method was used in 1962 to help detect the long-lost site of the ancient Greek city of Sybaris, the Greek colony in southern Italy, the name of which is preserved in our word "sybarite." The people of Sybaris were notorious for their idle and luxurious way of life.

The site is so heavily waterlogged that excavation of the whole area will be difficult and expensive. Powerful hydraulic apparatus is needed to pump dry even a small section. When, in 510 B.C., the neighboring city of Croton attacked and sacked Sybaris, they were so determined to obliterate all memory of it that they diverted the course of a river over the site. Sixty-seven years later a new city called Thurii was built on the old, silted-up site by Greek colonists, one of whom was the historian Herodotus. But in time this too was destroyed, and as for Sybaris, all that remained was the memory of its wealth and hedonism, preserved in Greek and Roman literature. One reads how its horses were trained to dance to the flute; of banquet contests where the winning chef was awarded a year's copyright on his prize dishes; of one citizen named Smindyrides who slept on a bed of rose petals but complained that it gave him blisters; of emancipated Sybaritic women who spent one year in preparing an elaborate toilette to be displayed at one annual festival; and so on. No wonder that Norman Douglas wrote "Who would not live long enough, if he could, to see what comes to light?"

As recently as 1959, this prospect seemed remote. The edition of the

MAIDEN CASTLE TELL AS SEEN FROM THE AIR

Encyclopædia Britannica published in that year stated that "Explorations have so far failed to lead to a precise knowledge of the site." But in 1962 two independent archaeological teams identified it beyond reasonable doubt, buried some twenty and more feet below the sodden ground near the coast of Calabria, in the "heel" of Italy. Yet nothing was visible at ground level or from the air.

During these investigations, one archaeological team, headed by Salvatore Foti, superintendent of antiquities for Calabria, used conventional methods, assisted by hydraulic engineers. Digging a pit to a depth of some twenty feet, he came upon remains of a fifth-century town which he has ascribed "with certainty" to Thurii. Below this level the archaeologists found potsherds of the sixth century B.C.—contemporary

479

with the last years of Sybaris. But it took seven days of continuous pumping to clear the test pit, and when the pumps had to stop, the pit filled with   ter again within six hours.

The other archaeological team, working independently of Foti, combined the efforts of F. G. Rainey of the University of Pennsylvania, with his helpers, and the staff of the Lerici Foundation headed by its president, Carlo Lerici, one of Europe's pioneers in the application of electronics to the study of geological substructures. Lerici, who began his career in Milan twenty-eight years ago, is an engineer-industrialist whose

THE MAGNETOMETER USED TO MAP UNDERGROUND SYBARIS

hobby is archaeology. It was Lerici who discovered oil at Gela in Sicily and gas at Ferrandina. His work on the location and examination of Etruscan tombs is well known, and his experts have worked in Egypt and Turkey, where, in 1963, using electronic methods, they located the tomb of the Seleucid king Antiochus.

At Sybaris Lerici's potentiometer traced a buried wall for more than one hundred yards, not far from Foti's excavation. Rainey then went into action with another apparatus, invented by the Oxford University Research Laboratory, which detects stone structures and other anomalies underground with a proton magnetometer. These anomalies can be detected by observing the movements of protons in a bottle of alcohol containing an electric coil. The device enabled Rainey to continue plotting the buried wall for a further three-quarters of a mile. This technique might be roughly compared with X-raying a human body so as to make the bones visible through the flesh.

These discoveries of things invisible to the eye tended to bear out the statement of the ancient writers that the walls of Sybaris extended over five miles. Yet all this lies deep under waterlogged ground—hence the effort and expense of draining and excavating it. Yet it might become another Pompeii, especially as its flooding and silting-up may have preserved objects that would otherwise have been looted.

Next, Lerici, not to be outdone, applied oil-drilling techniques. High-speed drills bored deep into the soil, bringing up cores embedded with datable fragments of pottery. (Here it is worth noting that if an earlier generation of archaeologists had not learned and taught the technique of comparative dating by pottery styles such fragments would have meant nothing.) To speed up the process, the Lerici team introduced a water tanker coupled to the drill, which spewed up pottery fragments which could then be allocated to their appropriate levels and dated. These confirmed a sixth-century date. It was now certain that below the remains of Thurii were those of an earlier city which could hardly be other than Sybaris. Thus Petrie's "sequence dating" method was accelerated by modern technology.

Lerici has had dramatic results from his electronic and photographic surveys of buried Etruscan tombs. The Etruscans, whom the Greeks called Tyrrhenians, created vast cemeteries near their cities, such as Cerverteri, Tarquinia, Vulci, and Fabriano. The Etruscans have always been something of a mystery and remain so. They created a high civilization in Italy long before the coming of the Romans, whom they fought and by whom eventually they were defeated. But no one can be sure where they came from; whether their culture grew up on Italian soil, or whether, as some ancient writers averred, they were immigrants from Asia Minor. Their cemeteries have been known for centuries and have been much robbed, but there are so many tombs that it seems possible that a few may have escaped plunder; also that some of the already plundered sepulchers may contain fine painted wall-frescoes. Inscriptions also would be important, since Etruscan writing has still not been fully deciphered, and archaeologists continually hope to find a bilingual clue.

Lerici used three interconnected methods in his surveys of Etruscan cemeteries: aerial reconnaissance and photography; earth resistivity tests for examination at close range; and finally camera examination. To save the labor of excavating a tomb, Lerici drills a small hole in the top of a chamber and lowers into it a tube, like a periscope, with an arrangement of mirror-reflected lights which enables him to survey the interior. A camera is incorporated, with flash equipment, so that if the initial sur-

GOLD FUNERAL WREATH OF THE HELLENISTIC STYLE FOUND IN AN ETRUSCAN
TOMB AT PERUGIA

vey reveals anything interesting this can be photographed in color. At
Fabriano, Lerici's team first tried this modern method. The Italian
archaeological authorities had excavated about one tomb per year using
conventional methods. Lerici located sixty at the rate of two per day.
At Tarquinia, one of the best-known Etruscan cemeteries, the new
methods approached mass production. Twenty-six hundred tombs were
located, among which were twenty-two painted tombs. The last painted
tomb to be discovered before Lerici arrived was found in 1894.

As *The Times* correspondent expressed it, "the known heritage of
Etruscan painting has been doubled by this one survey." And at least one
of these tomb chambers was inscribed in Etruscan, though, alas, no bilingual clue has yet been found.

However, these quick-fire methods have their disadvantages. They
make buried antiquities more and not less vulnerable, since once their
existence is established they are likely to attract illicit diggers, unless
adequately guarded. In fact, during recent years large numbers of Etruscan objects have appeared on the market to cater to a new, fashionable
demand. Most of these, one can be sure, were obtained illicitly.

To the writer, the most valuable aspect of electronic detection by
earth resistivity tests is that it enables preliminary surveys to be done
and sites preserved for future methodical excavation. At Sybaris, for

instance, there was grave danger that, if the site had not been located, it could have been built over, as new factories are being erected in the area. One wonders how many important sites throughout the world have been obscured in this way, when the application of electronic methods would have detected them in good time. But it should also be realized that these new methods cannot be applied to all archaeological sites which, in many cases, will continue to need excavation by the old, well-tried methods. Çatal Hüyük, for instance, was discovered not by electronics but by the shrewd and experienced observations of Mellaart, who, like Petrie and Papademetriou, has "a nose for a site."

Another technique, not applicable at all sites, is that of pollen analysis. It is well known (especially by sufferers from hay fever) that in summer the air is impregnated with minute grains of pollen carried by the wind. Under a microscope these grains reveal the plant from which they came, whether it is a tree, a blade of corn, or wild grass. But it is not generally realized that in a favorable climate these grains may be preserved for thousands of years in waterlogged soil, e.g., peat bogs. If an archaeologist digs out a site in which these pollen grains have been preserved, his colleague the paleobotanist can recognize the plant species and thus build up a picture of the flora and fauna that existed at the time the site was occupied. (He can recognize the fauna from the type of plant on which certain animals feed.) If this occupation extended over hundreds of years, the paleobotanist can even describe the climatic changes which took place, and hence deduce how the human inhabitants reacted to these changes.

This brings us to northern and western Europe, especially Great Britain, where climatic conditions are unfavorable to the preservation of wood and metal—which may survive in Egypt for five thousand years. Some objects, however, do manage to be preserved, especially in waterlogged ground, and these can be identified and examined by modern methods. A good example is the Mesolithic settlement at Star Carr in Yorkshire, England. This Mesolithic (Middle Stone Age) site illustrates the difference between the archaeology of today and that of a century ago; between the obvious excitement of digging up a buried city rich in works of art, and the synthesizing of a long-vanished human society from objects which an earlier generation would not have looked for, or known how to interpret if they had found them. At Star Carr there was nothing visible on the ground or from the air. It was an unattractive, waterlogged piece of ground about five miles from Scarborough on the bleak North Sea coast of England. But there were geological indications suggesting that in early postglacial times the area might have bordered a freshwater lake. Two other areas in northern Europe, Vig in Sjaelland and Klosterlund in Jutland, where a similar geological structure exists, had yielded remains of human settlements of the Maglemosian period (6800–5000

B.C.). Because of these finds, in the fifties, trial pits were sunk with some difficulty in the mud of Star Carr, pumps being used continuously to suck water from the deepening excavations.

The investigators' guess proved correct. They found the rotted remains of a huge wooden platform made of birch brushwood—a kind of mattress built over the marshes that had bordered an ancient lake. On this platform the settlers would have built huts, probably of skins or reeds which had perished. But under the platform lay food waste, an enormous accumulation of animal bones: elk, ox, pig, red and roe deer, and water birds. There were also over seventeen thousand stone tools of the proto-Maglemosian period, consisting of flint arrowheads, awls, saws, scrapers, hand-axes, etc. Bone implements had been made from deer antlers and elk bones.

Preserved in the slime were minute pollen grains which, under the microscope, enabled the paleobotanists to deduce what kind of vegetation had existed, and the type of climate that would have produced it. Carbon-14 analysis of a piece of birchwood yielded a date of 7488 B.C. plus or minus 350 years. In those days, after the glaciers of the last Ice Age had retreated, the climate had become warm and moist. Where today the North Sea breakers thunder beneath the cliffs, and in winter a bitter wind buffets the substantial hotels of Scarborough, human beings in considerable numbers had settled on the marshes beside a placid lake, hunting game for food, and fishing from skin canoes. A wooden paddle was found, the oldest navigational appliance yet discovered anywhere in the world.

These people did not grow crops—agriculture would not reach Europe for at least another four thousand years—but they gathered edible plants to supplement their food supply. And though they may possibly have domesticated the dog, they owned no other domestic animals. They probably observed some kind of religious ritual. Stag frontlets, still bearing the antlers, had been made into headdresses with holes for fastening straps. Twenty-one of these were found and may have been used for ritual dances connected with the hunting of game; or the headdresses could have been used for stalking.

The objects retrieved, housed in a museum, would hardly merit a passing glance from the average layman. Yet in their way they excite the imagination just as much as the gold-embellished furniture found by Carter at Thebes and by Woolley at Ur, cities that came into existence more than five thousand years after the hunter-fishermen of Star Carr had rotted in the lakeside marshes above which they lived some nine thousand years ago. I have chosen this example because it illustrates very vividly the strides which archaeology has taken during the past thirty years, and because it affords such a contrast with the treasure-hunting of a century ago.

JACQUES-YVES COUSTEAU, WEARING
THE SCUBA EQUIPMENT HE IN-
VENTED. THE MOBILITY WHICH UN-
DERWATER SWIMMERS GAIN WITH
THE USE OF THIS EQUIPMENT HAS
FACILITATED MANY NEW ARCHAE-
OLOGICAL INVESTIGATIONS

Another vast and potentially rich archaeological field has been opened by new techniques of underwater exploration. The offshore waters of the Mediterranean are littered with ancient wrecks, some dating from Greco-Roman and even earlier times. Though the timbers will usually have perished, the more durable parts of their cargoes, e.g., wine amphorae, statues and other works of art, and, in favorable conditions, metal objects, will often have survived. Occasionally in the past magnificent works of Greek art have been dredged up accidentally by fishermen, e.g., the bronze statue of Poseidon now in the Archaeological Museum in Athens. But today, thanks initially to Jacques Cousteau and his pioneering work in the field of underwater exploration, divers can move easily along the seabed, locating, marking, and eventually excavating ancient ships.

It is possible to train amateur divers to do reconnaissance work, thanks to the art of skin diving and the introduction of the aqualung. In time, more and more of the younger archaeologists can be taught to use their special skills and trained eyes in locating and examining objects on the seabed. Among these may be the "underwater Petries" of the future. The archaeologist Philippe Diolé is a noted exponent of this method, which he has described in his book *4,000 Years Under the Sea* (1954). Some remarkable finds have already been made by this method. For instance, in 1963 the Archaeological Society of Béziers in France, surveying the coastal waters of the Western Hérault division, found the cargo of a ship dating from about twenty-five hundred years ago. It was evidently that of a bronzesmith. From an area about seventy-five feet by forty-two feet the underwater archaeologists have retrieved thirteen hundred bronze ingots, in all 359 pieces, eight weighing between eleven and fifteen pounds. There were also ingots of tin and 660 objects of bronze and copper, including axes, pins, brooches, belt buckles, earrings, arms, and hunting equipment. Even the manufacturer's trademark was still visible on some of the ingots.

Near the Isle of Giannutri, off the coast of Tuscany, Italian divers retrieved a Roman shipload of plates, vases, and other tableware from under eighteen fathoms. Parts of the ship, which sank in about 100 B.C., are still under the mud of the seabed where they were scattered some twenty centuries ago. Other wrecks are being discovered every year, and there is already a danger, similar to the one which Petrie and other pioneers recognized, that indiscriminate plundering by amateur treasure-hunters may destroy valuable archaeological evidence. One hears disquieting stories of rich playboys diving from their yachts in the Aegean and coming up with Greek amphorae.

But although such incidents are bound to happen—one cannot protect the entire Mediterranean from these activities—the location of buried wrecks is normally so difficult and their excavation so expensive that one may be sure that this new field of submarine archaeology will continue to yield valuable results for generations to come. One of its most exciting possibilities is the recovery of great works of art which the Roman entrepreneurs exported from Greece during the centuries of Roman occupation. From time to time these have been recovered in the past—the well-known Poseidon masterpiece is an example—but always by accident. Usually fishermen bring them up in their nets, and on more than one occasion such finds have been flung back into the ocean, for superstitious reasons. Nowadays, however, we have reached the stage when deliberate and scientific search for sunken antiquities is possible, given the money and facilities. It has already reached the treasure-hunting stage, e.g., in the search for sunken Spanish galleons and other treasure ships off the coast of Britain. But there can be no doubt that now and in the future the new techniques will be applied in the cause of scientific archaeology.

After more than a century and a half of intensive exploration, the land is far from having yielded all the secrets of the buried past. And now that the seabed is becoming increasingly accessible, a new chapter is opening and one may confidently expect important and even sensational discoveries, especially under the Mediterranean, around which most of the earliest civilizations grew up, and in whose treacherous waters Egyptian, Cretan, Mycenaean, Phoenician, Persian, Greek, and Roman vessels must often have foundered. And not only ships or their cargoes await discovery. During the past five thousand years, earth movements have submerged ancient ports and harbors, e.g., off the coast of Crete where several are known to exist; and parts of ancient Alexandria, including the foundations of the famous lighthouse—one of the Seven Wonders of the World—now lie under water.

Generally speaking, the wrecks of ancient ships are more likely to be discovered under the clear waters of the Mediterranean than off the coasts of the North Sea and the Atlantic. But there have been exceptions. One of these was the remarkable reclamation, by Swedish archaeologists, of a great warship, the "Vasa," which sank off Stockholm in A.D. 1628. She was lifted, mainly intact after over three hundred years, and was found to contain not only her guns and cargo but such things as leather boots, clay pipes, pewter mugs, navigating instruments, and even casks of butter. The "Vasa" herself has been painstakingly restored and reconstructed, her ancient timbers bathed in water-sprinklers to prevent them shrinking when exposed to the air after more than three hundred years of immersion. But the "Vasa" is of yesterday compared with, for example, a ship that was wrecked near modern Cape Gelidonya in Turkey, estimated to be three thousand years old. Believed to be the oldest ship so far discovered under water, she contained more than a ton of Bronze Age objects, including plowshares, picks, shovels, adzes, and knives. There were even olive stones and fish bones, relics of the sailors' meals!

ARCHAEOLOGY IN GREAT BRITAIN

Finally, turning again to Great Britain, the training ground of so many brilliant archaeologists, one must begin by recognizing the contributions made by generation after generation of zealous investigators, from the "antiquaries" of the sixteenth and seventeenth centuries—Leland, Dugdale, Browne, and the rest—to the scientifically minded young scholars of today who have applied laboratory techniques to the investigation of ancient remains. One of Britain's most valuable exports, culturally speaking, has been her archaeologists, many of whom, such as Petrie and Woolley, have spent most of their most productive years in countries far remote from their own.

In Britain, where there was a long-established tradition of "antiquarianism," Roman roads were traced, villas and forts unearthed, and the writings of Tacitus, Suetonius, and others were combed for any clue which might assist archaeologists in tracing the pattern of the Roman invasion and occupation of the island. But these clues were scanty, for the Roman historians were vague on topographical detail; to this day no one has identified the battlefield where the British King Caractacus

487

made his last stand, or where Suetonius Paulinus destroyed Boudicca's rebel armies. But much was revealed in the excavation of the legionary fortresses such as York, Lincoln, and Caerleon, where long occupation had left not only the buried foundations of buildings but in some cases walls of considerable height. There were also many inscriptions and tombstones, especially near the forts along the seventy miles of Hadrian's Wall, the northernmost frontier of an empire which stretched from the River Tyne in the north to the Nile in the south and the Euphrates in the east.

From these it was possible to trace the careers of high officials of the Roman Empire, the names of army units which had built sections of Hadrian's Wall, and individual names of soldiers and their families who had known that lonely rampart more than seventeen centuries ago. However, the great breakthrough in our knowledge of Roman Britain had to await the twentieth century, when aerial photography and other modern methods have revealed roads, forts, and villas which the nineteenth-century excavators could not detect. But this again was "in-filling." More important were the researches of scholars who probed much further back than the period of the Roman Empire; those who excavated burial mounds of the Iron Age and the Bronze Age, in the Quantock Hills of Somerset, the Cotswold Hills, and the highlands of Derbyshire, Yorkshire, Cumberland, and elsewhere.

There were also the stone circles, of which the best known are at Avebury and Stonehenge in Wiltshire, and other examples exist in many places such as Great Rollright in Oxfordshire, Arbor Low in Derbyshire, and Keswick in Cumberland. Some of these, e.g., Stonehenge, date from the late Neolithic (New Stone Age) period, though they received additions in the Bronze and Iron Ages. Some date from the Bronze Age. There are also hilltop fortresses surrounded by earthworks of prodigious size, comparable in some ways with the work of the pyramid-builders of Egypt, since these earthworks were raised by men using picks made from deer antlers only. Similar camps and fortresses, stone circles, and stone-lined burial mounds have been excavated in France and Spain. Many of the hilltop camps date from the Iron Age (from about 300 B.C.), and it was these *oppida*—strong points—which the Romans had to attack when they invaded Britain, as described by Tacitus. But some go back to the Bronze Age and even earlier in time.

The stone circles, with their concentric rings of monoliths, usually approached by long avenues of standing stones, as at Avebury, appear to have been sun-temples, and some authorities think that this tradition of megalithic building began with the Mycenaeans in Greece and gradually spread along the northern coast of the Mediterranean through Spain to the Atlantic coast and thence to Brittany and Britain. Quite recently at Stonehenge, the most magnificent megalithic monument in Britain, the carving of a dagger was observed on one of the stones, and from the shape of this dagger some scholars have identified it as Mycenaean; but this in itself does not prove that the Mycenaeans themselves ever saw Britain, only that their trade-goods reached the island. This would not be surprising, since we know from the excavation of certain Bronze Age burial mounds in Britain that among the grave-goods were little cylindrical beads of faience which could only have been manufactured in Egypt about 1500 B.C.

"Antiquities," wrote Sir Francis Bacon early in the seventeenth century, "are history defaced, or some remnants of history which has casually escaped the shipwreck of time . . ."[16]

True enough; but what the great lord chancellor could not have known was that there is a link between the remote antiquities of Britain and the Neolithic settlements at Çatal Hüyük, at Jericho, and at many sites

---

16 Cf. *Advancement of Learning*, 2nd Bk. II. 3; *GBWW*, Vol. 30, p. 34d.

in the Levant. The opposite ends of the ancient world—the Fertile Crescent in the east and the barbarous northern island in the west—were connected, however remotely, by trade and cultural contacts long before the Romans entered Britain with their civilizing mission. The Neolithic Revolution, during which men ceased to depend entirely on the hunting of game and learned how to grow crops and domesticate animals, began in the Middle East between 10000 and 5000 B.C. At that time the peoples of northern Europe were still hunters. The new way of life, which enabled mankind to settle in favored areas without the need to move, was transmitted gradually across Europe, carrying with it religious beliefs and customs, of which the building of megalithic monuments was one; another was the custom of interring the dead under large burial mounds and accompanied by grave-goods needed in the afterlife. There is a connection between the pyramids of Egypt and the tholos-tombs of Mycenae and the chambered tumuli still to be seen on the Cotswold Hills, in Derbyshire, Wiltshire, Cumberland, and elsewhere.

"Towards the middle of the Third Millenium B.C.," writes Nicholas Thomas,

> groups of adventurers, farmers and herdsmen set sail from France and the mouth of the Rhine and settled in southern England. In a short time their revolutionary culture, in which food production and domestication of animals were the characteristic features, had spread over Britain. We have to visualise boatloads of men, women, and children disembarking upon our shores and unloading sheep, cattle and seed grain for their first sowing-time. They had come to a fertile island, the higher ground easy to clear and cultivate with polished stone axes and shoe-blades. A network of rivers and natural land routes enabled them to penetrate deep into the rivers they had braved the Channel to explore.[17]

The Iron Age peoples followed with more advanced agricultural techniques and more sophisticated military methods, in about 300 B.C. They gave the conquering Romans a lot of trouble, and at Maiden Castle, in Dorset, their mighty fortress with its high concentric banks of earth encircling a central enclosure seemed impregnable. Here is a point where classical literature and archaeology meet, because Tacitus describes how Vespasian (much later to become Emperor) led the Second Augustan Legion on a series of operations against what the historian calls *oppida*. One of these which has been positively identified is Maiden Castle, the result of the archaeological research of Sir Mortimer Wheeler, unaided by any substantial literary evidence apart from the vague reference to the *oppida* by Tacitus.

There were two main gates, one on the east, the other on the west,

---

17 Nicholas Thomas, *A Guide to Prehistoric England* (London: Batsford, 1960).

marked today by high turf embankments of complicated shape. Evidently the Legion decided to attack the weaker east gate; they first laid down a barrage of ballista-arrows, powerful projectiles fired from spring-guns. The body of one of the defenders was found with such an arrow embedded in his vertebrae, and it had entered from the front. The Second Augustan then advanced, setting fire to some huts near the entrance, and under cover of the clouds of smoke the gate was assaulted and the position taken. But the defense had been fierce, and once they had entered the Romans showed no mercy. There seems to have been an indiscriminate massacre of men, women, and children until the troops were called to order. The dead were buried where they fell; Wheeler found, within the east gate enclosure, bodies of the fallen Britons, buried in shallow graves, each with some small funerary offering. The bones of many showed how they had died, by sword, spear, or arrow. This, then, is the oldest British war cemetery known. The archaeologists also found "ammunition dumps" consisting of thousands of round pebbles used by the defenders in the sling-warfare for which they were famous, and for which their heavily ramparted camp had been designed.

More recently than Wheeler's excavation in the thirties, another Iron Age *oppidum* taken by the Romans has been identified at Hod Hill, also in Dorset. Here there was a concentration of ballista-bolts at one particular point, which may have been the site of the chief's dwelling within the enclosure. Later a Roman fort was built within the earthworks; units of a legion and some cavalry were stationed there, maybe to act as a police force while the people of the surrounding Cranborne Chase, a rich farming area, were being brought under subjection. It appears that the Romans did not have an easy time subduing this wild western country.

More has been discovered concerning the Roman conquest and occupation of Britain during the past thirty years than during the preceding two centuries. This is the result of a number of reasons: the increasing skill and numbers of British archaeologists, especially among the younger generation, armed with new knowledge and techniques; the increased use of aerial photography in locating sites usually invisible from the ground, especially roads, forts, and marching camps in north Britain and Scotland; and the use of earth resistivity tests—the proton magnetometer already described—in locating buried walls and filled-in ditches, thus cutting down the time needed for excavation. Another reason is the immense amount of road-building and other constructional work now taking place in Britain, which frequently leads to accidental finds not only of Roman but also of pre- and post-Roman remains.

To name all the important finds made even during the past two decades would require a complete article in itself, but here are a few random examples. At Hinton St. Mary in Dorset a large and elaborate villa

DURING THE BULLDOZING OF A GARAGE-SITE IN COLCHESTER, ESSEX, AN ANTIQUE
ROMAN MOSAIC PAVEMENT WAS UNEARTHED. BY APPLYING PLASTIC ADHESIVE, THE
ARCHAEOLOGISTS WERE ABLE TO TRANSPORT THE PAVEMENT TO A SAFER LOCATION

was recently discovered containing a magnificent mosaic pavement incorporating the Chi-Rho sign, one of the earliest symbols of Christianity,
and a portrait of a young bearded man believed by some authorities to
be a representation of Christ. The pavement has now been removed and
set up in the British Museum. Near the Roman city of Chichester another
even larger villa was unearthed and will be put on permanent display.
From its size and elaborate construction—more like a royal palace than
a nobleman's villa—it may well be the royal residence of Cogidumnus,
a Roman client-king who is known to have been on very friendly terms
with the invaders. A Latin inscription bearing his name and titles was
discovered at Chichester many years ago; he bore the same titles as a
much more famous client-king who ruled at the other end of the Roman
empire—Herod the Great—and these are the only two native, non-Roman
rulers who are known to have been so honored.

One of the most fascinating finds at the Chichester villa is the remains
of a Roman-type formal garden, the first to be found in Great Britain.
The paths and flower-beds can be distinguished, and from surviving plant
remains it will be possible to restock the beds with flowers and plants of
the same type which flourished there some eighteen hundred years ago.

Much excitement was generated recently when it was thought that the
site of King Arthur's Camelot had been identified at Cadbury Hill, a
hill-fort in Somerset. It has the most elaborate arrangement of ramparts
in that county, four complete rings of banks and ditches enclosing about
eighteen acres, the whole standing on an isolated hill some four hundred
feet in height. Although the structure is mainly of the Iron Age, probably
of the first or second century B.C., there is evidence from recent excava-

492

tion that it was occupied at a much later date, corresponding roughly to the period immediately following the end of the Roman occupation when King Arthur—if he had existed—would have been alive. The west country—Somerset, Devon, and Cornwall—is closely associated with Arthur in legend. In Somerset there is Glastonbury Abbey in which he was supposed to have been buried. There is a strongly held belief among many archaeologists and historians that King Arthur—though the name is surrounded by mythical accretions—had a historic existence and was probably a Romanized British cavalry leader who fought the invading Saxons during the chaotic period following the withdrawal of the legions. Cadbury Hill Castle would be an ideal site for a fortress such as Camelot must have been, but, to date, nothing has turned up which would enable archaeologists to identify it positively. The excavations are continuing.

The interest aroused by this excavation illustrates several points which I have tried to emphasize in this essay—the links between archaeology, literary history, and legend, of which Troy and Mycenae are other examples. Archaeologists, though not as naive as Schliemann was, are less liable nowadays to dismiss myths and legends out of hand. Very often myths are a form of folk-history, passed on from generation to generation by people who were either illiterate or who lived before the invention of writing. And in the future there is no doubt that where such strong traditions exist they will be taken seriously, if cautiously, by archaeologists.

One could go on quoting examples, all of which illustrate, in different ways and in varying degrees, the contribution which archaeology has made, and is making, to Western thought. But it is important to establish the true priorities. No matter how intriguing any individual discovery may be, whether it is a Paleolithic cave-painting of 20000 B.C. or a Roman villa of A.D. 200, a sunken wreck full of bronze ingots, an Egyptian royal tomb of the First Dynasty, or even the faint outline on an aerial photograph of a hitherto unknown hill-fort in France or Britain, the discovery in itself is only significant if it adds something, however little, to our knowledge of human development. The new technological skills that are being increasingly applied to archaeological investigation may fascinate us by their ingenuity, but if they are merely applied to treasure-hunting, we are no better than the ignorant plunderers who wrecked valuable sites in Egypt, Europe, and the Middle East one hundred or more years ago.

In the final analysis, archaeology is only an extension of the experience which poets, artists, historians, and philosophers have been gathering and transmitting through written records and oral tradition during the past five thousand years. In the words of *The Times* leader in 1922, announcing the discovery of the Tomb of Tutankhamen, "The earth holds in her recesses the rich memories of our race."

M. I. Finley

A widely read and highly respected
classical scholar who has done much to
revise our understanding of the ancient
world, M. I. Finley was born in New York
City in 1912. He had a distinguished
professional career in the United States
before moving to England, where since
1957 he has been a Fellow of Jesus College

and, since 1970, Professor of Ancient
History at the University of Cambridge. He
is the author of *Studies in Land and Credit
in Ancient Athens* (1952), *The World of
Odysseus* (1954), and *Early Greece: The
Bronze and Archaic Ages* (1970), and has
edited *The Greek Historians* (1959) and
Slavery in Classical Antiquity (1960),
among other works. His published articles
have appeared in literary reviews as well
as in professional journals. He lives in
Cambridge and since 1962 has been a
British subject.

New Developments in
Classical Studies[*]

W riting at the end of the pre-Christian era, the Sicilian Greek historian Diodorus told how in 384 B.C. Dionysius I of Syracuse raided the Etruscan port known in Greek as Pyrgi, took much booty and many captives, whom he sold as slaves, and so raised enough money to hire and equip a large army.[1] What Pyrgi was called in Etruscan is unknown; today it is an unimportant little bathing resort, Santa Severa, about forty miles west by north of Rome, but in Dionysius' time it was filled with wealth because it was the harbor of the powerful Etruscan town of Cisra (Caere in Latin, Cerveteri today).

In 1957 Massimo Pallottino, the outstanding Etruscologist, and his pupil, Giovanni Colonna, began to excavate Santa Severa systematically. They discovered the foundations of two temples, lying parallel to each other facing the sea, typically Etruscan in ground plan, the earlier dating about 500 B.C., the later two or three decades after that. Then, on July 8, 1964, came a spectacular discovery. In a niche between the two temples, carefully folded away, were found three tablets of pure gold, one-third to one-half millimeter in thickness. Tucked in the folds were bronze, gold-headed nails with which the tablets had originally been affixed to something, perhaps the doors of the older temple. Each of the tablets was beautifully inscribed, two in Etruscan and the third in Punic, the Phoenician dialect of Carthage (in modern Tunisia). The texts, no more than ninety words altogether, overlap, and there are doubts about some of the reading. The Punic text seems to say something like the following:

> *To the lady Astarte. This is the sacred place made and given by Thefarie Velianas, king of Cisra, in the month of the Sacrifice of the Sun in gift within the temple and sanctuary[?], because Astarte has raised [him] with her hand[?], in the third year of his reign, in the month of Krr, on the day of the Burial of the Divinity. And the years of the statue of the goddess in her temple [are as many] as these stars.*[2]

---

* A more precise title would be "Some new developments. . . ." I have touched only lightly on the Bronze Age in Greece and on the so-called Hellenistic period following the conquests of Alexander the Great. Science, philosophy, and the fine arts hardly appear; even under the subheadings I have introduced, I have permitted my own interests to carry undue weight. Nor are the references to books and articles meant to be exhaustive. In particular I want to disclaim any implication, in the deliberate concentration on publications in English, that there is little, or less, of importance in other languages.

This discovery is surprising in so many ways, and raises so many questions, that it makes an admirable introduction to the complexity of the idea of "new developments" in our knowledge of the ancient Greeks and Romans. First and most obvious is the question of language. Etruscan remains one of the few major linguistic obscurities in Europe—not, as is still widely and wrongly believed, because the alphabet of twenty-six letters is undeciphered, but because the language has no known affinity with other European (or Asiatic) tongues, and because all but a few of the more than ten thousand Etruscan texts now known are brief formulas, such as "I am the jug of Enotenus." What the experts have been waiting for is a larger bilingual text, which would open the way to completion of the now partial decipherment. Naturally it was an Etruscan-Latin bilingual that was hoped for; instead Pyrgi produced an Etruscan-Punic pair that do not translate each other literally. Since this is just about the oldest Punic text found anywhere, there are difficulties with it too.

The second big question is religious and political combined. Why did an Etruscan ruler near Rome go to such lengths to honor Carthaginian Astarte, the Ishtar of the Bible? Why, furthermore, does the longer of the two Etruscan tablets call her Astarte-Uni? That combination is of particular interest because Uni was identified with the Roman Juno and sometimes also assimilated to the Greek Hera, consort of Zeus. It was characteristic of ancient polytheism that gods and goddesses traveled to new shrines in new regions, that they were sometimes "identified" with each other, that they acquired new attributes, that, in sum, the pantheon was not something fixed for all time but rather a changing accumulation of divinities and functions responding to new needs and situations. But the changes were neither whimsical nor meaningless; there was always a reason, though it may be lost to us today.

Nothing in the Pyrgi tablets hints at an explanation directly, but we may draw some plausible inferences from the well-known Roman legends and traditions about early Rome. In particular, two events in that tradition are relevant. The first is that in 509 or 508 B.C. the Romans overthrew their Etruscan king and established a republic. The second is that the new, independent Roman regime immediately signed a rather complicated political-commercial treaty with Carthage. Many historians have in the past expressed doubt about the early date assigned to that treaty, because Rome was then too insignificant to warrant such recognition from powerful Carthage. But the Pyrgi tablets point the way to an explanation, namely, that Roman emancipation was part of a larger story of breakdown in the Etruscan league that had dominated central Italy and that the Carthaginians, who had had a *modus vivendi* with the Etruscans, thought it desirable, even necessary, to come to terms with petty Italian states now claiming independence. Hence the treaty with

Etruscan jug with painted figure of Lasa, a female Eros; fourth–third century B.C.

Rome; hence, too, a relationship with Thefarie Velianas of Cisra, symbolized by the (temporary) worship of Astarte in Pyrgi.

This is not the place for a full discussion of the implications of the Pyrgi tablets.[3] Enough has been said to reveal the frustrating condition that is chronic in classical studies: paucity of evidence (often in difficult and sometimes unintelligible language) forces heavy stress on every new scrap that comes to light, not only for its own sake but, as the Pyrgi tablets show, also for a reconsideration of older, generally accepted views of broad issues and major developments. It is therefore not surprising that university students, for example, frequently express the idea that ancient history is somehow qualitatively different from modern history. Certainly the ancient historian envies his colleagues who specialize in the American Civil War or Victorian England; for each of those short periods there is probably more documentation available than for the whole of the Greco-Roman world, from Homer to Constantine. In reality, however, the difference is one of degree rather than of kind. A treaty is still a treaty, even though we need the accident of the Pyrgi discovery to help assess the otherwise suspect tradition of a Roman-Carthaginian treaty as early as 508 B.C. It can also be argued that modern historians, with their wealth of written documents, do not make sufficient use of archaeology, of objects. It is only in recent decades that aerial photography has radically influenced our knowledge of late medieval and early modern agricultural field systems. It was in 1956 that the late Erwin Panofsky, in a brilliant series of lectures at the Institute of Fine Arts, New York University, expounded a new concept of the changing function of funeral monuments, from "prospective" to "retrospective," based on an examination of tomb

497

sculpture from the ancient Egyptians to the Renaissance, materials which had been very familiar long before he put new questions to them.[4]

A mere catalog of recent finds would therefore constitute only one aspect of "new developments" and, if left at that, would give a false image of what is happening in classical studies. "New," like "original," is a complex concept. In 1964 a committee on postgraduate instruction in Cambridge University reported that the old requirement that a Ph.D. dissertation must represent "original work" put "a premium on novelty for its own sake, with the result that many Ph.D. dissertations, though technically 'original,' are concerned with peripheral and even trivial subjects of study." The committee recommended, and the university adopted, a new definition: a satisfactory dissertation is one that "represents a substantial contribution to scholarship, for example, through the discovery of new knowledge, the connection of previously unrelated facts, the development of new theory, or the revision of older views."

This statement will serve to define the scope of the present survey. It is a commonplace, but nonetheless true, that every age rewrites history, Greco-Roman history included.[5] I shall be primarily concerned with some of the major issues and topics, rather than with individual finds, no matter how spectacular—with the counterpoint between discovery and interpretation (or "understanding"). However, in view of the important place of archaeology in classical studies, already noticed, it is first necessary to have a clear idea of the nature and number of new finds, of just what new raw materials are at the disposal of the student today for the process of interpretation.

The evidence of archaeology[6]

A crude but fundamental distinction must be drawn at the start: excavations, whether licensed or illicit, planned or accidental, produce two different kinds of material—written and unwritten, documents and objects.

Documents have to be divided in turn. On the one hand there are literary texts, a term I use broadly to include not only *belles lettres* but also historical, philosophical, and scientific writings, technical manuals, legal treatises, political pamphlets. The normal "paper" was made of dried thin strips of an Egyptian reed called *papyrus,* worked into sheets, which could be pasted together side by side to form a roll. Each new copy of such a book was handwritten on papyrus, like the original, and we must assume that few copies of any book were in existence at any one time. (The more durable *parchment* was a late invention and never in antiquity a serious competitor with papyrus.) The permanent danger was not merely that a book would go out of print, but that it would go out of existence altogether. What survives today is what was deemed worthy of being copied and recopied for hundreds of years of pagan history, and

498

then for more hundreds of years of Christian history, Byzantine in the east, Latin in the west, centuries during which tastes and values changed more than once, often radically. Thus, although the names of some 150 authors of Greek tragedies are known, plays by only 3 of them are extant in full: 7 of Aeschylus' 82 compositions, 7 of perhaps 123 by Sophocles, 19 of Euripides' 92. Of the rest, we are left with mere names or with occasional quotations (often misquotations) by later authors and anthologists. Nor are the surviving texts completely accurate. That would be too much to expect of centuries of copyists.

The search for medieval and Byzantine manuscripts has been so thorough ever since the Renaissance that the chance of finding new works from that source has become very remote. Everything must therefore be pinned on the peculiar climatic and historical condition of Egypt. There the absence of moisture permits papyrus to survive indefinitely if it is protected by sand or sealed tombs from the floodwaters of the Nile. After Alexander the Great conquered Egypt in 332 B.C., the country was controlled by a new, originally Greco-Macedonian ruling class, whose language and culture remained Greek until the Arab conquest in A.D. 642. In the excavated debris of that thousand-year period, complete or nearly complete books in the form of papyrus rolls can be counted on one's fingers, but fragments turn up year after year. A catalog published in 1965 runs to nearly twenty-eight hundred items (fragments of individual volumes, not separate titles), including commentaries or grammatical treatises but excluding school exercises and shorthand manuals.[7] Of these, Homer alone accounts for a third or more, followed by Euripides, Demosthenes, and Plato, with works by writers later than Alexander very much in the minority.

In assessing these statistics, one should bear in mind that they reflect the possessions of provincials. Alexandria, the capital of Egypt and also, in the centuries following Alexander the Great, the rival of Athens to the title of intellectual capital of the Greek-speaking world, has produced virtually no papyri, for physiographic and historical reasons. Given that qualification, the literary finds provide an interesting index of taste, a subject that needs more investigation than it has so far received. Otherwise, the importance of papyrus fragments of already known works stems from their age. Usually much older than the medieval manuscripts, they are helpful in the continuing struggle to get back to the exact original text of a poem, play, or book. Scholarly notes and commentaries, sometimes accompanying a literary text, sometimes written independently, also have their value. Though few can claim intrinsic interest as works of criticism, they add to our meager stock of information, occasionally in a sensational way. One such papyrus, published not quite twenty years ago, revealed that Aeschylus' *Suppliant Women*,[8] previously thought to be one of his earliest tragedies, was in fact quite late, probably written and performed in 463 B.C. That one new fact has undermined quantities of

499

modern scholarship about the development of Aeschylus' technique, such as his use of the chorus (and one hopes, probably in vain, will serve as a warning against the sandy foundations of certain kinds of literary history).

All this will be of greater interest to the scholar than to the layman. Not so those papyri that have rescued major lost works in whole or in part. Included are poems by Sappho and Alcaeus, who lived on the Aegean island of Lesbos in the years immediately before and after 600 B.C., among the most famous of all Greek lyric poets, in Rome as in Greece. Horace boasted that he was the first to fit the Aeolic lyric to Italian measures[9] (Aeolic was the dialect of Lesbos). Though the Alcaic meter was his favorite, the Sapphic next, his claim was not strictly true: Catullus had already used them; one of his poems, the fifty-first, is an adaptation of one of Sappho's; he called his ladylove Lesbia, though her real name was the good Latin Clodia. The scholars of Alexandria had published editions of Alcaeus in ten books, of Sappho in nine. As late as the fourth century A.D. Sappho was being quoted by orators, and we are told that her poems were still being taught in schools then. Afterward they disappeared, so completely that Sappho survived in some half-dozen long quotations (up to twenty-eight lines), a few short quotations, and a hundred-odd phrases and lines, Alcaeus in hardly enough lines to be worth adding up. Today, thanks to the papyri, we have a genuine appreciation of the poetry of Alcaeus (and of his political career), while the number of long selections from Sappho has more than doubled.

Another example, that of Menander, takes us from the realm of fragments to a complete work. An Athenian born in 342 or 341 B.C., Menander was the creator of so-called New Comedy, and its greatest artist. The availability of his plays in the original can be traced into the sixth or seventh century before the trail dies. Latin adaptations by Plautus and Terence of at least eight of his plays still exist, but the question remains controversial as to how close to the original they are. We also have the usual ragbag of quotations, particularly misleading in this case because they reflect the narrow interests of the two main anthologists—food and drink for the one, moral uplift for the other. Then, at the beginning of this century, longer sections of three of Menander's mature works were discovered on papyrus, and in the 1950s a complete play, the *Dyskolos* or *Misanthrope,* copied with considerable inaccuracy in a hand of about A.D. 300. This is an early play, produced in 316 B.C., and an inferior one. Yet one cannot carp: until the publication of the *Dyskolos* in 1959, Greek comedy had been really known to us only through the works of Aristophanes.[10] His genius does not lessen the importance of the new finds, introducing us directly as they do to the master of the later, extremely influential genre of New Comedy.[11]

My final example is of a different kind of book. Aristotle and his disciples, working as a research organization, produced short treatises on the "constitutions" of 158 states, Greek for the most part but a few of them "barbarian," such as Carthage. They became a quarry for later writers, for example, Plutarch, whose life of Lycurgus[12] drew heavily on the *Constitution of Sparta*. Eventually all 158 disappeared, save for the usual quotations, until the discovery of a papyrus, published early in 1891, of the complete *Constitution of Athens*, with only the first few chapters missing.[13] In seventy smallish pages (of modern print) the history was summarized first, and then the working of the Athenian government in Aristotle's own day was described in detail. No other work of its kind has come down from antiquity about the Greek world, and every modern account of Athens starts from there.

It need hardly be said that private records and letters as well as public documents were normally written on perishable materials, too, nor would they attract copyists in later ages unless they chanced to be quoted in a book, by a historian or an antiquarian. Happily, both the Greeks and the Romans inscribed certain types of document on durable material, usually stone, occasionally metal (the gold of the Pyrgi tablets being most exceptional), baked clay, or leather.[14] Boundary stones, tombstones, statue bases, helmets and other articles dedicated to gods, all commonly carried inscriptions—that is familiar enough to us—but the ancients went further and, to a degree unparalleled in other civilizations, employed inscriptions as a means of public notice for laws and decrees, treaties, public honors to individuals, financial statements, public leases and contracts, sacrificial calendars, and a variety of other activities. Practice was far from uniform: it was no accident, for example, that democratic Athens made extensive use of stone in this way, whereas oligarchic Corinth never did. Nor was there any uniformity in the length of time such inscriptions were allowed to stand. Inscriptions carved into the wall of a public building or temple would normally remain as long as the edifice itself, but most lost purpose in a matter of years. Besides, good stone was too valuable: it could be reinscribed, or it could be used in a pavement, a wall, or a cistern. With luck, the writing remains legible when and if an archaeologist recovers the stone two thousand or so years later.

By convention all such texts are known as "inscriptions," and they constitute the second subdivision of documents. By now, it would not surprise one if the number in Greek and Latin, plus a few bilinguals, runs to more than a hundred thousand, adding in the broken scraps and the names on tombstones along with the long major texts and everything in between. One example will give an idea of the tempo of new finds in this category. In 1933 the Clarendon Press published the first volume of *A Selection of Greek Historical Inscriptions*, edited with detailed commentary by Marcus N. Tod. That volume was limited to the earliest period, down to 400 B.C., during which the total number of known inscriptions is anyhow small. In 1969 a completely new selection was issued, on the same principles, edited by Russell Meiggs and David Lewis, with ninety-five documents (against Tod's ninety-six). Apart from different standards of selection, the many revised and corrected readings, and the vastly different commentaries, reflecting a generation of further study by scholars in many countries, the essential point for us is that the Meiggs-Lewis volume replaces seventeen inscriptions by sixteen texts that were unknown or unavailable when Tod prepared the first edition.

By their nature, even the longest inscriptions, considered individually, will be more limited in their appeal and in the significance of their contribution than the best of the literary papyri. However, there is one exception remarkable enough to merit special notice, though it is strictly speaking not a new find. When the first Roman emperor, Augustus, died in A.D. 14, he left among his papers an account of his stewardship during his forty-five-year reign. This document, occupying ten pages in modern print, was, on his instruction, inscribed on bronze tablets set up before his mausoleum in the city of Rome. The tomb and tablets have long since disappeared. What is surprising is that, though the original remained available in the imperial archives, and though its importance is obviously of a high order, there are only two references in the surviving literature of the Roman Empire, and not a single quotation. Outside Rome, the province of Galatia in Turkey received permission to repeat the text on a local monument, a temple to Augustus and Rome in the city of Ankara. The inscription is still standing, somewhat mutilated, written both in the original Latin and in a rough Greek translation (since Greek was the language of the eastern provinces). It was described by a number of European travelers from as far back as the year 1555, but the first publication was not until 1872. A generation ago, Greek fragments were also found in Antioch and in Apollonia, both in the district of Pisidia in southern Turkey. By a fortunate coincidence, all the gaps created by time in the Ankara text can now be filled in, so that with the publication of the latest finds in 1933 the complete *Res gestae* of Augustus is once more available to anyone who cares to read it.[15]

To consider even a sampling of the more important inscriptions and what has been learned from them, would involve us in a long, disjointed, and not very illuminating catalog. Essentially, there is nothing new about this aspect of classical studies, nothing fundamentally different from any other study of documents ever since historians, in every field, began to make use of them. What is really new and extraordinarily promising is the way "meaningless" inscriptions are now being forced to yield interesting information by a sort of statistical approach. In the purely linguistic field, that has been going on for a long time, simply because inscriptions provide detailed information about regional dialects, in Greek or in the Italic languages close to Latin, in a way that the polished literary language does not permit. In the study of institutions, however, scholars have been relatively slow to employ quantitative analysis, partly because the number of available inscriptions of any single type has first to be significant, but also because a new concept of archaeological research was needed (a point to which I shall return at the end of this section).

I begin with ostracism, that curious device employed in Athens on a number of occasions during the fifth century B.C. to remove a "dangerous" political leader by a ten-year exile, without loss of property or citizen rights (the consequences of penal exile, for example). Once a year there was a preliminary vote to decide whether or not there should be an ostracism that year. If the decision was in the affirmative, every citizen was invited to participate by handing in a broken bit of pottery (in Greek *ostrakon*) bearing the name of his candidate for exile. Provided the total number of "votes" cast reached six thousand, the man receiving the largest number was ostracized. Among the victims were such outstanding leaders as Aristides, Themistocles, and Cimon. This much was known, despite some uncertainties, from such writers as Herodotus, Thucydides, Aristotle (in the *Constitution of Athens*), and Plutarch. But somehow we had the picture askew from the literary sources, with their concentration on the great names and on picturesque stories. Excavations in Athens have so far turned up nearly two thousand ostraca, not at all interesting individually, just potsherds with names scratched on them, the kind of object that would have been discarded a century ago; 1,658 out of that number have been properly tabulated. Of these, 568 bear the name of Themistocles, which is accidental but not too surprising; next, with 263, comes Callixenus the son of Aristonymus, a man whose very existence had been unknown to us. He and the other unknowns who appear show that the "scatter vote" was far greater than the literary sources led historians to expect. One group of 191 ostraca found together, all with the name of Themistocles, clearly come from a single potter's stock and were inscribed by only 14 different hands. This lays to rest the traditional belief, expressed by Arnold W. Gomme in the *Oxford Classical Dictionary* (published in 1949 but largely written before the war), that "the name of the individual to be ostracized *was cut by the voters* on the ostraca" (my italics). On the contrary, with so much at stake, organized political factions carefully prepared for an ostracism, having the ostraca ready beforehand to pass round to prospective voters.[16]

Much more far-reaching in their implications were two studies published in 1952, one by J. V. A. Fine of Princeton, the other by myself, each of us working independently.[17] Our starting point was a group of inscribed stones from Athens known as *horoi,* many of them ordinary fieldstones roughly carved, which were posted on boundaries of farms or were set into the walls of houses, recording the fact that a piece of property was subject to a mortgage. A *horos* was originally just a boundary stone; thousands have been found throughout the Greek world, but this particular group represented a new, peculiarly Athenian practice of giving public notice about a legal encumbrance. At the time we were writing, 222 of them had been published, 182 in a sufficiently complete state

Red-figured Grecian vase; *c.* 475–465 B.C.

to be analyzed. They all seem to fall within the period 400–250 B.C., and they were all found within the territory of ancient Athens save for a few from four Aegean islands under Athenian influence. A longer-than-average text, translated literally with the addition in square brackets of words that do not appear on the stone, reads as follows:

> [*In the archonship*] *of Praxibulus* [*i.e. 315–314* B.C.]. *Horos of the land and house put up as security to Nikogenes of* [*the deme*] *Aixone, 420* [*drachmas*], *according to the agreement deposited with Chairedemos of* [*the deme*] *Rhamnus.*

Few of the stones have longer texts; most are shorter, for a date is given in only 27 or 28, a written agreement is mentioned in but 15, even the name of the creditor and the amount of the debt are sometimes omitted.

504

Thus, one marble block found in the city of Athens proper says merely: *"Horos* of a workshop put up as security, 750 [drachmas]"—three words and a numeral in the Greek.

No one will pretend that such texts are very informative. Nor do I claim that collectively they could lead to much understanding, not even by the most elaborate tabulation. However, when combined with the fragmentary information that had always been available, primarily in several court speeches by Demosthenes and others that have survived because of their literary interest, they enabled Fine and myself, in different ways, to throw new light on the Greek law of property and creditors' rights; on the emergence of a real estate market; on the shortage of liquid capital in the hands of richer landowners and the considerable indebtedness into which they could therefore be forced by social (rather than business) demands, such as expensive dowries for their daughters; on the financial activity of the many small private cult-associations that were a feature of Athenian life in this period. These may seem extravagant claims, given the unpromising nature of the stones, but the fact is that on the whole they have stood up to nearly twenty years of further study. And, with our imperfect knowledge of Greek law and economics, they are important claims.

My third and final example of this type of analysis pertains to a central development in the government of the Roman Empire—the creation of a civil service. Bureaucracy was a familiar institution in the older empires of the Near East, but it was long unknown to either Greeks or Romans (except where Alexander's successors took over Oriental monarchies, as in Egypt). They managed well enough with amateur administration, aided by a few clerks. But after Augustus put an end to the civil war that had riven Rome for decades, he needed a professional establishment to administer the stabilized empire. The top posts—provincial governors, legates, military commanders and the like—were reserved for the two highest "orders" or "estates," the senators and *equites.* For the rest Augustus turned to his own slaves and freedmen, and this group, the *familia Caesaris,* constituted the imperial civil service for the next two centuries. This much is well known and will be found in every history of Rome. The bald outline lacks vital, concrete detail, and it has been traditionally colored by the disdain with which the *familia Caesaris* is occasionally mentioned by Roman writers, a disdain that turned into savage hatred when, under Claudius and Nero, several freedmen attained personal positions of power and wealth at the very top of the ladder—this being attributed, naturally, to their ability to corrupt weak and debauched emperors.

The literary evidence is so meager that nothing new can be made of it, though one might have been a bit more suspicious of the picture of an empire not far short of two million square miles, with a population that reached perhaps sixty million, being run as if it were the Pasha-land of

Mozart's *Abduction from the Seraglio*. The only other source of information is again a group of brief inscriptions—tombstones recording in summary fashion the last post held, the marriages and children, and the age at death of members of the *familia Caesaris*. They have been found in various regions of the empire, though not equally distributed, and, as always with such documents, not all give the same information. Not even the age at death is always recorded; others are more detailed. Yet, thanks to the current work of one historian, P. R. C. Weaver, who has assembled the names of about four thousand individual slaves and freedmen of the emperors and analyzed every scrap of information possible about them, we now have a picture of this important Roman institution that adds a new dimension to our understanding of the hierarchical and status-ridden society of imperial Rome. Weaver has been able to show that the slave-freedman civil service had a regular bureaucratic hierarchy of its own, that promotion and status differed between the capital and the provinces, that the age at which the slaves were freed was closely linked with the posts they held, and that recruitment into the service was achieved by the surprising method of permitting, and probably encouraging, the men to take freeborn women as wives. Their children would nevertheless be slaves, automatically enter the *familia Caesaris,* and follow their father's careers if they were able enough. In this way much of the paper work of the empire was carried on successfully, though as a result there was created a dissonant segment within Roman society that added to the tensions when conflict arose between the emperor and the nobility.[18]

When we then turn from documents to objects, we find a parallel range of possibilities. At the one extreme there are such ruins as Mycenae, Pompeii, or the fourth-century Roman villa near Piazza Armerina in southern Sicily (with mosaic pavements that originally covered nearly an acre of floor space); and such individual works as the 4-foot bronze boy fished up from the Marathon Bay in 1925, or the unique bronze urn, 5 feet 4½ inches tall, of Greek manufacture of the sixth century B.C., discovered in 1953 in a Celtic grave at Vix near Châtillon-sur-Seine. They speak for themselves, in a sense; one can respond to them without lengthy commentaries. At the other extreme is the rubble that fills every archaeological site: pottery fragments, marble chips, twisted and corroded metal, food refuse. The practical question is where to draw the line beyond which the rubble is not worth studying. That line is not fixed. Specialists in the Stone Age have, of necessity, had to draw it near the lower end ever since the study of prehistory began, for the simple reason that they have little else to work with. Classical archaeologists, in contrast, have long permitted themselves the luxury of a different line, given the existence of books and documents, and the promise of new works of art to be found.[19]

Pyrgi symbolizes a new stage in the story. It required courage and dedication for Pallottino to set out on a lengthy excavation of Santa Severa.

506

Etruscan archaeology has been tomb archaeology: that is where the treasure lies, and no one knows how many thousands more remain to be explored. Most Etruscan cities are beyond reach because they have been continuously inhabited to this day. An exception such as San Giovenale, southwest of Viterbo, virtually deserted for some fifteen hundred years, produced miserable stuff and no treasure when a Swedish team excavated it. The gold tablets Pallottino found in Santa Severa were a bonus he could not have dreamed of—and was not looking for. He, like the archaeologists at San Giovenale, was posing questions about the life and history of the Etruscans that could not be answered from the tombs. All archaeology has been moving in this new direction in the past generation or so, the prehistorians perhaps more rapidly than the classicists, toward a greater interest in culture complexes as a whole, in the growth of communities and their institutions (including their economies), in their interrelations through trade, cultural interchange, migration, and war. New scientific techniques have helped, but so has the recognition that, when studied collectively, the most insignificant objects and documents acquire significance often greater than beautiful individual treasures. That seems to me to be the most important "new development" in this section of my subject, and that is why I have devoted so much space to it. One final, very simple example will serve to sum up the point.

For two hundred years, beginning about 550 b.c., Athens had a near monopoly in the production of fine painted pottery with human and mythological scenes, exported throughout the Greek world and to the Etruscans. This black- and red-figured ware is familiar in museums every-

Fragment of a Greek calendar (parapegma) found at Miletus

where. A number carry the signatures of the potters and painters, and starting from this basis, specialists led by Sir John Beazley have succeeded, through close stylistic analysis, in identifying the workshops in which virtually all known Athenian vases, jugs, cups, and plates originated (including the larger fragments). That was a remarkable accomplishment, enough to rest on for decades, until Robert M. Cook asked the question in the late 1950s (which appears so obvious in retrospect), What was the size of the Athenian fine pottery industry? His calculations, restricted to the red-figured ware, suggest that some 500 painters were active in the course of the fifth century B.C., or 125 in any one generation, and that the total work force in the trade was four times that number. Allow a fair margin for error, and these estimates are still a capital contribution to Greek economic history that could not have been squeezed out of any other source of information.[20] Contemporary Athenians would themselves not have known the precise totals.

Languages and scripts

A century ago Hittites were only a name, mentioned some dozen times in the Old Testament, distinguished from the Hivites or the Jebusites only because they supplied Esau and Solomon with wives, bought imported Egyptian horses from Solomon, and once helped the Israelites in a war against the Syrians. They began to emerge as a great nation in the last quarter of the nineteenth century with the identification of some of their monuments and their appearance in recently discovered Egyptian documents. In 1906 the German Orient Society started to excavate their capital at Bogazkoy in central Turkey and promptly found the royal archives. Decipherment went on during and immediately after the First World War, and by 1933 a serious account could be published of their history and civilization.[21]

The recovery of lost worlds has been one of the great intellectual achievements of the nineteenth and twentieth centuries, in which the archaeologist was joined by the decipherer in providing the basic raw materials—starting with Georg Grotefend's (neglected) paper of 1802 on the cuneiform script and Jean François Champollion's letter to the Academy of Paris in 1822 announcing his decipherment of Egyptian hieroglyphics.[22] There is now little that is wholly undeciphered in Europe and western Asia, and that little is represented by a tiny number of texts, most of them very short. However, room for progress is greater than we like to admit, and it is necessary to consider why that should be the case.

To begin with, the word *decipherment* covers a variety of rather distinct operations, or at least situations. There is first the case of Egyptian and Sumerian, in which both the language and the script were unknown at the start. Then there is Etruscan, an unknown language written in a well-known script (borrowed from the Greek). And the Linear B or Cypriot type explained below, a known language (Greek) in an unknown script. Cutting across all three there is the further distinction between a language belonging to a known "family" and one with no apparent connections. Indo-European Hittite and Semitic Babylonian or Assyrian are examples of the former, Etruscan and Sumerian of the latter. Hence Sumerian is much less perfectly understood than Babylonian, though both were written in the same cuneiform (wedge-shaped) script; so, too, Etruscan remains a major problem, as indicated at the beginning. There is finally the distinction based on the volume and nature of documentation: the chance of a complete decipherment increases with the number of individual texts and the amount of continuous writing they contain. An endless succession of short formulas, as in Etruscan or Linear A and B, leads to early frustration.

If that were all, one could draw up a simple correlation table and express the state of a decipherment and the prognosis in simple mathematical terms, barring future discovery of material of a new kind in any given language or script. What upsets the pattern is the fact that languages have a social history, too. The syntax, morphology, and phonetics of ancient Egyptian are better known than one might imagine from the number of question marks that still disfigure every translation of a hieroglyphic document (and still more so of a late Egyptian development, the rapid script known as *demotic*). Nor is it a weakness in grammar that leads to so much divergence among translators of the Hittite law code found in Bogazkoy. These were distant and alien societies, and we need to decipher their social structures and their values as much as their scripts. Had they produced a Thucydides, an Aristotle, or a Cicero, we should have clues and controls we now lack.

Much of the achievement, it will be noticed, touches the Greeks and Romans rather lightly; the recovery of lost worlds affects our knowledge of the classical world chiefly at or even before its dawn, and soon the Greeks and Romans were themselves the agents who drove the competing languages out of existence—in Europe below the Rhine-Danube line, in western Asia (except for Hebrew and Aramaic), in much of northern Africa. The major writing systems were invented outside, too, and the last of them, the Phoenician alphabet, passed to the Greeks about 750 B.C., from them to the Etruscans and Romans, and in time to most of the world. None of this is surprising: the need for writing was felt very much earlier in Mesopotamia and Egypt than elsewhere, for bureaucratic record-keeping (not literary) reasons, and then the superiority of the alphabet over pictographic and syllabic systems assured a monopoly. What is a puzzle is the exception of Crete, where at least three different, though relatively short-lived, scripts were created. First, perhaps before

2000 B.C., came a modified picture writing which Sir Arthur Evans labeled "hieroglyphic" on the analogy of the Egyptian script. There then emerged a more sophisticated script, called *Linear A* by Evans, in which most of the signs represented syllables. That gave way, in turn, to an outgrowth called *Linear B* (before 1500 B.C.), and it was diffused for a time to the mainland of Greece.[23]

These particular scripts offer a classic instance of the difficulties of decipherment when the documents are short and formulaic. Apart from signs engraved or scratched on seal stones, pottery, and miscellaneous objects, Linear A and B are known to us in bulk only from small, leaf-shaped clay tablets, a few hundred written in Linear A, several thousand in Linear B. No doubt perishable materials were also used, but we have no trace of them, and even the clay tablets have survived by accident. They were palace records (or lists) of property relationships, stocks of goods on hand, ration allocations, and the like, not meant to be kept for long periods and therefore inscribed on unbaked clay. Only the conflagrations that accompanied the destruction of the great palaces at Cnossus in Crete, Mycenae and Pylos in Greece, preserved whatever inscribed tablets happened to be on hand at the moment. Neither the hieroglyphic script nor Linear A has been deciphered, despite several claims to the contrary, and it seems likely that the language of those tablets, certainly not Greek, is not any known tongue. The suggestion that it is a Semitic language, among others, has found little support. The Linear B tablets, however, turn out to have been written in an early form of Greek, and the announcement in 1953 of their decipherment by Michael Ventris is the last great chapter in the story that began in 1802.[24] Further progress has been disappointingly slight (and a few scholars still refuse to accept the decipherment): there are, for example, too many words on the tablets that still cannot be reasonably shown to be Greek.[25] Nevertheless, the importance of Ventris's discovery for our knowledge of Bronze Age Greece cannot be overstated, though to go into that subject would take us outside the scope of this survey.[26]

The employment of the Cretan scripts was so closely and narrowly geared to the administrative needs of the palace-dominated society that, when that society was destroyed about 1200 B.C., the art of writing disappeared from both Crete and Greece. Only on the island of Cyprus was there a curious survival. There Greek was written as late as the fourth century B.C. in a syllabic script that included seven signs from Linear B and others that were modifications of that otherwise long-extinct script. Not only is the phenomenon itself an imperfectly understood puzzle, but the texts cannot be read with certainty.

In Greece proper when the art of writing returned, some four hundred or more years after the end of the palace society, it was in the new alphabetic form, and it found new uses—the writing of poetry, for one.

Literature: the spoken and written word

Plutarch relates that when an Athenian expeditionary force in Sicily was captured at Syracuse in 413 B.C., some prisoners were set free because they could recite by heart choruses from the plays of Euripides, "whose poetry, it appears, was in request among the Sicilians more than among any of the settlers out of Greece."[27] The story may or may not be true, but it is absolutely right. The Greeks were the first really literate people in history. That is to say, in all the more advanced, more urbanized regions of the Greek world (and of the Roman world), a majority, probably a large majority, of the males knew how to read and write.[28] This was not the case with the ancient Near Eastern peoples, as is shown by the high standing of the class of scribes among them, a class that simply did not exist in the Greco-Roman world. Paradoxically, it is correct at the same time to insist that Greek and Roman culture was as much one of the spoken word as of the written (and in some contexts more). That is the lesson of Plutarch's anecdote. Syracuse was a civilized, cosmopolitan city; no doubt copies of the plays of Euripides were available there, but the average Syracusan depended on their transmission by word of mouth. In Athens itself, where these plays originated, for every man who read a tragedy there were tens of thousands who knew the tragedies from performing in them or from hearing them. Lyric poetry acquired its very name from the fact that the poems were written to be sung to a stringed accompaniment, normally on ceremonial occasions—a wedding, a religious festival, a military celebration—and often by choruses rather than by individuals. Even the earliest political writings, those of Solon, and philosophical writings as late as the fifth century B.C. were in poetic form, partly at least because that facilitated memorization. Books, Plato said, are not to be trusted: they cannot be questioned, and therefore their ideas are closed to correction and further refinement; besides, they weaken the memory.[29]

Plato himself wrote books, to be sure, but he usually cast them in the form of "dialogues"—more precisely, of conversations, and very dramatic ones, in which real people argued, joked, cheated a bit, became angry. Oratory rapidly developed into a major art form in its own right, and rhetoric dominated higher education from the time Isocrates founded his school in Athens in the fourth century B.C. to the end of antiquity.[30] Orations were a feature of the Olympic Games and other such festivals; cities hired famous orators to honor them with an example of their art; Roman emperors patronized them: Marcus Aurelius endowed a chair of rhetoric in Athens. Oratorical skill was essential for a political career. Demosthenes and Cicero made their way into the political elite that way; their speeches were published, assessed, and criticized not merely as *political* speeches but as high literature. In their turn, historians, reflecting the realities and values of their time, interlarded their narrative with carefully composed speeches.

Closely linked was the public character of literature, thematically and institutionally. Thus, throughout the fifth and fourth centuries B.C., the classical period in Greece, it was almost the case that no one wrote a poem about love or any other private theme. That had been common among lyric poets from about 650 to 500 B.C., and then it ceased as if by fiat. In Rome we have to come down to Catullus for the first personal poetry; even the Roman writers of comedy on the model of Greek New Comedy, though they dealt with caricatured personal situations, were filled with ethical and social observations and lessons. What dominated choral odes or tragedy or prose (history and oratory) were religion, mythology, ethics, public affairs, war, politics, and humanity. Appropriately enough, the state itself was the chief patron of the arts, either through the numerous religious festivals or through imperial patronage in the periods when there were emperors.

Nothing I have said so far in this section is in the least new—except for the stress.[31] Formal classical study since the mid-nineteenth century was until recently dominated by the concept of *paideia,* intellectual and moral formation for life, for the life of an intellectual and social elite. (Scottish universities still have Departments of Humanity, elsewhere known as Departments of Latin.) That concept not only determined the selection of authors to be studied—Thomas Arnold at Rugby could not bring himself to read Aristophanes until he had reached the age of forty, found the tragedians overrated, Petronius unmentionable—but also led to basic misjudgments about the Greeks and Romans themselves. One misjudgment arose from a sort of evolutionary scheme, in which the introduction of literacy was regarded as symbolizing the movement from barbarism toward the life of reason, with the corollary that what really mattered appeared in books, in some books, especially the more highminded among them.

No one wishes to deny the significance of literacy, nor the legitimacy of selection, whether for reasons of *paideia* or for some other purpose. But it has become clear, at least to some of us, that such narrow focusing on one facet of Greco-Roman civilization is the wrong way to understand that civilization *in its own terms.* A world that relies as much on the spoken word as did the ancients will, for example, have a different view of its own past or of its religion from one that transmits such ideas primarily through books (let alone the Book). It cannot have the same canons of truth and falsity, orthodoxy and heresy, when the controls are one man's "memory" against another's. It cannot recover lost information about the past, except by inventing it. It can neither compose nor respond to poetry in the "individual" way familiar in the age of printed books—in the age, that is, in which the scholars who study the Greeks and Romans themselves live.

By far the outstanding example of a modern revaluation in this respect s the unique, and therefore unfair, one of Homer. "By the general con-sent of critics," wrote Dr. Johnson in his life of Milton, "the first praise of genius is due to the writer of an epic poem, as it requires an assemblage of all the powers which are singly sufficient for other compositions." Milton's *Paradise Lost,* he concluded, "is not the greatest of heroic poems, only because it is not the first," a place preempted by Homer, whom the Greeks themselves referred to simply as "the poet." Since Johnson's day an occasional voice has remarked on the puzzling fact that the earliest works in European literature, and particularly the *Iliad,* are of such towering genius. By and large however, that question was dismissed— how can one ever explain genius?—and critics, assuming that Homer was the first in the line of poets that includes Virgil, Dante, and Milton, examined, dissected, and criticized him in the same way.[32]

One of the central problems in Homeric criticism is the amount of rep-etition in the poems. The coming of day is nearly always "And when rosy-fingered dawn appeared, the child of morn." Athena is "owl-eyed," the island of Ithaca "sea-girt," Achilles "city-sacking." When a verbal message is sent (and messages in Homer are never in writing), the poet has the messenger hear the exact text and then repeat it to the recipient word for word. How do we explain this practice? The answer was given by Mil-man Parry in the late 1920s and early 1930s, first by an elaborate analysis of the two poems and then by extensive fieldwork among living bards in Yugoslavia. This is the technique, he demonstrated conclusively, of oral poetry, composed by illiterate bards during actual performance before an audience. The formulaic language serves like building blocks: about one-third of the *Iliad* consists of lines or blocks of lines that occur more than once in the work. The first twenty-five lines alone have some twenty-five formulaic expressions (or fragments of formulas). Yet this is no simple monotonous repetition: there are thirty-six different epithets for Achilles, and the choice is rigorously determined by the position in the line and the required syntactical form. These formulas were developed and modified, and a stock of heroic incidents and tales built up, during the centuries when not only the bards were illiterate but the whole society (which was not the case with the Yugoslavs). Homer came at the end of a long tradi-tion. After him, the more creative talents turned to other kinds of poetry, behind which there was also an oral tradition, though a different one.[33]

None of this explains the genius of Homer. One question, in particular, is currently the subject of considerable controversy. How could the *Iliad* and *Odyssey,* some sixteen thousand and twelve thousand lines long, re-spectively, each with an intricate and coherent structure, have been com-posed and transmitted orally? For me the reasonable answer is that each is the work of a poet who not only had a long tradition behind him but who also had the newly acquired (or reacquired) art of writing available to him.[34] Even so, the *Iliad* and *Odyssey* must be located, and therefore studied, with oral "heroic" poetry—a genre independently developed in many parts of the world—and not, as Dr. Johnson did, with Virgil or Milton. When Virgil sat down to compose the *Aeneid,* he had on his desk books of poetry, the *Iliad* and Greek tragedy among them; he was a man of learning surrounded by literate and learned friends and patrons; he could check and recheck, borrow and modify patiently, avoid "structural anomalies," inconsistencies in details, misplaced epithets, and all the "faults" that have distressed generations of Homeric scholars working from a fundamental misconception of the nature of the two poems. Nor is it only the literary quality of the *Iliad* and *Odyssey* that requires total reexamination after Milman Parry. The society in which they were created, the long "Dark Age" between the destruction of the Mycenaean world and the emergence of a new kind of Greek society in the eighth century B.C., has to be reassessed as well, in its institutions, its values and beliefs, its poetry.[35]

The very fact that Virgil wrote the *Aeneid* as late as the end of the pre-Christian era, I should add, is the consequence of the fact that the Romans produced no heroic poetry of their own in their preliterate period. They of course had their traditions, transmitted orally from generation to generation, and they had their singers of songs and tales. But it was a different tradition, as we can see in the largely fictionalized version in Virgil's contemporary, the historian Livy, culminating in the struggle for independence from the Etruscans. By then both Etruscans and Romans were at least partially literate, and much influenced by the Greeks intellectually and culturally, as they continued to be for centuries thereafter. To fix the relative time scales, it should be enough to note that when Rome achieved her independence, Sappho had been dead for nearly a century, Aeschylus was in his teens.

For all practical purposes, Aeschylus was the inventor of the drama. Even if Aristotle should prove not to be right in asserting that Aeschylus introduced the second actor into tragedy,[36] his *Persians* (472 B.C.) is the earliest play ever written that still survives. And we are at once plunged into a very complex problem, on which Frank R. Leavis has laid so much stress in English literature. Put succinctly, it is this: we cannot read Aeschylus as we can read Shakespeare, and we cannot read Aeschylus as if Shakespeare did not exist. Obvious as that may appear, it is remarkable how difficult the struggle still is to avoid sliding into "modernization" of the ancients, into reading and interpreting them as if they were near contemporaries, almost as familiar with our accepted conventions (of drama, for example) as we are. In an article on "Inconsistency of Plot and Character in Aeschylus," published in 1963, R. D. Dawe opened with a brutal protest:

> *The plays of Aeschylus contain many contradictions, and much recent criticism of the dramatic technique of this author has been*

514

directed at attempts to extract from these contradictions a unified picture of what the poet really intended us to understand in the case of each particular play.... All this may seem entirely praiseworthy; and yet, as we come to read more and more of these books and articles, the sensation may grow upon some of us that we are not so much learning about Aeschylus as witnessing the transactions of a private club.... Although the members of this club are willing to challenge each others' viewpoints, they are all agreed that no gentleman would venture to call in question the one great assumption that underlies all their discussions: namely that Aeschylus could not possibly have constructed plays in which such contradictions were deliberately intended; and only seldom can he be allowed to have contradicted himself by oversight.[37]

In a long and persuasive analysis, Dawe proceeded to demonstrate that the "inconsistencies" normally disappear when one considers only individual scenes, written for performance before a live audience under the "abnormal" conditions of an Athenian religious festival. The intent is deliberately to create a certain effect, for example, to lead the audience to anticipate something which then does not happen, or to plunge the audience into confusion, or to achieve some other dramatic objective. In the leisure of his study, a scholar (or any attentive reader) soon enough discovers the "inconsistencies," and he objects. He will not allow the poet, in Dawe's words, to "sacrifice consistency in order to purchase greater effectiveness in the individual scene."

Up to a point this is no more than the danger, familiar to all literary scholarship (witness that of Shakespeare), of living with a work or an author until one forgets that plays were written to be performed, to be heard and not read; and one forgets that great poets (or historians) are not necessarily, even not probably, systematic thinkers. But there is more to it. For us it is almost axiomatic that consistency and development of character are a necessary and major ingredient in plays and novels, so axiomatic that there is insufficient appreciation of the fact that our idea of character, our psychology, is radically different from the ancient Greek. Aeschylus could portray an inconsistent Agamemnon in the play of the same name without giving it a second thought. It is not even possible to answer definitively the question, Was Aeschylus' Agamemnon a good man or not? Impossible in a play which by universal consent is one of the greatest masterpieces in world literature! And Agamemnon, at least, was recognizably a tragic hero, which Oedipus was not. Indeed, we now know that the tragic hero, who has mesmerized critics of Greek tragedy for centuries, ever since he was wrongly attributed to Aristotle in the *Poetics*, is nothing but a hindrance to the understanding of tragedy. Oedipus was the central figure in more than one Greek play, but he was

515

no hero except in the most strained sense of that word. He committed no moral fault and had no "moral flaw." He was doomed before he was born, and nothing he could do, flawed or unflawed, could forestall the workings of fate.[38]

In my view, probably a minority view, stripping away the anachronisms imposed over the centuries is one of the more urgent tasks not only in classical literary study but in all classical study.[39] That requires great effort of the imagination, and the results are bound to be limited: not only are there the limits set up by the interposition of Shakespeare, to return to that example, but also those imposed by the alienness of much in the system of values. Consider Oedipus again. The audience that first saw and heard Sophocles' *Oedipus the King* had not just "taken in a show"; they were participants in a great public religious festival, at which the god himself was present and received the preliminary sacrifices. The starting point is an oracle warning King Laius of Thebes that his unborn son, Oedipus, would one day kill him and marry his widow (Oedipus' own mother). Do we believe in the oracle, in the strict sense of that verb? The audience did, and so did Sophocles. No evasion such as "dramatic device" will do. Midway through the play, the chorus of Theban elders says:

> *The old prophecies concerning Laius are fading; already men are setting them at nought, and nowhere is Apollo glorified with honors; the worship of the gods is perishing.*[40]

"Worship is perishing" not because of revulsion against a god who decreed such a terrible fate for a child still unborn but, on the contrary, because what a god had prophesied seemed not to be fulfilled; worse, seemed to have been successfully thwarted by human artifice. No wonder John Jones, who rightly insists that "we should allow them to mean what they say," finds it all "desperately foreign." We "know nothing," he continues, "in the least" like the "bottomless, relativistic insecurity" of the Sophoclean faith. "There can be no contact between Christianity or individualistic humanism and a cosmic Mutability which averages out rather as the weather does. And because no contact, no experience of Mutability's compensating application to this or that man's singular fate."[41]

Not all Greeks shared Sophocles' cool acceptance of such a value system. Greek intellectual history is one of conflict and struggle, not rarely within a single artist or thinker. But the struggle cannot be understood until we fully acknowledge both sides. "Euripides the rationalist," as he was once unhappily labeled, also wrote the *Bacchae* at the end of his life, a powerful and terrible demonstration of the perils of resistance to maenadic ecstasy and other "irrational" drives. One must accept the coexistence of "mythical" and "tragic" and "rational" modes of thought, some-

516

times in separate compartments, sometimes overlapping, sometimes in brutal conflict. Yet experience has shown that this is far from easy: there is a strong pull, at least among scholars, toward what they conceive to be "rational." When Eric R. Dodds published his fundamental *The Greeks and the Irrational* in 1951,[42] he turned for support and guidance to modern anthropology on shamanism and other taboo topics. In his Preface he wrote:

> *To my fellow-professionals I perhaps owe some defence. . . . In a world of specialists, such borrowings from unfamiliar disciplines are, I know, generally received by the learned with apprehension, and often with active distaste. I expect to be reminded, in the first place, that "the Greeks were not savages," and secondly, that in these relatively new studies the accepted truths of today are apt to become the discarded errors of tomorrow. Both statements are correct. But . . . why should we attribute to the ancient Greeks an immunity from "primitive" modes of thought which we do not find in any society open to our direct observation?*

There, I suggest, is the justification for the view I have expressed of what is one of our most urgent tasks in classical studies.

If, it is then legitimate to ask, Greek tragedy (by way of example) is "desperately foreign," how is it able to arouse in a modern audience "pity and fear, wherewith to accomplish its catharsis of such emotions," to quote from Aristotle's definition of tragedy?[43] No simple answer is available—this is in fact one of the most difficult questions in the history of art—and I shall not attempt one here beyond repeating the commonplace that there are several levels of response to a work of art. What I want to look at for a moment is one particular aspect of the broad question, and that is the special and inescapable problem of translation, which has its own history. In antiquity there was no "problem." That is to say, translations were made as a matter of course. We have already seen how Roman comedy was founded on avowed, if free, translations. Cicero translated several Greek works including Plato's *Timaeus*. The Renaissance translated like mad in all countries,[44] not always with the insouciance of one of the most influential Tudor translators, Sir Thomas North, whose *Plutarch* (without which we should not have had Shakespeare's *Julius Caesar, Antony and Cleopatra,* or *Coriolanus*), was based not on the Greek original but on Jacques Amyot's French translation. Dr. Johnson, no respecter of dilettantism, never read the whole of the *Odyssey* in the original; he also defended Pope's *Iliad* despite its free rendering. Another Homer translation, Chapman's, evoked a beautiful sonnet by Keats. Then, somehow, pedantry seized control, summed up in that wicked Italian pun, *traduttore traditore* ("to translate is to betray"); translations were labeled cribs (and too many began to read like cribs). More precisely, translations from Greek and Latin (and perhaps French) were

517

The Dead Sea Scrolls

"Dead Sea Scrolls" is a rather broad term referring to the groups of leather manuscripts and papyri discovered in caves and ancient ruins near the Dead Sea and the Wilderness of Judaea. Numerous documents, found in eleven caves in the vicinity of Khirbet Qumran, turned up evidence about an ancient Jewish sect that flourished there. These scrolls date from as far back as the third and early second centuries B.C., up to the first century of the Christian era. (Above) Fragments of papyrus discovered in a cave some one thousand feet above the Dead Sea; (above, center) manuscript roll, found near the Dead Sea in 1947, from which a page shedding new light on the Old Testament was separated; (above, far right) fragments of a blessing that was appended to the rules of the community; (below) the documents, from left, are three relatively well-preserved scrolls: "manual of discipline," Book of Isaiah fragment, and commentary on the prophet Habakkuk.

denigrated, while the same pedants, if they were also cultured, read their Ibsen and their Dostoevsky but not in Norwegian or Russian.

Cribs, let it be said, have a legitimate function, but it is not the function of a genuine translation. "Coming after the original," wrote Walter Benjamin, "translation makes for significant works, which never find their proper translator in the era of their creation, the stage of their continuing life." The word *continuing* needs underscoring. "Translation," Benjamin added, "is far removed from being the deaf, inert equation of two dead tongues. Translation is among all communicative modes, the one most concerned to mark the ripening process in a foreign language and the pulse of changing life in its own."[45] Just as every age must rewrite history, so it must make its own translations.

Myth and religion

In the second half of the sixth century B.C., the Greek philosopher Xenophanes protested that "Homer and Hesiod have attributed to the gods everything that is a shame and reproach among men, stealing and committing adultery and deceiving each other." In a loose way, that remark may be considered the beginning of the discussion, which still goes on and is indeed now more lively than ever, of the problem of myth. It is almost impossible to read an ancient author without coming across mythical elements. Not only did myths provide most of the themes for the tragedians, or for such poets as the Greek Pindar and the Roman Ovid, but they were frequently quoted by public orators and by the most austere philosophers in order to illuminate one point or another. Beyond that, Greek and Roman myths are so worked into the fabric of Western literature that Oedipus, Orestes, Jason, Aeneas are known to every literate person.

Myths, legends, and folktales are hard to define and distinguish (leaving aside fables of the type associated with the name of Aesop). They share certain elements: they are all narratives, they are supposed to have occurred in the past (usually no more clearly dated than "once upon a time"), and they have a strong touch of fantasy, of the impossible. However, we can separate myth from the others by a rough rule of thumb: it usually involves gods or other supernatural beings (though it need not be a story *about* gods), it frequently deals with origins (Prometheus and the use of fire, the Tower of Babel and the diversity of languages among the descendants of a common ancestor, the rape of Persephone and the foundation of the cult of Demeter at Eleusis near Athens), it tends to involve reversal of fortune (Oedipus) or physical transformation.

Almost to the end of the nineteenth century, the study of myth was concentrated on the Greeks, and secondarily on the Romans (whose stock of genuine original myths, as distinct from historical legends, is poor). That is easily explicable from the predominance of these myths in Western culture, but the result of this narrow concern was disastrous for at least two reasons. The first was the barrier set up by the insistence that "the Greeks were not savages." Myths were explained away as allegories (a game everyone can play, since there are no rules and no controls, and which was already played by sophisticated intellectuals in antiquity); or they were explained by fantastic theories, each short-lived and none worth repeating now. The second weakness was a failure to appreciate how distorted Greek myths are as we know them, through the trick lenses of great literature.[46] One obvious fact, at least, should have put students on their guard: the freedom with which myths were changed about. The ending of Aeschylus' *Eumenides,* the closing play in the Orestes trilogy, is a blatant invention by the playwright, reflecting on political developments in Athens at the time of writing. Or one may compare the fundamentally different ways in which Aeschylus, Sophocles, and Euripides deal with the story of Orestes and his sister Electra in three surviving plays.* Or, to turn to Rome, there is the untidy way the Aeneas myth (which is legend as well as myth) is woven into the Romulus myth about the foundation of Rome.

There was no hope for serious advance until anthropologists began direct observation of myth in action, as it was repeated and as it functioned among the preliterate "primitive" peoples still inhabiting parts of the Americas, Asia, Africa, and Australia. Archaeology also made its contribution with the rediscovery of the rich mythology of the Sumerians, Babylonians, and other ancient Near Eastern people, who were literate like the Greeks but who still retained a less distorted, less "sophisticated" store of myths. With this new body of raw material available, the problem of myth was raised to a new level of analysis, though it can hardly be said that anything like agreement has been reached. A recent survey has classified modern theories of myth into seven main types, and, since their proponents tend each to think of his theory as the only correct one, the seven become mutually exclusive.[47] Three are familiar outside specialist circles. One of these, most closely associated with Sir James George Frazer and his *Golden Bough,* is that all myths are attached to rituals. The weakness is that although some myths are thus attached, many are demonstrably not, despite desperate efforts to establish a connection. This theory is no longer seriously held as a general explanation, except, for some curious reason, among specialists in ancient Near Eastern myths.[48] The second is the psychoanalytic theory, or rather theories, as they diverge into two main streams, the Freudian and the Jungian, and from there into smaller branches. The popular model of the myth as an

---

* *GBWW,* Vol. 5, pp. 70–80, 156–69, 327–39.

expression of the unconscious is, of course, the Oedipus complex. Finally, and most recently, there is the subtle, complex, and difficult "structuralist" theory of Claude Lévi-Strauss: myth is a symbolic language which "mediates" the contradictions or opposites in human experience. One of the most important opposites for Lévi-Strauss is that between nature and culture, the point to the title of one of his major books, *Le cru et le cuit* [The raw and the cooked] (1964).[49] In place of Freud's Oedipus complex, we have the contradiction between nature's tolerance of incest and the cultural taboo against it, a point already noticed in antiquity, though in a very different context—for example, by Diogenes.[50]

The way out of these conflicting theories that seems to be emerging is a recognition that myths have different functions, that even a single myth often has more than a single function. Some myths do explain rituals: the example of the Demeter cult at Eleusis has already been mentioned. Others are "charters" (a term coined by the anthropologist Bronislaw Malinowski) giving sanction to authority, social order, rules and laws, ceremonies, and beliefs. Many of the symbols repeat themselves in dreams and are so universal that the psychoanalysts have a strong case. And the intricate myth-structures of Lévi-Strauss do sometimes appear without undue forcing of evidence. We are finally coming to realize that there is an intellectual, even speculative, side to many myths, that the narrative is in some ways an explanation; in other words, that there is a "mythical mode of thought" among Greeks as among "savages" for all the profound differences between them.

However *we* explain the phenomenon of myth, the point that must never be lost sight of is that myths were believed to be true. Otherwise a myth has little value or function (the example of the oracle about Oedipus has already been mentioned). This concrete quality of ancient religion, the tendency to answer questions about origins, rituals, even natural phenomena and beliefs—by a narrative involving gods and goddesses, either directly or indirectly, is very striking. The changes in the pantheon mentioned at the beginning of this essay normally took the form of yet another story, how Apollo came to Delphi or Heracles swam the Strait of Messina and wandered across Sicily. Neither the skepticism of Xenophanes and later philosophers nor the (to us) irreverent jokes of Aristophanes or Lucian about the gods invalidate the general formulation.

The skepticism of the few had its limits. There were no atheists in antiquity; the word *atheist,* which comes from the Greek, meant someone who does not accept the conventional, official religion of his society. Even Epicurus, whose name became the Hebrew word for *atheist,* did not deny the existence of the gods; he denied only that they concerned themselves with, and intervened in, man's daily affairs. That was shocking enough, for it was very rare, in all circles including the most advanced intellectual ones, to disbelieve in the techniques by which the will of the gods could be divined or in the efficacy of sacrifice. Socrates' last words were, "Crito, I owe a cock to Asclepius; will you remember to pay the debt?"[51] Asclepius was the healer god, into whose temples men went to be cured while asleep, in gratitude for which they then dedicated models of the diseased parts of their bodies. His worship was introduced in Athens at the time of the great plague of 430–426 B.C. One of the god's sacred snakes was brought from Epidaurus in the Peloponnese in solemn procession. Until a proper temple could be erected, the snake was housed and an altar was provided for it by the playwright Sophocles. Greco-Roman religion, in sum, did not divide neatly and simply, as modern "rational" accounts often tend to suggest, into "rational theology" and "popular superstition."[52]

One consequence of the concreteness of religion, with its stress on life on earth rather than on salvation and the hereafter, with its extreme localization, its profusion of myths and rituals, and with the absence of an organized, authoritative "church," was a wide measure of tolerance. Since there was not (and could not be) anything one could call orthodoxy, there was also no heresy. Tolerance ended only at the point where there was suspicion of blasphemy, of an act which openly flouted the gods. There were two closely related reasons for drawing that line: angry gods might, and sometimes did, take revenge on the whole community, not just on the individual; besides, the community felt itself flouted. Cases of persecution for ideas about the gods, as distinct from actions, were rare; the notoriety of the trial of Socrates, charged with "not believing in the gods in which the city believes," should not lead to a false generalization on this score.[53] Ironically, his admiring pupil Plato, in his last work, the *Laws*, in effect took up the position of the state against Socrates, when he proposed severe punishment for impiety "in word or deed," culminating in the death penalty for recidivists.[54] This was not the only one of Plato's ideas that did not become common practice.

The greatest test came in the Roman Empire, with its vast agglomeration of peoples and therefore of religious ideas and practices. As a matter of policy, the imperial state went to considerable lengths not to interfere, unless there was deemed to be a political (subversive) threat, most notably in the revolt of Judaea in A.D. 66–70. But then, Jews and Christians stood outside the whole Greco-Roman tradition. For them, there was true belief and false belief, so that conversion involved not the normal polytheistic accumulation of divinities but rejection of all others.[55] For complicated reasons the Roman state was able to accept, though it did not particularly like, Jewish exclusiveness; it would not accept Christian exclusiveness.

If myths with their sacral element could be believed, there was of course no difficulty in accepting the secular, often "historical" legends. The Trojan War provides the elementary example. Xenophanes started a line of doubt about the morality of the Homeric poems, but no one extended that skepticism to the narrative. Even the hardheaded historian

Thucydides, who thought that only contemporary history was really knowable and who warned his readers to turn elsewhere if they wished "romance,"[56] accepted without question the basic historicity of the *Iliad*.[57] And so throughout antiquity, with Jason and the Argonauts in their search for the golden fleece, the Seven against Thebes, the coming of Aeneas to Rome from Troy, Horatius at the bridge, and the rest of the long list.

What are *we* to make of these tales? That has been a bitterly disputed question since the beginning of the nineteenth century, and it remains so today. Psychologically, it is difficult to assign to the realm of fantasy some of the best-known characters and tales in the Western cultural tradition, all the more so for those periods of antiquity for which there is otherwise so little evidence or none at all. Nor is it easy to produce decisive arguments on either side of the debate. Again the Trojan War will serve as the first example. No one disputes the presence of much impossible and contradictory material in the Homeric poems, even on the strictly human side without reference to the continuous divine interventions. On the other hand, enough remains that is plausible, and the question is then simply, How can we know whether the plausible is in fact true? It need not be; after all, every good novel is plausible. Archaeology has contributed less than is commonly believed. Heinrich Schliemann found a place that roughly corresponds to what could be Troy, and the city he found was repeatedly destroyed, once at a date, about 1200 B.C., which coincides with the end of the Mycenaean period. However, nothing in the archaeological record informs us who the destroyers were, and that is of course crucial for a control over the Homeric tale of a great mainland coalition led by Agamemnon. For early Rome, as a second example, archaeology has done a bit better: it has supported the tradition that Rome was once under Etruscan domination and that it broke free about 500 B.C. But no more, nor can we expect archaeology to throw light one way or another on the massive detail that appears in Livy, neither the names of the kings nor the story of the rape of Lucretia nor anything else in that category. As with Troy, much of the tradition is impossible, some is plausible, and beyond that we cannot go except on subjective arguments.[58] In particular, it is poor logic to maintain that because a kernel of demonstrable fact has been discovered in one legend, there must be a similar kernel in every other legend.

Nor should we deny the Greeks and Romans as much imaginative power as we have. The novel as an art form was unknown to them until near the end, and then only in a very rudimentary sense. That implies not a lack of creative imagination but its divergence into other channels. To hold, as some do, that the Jason story is a mythical cover for hard reality —the metal trade with the Near East—is unnecessary, unprovable, and a denigration of Greek powers of invention. So is the supposed historical background to the story of Daedalus, the master craftsman who made wings with which he and his son Icarus fled from Minos, king of Crete. Icarus flew too close to the sun and died, but Daedalus landed in Sicily and entered the service of King Kokalos there. Minos came after him with an army and was routed by Kokalos. This tale, some historians believe, has behind it the colonization of Sicily in the Bronze Age (not later than 1500 B.C.) by "Minoan" Crete, and they continue to believe it despite the complete absence of any Minoan objects in Sicily, where archaeologists have been systematically exploring for many decades. Heracles' "grand tour" of Sicily provides no analogy. That myth was simply part of the continuing process of transporting gods and demigods to new places as the Greeks migrated to them, in Sicily beginning in the middle of the eighth century B.C. The details of Heracles' tour, it is of some interest to note, are nearly all wrong when matched against the known history of the actual colonization movement.

An extreme example is currently receiving much publicity—the myth of Atlantis as told by Plato,* a myth that everyone in antiquity agreed was a Platonic invention. It is now suggested that behind it lay a genuine occurrence, a staggering underwater volcanic explosion that destroyed much of the island of Thera (modern Santorin) in the Aegean Sea about 1500 B.C. Linking the two requires major surgery: Atlantis has to be removed from the Atlantic to the Aegean, Crete has to become Thera, Athens has to be removed from the myth, all the numbers in Plato have to be reduced by lopping off the final zeros, and much else. I find this wholly incredible and, what is worse, pointless.[59] Why should Plato, of all people, not be allowed poetic license? The creation of historical legends was not in his day a lost art. There is the famous case of Lycurgus, the legendary founder of the Spartan system. His name does not even rate a mention in the extensive surviving fragments of the Spartan poet Tyrtaeus, writing late in the seventh century B.C. By the middle of the fifth century B.C., Herodotus had heard of him, in a confused way, but no more than that he was a king's uncle and tutor and the great lawgiver. Herodotus had no idea when Lycurgus lived, nor did he know his patronymic, by which every good Greek was identified.[60] More than five hundred years later Plutarch wrote a full-scale biography of the same Lycurgus, all the details of which had been invented in the intervening centuries.[61] The growth of the Aeneas story in Rome is a comparable instance, again starting out with nothing (and indeed with the very different Romulus tradition which had to be knitted with it in the end).

A somewhat comic note seems appropriate as an ending to this section. In the closing centuries of antiquity, one question vigorously debated between Christian and pagan apologists was, Who came first, Homer or

---

* *Critias; GBWW*, Vol. 7, pp. 479b–485d. *Timaeus* 20D–25D; Ibid., pp. 444a–446b.

Stamped hieroglyphs on the Phaestus disc; Middle Minoan III, after 1600 B.C.

Moses? And often it was turned into the blunter question, Who plagiarized from whom? As an anonymous writer of about A.D. 200 phrased it,

> I think you are not ignorant of the fact. . . that Orpheus, Homer, and Solon were in Egypt, that they took advantage of the historical work of Moses, and that in consequence they were able to take a position against those who had previously held false ideas about the gods.

Among his many "proofs" were the "borrowing" of the opening of Genesis for one bit of the description of the shield of Achilles in the *Iliad;* the portrayal of the Garden of Eden in the guise of the garden of King Alcinous in Book VII of the *Odyssey;* and Homer's referring to the corpse of Hector as "senseless clay," copied from "Dust thou art and to dust thou shalt return."[62]

Politics and political theory

The Greeks created politics. That claim is to be taken literally (with one possible qualification). Before 600 B.C. it was accepted in many Greek communities that there were different, conflicting interests within a state, that public policy therefore required public discussion, which led either to the triumph of one interest or viewpoint over the others, or to a compromise, or, if it came to the worst, to civil war. Much of Greek history then became the history of political debates and maneuvers, in the course of which in many communities, though not all, the people as a whole finally won recognition as the holders of sovereignty. (The objection that the "people" excluded a majority—women and slaves—does not invalidate the significance of the Greek innovation, though it is correct as a statement of fact.)

The proposition can be stated in a different way. Politics is about authority and obedience. Every society must have a mechanism for decision-making; the decisions must be initiated from some source, they must be enforceable in some way, and they must have a sanction, a justification. One pattern is the ancient Near Eastern, that of a hierarchic and hieratic organization in which the orders travel down the line and obedience travels back up.[63] A text of the Hittite king, Hattusilis III, who reigned from about 1275 to 1250 B.C., begins with these words:

> *Thus speaks Tabarna Hattusilis, the great king, king of Hatti, son of Mursilis, the great king of Hatti, grandson of Suppiluliumus, the great king, king of Hatti, descendant of Hattusilis, king of Kussara. I tell the divine power of Ishtar; let all men hear it, and in the future may the reverence of me, the Sun, of my son, and of my son's son, and of my Majesty's seed be given to Ishtar among the gods.*[64]

In Mesopotamia, too, "the 'good life' was the 'obedient life'. . . . an orderly world is unthinkable without a superior authority to impose his will. The Mesopotamian feels convinced that authorities are always right."[65] Even among the ancient Hebrews, the prophets were the exception that proved the rule: they failed in the long run to unseat theocratic absolutism. The Greeks, in contrast, expected obedience only to the law and the community; the law could be changed, and more and more members of the community claimed freedom (*eleutheria*). Freedom is never a simple concept, and the tension between freedom and authority was a constant factor in Greek history, as in later history, but it is fundamental that the word *freedom* cannot be translated into any ancient Near Eastern language (or into any Far Eastern language). Greeks could lose their "freedom," for example to tyrants, but that implies they had something to lose (and to regain).

The importance of politics permeated Greek life and thought. Not only did Greeks accept political activity as a necessary kind of activity; they also attributed positive value to it, in the sense that they ranked it high among the activities to which a citizen should devote himself, even full-time when personal circumstances permitted. And the activity led to thinking about politics, at first in terms of vague concepts and ideological notions, by the end of the fifth century B.C. in more systematic and theoretical ways. Political behavior was a common subject of discussion and of moral judgment. That is apparent in the innumerable jokes, some of them earnest ones, in the comedies of Aristophanes; in Thucydides' *History,* which made politics and its extension, war, the central themes of historical writing, as they have continued to be almost to our day; above all, in the writings and teachings of Plato and Aristotle in the fourth century B.C. No other society before the modern era, Eastern or Western, produced a work like Aristotle's *Politics*—with its mixture of political and ethical analysis, the crowning touch to Greek originality in this respect.[66]

The one possible qualification I mentioned at the beginning of this section stems from our complete ignorance about life in the Phoenician city-states, Tyre and Sidon, and among the Etruscans. It is not impossible that Roman political activity, visible as soon as Rome broke away from the Etruscans about 500 B.C., had an Etruscan background. What is certain, anyway, is that the Romans then failed to develop on their own any systematic thinking about politics. The first Roman historian, the aristocratic Fabius Pictor, wrote during the crisis of the war with Hannibal, nearly two hundred years after Thucydides—and he wrote in Greek.[67] Another century was to go by before one can see a serious interest in political theory in Rome, and again the Greek influence was direct and undisguised. Men like Cicero naturally adapted Greek ideas to their own society, but it is difficult to find any original Roman political theory.

Cicero's influence on later ages was not diminished by his lack of originality. And it went in the direction laid down by his Greek models, in favor of an ethical approach to politics. The result has been paradoxical in modern classical studies. On the one hand, everyone approves of freedom, and everyone in the twentieth century, if not in the nineteenth, is for democracy, best represented in antiquity by Athens. On the other hand, ancient writers, drawn from the leisured classes, are almost unanimous in their condemnation of the actual behavior of Athens or of quasi-democratic Rome in Cicero's day. These writers are among the greatest moralists the West has produced, so we must accept their judgments. That leads to the odd situation in which many modern histories approve the principles of the best ancient states and condemn their practices. The contradiction is then customarily explained by greed, unbridled license, or some similar, and ill-defined, moral concept.

Closer examination reveals that Plato, Aristotle, Cicero were not being so paradoxical: they disliked democracy in practice and argued that it was also defective in principle. One cannot be prodemocratic and pro-Plato at the same time. A different approach is required and is slowly being introduced into the study of Greco-Roman society. This approach does not (and need not) withdraw politics from morality, but it does not see everything in blacks and whites, and, with the help of modern political science and political sociology, it raises a series of fundamentally new questions about the operational side. It goes beyond the traditional narrow constitutional study—the powers of the assembly and Senate, the duties and prerogatives of magistrates, and so on—to consider leadership and elites and the techniques of decision-making, to define more closely the different classes and "estates" and their psychology, to examine propaganda techniques and the creation of ideology, or the costs and benefits of empire in concrete terms.

A few illustrations are all that space permits. Ostracism provides a good starting point. It was a curious institution, depriving Athens of some of its most experienced political leaders at important moments, and it has regularly been criticized as nothing but a tool for the fickle populace and their demagogues. One has now learned, however, to distrust such loaded terminology: demagogues seem somehow to be restricted to the other side. If one translates suspicion into precise operational questions, interesting conclusions emerge. Athens was a direct (not a representative) democracy, in which the citizens voted directly on issues as well as at elections. The citizen body as a whole could not have the necessary expertise and had to rely on professional politicians, who were not paid and who were therefore drawn from men of independent means. No one else could afford the time required to become, and act as, a professional. This leadership was responsible directly to the people meeting in assembly, without the mediation (or buffer) of a political party. Those who had the ear of the people at any period were challenged by other potential leaders, with alternative policies (or just with a desire for places of authority). The same thing goes on today, but the techniques in a small, face-to-face community were necessarily different from ours, above all because of the direct, almost weekly intervention of the popular assembly. Hence there was more of an all-or-nothing quality about political battles: getting an opponent out of the city physically was clearly the best possible insurance for the opposition short of assassination, and that is how ostracism became a factional political instrument. Before one rushes to condemn, it is worth remembering that political assassination was almost unknown in Athens during its nearly two centuries of democracy, that the Athenians had no precedents to guide them and had to invent as they went along, that all political societies require leadership as well as ways of removing unsatisfactory leaders, and that the Athenians managed to make their system work, achieving the difficult combination of direct rule by the people as a whole on the one hand, and, on the other,

529

political leadership that was completely in the hands of the wealthy.[68]

Given the bias of our sources, the fact is not surprising that *demagogues* in its negative sense is regularly reserved for those leaders who spoke most directly for the lower classes. The word *democracy* is itself ambiguous: it means rule by the *demos,* and *demos,* like *the people* in English, means both the people as a whole and the lower classes. Antidemocratic writers were quick to seize on the possibilities of word-play. Eventually the Greek historian Polybius, who lived and wrote in Rome in the second century B.C., abandoned the game and coined the substitute word, *ochlocracy* ("mob rule"). Within a century after Polybius, the Roman "mob" took the center of the stage, paralyzed legitimate governmental functions, demanded bread and circuses, rioted frequently, and, together with corrupt politicians, destroyed the Roman Republic. At least that is the familiar picture, and it is not wholly devoid of truth. The vast Roman expansion after the defeat of Hannibal led, by various means, to the creation of the largest fortunes hitherto known in private hands, to the disappearance of a substantial portion of the Italian peasantry, and to a sharp increase in the population of the city of Rome, where the majority lived in frightful slums with little prospect of earning a regular livelihood by legitimate means. Many were therefore available for corrupt and riotous activities.

However, availability is only half an answer. Someone must make use of available instruments, and anyway "mobs" that have been observed in other countries and other times have never rioted continuously decade after decade. A close study of the Roman evidence, chiefly from Cicero who can scarcely be accused of bias in favor of the mob, has now proved what we ought to have been able to guess anyway, that there was continual manipulation, that the mob was being openly and flagrantly used by ambitious men from the highest social and intellectual circles.[69] That Roman society in the last pre-Christian century was wildly corrupt is clear beyond question, but this was true of all classes. To single out the mob and the demagogues is a distortion. Besides, to moralize about corruption, even when the target is correctly selected, is an evasion of historical explanation. Corruption never takes over a society for no reason at all.

One factor in Rome was imperial expansion and exploitation. Empire was a central institution in much of Greco-Roman history, as it had been in the Near East earlier. *Empire* is an umbrella word: there is more than one way of ruling over subject people, there are different reasons for doing so, and there are differences in the distribution of the benefits among the ruling population. Surprisingly, this remains one of the most neglected fields in ancient history. Endless study has been devoted to the details of the expansion with its innumerable wars, to the rules of provincial administration, to the tax collectors, to the colonial personnel who succeeded in rising into the ruling elite, and to "good" and "bad" emperors. But there has been insufficient comparative analysis and too little differentiation within each empire, among both the rulers and the ruled. Again the moralists have tended to take over, condemning the Athenian empire out of hand, singling out the publicans and corrupt individuals in Rome.[70]

The Athenian case is particularly interesting because the empire has been tied in with the demagogues and the people, to be condemned as the outstanding manifestation of wicked democratic practice. Thucydides put into the mouth of Pericles the improbable remark that our empire "is, to speak somewhat plainly, a tyranny,"[71] and he has not often been challenged by historians. In 1954, however, G. E. M. de Ste. Croix took a close look at Thucydides' own narrative, and the other available evidence, and discovered that among the 150-odd small subject communities in Asia Minor, Thrace, and the Aegean islands, there was a remarkable amount of loyalty to the Athenians even when the Peloponnesian War was turning badly against Athens. Why should that have been? His answer is that the subject communities were not homogeneous but factionally divided and that the democratic factions, often weak and threatened by oligarchy, frequently welcomed Athenian suzerainty because it supported them against their internal enemies. Liberty from imperial rule was a fine thing, but not when the price was subjection at home.[72] This was the inverse of the position taken by some French generals (and others) in 1939: Better the Boches than our own Reds.

The word *libertas* (the Latin for *eleutheria*) came easily to the lips of Roman orators and historians. We can hardly avoid translating it as *liberty,* thus introducing a false note. Shakespeare's *Julius Caesar** provides the model, but in fact what sort of liberty did Brutus stand for? Not the liberty of the provincial population: as a young man, Brutus had lent money to the city of Salamis in Cyprus at 48 percent interest and had then gotten the Roman army to squeeze the payments out of the Salaminians for him. Nor really the liberty of anyone else, save that of the Roman ruling class to live according to their lights and to retain a monopoly of government. This was Cicero's idea of *libertas,* as it was of the lost *libertas* that provided the historian Tacitus with his main theme under the emperors.[73] Not even the great edifice of the Roman law offered a fundamentally different conception, though it required a conscious break from the abstract juristic approach, dominant since the late Middle Ages, in order to establish an appreciation of the social bias of Roman law in practice.[74]

Reexamination of institutions and concepts has led to a reassessment of the main ideological spokesmen, such as Cicero and Tacitus.[75] The sharpest contemporary controversy, however, has not developed around any Roman thinker but around Plato. With the rise of the Nazis to power,

---

* *GBWW*, Vol. 26, pp. 568–96.

a number of philosophers, especially in England and the United States, saw a frightening kinship with Plato's political ideas, and they felt fortified in their view by the Nazis' own claim to Plato as a forerunner. The climax of the attack was reached in the first volume of Karl Popper's *The Open Society and Its Enemies,* published in 1945.[76] Defenders were quick to reply with equal heat; they were able to catch errors, and in particular they were right to object to the anachronistic labeling of Plato as a fascist. Where does the argument now stand? I find it difficult not to agree with Renford Bambrough, editor of a recent anthology of important contributions to the debate, a close and in many respects admiring student of Plato. He writes, "Plato's enemies mislead us when they say that he is a Fascist, but his friends cannot be allowed to rebut the charge with such force and in such terms as to obscure the fact.that his doctrine is totalitarian in the sense in which Fascism is totalitarian." The issues, we also conclude with Bambrough, "are still alive in everyday and political life."[77]

The masters and the slaves

When slavery was introduced into the Americas, both North and South, one interesting aspect of the story was the ease with which Europeans, who had had no contact with large-scale slavery for centuries, were able to establish the institution, provide the necessary laws, and find the moral justification. The explanation lies in the biblical and classical worlds, and in the accommodation made with slavery by the early Church Fathers. Roman law, the Bible, and classical literature were familiar to every educated Englishman, Frenchman, and Spaniard of the period, and no institution was mentioned so frequently, if not often systematically, in these writings as slavery.[78] Everything was there ready to hand. So were such pleas for benevolent treatment of slaves as Seneca's, borrowed by the Jesuits who sought to protect Amerindians in South America from enslavement, and by other humanitarian men, who, however, were at that time not challenging slavery as an institution.

On neither side was there a systematic inquiry into ancient slavery— merely a picking and choosing of suitable texts. The Enlightenment and the French Revolution saw the first analytical interest, but it was the nineteenth-century abolitionists who produced the first serious studies, in particular the three-volume history of slavery in antiquity by the Frenchman Henri Wallon. The first edition appeared in 1847, the second in 1879, when Wallon was Dean of the Faculty of Letters of the University of Paris. The three volumes, a work of genuine erudition and still

Section of Aristotle's *Constitution of Athens*, a papyrus manuscript found at Asyut, in Egypt; second century A.D.

the only history of ancient slavery on that scale, were at the same time an open tract for abolition, charged with emotion. By 1879 Marx had already published the first volume of his *Capital,* and numerous other works. Ancient slavery thus became an important historical element in another, widely unpopular, movement—Communism. A reaction soon set in. The counterattack was not a defense of slavery as such, but a two-pronged argument: first, that ancient and modern American slavery were so different that all comparisons are misleading (especially any projection of the horrors of modern Negro slavery back onto antiquity); second, that the extent and the impact of slavery in antiquity were grossly exaggerated anyway. The most influential voice in the counterattack was Eduard Meyer, the outstanding ancient historian of his day in Germany; but the fullest statement of that position will be found in a relatively recent book by an American pupil of Meyer's, William L. Westermann.[79]

Most ancient historians implicitly agreed with Meyer, at least to the extent of ignoring slavery. The exceptions were the Marxists and the Roman lawyers. The latter had no choice, because, as William W. Buckland pointed out in the preface to his 735-page *Roman Law of Slavery,* "There is scarcely a problem which can present itself, in any branch of the law, the solution of which may not be affected by the fact that one of the parties to the transaction is a slave, and, outside the region of procedure, there are few branches of the law in which the slave does not prominently appear."[80] If that is so, one might have thought, then students of ancient religion or social institutions also have no choice. And indeed, one German scholar has now published a four-volume monograph, totaling nearly 800 pages, on the religion of the slaves in Greece and Rome.[81] Nevertheless, the fact remains that this kind of thorough inquiry began only after the Second World War (barring the occasional exception), and the old neglect of the topic still persists. An extreme example is Martin P. Nilsson's standard, massive reference work on Greek religion, also in German, first published in two fat volumes in 1941 and 1950. It contains a single paragraph on the religious aspects of the slave revolts of the second century B.C., and other than that the word *slave* does not appear in the index.[82]

On balance, the Nilssons are losing ground, and slavery is today a major concern among classical students. In part, the change may be attributed simply to the diminishing pull of the old sentimental adulation of the Greeks and Romans. However, there is more to it, and that is the increasing recognition that classical studies have something to learn from other disciplines. From social anthropology we have learned that some form of bondage has been the most general form of labor (apart from self-employment and family labor) in early and more primitive societies; that wage labor is a relatively late, sophisticated institution; and that outright slavery, in which human beings are mere chattels, is only one of a range of servile forms.[83] Even within the Greco-Roman world, a more

534

complex analysis is necessary, distinguishing between slaves and so-called debt slaves (familiar from the Bible as from early Greece and Rome), for example, or between the helots of Sparta and the chattel slaves of Athens, between the slaves in industry and commerce and the slaves on the large landed estates of Italy and Sicily. We have also learned from the anthropologists that slavery has a profound impact not only on the economy but also on popular psychology and behavior in such areas as sexual ethics, attitudes to work, technology, even attitudes to human life (as symbolized by the cruel gladiatorial shows, for example). This side of the problem is extremely elusive when we can no longer observe the society in action and are dependent entirely on ancient writers, who, it should be stressed, were unable to test or judge their own experience against societies that did not possess slaves. Conjectural as our analyses are therefore bound to be, I nevertheless rate this group of problems high on any list of urgent research subjects in the classical field.

The old debate about the validity of comparisons with American slavery has also been taken to a new level, both because of the more intensive investigation of ancient slavery and because there has been an upsurge, within the last two decades, of very sophisticated new work on American slavery. It is now clear that there are at least three fundamental distinctions between the American institution and the ancient one. The first is the element of color, affecting not only the slaves but also the ex-slaves. By and large, slaves had a far higher chance of being freed in antiquity, and when that happened, their descendants melted into the total population, lacking as they did the permanent mark of color. The second distinction stems from the importance of slaves in the urban sector of antiquity, in particular in manufacture; plantation slavery was paralleled for only one period in Italy, and even then there was nothing like the monoculture of the cotton states. Finally, there is the fundamental distinction in the underlying economies and the corollary that modern slavery existed within a world that also included important non-slave economies. These are all limitations on comparative study, grounds for caution, but they do not warrant Eduard Meyer's total rejection of all comparisons.

The glory that was Greece and the grandeur that was Rome

These two lines from Edgar Allan Poe's "To Helen" were chosen as the titles for two of the most successful books ever written about the classical world, both by John C. Stobart. The Greek volume, published in 1911, went through fourteen printings before a posthumous fourth edition was issued in 1964, and the Roman book had nine printings from 1912 until its fourth edition in 1961. As the titles already warn us, the picture is idealized in the extreme, and explanation is reduced to little more than

535

reference to innate character and eternal verities. The break from an attitude summed up by Stobart has been one of my main themes. It would be a pity, however, if it were thought that I have been making a plea for "debunking," for chopping the Greeks and Romans down to size. The Parthenon still stands, Greek tragedy is still read and loved, Plato remains one of the towering figures in the whole history of philosophy, Tacitus a remarkable historian. Interpretation in place of sentimental adulation should make these men, and the whole achievement, more meaningful, not less so, precisely because it humanizes an otherwise wholly unreal civilization and because it seeks to explain what was accomplished, and why, and how, and where the limits were. If the study of dead civilizations is to be justified as an enrichment of contemporary experience, that is the way to achieve the objective.

When the rediscovery of the ancient Near East began in the latter part of the nineteenth century, the most powerful voices in the classical field were nearly unanimous in their contempt. Very interesting, they said, but let no one imagine that any new light would be thrown on classical history and civilization. East and West were each a closed compartment; when they met, it was only in mortal combat. And there could be no doubt where the victory would lie, since the "West" had total moral and intellectual superiority. In time other voices were raised, and in the past two or three decades there has been scrupulous examination of the flow of ideas and skills from the Near East to Greece during the Bronze Age, later in science, religion, and mythology, and in the fine arts. A considerable list of outright borrowings can be drawn up: metallurgy (not to go back earlier to agriculture), elementary mathematics, astronomy, individual myths, the Phoenician alphabet, possibly sculpture, decorative motifs on pottery and ivory. And why not? Why should the Greeks have refused such skills and knowledge when they became available? Any more than in a later age the early Christians borrowed the Greek philosophical concepts with which they were able to construct a systematic theology?

Except as miscellaneous facts, however, such lists of borrowings are not very interesting. What matters is what the borrowers made of their borrowings. Christian theology was Christian, not pagan Greek. And in every instance I have just given, the Greeks transformed what they took into something new and original. The Phoenicians invented the alphabet, but there were no Phoenician Homers. No Babylonian wrote the *Theogony* of Hesiod or the *Elements* of Euclid. That is "glory" enough.

---

1 *Universal History* 15. 14. 3–4.

2 Alternative translations should be noted: "because Astarte commanded [it] through him" instead of "because Astarte has raised [him] with her hand"; and "may the years . . . be as many" in the final sentence.

3 I have gone into further detail in *Aspects of Antiquity* (New York: Viking Press, 1968), chap. 9.

4 The lectures were later published in a handsome illustrated volume, *Tomb Sculpture,* ed. Horst W. Janson (London: Thames & Hudson, 1964) .

5 Some of the chapter headings in the recent book by Antony Andrewes, *The Greeks* (New York: Alfred A. Knopf, 1967), make the point succinctly. It would not be easy to find an earlier book on Greece with chapters entitled "Tribes and Kinship Groups," "Landowners, Peasants and Colonists," "Social Values and Social Divisions," or "Open Speculation," with "Outline of Political History" also a single chapter.

6 Recent advances in the application to archaeology of new scientific equipment and techniques will not be discussed.

7 Roger A. Pack, *The Greek and Latin Literary Texts from Greco-Roman Egypt*, 2nd ed., rev. and enl. (Ann Arbor: University of Michigan Press, 1965). The Latin items, not included in my figures, are a mere 110, of which 41 are treatises on Roman law. The explanation is that even after Egypt became a Roman possession in 30 B.C., the language of the educated classes remained Greek until replaced by Arabic.

8 *GBWW*, Vol. 5, pp. 1–14.

9 *Odes* 3. 30. 13–14.

10 *GBWW*, Vol. 5 pp. 449–649.

11 I say "finds" in the plural because since 1959 there have been published papyri containing three acts of the *Samian Woman*, two acts of the *Shield*, a group of long selections from the *Man from Sicyon*, and other important fragments.

12 *GBWW*, Vol. 14, pp. 32–48.

13 *GBWW*, Vol. 9, pp. 549–84.

14 They did not, however, use clay tablets, virtually indestructible, for day-to-day writing purposes, as was the practice in Mesopotamia for more than two thousand years, from the Sumerians to the Neo-Babylonians. The most important leather documents are the Dead Sea Scrolls, which fall outside this survey.

15 A convenient cheap edition, with English translation and notes, is that edited by Peter A. Brunt and John M. Moore (London: Oxford University Press, 1967).

16 This conclusion ties in with the larger topic of current reexamination of the workings of Athenian politics, discussed below. Photographs of the Themistocles ostraca are reproduced in *Hesperia* 7 (1938): 231–42.

17 J. V. A. Fine, *Horoi* (*Hesperia*, supp. 9, 1951); M. I. Finley, *Studies in Land and Credit in Ancient Athens, 500–200 B.C.* (New Brunswick: Rutgers University Press, 1952); "Land, Debt, and the Man of Property in Classical Athens," *Political Science Quarterly* 68 (1953): 249–68.

18 Weaver's most general statement of his results will be found in his article "Social Mobility in the Early Roman Empire," *Past & Present*, no. 37 (1967), pp. 3–20.

19 In writing *Early Greece: The Bronze and Archaic Ages* (New York: W. W. Norton & Co., 1970), I wanted to consider the gradual disappearance of swords, spearheads, and other military equipment from graves after the breakup of the Mycenaean palace society, but I was largely frustrated by the casual attitude, in much archaeological reporting, about such material once it ceased to consist of quality goods.

20 Robert M. Cook, *Greek Painted Pottery*, reprint with corrections (New York: Barnes & Noble, 1966), pp. 274–75.

21 The standard survey in English is Oliver R. Gurney, *The Hittites*, 2nd ed. rev. (Baltimore: Penguin Books, 1961), which begins with a good short introduction on "The Discovery of the Hittites."

22 The most reliable account, well illustrated but not interestingly presented, is Johannes Friedrich, *Extinct Languages*, trans. Frank Gaynor (New York: Philosophical Library, 1957). The 2nd German edition (1966) brings the story up to date.

23 I am ignoring the further complications created by several isolated objects, such as the Phaestus disk, with still different characters inscribed on them.

24 See John Chadwick, *The Decipherment of Linear B*, 2nd ed. (London: Cambridge University Press, 1967).

25 For a balanced statement of the position, see Geoffrey S. Kirk, *The Songs of Homer* (New York: Cambridge University Press, 1962), pp. 24–29.

26 It is equally impossible to enter into a discussion of the effects of more than 150 years of decipherment on linguistic study itself.

27 *Life of Nicias* 20; *GBWW*, Vol. 11, p. 190b.

28 The best presentation of the evidence is by F. D. Harvey, "Literacy in the Athenian Democracy," *Revue des études grecques* 79 (1966): 585–635.

29 *Phaedrus* 274–8; *GBWW*, Vol. 7, pp. 138c–140d.

30 *See* Henri I. Marrou, *A History of Education in Antiquity,* unreliably translated by George Lamb (New York: Sheed & Ward, 1956).

31 In the remainder of this essay I repeatedly contrast "new" with "old" or "traditional" approaches. If I rarely stop to discuss, or even to mention, scholars whose work represents alternative or exceptional views, that does not imply that they do not exist.

32 The poems of Homer are published in *GBWW,* Vol. 4, of Virgil in Vol. 13, of Dante in Vol. 21, of Milton in Vol. 32.

33 The best introduction is Kirk, *Songs of Homer.* There is a shorter, paperback version, *Homer and the Epic* (New York: Cambridge University Press, 1965). I am ignoring many difficult Homeric questions such as whether or not the *Iliad* and the *Odyssey* are the work of two different composers.

34 This view is most cogently argued by A. Parry, "Have We Homer's *Iliad?*" *Yale Classical Studies* 20 (1966): 177–216.

35 *See* my *World of Odysseus,* rev. ed. (New York: Viking Press, 1965).

36 *Poetics* 1449a16; *GBWW,* Vol. 9, p. 683b.

37 *Proceedings of the Cambridge Philological Society,* n.s., no. 9 (1963), p. 21.

38 *See* John Jones, *On Aristotle and Greek Tragedy* (London: Chatto & Windus, 1962).

39 It is worth noting the date of Jones's highly polemical book, cited in the previous note. Dawe was applying to Aeschylus a type of analysis that had already been made of Sophocles as far back as 1917 by a young German scholar, Tycho Wilamowitz, and that had been promptly and rudely rejected by most specialists.

40 *GBWW,* Vol. 5, p. 107c.

41 Jones, *On Aristotle,* p. 233.

42 *The Greeks and the Irrational* (Berkeley and Los Angeles: University of California Press, 1951).

43 *Poetics* 1449b27; *GBWW,* Vol. 9, p. 684a.

44 A long list is published in Appendix II of Robert R. Bolgar, *The Classical Heritage and Its Beneficiaries* (New York: Cambridge University Press, 1954; Harper & Row, Publishers, Harper Torchbooks, 1964).

45 "The Task of the Translator," *Delos,* no. 2 (1968), pp. 78 and 82, respectively. The existence of *Delos,* subtitled *A Journal on and of Translation,* is itself deserving of note.

46 This point is fully developed in Geoffrey S. Kirk, *Myth: Its Meaning and Functions in Ancient and Other Cultures* (Berkeley and Los Angeles: University of California Press, 1970).

47 P. S. Cohen, "Theories of Myth," *Man* 4 (1969): 337–53.

48 In view of the wide circulation of Robert Graves, *The Greek Myths* (London: Penguin Books, 1955), it should perhaps be said that he still clings to this theory, that he does not apply it consistently, and that his account of the myths is not always reliable.

49 A lively introduction is now available in Edmund Leach, *Claude Lévi-Strauss* (New York: Viking Press, 1970).

50 *See* my *Aspects,* chap. 7, on Diogenes.

51 Plato *Phaedo* 118; *GBWW,* Vol. 7, p. 251d.

52 As a model of the approach I am challenging, *see* Martin P. Nilsson, *Greek Popular Religion* (New York: Columbia University Press, 1940).

53 *See* my *Aspects,* chap. 5, on the trial of Socrates.

54 *Laws* 10. 907D–909C; *GBWW,* Vol. 7, pp. 769d–770c.

55 The fundamental book remains Arthur D. Nock, *Conversion* (London: Oxford University Press, 1933).

56 *The Peloponnesian War* 1. 22; *GBWW,* Vol. 6, p. 354c.

57 *Ibid.* 1. 8–11; *GBWW,* Vol. 6, pp. 350d–352b.

58 The reader should be warned that my own position is an extreme one on the side of disbelief. *See* my *Aspects,* chap. 2, and my article "The Trojan War," with comments by J. L. Caskey, G. S. Kirk, and D. L. Page, *Journal of Hellenic Studies* 84 (1964): 1–20. On early Rome, *see* Arnaldo Momigliano, "An Interim Report on the Origins of Rome," *Journal of Roman Studies* 53 (1963): 95–121, reprinted in his *Terzo contributo alla storia degli studi classici e del mondo antico,* 2 vols. (Rome: Edizioni di Storia e Letteratura, 1966), pp. 545–98.

59 The most sober statement of the Atlantis argument is that of John V. Luce, *Lost Atlantis* (New York: McGraw-Hill Book Co., 1969). My objections were published in *New York Review of Books*, May 22 and December 4, 1969.

60 *The History* 1. 65–66; *GBWW*, Vol. 6, p. 14b–c.

61 *GBWW*, Vol. 14, pp. 32–48.

62 A full account of the Moses-Homer debate will be found in Jean Pépin, *Mythe et allégorie: Les origines grecques et les contestations judéo-chrétiennes* (Paris: Éditions Aubier-Montaigne, 1958).

63 I am not concerned with "pre-state" systems, in which tribal or other kinship groupings organize the affairs of the community. Some historians believe that such communities continued to exist within Near Eastern kingdoms—a much debated question today.

64 Quoted from Gurney, op. cit., p. 175.

65 Thorkild Jacobsen in Henri and Henriette A. Frankfort et al., *Before Philosophy* (Harmondsworth, Middlesex: Penguin Books, 1951), pp. 217–18.

66 *GBWW*, Vol. 9, pp. 437–548.

67 See Arnaldo Momigliano, "Linee per una valutazione di Fabio Pittore," in his *Terzo contributo*, pp. 55–68. This article will be published in English in a collection of Momigliano's papers, probably not before 1972.

68 I have developed this analysis at length in "Athenian Demagogues," *Past & Present*, no. 21 (1962), pp. 3–24.

69 P. A. Brunt, "The Roman Mob," *Past & Present*, no. 35 (1966), pp. 3–27; idem, *Social Conflicts in the Roman Republic* (London: Chatto & Windus, 1971), chap. 6.

70 The gap has been partly filled by an important book, Ernst Badian, *Roman Imperialism in the Late Republic* (Ithaca, N.Y.: Cornell University Press, 1968).

71 *The Peloponnesian War* 2. 63. 2; *GBWW*, Vol. 6, p. 403c.

72 G. E. M. de Ste. Croix, "The Character of the Athenian Empire," *Historia* 3 (1954): 1–41. Attempts to challenge his main thesis have been unsuccessful.

73 *GBWW*, Vol. 15. See above all Chaim Wirszubski, *Libertas as a Political Idea at Rome during the Late Republic and Early Principate* (New York: Cambridge University Press, 1950).

74 See John A. Crook, *Law and Life of Rome* (London: Thames & Hudson, 1967).

75 Richard E. Smith's encomiastic *Cicero the Statesman* (London: Cambridge University Press, 1966) is a reminder that new trends are not universally accepted. One cannot leave this subject without mentioning the seminal work of Ronald Syme, *The Roman Revolution* (Oxford: Clarendon Press, 1939).

76 *The Open Society and Its Enemies*, 2 vols.; the fourth edition, including a reply to his critics, was published in 1962 (London: Routledge & Kegan Paul).

77 *Plato, Popper and Politics* (New York: Barnes & Noble, 1967), pp. 16–17.

78 The continuity in the history of slavery has been brilliantly analyzed by David B. Davis, *The Problem of Slavery in Western Culture* (Ithaca: Cornell University Press, 1966), pt. 1. On the early discussion in Latin America, see Lewis Hanke, *Aristotle and the American Indians* (London: Hollis & Carter, 1959).

79 Eduard Meyer, "Die Sklaverei im Altertum" (Lecture originally published in 1898), in his *Kleine Schriften*, 2nd ed. (Halle: Max Niemeyer, 1924), 1: 169–212; William L. Westermann, *The Slave Systems of Greek and Roman Antiquity* (Philadelphia: American Philosophical Society, 1955).

80 *The Roman Law of Slavery* (Cambridge: At the University Press, 1908).

81 F. Bömer, *Untersuchungen über die Religion der Sklaven in Griechenland und Rom*, published in the *Abhandlungen der geistes- und sozialwissenschaftlichen Klasse* of the Akademie der Wissenschaften und der Literatur, Mainz, 1957 no. 7, 1960 no. 1, 1961 no. 4, 1963 no. 10.

82 Martin P. Nilsson, *Geschichte der griechischen Religion*, 2 vols. (Munich: C. H. Beck'sche Verlagsbuchhandlung, 1941–50).

83 Space does not permit me to go into detail on any of the points that follow in this section, nor to cite the now voluminous bibliography, for which I refer to *International Encyclopedia of the Social Sciences* (New York: Macmillan Co. and Free Press, 1968), for my article "Slavery."

539